Land of Hope

WILFRED M. McCLAY

LAND OF HOPE

An Invitation to the Great American Story

First American edition published in 2019 by Encounter Books,
an activity of Encounter for Culture and Education, Inc.,
a nonprofit, tax-exempt corporation.
Encounter Books website address: www.encounterbooks.com

Manufactured in the United States and printed on
acid-free paper. The paper used in this publication meets
the minimum requirements of ANSI/NISO Z39.48–1992
(R 1997) (*Permanence of Paper*).

FIRST AMERICAN EDITION

LIBRARY OF CONGRESS CATALOGING-IN-PUBLICATION DATA

Names: McClay, Wilfred M., author.
Title: Land of hope : an invitation to the great American story / by Wilfred M. McClay.
Other titles: Invitation to the great American story
Description: New York : Encounter Books, [2019] |
Includes bibliographical references and index. | Audience: Grades 9-12.
Identifiers: LCCN 2018045970 (print) | LCCN 2018046473 (ebook) |
ISBN 9781594039386 (ebook) | ISBN 9781594039379 (hardcover : alk. paper)
Subjects: LCSH: United States—History—Juvenile literature.
Classification: LCC E178.3 (ebook) | LCC E178.3 .M143 2019 (print) | DDC 973–dc23
LC record available at https://lccn.loc.gov/2018045970

For Bruce Cole

Indispensable man, irreplaceable friend

Every generation rewrites the past. In easy times history is more or less of an ornamental art, but in times of danger we are driven to the written record by a pressing need to find answers to the riddles of today. We need to know what kind of firm ground other men, belonging to generations before us, have found to stand on. In spite of changing conditions of life they were not very different from ourselves, their thoughts were the grandfathers of our thoughts, they managed to meet situations as difficult as those we have to face, to meet them sometimes lightheartedly, and in some measure to make their hopes prevail. We need to know how they did it.

In times of change and danger when there is a quicksand of fear under men's reasoning, a sense of continuity with generations gone before can stretch like a lifeline across the scary present and get us past that idiot delusion of the exceptional Now that blocks good thinking. That is why, in times like ours, when old institutions are caving in and being replaced by new institutions not necessarily in accord with most men's preconceived hopes, political thought has to look backwards as well as forwards.

JOHN DOS PASSOS
"The Use of the Past,"
from *The Ground We Stand On:*
Some Examples from the History
of a Political Creed (1941)

CONTENTS

ONE LONG STORY

THERE ARE ALREADY DOZENS OF HIGHLY COMPETENT, lavishly illustrated, and meticulously detailed accounts of the history of the United States in circulation. Why the need for this book, then? That is a very good question. The short answer is that this book seeks to accomplish something different from the others. You the reader will have to be the ultimate judge of whether it has been successful. But let me first take a few words to describe some of its guiding intentions.

Its principal objective is very simple. It means to offer to American readers, young and old alike, an accurate, responsible, coherent, persuasive, and inspiring narrative account of their own country – an account that will inform and deepen their sense of the land they inhabit and equip them for the privileges and responsibilities of citizenship. "Citizenship" here encompasses something larger than the civics-class meaning. It means a vivid and enduring sense of one's full membership in one of the greatest enterprises in human history: the astonishing, perilous, and immensely consequential story of one's own country.

Let me emphasize the term *story*. Professional historical writing has, for a great many years now, been resistant to the idea of history as narrative. Some historians have even hoped that history could be made into a science. But this approach seems unlikely ever to succeed, if for no other reason than that it fails to take into account the ways we need stories to speak to the fullness of our humanity and help us orient ourselves in the world. The impulse to write history and organize our world around stories is intrinsic to us as human beings. We are, at our core, remembering and story-making creatures, and stories are one of the chief ways we find meaning in the flow of events. What we call "history" and "literature" are merely the refinement and intensification of that basic human impulse, that need.

The word *need* is not an exaggeration. For the human animal, meaning is not a luxury; it is a necessity. Without it, we perish. Historical consciousness is to civilized society what memory is to individual identity. Without memory, and without the stories by which our memories are carried forward, we cannot say who, or what, we are. Without them, our life and thought dissolve into a meaningless, unrelated rush of events. Without them, we cannot do the most human of things: we cannot learn, use language, pass on knowledge, raise children, establish rules of conduct, engage in science, or dwell harmoniously in society. Without them, we cannot govern ourselves.

Nor can we have a sense of the future as a time we know will come, because we remember that other tomorrows also have come and gone. A culture without memory will necessarily be barbarous and easily tyrannized, even if it is technologically advanced. The incessant waves of daily events will occupy all our attention and defeat all our efforts to connect past, present, and future, thereby diverting us from an understanding of the human things that unfold in time, including the paths of our own lives.

The stakes were beautifully expressed in the words of the great Jewish writer Isaac Bashevis Singer: "When a day passes it is no longer there. What remains of it? Nothing more than a story. If stories weren't told or books weren't written, man would live like the beasts, only for the day. The whole world, all human life, is one long story."

Singer was right. As individuals, as communities, as countries: we are nothing more than flotsam and jetsam without the stories in which we find our lives' meaning. These are stories of which we are already a part, whether we know it or not. They are the basis of our common life, the webs of meaning in which our shared identities are suspended.

This book is an invitation to become acquainted with one of those webs of meaning: the American story. It does not pretend to be a complete and definitive telling of that story. Such an undertaking would be impossible in any event, because the story is ongoing and far from being concluded. But it is also the case that this book has striven to be as compact as possible. As any author will tell you, the most painful task in writing a book of this kind is deciding what to leave out. It is always very easy to add things but very difficult to take them out, because every detail seems important. One is constantly committing cruel acts of triage, large and small, throwing details out of the lifeboat to keep the vessel from sinking – a harsh but necessary act, if what remains is to take on the shape of a story rather than a mere accumulation of facts.

As will be clear, I have chosen to emphasize the political history of the

United States at every turn, treating it as the skeleton of the story, its indispensable underlying structure. This emphasis is particularly appropriate for the education of American citizens living under a republican form of government. There are other ways of telling the story, and my own choice of emphasis should not be taken to imply that the other aspects of our history are not worth studying. On the contrary, they contain immense riches that historians have only begun to explore. But one cannot do everything all at once. One must begin at the beginning, with the most fundamental structures, before one can proceed to other topics. The skeleton is not the whole of the body – but there cannot be a functional body without it.

History is the study of change through time, and theoretically, it could be about almost anything that happens. But it must be selective if it is to be intelligible. Indeed, in practice, what we call "history" leaves out many of the most important aspects of life. It generally does not deal with the vast stretches of time during which life goes on normally, during which people fall in love, have families, raise their children, bury their dead, and carry on with the small acts of heroism, sacrifice, and devotion that mark so much of everyday life – the "unhistoric acts," as George Eliot wrote in the closing words of *Middlemarch*, of those "who lived faithfully a hidden life, and rest in unvisited tombs." There are a few moments, like the American holiday of Thanksgiving, or great public commemorations, at which the low murmur of those ordinary things becomes audible and finds a measure of public acknowledgment. But by and large, "history" is interested in the eruptions of the extraordinary into the flow of the regular. It must leave out so very much.

This book extends a come-as-you-are invitation, and as such, it attempts to be a friendly point of entry for all sorts of readers and students of history, whatever their background. As the best stories show us, simplicity and complexity are not mutually exclusive. Hence this book strives to be, as the ancient sage put it, a river shallow enough for the lamb to go wading but deep enough for the elephant to swim. I hope all those who are new to the subject will be so intrigued that they will want to venture into deeper waters and, eventually, turn to the many outstanding books and authors that can take them much, much further, and deeper, than this book possibly can. But I hope that I have also done some justice to the deeper waters, without sacrificing the book's accessibility.

For both sorts of readers, I try to keep before us the recognition that history is not just an inert account of indisputable and self-explanatory details. It is a reflective task that calls to the depths of our humanity. It means asking questions, and asking them again and again, and asking fresh questions as the experience of life causes fresh questions to arise. The past does not speak for itself, and it cannot speak to us directly. We must first ask. It may have things to tell us that we have not yet thought to ask about. But it can be induced to address some of our questions, if we learn to ask them rightly. That is one of the many subtle glories of the study of history.

Finally, I'd like to offer a word about the book's title, which forms one of the guiding and recurrent themes of the book. As the book argues from the very outset, the western hemisphere was inhabited by people who had come from elsewhere, unwilling to settle for the conditions into which they were born and drawn by the prospect of a new beginning, the lure of freedom, and the space to pursue their ambitions in ways their respective Old Worlds did not permit. Hope has both theological and secular meanings, spiritual ones as well as material ones. Both these sets of meanings exist in abundance in America. In fact, nothing about America better defines its distinctive character than the ubiquity of hope, a sense that the way things are initially given to us cannot be the final word about them, that we can never settle for that. Even those who are bitterly critical of America, and find its hopes to be delusions, cannot deny the enduring energy of those hopes and are not immune to their pull.

Of course, hope and opportunity are not synonymous with success. Being a land of hope will also sometimes mean being a land of dashed hopes, of disappointment. That is unavoidable. A nation that professes high ideals makes itself vulnerable to searing criticism when it falls short of them – sometimes far short indeed, as America often has. We should not be surprised by that, however; nor should we be surprised to discover that many of our heroes turn out to be deeply flawed human beings. All human beings are flawed, as are all human enterprises. To believe otherwise is to be naive, and much of what passes for cynicism in our time is little more than naïveté in deep disguise.

What we should remember, though, is that the history of the United States, and of the West more generally, includes the activity of searching self-criticism as part of its foundational makeup. There is immense hope implicit in that process, if we go about it in the right way. That means approaching the work of criticism with constructive intentions and a certain generosity that flows from the mature awareness that none of us is perfect and that we should therefore judge others as we would ourselves wish to be judged, blending justice and mercy. One of the worst sins of the present – not just ours but any present – is its tendency to condescend toward the past, which is much easier to do when one doesn't trouble to know the full context of that past or try to grasp the nature of its challenges as they presented themselves at the time. This small book is an effort to counteract that condescension and remind us of how remarkable were the achievements of those who came before us, how much we are indebted to them.

Land of Hope

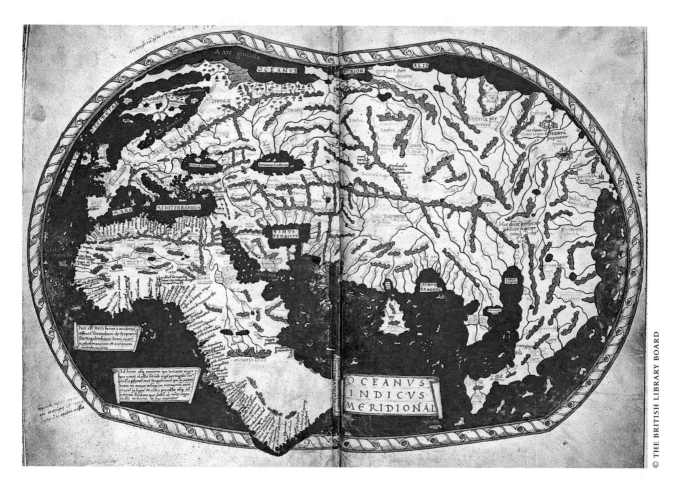

Henricus Martellus, Insularium Illustratum, *c. 1489. It is believed that Christopher Columbus studied this map as he prepared for his first voyage in 1492.*[*]

CHAPTER ONE

BEGINNINGS

Settlement and Unsettlement

HISTORY ALWAYS BEGINS IN THE MIDDLE OF THINGS. It doesn't matter where you choose to start the story; there is always something essential that came before, some prior context that is assumed. This is why the past can't be divided up into convenient self-contained units, with clear and distinct beginnings and endings, much as we might wish it were otherwise. Instead, the spectacle that lies before us when we gaze backward is more like a sprawling, limitless river with countless mingling branches and tributaries, stretching back to the horizon. Like a river, time's restless force pushes ever forward, but its beginnings lie far back, extending far beyond what we can see, fading into the mists of time at the edges of lands beyond our knowing.

Consider the story of your own life. The story didn't begin with you. You didn't call yourself into existence out of the void. You didn't invent the language you speak, or the foods you eat, or the songs you sing. You didn't build the home you grew up in, or pave the streets you walked, or devise the subjects you learned in school. Others were responsible for these things. Others, especially your parents, taught you to walk, to talk, to read, to dress, to behave properly, and everything else that goes with everyday life in a civilized society, things that you mainly take for granted.

But it's important to remember that those others didn't come into the world knowing these things either. Your parents didn't invent themselves any more than you did. And the people who taught them were just the same in that regard, taught by people before them, who were taught by people before them, and so on, in an ever-lengthening chain of human transmission that soon carries us back into the misty unknown. We carry the past forward into the present much more than we realize, and it forms a large part of who we are. Even at the moment of birth, we already find ourselves in the middle of things.

So how far back would you go in telling your own story? You could go back pretty far, if you wanted to. Many people are fascinated by tracing out their family histories, their genealogies. The details can be surprising and intriguing, and they may reveal unsuspected things about your ancestors. But too much of that will get in the way of relating the most important parts of the story and illuminating the pattern of your own life. Too much detail muddies the picture and defeats the ultimate purpose.

What we call "history" is the same way. It is not the sum of the whole past. It doesn't include everything, and it couldn't. Instead, it is a selection out of that expansive river of the past, like a carefully cropped photograph, organized wisely and truthfully, which allows us to focus in with clarity on a particular story, with particular objectives in mind.

The story that this book seeks to tell, the story of the United States, is exactly like this. It is not going to be the story of everything. It's a story about who we are and about the stream of time we share; it is an attempt to give us a clearer understanding of the "middle of things" in which we already find ourselves. And it is crafted with a particular purpose in mind: to help us learn, above all else, the things we must know to become informed, self-aware, and dedicated citizens of the United States of America, capable of understanding and appreciating the nation in the midst of which we find ourselves, of carrying out our duties as citizens, including protecting and defending what is best in its institutions and ideals. The goal, in short, is to help us be full members of the society of which we are already a part.

So where to begin? After all, there is a long, complex, and fascinating prologue to this story. We could go back many thousands of years, to the very edges of the mist, and examine what we know, or think we know, about the ancient origins of this country. And as in a family genealogy, we would find some surprises.

For one thing, it turns out that there are no peoples that could truly be called "native" to America, because all appear to have migrated there from other parts of the world. In other words, the entire western hemisphere, including both North and South America, was from the start populated by immigrants, by peoples who came there from someplace else, in search of something new and better.

Our best guess at present is that the first human settlers came over into the western hemisphere twenty thousand to thirty thousand years ago from northeastern Asia, probably by crossing over an icy land bridge or by island hopping across what is now the Bering Strait, the frigid waters that separate Russia and Alaska. From there, we believe that these first immigrants to America gradually filtered outward and downward, thinly populating all of North and South America, from the frozen Yukon to the southernmost tip of Patagonia, and east to the Atlantic coast and the forests and rivers and swamps of the American Midwest and South.

Some of those migrant peoples would long remain confined to the life of Stone Age nomads, for whom the elemental power of fire, along with crude implements made of stone or bone, were their chief shields against the pitiless ferocity of nature. Others, however, moved into more settled forms of habitation, adopting the practice of agriculture and, in some cases, eventually developing into highly advanced cultures. These cultures rose, flourished, and fell, blazing a trail across time but leaving behind for us little literature or history, only a few poignant material reminders of them. Most impressive of these to us today were the classic cultures of Middle and South America, the Mayas and Aztecs of Mexico and the Incas of Peru, which erected formidable civilizations featuring splendid cities filled with elaborate pyramids, temples, and courts, some of which survive to the present day.

Far less grand but just as intriguing are the remains of the North American settlements, such as those of the Adena and Hopewell cultures, that left large earthworks and burial mounds scattered across the landscape of the American East and Midwest, still readily visible today in ordinary places like Chillicothe, Ohio, or Romney, West Virginia. These, too, are eerily silent clues to a once-flourishing but now vanished way of life. Much the same can be said of the ancestral Pueblo peoples of the arid Four Corners region of the American Southwest, sometimes called by the Navajo name "Anasazi," a peaceful and highly organized people who left behind their startlingly modern-looking multistory cliff dwellings tucked in beneath overhanging cliffs, structures whose remnants can still be seen today in places like Mesa Verde, Colorado, and the Chaco Canyon area of northwestern New Mexico.

There is something haunting and melancholy about the remaining traces of these earliest civilizations. Hints of their once-grand presence still linger in the American landscape, like faded echoes of a distant drama. Their mysteries intrigue us. But they are in only the most remote sense a part of American history. They do not play an important role in this book, simply because they had no direct or significant role in the establishment of the settlements and institutions that would eventually make up the country we know as the United States.

Neither did the later discovery and exploration in the early eleventh century of a New World by adventurous Norse seamen like Leif Eriksson of Iceland, an enterprising fellow who sought to plant a colony on what is now the large Canadian island of Newfoundland. He and other Norsemen tried their best to establish a settlement in this newfound land to the west, to which he gave the cheerful name of "Vinland," but their efforts came to nothing and are generally counted as historical curiosities – interesting false starts on American history, perhaps, but no more than that.

But not so fast. Maybe this statement needs to be modified. Maybe the lost civilizations of the first Americans and the episodic voyages of Eriksson and other Norsemen, taken together, do point powerfully, if indirectly, toward the recognizable beginnings of American history. For they point to the presence of America in the world's imagination as an idea, as a land of hope, of refuge and opportunity, of a second chance at life for those willing to take it.

Perhaps that seems a fanciful statement. After all, we can never be sure exactly what forces and impulses led those earliest Asiatic peoples twenty thousand years ago to cross over into Alaska and make the dangerous and costly journey to populate a new continent. What was in their minds? Were they mainly pushed by dire necessity, such as war or scarcity? Were they hunters who were merely following their quarry? Or were they in part pulled into the new lands by a sense of promise or opportunity, or even adventure, that those lands offered?

We don't know. The answers to those questions will probably always remain beyond our reach. But we know that the Norsemen's brave impulse of over a thousand years ago, which drove them to go forth in search of new lands, came out of something more than mere necessity. They were drawn to cross the icy and turbulent waters of the North Atlantic by the lure of available western lands and by a restless desire to explore and settle those lands. And they were influenced by sentiments that were already widespread in their time, a thousand years after Christ and five hundred years before Columbus.

From the beginning, there was a mystique about the West. Leif's explorer father, Erik the Red, played upon that very mystique when he gave the alluring name of "Greenland" to the largely frozen island mass we know by that name today. He was appealing to an idea already long embedded in literature, myth, and religion that there were new lands of plenty and wonder and mystery out there – perhaps even an earthly paradise – waiting to be found, lying somewhere in lands beyond the western horizon. This message was especially alluring at the dawn of the new millennium, at a time when post-Roman Europe was stagnating, disorganized, and underdeveloped, still struggling to get back on its feet.

But the message itself was not new. The ancient Greeks had spoken this way a millennium and a half earlier. They sang of the Isles of the Blessed, where the heroes and gods of their mythology dwelled in a fertile land where there was no winter, and of the Elysian Fields, which the poet Homer located on the western edge of the earth, beside the stream of the world's seas. Centuries later, at the outset of a new age of exploration, Sir Thomas More's book *Utopia* (1516) described an ideal society located on an island in the West, as did Francis Bacon's *The New Atlantis* (1627), the very title of his book recalling one of the most enduring legends of the West – the strange story of the isle of Atlantis, a fully developed civilization with kings of great and mighty power that had been swallowed up by the seas and disappeared forever from view.

So the West had long been thought of, in Europe, as a direction offering renewal and discovery, a place of wealth and plenty, a land of hope – a vivid anticipation of what a New World could be like. And as we shall soon see, the shape taken on by this expectation would owe more to the yearnings of the Old World than to the realities of the New.

So, since we must begin in the middle of things, we will start our history of America in the middle of Europe's history. In fact, the two histories cannot be understood apart from one another. America is best understood as an offshoot of Europe; even the name "America" comes from the first name of the Italian-born navigator and explorer Amerigo Vespucci, who was among the first to speculate that the lands Columbus discovered were not the easternmost parts of Asia but part of an entirely new landmass.

But America would prove to be an unusual kind of offshoot. It was not like a new branch emerging out of the trunk of a great tree, duplicating the appearance and structure of the trunk and the tree's other branches, nor was it a careful and deliberate transplant, a smaller spin-off of what had already been established in Europe. Instead, it would receive certain parts of Europe, certain fragments that had been broken off from the whole – particularly English laws and customs – and would give those fragments a new home, in a new land, where they could develop and flourish in ways that would never have been possible in their native habitat. But so much of it was unpredictable, unplanned, unanticipated. The writer Lewis Mumford expressed this surprising process in a single brilliant sentence: "The settlement of America had its origins in the unsettlement of Europe."

What did Mumford mean by this? He meant that by the time of Christopher Columbus's famous voyage in 1492, which was one of the signal events in the making of America, Europe was becoming a dramatically different place from what it had been for the three preceding centuries, during the relatively stable and orderly years we now call the High Middle Ages (1000–1300). By the Late Middle Ages (1300–1500), Europe was entering the modern age, in the process becoming a place of pervasive change and innovation of all kinds. A great upsurge in fresh energies and disruptions, converging from many different directions at once, was unsettling a great deal of what had become familiar in the older world.

If any one of these innovations or disruptions had come along by itself, without the company of others – say, if the desire for an expansion of global commerce had not been accompanied by breakthrough inventions that provided the technological means to make such commerce possible – its effects would have been far less pronounced. But by coming together at once, these innovations gathered strength from one another, so that they contributed to a more general transforming fire, as when many small blazes fuel a greater conflagration. Such is the case with all great historical transformations; they arise not out of a single cause but out of the confluence of causes. This unsettling transformation of Europe that was already well under way in 1492 was throwing off flames that would land in other places and set off transformations there as well. The exploration and settlement of America would be one of the most consequential of these flames, the product of a host of great European disruptions: economic, social, religious, technological, and cultural.

What makes the story even more surprising is the fact that the movement toward the West actually began with a movement toward the East. Some key changes for Europe were wrought unintentionally by the Crusades, which were a Church-sanctioned military effort in the eleventh to thirteenth centuries to free the Holy Lands from their Muslim occupiers, who had in the four centuries since the death of Mohammed in 632 conquered two-thirds of the Christian world. Far from being intended as an early act in the unsettlement of medieval Europe, or as an act of unprovoked aggression, the Crusades were meant to be part of Europe's ongoing work of self-restoration. They were in many ways a perfect expression of the high medieval spirit in Western Europe, a world that was dominated by the Roman Catholic Church as a spiritual, political, and military power.

But we are more concerned here with one of the indirect effects of the Crusades, which was to bring Europeans into contact with the riches of the lands along the eastern shores of the Mediterranean Sea, consequently opening up overland trade routes to Asia, from which many desirable goods, such as rugs, silks, gold brocade, perfumes, teas, precious stones, dye-woods, and unusual spices such as pepper, nutmeg, and cloves, could be imported.

Small wonder that the East came to hold such a cultural fascination for many Europeans. A widely read memoir by the Venetian traveler Marco Polo, featuring spellbinding stories of his adventures along the Silk Road and in the lavish court of the Mongol emperor Kublai Khan, gave Europeans their first direct knowledge of the fabled wealth of China and Central Asia and sparked the restless imaginations of future explorers like Columbus and Ferdinand Magellan. The benefits of commerce with Asian cultures were obvious and enticing.

There were many obstacles, however. Overland trade with the East along the legendary Silk Road was slow, costly, and dangerous, and became more so after the fall of Constantinople to the Ottoman Turks in 1453. It could take a year to go from Venice to Beijing by land, traversing mountains and deserts on narrow trails with cargo packed on the backs of horses and camels. Muslim Turks and other unfriendly groups controlled the land routes to the east, so that even if travelers were able to elude bandits, there would be levies to be paid to local potentates and middlemen along the way, making the goods very expensive by the time they finally arrived at markets in Europe. As consumer demand for these luxuries grew and interest in trade with the East swelled, it became more and more urgent to find a better way of getting there, and back. The search was on to discover an all-water route to the East, which, if found, would go a long way toward solving these problems.

This search helped more generally to boost the era's attention to oceangoing exploration and stimulate a thoroughly modern passion for extending and mapping the contours of the known world. Fortunately, vital technological inventions and improvements in navigation and ship design became available that made such expansive voyages possible – advances in mapmaking and astronomical navigation, the dry magnetic compass, the astrolabe, the quadrant, the cross-staff, and other such instruments, as well as the development of new ships, such as the oceangoing Genoese *carrack* and the fast and maneuverable Portuguese *caravel*, whose ingenious combination of differently shaped sails enabled them to move easily against the wind.

Innovation did not stop there, though. The rapid expansion of trade was remaking the social and political map of Europe, at the same time that explorers were redrawing the physical map. In earlier eras, wealth and power had rested in the hands of those who owned land, but that was about to change. The years of expanding seaborne travel saw the rising economic and political power of a merchant class made up of those traders who had become wealthy from the risks and rewards of expanding commerce. Those years also saw the steadily growing importance of bustling market towns and port cities where the merchants' commercial activities would come to be concentrated and where a host of ancillary middle-class businesses and professions – bankers, lawyers, insurance providers, outfitters and suppliers of goods and services, teachers – would set up shop and thrive.

These changes would have far-reaching effects, further unsettling the existing order. The spectacular rise of the new merchant elites in places like Lisbon, Seville, and Venice challenged the power of old local and regional aristocracies, whose power had been based on their possession of land in a relatively closed and stationary feudal economy. Such older elites either had to accommodate themselves to the newcomers or be swept aside. The older ways were no match for the dynamic, wealth-generating, and disruptive new economics of trade.

Such changes would give rise in turn to new and unprecedented political structures. In Italy, ambitious merchant-princes used their new wealth to create powerful city-states, such as Florence and Venice, which featured glamorous palaces, churches, and other architectural and artistic wonders echoing the glories of Greek and Roman antiquity. In other places, the changes would lead to the emergence of great national monarchies, unified and centralized kingdoms over which individual rulers would be able to govern with vast authority and power. Such monarchs managed to break the hold of the local nobles and regional aristocrats who had dominated the feudal system and to create larger and more cohesive nations featuring a new kind of national-scale order, with a uniform national currency, a removal of internal barriers to trade, a professional standing military that kept internal order and supported the nation's interests abroad – all innovations that would further the interests of the merchant and middle classes, even as they helped to build the nation.

By 1492, four such national states were emerging in Europe: France, England, Spain, and Portugal. All four had both the wealth and the motivation to support the further exploration that would be needed to find a water route to the East and to expand the reach of their commerce and their growing power.

It was Portugal, though, that took the initiative in this Age of Discovery, early in the fifteenth century, under the guidance and patronage of Infante Henrique, later to be known as Prince Henry the Navigator (1394–1460). Portugal was a small country, but as the westernmost country of mainland Europe, with an extensive Atlantic coastline and the magnificent ports of Lisbon and Porto, it was perfectly situated to become an oceangoing power, and eventually the first global empire in the history of the world. Under Henry's leadership, Portugal became a magnet for the most able and advanced navigators and seamen from all over Europe, who were drawn to take part in the expeditions he sponsored. Step by step, skilled Portuguese crews charted the entire west coast of Africa, opening it up to commerce, and eventually, explorers like Bartolomeu Dias and Vasco da Gama would round the southern end of the African continent and, by 1498, establish the long-sought waterborne path to India.

The example of such Portuguese exploits drew Christopher Columbus away from his native Italian city-state of Genoa to settle in Lisbon at the age of twenty-six. He was already a highly experienced and capable sailor who had been to ports in the Mediterranean and northern Europe and, in partnership with his brother, voyaged under the Portuguese flag as far north as the Arctic Ocean, south along the coasts of West Africa, and west to the Azore Islands. Like everyone else of the time, he was obsessed with the idea of discovering an all-water route to "the Indies," as the Far East was called; but he had his own ideas about the best way of doing it. Everyone else was confident that going east and rounding Africa was the key; Bartolomeu Dias seemed to have confirmed that when he rounded Africa in 1488. But Columbus became convinced that going west would be both faster and more direct, and he formulated a plan for an expedition that would prove it.

When he took the plan to the King of Portugal in search of financial support, however, he was turned down – twice. Then he appealed to leaders in Genoa and Venice, and in England, and then in Spain, and had no luck with any of them. All of them said the plan was impractical and grossly underestimated the distances involved. Finally, however, after determined negotiations, Columbus was able to persuade the Spanish monarchs Ferdinand and Isabella to support him, and they signed an agreement called the Capitulations of Santa Fe. On August 3, 1492, he set sail from Palos de la Frontera in Spain aboard a large *carrack* called the *Santa Maria*, accompanied by two *caravels* and carrying a Latin passport and a sheath of letters of introduction, including a letter of introduction from Ferdinand and Isabella to the Emperor of China, just in case. He also brought along a Jewish scholar who was conversant in Arabic so that he would be able to communicate with any Muslims he encountered at his Oriental destinations. What may have been lacking in hard evidence for Columbus's theories he more than made up for by the fervency of his faith. He fully expected that he would end up in the Far East.

Not only was Columbus fiercely determined but he was a superb and knowledgeable sailor, with all the latest navigational tools in his arsenal. But a spirit of almost unimaginable daring was required to face the perils of a transatlantic voyage in his time, since it meant placing oneself at the mercy of harsh elements that could crush and drown one's fragile enterprise at any moment. Nor could Columbus really know exactly where he was going. Despite all his calculations, most of which were wildly inaccurate, his voyage would be a giant leap into the unknown. The shape of the larger world was still a murky mystery, as can be seen in the crude maps at Columbus's disposal, such as the 1491 Henricus Martellus map that he very likely studied in advance of his voyage. After a month at sea without sight of land, his crew began to feel overwhelmed by the dread of a watery death, and they threatened to mutiny. Yet Columbus stood adamant, and his commanding determination prevailed over their worries. The three ships sailed on.

On October 12, his party spotted land, one of the islands of the Bahamas, which Columbus named "San Salvador," meaning "Holy Savior." What they had found was in fact an outpost of a new and unexplored landmass. But Columbus refused to believe that these lands could be anything other than the "Indies" he had counted upon finding, and he accordingly called the gentle Taíno natives who greeted them by the name "Indians." To be sure, he found none of the plentiful spices, jewels, gold, silver, and other precious goods that Marco Polo's account had led him to expect. The Caribbean islands were beguilingly beautiful, but they were full of exotic plants and trees that did not correspond to anything he knew or had read about. He was able to admit that he did not recognize them. But he was not able to imagine that he was looking at an altogether New World.

Between 1492 and 1503, Columbus commanded four round-trip voyages between Spain and the Americas, all of them under the sponsorship of the Spanish Crown. He was not the first European to reach the Americas, but he was the first to establish enduring contact between the Old World and the New. Hence his voyages are of great significance in the history of Europe and mark a proper beginning for our story as the first elements of Europe's unsettlement that would reach western shores and begin to give rise to the settlement of America.

But Columbus was not able to see it that way. He insisted, in the face of all evidence to the contrary, that the lands he visited during those voyages were part of Asia. He was possessed by an iron resoluteness that his initial theory *had* to be true. By his third voyage, which took him to present-day Venezuela, he came to believe that, while that land was not the Indies proper, it was merely a barrier between him and them and that all that remained was to find a strait or other passage through. His final voyage was an unsuccessful effort to find that strait, a journey that took him even to what would later be the site of the Panama Canal, just a few miles away from the immensity of a Pacific Ocean that he never knew was there. But he returned home in disgrace and was regarded as a failure.

What a strange irony it is. He had made one of the most important discoveries in human history, and yet he didn't quite realize it. He was never able to understand the meaning of what he had discovered. His preoccupation with finding a new way to reach the riches of the East was the force that had propelled him into a far more momentous discovery in the West, the mysterious land of mythic renewal. And yet he could not see what was before him with fresh and open eyes. He was blind to its possibilities.

In 1951, almost five hundred years later, the American poet Robert Frost would capture this irony in a witty poem about Columbus called "And All We Call American":

> *Had but Columbus known enough*
> *He might have boldly made the bluff*
> *That better than Da Gama's gold*
> *He had been given to behold*
> *The race's future trial place,*
> *A fresh start for the human race.*
>
> *America is hard to see.*
> *Less partial witnesses than he*
> *In book on book have testified*
> *They could not see it from outside –*
> *Or inside either for that matter.*

America is hard to see. Columbus had trouble seeing America for the new thing that it was, and could be, and eventually would become. He was not the first, and he would not be the last. It is part of the human condition, and a recurrent feature of human history, that what we find is not always what we were looking for, and what we accomplish is not always what we set out to do.

Hence, too, the reality that Columbus's journeys were also the beginning of a great collision of cultures, a process that nearly always entails tragic and bitter consequences. Hence the cruel irony, as we shall see, that the settlement of America by newcomers would also produce a profound unsettlement for those who were not newcomers. The fresh start for the world came at a heavy price for those who were already settled on the land, men and women for whom San Salvador was not a New World being discovered but an old and familiar world about to be transformed.

CHAPTER TWO

THE SHAPING OF BRITISH NORTH AMERICA

O F ALL THE UNSETTLEMENTS THAT EUROPE EXPERIENCED in the years leading up to the establishment of the North American colonies, the most consequential of them involved changes in religion. This is not surprising, because in most human societies for most of human history, religion has served as the shared touchstone of life's meaning and the foundation of culture, the chief vessel bearing the common values and vision of a whole society. Whenever religions change, it means that a great many other things are changing too.

The Western European civilization of the High Middle Ages, which reached its zenith around the year 1300, had been unified around religion, in the form of an almost universally shared Roman Catholic faith. There was only one Christian Church in the western lands in those years, and its power and authority permeated all aspects of life, both spiritual and worldly. Religion's presence was everywhere. The obligations of lords and vassals alike under the feudal system were underwritten by religious oaths. Kings were crowned by churchmen, guilds chose patron saints to represent them, and every town sought to erect its own magnificent cathedral as testimony to its faithfulness.

At the time they were built, the great medieval cathedrals that still dot Europe's landscape served as the focal points of their towns, architectural expressions of the age's confidence in its having found a harmonious union of the sacred and the secular. Like the newly empowered papacy itself, and like the impressively systematic scholastic philosophy of Thomas Aquinas, so too the great cathedrals of Europe expressed the powerful and unified structure of order and authority at which western Europe had arrived. They were an expression of the high tide of Christendom.

That high tide, though, like all such tides, was not destined to last. It would all be undermined and banished by a series of rude disruptions, including massively death-dealing plagues, fierce intrachurch quarrels, and growing secular and national sentiments, conditions culminating in the great upheaval of the Protestant Reformation, which shattered the religious unity of Europe forever.

To understand these revolutionary unsettlements fully, of course, one has to take into account a great many other factors besides religion itself. Religion always exists in the larger context of its times, and it cannot help but be responsive to the political, economic, and social conditions in which it finds itself. Moreover, great historical changes are never attributable to any one single cause alone. There were many reasons why the impressive unity of the High Middle Ages became so deeply unsettled and unable to sustain itself. Religious conflict was often mixed in with other forms of conflict and protest that had little or nothing to do with questions of theology or belief. But the emergence of bitter religious differences would nevertheless serve as a powerful catalyst for conflict and discontent from other sources.

A common theme was a simmering anger and resentment at the worldly grandeur, wealth, and power of the Roman Catholic Church. Peasants and poor laborers felt aggrieved by the Church's unabashed displays of opulence, which seemed to them to be deeply contrary to the humble teachings of their faith's Founder. Middle-class businessmen in the urban areas had other motives: they wanted to be free of the Church's interference in economic life, free to run their own churches and congregations, rather than others governing them from afar. Monarchs and princes, secular leaders who were steadily gaining in power and wealth, also wanted to become more fully masters of their own territories rather than battling with the Church about matters of taxes, property, and legal jurisdiction. And a growing number of religious reformers were increasingly convinced that the Church was guilty not merely of correctable abuses but of terrible doctrinal errors. The stage was set for an eruption.

The first and perhaps most famous of all the catalysts for reform was the German monk Martin Luther, a pious and passionate man who, in 1517, took offense at the Church's practice of selling indulgences, grants of remission understood to ease the path through the afterlife for one's deceased relatives. Luther was especially offended by the sale of indulgences as a way of financing the construction of St. Peter's Basilica, the grand home church of the Pope in Rome. Not only did this practice strike him as unseemly but he found in it the seeds of even more profound errors, which he went on to proclaim to the world in his famous Ninety-Five Theses.

His objections went to the very heart of Christianity's self-understanding as a religion of redemption and salvation. What "justified" a Christian believer in God's eyes and rescued sinners from damnation? It could not be some number of good "works" that the believer was thought to have performed in atonement for sins committed, because no number of good works could be enough to offset that person's transgressions. No, Luther insisted, the grant of salvation was not something humans could ever deserve, let alone work to earn. Only their faith in Christ, granted to them by God through an act of sheer grace, could secure their salvation. Importantly, too, this was not something that could be bestowed on the individual by a priest, or by the institution of the Church, or by any external actions whatsoever. It was a transaction between the soul of the individual believer and God.

The larger implications of this doctrine of "justification by faith" were enormous, and radically unsettling, not only to the Church but to society as a whole. The Catholic understanding of the priesthood had insisted upon the priest as a necessary mediator between individual believers and God. The holy sacraments, such as Holy Communion and Baptism, which only the priest could administer, had been understood as the authentic avenues of God's grace, not available outside the Church or apart from the ministry of an ordained priest.

But if Luther was right, that meant that the Church had been wrong and the priesthood did not perform a necessary function. And Luther went even further, arguing that a great deal of the theology and structure of the Church, including the authority of the Pope, had been invented without reference to the Bible – a grave error, because only the words of the Bible, he insisted, were authoritative in matters of Christian faith. Hence much of the current structure of the Church was deemed fraudulent and corrupt, because any offices or practices that were not grounded in biblical texts were illegitimate. Individuals did not need the guidance of their priests and bishops and popes; they could read the Bible for themselves, making a direct and unmediated contact with God's word and freely arriving at their own interpretation of the text's meaning, according to the dictates of their consciences.

Despite the radical challenge represented by these assertions, Luther did not set out to produce a split in the Catholic church. Nor was he at all interested in fomenting political or social revolution. He was quite conservative in such matters, in fact, and consistently emphasized the importance of obedience to established worldly authority. But the forces he had set into motion could not easily be stilled or slowed. Like a snowball rolling down a mountain slope, they gradually became transformed into a fearsome avalanche. Lutheranism swept through Germany with immense force, drawing some of its strength from dissident groups seeking political and social revolution, such as rebellious

knights and impoverished peasants, and along the way stimulating the formation of more radical religious sects, known collectively as Anabaptists. Lutheranism also became associated with the political efforts of the princes who ran
the free cities and states of the Holy Roman Empire to resist the authority of
Catholic emperor Charles V and claim more of that authority for themselves.
This led to war and to the eventual fragmentation of Germany into a loose collection of increasingly separate states.

The other great theological reformer of the time, the French lawyer John
Calvin, came two decades after Luther, publishing his *Institutes of the Christian
Religion* in 1536. Calvin's critique of the Church resembled Luther's in many
respects, but diverged in several critical ways. For one thing, whereas Luther's
appeal was strongest in the German-speaking world and northern Europe, Calvin's audience embraced the reform minded all over Europe, including places
like the British Isles, where Lutheranism was never to make much headway.

There also were notable theological differences. Calvin strongly emphasized the doctrine of predestination, arguing that God's omnipotence and
omniscience meant that he had willed from all eternity those who would be
saved, the elect, and those who would be damned. Curiously, the rigidity of this
doctrine had a powerful effect on its adherents, quite opposite to what one
might think. It did not make them fatalistic or complacent. Instead, it made
those who were persuaded of its truth, and convinced of their own election,
into paragons of burning conviction, uncompromising perfectionists intent
upon living exemplary lives and comprehensively reforming the world, including the Church. In fact, Calvinists understood each person's labor, no matter
how humble or worldly, as a "calling," a task to be performed as if in service to
God, every bit as much as the tasks of clergy would be. In addition, the Calvinists wanted to strip away all that they believed had been wrongly superadded to
the Church over the course of its history and thereby restore the Church to
something purer and simpler. They wanted the Church to be a community
closer to the laity, closer to what it had been in the time of Jesus.

Reflecting this quest for simplicity, Calvinism rejected the hierarchical
church-governance structure that Lutheranism had taken over from Catholicism. It abolished the institution of bishops in favor of elected bodies made up
of ministers and laymen, bringing a measure of democratic self-governance to
the church. And yet Calvinism also rejected any hint of subordination of the
church to the state, seeking instead to model the state on religious principles
and remake the community itself along religious lines. There was in Calvinism
a revolutionary energy, a desire to transform the world, that spilled over into
all other aspects of life.

John Calvin himself enjoyed remarkable success in establishing just such a prototypical community in the Swiss city of Geneva. It became for a time the Protestant Rome, a destination for reformers of all nationalities who came to witness the living example of a true scriptural community, one whose way of life and forms of worship were regulated by the Bible alone. All over Europe, in places as different as Poland, France, Holland, and Bohemia, dissident groups within established churches found inspiration in Calvin's *Institutes*. In Scotland and England, and then later in America, these zealous reform-minded Calvinists would become known as Puritans.

Luther and Calvin were not the only important figures of the Protestant Reformation. Much more could be said about the profusion of other religious sects emerging at this moment of profound unsettlement in the history of Europe. It is sufficient for our present purposes to make the broader observation that Western Christianity was fracturing and fragmenting into a great many pieces, often along lines that supported the growth of nationalism. The Reformation was like an earthquake whose tremblings radiated out in unpredictable ways through much of the world. Nearly all the forms of fracture it induced would eventually find a home in the New World, which would become an asylum for religious dissenters and nonconformists.

But let us narrow our focus a bit. To understand the eventual character of American religion, as well as American political life, we need to pay special attention not just to the Reformation but to the specific features of the Reformation as it unfolded in England. Like so much else about England, its Reformation unsettlement followed a path all its own, different from that of Continental Europe.

At the time that the Reformation was getting under way in Germany, King Henry VIII of England (who reigned from 1509 to 1547) ranked among its fiercest opponents. He was a strong supporter of orthodox Catholicism and an implacable foe of Lutheranism, so much so that when he penned in 1521 a rousing polemic against Lutheran ideas, Pope Leo X gratefully bestowed upon him the title "Defender of the Faith." But Henry was also a king and faced a looming political problem. His father, Henry VII, whose reign had lasted from 1485 to 1509, had founded the Tudor dynasty that had rescued the English monarchy and nation from years of bitter civil wars and anarchy. The son did not want to see his father's work undone by permitting that violent and divisive history to be repeated. He was intent upon sustaining the benefits of Tudor rule and building a strong and durable monarchy. To do that, he needed a male heir to serve as his legitimate successor. Unfortunately, his first wife, Catherine of Aragon, had not been able to give him a son in twenty-three years of marriage, so he asked Pope Clement VII to grant him an annulment, which would free him to marry a second wife, Anne Boleyn, and try again for a son.

The pope refused the request for complicated political reasons, including the inconvenient fact that Catherine was the aunt of the Holy Roman Emperor Charles V (Charles I of Spain), someone whom Clement dared not offend. Henry responded to this rejection angrily, with lightning speed and brutal decisiveness. He separated the Church of England from the Roman Catholic Church; made himself its supreme head; replaced the archbishop of Canterbury, who then granted his annulment; and married young Anne Boleyn. He then went on to solidify the change by directing Parliament to pass an Act of Supremacy, to which all subjects were thenceforth required to pledge their obedience. He proceeded to close the monasteries in England and seize their extensive lands, which he then parceled out to his followers as a means of securing their loyalty. In the blink of an eye, he had stripped the Roman Catholic Church of all meaningful power in England.

In a sense, this English Reformation that Henry initiated was the exact opposite of Luther's. Questions of theology, not politics, were what had most exercised Luther. But that was not the case with Henry. In fact, aside from his challenge to the pope's authority, Henry had no complaints about the doctrines of the Catholic Church. He would have been happy to keep things just as they had been in every respect other than the magisterial status of the pope. It was politics, not theology, that provoked Henry's break from Rome.

Ironically, Henry never managed to obtain the male heir he sought, despite his marriage to Anne Boleyn (whom he would put to death after three years), and despite Anne being followed in rapid succession by four other wives. After Henry's death in 1547, a turbulent period ensued for English royal politics, in the course of which Catherine's fiercely Catholic daughter Mary came to the throne and attempted to reimpose Catholicism on England. She failed, but it was only when she was succeeded in 1558 by Henry's daughter Elizabeth that stability came at last, and England became firmly committed to an official form of Protestantism, which was called Anglicanism, embodied in a state church to which all English subjects were obliged to belong.

But what kind of Protestantism would this be? That would be ambiguous, by design. Elizabeth, an extraordinarily canny woman who would prove to be one of the greatest monarchs in English history, did not want to heighten the religious strife that had overtaken her country in the years before her ascent to the throne; she wanted to end it. But doing so meant leaving room for all varieties of Anglican faith and practice to coexist peacefully, to the greatest extent possible. There were, for example, a great many High Church elements that emphasized the persisting Catholic aspects of the Anglican faith rather than the Protestant innovations. But there were also many younger bishops and other clergy coming into the church who had been trained on the Continent, where they had been exposed to Calvinist ideas. They sought to bring these ideas to bear on the work of reforming the Church of England.

There was therefore a strong tension between the inherited Catholic-style orthodoxy with which the newly independent Church of England had begun its institutional life and the reforming zeal Calvinist-influenced clergy and laity now brought to church life. This particular form of compounded unsettlement – division between the Church of England and Rome, plus division between and among the factions within the Church of England – would not only shape English and British history for years to come but lie at the heart of the distinctive shape that American religion would assume a century or more later.

These developments matter so greatly to our story because of the eventual prevalence of the English influence in the settlement of North America. But there was nothing inevitable or foreordained about that dominance. In fact, the Spanish were the overwhelmingly dominant colonial power in the western hemisphere for more than a hundred years after Columbus's first voyages of discovery. At a time when the English were too preoccupied with their own internal divisions and near-constant conflicts with the French to explore empire building, the Spanish were rising to their greatest political and civilizational heights, enjoying a period of unprecedented flourishing in the arts and literature as well as a free hand to explore and exploit the resources of the New World.

Beginning with Columbus's ventures in the Caribbean, and then with the explorations of Vasco Núñez de Balboa, Ferdinand Magellan, Hernando Cortés, and others, an intrepid group of explorers in the employ of Spain would establish a Spanish presence and a distinctively Spanish pattern of settlement in the New World and would help to make the Spanish Empire into the most powerful on the globe.

The motives behind Spain's imperial push into the New World were very mixed, and cannot be reduced solely to exploitation and greed. There was a strong element of high-minded and passionate religious conviction behind the efforts of Catholic missionaries. These were men and women whose desire to serve God by spreading Christianity to the populations of the Americas meant their venturing into even the most remote and forbidding places and their willingness to endure extreme privation and suffer martyrdom, if necessary, for the sake of their cause. And even the Spanish *conquistadors* could not have been effective without help from indigenous allies, who saw them as liberators overthrowing the rule of indigenous despots.

But there was also a powerful element of naked materialism driving the colonization effort, a readiness to plunder the land for its gold and silver and other riches, without regard for the needs or wishes of the native populations. Indeed, the Spanish treatment of native populations, beginning with the troubling rule of Columbus himself in the Caribbean islands, and extending to that of the *conquistadors* who undertook the pillaging of the Aztec and Inca civilizations, was often brutally tyrannical and cruelly exploitative, and the Spanish put into effect laws and institutions of colonial governance that froze into place extreme inequalities of wealth and power and reduced the indigenous peoples to the status of subhuman laborers.

It is crucial to keep in mind, though, that the single most important factor leading to the extinction or dramatic reduction of various indigenous peoples after contact with the Spanish was not the cruelty of Spanish rule, but the epidemic spread of Old World diseases such as smallpox, measles, and malaria, to which people in the Americas had never been exposed, and therefore to which they had no natural immunity. Such afflictions would often run rampant through indigenous communities, wiping out entire populations with astonishing speed. This spread of deadly disease was not intentional. It was part of a large, unanticipated, and ultimately mysterious encounter, sometimes referred to as the Columbian Exchange, an encounter between plants, animals, and microbes, that was occasioned by the cultural contact between the Old and New Worlds that Columbus's voyages had initiated.

From the outset, the Spanish government attempted to regulate colonial administration as much as possible, with a view toward making the colonies as profitable as possible for the interests of the mother country. Colonization for the Spanish was an entirely centralized undertaking, following the economic principles of mercantilism and serving the purposes of the Crown, leaving little, if any, room for independent entrepreneurship. There was simply no thought of developing free commerce with the native populations, or more generally of promoting market economies, or otherwise enabling those colonies to mature into free and self-governing societies whose subjects could aspire to the status of citizenship.

So although the riches extracted from the Americas helped make the Spanish Empire fabulously wealthy, the colonies themselves would not be permitted to stray far from the control of centralized Spanish authority. In any event, the Spanish dominance over the New World was not to go unchallenged for long. Beginning in the 1520s, French privateers set their sights on raiding and plundering Spanish treasure ships returning from the colonies with their precious cargo. By the mid-1500s, both the Dutch and the English were supporting privateers of their own, such as the "sea dogs" John Hawkins and Francis

Drake, cunning independent operators who sought to wreak havoc on Spanish shipping in the Atlantic and otherwise defy and undermine Spain's power and influence over its American colonies.

Eventually, the disruptive effects of these raids, many of which were being quietly supported by Elizabeth, took a toll. So too did the grave offense taken by Spain over Elizabeth's execution of her arch-Catholic relation Mary, Queen of Scots, who was found to be plotting to overthrow her. These outrages would lead the Spanish ruler Philip II to seek a large-scale military confrontation with England, through which he was confident he could crush her ambitions once and for all and reinstate Catholicism as England's state religion.

In 1588, Philip assembled an "Invincible Armada" of 130 ships, the largest such fleet ever seen in Europe to date, which would escort an army of some fifty-five thousand men to invade England. Considering these formidable numbers, the battle could have been highly one-sided. But through a series of favorable developments, including the English fleet's brilliant strategists and more maneuverable vessels and superior seamanship, as well as an unexpected "Protestant wind" that swept the Spanish fleet out into the North Sea, the English were able to defeat the Armada soundly and decisively. In doing so, they accomplished far more than merely averting any contemplated invasions of England; they changed the balance of power in Europe irreversibly. From 1588, the star of England was in the ascendant, and the star of Spain was in irretrievable decline.

The defeat of the Armada had an enormous effect on the kind of culture that North America would come to have, if only by determining the kind of culture it would *not* have. That is not to say that North America would ever be exclusively English and that all traces of Spanish heritage and influence would disappear from it overnight. Far from it. All one has to do is notice the many Spanish place-names – Los Angeles, Santa Fe, San Antonio – that persisted across the continent to see that this did not happen. But the defeat of the Armada opened the way for England to take the lead in settling North America, and the result would be a continent and nation whose institutions, laws, and government were determined by their English antecedents.

What were the implications of this English dominance? What shape did the English colonies take as a consequence of it? England itself, as an island nation that developed in comparative isolation from other nations' influences, devised institutions and customs that were very different from those on the European continent. It had a far weaker feudal tradition than its continental rivals, and a far stronger commitment to property rights. As in religion, so in politics and society, the English way of doing things was distinctive.

The monarchies of early modern France and Spain embraced absolutism, which meant greater and greater centralization of power in the hands of a single sovereign whose royal prerogatives were grounded in divine right. But the English followed a very different route, creating a system in which the ruler was limited by forces that divided and restrained his power. The Crown had to share power with aristocrats and gentry, who convened independently in a legislative body called the Parliament that, among other things, held the "power of the purse," the ability to authorize taxes and control the Crown's access to public monies. The Crown did not control government on the local level, which was handled by counties and towns, each of which had its own roster of local public officials – justices of the peace, sheriffs, magistrates, and the like.

And most important of all, the Crown's power was limited by a generally held conviction that the people possessed certain fundamental rights that no monarch could challenge or violate. Such rights were believed to be grounded in something more permanent than the wishes of rulers. They were seated deep in the unique English tradition of common law, an approach to law that relied on judicial precedents built up over many years by generations of judges. Rights such as the right to trial by jury or protection from unwarranted search and seizure were inviolable because they were enshrined in both law and custom, liberties woven into the warp and woof of English historical development.

Another marked difference was the English approach to colonization. Unlike the Spanish, the English tended to approach the project as settlers in the full sense of the term, generally seeking to transplant a recognizably English way of life to the New World. Just as importantly, though, the English approach to colonization was amazingly decentralized and freewheeling, in ways that reflected the English penchant for enterprise and commerce. In short, English colonization of the New World was not a centrally directed government project. The Crown was, of course, involved in various ways, since it was the Crown that granted licenses to colonize Virginia, as the whole area of North America claimed by England was then known, and there was a recognition that the nation as a whole had a stake in these settlements.

But in the end, English colonization was a largely private undertaking. Or rather, it was a haphazard collection of uncoordinated private undertakings, taken on by a diverse group of entrepreneurs, visionaries, and zealots, each seeking the fresh opportunities of the New World for his own purposes, and each being given an extraordinary degree of freedom in pursuing those ends without being steered by a larger national vision. Such initiatives were also facilitated by the ease with which English investors could form joint-stock companies, forerunners of the modern business corporation, which allowed stockholders to pool their capital resources, maximizing their assets while minimizing their potential liabilities, sharing in both the risks and the rewards of colonization.

Each of these undertakings, then, had its own profile, its own aspirations, its own distinctive way of understanding America as a land of hope. Hence the contrasts among them could be very striking, and very instructive. Perhaps the sharpest contrast of all came at the very beginning, between the colonies of Virginia and New England. It is a contrast worth exploring in some detail.

Virginia came first. The first permanent English colony would be established in 1607 at Jamestown, named for James I, Elizabeth's successor. The initial inhabitants consisted of some 105 men sent by the Virginia Company, a joint-stock company, in search of lavish material wealth. Their charter from the King could not have been clearer about that central objective: they were empowered "to dig, mine, and search for all Manner of Mines of Gold, Silver, and Copper." They also located themselves next to a river taking a northwestern direction, a faint indication that they still hoped they might yet in the course of things stumble upon that elusive passage to India.

Unfortunately, nearly all of them were men who had lived their previous lives in town settings and were thus spectacularly ill equipped for almost every aspect of pioneering colonial life. Not only did precious few of them have the requisite knowledge of building, farming, hunting, woodlore, and the like, but the more well-off among them harbored a visceral disdain for most forms of manual labor. They were primarily interested, as was the Virginia Company, in profitable ventures, searching for gold and other precious metals, as well as such absurdly impractical sideline activities as glassblowing and wine production. But they were employees of the Company working for absentee stockholders, and they could not hold private property, so there was no incentive for them to work hard and accumulate wealth. It was a comedy of errors, in a sense, but the results were bitterly tragic. More than half the settlers died during the first winter. Even more of them would have died had it not been for the generous gifts of food made to them by the Powhatan Indians in those early days.

The colony was saved from ruin on that occasion by the heroic leadership of Captain John Smith, who imposed military-style discipline on the colonists, declared that only those who worked would be allowed to eat, put down rebellions and mutinies, and established a semblance of peace and harmony – but only temporarily. Such was the pattern of the early years at Jamestown, characterized by constant struggles with disease, starvation, ignorance, and eventually Indian attacks, when the relationship with the Powhatans went sour. Things seemed always on the edge of breakdown, and the absence of women from the colony reinforced the sense of impermanence, since motley groupings of unattached males were not likely to build families or nurture stable social structures. As of 1624, despite in-migration of more than fourteen thousand souls since 1607, the population of Jamestown stood at barely a thousand. In that year, the Virginia Company was dissolved, and Virginia became a royal colony.

By then, though, changes were afoot that would lead to genuine stability. For one thing, the institution of private property in the form of the freehold had finally been firmly established, so that men who had come over as servants could now be landowners and potentially enjoy the status of freemen. This change meant, as John Smith said, that the indolent man who used to "slip from his labour or slumber over his taske" now worked harder in a day than he used to work in a week.

What finally saved the colony from certain collapse, though, was the discovery of tobacco, a cash staple crop whose export to the home country and the rest of Europe would buoy up the floundering local economy. By 1639 Virginia's tobacco production had soared to three million pounds per year, providing a solid, if somewhat less than entirely admirable, source of general prosperity. With prosperity came more orderly political institutions, including a governor and legislative assembly, as well as the construction of roads and other internal improvements and the establishment of the Anglican church. With prosperity, though, came also ever more conflict with the Indians, whose land many settlers coveted as potential fields into which they could expand the cultivation of tobacco. Conflict over these and other matters eventually led to pitched battles, the most famous of which, Nathaniel Bacon's Rebellion in 1676, pitted the wealthiest planters against the less advantaged people of the colony over an anti-expansionist Indian policy that thwarted access to land on the western frontier.

By this time, the colonies of New England had emerged, beginning with Plymouth Plantation in 1620 and then Massachusetts Bay in 1630, and they could hardly have been more different from Virginia. Whereas the earliest settlers of Virginia had been motivated primarily by material considerations, the New Englanders were driven almost entirely by religious zeal. Most of them were Puritans, men and women who believed the Church of England had not gone far enough to purge itself of its Catholic corruptions, and despaired of such a cleansing renewal ever taking place in their lifetimes. Most were at least comfortably middle class and thus were not impelled to undertake the perilous voyage to the New World by the spur of material need. Instead, they endeavored to make a fresh new start for the life of the Christian Church, a New Zion in a new land. More than that, they understood themselves as on a divinely ordained mission, an "errand into the wilderness," in which they would seek to create "holy commonwealths," models for the reformation of the Church they left behind.

There were important differences in the origins of the Plymouth and Massachusetts Bay colonies. The Plymouth colonists, a group sometimes referred to as the "Pilgrims," were a small group of Separatists who had abandoned the Church of England altogether as a hopelessly corrupted body, preferring to worship in independent congregational (i.e., self-governing) churches. After eleven years of living in exile in the Netherlands, they secured a land patent from the Virginia Company permitting them to establish an English colony where they could practice their faith freely. Over the ocean they came in the *Mayflower* and made landfall at what is today Cape Cod – outside of the Virginia Company's jurisdiction and, indeed, outside the jurisdiction of any known government.

The leaders of the group were aware of the potential dangers in their situation and were especially worried that the colony might not be able to hold together as a law-abiding entity in the absence of any larger controlling authority. In response, they drafted and signed a short document called the Mayflower Compact, which constituted them as a body politic and committed all the signatories to obey the laws and authorities.

It was an important milestone in the development of self-governing political institutions, and it followed the same pattern by which the New Englanders were organizing their self-governing churches. Just as in the Congregational churches, ordinary believers came together to create self-governing churches, so with the Mayflower Compact, a group of ordinary people came together to create their own government. It was an astonishing moment in history, though, because it amounted to a real-world dramatization of the increasingly influential idea that civil society was based upon a "social contract" among its members. Here was a case where a group had actually covenanted with one another, and with God.

Massachusetts Bay came ten years later but would be much larger and more organized and would have more influence over the eventual shape of colonial New England. The Massachusetts Bay Company, a group of Puritans led by the wealthy lawyer John Winthrop, received a charter from King Charles I, James's son. Winthrop and his group were Nonseparating Congregationalists, meaning that, unlike the Pilgrims, they had not yet given up entirely on the Church of England. Nevertheless, in 1630, they undertook the voyage to America with a small flotilla of seven ships, led by the *Arbella*, aboard which was Winthrop and the charter, which he had shrewdly brought along with him rather than leaving it in England. This would give the colony much more independence, because, unlike Virginia, they would not be controlled by a company board of directors located across the sea.

Before they made landfall in America, Winthrop delivered a lay sermon called "A Modell of Christian Charity," in which he laid out the settlement's mission and guiding purposes. This speech leaves one in no doubt about the fundamentally religious intentions behind the colony's existence and the hope that the godly community they were creating could eventually serve as a means of renewal for the Old World they had left behind. Said Winthrop, "We are entered into Covenant with [God] for this work.... For this end, we must be knit together, in this work, as one man.... We must delight in each other; make others' conditions our own; rejoice together, mourn together, labor and suffer together, always having before our eyes our commission and community in the work, as members of the same body.... We must consider that we shall be as a city upon a hill. The eyes of all people are upon us."

It was an audacious statement under the circumstances. Here they were, countless miles away from anyone or anything that was familiar to them, having just crossed a vast and turbulent ocean, cut off from the civilized world and stranded by their own choice, looking out at a land that must have seemed like little more than an inhospitable wild land to them. These were not reckless adventurers but pious families, most of them comfortably situated middle-class people from East Anglia.

And now? Who could possibly imagine that the eyes of all people were upon them? On the contrary, they might as well have been landing on the surface of the moon. No one was watching; no one could know what they were doing. Surely there must have been some among them who quaked a bit, silently and inwardly, and wondered for a moment if it had not all been an act of madness rather than faith that carried them so far away from all they had known, into the terrors and uncertainties of a strange and forbidding land.

Some of the desolation they must have been feeling was well expressed by William Bradford, who led the Pilgrim settlers when they arrived at Cape Cod ten years before:

> *Being now passed the vast ocean, and a sea of troubles before them in expectations, they had now no friends to welcome them, nor inns to entertain or refresh their weatherbeaten bodies, no houses, or much less towns, to repair to, to seek for succor.... Besides, what could they see but a hideous and desolate wilderness, full of wild beasts and wild men? and what multitude of them there were, they knew not: for which way soever they turned their eyes (save upward to Heaven) they could have but little solace or content in respect of any outward object; for summer being ended, all things stand in appearance with a weatherbeaten face, and the whole country, full of woods and thickets, represented a wild and savage hew.*
>
> *If they looked behind them, there was a mighty ocean which they had passed, and was now as a main bar or gulf to separate them from all the civil parts of the world.... What could now sustain them but the spirit of God and his grace?*

What, indeed, but their religious faith could have sustained them, just as it had propelled them across the sea? John Winthrop's words could hardly have been more commanding in that regard. They do not betray any shred of doubt or shadow of turning. The point of calling the colony-to-be a city upon a hill, an image that came straight out of Jesus's Sermon on the Mount in Matthew 5:14–16, was to declare something beyond the mere declaration that this Puritan settlement would strive to be a godly commonwealth and a beacon of light to the world. It was also saying that the colony would be judged by that same high standard, by the degree to which it faithfully carried out the terms of the "commission" that God had assigned it.

We might be tempted to read this as an expression of religious pride, as perhaps it was. But it was equally an expression of religious humility, of a people choosing to subordinate their selfish desires to the accomplishment of their mission: to make a godly place in the New World, for the sake of the renewal of the Old.

So we can see in the contrast between Virginia and New England two of the contrasting aspects of the people and nation that were to come. In Virginia, the motives for settlement were largely material ones, while in Massachusetts Bay, they were frankly religious ones. This is not to say that there were no areas of overlap between the two; Virginia had its distinguished churchmen and Massachusetts Bay its prosperous merchants. But it is fair to say that in the contrast between the two, we can see two very different principles – two different ways of understanding what is meant by the "good life" – on display.

Other British North American colonies were to come, and taken together, they formed a remarkably diverse group, covering a wide spectrum of possibilities. But many of them had in common an intentional quality. They were formed with a larger purpose in mind.

For example, in New England, the intense rigors of the religiously formed regime that Winthrop sought to establish in Massachusetts naturally created friction and dissidents. Under the leadership of Roger Williams, an intense Puritan minister who argued that church and state should be kept completely separate, and that neither Massachusetts nor any other government had the right to coerce men's consciences in matters of faith, the colony of Rhode Island was created as an asylum for dissenters. Connecticut, by contrast, was a Puritan offshoot of both Plymouth and Massachusetts, which contained the New Haven colony, the most rigorously Puritan settlement in all New England.

The middle colonies of New York, Pennsylvania, New Jersey, and Delaware would all be different: more ethnically, economically, and religiously diverse. The colony of Pennsylvania was founded in 1682 to be a common-wealth of the Quakers, a radical nonconforming religious group that arose out of the English Civil War. The Quakers, more formally known as the Society of Friends, went even further than the Puritans in their abjuring of the formal rituals and hierarchies of the Catholic church. They eliminated the clergy altogether, eliminated formal services, and eliminated slavish reliance on the text of the Bible. William Penn, its wealthy founder, considered his colony a "Holy Experiment" and offered freedom of worship to Christians, including Catholics and Jews. He promoted the colony tirelessly and encouraged the immigration of Germans and other non-English-speaking groups. His capital city was called Philadelphia, a Greek name taken from the biblical book of Revelation meaning the "City of Brotherly Love."

The last of the continental colonies, Georgia, founded in 1732 with lands carved out of the province of South Carolina, was similarly motivated by brotherly love. It was the brainchild of a group of London philanthropists who were concerned over the problems of urban poverty, and particularly of debtors who were imprisoned for failure to discharge their debt obligations. The philanthropists sought to obtain a grant of land from the King where these unfortunate debtors could be resettled to start their lives anew. King George II saw the advantages of a buffer colony protecting other British holdings from Spanish Florida; he agreed, the land was granted, and General James Oglethorpe took charge of the project.

An idealistic if somewhat rigid man, Oglethorpe envisioned Georgia as a utopian experiment, in which there were tight restrictions on landholdings and sales, in which rum and other alcohol was banned, and in which the economy was devoted to producing luxury products like silk and wine, which (as it happened) the Georgia climate did not favor. The experiment collapsed within a few years, and Georgia became an ordinary royal colony.

Not all the British colonies reflected such grand intentions on the parts of their founders. The sprawling province of Carolina, for example, was established in 1663 as a payoff by King Charles II to eight nobles who had helped him regain the throne in 1660. The sugar colonies in the Caribbean, such as Jamaica and Barbados, were sources of great wealth and relied heavily on a particularly harsh form of plantation slavery to produce it.

But a striking number of the colonies did reflect idealistic aims, and in that respect they recall the continuing influence of the earliest, most primal impulses that led to the exploration and settlement of the Western world in the first place. The desire to renew the world, to restore it, to recover some portion of the unity that had been lost in the great unsettlement of Europe, to implement more fully some of the ideals that had been set loose in the world by that same unsettlement – all of these hopes and more found ample ground for their further exploration and elaboration in the New World.

Most such attempts failed in important respects to fulfill their original intentions. They started out with one vision, but time and chance happened to them all. Puritan New England could not sustain itself; it had lost most of its religious zeal by the end of the seventeenth century. Quaker Philadelphia was no longer dominated by the Quakers by the time of the American Revolution, a victim of its own policies of toleration. Maryland was established to be a refuge for Catholics but quickly became dominated by Protestants. Georgia's experiment was a grand humanitarian plan that would renew the lives of men, but it fell apart before the expiration of its royal charter, a victim of its own folly and excess, its unrealistic aspirations, and its underestimation of the appeal of sheer human freedom.

It is because of stories like these that the historian Daniel Boorstin declared mordantly that "the colonies were a disproving ground for utopias." There is ample ground for his saying so; it is the ironic side of being a land of hope. Being a land of hope may also mean, at times, being a land of disappointment. The history of the United States contains both. It is hard to have one without the other.

But it would be a mistake to leave it at that. The impulse to hope, and to seek to realize one's hopes in the world, is the inmost spark of the human spirit, every bit as precious as life itself. Much would be learned in the nearly two centuries of British North American colonial life, and much of what was learned came out of the interplay between high hopes and hard realities, and the way in which the one had to learn to accommodate itself to the other. Colonial life was experimental, and even when experiments fail, something important is learned from them. Above all else, what was being learned and acquired in the English colonies was the habit of self-rule, developed in the lives of free colonists who were too distant from their colonial masters to be governable from afar. That habit of self-rule, grounded in English law and custom, but intensified by distance from England itself, was becoming an indelible part of the colonists' way of life.

CHAPTER THREE

THE REVOLUTION OF SELF-RULE

THE HABIT OF SELF-GOVERNMENT IN THE ENGLISH COLONIES of North America was helped along by the fact that the English ran into so many difficulties in imposing an overall colonial policy. The historian Sir John Seeley would quip in later years that his countrymen had managed to create a great empire "in a fit of absence of mind." That was an exaggeration, but it captured an important truth: there had been no master plan at the outset of the British Empire, which meant no blueprint to dictate how the British colonies should be organized and arranged.

Instead, as we have seen, British colonial settlement had been a haphazard and piecemeal thing, left largely in the hands of private entrepreneurs operating independently of one another, pursuing their own goals. But as it turned out, this very "planlessness" would be a major asset and a source of the English colonies' success, both economically and politically. Self-government and economic growth are more likely to flourish in circumstances in which people are free of remote external governance and ambitious entrepreneurs are allowed to operate freely, without the constraints imposed by the stifling hand of centralized governmental direction.

As has already been observed, the English approach differed markedly in this respect from that of the Spanish, and the difference was not entirely a matter of conscious English choice. It had a lot to do with the general circumstances. England was distracted by its own deep and fundamental internal political turmoil, especially during the extended periods of struggle over the course of the seventeenth century between the English kings and the Parliament for political supremacy. It was not possible to formulate an organized governing strategy for overseas colonies in those days, when the most important matter at hand

An eighteenth-century map showing British possessions in North America following the French and Indian War.

was something even more basic: determining what sort of government England would have at home.

The English system of constitutional governance was one of the world's wonders, but it was not established at one stroke, as the product of some one person's or one group's vision. Instead, it evolved organically through a process of many struggles and settlements, the collisions and accommodations between contending parties that are the stuff of historical change. Dramatically different philosophies of government were being played out and fought over in the various parts of Europe during those years.

England was not typical of the times. In much of Europe, it was an age of absolutism, in which the kings of the continent's increasingly unified and powerful nation-states asserted that they ruled by divine right, as absolute monarchs with supreme authority granted them by God. This meant, in the purest version of the theory, that kings were above the law, not under it – not answerable to constitutions or laws, not to legislative bodies, and not to inherited customs or traditions. Mercantilism, the era's most influential economic theory, was entirely consistent with this absolutism. Working from an assumption that a nation's wealth was finite and directly related to its stores of precious metals, mercantilism promoted a high degree of direct governmental intervention in the economy. It used tariffs, trade restrictions, and other forms of centralized control of trade and economic life as ways to protect and promote domestic industries and maximize the flow of gold and silver into the coffers of the mother country.

Such absolutist ideas had great appeal to England's colonial rivals France and Spain and shaped their policies toward their overseas holdings. But absolutism ran flatly against the deepest political and economic traditions of the English, for whom there had long been well-established limits to the power of any king, going back at least to the restraints placed upon King John in the Magna Carta of 1215, and embodied in the practices of the common law and the institution of Parliament. Efforts to impose absolutism in England always had to battle against fierce headwinds. When the Stuart King James I ascended to the throne of England in 1603, and brought with him a belief in divine right, he thereby initiated several generations of heated and often violent conflict between the English kings and their parliamentary opponents.

These struggles went on through much of the seventeenth century, seesawing back and forth through years of a bitter and bloody civil war from 1642 to 1651; through the overthrow and execution of James's successor, Charles I; through the interlude of Oliver Cromwell's dictatorial Puritan Commonwealth; through the Restoration of the Stuart monarchy; and finally culminating in the Glorious Revolution of 1688. That signal event overthrew James II, thereby discrediting the divine right of kings; established parliamentary supremacy and a far-reaching Bill of Rights; and, along the way, provided a vital precedent for the American Revolution of 1776.

During those turbulent years, colonial affairs in the North American mainland languished on the back burner of English policy. Efforts to control trade and impose mercantile controls that would make these colonies more profitable to England were fitful and ineffective. A series of Navigation Acts were passed by Parliament during those years, but none of them were ever enforced consistently or convincingly. Regulating trade was a big and complicated task, especially when it involved colonies an ocean away, and the English lacked both the means and the will to create the complex bureaucracies needed to do the job. Hence North Americans became accustomed to receiving something less than a firm hand of direction from the mother country. Distance was their friend. By the 1720s, a "wise and salutary neglect" (to use the words of Edmund Burke) became the all but explicit spirit of British colonial policy.

Given the absence of any master plan, and the protective buffer of an ocean, experiments in American colonial self-government were free to flourish. To a remarkable degree, the colonies individually repeated struggles very similar to the grand struggle being enacted in English politics. Colonial governors wrestled with their colonial assemblies, just as if they were kinglike executives contending with Parliament-like legislative bodies. They worked toward achieving a balanced equilibrium of forces, establishing little by little the laws and practices and rights that would prevail in each of those particular colonies. Their governments, too, just like that of England, evolved organically, out of conflict and circumstances over many years. Each colony was distinctive; but in many respects, each was an England in miniature. Each had become entirely accustomed to ruling itself.

Of course, citizenship and the ability to participate in the political process in these colonies were severely restricted when measured by our present-day standards, since women, Native Americans, and African Americans were not permitted a role in colonial political life. But it is important to keep that fact in correct perspective. Such equality as we insist upon today did not then exist anyplace in the world. That said, no other region on earth had such a high proportion of its adult male population enjoying a free status rooted in the private ownership of land. A greater proportion of the American population could participate in elections and have a role in selecting their representatives than anyplace else on the planet. These colonists were acquiring the habit of self-rule, and they were not likely ever to want to give it up easily or willingly.

Contrast that development with the steadily ebbing Spanish presence in Mexico and Florida, where fractious settlements suffered from the colonial leaders' need to exert tyrannical control over the native and *mestizo* (mixed-race) populations, even as they were mesmerized by the endless (and often fruitless) search for gold and silver and other resources they could extract from the land. Like desert travelers hypnotized by a shimmering mirage, they pursued mineral wealth obsessively, showing a near-complete incomprehension of the entirely different forces – freedom, enterprise, room for ingenuity, rule of law, private property rights – that were leading to broad economic success and thriving long-term settlements in the British colonies. Or consider the French in the New World, who formed friendlier relationships with native populations but never got beyond thinking of their thinly populated and widely disbursed settlements as little more than glorified French trading posts. The English approach, propelled by an uncoordinated multitude of private investors who were allowed to pursue their interests as they saw fit, was distinctive, and that distinctiveness would make all the difference.

It was not long before these different approaches to colonization came into conflict. The rival European powers had largely been able to steer clear of getting into fights with one another in the New World for most of the seventeenth century; there had been room enough for everyone. But that peaceful state of affairs could not last. In the seventy-five years after the Glorious Revolution there would be four great European and intercolonial wars, the last of which, the Seven Years' War, would be particularly important to the future of America, where it came to be referred to as the French and Indian War, and would last from 1754 to 1763.

The French and Indian War was enormously consequential. It would dramatically change the map of North America. It would also force a rethinking of the entire relationship between England and her colonies and bring to an end any remaining semblance of the "salutary neglect" policy. And that change, in turn, would help pave the way to the American Revolution.

The French and Indian War began to take shape in North America in the early 1750s, when Pennsylvania fur traders and land-hungry Virginians began to venture into new territory, across the Allegheny Mountains and into the Ohio River Valley. Their incursion brought them into contact with French settlements and trading interests and produced an angry reaction from the French, who drove the British interlopers back and proceeded to construct forts in western Pennsylvania to protect their interests.

A British delegation, including a twenty-one-year-old militia officer named George Washington, was sent to the French to mediate the conflict, but it returned empty-handed. A subsequent mission to the area, led by Washington, with the goal of building a fort at the site of present-day Pittsburgh encountered armed French resistance and suffered a humiliating defeat. Then, in 1755, British general Edward Braddock was dispatched to Virginia to take care of the situation. After hacking his way through the wilderness of the upper Potomac, though, he found himself soundly defeated by guerrilla forces made up of a combination of Ojibwa Indians and French soldiers. Braddock's forces sustained some nine hundred casualties, which included the loss of Braddock's own life.

Such disappointing results induced British prime minister William Pitt to dial up the power and make America the principal field of conflict with France in the Seven Years' War. He recognized far better than most of his contemporaries the enormous ultimate value of North America, and accordingly, he poured

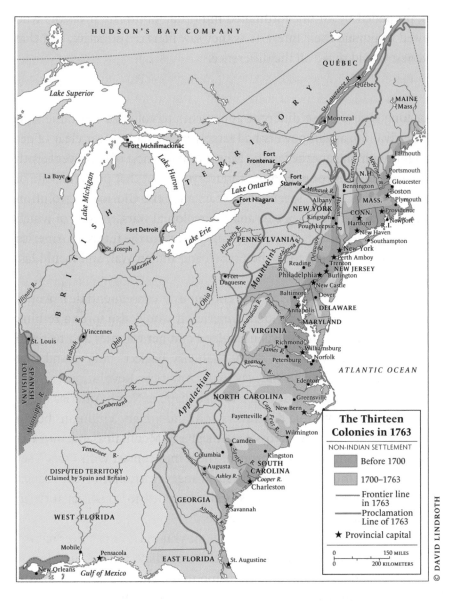

A schematic of the territorial results of the French and Indian War, including the proclamation line of 1763. The map overlies boundaries of present-day states.

resources from the national treasury into the cause – lavishly, even recklessly, in ways that would weigh on the country's future. He mobilized forty-five thousand troops for the purpose and invested a lot of money – the economist Adam Smith estimated it at £90 million – all the while treating the colonists as partners in the war enterprise. His efforts bore fruit in 1759 with a series of military victories, at Fort Niagara, Lake Champlain, and most decisively of all, on September 13, 1759, at Quebec City, where General James Wolfe made short work of the French infantry on a plateau known as the Plains of Abraham, an hour-long battle that effectively put an end to French ambitions in North America.

The war was formally concluded with the Treaty of Paris in February 1763, making French North America a thing of the past, except for two tiny islands off the coast of Newfoundland and a few remaining islands in the Caribbean. England, now more properly called Great Britain, took over Canada and the eastern half of the Mississippi Valley. It was a great victory and seemed to cement British dominance in the New World.

But every great victory in war means the creation of a new set of problems in peace, and the French and Indian War was no exception to the rule. This victory would mean the end of the era of "benign neglect," the source of so much creativity and freedom in the British colonies. Such loose-jointed independence could not be allowed to continue. This outcome was doubly ironic, because the war's waging and results had produced a surge of pride among American colonials, and the shared experience of war generated in many of them the first stirrings of American national sentiment, the feeling that there was something more than just their shared British language and cultural heritage that bound them together. There were even tentative explorations of some manner of colonial union. That took the form of a meeting held in Albany, New York, in 1754, dubbed the Albany Congress, at which representatives of seven of the thirteen British colonies considered a Plan of Union, proposed by a committee headed by Benjamin Franklin.

But it was the British who had won the war, not the Americans, and it was the British who had to pay for it – a mammoth expense, which included putting the nation under the burden of some £58 million of additional debt. As a result, it seemed inevitable that there would have to be a tightening of imperial control over the colonies. As Adam Smith observed, it was no longer possible for the colonies to be considered "provinces of the British empire" which "contribute neither revenue nor military force toward the support of the empire." In other words, the days of the colonies enjoying a free ride, not being required to pay taxes as British citizens, were over. It made sense to devise an imperial system within which the Americans would pay their fair share. But how to do this? How to go about the business of consolidating the British Empire, while maintaining the profoundly English tradition of self-rule in its constituent elements? This was not going to be an easy problem to solve.

War was not the only common experience beginning to draw the disparate colonies together, laying the groundwork for a national form of consciousness and a commensurately national form of self-rule. Religion, which had from the beginning been one of the mainstays of American colonial life, provided another. It is true that, by the beginning of the eighteenth century, there had been an ebbing of the religious zeal that had motivated the first Puritan and Quaker settlers, as the colonies became more settled and more wealthy and comfortable, less convinced of their dependency on God. But that period of religious lassitude did not last.

Beginning in the 1730s, waves of religious and spiritual revival began to sweep up and down the British colonies along the North American coast, a mass movement led by gifted and charismatic evangelical preachers that came to be called the Great Awakening. The coming of what would be called "revivalism" would transform the church life of the colonies and introduce a new, more emotional and experiential approach to worship: the evangelical style.

The fuse for this explosion of religious energy was lit by the itinerant minister George Whitefield, a powerfully dramatic and golden-voiced British preacher who arrived in Philadelphia in 1739 and traversed the colonies, everywhere drawing huge crowds of enthusiastic believers who were seeking the "new birth" of sudden religious conversion. Whitefield's success was a measure of the depth and breadth of the colonies' religious hunger. But his efforts had been preceded by those of the brilliant American-born theologian Jonathan Edwards, whose preaching at the Congregational church in Northampton, Massachusetts, in the earlier years of the 1730s become famous and, according to many accounts, had transformed western Massachusetts from a spiritual desert to an oasis of piety and spiritual joy.

Edwards was a profoundly learned man and a gifted and original thinker who sought to restore the rigor and depth of New England's original Calvinism. He wanted to produce repentance in the hearts of his torpid, backsliding listeners, and to do so, he adopted an approach to preaching that was not only intellectually rich but emotionally compelling, filled with extraordinarily vivid and concrete imagery that would use the senses to make tangible the ideas and principles about which he was teaching. He is particularly famous today for his 1741 sermon "Sinners in the Hands of an Angry God," delivered to the congregation at Enfield, Massachusetts, which is notable for its fiery depiction of the fearful torments of damnation and the greatness of human dependency upon God. But such "fire and brimstone" is not typical of Edwards, and some of his finest sermons were devoted to the experience of spiritual awakening and the workings of divine grace. For example, he concluded "A Divine and Supernatural Light" (1734) with these mystical words: "This light, and this only, has its fruit in a universal holiness of life. No merely notional or speculative understanding of the doctrines of religion will ever bring to this. But this light, as it reaches the bottom of the heart, and changes the nature, so it will effectually dispose to a universal obedience."

There were other important transformative effects of the Great Awakening. It was, to begin with, an event that had been experienced throughout the colonies as something fresh and new – a form of religious expression that was dramatically different from the inherited and transplanted religious beliefs and practices that the colonists' forebears had brought with them. It emphasized individual conversion and behavior more than adherence to orthodox doctrine and forms. It appealed directly to the common people – to laborers, servants, farmers, and the like. It caused, in church after church, challenges to the established clergy and old, entrenched leadership class of those churches, often leading to congregational divisions and bitter institutional splits between the old and the new – Old Lights versus New Lights, Old Side versus New Side. In the end, it established a freewheeling evangelical individualism, operating independently of church discipline and authority, that became one of the hallmarks of American religion, especially in the North. All across the colonies, something like the principle of self-reliance was penetrating even to the inmost life of religious believers.

Similar currents of thought were evident, though, in secular channels of early American thought. If religion was congenial to colonial America, so too were the ideas of the Enlightenment, a diverse and powerful intellectual movement whose chief figures understood the world as a rational and orderly place governed by natural laws that could be discovered and made fully intelligible to the human mind through the careful and disciplined methods of modern experimental science.

America would prove to be especially fertile ground for the Enlightenment, since it was a new land, a land of new societies – a land of nature rather than culture. What it lacked in the rich traditions and vast historical background of the mother country, it made up precisely in its freedom from the weight of historical baggage, its openness to experiment, its can-do optimism, and its ability to set aside whatever was customary, instead taking a fresh look at things, starting from no authority but reason. It was not a coincidence that America would become the first place on earth where the idea that each individual possessed natural rights – rights that derived from nature or God, not from the hand of any king or agency of government – would take hold strongly.

The Enlightenment would be yet another expression of Europe's unsettlement, every bit as powerful and important in its effects as the Reformation. It arose out of the Scientific Revolution of the seventeenth century, which overthrew the ancient earth-centered view of the cosmos, enshrined since the time of Aristotle, and all the antiquated preexperimental science that came with it. The revolution was aided by certain crucial inventions, such as dramatic improvements in optical devices like telescopes and microscopes, but above all else, it was a revolution in thought. Through the work of distinguished scientists, such as Sir Isaac Newton, who developed modern calculus as a tool for the measurement of continuous change, this revolution established universal laws of motion that could be formulated in precise mathematical language.

Before Newton, there was no *dynamic* theory of motion – one that could, for example, explain what physical forces were at work causing the moon to orbit the earth rather than merely career out into space and causing other celestial bodies to move in more or less circular paths. After Newton, gravitation entered the world picture as an explanation and as a force that could be quantified and precisely calculated: the attractive force of gravity between two objects was directly proportional to the product of their masses and inversely proportional to the square of the distance between them. The laws of motion that Newton propounded applied as much to earth-bound things as to celestial ones; there was one set of laws for all physical reality.

But this intellectual revolution had further repercussions. It provided a way of thinking about the world – as law based, orderly, and intelligible, its secrets fully accessible to the mind of man – that seemed to have unlimited application. Similar explanatory principles could, in theory, be extended to all other subjects of human inquiry: not just astronomy, not just the physical sciences, but also politics, society, economics, and all other forms of human activity and relationship. If clear and understandable natural laws could be found to undergird the movement of the planets and all other physical objects, there seemed no reason why similar laws could not be discovered at the root of everything else.

No American figure epitomized the Enlightenment more fully than Benjamin Franklin. None better exemplified the opportunities that America provided an energetic and self-reliant young man, who came into the world without any credentials or pedigree, to rise in the world by the sheer power of his ambition, pluck, and innate genius.

Born in 1706 to a pious Puritan candlemaker in Boston, Franklin ran away from home at the age of seventeen and came to Philadelphia, where he quickly established himself as a printer. It did not take long for him to begin making his mark. By the age of twenty, he was publishing the *Pennsylvania Gazette*, an influential forum for political and social commentary. Then, a few years later, he began publishing the yearly *Poor Richard's Almanack*, an entertaining collection of weather forecasting, poems, witty aphorisms ("Lost time is never found again" or "Three may keep a secret, if two of them are dead"), and puzzles that made his larger reputation and became a mainstay of colonial life.

In his early forties, Franklin retired from business and devoted himself instead to his many other interests, which included the scientific study of electricity and other phenomena. He won international fame for his work in these areas and also as a fountain of practical inventiveness, with innovations such as the Franklin stove, the glass harmonica, the lightning rod, bifocal glasses, and countless other creations to his credit.

His creativity also extended to social and institutional inventions: he founded the first circulating library in America, one of the first volunteer fire departments, the American Philosophical Society, and the first hospital in Philadelphia and the forerunner of the University of Pennsylvania. Perhaps most important of all, his wise and pragmatic guidance and diplomatic skills would be of crucial importance to the greatest social innovation of his day: the United States of America.

In a sense, Jonathan Edwards and Benjamin Franklin could be taken as contrasting symbols of the two most distinctive intellectual currents of the time in British colonial America. But they are not as contrasting as they might look at first glance. It might seem logical to us today that there would be a necessary incompatibility and antagonism between the passionate Bible-based Protestant religious faiths of colonists like Edwards and the methodical new science embraced by the likes of Franklin – particularly when the logic of Newton's mechanistic model of the cosmos was pressed to its limits. But this was not quite the way things looked to Americans of the time.

In the Anglo-American world of the eighteenth century, the spirit of Protestantism and the spirit of science were not seen to be in fundamental conflict with one another. Belief in some version of the biblical God and belief in an ordered and knowable universe were not seen as at all incompatible. There was a high degree of tolerance of religious differences, a by-product of the remarkable religious diversity of the colonies. Beliefs easily intersected; Edwards himself had a keen interest in Newton's new science and saw the orderliness of nature as evidence of God's masterly design, while Franklin, who tended toward Deism in his own beliefs, was captivated by George Whitefield's preaching, and by its salutary effects upon his listeners, when the latter came to Philadelphia.

It is also the case that, despite their differences, these two currents had certain important features in common. They shared a skepticism about received or traditional institutions and a lack of deference to established forms of authority, whether in the church or in politics. Both understood themselves as an expression of the spirit of liberty. No less than the Enlightenment, the Great Awakening and the Protestant revivalism it embodied weakened the power of all traditional churches and clergy, Protestant and Catholic alike, and indeed of all figures of authority, while making the emerging forms of religious life dependent upon the judgments of each person's free and uncoerced conscience.

Such changes would have effects far beyond matters of religion. Among other things, they would make it easier for the American colonists, who were beginning to think of themselves as a distinct people, to contemplate an act of rebellion against King and empire.

In the wake of the French and Indian War, a huge new British Empire now encircled the globe – which meant that the long-deferred problem of imperial organization, or disorganization, finally had to be faced, particularly with respect to the American colonies. Theoretically, those colonies were entirely subject to the King and Parliament, but in practice, that authority had never been effectively exercised. Parliament had never tried to raise revenue in America, and Benjamin Franklin himself firmly opposed the idea, stating that doing so without the colonists' consent would be tantamount to "raising contributions in an enemy's country" rather than "taxing Englishmen for their own benefit." And that was precisely how many of the colonists saw the matter. But that did not mean that Parliament did not have a legal and legitimate right to raise such taxes, should it ever choose to do so. Under the policy of "salutary neglect," the matter had been left dangling. That would not continue to be the case much longer.

Even before the formal conclusion of the war, with the signing of the Treaty of Paris in 1763, the British were moving toward consolidating the empire. One notable example occurred in 1761, when the use of general search warrants (known as writs of assistance) was authorized as a way of allowing British customs officials to crack down on colonial smugglers who were trading with the French in the West Indies. They could enter any place for any reason, in search of evidence of illegal trade.

Americans reacted in horror to this invasion of their privacy and violation of their rights, and a group of merchants hired Boston lawyer James Otis to fight the writs in court. Otis lost the case, but his argument that the very institution of the writs violated the British constitution was an argument that made great sense to his clients and supplied an important precedent for the years ahead.

Another burdensome issue facing the British was what to do about the lands west of the Appalachian Mountains, which were still inhabited by Indian tribes. The victory over the French had given British colonial settlers new impetus to westward expansion into Indian lands; such intrusions had in turn precipitated a bloody reaction, known as Pontiac's Rebellion, in which the embattled tribes attempted to push white settlers back across the mountains and toward the ocean. The rebellion failed, but the British wanted to forestall any repeat experience and thus, in response, adopted a new western policy: by the terms of the Royal Proclamation of 1763, no settlers were to cross an imaginary line running across the tops of the Appalachian Mountains.

This edict was understandably unpopular with Americans, but the public response to it was relatively subdued, partly because it did not directly involve taxation and settlers felt free to defy it. It appeared to be yet another grand but ineffective measure, like those that had been tried and failed in the past. But there was a far more intense reaction against other measures soon put forward under the leadership of Prime Minister George Grenville, a flinty, hardheaded accountant who was determined to make the prosperous Americans pay some of the cost for their own protection.

The Sugar Act, proposed in 1764, placed tariffs on sugar, tea, coffee, and wine, all products that Americans needed to import. Smugglers who were accused of violating the act were to be tried before British naval officers in a maritime court based in Halifax, in which they would not enjoy the presumption of innocence. And in a further intrusion into the colonies' customary practices of self-governance, the Currency Act of 1764 sought to end the colonies' practice of printing their own paper money as a means of easing currency shortages.

Neither measure had a positive effect. The Currency Act only deepened the postwar economic decline from which the colonies were suffering, and the Sugar Act failed to produce any additional revenue, since whatever monies it took in by more rigid enforcement of the Sugar Act were more than offset by the bureaucratic costs of administering it. But the message was clear: after the French and Indian War, and under the leadership of Grenville, the era of Britain's easygoing inattention to the colonies was screeching to a halt. And there was much more to come.

The pace of intrusion quickened even more in 1765, when Parliament produced the Stamp Act, which required that revenue stamps be purchased and affixed to legal documents and printed matter of all kinds, ranging from newspapers to playing cards. The same year, Grenville directed Parliament to pass the Quartering Act, which required the colonial legislatures to supply British troops with barracks and food wherever they were – in effect, another form of taxation. The justification offered for both measures was that they legitimated means by which the colonists could be induced to help pay for their own defense. But the Stamp Act did not work either; in fact, it did not produce any revenue at all. The colonists simply refused to abide by it.

Why did they react so strongly? For one thing, it was because this Act involved direct taxation rather than trade policy and as such raised the specter in colonists' minds that the whole fabric of their relatively free existence might be in eventual jeopardy. In the words of Boston clergyman Jonathan Mayhew, almost every British American "considered [the Act] as an infraction of their rights, or their dearly purchased privileges." Virginia's Patrick Henry insisted that his colony's House of Burgesses had "the only and sole and exclusive right and power to lay taxes" and that Parliament had no such right or authority. Protests against the Stamp Act were everywhere, a veritable flood of pamphlets, speeches, resolutions, and public meetings in which the cry of "no taxation without representation" was heard far and wide. Some protests turned violent, with British stamp officials being harassed, vandalized, and hanged in effigy, the stamps themselves confiscated and burned. By the time the law was to take effect in November 1765, it was already a dead letter.

Once again, Grenville and Parliament had grossly misjudged the situation. Grenville concocted a doctrine called "virtual representation" to explain how it was that the colonists could be represented in Parliament even if they could not send their own popularly elected members to take part in it. Some Britons found this idea persuasive, but the colonists, deeply rooted as they were in the habit of self-rule, and already thoroughly accustomed to using their own colonial representative assemblies, dismissed it as rubbish and sophistry, incompatible with the principle that government derives its just powers from the consent of the governed.

Grenville's aggressive actions portended a radical overturning of their accustomed way of life and an imposition of the very same royal tyranny that the English themselves had fought against so valiantly in the seventeenth century, and from which Parliament had finally saved them in the Glorious Revolution. It was as if the same history was being reenacted, with many of the same danger signs in evidence.

Why were the British imposing a standing army in the western lands, if not to confine and suppress the colonists? Why were the new vice-admiralty courts overriding the primordial English commitment to trial by jury, if not for the purpose of imposing the heavy hand of empire upon local liberty? Why was Parliament infringing upon the colonial assemblies' power of the purse, thereby depriving them of one of the most fundamental of English rights? The colonists had a pattern close at hand in their own history that could make sense of these questions.

Finally, the British appeared to pull back from the brink. In 1766, Grenville was dismissed from office and replaced by the more flexible and sympathetic Marquis of Rockingham. In addition, Parliament repealed the Stamp Act. But what Parliament was giving with one hand it was taking away with the other. On the same day that it repealed the Stamp Act, it passed a Declaratory Act stating that Parliament's power over the colonies was unlimited in principle and that it could enact whatever law it wished "to bind the colonies and people of America." This assertion was more than just a face-saving gesture. It was stating, under the cover of reconciliation, an unambiguous principle of sovereignty to which Parliament could turn and which it could invoke decisively in future battles.

For the British had not abandoned the goal of consolidating the empire, and that inevitably meant finding a way to tax the colonies. The next nine years of fractious history represented a steadily intensifying effort on Britain's part to establish the imperial control that had so far eluded them, met by a steadily mounting resistance on the colonists' part, and accompanied by a growing awareness on the colonial side that the issues separating them from the mother country were becoming deeper by the day and were perhaps even irreconcilable.

The Declaratory Act offered clear evidence that lurking beneath all the particular points of conflict between England and America were fixed and sharply divergent ideas: about the proper place of America in the emerging imperial system, about the meaning of words like *self-rule*, *representation*, *constitution*, and *sovereignty*. It was a genuine debate, in which both sides had legitimate arguments. But it did not help that, as time went by, British leaders seemed less and less inclined to listen to the colonial perspective and more inclined to crush it.

What followed, in the years after the Stamp Act contretemps, was a series of inconclusive conflicts that seemed, in retrospect, to do little but heighten the inevitability of armed conflict. The next round began in 1767, when the chancellor of the exchequer, Charles Townshend, introduced a new revenue plan that included levies on glass, paint, lead, paper, and tea imported into the colonies. To this the colonists responded with boycotts of British goods, with efforts to promote colonial manufacturing and with a growing radical resistance movement, headed by firebrand agitators like the brewer Samuel Adams of Boston. Eventually, after the 1770 Boston Massacre resulted in the deaths of five Americans at the hands of British soldiers, Parliament repealed all the Townshend duties, except the one on tea. Things settled down somewhat until 1773, when a group of sixteen disguised colonists dumped a load of East India Company tea into Boston Harbor, thus carrying out the famous Boston Tea Party. This incident immediately elicited an enraged response from Parliament in the form of four Coercive Acts, or as the colonists called them, Intolerable Acts. They annulled Massachusett's charter, closed Boston harbor, forced colonists to quarter British troops, and moved trials for capital crimes outside of the area in which the crimes were committed. These actions were designed to take control of the legal and economic system, turn Boston into an occupied city, and thereby single it out for visible humiliation, making it an ominous example to all the others.

This divide-and-conquer strategy did not work either. Instead, it caused the other colonies to rise up and rally to Boston's cause, not only by sharing supplies and intensifying boycotts of British goods but by inducing them to convene a first-ever Continental Congress that would represent the interests of all the colonies – a clear step in the direction of a political union.

When the Continental Congress met in Philadelphia in September 1774, it formally endorsed the various forms of lawful resistance to the Coercive Acts, particularly the boycotts, and endorsed a Declaration of American Rights, which expressed the colonial view as to the limited authority of Parliament. Exactly how to define the extent of that limitation, however, was a matter about which there would be disagreement. Did Parliament retain the right to regulate trade alone – or was even that right now in question, as the Boston lawyer John Adams, a cousin of Sam Adams, asserted?

In the meantime, the boycott movement was becoming more effective, tapping into the patriotic passions of thousands of ordinary Americans who were willing to express their alarm at the British threats to American liberty. It was the same common people – farmers and working men – who volunteered to serve in militias, such as the Minutemen of Massachusetts, for the same reasons. This was no longer the behavior of loyal subjects but increasingly that of liberty-loving citizens yearning to remain free and restore their customary practices and legal rights.

A profound shift of sensibility was taking place. As John Adams asserted, reflecting many years later on the events he had lived through, "The Revolution was effected before the war commenced. The Revolution was in the minds and hearts of the people; a change in their religious sentiments of their duties and obligations." The people of America were disposed to revere their King and their British institutions; but when they saw their King, and all in authority under him, renouncing "the laws and constitution derived to them from the God of nature and transmitted to them by their ancestors" and behaving like tyrants, "their filial affections ceased, and were changed into indignation and horror.... This radical change in the principles, opinions, sentiments, and affections of the people, was the real American Revolution." It was a revolution of the mind and heart they had begun.

The direction of this gathering storm was clear to the British leadership, which was more disposed than ever to have a showdown with the colonies. Britain's King George III put it bluntly: "The New England governments are in a state of rebellion. Blows must decide whether they are to be subject to this country or independent." In this respect, he faithfully reflected the general state of British opinion, which wanted to bring to a swift end what looked increasingly like sheer insurrection on the part of a maddeningly ungrateful people.

The fuse of war was lit at last in April 1775, when orders reached the royal governor of Massachusetts, Thomas Gage, to move aggressively to stop the rebellion. Gage decided to march seven hundred red-coated British troops to Concord, a town about twenty miles west of Boston, where he would seize a militia supply depot that had been established by the Patriot forces. Along the way, in the town of Lexington, the British encountered a rag-tag group of seventy Minutemen in the town common. It was dawn, but the men were there because they had been warned, by the famous midnight ride of Paul Revere, that the British were coming.

After some taunting shouts and argument, the Patriot militiamen were beginning to withdraw – but then a shot was fired, leading the British to fire on the group, killing eight of them. Then the British marched on to Concord, where they encountered half-empty storehouses and stiff resistance, as alerted militiamen swarmed into the area. After losing fourteen men in a skirmish at Concord's North Bridge, the British began to retreat to Boston and faced withering and deadly fire along the entire bloody way back. In the end, the British lost three times as many men as the Americans.

So the war had begun, and the conflict spread to Fort Ticonderoga in upper New York, and to the hills overlooking Boston, where the Americans again showed their military mettle, inflicting over a thousand casualties on a startled British Army in the Battle of Bunker Hill. But the war's objectives were not yet clear, since independence had not yet been declared.

Even some who identified wholeheartedly with the Patriot cause still found it impossible to contemplate such a final break from Britain. John Dickinson of Pennsylvania had poignantly expressed their anxieties at the time of the Townshend Acts: "If once we are separated from our mother country, what new form of government shall we accept, or when shall we find another Britain to supply our loss?" It seemed to him that the American colonies were too weak and divided to constitute themselves as a nation and that the ties of common culture with Britain were too many and too strong to be broken without incalculable and fatal loss. "Torn from the body to which we are united, by religion, liberty, laws, affections, relations, language, and commerce, we must," he feared, "bleed at every vein." And that was not all. There might be even worse fates in store than being tyrannized by the British Crown. There might be domination by other hostile powers. And the disturbances in Boston and elsewhere suggested the possibility of mob rule and anarchy.

Several more things had to happen for the movement to independence to become unstoppable. First, the British government refused to consider any form of compromise. King George III summarily rejected a conciliatory appeal known as the Olive Branch Petition, written by Dickinson, refusing even to look at it, and choosing instead to label the colonists "open and avowed enemies." Then the King began to recruit mercenary Hessian soldiers from Germany to fight the Americans, a gesture that the colonists regarded as both insulting and callous, a way of signaling that they were no longer fellow Englishmen.

Finally, there was the publication in early 1776 of Thomas Paine's pamphlet *Common Sense*, which argued with bracing logic for the "necessity" of independence, artfully directing colonial grievances away from the impersonal Parliament and focusing them instead upon the very personal figure of the King himself, whom Paine then attacked not only in the form of the current monarch (whom he mocked as a "Royal Brute" and a "Pharaoh") but in the very idea of monarchy itself. Oddly, Paine himself was a Briton who had only been in America a year, a rootless and luckless soul in his late thirties who had failed at nearly everything else he had attempted. But he proved to have a talent for political agitation and stirring rhetoric.

He had brought with him a deep commitment to the idea of natural rights and the republican ideal of self-rule, along with a vivid and explosive prose style that made the case for complete independence with greater power and grace than anyone before him. His pamphlet was read by or known to virtually everyone in the colonies and sold more than 150,000 copies (roughly the equivalent of three million copies today) within the first three months of 1776. Its effect was electrifying. "*Common Sense* is working a powerful change in the minds of men," admitted George Washington, who would soon be a leader of the Patriot cause. Paine had connected the dots as no one before him had done and had brought sharp definition to an unsettled situation. He made the path forward unmistakably clear.

Finally, at the urging of the provincial governments, the Continental Congress began to move decisively toward independence. Richard Henry Lee of Virginia introduced a motion on June 7 "that these United Colonies are, and of right ought to be, free and independent states." The resolution passed on July 2, which really should be the day that Americans celebrate Independence Day. But it was two days later, on the Fourth of July, that the Congress adopted the Declaration of Independence, a remarkable document, drafted mainly by the thirty-three-year-old Thomas Jefferson of Virginia, that served at once as a press release to the world, listing the specific reasons for the Americans' actions, but also as a presentation of the key elements of a foundational American political philosophy. It was, and has continued to be, a document that had both practical and philosophical dimensions and that carried both particular and universal meanings.

Reflecting on the matter nearly fifty years later, a year before his death in 1826, Jefferson explicitly and rightly disclaimed any great originality in his ideas. "I did not consider it any part of my charge to invent new ideas," he insisted; his goal in writing the Declaration was "not to find out new principles" but to "place before mankind the common sense of the subject" and formulate "an expression of the American mind" that would draw its authority from "the harmonizing sentiments of the day." In other words, he sought to articulate the things about which nearly all Americans agreed rather than staking out territory that might be regarded as controversial. In some of his text, he drew upon his own political writings and on those of his fellow Virginian George Mason, but the deep structure of the argument came straight out of John Locke's *Second Treatise of Civil Government*, particularly the idea that civil society was best understood as a contract between and among its constituent members.

Accordingly, Jefferson proclaimed it a "self-evident" truth that all men were created equal and were endowed by their Creator – and not by their government or any other human authority – with certain rights, including "life, liberty, and the pursuit of happiness." Governments existed to secure these rights and derived their powers from the consent of the governed – a crisp statement of the basic principle of self-rule. When a government failed to secure those rights and failed to sustain the consent of the governed, when it evinced a "design" to deprive the colonists of their liberty, it was no longer a just regime, and the people had the right to abolish and replace it – which is to say, they had a right of revolution.

A long list of grievances followed, laying nearly all the blame at the feet of the King, following the personalization strategy that Paine had so expertly deployed in *Common Sense*. "He has refused his Assent to Laws.... He has dissolved representative houses.... He has obstructed the Administration of Justice.... He has kept among us standing armies.... He has plundered our seas, ravaged our Coasts, burnt our towns, and destroyed the lives of our people.... A Prince whose character is thus marked by every act which may define a tyrant is unfit to be the ruler of a free people."

The grievances built forcefully to the Declaration's inescapable conclusion, echoing the words of Lee's motion: "That these United Colonies are, and of Right ought to be free and independent states; that they are absolved from all Allegiance to the British Crown, and ... have full power to levy War, conclude Peace, contract Alliances, establish Commerce, and to do all other Acts and Things which Independent States may of right do."

The Declaration was a magnificent and enduringly influential document, read and admired around the world as one of the greatest of all charters of human dignity and freedom. Its eloquence gave immense impetus and plausibility to the colonial cause, while at the same time strengthening the cause of liberty in France and other places around the world. Yet many questions remained unanswered. The document was very clear about the form of union it was rejecting. But what kind of union was it embracing? What would it mean to have a colonial union of free and independent states – was that not a contradiction in terms? How was it possible to be both united and independent?

And then there were those pregnant words, "all men are created equal." What did they mean? Did they contemplate equality in only the narrowest sense – that the colonists were in no way politically inferior to the arrogant Britons who were trying to deprive them of their rights? Or was there a larger and more universal sense to those words? Did they apply only to males, or did the term *men* tacitly include women? Were they compatible with the obvious forms of inequality, of wealth and ability and status, that had existed in all previous human societies?

And what about the institution of slavery, the very existence of which in all thirteen colonies in 1775 would appear to call into question the legitimacy of Jefferson's most resonant words? Jefferson himself owned slaves, despite his moral misgivings about the institution of slavery and his consistent denunciation of the Atlantic slave trade as an "abomination." What did he think he was saying when he wrote those words about "all men"? How could those words accommodate an institution that permitted ownership in human flesh? How to answer the gibes of men like the English theologian John William Fletcher who sneered that the Americans were "hypocritical friends of liberty who buy and sell and whip their fellow men as if they were brutes, and absurdly complain that *they* are enslaved"?

But all these questions lay in the future, and answering them would be one of the principal tasks facing the new nation for the next 250 years. The Revolution was prosecuted by imperfect individuals who had a mixture of motives, including the purely economic motives of businessmen who did not want to pay taxes and the political conflicts among the competing social classes in the colonies themselves. Yet self-rule was at the heart of it all. Self-rule had been the basis for the flourishing of these colonies; self-rule was the basis for their revolution; self-rule continued to be a central element in the American experiment in all the years to come.

Perhaps nothing better illustrates that centrality than an interview given in 1843 by Captain Levi Preston, a soldier who fought the British at Concord in 1775 and was interviewed at the age of ninety-one by a young Mellen Chamberlain.

> "Captain Preston, why did you go to the Concord Fight, the 19th of April, 1775?"
> The old man, bowed beneath the weight of years, raised himself upright, and turning to me said: "Why did I go?"
> "Yes," I replied; "my histories tell me that you men of the Revolution took up arms against 'intolerable oppressions.'"

"What were they? Oppressions? I didn't feel them."

"What, were you not oppressed by the Stamp Act?"

"I never saw one of those stamps, and always understood that Governor Bernard put them all in Castle William. I am certain I never paid a penny for one of them."

"Well, what then about the tea-tax?"

"Tea-tax! I never drank a drop of the stuff; the boys threw it all overboard."

"Then I suppose you had been reading Harrington or Sidney and Locke about the eternal principles of liberty."

"Never heard of 'em. We read only the Bible, the Catechism, Watts's Psalms and Hymns, and the Almanack."

"Well, then, what was the matter? and what did you mean in going to the fight?"

"Young man, what we meant in going for those red-coats was this: we always had governed ourselves, and we always meant to. They didn't mean we should."

And that, concluded Chamberlain, was the ultimate philosophy of the American Revolution.

CHAPTER FOUR

A WAR, A NATION, AND A WOUND

ECLARING INDEPENDENCE WAS THE EASY PART. IT WAS NOT hard to produce a convincing manifesto and advance the glorious cause in elegant and ringing words. It was not hard to manage a few small and scattered military triumphs, even if they depended on the element of surprise and were little more than pinpricks that served to annoy the British and frustrate their intentions. But soon the immensity of the task ahead became clear and the warnings and admonitions of men like John Dickinson – a Patriot who had nevertheless opposed the Declaration, deriding it as a "skiff made of paper" – began to seem prophetic. How on earth did the American revolutionary leaders imagine that they could prevail against the greatest military power and most powerful empire in the world?

They went into the struggle with huge disadvantages. To begin with, the country, which was hardly even a country yet, was not fully united in embracing the revolutionary cause. We often assume that everyone in the colonies was solidly on board for independence, but that was very far from being the case. It is hard to know for sure, but perhaps as many as one-third of Americans remained loyal to the Crown and opposed the Revolution; another third seemed to be indifferent as to the outcome. Even the remaining third who supported independence had divergent motives for doing so. And the emerging country did not yet have a coherent or effective national political organization; as we have already seen, the Declaration itself was carefully ambiguous as to exactly what kind of national union these "free and independent states" were going to form together.

In addition, there could be no guarantee that such unity as could be summoned in the summer of 1776 would survive through the years of a rigorous, punishing war. The Americans could field only the most rudimentary, ill-trained, and poorly supplied army; they had no navy to speak of, little money, and no obvious means of raising funds to build and support these essential military components. The deck seemed to be stacked against them. On the very day in which independence was voted on by the Continental Congress, the British were easily able to land, facing no resistance, a large contingent of troops on Staten Island at the mouth of New York Harbor, the first installment in what would by August swell to a siege force of more than thirty thousand. They were not impressed by the Americans' brave and high-flown words. An American victory under such circumstances seemed a pipe dream.

But the Americans enjoyed certain very real advantages, and those would soon become clear. First, there was the fact that they were playing defense. They would not need to take the war across the ocean to the motherland of Britain to win. They needed only to hold on long enough at home to exhaust their opponent's willingness to fight, to drag things out long enough to saddle the British with an economically draining, tactically difficult, and logistically challenging war, conducted half a world away. In such a conflict, with time on their side, the Americans could lose most of the battles but still win the war. Given the desire of other European powers – notably the French, who were still licking their wounds after their costly defeat in the French and Indian War fourteen years before – to see an ever more dominant Britain dealt a severe blow and put in its place, it was entirely possible that the colonies could find allies among Britain's enemies. If France, Britain's perpetual foe, could be persuaded to support the American cause, that could make all the difference and compensate for the inherent weaknesses of the American position.

The Americans also had a second advantage. They were blessed with an exceptional leader in the person of George Washington, a man of such fine character that he automatically commanded the admiration and loyalty of nearly all Americans and thereby served as a unifying force. He was a proven Patriot, as he had from the beginning strongly opposed the various coercive acts of the British Parliament, and was thoroughly committed to the preservation of the colonists' rights and freedoms. Moreover, he was willing to leave a pleasant and comfortable life at his Mount Vernon estate to lead the colonial opposition. When he showed up at the Second Continental Convention in Philadelphia, he was wearing his military uniform, signaling for all to see that he was ready to fight for the colonial cause. The Congress acted accordingly, making him commander in chief of the Continental Army in June 1775. He accepted the position, on condition that he receive no pay for it.

His insistence upon that condition tells us a great deal about the man. Intrepid, courageous, charismatic, wise, tireless, and always learning, George Washington was the indispensable man to lead the war effort. He had extensive military experience and looked the part of a natural leader, impressively tall and muscular, with a dignified gravity in his bearing that led all to treat him with instinctive respect. But even more, he was known and admired as a man of exceptionally noble character who self-consciously modeled himself on the classical republican ideal of the unselfish, virtuous, and public-spirited leader, a man who disdained material rewards and consistently sought the public good over private interest. Like a great many other Americans of his day, Washington was deeply influenced by Joseph Addison's 1713 play *Cato, a Tragedy*, a popular and powerful drama about the meaning of honor. The play depicts the virtuous life of its subject, the ancient Roman senator Cato the Younger, who sacrifices his life in opposing the incipient tyranny of Julius Caesar. It was an example Washington took to heart. He saw the play performed a great many times and frequently quoted or paraphrased it in his correspondence and had it performed in front of his soldiers. Cato's lofty example was the example he wished to emulate; much of the American public shared his admiration and would respond well to the prospect of his leadership.

The greatest immediate challenge facing Washington was to recruit and deploy a disciplined and effective American army. This was no easy task, and it would continue to be a problem through the entire conflict. Even at the very outset, Washington experienced a taste of what was to come, with the constantly fluctuating numbers of troops at his disposal. In August 1776, he had twenty-eight thousand men under his command; by December, that number had shrunk to a mere three thousand. What had happened? Washington's troops had been driven from New York City by British regulars under the command of Major General William Howe and were forced to flee into New Jersey and, eventually, Pennsylvania. Along the way, a great many militiamen had simply deserted and gone home. The army's morale and numbers were always unstable, hostage to successive emotional peaks and valleys of hope and despair, depending on how the war effort seemed to be going at any given time. Washington would need to keep a cool and determined head through these constant fluctuations and frustrations.

The winter of 1776–77 that lay ahead would be an exceptionally harsh one, a gloomy valley of discouragement. But the Patriots' morale would be lifted immensely by the timely intervention of another pamphlet from the pen of Thomas Paine, the first in a series of pamphlets called *The American Crisis*, tailor-made for the discontents of that moment. It began with his famous inspirational words: "These are the times that try men's souls: The summer soldier and the sunshine patriot will, in this crisis, shrink from the service of his country; but he that stands it NOW deserves the love and thanks of man and woman." Yes, he conceded, the immediate future looked grim; but that was even more reason to hunker down and push ahead, because "the harder the conflict," he insisted, "the more glorious the triumph." Once again, Paine's words worked their magic. Washington ordered that they be read aloud to the army encampments, and they had the desired effect in rousing once more the fighting spirit of his men. For a second time in one year, Paine had made an inestimable gift to the colonial cause.

On Christmas night 1776, Washington struck back, leading a force through snow and sleet across the icy Delaware River and surprising at dawn a sleeping force of Hessians at Trenton, New Jersey. A week later, his forces enjoyed a similar triumph, repulsing a British force at Princeton. Two small victories, but one could hope that they were auguries of good things to come. They made it possible for the American soldiers to go into the winter months, which they spent at Morristown in the hills of New Jersey, with a sense of momentum and reason for hope. The American forces, it appeared, would not be defeated quickly, a fact that not only greatly encouraged the Patriots and aided their recruiting but discouraged their British and Loyalist foes. Despite a brutal, smallpox-ridden winter at Morristown, during which the army shrank to a mere thousand men, the coming of spring brought a flow of fresh recruits, lured by the promise of generous bounties, and Washington could resume the fight against Howe.

As it turned out, the coming year of 1777 would be crucial in determining the outcome of the war. The British had formulated a complex plan that aimed at cutting New England off from the rest of the colonies, by launching three coordinated assaults on American positions. Had the plan succeeded, they might have ended the colonial insurrection then and there. But all three assaults failed miserably. The most important of them involved the colorful British General John "Gentleman Johnny" Burgoyne, commanding the northern forces, who was to move his men down from Canada and across Lake Champlain toward Albany. He successfully traversed the lake and occupied the abandoned Fort Ticonderoga on the lake's southern end. But when he tried to go further, the effort, slowed by an immense baggage train that included thirty carts carrying Burgoyne's lavish wardrobe and his supplies of champagne, became bogged down in the dense woods north of Saratoga. The American forces swelled in numbers and enthusiasm as volunteers and militia flocked to the area, and eventually Burgoyne found himself hopelessly surrounded and forced to surrender on October 17. Some fifty-seven hundred British troops were taken prisoner. It was an enormous triumph for the Americans.

The victory at Saratoga was the signal the French had been waiting for, a clear indication that the Americans were up to the fight, and that it might therefore be in the interest of the French to involve themselves on the side of the Americans and help them administer a bitter setback to their old enemies. After having lost their North American empire to the British just a few years before, now there was a chance of returning the favor, a sweet revenge that would deprive the British of their North American colonies and thereby greatly diminish their power in the world.

Fearing this very prospect, Lord North made a desperate last-ditch offer to the colonies, offering to repeal all the offensive acts promulgated in the years before 1775 and promising never to tax the colonies. But it was too little too late, and the offer was flatly rejected. Instead, as a direct consequence of Saratoga, the French extended diplomatic recognition to the United States and concluded a commercial agreement and a treaty of alliance between the two countries that obligated both parties to see the war through, should France decide to enter it. The French had already been aiding the colonial cause with gunpowder and other supplies; in 1778, they would join the war effort on the American side, as would the Spanish and the Dutch. This support would mean not only additional trained troops but the assistance of the French Navy, which could make it possible to challenge British near-impregnable naval superiority.

But that lay in the future, just over the horizon. In the meantime, the horrendous winter of 1777–78 represented a low point for Washington's army, which found itself encamped at Valley Forge, eighteen miles outside Philadelphia, and beset by exposure, hunger, and disease. Conditions were horrifyingly difficult, and the army's very existence hung by a thread. The Marquis de Lafayette, a French aristocrat who had volunteered to fight with the Americans, observed that "the unfortunate soldiers … had neither coats, nor hats, nor shirts, nor shoes; their feet and legs froze till they grew black, and it was often necessary to amputate them." More than twenty-five hundred soldiers had died by the end of February 1778, and another one thousand had deserted. Another seven thousand were too ill for duty. Faith in Washington's leadership ability was put to a severe test. But after the arrival of General Friedrich Wilhelm von Steuben on February 23 to begin training the army, things began to turn around, and the army miraculously regained its fighting spirit. Von Steuben was a pro; he had been a member of the Prussian Army, had served on the General Staff of Frederick the Great, and was a believer in the revolutionary cause. He immediately began to put the American troops through an intense regimen of drilling. By May, he had made them into a reasonably cohesive military force.

Encouraged by news of the French military alliance, and by a promise of extra pay from the Congress, the Continental army was ready to move ahead.

In summer 1778, Washington's forces were strong enough to go after the withdrawing British forces across New Jersey. After an inconclusive engagement at Monmouth Court House, the middle region of the colonies settled into stalemate – and stalemate was nearly as good as victory, under the circumstances. In the meantime, there was good news on the western frontier. The daring young Virginia militiaman George Rogers Clark led 175 frontiersmen down the Ohio River in flatboats and, on July 4, surprised the British-held Kaskaskia and captured it without firing a shot; he then in short order took the garrison at Cahokia, both in present-day Illinois, and then occupied Vincennes in present-day Indiana. Washington enthusiastically hailed these victories, which offered further proof to the French of the fighting effectiveness of their new American allies and laid the groundwork for eventual American settlement of the Northwest Territory.

But not everything went so well. In late 1780, the British turned their attention to the southern colonies (which were after all more important to them as sources of staples and raw materials) and captured Savannah and Charleston, the latter debacle representing the worst American defeat of the war. Then, seeking to secure the Carolinas further and cut them off from external sources of aid, British General Charles Cornwallis took his force of seventy-two hundred men northward, heading toward Virginia and ending up in Yorktown, a small port city strategically located near the mouth of the Chesapeake Bay. They would be safe and secure from siege there, he believed, since the Americans lacked a serious navy to challenge him by water and sufficient troops in the area to threaten him by land.

Both those assumptions proved to be dead wrong, and the assistance of the French Navy was the main reason why. Cornwallis soon found himself trapped in the pincers of a combined operation, coming at him from both sea and land. First, French Admiral Comte de Grasse's fleet came up from its Caribbean base to decisively defeat the British Navy in September 1781 in the Battle of the Chesapeake. De Grasse was then able to blockade the coast while in the meantime ferrying in troops to join those already in place outside the town. In time, the American and French troops gathered outside Yorktown numbered more than sixteen thousand, more the twice the size of Cornwallis's army. He was trapped and hopelessly outmaneuvered, with no choice but to surrender.

On October 19, he did so. It is said that, as his forces marched out, the British band struck up a familiar English ballad, "The World Turned Upside Down," many of the words of which must have seemed hauntingly appropriate to Cornwallis and his men on the occasion:

Listen to me and you shall hear, news hath not been this thousand year:
Since Herod, Cæsar, and many more, you never heard the like before.
Holy-dayes are despis'd, new fashions are devis'd.
Old Christmas is kickt out of Town.
Yet let's be content, and the times lament, you see the world turn'd
upside down.

The world turned upside down. With Cornwallis's surrender, the war was effectively over, and the impossible had happened: America had won. Peace talks would begin soon thereafter, eventuating in the Treaty of Paris, signed on September 3, 1783, which granted and codified the American independence that had been declared in 1776 and that had been persistently and courageously sought, despite great odds, in the seven long and hard years thereafter.

We don't know for certain whether the band played "The World Turned Upside Down." It might just be a well-established legend. But if it was, it was an exceptionally meaningful one. The words of the song not only served to haunt the defeated British. They also raised unsettling questions for the Americans about the revolutionary journey on which they found themselves embarked. What sort of effect was this war having on the social and political life of the colonies-becoming-a-nation? How was it changing things? If this was to be a revolution, how thoroughgoing a revolution was it to be? Was, in fact, the world being turned upside down – or merely right side up?

The latter might have seemed more likely. As we've seen, the most influential justifications offered in favor of revolution invoked not radical change but rather restoration – restoring and protecting the colonists' customary rights as Englishmen – as the pretext for revolution. But like any great historical event, the American Revolution was complicated, with many aspects. Even those fighting on the same side sometimes saw the cause differently. To a greater extent than many of us appreciate today, the Revolutionary War took on many of the aspects of a civil war, pitting Loyalists against Patriots; dividing families, towns, regions, and social classes; and producing fierce struggles over fundamental political and social values. Loyalty to the Crown had been the instinctive response of a sizable minority of Americans. But for some, the resonant words of the Declaration of Independence pointed toward a larger aspiration, something more than mere restoration. Such an interpretation pointed toward the emergence on the world stage of something genuinely new: a republican order built upon a principled commitment to both equality and liberty.

Historians have been arguing for generations which of these different tendencies was dominant and hence which offers us the best way to think about the Revolution. Was the Revolution essentially conservative in its objectives, merely seeking to separate America from Britain to return the political order to what it had been before the disruptions caused by clumsy and wrongheaded British colonial policies? Or was it something radical, in the sense of wishing to shake things up, dramatically and fundamentally upending the entrenched inequalities and hierarchies in society, and not merely changing the names and faces of those at the top of the political structure? As the American historian Carl Becker, who strongly advocated for the latter view, put it memorably more than a hundred years ago, "the war was not about home rule, but about who would rule at home."

There is evidence for his claim. Certainly the war was not *only* about home rule, and certainly it reflected some radical democratizing currents that had been operating in the society for many decades. Just as the Great Awakening had in many places weakened the authority of established clergymen, while unleashing a sense of individualism and self-reliance and willingness to question authority, so the war against British colonial authority placed all forms of settled authority under suspicion, including the homegrown class distinctions that were a fairly settled part of colonial life. The Revolution was not just a matter of lawyers and patricians; it had drawn freely upon the enthusiasm and energy of laborers, farmers, mechanics, servants, and common people of every type to propel the public demonstrations, support the consumer boycotts, and fight the battles that ultimately made independence possible. Five thousand African Americans fought in the Revolution. Did not all of these groups deserve some share of the triumph? How could this great freeing-up of energy, buoyed by idealistic talk of liberty and equality, not have an effect upon the traditional political and social arrangements and call into question the right to rule of the wealthy and well-born? How could it not ultimately call into question the existence in the new nation of an institution that most glaringly stood in contradiction to both liberty and equality: the institution of chattel slavery?

Such questions could not be easily set aside. But the immediate task at hand was how to devise institutions that could fulfill the republican aspirations that had inspired the revolutionary effort in the first place, while providing the unity needed to carry out the functions of a national government. The newly independent Americans were determined to get along without a monarch and to vindicate the possibility of republican self-rule. But how to do it? Those among the Founding generation who were conversant in the history of previous republics, especially those in classical antiquity, knew that the single most common characteristic of a republic was its fragility. Everything depended upon the virtuous character of the citizenry, on their willingness to live as

George Washington had done and place the public's well-being over and above their own personal interests. Such civic virtue was exceedingly rare and hard to sustain in a whole society.

The size and scale of a republic also mattered. Philosophers such as Aristotle and Montesquieu had argued that a republic had to be relatively small if it were to maintain itself as a republic. Large nations tended either to fall apart into discord or to be transformed into empires under monarchical rule. The historical example of Rome haunted the early Americans for that very reason. The Roman Republic had become strong through the martial and civic virtues of its hardy citizenry; the Roman Empire had fallen into dissolution from the decadence and corruption of its spoiled and self-interested inhabitants. Many Americans feared that Great Britain in the age of George III was following that same downward path, and they wanted above all else to spare themselves that fate.

Hence the emphasis in American constitution making, starting in 1776, would be on the state level. Most everyone agreed that the states should continue to be the principal sources of political power and authority, guarantors of individual rights and exemplars of the principles of separation of powers, which they employed to protect against abuses of power by any particular individuals or groups. Generally this meant limiting the power of governors in preference to legislatures, and it most certainly meant reserving for the national government only the most essential elements of power. The state governments would serve as laboratories of experimentation, whose experiences and findings would profitably inform the eventual shape of the U.S. Constitution.

There hadn't even been a national constitution properly in place during most of the war years. The Articles of Confederation had been drafted in 1777 but had not been ratified by all the states until 1781. It mattered very little; the Continental Congress had already been operating as if the Articles were in place anyway, so that their formal adoption didn't change much.

An examination of the Articles sheds considerable light on what kind of union these newly "free and independent states" had in mind. The Articles conceived of the combination of states as a "league of friendship" rather than a national union. The primacy of the states was spelled out in Article II, which specified, "Each state retains its sovereignty, freedom, and independence, and every Power, Jurisdiction, and right, which is not by this confederation expressly delegated to the United States, in Congress assembled." Each state, irrespective of its size, would have a single vote in Congress, and for the passage of the most important measures (currency, tariffs, military matters), either a unanimous vote or a supermajority was required. And the national government was not to be given any coercive tools – no courts, no executive power, no power of taxation – that would allow it to act independently or to force the individual states to do anything they didn't want to do.

In retrospect, it's easy to see why the Articles' approach was unlikely to succeed in providing a stable and unified political order. But it also is important to try to understand why the revolutionary generation overwhelmingly favored it at first. For one thing, the war itself was still under way in the 1770s and early 1780s, and there was simply no time to engage in laborious and possibly bitter debate about a dramatic change in the form of government. But there was a far deeper reason. These historical actors had an intense but understandable preoccupation with their immediate history. No one wanted to replicate the same horrors of overcentralized government that they had just overthrown. That outcome was to be avoided at all costs. But this preoccupation blinded the Framers of the Articles to the larger range of issues that a new government would have to confront, if it were to be effective. They overreacted, going too far in the opposite direction and creating for themselves an impossibly weak and unworkable central government: one that eschewed centralization, yes, but did so to such an extent that it could neither conduct foreign policy nor regulate interstate trade nor defend the nation's borders nor put the nation's economic and financial house in order.

Before taking note of these failings, though, we must take note of one major exception, a singularly impressive and enduring accomplishment of the Congress under the Articles. That was the establishment of wise and farsighted policies for the development of western lands, formulated in a series of land ordinances culminating with the great Northwest Ordinance of 1787. These ordinances laid down the procedures by which the inestimable treasure of the western territories, which had been acquired by Britain in the French and Indian War and was awarded to the Americans through the Revolution, could be settled and organized and incorporated into the nation, in a way that not only extended fundamental American principles and promoted stability but also generated precious revenue for the national treasury.

The Northwest Ordinance provided a clearly defined process by which the western lands would, in several stages, eventually be "formed into distinct republican States." The historian Daniel Boorstin called it "the add-a-state plan." It ensured that the western lands would not be held as permanent colonial dependencies but would gradually enter the Union on terms exactly equal to those the already existing states enjoyed. The result would be a steadily growing country, not an empire, and a union that grew more and more imbued with a spirit of national unity. And that was not all. The ordinance contained language prohibiting the introduction of slavery or involuntary servitude into the territory and took a strong stand favoring the creation of public educational institutions. "Religion, morality and knowledge being necessary to good government and the happiness of mankind," it stated, "schools and the means of education shall forever be encouraged."

But in most other respects, the nation's interests were poorly served by the Articles. In the western frontier areas, the British refused to withdraw from the several military posts they had established, even though the terms of the Treaty of Paris had required it. Who was going to force them? In the southwest, the Spanish similarly refused to yield their control over the Mississippi River, the commercial lifeline to the country's midsection. Such actions were a blatant thumb in the eye of the Americans, who simply lacked the means to respond effectively to them.

But that was not all. The British succeeded in badly damaging American economic interests by severely restricting American imports and flooding American markets with their own low-priced manufactured goods. This wave of British hypermercantilism came as the United States was already reeling from a postwar economic depression and struggling to recover from wild alternations of inflation and deflation that had thoroughly debased the currency and badly distorted prices and wages. The sharp deflation in commodity prices meant that debtors, especially farmers, suddenly found themselves with insufficient income to meet their fixed obligations, including the mortgages on their property. Foreclosures on mortgaged property became more and more common. Debtors pleaded for relief in the form of credit extension and currency inflation – which meant printing more and more paper money, exactly what the bankers and politicians felt they could not do, as they tried to pay down debts and stabilize the currency. Conditions were ripe for an eruption. In several places, desperate mobs attempted to stem the tide of foreclosures by force, blocking courts from meeting and preventing them from doing their business.

Such conflicts escalated to an alarming level of raw class conflict between debtors and creditors, between haves and have-nots. The state governments were levying ever higher taxes, trying their best to pay off the massive debts they had accumulated in the conduct of the war. Many of the holders of that debt were wealthy creditors comfortably ensconced in places like Boston. Many of the debtors were struggling farmers who had fought in the war and who returned to find their livelihoods and their homes in peril.

One particularly notable uprising took place in western Massachusetts in summer 1786, when Revolutionary War veteran Daniel Shays led a march on Springfield to shut down the state supreme court and then attack the Springfield arsenal. Although the incident died down quickly and had little lasting effect in Massachusetts, it was widely noticed by some of the nation's leaders, who saw it as an alarming indication that the liberatory energies released by the

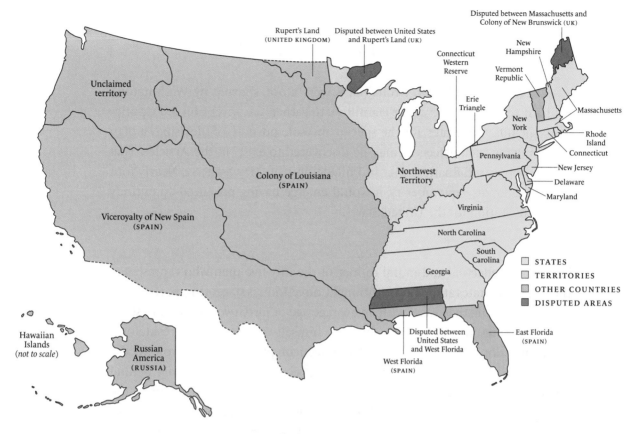

States and territories of the United States in 1790, including the Northwest Territory.

war were starting to run riot. Liberty was turning to license; "we are," worried George Washington, in a letter to James Madison, "fast verging to anarchy and confusion!" (Jefferson, in Paris at the time, disagreed. "[A] little rebellion now and then is a good thing," he declared to Madison, "as necessary in the political world as storms in the physical.")

The deficiencies of the Articles had long been apparent; the importance of Shays' Rebellion was in clarifying that perception and imparting a sense of urgency to the task of institutional reform. As Washington wrote to John Jay of New York on August 1, 1786,

> Your sentiments, that our affairs are drawing rapidly to a crisis, accord with my own. What the event will be, is also beyond the reach of my foresight. We have errors to correct; we have probably had too good an opinion of human nature in forming our confederation. Experience has taught us, that men will not adopt and carry into execution measures the best calculated for their own good, without the intervention of a coercive power. I do not conceive we can exist long as a nation without having lodged some where a power, which will pervade the

whole Union in as energetic a manner, as the authority of the State Governments extends over the several States.

Even as Washington wrote, plans were afoot, spurred by Washington's brilliant young aide Alexander Hamilton, to gather "a Convention of Deputies from the different States, for the special and sole purpose of [devising] a plan for supplying such defects as may be discovered to exist" in the Articles. That convention would finally gather in Philadelphia on May 25, 1787. Nearly four months later, on September 17, it would emerge having produced an entirely new Constitution for the United States.

The high intellectual and moral caliber of the fifty-five men who represented the respective states at the Constitutional Convention is staggering, particularly given how young they were, with an average age of forty-two. There were some older men present – George Washington himself was elected to preside over the convention; Roger Sherman of Connecticut played a major role in the debates; and Benjamin Franklin, then in his eighties, worked mainly behind the scenes – but most of the work was done by a handful of delegates under the age of fifty, men such as James Wilson of Pennsylvania (age forty-two), Gouverneur Morris of New York (age thirty-five), and, perhaps most important of all, James Madison of Virginia (age thirty-six), who was a driving force at the convention and the principal architect of the Constitution itself.

Unlike the physically imposing Washington, James Madison did not look the heroic part he was given by history to play. His nickname was "Little Jemmy," because he was such a tiny, frail man, a mere five feet tall, with a squeaky voice and a reticent, bookish manner. But no one doubted his high intelligence, his encyclopedic knowledge of political history, and his eloquence and persuasiveness in debate. His intelligence was of the rarest sort, combining the shrewdness of an effective practical politician with the reflectiveness of a philosopher. His knowledge of the past gave him a particularly keen appreciation of the possibilities inherent in the moment in which America found itself, and he intended to make the most of those possibilities. Getting the Constitution right would be a high-stakes affair. America, he asserted, would "decide for ever the fate of republican government."

Such weighty words reflected the Framers' remarkable combination of soaring ambition and practical humility. They were excited by the possibilities that lay before them and felt a determination to lay hold of them. As John Adams exulted, they were living in a time in which "the greatest lawgivers of antiquity would have wished to live," with a chance to establish "the wisest and happiest government that human wisdom can contrive." Hence they were emboldened to expand their mission beyond the narrow one of merely correcting the Articles and instead to create something far better, something that could be an example to the world. But their ambition was always tempered by prudence and sobriety. They were exceedingly careful, always mindful of the ominous example of Rome, always suspicious of the utopian turn of mind, and always intent upon keeping the frailty and imperfection of human nature in mind. They understood politics as the art of the possible and the best constitution as one built with the crooked timber of selfish humanity in mind – one that took to heart Washington's warning not to have "too good an opinion of human nature."

The debates that emerged at the Philadelphia convention would often revolve around the divergent interests of the various states. But there also was a great deal of consensus about certain fundamental points of political philosophy. There was agreement that the new government should continue to be republican, meaning that it would rule out the possibility of any kind of monarch or monarchical office. They agreed on the basic principle, worked out in the political turmoil of seventeenth-century England, that power, being prone to corrupting and misleading its fallible possessors, should never be concentrated in any one person or office but should be divided and distributed as widely as possible: in a parliament, in state and local governments, in common law and tradition, and in the conviction that every person possessed certain fundamental liberties and rights that no government could legitimately suppress or violate. The chief challenge of constitution making was to ensure that these different sources of power be so arranged that they could check and balance one another, ensuring that even with a more powerful national government, no one branch or faction or region would dominate over all the others.

The delegates favored a federal system that would maintain a large measure of autonomy for the states, while turning over to a national government only those things that had to be undertaken in common. Ideally, this federal system would reconcile opposites, combining the advantages of self-rule with the advantages of union, the cohesiveness and diversity of smaller-scale local organization with the greater resources and power of a unified national state. It would be a difficult balance to strike, though, and even more difficult to hold.

In a sense, the history of the British Empire to date had already demonstrated how difficult such a federal reconciliation would be, particularly in the absence of a written constitution to spell out how power was to be distributed through the imperial system. Consider, for example, the bitterly divisive question of taxation for the colonies, which would always remain insoluble so long as there was no shared overarching vision of how the pieces of the empire would be related to one another as parts in a whole, even as they retained much of their individual autonomy, their own capacity for self-rule. Might a more creative brand of leadership in Great Britain and America have devised such a vision, a federal understanding of the British Empire that could have kept the empire intact? It seems highly unlikely, but who knows?

In any event, the Philadelphia convention would have to address itself to remarkably similar questions and incorporate its answers into the document they were drafting. After electing George Washington to preside over the convention, and voting to close the proceedings and meet in secret, the delegates faced two fundamental decisions: How much power needed to be given to an expanded national government? And how could they ensure that this empowered national government would itself be fully accountable, and would not become *too* powerful?

Thanks to Madison's copious notes on the proceedings, we know a great deal about how the convention proceeded, despite the veil of secrecy under which it met. Early on, the delegates agreed that the Articles had to be scrapped and a new, more truly national arrangement substituted for it. They also agreed readily on most of the new powers that would be granted to the national government: the right to levy taxes, regulate interstate and foreign commerce, raise and maintain the army and navy, call up the state militias, regulate currency, negotiate treaties, assess tariffs, and supersede the states' claims to do these things.

In light of the distrust of executive power that had manifested itself in the Revolution, the powerful new office of the presidency has to be accounted as the most striking departure of all from the decentralized Articles. One may well wonder whether the delegates would ever have been willing to take a chance on such a dramatically expanded office had they not been able to rely on the availability of George Washington to fill the position and establish precedents that would make the position both effective and deserving of the nation's trust. Once again, Washington showed himself to be the indispensable man. Even so, the leap of faith being made, and asked for, was considerable. The president would have responsibility for executing the laws and directing the diplomatic apparatus of the nation. He would serve as commander in chief of the armed forces. He would appoint federal judges and secretaries of executive branch agencies. He would have the power to veto congressional legislation, and his veto could only be overridden by a supermajority of two-thirds. There was no precedent for this in the colonial experience – aside, that is, from the figure of the King.

But debates emerged over other issues, particularly the question of how representation in Congress would be determined. There were two competing approaches under consideration. Madison's initial plan, which came to be called the Virginia Plan, called for representation by population. The smaller states, which rightly feared this arrangement would render them second-class citizens under the new Constitution, fought back and, under the leadership of William Paterson, proposed what came to be called the New Jersey Plan, which would maintain the Articles' pattern of representation by states.

This clash was a question not only of contending powers but of competing principles. Representation by state, in which each state had equal representation, seemed to violate the very principle of democracy itself, rendering the votes of those in the populous states less valuable than those in the small states. Why should tiny Rhode Island have the same legislative power as large and populous Virginia? But representation by population had its problems, too, for it violated the principle that the country was, as its name implies, a union of *states*, in which the states remained the fundamental unit upon which the national polity was built.

The Convention settled on a compromise between these two positions. This Great Compromise, engineered by Roger Sherman, was, like all such compromises, a political deal. But it ended up being something much more than that. Instead of favoring one principle over another, it acknowledged the legitimate aspects of both principles, giving both their due, and putting them into fruitful tension with one another. The key was the use of a bicameral or two-house structure, patterned after the British division of Parliament into a House of Commons and an aristocratic House of Lords. In the American version, the more populous states would be accorded representation by population in the House of Representatives, the lower house in the new Congress; the smaller states would retain their equal footing in the Senate, the upper house, where each state would be accorded two representatives, no more and no less, irrespective of its size or population.

Legislation would have to clear both of these very different houses, with their different principles of representation, and be signed by the president to be enacted into law. The interests of varied and conflicting groups could thereby all have a role in determining the fate of important legislation. The lower house would be closer to the great mass of ordinary citizens, with its members apportioned by population and chosen by popular vote for short, two-year terms. The upper house was designed to be more aristocratic and somewhat shielded from the winds of popular will, with its members standing for staggered six-year terms and elected by the state legislatures rather than by the people at large. The lower house would be a "commons," more responsive and more democratic, while the upper house would be, if not quite a chamber of "lords," a more aloof, more deliberative, and more rarified body, with built-in insulation from passing enthusiasms and passions. The lower house would be entrusted with the sole power of introducing revenue bills; the upper house would be entrusted with foreign relations, the ratification of treaties, and confirmation of executive branch appointments.

The result of this compromise was a structure that was arguably better than either of the alternatives it attempted to reconcile. It quickly took its place as one of the chief elements in the Constitution's famously intricate network of checks and balances, a system by means of which each power granted to one unit of government is kept within safe limits by countervailing powers vested in some other unit. This pattern played out on multiple levels. The newly established national government would have unprecedented powers. But its powers would be enumerated, spelled out, and thereby limited by the Constitution itself, and the state governments would remain strong, serving as an additional check on the national government. The national government was further checked by being subdivided into executive, legislative, and judicial branches, each of which was in competition with the others, and each of which had some ways of thwarting the other branches in cases of injudiciousness or overreach. The president could reject a bill of Congress with a veto. Congress could override that veto by repassing the bill with a two-thirds majority. Congress could remove the president and members of the executive branch through impeachment. The Senate could reject executive branch appointments. The president could command the armed forces and negotiate treaties, but only Congress could declare war, and only the Senate could ratify treaties. And so on.

Behind all these particulars was a powerful idea. Conflict is part of the human condition and can never be eliminated. Neither can the desire for power and the tendency to abuse it. Therefore a workable constitution has to provide a structure within which conflict can be tamed, institutionalized, and thereby made productive, while the search for power can be kept within bounds. Like an internal combustion engine, such a constitution should be designed to redirect the energies released by the explosions that take place within its chambers, using those energies to drive the work of American governance and enterprise. It should be designed to work with the grain of human nature, not against it; but in doing so, it should also counteract the worst tendencies of human nature rather than encourage them. For that very reason, it is not conducive to easygoing peaceableness. The only thing all contending parties need to agree on is the authority of the Constitution itself and the rules of engagement it sets forth.

So this was the document that the delegates agreed on in Philadelphia and signed on September 17, 1787. Let us pause here for a moment to step back and reflect on the larger picture. Constitution Day, which we observe every September 17, is a singularly American holiday, even more unique than the Fourth of July. After all, many nations have their great leaders and laborers, their war heroes, their monuments, and their days of independence. But there is only one nation on earth that can point with pride to a written Constitution that is more than 230 years old, a continuously authoritative expression of fundamental law that stands at the very center of our national life.

As such, the U.S. Constitution is not merely our most weighty legal document; it is also an expression of who and what we are. Other countries, such as France, have lived under many different constitutions and kinds of government over the centuries, so that for them, the French nation is something separable from the form of government that happens to be in power at any given time. No so for Americans, who have lived since the 1780s under one regime, a remarkable fact whose significance nevertheless seems to escape us. Yes, we do revere our Constitution, but we do so blandly and automatically, without troubling ourselves to know very much about it, and without reflecting much on what our Constitution says about our national identity.

That identity is a complicated one, and there are elements of it about which we all will probably never agree. Ties of blood and religion and race and soil are not sufficient to hold us together as Americans, and they never have been. We think of "diversity" as something new in American history, but in fact the conduct of American life has always involved the negotiation of profound differences among us. We are forever about the business of making a workable unity out of our unruly plurality, and our Constitution accepted the inevitability of our diversity in such things, and the inevitability of conflicts arising out of our differences. In addition, it recognized the fact that ambitious, covetous, and power-hungry individuals are always going to be plentifully in evidence among us and that the energies of such potentially dangerous people need to be contained and tamed, diverted into activities that are consonant with the public good.

Hence we have a Constitution that is not, for the most part, a document filled with soaring rhetoric and lists of high-sounding principles. Instead it is a somewhat dry and functional document laying out a complex system of markers, boundaries, and rules of engagement, careful divisions of function and power that provide the means by which conflicts that are endemic and inevitable to us, and to all human societies, can be both expressed and contained; tamed; rendered harmless, even beneficial. Unlike the Declaration of Independence, the Constitution's spirit is undeclared, unspoken; it would be revealed not through words but through actions, through processes, and through events that would express the unfolding demands of history.

That history has been largely successful – yet not entirely so. The Constitution the Framers wrote fell short, and grievously so, in one important respect:

in its failure to address satisfactorily the growing national stain of slavery. As we will see, there were understandable reasons for that failure. But the trajectory of history that was coming would not forget it, and would not forgive it.

Slavery is as old as human history. It has existed on all habitable continents, and all the world's great religions have given it, at one time or another, authoritative approval. In the New World, its introduction was pioneered by the Portuguese and Spanish, beginning in the sixteenth century, and only later picked up by the English (as well as the Dutch and French). It was not a part of any larger plan for English colonization, and it did not take root immediately in colonial English America, although the forced labor system known as indentured servitude was common in the colonies from the start and it could be said to resemble slavery in its coerciveness and harshness. In fact, indentured servitude was so common that some historians have estimated more than half of the white immigrants to the American colonies up to the time of the Revolution had come to the New World under indentures, and even the first black Africans to appear in North America, dropped off at Jamestown, Virginia, in 1619 by a Dutch ship, may well have been indentured servants rather than slaves.

Although often a brutal institution, indentured servitude served a real purpose. The colonies were desperately in need of a steady supply of immigrant labor, especially in the agricultural areas near the Chesapeake and in the low country of South Carolina, which suffered from a high mortality rate due to disease, food shortages, and constant Indian conflicts. But a great many desperately poor Europeans who were otherwise willing to emigrate to America and endure such harsh conditions lacked the means to pay for their own voyage. Indentured servitude allowed them to solve that problem, temporarily trading their freedom for the cost of their passage, signing contracts of indenture lasting from four to seven years with masters or landowners who would pay for their transportation and upkeep in exchange for their work, usually on a farm. At the termination of their contracts, they would be free to go their own way, working for wages or acquiring their own land.

The first Africans experienced conditions similar to those of indentured whites, and the African population in the Chesapeake grew slowly, to about four hundred laborers by 1650. But as it grew, so too did the practice of discrimination against Africans because of their race, and by the 1660s, such practices had hardened into laws or slave codes enacted by colonial assemblies, which dictated that Africans and their offspring be kept in permanent bondage. In other words, the Africans were being made into chattel, the legal property of their owners. The interest in using slaves began to grow as the agricultural economy grew and as the improving British economy meant that fewer white indentured servants were available, and those who were available were more expensive. Little by little, the cheaper labor supplied by slavery became an essential part of the agricultural economy in states like Virginia and South Carolina. By 1750, half the population of Virginia and two-thirds of South Carolina were enslaved. Yet it should be remembered that slavery was not exclusively a southern phenomenon; at the time of the Revolution, every state in the union permitted it.

Hence, by the time of the Constitutional Convention, the institution of race-based slavery was deeply enmeshed in one segment of the national economy, despite all the ways that its very existence seemed to stand in glaring contradiction to the national commitment to liberty, equality, and self-rule. There was real bite to the mocking question fired at the Americans in 1775 by the British writer Samuel Johnson: "How is it that we hear the loudest yelps for liberty among the drivers of negroes?" It was an excellent question, particularly if one kept in mind how many of the most prominent Founders, including Thomas Jefferson and George Washington, were themselves owners of slaves. Indeed, more than thirty of the fifty-five Framers of the Constitution owned slaves. How, we wonder today, could such otherwise enlightened and exemplary individuals have been so blind to the fundamental humanity of those they confined? How could they have made their peace with practices so utterly contradictory to all they stood for?

There is no easy answer to such questions. But surely a part of the answer is that each of us is born into a world that we did not make, and it is only with the greatest effort, and often at very great cost, that we are ever able to change that world for the better. Moral sensibilities are not static; they develop and deepen over time, and general moral progress is very slow. Part of the study of history involves a training of the imagination, learning to see historical actors as speaking and acting in their own times rather than ours and learning to see even our heroes as an all-too-human mixture of admirable and unadmirable qualities, people like us who may, like us, be constrained by circumstances beyond their control.

What made the American situation especially intolerable was not the wrongs these earliest Americans perpetrated but the high and noble ideals they professed, which served to contradict and condemn those very practices. They were living an inconsistency, and they could not be at ease about it. Washington freed his own slaves upon his death. Jefferson did not, but he agonized over his complicity with slavery and later in life foresaw slavery as an offense against God and a possible source of national dissolution. What these two examples tell us is that the seeds of a more capacious ideal of liberty were already planted and had begun to take root but still were far from being ready to blossom.

It is also true that a considerable number of the Framers sincerely believed that slavery was already on the wane, that it had been on the wane since the Revolution, and that it would eventually disappear of its own accord. They therefore were willing to accept the compromises in the Constitution for the sake of a brighter future of whose coming they were very confident. Roger Sherman observed "that the abolition of slavery seemed to be going on in the United States, and that the good sense of the several States would probably by degrees complete it." Similarly, his fellow Connecticut delegate Oliver Ellsworth predicted that "Slavery, in time, will not be a speck in our Country."

The results of the Convention reflected this mixed and ambivalent condition. Sadly, there was little serious consideration given to the idea of abolishing slavery at the time. Indeed, some delegates were too bound by their states' economic interests to oppose any measure that would even inhibit slavery; one delegate from South Carolina threatened that his delegation and the Georgia delegation would never agree to a Constitution that failed to protect slavery. In other words, the price of pursuing abolition of slavery at that time would almost certainly have been the dissolution of the American nation, which would probably have rendered the resulting nation-fragments highly unstable and unable to defend their interests. Would that have been worth the price? This is a far different question for us to ask today than it was for them to answer at the time.

In any event, the defenders of slavery got a concession, through an idea carried over from a proposed amendment to the Articles, that three-fifths of the slave population would be counted for representation and taxation purposes, even though slaves had none of the rights of citizens. (Northern delegates had wanted slaves to be counted at 100 percent for taxation purposes but at zero for representation purposes; they were forced to compromise.) They also got a concession allowing the transatlantic slave trade to continue until 1808 and installed a fugitive slave clause, which required that a "person held to service or labour" (a term that could include indentured servants) who escapes to another state must be "delivered up on claim of the party to whom such service or labour may be due."

So slavery would be protected. But the Constitution was otherwise notably reticent on the subject. Note, for example, the unwillingness, in the Fugitive Slave Clause, to use the words *owner* or *master*. The words *slave* and *slavery* never appear in its text, whether out of delicacy or diffidence; either way, the Framers showed by their silence that they were not at ease with slavery and preferred euphemisms such as "persons held to Service or labour." And it is also indicative that the final document did open the way to an ending of the transatlantic slave trade after the year 1808, a move inspired by a resounding speech from

George Mason of Virginia, himself a slaveholder but also a Christian who labeled the trade an "infernal traffic." Mason feared the corrupting spread of slavery through the entire nation, which would bring "the judgment of Heaven" down severely upon any country in which bondage was widespread and blandly accepted. His own state of Virginia had been one of the first jurisdictions in the world to stop the importation of slaves for sale, doing so in 1778 under the leadership of its governor, Thomas Jefferson. These things speak volumes about the Framers' conflicted consciences.

The legal importation of African slaves into the United States did end in 1808, but slavery itself persisted and grew in the American South, since the conditions of life in the United States would prove highly favorable to a steady natural increase in the slave population, in comparison to the harsher conditions in Brazil or in the sugar-producing islands of the West Indies. In fact, slaves in the antebellum South would have the highest rate of natural increase of any slave society in history. Ironically, that more favorable environment meant that the institution would prove difficult to eliminate, contrary to the confident hopes of men like Sherman and Ellsworth.

The ambivalences regarding slavery that had been built into the structure of the Constitution were almost certainly unavoidable in the short term in order to achieve an effective political union of the nation. What we need to understand is how the original compromise no longer became acceptable to increasing numbers of Americans, especially in one part of the Union, and why slavery, a ubiquitous institution in human history, came to be seen not merely as an unfortunate evil but as a sinful impediment to human progress, a stain upon a whole nation. We live today on the other side of a great transformation in moral sensibility, a transformation that was taking place, but was not yet completed, in the very years that the United States was being formed.

Hence it would be profoundly wrong to contend, as some do, that the United States was "founded on" slavery. No, it was *founded* on other principles entirely, on principles of liberty and self-rule that had been discovered and defined and refined and enshrined through the tempering effects of several turbulent centuries of European and British and American history. Those foundational principles would win out in the end, though not without much struggle and striving, and eventual bloodshed. The United States enjoyed a miraculous birth, but it was not the product of an unstained conception and an untroubled delivery. Few things are.

CHAPTER FIVE

THE EXPERIMENT BEGINS

THE NEW U.S. CONSTITUTION HAD NOW BEEN DRAFTED AND approved by the Philadelphia Convention – but it still would have to be ratified by the states before it could become the supreme law of the land. The Framers knew that the road to that goal was not going to be easy or certain. As was the case with the Revolution, so with the Constitution: a great many Americans were not yet on board with the idea of abandoning the status quo, especially if it meant a great expansion of national power. High principles were at stake, but so too were entrenched political and economic interests. Local elites feared being overtaken and superseded by national ones. State legislatures were likely to look with suspicion on any new national constitution that would reduce their powers. Even in the fragile and tenuous new American republic, there were already enough vested interests to ensure that there would be stiff resistance to change.

Anticipating these obstacles and wishing the new charter to get the strongest possible endorsement from the people, whom Madison lauded as "the highest source of authority," the Framers of the Constitution specified in Article VII that this Constitution would become law automatically upon ratification by conventions from nine of the thirteen states. The specifying of "conventions" was very important. In requiring that the ratification be the work of state conventions created for the occasion, rather than the existing state legislatures, the Framers followed a method already pioneered successfully in 1780 by the state of Massachusetts when it submitted its new constitution to the voters for ratification. It was a shrewd move, because it improved the chances of success by allowing the process to work around the existing officialdom, which might be expected to be resistant to any change that challenged the status quo.

But in every state, there would be heated debate pitting supporters of the new Constitution, who called themselves Federalists, against opponents, who came to have the ungainly name Anti-Federalists, and who for various reasons favored retaining the loose and decentralized approach of the Articles and distrusted the Constitution's more nationalist orientation and its concentration of power in the national government, and especially the presidency. It is not easy to generalize about the sort of people who took either side. The Federalists, many of whose leaders had been participants in the Convention, were likely to be well-off professional people, knowledgeable, organized, worldly, and articulate, adept at producing the kind of sophisticated arguments and publicity that could sway delegates to vote their way. The Anti-Federalists were a more varied lot, and although a few were quite wealthy, a great many others were small farmers and debtors of modest means. In any event, the issue of ratification was very much in doubt; it was not a forgone conclusion which side would prevail.

The Federalist versus Anti-Federalist debates were a vivid and important instance of a persistent tension, one we have already seen in action before, between those who favored a strong and activist central government and those who deeply distrusted all forms of centralized power. This division would run through a great many of the conflicts in the American nation's early history, from the Anglo-American imperial debates of the 1760s through to the early years of the nineteenth century and beyond, even unto the present day. Both sides had compelling arguments to make, and indisputable patriots were making them, which is why in so many states the convention votes would be exceedingly close.

Political debate stimulates political reflection and political expression, and in this regard the debates over the Constitution proved to be very productive, giving rise to a profusion of spirited and thoughtful writings on both sides: pamphlets, broadsides, editorials, and articles whose authors, their identities often disguised behind Roman pseudonyms like Brutus and Cato, reflected with remarkable breadth and insight on the issues at hand. It was a great process of public self-education. Arguably the most distinguished of these writings were the eighty-five articles written in support of ratification by three of its chief proponents: Alexander Hamilton, James Madison, and John Jay. These fascinating essays, historically informed and erudite in ways that reflected the Founding generation's remarkable combination of intellectual maturity and political savvy, were published serially over a ten-month period beginning in October 1787, in the New York newspapers, always appearing under the collective pen name of Publius. The collection of all eighty-five essays into a single volume has been known ever thereafter as *The Federalist* or *The Federalist Papers*, and it is still generally regarded today as the single best interpretation of the Constitution as the Framers themselves intended it and understood it. Jefferson even called them "the best commentary on the principles of government which ever was written."

Many of the papers in *The Federalist* showed considerable originality and went on to become minor classics in the history of political thought – an improbable fate for mere newspaper columns. In *Federalist* 10, for example, James Madison put forward an incisive discussion of the problem of factions in political life – whence they come, how they can be controlled – and showed how a large and diverse republic like the United States could solve the factionalism that besets small republics by "extending the sphere," that is, by enlarging the republic to encompass so many different varieties of faction that no one of them would be able to predominate. In *Federalist* 51, he put forward a compelling account of how the Constitution's complex federal system could afford a "double security" for the rights of the people, pitting the states against the national government and dividing the national government against itself.

Beneath it all was a darkly realistic view of human potentialities, reflecting the chastened Calvinist view of human nature that permeated eighteenth-century America and informed the thinking of the Framers themselves, making them suspicious of concentrated power. "Ambition must be made to counteract ambition," Madison warned, because although a society needed the energy of its ambitious men, the most ambitious men were likely also to be the worst if they became corrupt, and the causes of faction were everywhere "sown into the nature of man." Hence the need for a Constitution that would not only create and bestow additional powers on officials of the central government but would see to it that those powers were incorporated in a larger design whose elements were carefully arranged so as to check and counter one another.

But perhaps the most portentous statement offered in the *Federalist* was penned by Hamilton and appeared at the beginning of *Federalist* 1:

> It has been frequently remarked that it seems to have been reserved to the people of this country, by their conduct and example, to decide the important question, whether societies of men are really capable or not of establishing good government from reflection and choice, or whether they are forever destined to depend for their political constitutions on accident and force. If there be any truth in the remark, the crisis at which we are arrived may with propriety be regarded as the era in which that decision is to be made; and a wrong election of the part we shall act may, in this view, deserve to be considered as the general misfortune of mankind.

In other words, the proponents of the new Constitution believed the stakes were very high. They saw their fight for a viable and effective constitution, created not by the collision of brute forces but by calm and patient reason, as an effort on behalf not only of the American people but of the whole world. They were echoing the Puritan idea of "commission," of a quasi-covenantal responsibility, both grand and grave, even though they were doing something quite different from what John Winthrop had sought to do. They were not establishing a Zion in the wilderness; they were trying to establish a constitution, a charter of fundamental law that could sustain a great republic built on the foundations of liberty and self-rule, for ages to come. They were engaged in one of the great experiments in the annals of politics, attempting to use the example of previous republics to avert those republics' fate. They used the new science of politics in trying to remedy the fatal flaws of republics past. They used history to defy history.

The ratification debates are well worth studying in great detail. But suffice it to say that the better organized Federalists were able to carry the day in the end, even winning ratification in the difficult and contentious state of New York. But the Anti-Federalists, despite their defeat and their awkward name, deserve credit for making a vital contribution to the eventual shape of the nation. They had feared, not without reason, that a more powerful central government might turn out to be tyrannical and become abusive of the fundamental rights and liberties for which Americans had fought their revolution. No one expressed that fear more memorably than the revolutionary hero-patriot Patrick Henry, who rose to speak vehemently against the Constitution at the Virginia State Ratifying Convention, decrying it as a document that "squints toward monarchy," aiming to make the country "a great and mighty empire" whose passion for grandeur and vainglory would prove "incompatible with the genius of republicanism." Many Virginians preferred the republican simplicity of agrarian life, and Henry's powerful words touched deep anxieties in them and convinced them and many Americans of the need for a bill of rights. In response to these legitimate fears, the victorious Federalists promised to add a bill of rights to the Constitution as one of the first acts of the new government.

They were true to their word, and the result was the first ten amendments to the Constitution, which have ever thereafter come to be regarded as integral to it. These were passed almost immediately by the First Congress and adopted by the states in 1791, with the goal of guaranteeing that the new Congress would make no laws infringing upon such rights as the freedom of religion, the freedom of speech and press, the right to bear arms, the right to a trial by jury, protection against unreasonable search and seizure, protection against the requirement to offer self-incriminating testimony, protection of due process rights, and other similar rights. In addition, the Tenth Amendment provided that any rights not explicitly delegated to the national government, or prohibited by it to the states, remained in the hands of the states or individuals.

The adoption of the Bill of Rights calmed all but the most determined critics of the Constitution. And although Madison and others had thought such a bill of rights was unnecessary, subsequent history showed them to be quite wrong about that and the Anti-Federalists to have been quite prescient, even prophetic, in many of their anxieties. Few today would ever want to contemplate the Constitution stripped of its Bill of Rights. It is one of the glories of the American constitutional system and, despite its added-on status, has become part of the very heart of the Constitution. It is one of the ironies of history that some of the fiercest opponents of the Constitution turned out to be among its chief benefactors. Although maybe that was not as ironic as it might seem, since the Constitution itself was consciously designed as an instrument to harness the energies of contending factions and groups, and since the Framers themselves incorporated their own quarrels into a Constitution that was in many ways better than what either side would have sought on its own.

Countless skeptics at the time were convinced that the Constitution could not last very long. Even George Washington confided to one of his fellow delegates that he did not expect it to last more than twenty years. He would have been as shocked as anyone to find it still functioning more than 230 years later.

That pessimism was not completely unwarranted, though. The Constitution itself was a remarkable achievement and a harbinger of hope. But it was also very much an experiment: a rough outline rather than a detailed plan, an architect's rendering rather than a finished building. No one could know for sure whether it would work. It had an elaborate system of checks and balances, but who could know for sure what that system would look like when put to use? It laid down some of the procedures by which decisions were to be arrived at, but it offered little guidance as to what the content of those decisions should be. It featured a much-empowered presidency, but offered little insight into how and where the president ought to exercise that power.

If the Constitution could be compared to a work of music, it could be said that in early 1789, it was nothing more than sheet music, elaborate musical notation printed on paper: artfully composed, perhaps, but meaningless until translated into actual sound – and no one yet knew what it would actually sound like. So many things remained to be filled in, connected, made concrete, actualized – and fought over. The new nation was moving into uncharted territory, while still carrying on its back the same crushing problems that had led it to turn in near-desperation to an entirely new Constitution. Each decision in the days ahead would be consequential, because each would fill in the picture, establishing practices and precedents and experiences that would steer the institution one way rather than another, as the experiment was little by little put to the test.

All this was happening, too, at a moment at which the nation had not yet had time to draw together, catch its breath, and develop a strong and cohesive sense of itself. History just kept coming at it. More than ever, it struggled to manage its considerable internal diversity – social, economic, cultural, religious – reflecting the regional tensions between the northern, southern, and middle sections that had already become evident in the colonial era, as well as a distinctive outlook emerging in the rowdy and expanding western areas, into which nearly uninterrupted streams of migrants were flowing and in which the pressures for further territorial expansion were ceaseless. But even with all these differences pulling it in different directions, it was also true that the United States remained an overwhelmingly agricultural and rural society, hugging the Atlantic seaboard, with only a handful of small cities and only the most rudimentary institutions and systems of transportation and communication to knit the nation together.

It made all the difference, though, that the dignified and universally trusted figure of George Washington would be available to serve as the first president. It had been in fact presumed by many at the Convention that he would be the one to hold that office. Sure enough, when the ballots of the first presidential electors were counted in the Senate on April 6, 1789, Washington was unanimously elected. On April 30, he took the oath of office at Federal Hall on Wall Street in New York City, which would be the seat of the national government for the next year. In his inaugural address delivered in the Senate chamber that day, Washington clearly and crisply echoed the vision that Hamilton had put forward in *Federalist* 1: "The preservation of the sacred fire of liberty, and the destiny of the Republican model of Government, are justly considered as deeply, perhaps as finally staked, on the experiment entrusted to the hands of the American people." The very future of liberty and self-rule: the stakes entailed in the American experiment would be nothing less.

Truth be told, though, Washington did not want the job. Even observers at his inauguration noted a certain hesitancy in his manner and modesty in his words, notwithstanding the military bearing of his tall, impressive figure and the ceremonial army sword he held. Nearing the age of sixty, after enduring two grinding decades of war and politics in which he always found himself thrust into a central role in determining the direction of his country, he wanted nothing so much as to be free of those burdens – and to retire from public life and return to Virginia, where he could enjoy the private joys of a gentleman farmer at his beautiful estate at Mount Vernon.

But it was not yet to be. Washington was blessed and cursed with the destiny of being the American nation's "indispensable man," as his biographer James Thomas Flexner rightly called him, the natural leader to whom everyone looked again and again for his judicious wisdom, his impartiality, and his selfless ability to rise above faction and partisanship to inspire and embody the guiding spirit of the fractious new nation. If the task before the country was a great experiment on behalf of all humanity but entrusted to the American people – a hugely consequential experiment that, like all experiments, could fail – how could he refuse to do his duty, particularly when he knew that he could discharge the tasks ahead more effectively than anyone else, at the nation's hour of greatest need?

His enormous sense of personal responsibility also made him acutely self-conscious. He knew that every decision he made and every action he took would have consequences, and this made him uncomfortable. "The eyes of Argus," the mythical giant of a hundred eyes, "are upon me," he complained, "and no slip will pass unnoticed." He told his friend Madison that "everything in our situation will serve to establish a Precedent," and for that reason, "it is devoutly wished on my part, that these precedents may be fixed on true principles." And so they were. Every one of his actions was carefully thought through, from his cautiously distant relations with Congress to his scrupulous avoidance of any hint of favoritism and nepotism in his appointments to his extreme care to project the right kind of public image, with a dignified and tasteful magnificence untainted by excess, as he thought appropriate to the republican leader of a great country.

His leadership style was reflected in the choices he made for his executive branch appointments. These men were chosen for their general competence and loyalty, not for their membership in any particular faction, for like so many military men Washington disliked political parties, and like so many of the Framers, he hoped that the new nation could avoid having them altogether. Following that pattern, he picked Thomas Jefferson to be his secretary of state, Alexander Hamilton as secretary of the Treasury, General Henry Knox of Massachusetts for secretary of war, and Edmund Randolph of Virginia as attorney general. He also established the precedent, not mentioned in the Constitution, of bringing these advisors together as a "cabinet," for the purpose of offering general advice to him, even outside their assigned areas.

Among the most urgent of the problems that Washington's new administration would have to face immediately was the country's parlous financial state. His Treasury secretary Hamilton, a brilliant and forward-thinking young leader with boundless energy and a firm commitment to the ideal of national greatness, addressed those problems head-on. Hamilton was a self-made man who had risen from a lowly birth on the tiny Caribbean island of Nevis to become Washington's personal aide during the Revolutionary War, and then one of the most successful lawyers in New York, as well as a political operator extraordinaire in the struggle to draft and then ratify the Constitution. He had vast ambitions for the American economy. America, he enthused, was a "Hercules in the cradle" that would flourish extravagantly if it could attract sufficient capital to develop its tremendous resources. To that end, he had devised and presented to Congress an ingenious three-part plan for bringing the nation's finances into a healthy order and igniting dynamic growth in the American economy.

First, the national government would pay off the national debt at face value and would assume all the war debts of the states. This bold action would at a single stroke demonstrate to the world the nation's creditworthiness and attract investors, even as it strengthened the union by shrewdly binding the self-interest of the grateful states to the union's general success. Second, high tariffs would be imposed on imported goods, which would protect the development of American industries by driving up the price of imports, even as it provided revenue for the Treasury from those very tariffs. Third, Congress would create a national bank for the storage of government funds and the printing of bank notes, which would provide a basis for a stable U.S. currency.

These initiatives all were adopted, although none without some measure of controversy. The debt-assumption idea, for example, was not universally applauded. Southern states, which generally had far less accumulated debt than the northern ones, saw the national government's assumption of state debts as inequitable. That was not an insuperable problem, though; the southern states would be mollified by the northern promise to locate the permanent capital of the country in the middle south on the Potomac River and dropped their objections. But a very fundamental debate, the first great debate about constitutional interpretation, was to erupt over the creation of a national bank.

Madison and his fellow Virginian Jefferson strongly opposed the idea, arguing that there was no basis in the Constitution for the creation of such a bank and that such a bold move would violate both the letter and spirit of the Constitution as a charter of limited and enumerated powers. Hamilton disagreed. He believed that justification for such expansive power was implicit in the Constitution's very essence and was stated fairly directly in Article I, section 8, which granted Congress power to "make all Laws which shall be necessary and proper" for carrying out the functions of government, as listed in that same section of the article. "The criterion," Hamilton said, "is the *end*," the larger purpose that the Constitution was meant to serve, "to which the measure relates as a *mean*." To Jefferson, though, this was tantamount to saying that the end justifies the means – and that inevitably meant the creation of "a boundless field of power, no longer susceptible of any definition."

As in many of the most bitter struggles, there was something to be said for, and against, both positions. But in the end, Washington sided with Hamilton, and the bank became a reality – and an instant success. Similarly successful was the bulk of Hamilton's entire bold economic program, which liberated the nation from its heavy debt burdens in surprisingly short order and established a sound and solvent basis for the capital accumulation and rapid economic growth that were the hallmarks of a dynamic capitalism. But the philosophical difference between Jefferson and Hamilton, and particularly the difference between "strict" and "loose" interpretations of the Constitution, was something that went very deep and would not go away so easily. In fact, it was a difference that would become one of the central points of contention in the nation's subsequent history. For many years to come, the opposition between Jefferson and Hamilton would define the field of debate in much of American political thought.

That opposition went far beyond the two men's different views of the Constitution, beyond their intense rivalry and personal antagonism, and beyond their frequent policy jousting within the Washington cabinet. The two men symbolized two different ways of thinking about the kind of republic that the United States should become. Hamilton was an urban man, a patron of business interests, a New Yorker intent on building an expanding economy featuring extensive trade and manufacturing and using a powerful and active central government to help create the conditions favoring such an economy. Jefferson, by contrast, was an agrarian gentleman farmer from Virginia, a brilliant and cosmopolitan intellectual who nevertheless disliked cities and distrusted commerce and financial wizardry and regarded government as a necessary evil, at best, to be kept as small as possible. He favored a decentralized republican form of government, overseeing a society inhabited primarily by a multitude of small, self-sufficient farmers. Farming, he believed, was the way of life most conducive to the development of virtuous character in the citizenry. "Those who labor in the earth," he wrote, "are the chosen people of God ... whose breasts He has made His peculiar deposit for genuine and substantial virtue." By contrast, he feared that if Hamilton were to get his way, the result would be a large class of wage laborers and other landless and propertyless men concentrated in the cities, highly dependent on others for their well-being and highly susceptible to the snares and deceptions and promises of demagogic politicians.

Nor were domestic matters the only source of the two men's opposition. When the French Revolution, which had begun in summer 1789, led to a major war between France and England, President Washington was presented with a sticky foreign-policy problem: should the United States give assistance to the French, who had, after all, been indispensable allies in the American Revolution, who continued to be technically in an alliance with the United States, and whose desire to establish a republican form of government was something that most Americans were inclined to support enthusiastically, as a movement resembling their own? Jefferson, who deeply sympathized with the revolutionary cause in France, and thought the British corrupt and decadent by comparison to the noble republicans on the other side of the English Channel, believed that American foreign policy should show a preference for the French. Hamilton, by contrast, was known to be pro-British and an admirer of the stable hierarchy of British society; he broke with the French Revolution by 1794, decrying the chaos into which the Revolution in France had so quickly descended.

In the end, Washington followed neither advisor entirely, insisting on a neutral course until the United States could grow stronger. He issued a proclamation to that effect on April 22, 1793, declaring the United States to be "friendly and impartial toward the belligerent powers" and cautioning American citizens against "aiding or abetting" either side. Jefferson was highly displeased with this formulation, which he believed effectively favored the British, and resigned his position as secretary of state in furious opposition. But Washington understood that the needs of the nation, which was in no position to contest the doings of a great power like England or France, dictated a near-extreme reluctance to allow the nation to be dragged into European conflicts on either side.

Washington went to great lengths to stay steady on the path of neutrality, even risking popular discontent with his leadership from a volatile public that failed to understand how damaging a war could be at this time. There is no better example of this costly prudence on Washington's part than the controversial and deeply unpopular Jay Treaty (1794), negotiated with the British by Supreme Court chief justice (and Publius co-contributor) John Jay. The Jay Treaty was admittedly a very mixed bag, falling far short of what most Americans, and even Washington himself, had hoped for. The good news was that it pried the British out of their western frontier forts at last, eliminating a persistent and insulting thorn in the nation's side, and it settled some compensation claims related to British seizures of American ships in the West Indies. It worked in the direction of helping the nation consolidate its control over its own lands. But it did so at the price of leaving in place terms of trade that were highly favorable to the British and letting the British off the hook for a great many legitimate claims against them.

Much of the American public reacted with fury at this rather one-sided treaty, and Washington himself privately hesitated before signing it. In retrospect, though, it was an act of wise statesmanship to accept it, since nothing was more important to the future of the country than the calming and regularization of relations between the United States and Britain. But because of its political unpopularity, it had the unsought side effect of drawing more Americans into the Jeffersonian camp and thus contributing to the polarization that would lead to an eruption of political partisanship.

Given the comprehensive range of the Jefferson–Hamilton feud, it is no wonder that it turned out to be the seedbed of the first system of opposing political parties in the history of the United States. In addition, it is no wonder that a national beginning as fraught with large expectations as the American one would be productive of immense anxieties, constant worries that the great national experiment was being destroyed from within, by those of the opposing faction. We already saw these kinds of concerns come to the fore during the debate over ratification, but the French Revolution sharpened these concerns to a razor's edge. There was exaggeration and misperception on both sides. The Hamiltonians feared that Jefferson's followers were soft on mob rule and the violent overthrow of elites; the Jeffersonians feared that Hamilton and his followers really wanted a monarchy and that Hamilton's admiration for a vigorous central government and his admiration for Britain went hand in hand. Both sides feared, perhaps excessively, at times even hysterically, that the other side did not have the country's best interests at heart.

Under such circumstances, the formation of political parties was almost inevitable. Nevertheless, this development would be a bitter disappointment to a great many of the Framers. Nearly all of them, particularly Washington himself, had hoped that political parties would never have a chance to arise under the new government, a position that in retrospect seems more than a little bit utopian. In any event, the party lines that were steadily forming, pitting Hamilton's Federalist Party against Jefferson's Democratic Republicans*, did not become overt and hardened until after Washington stepped down from the presidency. This was out of deferential respect for the indispensable man himself, who continued to be a compelling figure of national unity, like a great dam holding back flood waters, even as the fierce quarrel between the two opposing camps gathered strength and looked for opportunities to manifest itself.

By the end of a second term of office, however, Washington was ready to retire and at long last to return to Mount Vernon for good. He announced his

---

* Hereinafter referred to as "Republicans," but not to be confused with the Republican Party formed in 1854.

decision to do so in a "Farewell Address" to the nation, delivered on September 17, 1796, the ninth anniversary of the adoption of the Constitution in Philadelphia, and then published in the nation's newspapers in fall 1796. But the title was deceptive; the speech did much more than say good-bye. It was a profound reflection on the national condition, containing the "disinterested warnings of a parting friend." It was an effort on Washington's part to project his wise and stabilizing influence forward into the American future, informing the thinking of future leaders, summarizing in durable form his wisdom about questions of statecraft, and voicing his worries about the new nation's presenting challenges. As such, it became an instant classic in the annals of American oratory and a point of reference in the centuries to come. Even today, the speech has much to tell us and richly repays careful study.

If its theme could be summed up in a single term, that term would be *national unity.* All around him, Washington saw evidence of growing divisions, which presaged troubles to come. Washington began by making it clear how much he deplored "the baneful effects of the spirit of party," the acrimony that was pushing the nation into the institutionalizing of partisan politics. He expressed his concern about the related rise of sectional conflict, in which northerners and southerners and easterners and westerners all seemed to be placing their local interests above those of the country as a whole, thereby forgetting all the ways in which their differences were mutually beneficial and necessary for the thriving of the whole.

The most enduringly influential part of the speech dealt with foreign affairs and America's proper disposition to the rest of the world. In such matters, Washington advised being discreet, dispassionate, and carefully aloof, always placing the interests of the nation over other considerations. He firmly cautioned against American citizens allowing "passionate attachments" to foreign nations and causes to override their commitment to their own nation's unity and interests. In addition, he urged American citizens to be constantly on their guard against efforts by foreign countries to infiltrate and destabilize and otherwise manipulate American politics to their own advantage. The new American nation had an inestimable advantage over all others in its remoteness, an existence buffered by a vast ocean. That advantage should not be forfeited, Washington cautioned, out of misplaced passion. The controversies that had been roiling Europe since 1789 were "foreign to our concerns," and America should stay clear of them, avoiding all "permanent alliances," a formulation that well reflects the thinking behind his neutrality policies. That admonition, that the United States should avoid foreign entanglements, especially permanent ones, remained a touchstone of American foreign policy for a century to come.

In the election of 1796, the first contested election in American history, Washington's vice president, John Adams narrowly defeated Jefferson. The closeness of his victory was a sign of the growing strength of the Republican faction and the corresponding discontent with the Federalists, who had been in power since 1789. So Adams began his administration with some disadvantages. Perhaps the greatest disadvantage of all was the extent to which he was doomed to suffer from comparison to his illustrious predecessor. If the default sentiment toward Washington was respect bordering on reverence, Adams excited something like the opposite emotions. He utterly lacked Washington's imposing stature and stately reserve; instead, he was a short, stocky, and voluble man, transparently vain, peevish, and easily roused to anger.

But Adams was also incorruptibly honest and public spirited, one of the greatest of the patriots, having been a revolutionary leader, a member of the Continental Congress, an effective diplomat who served the new nation with distinction in Europe, and a man of impressive intellectual sophistication and stubborn independence of mind. We know a great deal about his long and unusually affectionate marriage to Abigail, a formidable and witty woman who was fully his partner and equal, thanks to the survival of their extensive correspondence, a by-product of the months and years they were forced to spend apart because of his tireless service to his country. Through thick and thin, Abigail would be his soul mate and his most trusted advisor. In retrospect, this quirky and flawed but compulsively truthful man may well be the most lovable of all the Founders.

As president, though, he was dealt a very tough hand. The spillover from the ongoing French problem, which had been greatly exacerbated by public outrage over the Jay Treaty, threatened to engulf Adams's administration from the outset. French attacks on American shipping had long been a problem, and they were now escalating. When Adams attempted to negotiate with the French about the matter, his commissioners were presented with a crude demand from three of French foreign minister Talleyrand's intermediaries (known only as X, Y, and Z) for a very large bribe as the precondition of their even being permitted to begin such negotiations. The Americans curtly refused, and when Adams released the commissioners' report to the public, publicly revealing the French agents' outrageous and insulting demand, it caused an uproar and an abrupt reversal in the public's formerly affectionate view of France. "Millions for defense, but not one cent for tribute!" was the cry that went up throughout the country, and even some Republicans joined in the demand for war against the French as the only suitable answer. Yet Adams resisted the feverish cries for a declaration of war, soberly recognizing that the nation, which lacked even the semblance of a navy and had a grand total of thirty-five hundred men under arms, was spectacularly ill equipped for any such venture. It was a wise move, but one that did not endear him to the public. But then, making himself endearing to his own public was not one of John Adams's talents.

All this foreign turbulence also rocked the nation's internal politics and led it into a season of instability and genuine peril, in which the fragility of its unity was made all too alarmingly clear. The Republicans had always favored friendly relations with France, but now they found themselves on the defensive about that, having to choose between appearing to favor the revolutionary objectives of one of their nation's external adversaries (the French) or endorsing the position of their own internal political enemies (the Federalists). Meanwhile, some of the more extreme elements among the Federalists saw in this situation a rare opportunity to corner and demolish their ideological opponents. They allowed themselves to be persuaded, whether rationally or not, that the Republicans might well decide to side with the French in the event of war. If that were to happen, it would represent a clear threat to the nation, and so it should be prevented at all costs.

The specter of such treasonable potential acts, accompanied by a veritable flood of wild fabrications and misrepresentations filling the public press – the 1790s version of "fake news" – enraged the Federalists. Adding to their rage was the fact that Jefferson himself proved such a skilled and ruthless practitioner of hardball electoral tactics, attacking his enemies indirectly by planting rumors about them in the press or publishing anonymous editorials against them – or hiring writers to portray opponents like John Adams in a harshly negative light, as secret monarchists who longed to reign as kings. The Federalists were not above doing the same thing, but they did not do it nearly as well. In any event, the polarized and overheated atmosphere allowed the Federalists to push through Congress and obtain Adams's signature for legislation designed to suppress discordant or defamatory voices and prevent foreign infiltration of American politics.

These were the infamous Alien and Sedition Acts of 1798, which authorized the president to expel "dangerous" aliens at his pleasure and severely limited freedom of speech and the press. Adams did not originate the acts, but he did not hesitate to support them, and that proved to be a grave error on his part, both substantively and politically. The First Amendment's guarantees of freedom of speech and press were regarded by most Americans as fundamental to their way of life and therefore sacrosanct, and yet those sacred guarantees were seemingly being casually set aside so that the party in power could go after its opposition more readily. It now became a crime to publish what someone else might judge to be "false, scandalous, and malicious" criticism of high government officials; twenty-five Republican newspaper editors were prosecuted in the run-up to the election.

In angry response, Jefferson and Madison drafted the Kentucky and Virginia Resolutions, which denounced the Alien and Sedition Acts, and declared that because the Constitution was a "compact" among previously existing states, the individual states had the right to interpose themselves against, or to nullify outright, unconstitutional acts of the national government. Such propositions were every bit as dangerous as the Alien and Sedition Acts, for if implemented, they would have the effect of undermining the nation's entire constitutional structure. George Washington was appalled by them and warned Patrick Henry that, if pursued, such measures would "dissolve the union." The conflict had ratcheted up several notches, into extremely dangerous territory.

Clearly both parties were veering out of control, supplying an object lesson in the reasons why Washington loathed political parties. If the Alien and Sedition Acts had been excessive and dangerous, so too were the doctrines of interposition and nullification being offered by Jefferson and Madison. It seemed that in the heat of the moment, both sides of this controversy were losing their bearings and introducing ideas and practices that were inimical to the heart and soul of American constitutionalism. As the election of 1800 approached, the Federalists painted their opponents as wild-eyed Jacobins, atheists, and revolutionaries bent upon plunging the nation into a bloody French-style social revolution. Meanwhile, the Republicans depicted the Federalists as cryptomonarchists and would-be aristocrats, rabid enemies of liberty and friends of the wealthy who were using the instruments of government to consolidate their power and negate the effects of the Revolution. To top it all off, Adams's statesmanlike but politically costly decision to seek peace with the French rather than go to war against them lost him essential political support from members of his own party.

It was a volatile situation in which anything could happen. All was in readiness for an extremely contentious, and close, election. It seemed both unutterably sad and eerily ominous when the news came, in December 1799, of the death of George Washington, the august unifier whose presence had always pulled the nation together in the past. Had something vitally important gone out of the nation's life and spirit along with him? Who or what in the current madhouse of contention could possibly arise to take his place as a national unifier?

Such worries turned out to be unwarranted, at least in the short term. In the end, Thomas Jefferson defeated Adams by a small but decisive margin, seventy-three electoral votes to Adams's sixty-five. The outcome was complicated by the fact that, owing to a defect in the Constitution, which would soon be corrected by adoption of the Twelfth Amendment, Jefferson's vice presidential running mate Aaron Burr received the same number of electoral votes as Jefferson, and the matter of who became president had to be decided by a contested vote of the House of Representatives. That vote became a great drama, requiring the intervention of Hamilton on his arch-rival's behalf to thwart the candidacy of the disreputable Burr – an act of great statesmanship on Hamilton's part, but one that would eventually lead to a duel between Hamilton and Burr, in which Hamilton would be killed. But none of this baroque complexity and legislative melodrama altered the fact that the outcome of the election was decisive, that it was accepted by all parties as decisive, and that it therefore represented a very important inflection point in the development of American government and society.

This was so for several reasons. Perhaps most importantly, the inauguration of Jefferson in 1801 was the first time that the orderly, peaceful, and legitimate transfer of power from one political party to another had taken place in the United States under the new Constitution. The importance of this achievement is hard to exaggerate. Almost every kind of political regime stumbles when it arrives at the threshold of a major transition, and one of the best measures of stability in such a regime is precisely in the ease, or difficulty, with which it surmounts that challenge and replaces one leader with a new one. Even under the best of circumstances, that can be difficult. Even the best ruler can be followed by a bad one who undoes the good his predecessor had achieved. Even the best regime can buckle and bend under the pressures of war, social unrest, or economic deprivation. Even under the best of times, a transfer of power is a dicey proposition, because it necessarily takes place outside the guardrails of what is unusual and habitual and requires the initiation of something new, something that has not existed before.

And these were not the best of times. Given the frenetic circumstances under which the 1800 election took place, and the relative newness of the institutions that the Constitution had created, it could hardly have been a worse time to put the new Constitution to the test. How stable was this post-Washington America? How sturdy could those institutions be – and how deeply had they been sunk into the hearts of the people? The fact that the electoral outcome might mean the defeat and removal from office of an incumbent president, John Adams, made the question even more challenging. For what if, as many people feared, there was armed resistance?

All these were legitimate questions. If one had set out purposely to design things so that the divisions in society were so deep that Americans' respect for the rule of law would surely be defeated by their passions and their fears, one could hardly have improved on this scenario, short of imagining a fully launched and bloody civil war. That the nation did surmount this challenge, and did so not only peacefully but with surprising finesse, was quietly astonishing – and the best augury imaginable for the future success of the American experiment.

In addition, the election of 1800 was an important transition because it marked a change of direction. The Republican victory would mean a movement in the direction of somewhat greater democratization, wider political participation, a permanent place for political parties in the American system, and a shift in the tone and direction of many elements of both domestic and foreign policy.

But one should not exaggerate the extent of these changes. Jefferson himself grandly referred, in an 1819 letter written long after his retirement from public life, to "the revolution of 1800," and many historians have followed him in employing that expression. But Jefferson was referring in those words not to his implementation of transforming revolutionary policies but merely to the peaceable transfer of power itself: the nation's success in producing change "not effected indeed by the sword . . . but by the rational and peaceable instrument of reform, the suffrage of the people."

Indeed, Jefferson as president turned out to be a far less revolutionary leader than his enemies had feared or his friends had hoped. He signaled this would be the case in his First Inaugural Address, a speech nearly as masterly as Washington's Farewell Address, marked by its humility ("the task is above me. . . . I approach it with anxious and awful presentiments"), its respect for the losing side ("the minority possess their equal rights, which equal law must protect"), and above all, its desire to heal and unify the country ("Every difference of opinion is not a difference of principle. . . . We are all Republicans – we are all Federalists"). He also signaled a generous tolerance of dissent and varied opinion: "If there be any among us who would wish to dissolve this Union or to change its republican form, let them stand undisturbed as monuments of the safety with which error of opinion may be tolerated where reason is left free to combat it." He concluded with a list of principles he would follow, none of which could be seen as controversial and some of which echoed Washington's warnings against foreign entanglements very closely, repeatedly invoking the same rights of Englishmen that had been respected since time immemorial, products of "the wisdom of our sages and the blood of our heroes," nearly all of them enshrined in the Bill of Rights.

It is hard to imagine a more winning and conciliatory speech for the occasion and a more welcome balm to jangled public nerves after a season of near-hysteria that threatened the Union itself. Jefferson continued in the same calming and moderate vein during his early days as president. While he would go on to make some policy changes, there were but few that could be called dramatic, let alone drastic. He made modest reductions in military expenditures, reduced excise taxes that the Federalists had imposed, and worked hard to pay down the national debt. But he accepted that the Hamiltonian financial program, which he had fought tooth and nail while in Washington's cabinet, was here to stay, and he made a point of indicating his support for it.

The "revolution of 1800" is better thought of, then, as a significant step forward in the unification and maturation of the fledgling republic. The Constitution itself was a great achievement, but from its ratification debates forward, it was in the process of being worked on, and worked out, in actual political practice. Jefferson was an intellectual, but he was not an ideologue. The party system that the Framers had not wanted had arisen anyway, inexorably, and it served the Constitution well, as a way not only to express and channel controversy but to organize it and contain it.

An important outward sign of this maturation was the very venue at which Jefferson took the presidential oath of office and delivered his address. It did not occur in New York or Philadelphia but rather, for the first time, in the brand-new capital city of Washington. The Washington of that time, of course, only faintly resembled the grand capital city of today. But even then it possessed the bones of its later body, in the form of the grand urban design that French military engineer Pierre L'Enfant had been commissioned in 1791, by George Washington, to produce.

L'Enfant was a genius, but a temperamental one, and in the end he did not stay to finish his project. But thanks to the fundamental design he provided, Washington was to be unique among American cities. Most of those cities would be laid out to the extent possible as simple functional grids; one might think, for example, of the central business districts of such cities as Chicago or New York. L'Enfant's Washington would include such a functional grid but also would superimpose upon it a graceful latticework of wide diagonal avenues that interconnected through circles and squares, providing for an endless array of dramatic and unexpected vistas as well as numerous park sites for the erection of statuary and monuments to celebrate and memorialize the unfolding national story. Capitol Hill, site of Congress, would be the center of the Federal City, and diagonal boulevards named after the states of the union would radiate out from it, from the President's House, and from a few other important nodes. Under L'Enfant's plan, the area west of the Capitol was to be a garden-lined public promenade, a "grand avenue" open to all comers, something that would have been unthinkable in L'Enfant's France but seemed to him perfectly appropriate to the more democratic ethos of the new United States – as indeed it was.

But the "grand avenue" L'Enfant envisioned was not built, and it was not until the twentieth century that the area, now known as the Mall, would be made into an open space, eventually to become home to the Smithsonian Institution and a distinguished collection of museums, as well as being a national stage and premier site for public celebrations and civic protests. As such, it would realize L'Enfant's essential intention, but in a way very different from what he had in mind.

All that would still be many years into the future, though. At the time of Jefferson's inauguration, it was not uncommon to find farm animals grazing on the verdant land, content as if they were in the countryside. At this outwardly bucolic moment in the city's history, a mere ten years into its construction, Washington, D.C., was still a very rough work in progress, like the largely agrarian nation itself. But like the nation, the city had begun life with a brilliant founding plan, and like the nation, it would now take shape according to that plan.

CHAPTER SIX

FROM JEFFERSON TO JACKSON

The Rise of the Common Man

THE CONTRAST BETWEEN THOMAS JEFFERSON'S PRESIDENCY and the two Federalist presidencies that preceded it was as much a matter of style as of substance. Washington and Adams both believed it important to surround the presidency with an aura of grandeur and high dignity; think, for example, of Washington's insistence on traveling in a carriage drawn by a team of impressive white horses. Such elevated self-presentation was not for the sake of leaders' egos but instead was meant to serve an important public purpose. But it troubled those of a more republican sensibility, who feared the infiltration of monarchical ideas and practices into the new office of the presidency. Jefferson accordingly chose to depart from his predecessors' example. In pointed contrast with them, he decided to walk rather than ride to and from the Capitol for his inauguration, and he went on to establish a tone of low-key, unpretentious republican informality in his dress, his manners, and his way of entertaining visitors to the brand-new presidential residence known as the White House.

But the Jefferson administration had its own kind of glamour. Jefferson was not an especially gifted public speaker, but he was well known for his dazzling intellect, personal magnetism, and singular charm, all which he put to effective use in intimate dinner parties at the White House with carefully chosen members of Congress, Federalist and Republican alike. On these occasions he would serve his guests the superb cuisine produced by his French chef and ply them with excellent wines, all the while engaging them in brilliant conversation, getting to know them better than they realized, and subtly working his influence on them.

There was an iron fist beneath this velvet glove, however, for Jefferson was also a far more partisan figure than his predecessors. Indeed, he consciously embraced the role of party leader and, unlike Washington and Adams, appointed only men of his own party to the top cabinet positions. He excelled at this kind of strategic discipline, and over the two terms of his presidency, he enjoyed remarkable success in firmly establishing Republican dominance and putting the Federalist party out of business and on the road to extinction. Even so, despite his manifold skills, there was one area of the national government that eluded his control and remained in the hands of the Federalists: the judiciary.

This was extremely frustrating to Jefferson. Like many of his Anti-Federalist and Republican allies, he had a visceral dislike for judges and the exercise of judicial power and authority. The judiciary was, after all, the least democratic branch of government, deliberately insulated from the influence of political majorities and more generally from the current wishes of the people, which could often be inflamed by fleeting passions or passing circumstances. Instead, it drew its authority from the objectivity and permanence of laws and precedents that living people had little or no role in formulating or approving. And that chafed at Jefferson's democratic sensibility. "No society," he wrote to Madison in 1789, indicating his skepticism about the Constitution that Madison himself had largely drafted, "can make a perpetual constitution, or even a perpetual law. The earth belongs always to the living generation." In addition, Jefferson distrusted the tendency of judges to seek expanded influence, by using the questions before them to establish new precedents and extend their powers – or, in his colorful phrase, "to throw an anchor ahead, and grapple further hold for future advances of power" – all of it in ways designed to circumvent the will of the people as expressed in their democratic institutions.

These complaints were not only abstract and philosophical. Once Jefferson became president, they became practical and immediate. He was infuriated that Adams had, in the last days of his presidency, appointed the Virginia Federalist John Marshall, a distant cousin for whom Jefferson had little personal or political use, as chief justice of the Supreme Court; and then Adams had gone on, by means of the hastily passed Judiciary Act of 1801, to create six new federal circuit courts and staff them entirely with Federalists, from the judges down to the clerks. Thanks to these rather crafty court-packing moves, the judiciary would remain a Federalist redoubt for years to come, with Marshall serving as an exceptionally commanding chief justice for an astonishing thirty-four years, until 1835.

Much of the Court's enduring influence owed to the brilliant and savvy leadership of Marshall, who was not widely read in the law and had no previous judicial experience but made up for those liabilities with his strong sense of the

Court's proper place in the constitutional order and his uncanny ability to maneuver events and cases toward the Court achieving that status. It was clear to a great many Americans after their experiences with the Alien and Sedition Acts that there needed to be some check on the executive and legislative branches, to serve as insurance against another such time when those two branches again combined to pursue an unconstitutional end or pursue a legitimate end by improper means. It seems fairly certain that the Framers had wanted for the Supreme Court to play such a role, but they failed to spell out exactly how the check would operate. Marshall succeeded in establishing just such a check, the Court's right of judicial review, through the 1803 case of *Marbury v. Madison*, the first important case to come before his Court and a truly impressive example of Marshall's skillfulness in pursuing his goals.

It was a crafty decision, just the kind of judicial move that made Jefferson's blood boil. The roots of the case involved Adams's "midnight" appointments to the circuit courts that had so angered Jefferson. When he discovered that several of the documents commissioning justices of the peace in the District of Columbia had inadvertently not been sent out, even though they had been duly signed by Adams, Jefferson decided to hold on to them, thus effectively stopping the appointments themselves. In response, one of the appointees, William Marbury, sued for a Court order, or writ of mandamus, that would compel Madison, who served as Jefferson's secretary of state, to deliver his commission.

This situation presented Marshall with a sticky problem. If he refused to issue the order, it would avoid a collision with the new administration, but it would appear that he was kowtowing to Jefferson, a perception that would set a bad precedent, greatly damaging the prestige and independence of the Court and undermining the separation of powers, even as it deprived the judiciary of another Federalist judge. And besides, Marbury had a rather strong and substantial claim to the position, which fact made the avoidance strategy seem all the more untenable. But if Marshall agreed to issue the order to grant Marbury his commission, it was likely that Madison would ignore him, and the mood of the country, still very sour toward the Federalists, would likely back Madison up. Such a turn of events would be a disaster for the Court, because it would amount to an advertisement of the Court's impotence and yet another way of undermining the separation of powers. What, then, was he to do?

The strategy at which he arrived was ingenious. First, he argued that yes, Marbury had a right to his commission, under his reading of the thirteenth article of the Judiciary Act of 1789, which had set up the federal court system in the first place. But the article that Marbury invoked was, Marshall argued, unconstitutional. Congress could not legally grant the Supreme Court the power to issue writs of mandamus. This problem of jurisdiction in turn meant that the law

Marbury was invoking was null and void and could not be used to further his claims. Marbury therefore would not be able to receive his commission.

The brilliance of this solution might not be immediately apparent. But it is important to keep in mind that the work of courts, and especially courts of appeal, is built around the authority of legal precedents. And like a chess master who sacrifices his pawns to get at his opponent's queen, Marshall sacrificed Marbury's commission to take possession of something much larger. He in effect refrained from pursuing a small and unimportant potential Federalist gain (Marbury as a single Federalist judge) in exchange for a much larger gain: establishing a precedent that could be used again and again, because it served to underscore the independent power of the Supreme Court to rule an act of Congress unconstitutional. He gave Jefferson the decision Jefferson wanted, but he did so by means of reasoning that Jefferson did not want at all. But there was nothing that Jefferson could do about it, since the actual result of the decision was completely in line with his wishes. It was the reasoning, not the result, that would prove to be consequential in the end, allowing the case to establish a vital argument for limited government. The precedent and long usage of *Marbury* placed a very important circumscription on the power of Congress.

Talk about throwing an anchor ahead, and grappling toward future advances of power! And this gain was made all the more annoying to Jefferson because of the Federalist domination of the courts. Jefferson was not through fighting yet and went on to resist judicial Federalism by pressing for the impeachment and removal of judges whom he considered particularly noxious and partisan. But that campaign failed miserably – Jefferson badly overreached in trying to remove Samuel Chase, a revolutionary-era patriot and associate justice of the Supreme Court – and with only one exception, the Federalist judges remained in place. Marshall was left largely unscathed and, through a series of landmark decisions passed down during his many years in office, was able to strengthen the hand of the Court and of the central government – notwithstanding the dominance of Jefferson's party and the Federalists' banishment from executive and legislative power.

He would manage this by proceeding in a steady, methodical, case-by-case way, along the path that he had already pioneered with *Marbury v. Madison*. In *Fletcher v. Peck* (1810), the Court established that a state law could be declared unconstitutional. In *Martin v. Hunter's Lessee* (1816), the Court rejected the idea of a compact theory of union and established its jurisdiction over state courts on matters of constitutional interpretation. In *Dartmouth College v. Woodward* (1819), it declared that the Constitution prevented a state from altering a contract for a private corporation. In *McCulloch v. Maryland* (1819), the Court forbade a state to tax a federal institution (in this case, the Bank of the United

States) and confirmed the constitutionality of the Bank – and, in the process, once again rejected the "compact theory" of the Constitution's origins, resting them instead upon the sovereignty of the people acting in aggregate. He thus endorsed a strong doctrine of the federal government's "implied" powers under the "necessary and proper" clause. In *Cohens v. Virginia* (1821), the Court established the principle that the Supreme Court could review a state court's decision on any matters touching upon the power of the national government. And in *Gibbons v. Ogden* (1821), the Court asserted the federal government's primacy in the regulation of interstate commerce.

So even despite his popularity, Jefferson had to accept a measure of compromise with the opposition on the Court, just as he had accepted most of the Hamiltonian economic program to achieve national peace. Jefferson came into office with his own vision of the American future and well-developed ideas and firm convictions about the right ordering of political society. But like every American president in the nation's history, he had to adjust his ideas to the realities of practical politics in a complex and changing world.

Nor were these aspects of the Federalist legacy the only ways that Jefferson's administration had to depart sharply from Jefferson's principles to govern effectively. Perhaps the single greatest achievement of his first administration, and quite possibly of his presidency, was the American acquisition in 1803 of the Louisiana Territory, more than eight hundred thousand square miles of land west of the Mississippi River, an act that more than doubled the size of the country and at the same time removed the possibility of a dangerous foreign presence at the mouth of a great river crucial to western commerce. It opened the way for the United States to go from being a coastal nation to a sprawling continental one.

But it was also an act that involved Jefferson in what was arguably a violation of the Constitution – and certainly a violation of Jefferson's own understanding of the Constitution and of the principles of constitutional interpretation, as he had insisted upon them in his fierce battles with Hamilton during the Washington administration.

The lands in question had in 1800 been secretly reacquired by the French from the Spanish, reflecting Napoleon's interest in possibly reviving the French empire in the New World. This possibility rightly alarmed Jefferson, and he sent his protégé James Monroe, then governor of Virginia, to join ambassador Robert R. Livingston in France, with authorization from Jefferson to spend up to $10 million to purchase the city of New Orleans, which controlled commerce on the Mississippi and thus represented a potential chokepoint for American trade.

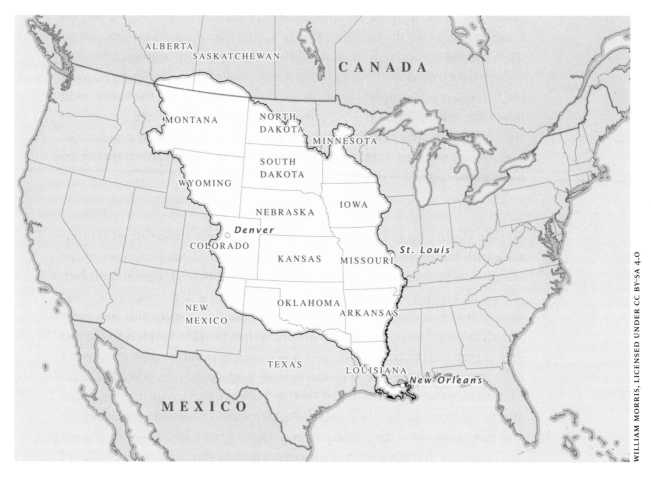

The Louisiana Purchase, superimposed upon the boundaries of the present-day states. At the time of the acquisition of Louisiana, most of the area to the south and west was owned by Spain.

Monroe joined Livingston in Paris in April 1803. Much to the two American ministers' surprise, they found that the French had experienced a change of heart about reviving their North American empire. Given Napoleon's inability to put down a bloody slave revolution in the French colony of Saint-Domingue (modern Haiti), and his need for money to support an impending war with Great Britain, he was only too happy to unload the territory at a bargain price. They offered to sell all the Louisiana Territory, a huge swath of land between the Mississippi River and the Rocky Mountains, extending north from the Gulf of Mexico to present-day Montana and west as far as Colorado and Wyoming, for a mere $15 million, or 60 million francs. Livingston and Monroe did not hesitate. Even though it meant exceeding their instructions, they said yes to the offer and signed a treaty.

Clearly they were right to do so; it was the deal of the century, if not the millennium. But it left Jefferson with a dilemma. He and nearly all Americans clearly saw the benefit of the Louisiana Purchase to the nation's future. For Jefferson, who wanted the United States to stay a primarily agricultural polity as long as possible, the purchase was a godsend, making available vast tracts of land that could enable the nation's development to take just such an agrarian track, and to do so at negligible cost. He could not say no.

There was a problem, though: there was no provision in the Constitution authorizing a president to add new territory to the United States by the purchase of land. Strict-constructionist Jefferson was now caught between high principle and high-stakes governance. It would have been unthinkable to pass up this offer – but how could it be justified within a strict-constructionist reading of the Constitution? He dithered for a while and tried to come up with a constitutional amendment, either before or after the Senate ratified the treaty, but finally concluded that the best path ahead would be to ignore the "metaphysical subtleties" of the issue; "the less we say about constitutional difficulties the better." Congress ratified the treaty, and that was that. Jefferson would cruise to a landslide reelection in 1804, and his popularity would soar as never before.

Observe the many layers of irony here. Just as Jefferson consolidated the Hamiltonian economic program rather than reversing it, so too he more than reinforced the Hamiltonian interpretation of the Constitution, rather than reversing it, by means of the single greatest exercise of executive power in the country's history to that point. And at the same time, he consolidated his own power, and the power of his party, for a generation to come. The fortunes of the Federalist Party sank further and further – even though some of the most consequential actions taken by Jefferson, actions that greatly bolstered his popularity, would seem to have supported their principles far more than they did his. It would not be the last time that a president would find it necessary to consolidate and secure some of the very initiatives and ideas he had opposed before taking office – not out of cynicism or opportunism but out of political and pragmatic necessity. It only added to the irony that a bitter rump group of defeated Federalists in New England, known as the Essex Junto (because so many of them were from Essex County, Massachusetts), began hatching schemes to secede from the Union and tried, unsuccessfully, to get Hamilton to join them. Federalists as secessionists and Republicans as nationalists: the world did seem to be turning upside down again.

But with the acquisition of the vast Louisiana Territory, it was as if a page of history was being turned and a new chapter begun, with a whole rich field of activity in the American interior being opened up for the American people. Jefferson, whose lively intellectual interests included a passion for scientific knowledge and research, could hardly wait to find out what mysteries and wonders awaited the nation in its new uncharted territory. In fact, he had already been planning a transcontinental expedition even before the chance to acquire all of Louisiana fell in his lap; among other things, he hoped to find a waterway linkage between the Missouri and Columbia rivers, yet another iteration of the old dream of a Northwest Passage. He had already been organizing an exploratory mission, called the Corps of Discovery Expedition, led by his private secretary Captain Meriwether Lewis and Second Lieutenant William Clark, both of them army officers with a record of frontier service, to study the area's topography and animal and plant life, establish relations with the indigenous peoples, and inventory the available natural resources – and to deliver a full and comprehensive report of their findings, complete with maps, sketches, and journals. They set out from St. Louis in May 1804, a party of some fifty men in a large keelboat and two dugout canoes, and, after traveling up the Missouri River, crossing the Continental Divide, and proceeding to the Pacific Ocean by way of the Columbia River, reached the site of present-day Portland, Oregon, in November 1805. After accumulating an amazing record of adventures, and an even more amazing treasury of information and artifacts relating to the lands through which they had passed, they finally returned to St. Louis in September 1806 under national acclaim, their assigned mission more than accomplished.

The national celebration attending the triumphant return of Lewis and Clark underscored the extent to which the exploration and settlement of the vast and ever-growing American interior would become an important focus of the nation's energies in the years of the nineteenth century. But there were still nagging questions of foreign relations to be resolved before that focus could be brought into a commanding role. Most of these problems revolved around the American effort to protect its neutral status and assert the principle of free trade in the larger world.

First, Jefferson sought to reverse his predecessors' practice of paying tribute to pirates from the Barbary States of North Africa as a way of buying protection for American shipping in the Mediterranean. By dispatching a small fleet of the U.S. Navy to the region, he gained a measure of respect and protection for American trade in the area.

Much more difficult were the problems with the British. The United States still found itself caught in the middle of the struggle between the British and the French, at a time when British control of the seas and French control of the landmass of Continental Europe were near-complete and each nation was trying to use economic warfare to cripple or disable the other. The American doctrine of neutral rights, permitting the United States to trade with all belligerents equally, was not tenable under the circumstances. The British especially made a mockery of American neutral claims with the practice of seizing American sailors whom they claimed to be British subjects and "impressing" them into service in the British Navy.

Like Washington and Adams before him, Jefferson did not want war, and in fact his reductions in military spending had made the weak American military even weaker. As an alternative, he persuaded Congress to pass the Embargo Act in 1807, which prohibited American merchant ships from sailing into foreign ports. He hoped that British dependence on American goods and shipping would force their hand and lead to a peaceful settlement of the issue. But unfortunately, the embargo backfired disastrously and caused far more hardship at home than it did to Britain, which was easily able to find substitutes for the lost American trade. After causing a near-depression in the New England states, Jefferson was succeeding in nothing so much as giving the Federalists, and the Essex Junto, a new lease on life by rallying public opposition to a much-hated law. Finally, as one of his last acts as president, he called for the repeal of the embargo.

Jefferson could have run for election a third time; there was no constitutional prohibition against it. But he believed in the importance of following Washington's example of retiring from office after two terms, as a practice befitting a genuine republican form of government. Even if he had not believed that, though, he would have been likely to retire. Four years after winning reelection by a lopsided margin, his fortunes had turned for the worse, and he was leaving office a weary man, debt-ridden, exhausted, defeated by seemingly insoluble problems, and overwhelmed with rheumatism and persistent headaches and other physical ailments. He came to refer to his presidential experience as "splendid misery" and even seemed to wonder for a time whether he had been miscast for his role in politics, whether he was made for a more contemplative existence. He wrote to a French economist friend just before the end of his second term, "Never did a prisoner, released from his chains, feel such relief as I shall on shaking off the shackles of power. Nature intended me for the tranquil pursuits of science, by rendering them my supreme delight. But the enormities of the times in which I have lived, have forced me to … commit myself on the boisterous ocean of political passions. I thank God for the opportunity of retiring from them."

But the sixty-five-year-old Jefferson was irrepressible, and his energies were soon restored by leaving politics behind and returning to his beloved home of Monticello outside Charlottesville. Not only he did he busy himself with scientific work, one of his life's unalloyed joys, but he would go on to establish the University of Virginia, an important step toward the fulfillment of his grand democratic dream of a free public education for all comers, irrespective of their social class or economic level. If there was a central feature of Jeffersonian democracy, it was this belief in education as the great equalizer, the force that could potentially raise any man to the level of any other – and education as the essential factor in forming citizens who would be capable of self-rule. "The qualifications for self government in society," he wrote to Edward Everett in 1824, "are not innate. They are the result of habit and long training." Or, as he had said several years before, in rather more ominous tones, "if a nation expects to be ignorant and free, in a state of civilization, it expects what never was and never will be."

With the election of 1808 and Jefferson's retirement, the problem of the British was now passed to his successor, James Madison, whose two terms as president would be dominated by that problem and would, despite all efforts to the contrary, result in war. And as had so often been the case before, the sources of conflict were the violation of neutral rights at sea, which now involved the French as well as the British, and conflicts with the British on the western American frontier.

This time around, however, things were different. For one thing, the diminutive, reflective, and soft-spoken Madison was no match for the impatient forces that were gathering on all sides and making the movement toward war nearly irresistible. Madison found himself unable to restrain the British, unable to arrive at a coherent and effective trade policy with the warring parties, and unable to control expansionist and insurgent forces at home. Settlers and land speculators on the frontier continued to press for expansion and provoked resentment and violence among the Indian tribes, who were losing more and more of their land. In response, the Shawnee warrior leader Tecumseh attempted to unite all the tribes east of the Mississippi into an Indian confederacy. Indian attacks were blamed on the British influence, operating especially from the Canadian province of Ontario. And a group of young and intensely nationalistic Republican congressmen, dubbed the "War Hawks," would be satisfied with nothing less than an invasion of Canada. Madison was overwhelmed.

Thus, despite the continued low level of American military preparedness, Madison yielded to the accumulating pressure and reluctantly asked for a declaration of war on June 1, 1812. Ironically, the British had decided at the same time to revoke the orders in council that had sustained their interference with American shipping. But thanks to the difficulties of transatlantic communication, their decision was not known until it was too late; war had been declared, and the requirements of war had taken on a momentum of their own.

About the war itself, the best that can be said for the United States is that it was lucky to get out of it intact. Had the British not been preoccupied with the war against Napoleon in Europe, the war would almost certainly have had a catastrophic effect upon the Americans. Indeed, after Napoleon's defeat in 1814, the British began to win a string of victories, including the capture and burning of Washington, D.C., that could easily have led to the war being a humiliating and permanently damaging setback for the United States. In addition, the war was deeply unpopular in the Federalist northern states, where it was disparaged as "Mr. Madison's War," and very nearly led a convention of New England states meeting in Hartford, Connecticut, in December 1814 to consider seriously the possibility of secession from the Union.

Fortunately, by then, there had been a few significant American triumphs, notably the defense of Fort McHenry in Baltimore against British bombardment, where the proud survival of the American flag inspired a lawyer named Francis Scott Key to write the lyrics to what would become "The Star-Spangled Banner," the eventual national anthem. More importantly, a war-weary Britain was ready to call it quits and find a settlement that would save face for all. The Treaty of Ghent in December 1814 was the result, a treaty that simply restored the status quo at the war's start without making any determination about neutral rights or any of the other questions that had been at issue. There were no territorial concessions on either side. It was to be as if nothing had happened. Of course, with Napoleon out of the picture, the very reason for the struggles over neutral rights at sea had largely disappeared.

But there was one unexpected bright spot for the Americans, again a result of the slow speed of transatlantic communication. A British force had been sent to New Orleans to capture the city and cut off the West from the rest of the country. It was met by General Andrew Jackson and his motley force of frontier militiamen, pirates, free blacks, and French Creoles. The British regulars regarded the Americans with contempt and made a frontal assault directed at them on January 8, 1815. But Jackson's men, who included some highly skilled marksmen and artillerymen, had managed to create well-fortified positions, from which they were able to rain down deadly fire upon the British and defeat them resoundingly. While U.S. forces suffered little more than a hundred killed, wounded, and missing, British losses exceeded twenty-five hundred. It was a smashing, thoroughly impressive American victory, perhaps the most impressive such in the nation's history to date. For many Americans, the glory of it more than made up for all the humiliations that had come before.

Even so, the great victory at New Orleans came after the peace treaty had been signed at Ghent. which meant that it could not have influenced the treaty deliberations. But that did not mean that it was of little importance – far from it. For one thing, the resounding victory ensured that the treaty would be ratified quickly by both governments; there would be no dilly-dallying or revisiting of the issues. But more importantly, this conspicuous win allowed the United States to come out of an ill-considered, badly waged, and carelessly misconceived war – a war that began as a result of miscommunication, teetered on the edge of debacle, and whose most significant battle occurred after the war had ended – with something to be proud of, with demonstrated military prowess and a greatly heightened sense of national pride – not to mention a new national hero.

There was yet another consequence. It is worth noting that the Republicans and Federalists once again had switched roles, the former playing the role of the vigorous nationalists and the latter taking the role of those advocating for states' rights and strict construction of the Constitution – much as it had happened before, at the end of Jefferson's administration. This time around, however, the Federalists' position assumed a darker countenance than before. It would become associated in the public mind with the wartime disloyalty of the Hartford Convention, a near-treasonous stigma from which a once-great party would never recover. Jackson's great triumph at New Orleans was the icing on that unlucky cake, and the many songs, speeches, celebrations, and commemorations of that victory nearly all contained a rebuke, open or implicit, of the Federalists.

It soon became clear that the Federalist Party was perhaps the greatest casualty of the War of 1812. Its days as a national party were numbered. It managed to field a presidential candidate in 1816, but that would be its last such effort. The "Virginia Dynasty" that had dominated the presidency since 1789, interrupted only by Adams's single term, would continue with little or no opposition. James Monroe ran unopposed in 1820, and by 1824, the Federalist Party had collapsed altogether. With its collapse came also an end to the first party system of the United States and a period of complete Republican dominance.

Thus the War of 1812, for all of its military inconclusiveness, had major effects on the domestic politics and economy of the United States. With the war's conclusion, the nation was soon on the road to being largely free of its chronic entanglements in European affairs and would be able to concentrate – at last! – on the pursuit of its own internal ambitions without major distractions, following the path laid out in Washington's Farewell Address.

A few issues remained to tidy up before that objective could be reached. A series of agreements with the British in the immediate wake of the war brought resolution to nagging issues relating to the demilitarization of the Great Lakes, fishing rights in Canadian waters, and boundary questions in the Pacific Northwest. Then, through a combination of diplomatic skill and aggressive military action by the now-celebrated General Andrew Jackson, the United States was able to acquire all of Florida from Spain in 1821. There could be no doubt: it had taken nearly a half-century, but the United States was at last moving into a position where it could exert control over its part of the world.

These changed circumstances would be expressed as U.S. policy two years later as part of President Monroe's last message to Congress in December 1823, in a statement that came to be known as the Monroe Doctrine. The gist of the Doctrine was fairly simple: the western hemisphere was henceforth to be considered off limits to further European colonization, and any effort to the contrary, including European meddling or subversion in the newly independent former Spanish and Portuguese colonies of Latin America, would be regarded as "the manifestation of an unfriendly disposition toward the United States" and "dangerous to our peace and safety." The western hemisphere had been a battleground of the European powers for centuries; it was now time for that to come to an end, as the New World ascended to a status equal to, but independent of, the Old World. The statement also included a promise not to interfere in the internal concerns of any of the European powers; the United States would stay clear of European wars and would not meddle in European internal affairs, just as it expected Europe to stay out of American affairs. Responding in 1821 to a request for help from Greek revolutionaries rising up to fight the Ottoman Empire, John Quincy Adams proclaimed that the United States "goes not abroad in search of monsters to destroy. She is the well-wisher to the freedom and independence of all. She is the champion and vindicator only of her own.... Her glory is not dominion, but liberty."

The Monroe Doctrine, the drafting of which was Adams's handiwork as Monroe's secretary of state, was in one sense merely a codification of the American doctrine of neutrality toward the European powers. As such, it looked back to Washington's Farewell Address. But in a practical political sense, it was rather daring, even presumptuous, akin to a poker-player's bluff. Such a proclamation, after all, could have no standing in international law or treaty arrangements, so other nations were not required to respect it. And the United States lacked the capacity to enforce it on its own, had it been challenged to do so. Such a challenge would likely have exposed the Doctrine as sheer bluster, and sent the Americans scurrying to the arms of the British Navy for protection.

But timing is everything in history, and the Doctrine was pronounced at a moment when the European powers had no desire to undertake any such challenge, so the principles it asserted were allowed to stand. Like *Marbury v. Madison*, the Monroe Doctrine established a vital and enduring principle at just the right moment, when it was least likely to be successfully challenged. The Monroe Doctrine would go on to become a cornerstone of American foreign policy, its influence lasting through the high tide of European colonialism and well into the twentieth century. In addition, it gave sharp definition to a distinctively American way of understanding the relationship of the Old World and the New World, asserting that the former's political systems were "essentially different" from that of the latter.

The position was not new. It had already been limned by Washington and Jefferson, and one can find hints of it even earlier, in the pre-national heritage of Winthrop's Puritanism and, of course, in the 1776 Declaration of Independence, which asserted the American strand's "separate and equal station." Adams and Monroe had now merely given it a more codified status. In addition, it would presume an American dominance within the western hemisphere that also would continue to stand, even as it became a chronic point of friction with Latin American countries.

Most of all, it expressed a sense of freedom that the country would finally be able to pursue its own destiny, develop and flex its own muscles, and embody more fully the fresh hope for renewal that had always been, since long before even Winthrop's time, the defining aspect of that westward magnetic pull that animated the American enterprise, now free (at least for a time) from compromising and distracting Old World concerns. A strong sense of national identity was beginning to permeate every sphere of American life, from the surging economy to the rising sense of America as a distinct, if not yet fully realized, culture of democracy.

The postwar economy was growing into a truly *national* economy. In the years immediately after the War of 1812, Representative Henry Clay of Kentucky proposed what became known as the American System as an instrument for fostering economic growth. Although Clay, like most Kentuckians, was a member of Jefferson's Republican Party, his ideas unmistakably echoed Hamilton's, calling for protective tariffs, the rechartering of the National Bank, and internal improvements, which mean what we today might call "infrastructure": roads, canals, and other improvements designed to create an ever more efficient system of national transportation.

The idea of federal support for internal improvements, while extremely popular in the west, was too controversial in the older eastern states and did not enjoy much success until the twentieth century. In 1817, President Madison vetoed a bill that would have established a fund for internal improvements, finding the idea to be attractive but unconstitutional. The federal and state governments provided indirect support to private concerns trying in various ways to improve transportation, but only the Old National Road, which ran from Cumberland, Maryland, to Wheeling, in what was then western Virginia, and eventually west to Vandalia, Illinois, was constructed by the U.S. government. (Today that same road is U.S. Route 40 and has been designated the Historic National Road.)

So the building of turnpikes and other internal improvements would be chiefly the responsibility of states and private concerns for the foreseeable future. That did not slow things down appreciably, because there were many such projects being built, with networks of privately funded toll roads arising to connect the nation's major cities. There was also a veritable boom in the construction of inland waterways such as New York's 363-mile-long Erie Canal, completed in 1825, a remarkable engineering feat strongly supported by Governor De Witt Clinton, who predicted that such a canal would make New York City "the granary of the world, the emporium of commerce, the seat of manufactures, the focus of great moneyed operations. . . . [T]he whole of Manhattan, covered with habitations and replenished with a dense population, will constitute one vast city."

Rarely has a politician's prophecy been more grandiose, and never more on target. The Erie Canal connected the Great Lakes to New York City, the economies of western farms with those of eastern port cities, and ignited a period of intense economic growth and fervent emulative canal building, often in the form of public–private partnerships, all over the country. The cities of Buffalo, Rochester, Syracuse, and other towns along the canal flourished, and New York rose to become "the Empire State." As Governor Clinton predicted, New York City, the eastern terminus for most of the canal's traffic, secured its emerging status as the nation's largest city and greatest commercial center.

Nor was that all; the first railroad lines were built in the 1820s and, by the 1830s, were beginning to give the canals a run for their money, transforming western towns like Chicago into major centers of commerce and population. That was a trend that would only continue and grow as the century rolled on. And in tandem with these improvements in transportation, a cluster of inventions and other innovations helped to spur economic growth. Some of these were products of the nation's first years, whose potential was finally being realized in the freer and more energetic postwar environment. There was immigrant Samuel Slater's development in the late eighteenth century of the factory system, which revolutionized textile manufacturing in New England; Eli Whitney's invention in 1793 of the cotton gin, which made possible the development of cotton as a highly profitable commercial export commodity; John Fitch's and Robert Fulton's pioneering development of steamboat technologies and services; Oliver Evans's mechanization of flour milling; and the list goes on.

And the innovations were as much legal and cultural as they were technological. Changes in state laws fostered entrepreneurship. They made possible the raising of large amounts of capital by corporations through stock sales, an important development because the burgeoning industrial economy needed large amounts of capital, if it was to finance the construction and operation of expensive factories, such as the textile mills that were making New England a preeminent textile manufacturer, as well as the canals, roads, and railroads that would be the veins and arteries of the emerging national economy.

The cumulative effect of all these developments, accompanied as they were by the country's rapid population growth (from four million in 1790 to almost thirteen million in 1830, at a steady rate of around 35 percent) and the physical expansion of the American range of settlement, involved something more than the increase of the gross domestic product or some other purely economic index. It was causing a more subtle, more profound change in the national self-image. Jefferson had hoped for an America of independent and self-sufficient farmers, who would live in sturdy, dignified, and self-reliant separateness from one another. But the America coming into being was being knit together, bit by bit, piece by piece, with every road that was constructed, every canal that was dug, every new city that established itself, and every product that found its way into a growing national marketplace – including the specialized cash-crop farming that was directed toward that market rather than toward providing for the subsistence of a single household. It was becoming as much a land of growing economic interdependence as one of sturdy self-reliance.

All these things helped make possible the coming together of a national spirit. But as the nation at long last turned its gaze inward, and westward, it soon saw, gazing back at it, the great problem it had failed to resolve in Philadelphia in 1787. The expansion of the nation inevitably raised the problem anew by forcing a decision about whether slavery would be permitted in the nation's newly created states. Each decision would entail, in some measure, revalidating the original decision, an act that became steadily harder for some and more inescapable for others.

But at least there had been an effort, ever since Vermont joined the union as a free state and Kentucky as a slave state, to keep the number of northern free states and southern slave states in balance. By 1819, there were eleven of each category, so that members in the Senate would be equal, and each section had the power to check the other. This was not a solution to the problem; it was at best a way of holding the problem at bay and keeping the growth of slavery within bounds.

Then the territory of Missouri applied to be admitted as a state, and the problem was immediately elevated to crisis level. Thanks to the preponderance

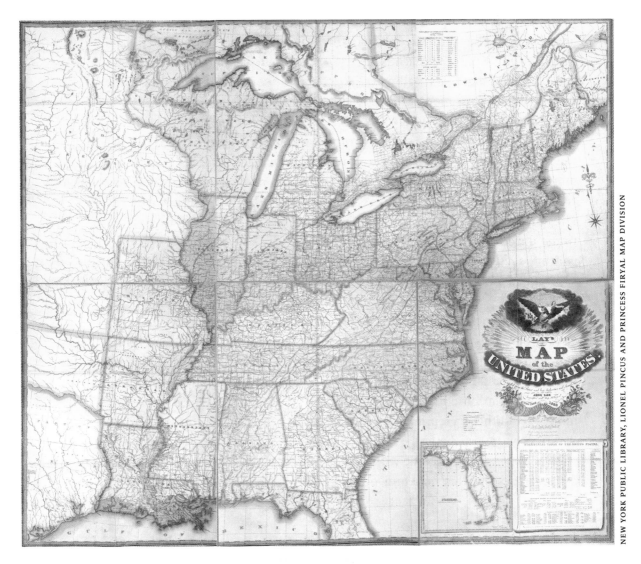

The United States circa 1827 by New York mapmaker Amos Lay.

of land-seeking southern migrants to the Missouri Territory, who had brought their slaves with them, slavery was already well established in Missouri, numbering about 15 percent of the population, and there was no doubt that Missouri would seek to be admitted as a slave state. But doing so would disturb the balance of states.

What ensued were a series of fiery debates in Congress over the merits of Missouri's case and whether restrictions on slavery could be imposed by Congress as a condition of its admission to the Union. Yet the debates also touched upon profound philosophical matters, becoming the most important and far-reaching debates about slavery since the time of the Constitution's drafting and adoption. They illustrated the gap that was opening up between men like Senator Rufus King of Massachusetts, who spoke on behalf of the Declaration's "law of nature" that "makes all men free," and John Randolph of Virginia, who dismissed the Declaration of Independence as a "fanfaronade of abstractions."

The philosophical differences could not be resolved then. But the immediate problem was solved by a compromise; the state of Maine, carved out of the northern part of Massachusetts, would be admitted as a free state, and slavery would be excluded from the rest of the Louisiana Territory north of the 36° 30′ line, which was Missouri's southern boundary extended westward. Thus the senatorial balance would be maintained, and this sudden flashpoint would die down, for the time being, with the 36° 30′ line providing a rule by which the rest of the Louisiana Territory could be organized on the question.

But a problem deferred is not a problem solved, and wise observers knew it. Nor was it possible to have the easy confidence of some of the Framers in Philadelphia, such as Sherman and Ellsworth, that slavery was an institution already on the path to extinction. Thomas Jefferson, writing to his friend John Holmes from his peaceful Monticello retirement, confessed that "this momentous question, like a fire bell in the night, awakened and filled me with terror. I considered it at once as the knell of the Union. It is hushed indeed for the moment. But this is a reprieve only, not a final sentence." He never spoke more darkly, or more prophetically. And he went on to express his sense of the difficulty of moving past the issue with a colorful image: "We have the wolf by the ear, and we can neither hold him, nor safely let him go."

Over the course of the five presidential elections after the epochal election of 1800, the nation's first two-party system had gradually disappeared, as the Federalist Party disintegrated and Jefferson's Republican Party became utterly dominant: so much so that James Monroe would run for his second term as president in 1820 without facing any organized opposition. It was nicknamed the Era of Good Feelings, and certainly it was a good time for the triumphant Republicans and a relatively peaceful time for the nation. For a stretch of twenty-four years, or six elections, every president had been from Virginia, and each of Jefferson's successors had served as secretary of state to the man who had preceded him. The process was so orderly as to resemble the workings of a mechanism.

Such stability and party unity could not last forever, though, especially not in such a dynamic and ever-expanding country. Madison himself had explained why it could not last, in his insightful *Federalist* 10: the causes of faction were sowed in the hearts of men and in the divergent material interests that came with their diverse situations in life. The year 1824 would mark the point of departure in the direction of an entirely new kind of politics, catalyzed by a bitterly contested presidential election.

The election would be fought out among four candidates, all of them Republicans: John Quincy Adams, Henry Clay, William Crawford, and the political outsider, Andrew Jackson. The results were accordingly chaotic; Jackson seemed to have the most popular votes and votes in the Electoral College, but he did not have a majority of either. That meant that the House of Representatives would have to choose the president from among the top three candidates. Henry Clay had been eliminated as the low vote-getter, but he had great influence in the House and could use his influence to turn the vote in the direction of either Adams or Jackson (Crawford had to withdraw due to health problems). When Clay chose Adams, which made possible his narrow election, and then was subsequently selected by Adams to be his secretary of state, Jackson and his followers were outraged. "Corrupt bargain!" they cried. That accusation seemed to stick with Adams for the next four years of what must be deemed an unsuccessful presidency.

Adams himself was a remarkable man, as befitted his status as the son of the second president, a man of aristocratic bearing, high moral probity, and superb intelligence who had been an outstanding secretary of state for James Monroe. Few men would seem to have been better equipped for the presidency. But he had the misfortune to rise to the office at a moment when his own party was fracturing, and he lacked the personality and the political acumen to adjust to the democratizing times. He would be easily and soundly defeated by Jackson in their 1828 rematch, by which time Jackson had rallied around himself a new political party, drawing on the boisterous political energies of the West and South and a growing spirit of egalitarian democracy in the land. He called the party the Democratic Republicans, but it would become known as the Democratic Party, the ancestor of today's party of that same name.

It was an ugly campaign, in which those running Adams's campaign mocked Jackson as an uncouth and ill-tempered brawler who was pitifully ignorant about the issues, and the Jacksonians returned the favor by depicting Adams as a haughty pseudo-aristocratic parasite who had been corrupted by his time in the courts of Europe and felt nothing but disdain for the common man. But Jackson had the advantage of being a certifiable military hero, whose rise to glory had coincided with the surge of American nationalism and whose appeal to the common man had coincided with the rising tide of an ever-expanding electorate, which was broadening year by year to include more and more eligible voters – not just landholders but workers, artisans, tenant farmers, and others who had previously been excluded.

In a sense, the unseemliness of the campaign and the broadening of the electorate were related to one another. Politics would be different in the Age of the Common Man. Previous campaigns had always been waged between candidates drawn from the upper classes; there was a more decorous "politics of deference" operating, in which potential officeholders were always drawn from the "better sort," those who were well-born, refined, and educated, and the voters to whom they had to appeal were drawn from a similarly limited spectrum of the citizenry. The broadening of the franchise meant that politicians needed to find a way to appeal directly to relatively new voters who had not been accustomed to being consulted that way in the political process. The results were bound to be visceral and messy, and popular campaigning was often as much a matter of popular entertainment as of serious discussion of issues, with parades, marching bands, and rallies featuring free food and drink. The worst thing a candidate could do would be to come off as aristocratic.

The chaotic scene at Jackson's inauguration on March 4, 1829, is legendary in this regard, with the crowds of his rowdy, unkempt admirers lining Pennsylvania Avenue and later thronging into the White House, tracking mud on the rugs and standing on the chairs to get a glimpse of their man. And to be sure, Jackson was unlike any major candidate ever seen before in American presidential history. He was a self-made, brawling, dueling, and tobacco-chewing frontiersman who had come from hardscrabble beginnings and had risen through the ranks of society without the benefit of a college education to become a wealthy, accomplished, and powerful man, a national hero, while never losing his common touch, or his rough manners, or his ability to project sympathy for those of lower station. John Quincy Adams disparaged him as a "barbarian," but his many admirers begged to disagree.

This combination of traits not only suggests the breadth of his political appeal but points to one of the chief ways that Jacksonian democracy differed from Jeffersonian democracy. If Jefferson had believed that education could raise the commonest man to the same station as the well-born, then Jackson believed that the common man was already where he needed to be and needed no raising – that his innate capacity for deciding questions of politics and economy on his own was sufficient, the hallmark of democracy. Indeed, Jackson can be said to be America's first leader deserving of the title *populist*, meaning that opposition to (and resentment of) rule by privileged elite classes was one of the most important forces behind his political appeal.

In some respects, one could argue that Jackson's symbolic significance as the representation of a new Age of the Common Man turned out to be far greater than his actual importance as president. He came into office without great plans, and much of his achievement was negative, meaning that it consisted in preventing things from happening: by his frequent use of the veto power (he vetoed more bills than all six of his predecessors combined), his firm rejection of the idea of nullification (of which more in a moment), and his fierce opposition to the rechartering of the Bank of the United States. In many respects, his political instincts represented a throwback to the views of Jefferson regarding strict construction of the Constitution and limited government, and Jackson had a particularly strong animus toward the alliance of government and business, manifested in his near-maniacal hatred for the Bank. But he was inconsistent, sometimes favoring internal improvements like the National Road and sometimes opposing them, as in his veto of the Maysville Road bill (which just happened to involve a project entirely within Kentucky, the state of his hated rival Clay).

But Jackson brought several interesting ideas to the presidency. He rightly identified the president as the only individual in the entire American system of constitutional government who could be said to be the representative of *all* of the people, a fact that he took to mean that he also was meant to be the guardian and protector of the common man against the abusive power of the wealthy, powerful, and well connected. This was an important step in the further definition of the presidential office. He also insisted, consistent with his confidence in the untutored abilities of the common man, upon the principle of "rotation" in staffing his administration, which meant that the terms of officeholders would be strictly limited. Rotation in office would, he believed, ensure that the federal government did not develop a parasitic class of corrupt civil servants who were set apart from the people and could make hay out of their monopolistic control of special knowledge. His sentiments marked one of the earliest expressions of what would become the populist strain in American political culture.

Jackson also played a key role in handling the eruption of a key constitutional issue in the Nullification Crisis of 1832–33, a conflict that has often been seen, rightly, as a prelude to the Civil War. The immediate controversy revolved around the federal use of protective tariffs, specifically the Tariffs of 1828 and 1832, which many Southerners opposed as unfair and injurious to their interests. But the underlying issue was whether the individual states had the right or the ability to set aside, or nullify, acts of the national government, if they deemed those acts to be unconstitutional. It marked a collision point between the enduring idea of state sovereignty and the idea of federal supremacy, both of which ideas the Constitution had sought to enshrine to the extent possible, but whose prerogatives were bound to come into conflict.

The crisis opened up a split between Jackson and Vice President (later Senator) John C. Calhoun of South Carolina, the latter becoming the most articulate defender of the concept of state nullification. The concept was not new; we have already seen it floated in the Kentucky and Virginia Resolutions of 1798 by Jefferson and Madison, and it could easily be derived from the "compact" theory of the Constitution's origins. But Calhoun developed the idea much further in his 1828 *South Carolina Exposition and Protest*, arguing that a state had the right to judge the extent of its own powers and the allocation of power between the state and the federal government. "The right of judging, in such cases," he remarked, "is an essential attribute of sovereignty, of which the States cannot be divested without losing their sovereignty itself." Hence, he concluded, the states must be deemed to have a "veto," or a "right of interposition," with respect to acts of the federal government that the state believes encroach on its rights. Otherwise, its sovereignty would be a sham.

It was a powerful argument, but others disagreed. Senator Daniel Webster argued that the matter had been settled definitely by the supremacy clause of the Constitution (Article 6, clause 2), which stated, "This Constitution ... shall be the supreme Law of the Land ... any Thing in the Constitution or Laws of any State to the Contrary notwithstanding," and that the Constitution made no provision for states to play a role in constitutional interpretation. In other words, he rejected the compact theory, seeing the Constitution as the product of "we the people," rather than the states, and seeing the national union as perpetual, not contingent. Even the aging James Madison agreed with him, arguing that the arrangements Calhoun envisioned would produce nothing short of chaos.

Jackson's own position on the matter was more guarded but began to become visible at the Democratic Party dinner in Washington honoring the late Thomas Jefferson's birthday, on April 13, 1830. It emerged not in a speech but in a dramatic succession of toasts. Given Jackson's generally strong support for state's rights, and Jefferson's own earlier support for nullification, it seemed an opportune moment for the nullifiers to claim the higher ground and perhaps draw the current president in their direction. First with a raised glass was Robert Y. Hayne of South Carolina, who proposed, "The Union of the States, and the Sovereignty of the States!" Jackson rose to offer a stiff rebuke: "Our Federal Union: It must be preserved!" Then Calhoun would respond with his own subtle defiance: "The Union. Next to our liberty, the most dear!" Finally Jackson's vice president, Martin Van Buren, would offer these conciliating words: "Mutual forbearance and reciprocal concession. Through their agency the Union was established. The patriotic spirit from which they emanated will forever sustain it." Thus did these wary politicians maneuver, signal, and size one another up, in advance of the coming conflict.

That conflict was not long in arriving, and when it did, this time over the 1832 Tariff, the result would be decisive. States' rights was one thing, but talk of secession was quite another for Jackson; and such talk had turned Jackson against the nullifiers and led him to believe that their revolt must be unceremoniously crushed. When an Ordinance of Nullification was passed by South Carolina on November 26, 1832, seeking to nullify the two offensive tariffs and prevent their enforcement within its boundaries, Jackson responded on December 10, dismissing the doctrine of nullification as "incompatible with the existence of the Union, contradicted expressly by the letter of the Constitution, unauthorized by its spirit, inconsistent with every principle on which it was founded, and destructive of the great object for which it was formed." It was clear that Jackson was fully prepared to use force to prevent the nullifiers from advancing their cause.

So were the South Carolinians, and the confrontation could have led to violence had it not been for the legislative skills of Henry Clay, who managed to pass a renegotiated version of the offensive tariff. That led in turn to a repeal of the Ordinance, and all sides stepped back to claim a partial and face-saving victory. But nothing had been resolved. Jackson himself brooded in the aftermath that "the tariff was only a pretext," with "disunion and southern confederacy the real object." But at least that had been averted, for a time.

Jackson also left an indelible mark on Indian policy, and there the mark was and is far more enduringly controversial. Jackson's inclusive democratic spirit did not extend to America's indigenous peoples, whom he regarded, as many western settlers did, with a mixture of fear and condescension, and whose claims to their homelands he flatly rejected. But he insisted that he did not hate them and sometimes adopted a paternalistic tone toward them, as if he were their father and they his children. He believed the best and most humane solution to the problem that these aboriginal inhabitants represented was to remove them from their homelands and resettle them in the lands west of the Mississippi River. And it was done. In 1830, the Indian Removal Act was signed into law, and by 1835, most eastern tribes had relocated to the West, some forty-six thousand individuals. Later, in 1838, after Jackson's term of office had ended, the U.S. Army forced fifteen thousand Cherokees in Georgia to leave for the Oklahoma Territory, on a difficult and humiliating eight-hundred-mile trek along what became known as the Trail of Tears. Some four thousand died along the way.

Few aspects of American history are more troubling than the story of how matters came to this dismal pass. Nor does it improve the picture to point out that the policy was a long time in coming and that the die had been cast well before Jackson was anywhere near the presidency. Removal was not Jackson's idea; it was the product of a far more consistent and long-standing pattern of national sentiment.

It was also in part a failure of imagination. From the very beginning of the new nation, leaders could not decide whether the American Indians should be treated officially as individuals or as distinct nations, and whether federal policy should be directed toward their assimilation or their displacement. It was never clear, in short, how the indigenous population either might be incorporated into the American experiment or humanely left out of it, and there can be no doubt that entrenched anti-Native racism played a key role in that indecisiveness. Yet what makes the story all the more exasperating is that there also were good intentions in the mix, which could be equally deadly in their effects.

Washington and Jefferson both had pondered this issue and had concluded that coexistence was possible only if Indians became "civilized" by making wholesale adaptations to the European settlers' culture, which meant adoption of their religion, language, and economic practices, including the ownership of private property. But it also was Jefferson who first proposed the idea of a land exchange, in which eastern tribes would give up their lands in exchange for western lands in the newly acquired Louisiana Territory. His idea was picked up by President Monroe, who, with the assistance of his war secretary Calhoun, sought to create a western Indian Territory and remove the eastern tribes there. President John Quincy Adams took a similar stand in favor of removal. So the table for removal had already been set by the time Jackson assumed the office.

There were also powerful raw material motives in play, ones that hinted at the forces behind the impending sectional conflict. Removal would take place mainly in the South, where the hunger for Indian lands was driven by the relentless expansion of an economy built upon cotton, a crop whose intensive cultivation rapidly led to soil exhaustion and hence the need for constant territorial expansion. Still, the Indian Removal Act was intensely controversial, encountering significant opposition even in the South, notably from Tennessee Congressman Davy Crockett, and it passed only after bitter debate in Congress.

Jackson was not alone in viewing the displacement of Indian tribal nations as inevitable, and he pointed to the American northeast, where the tribal nations had all but ceased to exist as genuine forms of governance and culture, as evidence of his view. He dismissed any other view as sentimental romanticism: "What good man," he asked, "would prefer a country covered with forests and ranged by a few thousand savages to our extensive Republic, studded with cities, towns, and prosperous farms, embellished with all the improvements which art can devise or industry execute, occupied by more than 12 million happy people, and filled with all the blessings of liberty, civilization, and religion?" Removal was, in his view, an act of mercy, protecting a vulnerable people from complete obliteration.

It should be noted, too, that Chief Justice John Marshall suffered a notable setback in the matter of the Cherokee removal from Georgia, which he opposed. In the case *Worcester v. Georgia* (1832), the Court ruled that the laws of Georgia had no force within Cherokee territory. Jackson, however, sided with Georgia and simply ignored the ruling, thereby rendering it impotent and futile. It was an act of presidential nullification, in a sense, and served as a powerful illustration of the limits of the Supreme Court's power when an executive is determined to reject its dicta.

A European traveler witnessed the effects of the Indian removal firsthand, as he happened by chance upon a group of Choctaws crossing the Mississippi River at Memphis in December 1831. That observer was the great French writer Alexis de Tocqueville (1805–59). "One cannot imagine the frightful evils that accompany these forced migrations," he remarked, and he went on to describe in compelling detail the frigid winter scene, the ground hardened with snow and enormous pieces of ice drifting down the river, as the Indian families gathered in silent and sorrowful resignation on the east bank of the river, proceeding without tears or complaints to cross over into what they knew to be an erasure of their past. It was, Tocqueville said, a "solemn spectacle that will never leave my memory."

Tocqueville, who would eventually become one of the most eminent European social and political thinkers of the nineteenth century, had come to America for other reasons. He was only twenty-six years old and as yet almost completely unknown when, accompanied by his friend and sidekick Gustave de Beaumont, he came to America intent upon "examining, in details and as scientifically as possible, all the mechanisms of the vast American society which everyone talks of and no one knows." The result, his two-volume book *Democracy in America* (1835–40), is perhaps the richest and most enduring study of American society and culture ever written. If one were permitted to read only one book on the subject, *Democracy in America* would almost certainly be the best choice – a surprising statement perhaps, given the fact that nearly two centuries have passed since its initial publication.

As the preceding depiction of the Choctaw removal illustrates, Tocqueville did not seek to exalt or excuse the moral defects of Jacksonian America. He called Jackson himself "a man of violent character and middling capacity." He was an unusually penetrating foreign observer, not an American cheerleader. But his book also vividly captured the era's ebullient and enterprising spirit and the energies that the democratic revolution in America was setting loose in the world. It is precisely because of its balance, its detachment, and its philosophical depth that *Democracy* continues to be almost uniquely valuable among books about America.

Tocqueville saw the United States as a nation moving in the vanguard of history, a young and vigorous country endowed with an extraordinary degree of social equality among its inhabitants and with no feudal or aristocratic background to overcome. In America, he believed, one could see embodied, in exemplary or heightened form, the condition toward which all the rest of the world, including France, was tending. In America, the only example the world then afforded of an expansive and expanding republic, one could gaze upon "the image of democracy itself, of its penchants, its character, its prejudices, its passions" – and having so gazed, could perhaps take away lessons that would allow leaders to deal more intelligently and effectively with the democratic changes coming to Europe.

Although an aristocrat himself, he was firmly convinced that the movement toward greater equality represented an inescapable feature of the modern age, a fact to which all future social or political analysis must accommodate itself. There would be no going back. Indeed, one could say that the one great idea in Tocqueville's writing was this huge sprawling historical spectacle, the gradual but inexorable leveling of human society on a universal scale, a movement that he identified with the will of God, so pervasive and so unstoppable did it seem to be.

Tocqueville's portrait of America was of a strikingly middle-class society: feverishly commercial and acquisitive, obsessively practical minded, jealously equality minded, and restlessly mobile, a constant beehive of enterprise and activity. It was also a surprisingly religious society, in which the spirit of liberty and the spirit of religion were understood to be complementary to one another, so that religious belief supported democratic practice – a very different state of affairs from what he had found at home in France. Tocqueville saw many things to admire in this energetic, bumptious democracy. But he also saw some things to fear.

Chief among the dangers was its pronounced tendency toward individualism – a new word at that time. Tocqueville saw in America the peril that citizens might elect to withdraw from involvement in the larger public life and regard themselves as autonomous and isolated actors, with no higher goal than the pursuit of their own material well-being. He acknowledged that in a modern commercial democracy, this was a particularly strong possibility, because self-interest would inevitably come to be accepted as the chief engine of all human striving. But where, then, would the generous and selfless civic virtues needed for the sustaining of a decent society come from? How could the individualistic Americans of the 1830s prevent self-interestedness from overwhelming all considerations of the public good and undermining the sources of social cohesion? Why, he asked, in a chapter that reads as if it were written today, are prosperous Americans so restless in the midst of their prosperity? And why, he asks later, are these same individualistic Americans so vulnerable to accepting the "soft despotism" of the state?

We may perhaps hear a faint echo in these questions of the Anti-Federalists' worries, and Jefferson's, about the fate of virtue in a commercial society. And even though nearly every outward feature of the Jacksonian-era world that Tocqueville described in his book has changed, and altered beyond recognition, the inward traits and tendencies he describes have remained remarkably consistent. The questions, too, remain as current as ever.

CHAPTER SEVEN

THE CULTURE OF DEMOCRACY

I N *DEMOCRACY IN AMERICA,* TOCQUEVILLE WAS NOT MERELY
interested in studying democracy as a political form. He argued that a democratic regime would manifest itself in every facet of human life: not merely
in public institutions but also in family life, in literature, in philosophy, in manners, in language usage, in marriage, in mores, in male–female relations, in
ambition, in friendship, in love, and in attitudes toward war and peace. He
grasped the fact that a society's political arrangements, far from being matters
that merely skate on the surface of life, are in fact influences that reach deep
down into the very souls of its inhabitants. Democracy is not just about politics; it is also a matter of culture, of a people's sensibility and way of life: their
habits, convictions, morals, tastes, and spiritual life. What, then, did this emerging culture of democracy look like?

Since religion lies at the very roots of culture, an examination of this
question should begin with a look at the path of religion's development in the
years after the Revolution. The first thing to notice is that the remarkable partnership of Protestantism and Enlightenment rationalism, that easy harmony of
potential antagonists that had been such a notable feature of the latter years of
the eighteenth century, was beginning to fray in the nineteenth, as the former
partners began to go their separate ways – although, as we shall see, it is also
notable that there remained important points of similarity, even as the separation was occurring.

On the elite level, more and more of those in the established churches of
the North found the Calvinist belief in innate human depravity to be too dour
and negative and, moreover, out of phase with the steadily improving world
that they saw emerging around them. They were increasingly drawn to more

rational and Enlightened offshoots of Christianity, such as Deism and Unitarianism, both of which declined to affirm the divinity of Christ and other supernatural elements of Christian orthodoxy and stressed instead the unity of God, the intelligibility of the universe, and the innate goodness of human beings, along with their ability to improve their own lot in life by the exercise of their reason and by taking greater care in the nurture of the young. Some of the most important leaders of the revolutionary generation, such as Jefferson and Franklin, had already been drawn in that direction, and in the early years of the new nation, rationalist religion grew, although it always remained largely an upper-class taste. By the 1820s, Unitarianism had become the overwhelmingly predominant faith of the elite classes in Massachusetts and dominated the outlook at bastions like Harvard College.

But there was far more intense and interesting activity happening on the other side of the religious divide – the revivalist side. A Second Great Awakening had already begun in the years around 1800, led by men like Yale's president Timothy Dwight, a Jonathan Edwards–like figure who attempted to return that campus, which had declined into a "hotbed of infidelity," to something closer to its uber-Puritan beginnings. A brilliant and charismatic speaker, Dwight led campus revivals that inspired a significant cohort of young Yale men to become evangelists.

Meanwhile, revivals on the southern and western frontier were far greater in number and far less decorous. In fact, they tended to be wildly enthusiastic, to an extent that was somewhat frightening to observers like Tocqueville, who referred to the Americans' penchant for "an exalted and almost fierce spiritualism." One such revival, a legendary camp meeting at Cane Ridge, Kentucky, in summer 1801, came to be known as the Second Pentecost; it was a kind of evangelical Woodstock, a fervent gathering of souls featuring ecstatic and emotional outpourings from the many lonely and unchurched individuals who lived in poverty and isolation and yearned for spiritual uplift and a sense of belonging. Events like Cane Ridge, too, played a crucial role in the launching of the Second Great Awakening.

The ministers who worked the frontier had adapted their message to the circumstances; instead of preaching sophisticated Calvinism, they offered a simple and direct message of personal salvation, easily grasped by anyone. Traveling revivals became a fixture of frontier life, and tireless Methodist "circuit riders" such as Francis Asbury and Peter Cartwright provided a moveable evangelism in which the church came to the people themselves. Cartwright, a man of astonishing stamina, delivered a sermon a day for more than twenty years, all the while riding a circuit that took in several states and presented all the rugged challenges and perils of frontier travel. The heroic efforts of him and others like him soon built Methodism into the largest Christian denomination in America.

By the 1820s, the currents of revivalism spread to upstate New York, in the region between Lake Ontario and the Adirondack Mountains, from Buffalo to Albany. It was the very region traversed by the Erie Canal, an area in which swift economic development had brought with it rapid and disorienting changes in the pattern of life, raising anew questions about the maintenance of virtue, which was seen as so essential to the survival of a republic. Perhaps that anxiety is why the region showed such an unusual openness to spiritual things, becoming known as the Burned-Over District because of the frequency with which the flames of revival had swept through it.

It was there in upstate New York, in 1821, that a young lawyer named Charles Grandison Finney underwent a "mighty baptism of the Holy Ghost" that enveloped him in "waves and waves of liquid love" and came out of the experience with the clear conviction that he was to become an evangelist: "I have a retainer from the Lord Jesus Christ," he announced, ever the lawyer, "to plead his case." He immediately began to study to become a Presbyterian minister and, by 1823, was ordained and began pleading the case in his inimitable prosecutorial way, combining unabashed showmanship with a rather flexible form of Christian theology to produce confessions and conversions aplenty among those in his audiences.

Finney would become the greatest revivalist of his day, and in his style, he could be seen as the prototype of the modern American evangelical preacher, in the mold of Billy Graham and his stadium-sized open-air revivals. Yet Finney's theological convictions were very far from the Calvinism in which figures like Graham would be educated. Finney believed that the saving of souls did not have to wait upon a miraculous infusion of grace; nor was it a question of a proper theological education. Instead, it was possible to induce conversion of everyone, black and white, male and female, young and old, by the careful use of "new methods" designed to elicit the proper emotional state and receptivity. Indeed, Finney was a master of the art, and using such innovations as the "anxious bench," where those called forward would publicly confess their sins and seek forgiveness, while surrounded by family and friends, he was able to transform his revivals into spectacular and cathartic emotional experiences. When accused of manipulation, Finney bluntly replied that "the results justify my method."

Certainly Finney's theology and practices were a clear departure from Christian orthodoxy. Lost, too, was any notion of the historic church and an authoritative clergy as essential elements in the life of the Christian. But such changes were an accommodation not only to the frontier but to a new democratic age and faithfully reflected the can-do optimism and expansive individualism of the Jacksonian moment. In an odd sense, Finney's transformation of Christianity into a positive creed of salvation that could be achieved through human exertion, for all its obvious differences from the highly intellectualized rational faith of the Unitarians, had a lot in common with it. In both cases, the Calvinist doctrine of human depravity, with its insistence upon the inability of the individual person caught in the snares of sin to free himself without divine grace, was being set aside as something outdated and out of phase with the rising spirit of optimism about human capabilities that pervaded the age. In certain respects, then, the two sides of America's religious divide were not as different as they might have seemed.

Finney's innovations were not the only ones to arise in the Burned-Over District and were far from being the most innovative. Indeed, this rapidly changing region proved to be exceptionally fertile ground for the growth of inventive, adventurous, and often quite heretical ideas, arising out of the collision between the weakening inherited faiths and the expansive spirit of the age. There were millennial cults like the Millerites, who preached the end of the world in 1844 and the imminent establishment of God's Kingdom. There was the spiritualism of the Fox sisters, who claimed the ability to communicate with the dead. There were utopian experiments in communal and perfectionist living. There were redoubled efforts to restore the purity of the apostolic church. Probably the most enduringly important of these innovations was the Church of Jesus Christ of Latter Day Saints, otherwise known as the Mormons. Today, some two centuries after the founding of Mormonism, we are unlikely to see this sturdy and conservative church as an expression of Burned-Over-District religious radicalism in its origins. But it was.

It all began with a teenaged boy named Joseph Smith Jr., whose family had moved from Vermont to the small town of Palmyra, New York. Smith had experienced a series of compelling supernatural visions, the eventual result of which was his production of the Book of Mormon, a narrative account of ancient Hebrews who were said to have inhabited the New World and had an encounter with Jesus Christ. This six-hundred-page tome was represented as an addition to the canon of Christian holy scripture – Smith regarded it as a lost section of the Bible – connecting the world of the Hebrew Bible with the aboriginal inhabitants of North America, and the current ones as well. In 1830, Smith began to form his own church, attracting converts by the dozens, and then by the hundreds, who were drawn to the church's novel theology and its strong sense of community.

Like so many strains of Protestant Christianity, Mormonism reflected a desire to recover the purity of the primitive church as it had been established by Jesus and the first apostles. But its theological differences from the mainstream of Protestantism were striking. It understood God as a personal being, Jesus as his literal son, and the church was headed by a Prophet who administered a lay male priesthood. While it accepted the Old and New Testaments of the Bible as sacred scriptures, it gave equal weight to the Book of Mormon and the revelations of the Prophet. It envisioned human beings as ultimately aspiring not merely to eternal life but to the status of gods. Above all else, Mormonism demanded of its members a very tightly organized community life, emphasizing a strong dedication to family, hard work, and personal discipline, including abstention from alcohol, tobacco, and drugs. It was perhaps the remarkable cohesiveness of Mormon community life, the strong sense of being a people apart, a "chosen" people who had rejected the practices of the "gentiles" around them, that most deeply characterized them – and most deeply irritated and alarmed their neighbors. If Mormonism could be said to be a product of the intellectual and spiritual ferment of the Jacksonian era, it might with equal justice be said to be a reaction against the era's sometimes chaotic individualism.

In the longer run, Mormonism showed the staying power to survive and thrive, when so many of the other religious innovations of its era faded away or transformed themselves into something else. And yet its insistence upon strong and exclusive group solidarity made it certain that its adherents would always clash with their neighbors. Matters were made far worse by Joseph Smith's adoption of the practice of "plural marriage," or polygamy, in which men were permitted to have more than one wife. That no doubt helped the sect grow more quickly, but it made the Mormons notorious, even reviled, and probably ensured that the subsequent history of Mormonism in American history for much of the century would be one of nearly uninterrupted persecution. The Mormons moved from New York to Ohio to Illinois, but violence and hostility followed them wherever they went.

Finally, in 1844, after an anti-Mormon mob killed Joseph Smith and his brother Hyrum, they made a decision to leave the country for land in Utah, which was then part of Mexico. Led by Brigham Young, who would make a strong and highly intelligent successor to Smith, the entire community of fifteen thousand made the great trek to the Great Salt Lake basin, the "Promised Land," beginning in 1846. They arrived to find an unpromising desert, friendly to nothing but crickets and snakes. But they wasted no time in developing an irrigation system, which was in place by 1848. And then, putting their customary industriousness to work, they proceeded to make the desert bloom.

Mormonism was more than a religion. It also was an experimental community – and far from being the only important communitarian experiment going on in America during the antebellum years. "We are all a little mad here with numberless projects of social reform," wrote Ralph Waldo Emerson in 1840. "Not a reading man but has a draft of a new community in his pocket." He exaggerated only slightly, for there were more than a hundred identifiable utopian communities launched in the United States during the nineteenth century. It stands to reason that this would be so. It was an optimistic and prosperous age, full of expectancy that the millennium, the long-prophesied return of Christ to rule the earth, was coming soon – or perhaps had already begun. What better time for such experiments in living to flourish?

Nor is it surprising that, in an age of individualism, the pursuit of an intensified communitarian ethos would have great appeal. We are social beings, and the disintegration or loosening of traditional sources of authority is not only liberating for us. It may also be disorienting, even frightening, as it clearly was for many inhabitants of the Burned-Over District and others who were experiencing the rapid changes of a dynamic and growing economy. Many of the earliest Mormons were New England farmers who were attracted to the faith precisely because it served as a clear alternative to the rootless materialism and self-seeking that the dramatic economic changes seemed to be bringing along with them. Both the Finneyite brand of evangelical Protestantism and the elite Unitarianism of Boston had in common a belief that the reform of institutions could lead to the reform of the person and the amelioration of his or her tendency toward sin. If human beings now had it in their power to effect comprehensive reform of those institutions, then the way was open for transformative change, for those with the boldness to seek it.

Some of those communities were short-lived, like the quixotic Brook Farm experiment in Massachusetts, promoted by Unitarian minister George Ripley; New Harmony, Indiana, started by the British industrialist Robert Owen; and the "phalanxes" of the French socialist Charles Fourier, which sought, and quickly failed, to overcome the force of competition in society. But others proved surprisingly durable, and the most durable ones generally had a strong religious dimension, as the Mormons had. The Rappites, a group of German Lutherans who fled persecution and settled in Butler County, Pennsylvania, lasted until the end of the century, holding their possessions in common, advocating celibacy, and waiting for the imminent second coming of Christ. Similarly, the Shakers, who believed God to be a dual personality, and believed their leader, Ann Lee Stanley, to be the second coming of Christ, lived lives of communal simplicity and kept celibate, joyfully anticipating that the consummation of the universe was near; their movement flourished in the 1830s and

1840s and lasted into the twentieth century. The Oneida Community, led by John Humphrey Noyes, went in the opposite direction, instituting the doctrine of "complex marriage," which meant that every man was married to every woman and the goal of community life should be the achievement of perfect release from sin. It lasted until the 1880s, when Noyes abruptly left the country to avoid prosecution for statutory rape; the community became a flatware and cutlery business, which still exists under the Oneida name today.

These utopian communities that sprang up, mainly in the North, like mushrooms across the American landscape, were only one sign of a much more general tendency of the time: it was a culture that exalted the idea of reform and the boundless possibilities for moral and spiritual reformation. As Emerson declared, writing in 1841, "in the history of the world the doctrine of Reform had never such scope as at the present hour ... and not a kingdom, town, statute, rite, calling, man, or woman, but is threatened by the new spirit." There was not only an embrace of the reshaping of society through disciplined communal living but also a strengthened commitment to the idea of a free public education for all young people, and a keener awareness of and concern for society's forgotten or unrepresented, such as blacks, Native Americans, the laboring classes, women, children, and the disabled. Behind this rising humanitarian sensibility was the concept of human perfectibility and the confidence that the place and the moment for its full-bore pursuit had arrived in America, then and there.

Perhaps the most visible and popular of all these causes was the temperance movement, which grew out of a belief in the possibility of moral perfectionism but also addressed itself to a very real problem: the many deleterious effects of alcohol consumption on workers, families, and children. It has been estimated that in 1830, the average American over the age of fifteen consumed the equivalent of 7.1 gallons of pure alcohol per year, about three times what we consume today. It is not hard to imagine the ill effects of such mammoth consumption on worker safety and productivity and on diminished standard of living. Drink, said a temperance pamphlet, was an enslaver, "the prolific source (directly or indirectly) of nearly all the ills that afflict the human family." It was not an implausible claim. Small wonder that a group of Boston ministers organized the American Society for the Promotion of Temperance, to campaign for pledges of "total abstinence" – those who took the pledge had a T by their names and were therefore called "teetotalers" – and ultimately for the restriction or prohibition of the sale of alcoholic beverages.

There were other humanitarian causes aplenty. Women's rights were another area of growing concern, as women's roles in the workplace and in public life expanded beyond the strictly domestic sphere, and as women active in reform movements like temperance and antislavery became anxious to play a more equal role in policy decision-making and governance. Public education for all, with a strong admixture of moral instruction, was the goal of Horace Mann, secretary of the Massachusetts Board of Education. Higher education began to flourish too, as a bevy of small colleges were founded beginning in the 1830s by churches and religious groups. The cruel and careless treatment of the mentally ill drew the attention of Dorothea Dix, a former schoolteacher who mounted a national campaign to publicize the problem and press for more humane treatment and facilities. Thomas Gallaudet opened a school for the deaf in Connecticut and Samuel Gridley Howe a school for the blind in Massachusetts. Reform was buzzing and blooming everywhere.

But the greatest of all reform causes, and the one that eventually enveloped all the others in the North, was the cause of antislavery. Opposition to slavery had grown steadily since the 1780s and had surfaced again in the controversy over Missouri; by the 1830s, when the movement finally began to coalesce, it was being pursued largely as a religious cause rather than a secular one – a grave and soul-imperiling national sin rather than a mere withholding of rights. The great revivals of the Second Great Awakening, while encouraging the reform of slavery in the South, had awakened in the North an uncompromising desire to eliminate it as soon as possible. That moral sharpening of the issue made gradual emancipation, or any other compromise with the defenders of slavery extremely difficult. The leading abolitionists, such as William Lloyd Garrison, publisher of the abolitionist newspaper called the *Liberator* and a fervent Quaker, were nearly all evangelical Protestants of some sort; they included among their numbers Theodore Dwight Weld (a protégé of Finney), Arthur and Lewis Tappan, and Elizur Wright Jr. Few were as radical as Garrison, however, a forceful and steel-spined man who demanded "immediate" emancipation and publicly burned a copy of the Constitution and condemned it as a "proslavery" document, a "Covenant with Death," and "an Agreement with Hell." Others were willing to work for gradual emancipation, carried out through existing political institutions; the black abolitionist Frederick Douglass, himself a former slave, supported that position.

Conflicts among antislavery proponents as to both means and ends had the effect of undermining the movement's practical effectiveness by the 1840s. Garrison in particular became convinced that slavery had so completely corrupted all of American society that only a revolutionary change could effect emancipation. His position was too extreme for most and precipitated a split in the movement, leaving it too weakened to have much political influence when the nation's sectional crisis heated up in the 1850s. By then it was clear that even the mild meliorist policies of figures like Abraham Lincoln would be unlikely to reverse the drift toward polarization and war between the North and the South.

So how are we to evaluate their success? Some scholars have argued that the antislavery movement, particularly in its Garrisonian abolitionist form, made things worse rather than better, by amplifying southern fears and alienating northern allies. Others argue that, without their having taken a strong and intransigent position challenging the practice of slavery, and insisting upon its incompatibility with American and Christian convictions, nothing would have changed, and the nation would have drifted forward indefinitely, with the moral blot of slavery still unaddressed well into the twentieth century. This is a debate worth having, since it connects in some way to the perplexities in almost every great moral cause in human history. Which voices are more deserving of our honor and our emulation?

Something that might be useful to introduce here is a distinction that the German sociologist Max Weber made between the ethic of moral conviction and the ethic of responsibility, two different ways of thinking about how leaders address moral problems in politics. The ethic of moral conviction was what propelled Garrison; it is the point of view that says one must be true to one's principles and do the right thing, at whatever cost. It has a purity about it that is admirable. The ethic of responsibility takes a different view. It guides moderates (and, as we shall see, Lincoln himself) to the belief that leaders must take responsibility for the totality of effects arising out of their actions. It takes into account the tragic character of history, the fact that one can easily do the right thing at the wrong time, in the wrong way, and do an immense amount of damage to good and innocent parties in the process. Such a distinction does not decide the question, but it does clarify it.

But one more thing remains to be pointed out. One of the chief forces that shifted northern antebellum American public opinion about slavery was not a treatise or a sermon or a speech or a work of political theory. It was a work of fiction: Harriet Beecher Stowe's *Uncle Tom's Cabin: or, Life among the Lowly*, published in 1852, which became the best-selling American novel of the nineteenth century. Stowe herself was an evangelical and a member of one of the leading evangelical families in the nation, and she used the novel to depict the life of its title character, a slave who was sold by his owner and torn from his family, but who retained his loving spirit and Christian decency through a horrendous sequence of cruel and violent acts eventuating in his death. It left an indelible mark on all who read it.

The book succeeded in people's minds not because of its cogent preaching on questions of abstract individual rights or abolitionism but because it appealed, vividly and emotionally, to antebellum Americans' sense that no institution could be defended if it so brutally and pitilessly violated the sanctity of the family. It succeeded because it endowed its black characters with undeniable dignity and brought the reader to identify with their suffering, and to feel the injustice of bondage as a denial of personal freedom, one of the central features of the American experiment. And it succeeded all the more because it showed that one of the worst aspects of slavery was its degrading effect upon the master class itself. In other words, it demonstrated the comprehensive wrongness of the institution by showing, in a powerful and plausible way, its awful consequences to everyone involved in it.

This observation about slavery's reciprocal effects was one that many others, including Thomas Jefferson himself, had already made about slavery in the past, and a point that Lincoln was fond of making also. But it was the vividness of Mrs. Stowe's novel that gave the point enough moral weight to change people's minds. This is to say that her contribution was not to argument but to vision, and its vividness moved its readers, not forward from abstract premises, but backward from visible consequences. It brought slaves inside the affective circle of its readers' minds, and it did so not with harsh sermons or shrewd political maneuvering but with an appeal to the moral imagination.

The influence of *Uncle Tom's Cabin* was undeniable – and that influence may well have been greater than the influence of all the Garrisons and Tappans combined. Its success testifies to the power of imaginative literature to alter the moral horizons and humanitarian sympathies of readers and to enlarge their sense of the possible. Curiously, however, Stowe's great novel has never been accorded high status for its literary qualities. That fact leads us back to consider what might have been happening in post-Jacksonian America in the other sense of the word *culture* – not popular culture, but high culture, such as literature, arts, and drama.

For anxious questions still lingered in the thoughts of many Americans, questions that had begun being posed at the very beginning of the American experiment and had never gone away for long. Yes, America had produced political institutions that, for all their faults, were the freest and most democratic in the world. But could that success be replicated in the sphere of culture? Could America ever shed its colonial mentality and generate a culture – a *high* culture – that was as fresh, distinctive, and admirable as its novel political institutions? Could it produce art, literature, music, drama, architecture, and so on, that could stand comparison to the similar products of Europe, while at the same time bearing the distinguishing marks of a genuine American originality?

Tocqueville saw little immediate evidence that it could. Looking at the literary culture of the country, he was decidedly unimpressed. He noticed that Americans seemed only to read English books, rather than books by their own authors, and speculated that the longer-run effect of democracy on literature would be to foster mediocrity, a great many small-scale works, hastily scribbled with the marketplace in mind, often gimmicky or sensational, tailored toward the sensibility of a busy, impatient, practical-minded people. His attitude was a milder version of the famous disdain expressed by the British literary critic Sidney Smith, writing in the *Edinburgh Review* in 1820, when he posed the rhetorical questions, "In the four quarters of the globe, who reads an American book? or goes to an American play? or looks at an American picture or statue?"

As harsh as such words may sound, they carried a sting of truth in them. The progress of American culture had in fact trailed far behind the progress of American politics. Some of this deficiency was surely attributable to the nation's youth and rawness and the absence in America of the long historical memories and deep cultural roots upon which European writers could draw in their own work. The freshness of America, such an advantage in the creation of its political institutions, was a disadvantage for its artists and writers, who had few reserves of tradition and allusion to draw from in nourishing their imaginations.

As the novelist Nathaniel Hawthorne would later complain, an American writer had to make his way writing about a new country, one too new to have accumulated the rich loam of a long and complex history. "No author, without a trial," Hawthorne said, "can conceive of the difficulty of writing a romance about a country where there is no shadow, no antiquity, no mystery, no picturesque and gloomy wrong, nor anything but a commonplace prosperity, in broad and simple daylight, as is happily the case with my dear native land." There had been a handful of talented minor writers in the early American years, such as the novelists Charles Brockden Brown and Washington Irving, but they produced little of enduring consequence and were not successful in placing the form and texture of American life at the center of their work. In the years before 1830, only James Fenimore Cooper managed to find a literary vein to work in his Leatherstocking tales, which reflected (albeit in highly romanticized terms) the distinctive drama of life on the American frontier. And only the melancholy southern mystery writer Edgar Allan Poe, whose macabre tales, detective fiction, and literary criticism were far ahead of his time, would be read with respect overseas.

But some of the problem began with Columbus: America can be hard to see, especially when one sees only what one has been looking for. It was hard to make out the distinctive and new American thing if one was burdened with a wrong set of expectations and was too preoccupied with the imitation and emulation of others. By the 1830s, that was beginning to change, as American writers started to find their voice, and as the elements of a distinctive national culture began to come into being. By the 1850s, an incontestable breakthrough had taken place. How and why did that happen?

We have seen that the flood of energy and innovation animating American religion in the early nineteenth century reflected the rising sense of American uniqueness and possibility, and it did so in a way that was thoroughly democratic – sometimes, perhaps, dismayingly so. But what about the realm of the arts and literature? Did that realm share in this larger cultural surge and show a similar inclination toward democracy? Were American writers and thinkers able at last to realize their dream of an American culture that was worthy of comparison to the products of Europe, while standing proudly as something new, something freshly and distinctively and inimitably American?

The usual starting point for thinking about American literature and art in this time is to stress the tremendous influence of the European romantic movement in the realm of ideas, literature, and the arts. That starting point is useful, even if *romanticism* is a complex term, very hard to define, and containing contrary and even contradictory impulses within it. That is perhaps why it is always easier to say what romanticism is against rather than what it is for.

But one can observe at the outset that romanticism played a similar role among the intellectual classes in America that the growing role of piety and emotionalism played in more popular evangelical religious practice. That similarity might be said to derive from a shared suspicion of, or weariness with, the intellectualism of the Enlightenment – if the Enlightenment is understood as a tidy and sterile view of the world that emphasizes logic and rationality over intuition and sentiment, prudence and utility over passion and fancy, a view of the world that makes no room for mystery, spontaneity, imagination, fantasy, creativity, or the deepest and most inexpressible needs of the soul. "The heart has its reasons that reason does not know," wrote the seventeenth-century French philosopher Blaise Pascal, a distant precursor whose words could well have served as a romantic manifesto a century and a half after he penned them.

Romanticism was established in Europe by the 1780s and was later in coming to America, but once it arrived, it found a very welcoming environment. Indeed, so many of the key ideas associated with romanticism – the exaltation of the individual person, the love of nature, the distrust of sophistication and the love of the primitive, the preference of the organic over the mechanical, the extolling of folk cultures, the glorification of the ordinary and everyday – sound like many elements of the Jacksonian-era persuasion. But romantic ideas made their greatest impact through the works of a few very specific thinkers, a circle of writers and thinkers who were very much a product of the religious and intellectual culture of New England, at a particular moment, in a particular place.

A century and half ago, bucolic little Concord, Massachusetts, was a hub of the American literary and cultural universe. One could hardly think of a more illustrious circle of American writers than Ralph Waldo Emerson, Nathaniel Hawthorne, Henry David Thoreau, Bronson Alcott, and Margaret Fuller. All of them knew one another, lived in or near Concord at roughly the same time, and wrote many of their most important works there. Indeed, all of them (with the exception of Fuller, who died in a shipwreck) are also buried there today. There is perhaps no single location in all of American literary history weightier in literary lore and more alive with the sense of possibility – precisely the sense of possibility that has always been one of the chief glories of American life.

These writers shared a fascination with the cluster of ideas and ideals that go under the rubric of Transcendentalism, a romantic variant that stressed the glories of the vast, the mysterious, and the intuitive. It sought to replace the sin-soaked supernaturalist dogma of orthodox Christianity and the tidy rationality of Unitarianism with a sprawling romantic and eclectic form of natural piety that bordered on pantheism. It placed the ideal of the majestic, isolated, and inviolable Self at the center of its thought, and at the center of Nature itself. Indeed, Nature and the Self were two expressions of the same thing. "Nature is the opposite of the soul," Emerson wrote in 1837, "answering to it part for part. One is seal, and one is print. Its beauty is the beauty of his own mind. Its laws are the laws of his own mind." The vastness of Nature's external panorama was exactly matched by the vastness of the soul's interior estate. Both were part and parcel of the Universal Soul that superintended all things.

Such a view of both Nature and subjective experience accorded little or no respect to older sources of commanding human authority and wisdom. The past was only raw material to be fed upon selectively, with only the needs of the moment (and of the feeding individual) in view. It also was rather sketchy on details of political and social thought. Emerson himself was notoriously contemptuous of "society," which he disparaged as a "conspiracy against the manhood of every one of its members," and was distrustful of all social movements, even those for undeniably good causes.

Instead, the Transcendental Self enjoyed an absolute liberty, free of any external restraint or law other than that of its own nature. In the Transcendental vision, individuals perfected themselves in unfettered liberty, in order that they might form a community that thrives without authority or traditions. Transcendentalism promoted a social and ethical theory that amounted to little more than the principle of self-trust.

Transcendentalism would have been unthinkable without its many transatlantic additives, including a nice helping of German romanticism. But it also was a movement as American, and New England, as apple pie, a movement marking a distinct phase in the strange career of American Puritanism. In Transcendentalism, the mysticism of Jonathan Edwards was turned loose in an un-Edwardsian universe, one in which Nature took the place of God and the sense of sin itself had begun to evaporate. This sounds very much like a highbrow version of Finney's theology.

The comparison is apt. Transcendentalism was, in effect, the evangelicalism of the New England intellectuals. Like mainstream evangelicalism, it sought to overthrow the established authority of denominational hierarchies and social elites and to ground religious affirmations in the authority of individual experience.

To be sure, in taking such a position, it subtracted such inconvenient evangelical distinctives as, say, a belief in the divinity of Christ, in born-again conversion, in the sacred and binding authority of the Bible, and in the imperative to work actively for social reform. It was too free-floating, skeptical, and self-satisfied for any of that. But still, the Transcendentalist movement needs to be understood as part of the expansive, hopeful, experimental, and sometimes utterly cockamamie spirit of antebellum American reform – a moment when America seemed ready to reconsider all existing social arrangements and precedents.

The specific establishment against which Transcendentalism was rebelling was Unitarianism, which was itself an intellectually liberal (though politically conservative) rebellion against the old-line official Calvinism of the Congregational church, and as idiosyncratic a New England institution as one could ever hope to find. Emerson's own family had faithfully traced the path of this portion of religious history. Emerson himself was the offspring of a long line of ministers in that tradition, including his Unitarian-minister father William, whom Emerson followed into the Unitarian ministry after first attending Unitarian-controlled Harvard College and Harvard Divinity School. Not long after moving into the pulpit, however, Emerson found himself restless and discontented with the airless rationalism and empty formalism of "corpse-cold" Unitarian theology and worship.

Unitarianism, which itself started out as an insurgency, had with amazing speed become a byword for smug complacency and conformity. "Nothing," remarked the acerbic historian Henry Adams, who knew that old Bostonian world well, "quieted doubt so completely as the mental calm of the Unitarian clergy.... They had solved the universe, or had offered and realized the best solution yet tried. The problem was worked out." They were too self-satisfied for their own good, too obsessed with outward form, too inattentive to the spark of inner life. Unitarianism had come to power with the promise of a greater theological freedom than what hard-shell Calvinism offered, but by defaulting to outward form, it failed to deliver on the expectations it had aroused. It would quickly be devoured by the very revolution it had started.

Emerson's discontent with this state of affairs finally led him, in 1832, to resign his clerical position at Boston's prestigious Second Church, even without any clear notion of what was to come next. But a substantial legacy left him by his recently deceased wife, Ellen, gave him breathing room and a chance to reorder his life. After a period of travel in Europe, in which he met Thomas Carlyle, William Wordsworth, and some of his other intellectual idols, Emerson resolved to set himself up as an independent writer and speaker, whose efforts would gain support and sustenance from the widening public interest in self-improvement and unconventional religious and spiritual explorations. He was America's first freelance intellectual.

A critical moment in his development was his delivery in 1837 of the annual Phi Beta Kappa address at Harvard, a challenging, occasionally taunting speech which would become known as "The American Scholar" and which would finally launch him in his newly conceived role. A memorable plea for American cultural independence and originality, a blunt challenge to the sodden academicism of Harvard, and a life plan for passionately independent minds like his own, "The American Scholar" would in due course become one of the most celebrated academic lectures in American history. "Mr. President and Gentlemen," it concludes,

> this confidence in the unsearched might of man, belongs by all motives, by all prophecy, by all preparation, to the American Scholar. We have listened too long to the courtly muses of Europe. The spirit of the American freeman is already suspected to be timid, imitative, tame.... Not so, brothers and friends, please God, ours shall not be so. We will walk on our own feet; we will work with our own hands; we will speak our own minds.... A nation of men will for the first time exist, because each believes himself inspired by the Divine Soul which also inspires all men.

It helps to imagine that the leading lights of the Unitarian elite were staring back at him from the audience, an audience that included such establishment dignitaries as Supreme Court justice Joseph Story and Massachusetts governor Edward Everett. The bold act of delivering such a speech before such an august group was a brave assertion of what Emerson would soon call "self-reliance," a deed of self-definition that validated Emerson's new role in the very act of presenting it to the world.

Oliver Wendell Holmes Sr., the father of the famous Supreme Court judge, referred to "The American Scholar" as America's intellectual Declaration of Independence, and the comparison was very apt. Emerson saw the American Revolution as a beacon to all of humanity and believed that the embattled farmers of his beloved Concord had indeed fired "the shot heard round the world," in the words of his own patriotic poem called "Concord Hymn" – probably the best-known words Emerson ever wrote. Hence, when he called for Americans to cease taking their cues from "the courtly muses of Europe," he was not advocating a withdrawal into provincialism. He was urging that America find its distinctive voice at last. He thought that America was uniquely situated, by virtue of its history and current circumstances, to achieve something new under the sun – politically, socially, intellectually – and to do so for the sake not only of itself but of all humanity.

But it would fulfill its mission to humanity precisely by being most fully itself – a principle that Emerson also saw reflected in individual life, where he sought to promote the ideal of expansive, unfettered liberty. See, for example, the swaggering energy of these words extracted from his 1841 essay "Self-Reliance":

> *Whoso would be a man, must be a non-conformist. He who would gather immortal palms must not be hindered by the name of goodness, but must explore if it be goodness.*
>
> *No law can be sacred to me but that of my nature. Good and bad are but names very readily transferable to that or this; the only right is what is after my constitution; the only wrong what is against it.*
>
> *The great man is he who in the midst of a crowd keeps with perfect sweetness the independence of solitude.*
>
> *Ah, then, exclaim the aged ladies, you shall be sure to be misunderstood! Misunderstood! It is a right fool's word. Is it so bad then to be misunderstood? Pythagoras was misunderstood, and Socrates and Jesus, and Luther, and Copernicus, and Galileo, and Newton, and every pure and wise spirit that ever took flesh. To be great is to be misunderstood.*

If there is brag and bluster in these words, they also are very American words. So too, though, were Emerson's entirely different words in the Harvard speech, calling for a new understanding of ordinary life, one that reflected unprecedentedly democratic and capacious norms. "I ask not for the great, the remote, the romantic," he wrote. "I explore and sit at the feet of the familiar, the low." Instead of the elite European emphasis upon the doings of heroes and kings and queens and aristocrats, he pleaded for something new: a literature that exalts the people and things that the courtly muses had never deigned to take notice of, a literature "of the poor, the feelings of the child, the philosophy of the street, the meaning of household life." It was the thrilling paradox of Emerson's idea of democratic culture that it could include both the grandeur of the uncoerced and nonconforming mind and a tender respect for the ordinary details of everyday existence, admitting no contradiction between the two.

Others in the Concord circle who felt Emerson's influence also became influential in their own right. Henry David Thoreau, who was Emerson's neighbor and something of a protégé, tried to put Emerson's ideas of self-reliance to the test and spent over two years living alone in a cabin on Walden Pond, spending most of his time in reflection and writing. Out of that experience of enforced simplicity and economy came one of the finest books in the American literary tradition, his *Walden; or, Life in the Woods* (1854), a wondrous blend of spiritual reflection, hard-edged social criticism, and keen naturalistic observation. Thoreau announced his intentions with these opening words: "I went to the woods because I wished to live deliberately, to front only the essential facts of life, and see if I could not learn what it had to teach, and not, when I came to die, discover that I had not lived."

Nathaniel Hawthorne was also a product of the same circle, even if in some ways a contrarian participant. Ever since his student days at Bowdoin College, where he had become friendly with classmate Henry Wadsworth Longfellow, and after hearing Longfellow's 1825 commencement address, "Our Native Writers," he had been afire with the idea of realizing the dream of creating a truly American literature. And indeed Hawthorne was arguably the first to achieve it; his 1850 novel *The Scarlet Letter* was a great breakthrough, the first great American novel, a work that would be read and respected world over. He shared an enthusiasm for many aspects of the romantic rebellion, questioning the scientific worldview and delighting in stories that were replete with supernatural and uncanny elements.

But Hawthorne dissented from the optimism of the others. Instead he stalked the era's official optimism like a shadowy apparition, propelled by a spirit of inherited Puritan skepticism, and he did so all the way up to the cataclysm of the Civil War. His early stories, collected as *Twice-Told Tales* (1837), made use of the New England past to explore issues of sin and guilt, the issue to which he brought a master's touch in *The Scarlet Letter*, a penetrating analysis of a Puritan community's sinfully cruel treatment of an adulterous woman. He wrote his novel *Blithedale Romance* (1852) as a wry put-down of the utopian delusions behind the Brook Farm experiment in communal living, in which he participated. His entire oeuvre can be thought of as a stern and consistent rebuke to the giddy optimism of his age and the false hopes and hidden terrors it failed to recognize. And yet he, too, was quintessentially American: as American as Emerson, as American as the Puritans.

And then there was Herman Melville. Although a New Yorker by birth and only occasionally a member of the Concord circle, Melville was a friend and an enormous admirer, to the point of adulation, of Nathaniel Hawthorne. It was under the influence of Hawthorne that he took the fateful turn in his writing that led him to produce *Moby-Dick* (1851), arguably the greatest of all American novels. That sprawling, melodramatic, rollicking, and searingly tragic drama of the voyage of the whaling ship *Pequod* in search of the Great White Whale under the direction of the mad and relentless Captain Ahab was based upon Melville's experience. He had gone to sea as a young man – "a whale ship was my Yale College and my Harvard," he said – and learned much about the extremities of life. On one voyage to the South Sea islands, he jumped ship, had many adventures, was captured by cannibals, participated in a mutiny, and came home with a huge treasury of stories and experiences. He drew on this treasury for a series of novels that were commercial successes but not especially memorable or enduring.

Then, after meeting Hawthorne, he changed his objectives, and the result was *Moby-Dick*, a masterpiece of psychological insight and metaphysical ambiguity, in which everything from the anatomy of whales to the existence of God is up for discussion. Unfortunately, Melville drove off his sea-yarn-loving audience; *Moby-Dick* became a commercial failure, and it sank like a stone, remaining forgotten for the next seventy years, until it was rediscovered by scholars. Melville too sank into obscurity, although writing some excellent poetry about the Civil War and a posthumously published novella called *Billy Budd*, in which he returned to the subject of shipboard life and studied, to profound effect, how a ship captain very different from Ahab – he is named Vere, the "truth" – handled the ethic of responsibility, with all its tensions and terrors.

Finally, the 1850s sees the emergence of the poet Walt Whitman, who is the most Jacksonian American writer of all. Unlike the Concord circle, he was a man of the city who adored the jagged contours and bustling crowds of the modern Brooklyn and Manhattan and wrote poetry about riding the ferry between them. There was not an ounce of snobbery in him, and he enjoyed mingling with all kinds of people, from the roughest street toughs to the habitués of grand opera houses. He worked for years as a journeyman editor for newspapers in Brooklyn, New York, and New Orleans, signing his material as "Walter" Whitman and showing little of the astonishingly original literary flair that would become his trademark. He had, however, read and digested Emerson, and when his first book, *Leaves of Grass*, appeared in 1855, he sent it to

Emerson, who hailed it as "the most extraordinary piece of wit and wisdom that American has yet contributed."

The book featured a frontispiece with a picture of Whitman, dressed in worker's garb, with his undershirt visible and his hat cocked provocatively at a rakish angle.

He was, he went on, "not a bit tamed – I too am untranslatable; / I sound my barbaric yawp over the roofs of the world." Writing in free unrhymed verse, using uncustomary and even startling images – the odors and passions of the body, the occupations of bricklayers and prostitutes – he presented all of reality as equally worthy of his attention, the ultimate democracy of the mind and heart and spirit.

At times, it could all seem like an undifferentiated mess, and Whitman, too, took many years to find his proper audience. He was, and is, easy to mock. But the British writer and critic D.H. Lawrence recognized in Whitman an achievement going beyond the literary, expressing the emerging culture of democracy, not only as it was but as it could be, better than anyone else had yet done:

> *Whitman's essential message was the Open Road. The leaving of the soul free unto herself, the leaving of his fate to her and to the loom of the open road. Which is the bravest doctrine man has ever proposed to himself.... The true democracy, where soul meets soul, in the open road.*

It is finally a doctrine of human dignity, of the infinite worth of the single and individual soul – the deepest aspiration of the age it represented.

CHAPTER EIGHT

THE OLD SOUTH AND SLAVERY

I T IS HARD TO IDENTIFY THE MOMENT WHEN "THE SOUTH" crystallized as a distinct region within the new nation. Regional tensions over slavery were already evident, as we have seen, at the Constitutional Convention in 1787, but they were not appreciably greater than East–West tensions over other issues, and certainly not strong enough to overwhelm the desire to establish a strong and stable national union. Indeed, the earliest serious movements in the direction of state secession from the Union would come from New England states, as in the Hartford Convention, rather than from southern ones. All but two of the first seven presidents of the nation were southerners, a fact that did not cause undue alarm or distress to the rest of the nation. Regional tensions flared up over tariffs, which tended to favor northern industrial and commercial interests over southern agricultural ones. But it may not have been until Jefferson's "fire bell in the night," the 1819–21 crisis over the admission of Missouri to the Union, that the possibility of the two sections, North and South, evolving into dramatically and enduringly different cultures loomed.

Yet the South had a certain unifying distinctiveness from the beginning. At the bottom of it all was a certain combination of climate and economics, a combination both felicitous and fatal. Commercial agriculture had been the bulwark of the southern economy from the discovery of tobacco onward and continued to be well into the nineteenth century. The South's climate was warm, humid, even in places subtropical, and the region enjoyed an almost year-round growing season, along with its being favored with numerous navigable waterways. Fertile bottomland made it ideal territory for the profitable cultivation of cash crops, such as cotton, tobacco, rice, sugar, and indigo, which could in turn be exported as a source of income.

By the early 1800s, there could be no doubt which of these crops was the most lucrative and most important: by the 1850s, cotton accounted for two-thirds of all U.S. exports and linked the South's burgeoning agricultural economy with Great Britain's preeminence in the textile industry. The mass cultivation of such crops in quantities large enough to be commercially profitable required a continuing supply of vast tracts of land, and an equally large supply of inexpensive unskilled labor to do the tedious and exhausting work that large-scale agriculture required. The economic incentives to expand westward were strong and unrelenting, and the plantation system and institution of chattel slavery, which were well suited to the mass production that cash-crop agriculture entailed, became central features of southern life. Much of the distinctiveness of the antebellum South can be traced back to the diverging character of the nation's regional economies and labor systems.

The South also was more self-contained, more drawn in upon itself, more conscious of its own identity, and increasingly aware of its potential minority status within the nation. Unlike the North, it did not experience great waves of immigration from Europe, such as the influx of Irish and German refugees who streamed into northern cities during the 1840s, fleeing from poverty, famine, and political instability in their native lands. As time passed, these trends tended to perpetuate one another; European immigrants avoided the South because there was so little nonagricultural work, and the status of agricultural labor was tainted by the existence of slavery. And so the South became ever more committed to slave labor, in what turned into a self-reinforcing cycle. As a consequence, the region's population growth would come mainly from internal sources.

Thus the South became a strikingly biracial society, underwritten by stark differences of power and status, although strangely, underneath it all was also a certain commonality of culture. This is a paradox not easily unraveled, although it may well derive in part from the specific texture of agricultural life, where there is likely to be a stronger sense of place, and where human relationships are more likely to be casual and organic in character, less guided by strictly instrumental or impersonal concerns. Another important commonality was that, aside from south Louisiana, which retained much of its Catholic character, the population of the South was almost entirely Protestant Christian in its religion, with Anglicanism dominant in the white upper classes and various forms of low-church evangelical Protestantism presiding in the lower classes, both white and black. The amount of exchange and interchange between and among white and black Southerners, in speech patterns, foodways, music, worship, folklore, and literary expression, was enormous.

Yet, at the same time, the mounting economic importance of slavery led, little by little, to a stiffening determination among southern whites to defend their "peculiar institution," as they came to call it, though even at the height of southern slavery, only a minority of southern whites were slave owners, and only a tiny number of those were plantation owners with large numbers of slaves under their command. This defensiveness of southern slaveholders would find its way even into their religion, with a strict interpretation of the Bible as the single most important method of defense. As the historian U.B. Phillips argued, "the central theme" of southern history became the "common resolve indomitably maintained" that the white population should maintain its dominance. This determination had the effect of muting the sort of class conflict among whites that was becoming all too common in industrializing northern centers like Boston, where the native born and the immigrant Irish constantly clashed. Such unity would, however, exact an awful price from enslaved black southerners with little or no access to freedom.

There were other distinctives about southern culture, although it is difficult in discussing the South to separate myth and legend from fact, and perhaps it is not even desirable to try too hard. For a myth that is widely believed may be itself a very powerful cultural reality – not in the sense that it describes reality accurately but in the more limited sense that it reflects a widely shared aspiration or formative belief that is as much a part of the historical landscape as any fact. Nothing was more distinctive about the South than the fact that southerners *believed* their region to be distinctive. So too did other Americans – and such a belief, when widely shared, becomes a fact in itself, a fact of culture.

To live enveloped in myth is, to say the least, a mixed blessing. Jonathan Daniels, a prominent North Carolina journalist, wrote in his 1938 book *A Southerner Discovers the South*, "We Southerners are a mythological people, created half out of dream and half out of slander, who live in a still legendary land." What he meant by that statement was exemplified the following year, when the 1939 movie *Gone with the Wind* was released and enjoyed an enthusiastic national reception, thus immortalizing a dreamy view of the Civil War–era South as a stable and dignified aristocratic society that looked out for its happy-go-lucky and compliant, childlike slaves as a benevolent father would watch over his lovable but immature brood. "Moonlight and magnolias," a tagline used in the movie by the hard-boiled character Rhett Butler, came to stand for this wistful sentimental vision of the Old South.

And yet equally vivid was the reverse portrait of the Old South as a sinkhole of the utmost depravity and cruelty of which humanity is capable, an image sketched unforgettably in Harriet Beecher Stowe's portrait of the vicious and violent slave owner Simon Legree in *Uncle Tom's Cabin*. This, too, is an overdrawn and exaggerated picture if it is made to stand for all the Old South, which had many elements of beauty and graciousness, learning and high culture, piety and devotion, all mixed in with elements of ugliness and brutal dehumanization. If one tries to view the Old South whole, it makes for a deeply baffling picture.

The most distinguished students of the subject, the historians Eugene Genovese and Elizabeth Fox-Genovese, asked poignantly in their 2005 book *The Mind of the Master Class*, how civilized people who were admirable in so many ways could also have embraced a cruel social system that inflicted horrors upon those subordinated to it. This is a haunting question that lingers in the mind and is not easily answered or set aside. It is a question that history often poses to us when we encounter times and peoples whom we esteem in many ways but whose values and circumstances are in other respects so different from our own. In any event, with mythic extremes making up so much of our image of southern life, it has been hard to find our way to something more closely approximating the reality in all its complexity.

Certain generalizations about the Old South are indisputable, however. It was an overwhelmingly agricultural society in which the production and sale of cotton constituted the central form of economic activity and in which cities were few and far between and economic diversification outside of agriculture was almost nonexistent. It was also a very wealthy region, but with wealth concentrated in a very few hands, individuals who were perched atop a very precarious social and economic structure, ultimately dependent on the price of cotton and the use of forced labor for their lofty standing.

Cotton enjoyed phenomenal success in establishing itself as a commodity avidly sought around the world, and especially in Great Britain, where southern cotton became the force powering the British textile industry. That success made the planter class overconfident about their standing and their prospects. As world demand for cotton continued to rise inexorably, the South's future prosperity seemed assured, so long as it was firmly wedded to cotton. With cotton as its chief weapon, the southern economy appeared to be unbeatable and could call the tune for the rest of the world, for long into the foreseeable future. As the South Carolina planter James Henry Hammond boasted, if the South were to choose to deprive England of a steady supply of southern cotton, "England would topple headlong and carry the whole civilized world with her.... No, you dare not make war on cotton. No power on earth dares to make war upon it. Cotton is king."

Such words smacked of hubris, the excessive pride that goes before a fall. And so they would turn out to be, expressing a mistaken vision that would lead to cruel and tragic consequences for the South. Lulled into a false sense of economic security by the illusion that cotton was invincible and its prices would never fall, the South would become fatally committed to a brutal social and economic system that was designed for the lucrative production of cotton on a massive scale but that achieved such productivity at an incalculable cost in human and moral terms. It placed the region on a collision course with changing moral sensibilities in the world, and with fundamental American ideals.

The system was not a machine, however. It evolved into a complex and many-faceted society whose contours would be as unique and varied as the South itself. As has already been pointed out, the elite planter class was small in number, constituting only about 4 percent of the adult white males in the South, and only a relative handful of those planters (around twenty-three hundred of them) owned at least one hundred slaves. The majority of slaveholders were ordinary farmers who owned fewer than twenty slaves and worked in the fields with their slaves. The majority of whites, three-fourths of them by 1860, were not slaveholders at all and were unable to afford the rich low-lying farmland favored by the planters, who lived instead in the upcountry, and got their living largely as subsistence farmers. The growing concentration of slaves in fewer and fewer southern hands and the decline of slavery in border states indicated to many Southerners that an end to slavery within the Union was coming. Yet the large planters continued to set the tone for the whole, exercising a disproportionate influence on their societies and the legislatures of their states. Far from resenting them or begrudging them their wealth, most poor whites tended to be loyal to the planters and hoped someday to be able to emulate them.

Dominated as it was by an aristocratic planter class, the Old South in some ways resembled a feudal society, with all the strict social hierarchy that implies. Over time, the resemblance became increasingly self-conscious and was actively embraced by those at the top of the social pyramid. Many planters adopted a code of conduct that they associated with the chivalric codes of medieval times, with a strong (and often prickly) sense of masculine honor, a respect for culture and learning, a taste for grand estates and lavish hospitality, a strong loyalty to family and locality, fierce veneration of womanhood and feminine purity, and strict deference to elders, a pattern of dutiful respect toward one's "betters" that would also be reflected (if less consistently) in patriarchal and paternalistic attitudes toward social subordinates, including slaves. Even if the economic basis of southern life revolved around a harsh form of commercial agriculture, the society that grew up around that economic basis increasingly conceived of itself in very different terms, as a variation on a very old theme: the belief that there is a great chain of being that links and orders all things, from the highest to the lowest, and that harmony and well-being derive from the preservation of the elements of degree and rank in that given order. As in feudal Europe, so in the American South: there was much that could be considered graceful and orderly and humane in that ideal.

The trouble was that it was not at all obvious how such a vision could be rendered compatible with the idea that all men are created equal or with the energetic individualism and entrepreneurship that Tocqueville had observed. "In the great Anglo-American family," wrote Tocqueville, "one can distinguish two principal offshoots … one in the South, the other in the North." How had the South become so different in such a short period of time? In later years, the writer Mark Twain claimed that books like Sir Walter Scott's 1820 historical romance *Ivanhoe*, which glorified the world of medieval England, had been the cause of the American Civil War, by filling the southern mind with "dreams and phantoms" of a "long-vanished society." The claim was wild and farfetched, as Twain tended to be, and just as fanciful as anything in Scott's romantic prose. But there was an important element of truth in it. The steady divergence of the antebellum South from the northern states was not just a matter of differences over nitty-gritty issues of economics and politics. Such differences were extended and hardened by the emergence of divergent social ideals. By the time the sectional conflict came to a head in the 1850s and 1860s, the depth and width of these cultural differences would make political compromise even more difficult to achieve.

Twain's observation conveyed another truth: "the South" was not merely the South of the planter class. To see it otherwise was to buy in to the very fantasy of a revived feudalism that Twain believed had led the South into catastrophe. Nor was it merely the South of white people. By the middle of the nineteenth century, the institution of slavery so completely undergirded the Southern way of life that it was impossible to consider southern culture apart from it. And that meant that black southerners, most of whom were enslaved, constituted a massive presence in southern life, from the very beginning, and exerted a constant and reciprocal influence on the culture of the South. To see the South whole means telling their story also.

That is not a simple matter. For one thing, the practice of slavery in North America was resistant to easy generalizations. Slavery in North America had begun in 1619 in Virginia as something approaching a casual afterthought, not always clearly distinct from indentured servitude, and as it spread, it changed and adapted to circumstances. For the century and a half of British colonial rule, it existed as a system of forced or coerced labor that had not been thoroughly defined and codified, a feature of "benign neglect" with a wide and informal variety in the way it was practiced – and it was practiced in all the colonies, New England as well as the South. After the Revolution, however, it became more regularized and regulated, and its practice became localized to the South, as the northern states gradually abolished it.

Yet even after these changes had taken place, the working and living conditions of slavery could still vary dramatically, depending on the historical moment and geographical location – and the disposition of individual masters. The living conditions of slaves on small farms in states like Kentucky in the Upper South, where they often found themselves living more like hired hands and working beside their masters in the fields, were very different from life on the giant sugar and cotton plantations of Louisiana and Alabama in the Deep South, where hundreds were living and laboring together, confined under strict and often oppressive discipline.

The plantations formed complex slave mini-societies, with intricate divisions of labor and gradations of rank and status. At the top of the slave pecking order were the household servants and skilled workers, who worked in more refined circumstances, coming into contact frequently with the planter's family and generally having better quarters and better treatment. At the bottom were the field hands, who typically worked in tightly supervised gangs from dawn to dusk. They slept in crude wooden shacks with dirt floors, poorly fed, poorly clothed and shod, and dwelling always in fear of the master's punitive lash.

Wherever there were larger concentrations of slaves, there one would find pronounced surviving elements of African cultural and religious beliefs, often manifesting themselves as hybrids and combinations of the distinct African tribal and regional cultures from which the slaves had originally come. The slaves' religion took on a distinctive flavor, blending Christianity with enthusiastic music and ecstatic African elements in ways that would come to distinguish much of African American worship in the years to come. Slaves found that many of the stories of the Bible spoke directly to their condition, in ways that their masters could not perceive, and they especially took heart from the story of the Israelites' exodus from slavery in Egypt – just as John Winthrop and the Puritans had done, two centuries before – seeing it as a figure and metaphor for their own tribulations and sufferings, and for the hope of their eventual liberation and redemption. Similarly, they could see their condition and their hopes mirrored in the humility of Christ, the God who came into the world incognito, in the guise of a lowly suffering servant, who took the side of the poor and oppressed of the world and proved himself more powerful even in his earthly humiliation than anything the existing authorities could do to him. His example gave them heart.

Religion was at the center of slaves' communal life, and it was the crucial resource that made it possible for them to sustain communities and families at all under such harsh conditions. The forces against their doing so were immense, especially in the closed circumstances of the large plantations. Slave marriages had no legal validity and no protections against the invasive force of the slave market, which often dictated that families could be torn apart at any moment by an owner's decision to sell a husband, a wife, or (more often) a child. (The plot of *Uncle Tom's Cabin* revolves around a series of such family dismemberments.) Ironically, the end of the legal slave trade in 1808 made such transactions more frequent, since the offspring of existing slaves had become even more valuable, particularly since the demand for slaves only increased as planters moved west, expanding cotton cultivation into the rich lands of the lower Mississippi Valley. In addition, slave women had an added source of humiliation and anguish, being subject to sexual abuse and exploitation by masters and other powerful whites in the plantation system. The immense sadness and longing one hears in the great spiritual songs that came out of the slave experience – songs like "Sometimes I Feel Like a Motherless Child" and "Nobody Knows the Trouble I've Seen" – were cries of the heart, products of that crucible of harsh and near-hopeless circumstance.

But those were not the only such products. There were also songs of exuberance and joy, such as "Rock My Soul in the Bosom of Abraham." And there were songs hinting at the possibility of this-worldly deliverance, such as "Steal Away to Jesus" and "Go Down, Moses," the latter of which was used by the black abolitionist Harriet Tubman as a coded signal to slaves thinking of fleeing to the North. Such songs, and the profound religious assurances that lay behind them, gave slaves the capacity to resist being completely overwhelmed by the circumstances of near-total domination in which they found themselves. The slave religion taught the same lesson that many previous generations of Christians, as well as Stoics like the Roman slave Epictetus, had learned: the soul can remain free even when the body is bound. While it would be wrong to minimize the psychological ravages of slavery, it would be equally wrong to exaggerate them and thereby deny the heroism and resiliency that slaves showed, guarding their hearts and keeping hope alive under hopeless conditions.

Slaves resisted their enslavement both passively and actively. Some of their most effective methods were "day-to-day" acts of passive or indirect resistance: work slowdowns, malingering, feigned illness, deliberate sabotage, breaking of farming implements, setting fire to buildings, and a range of other acts of obstruction. But given the tight grip in which slaveholders held their charges, and laws favoring the capture and return of fugitives, slaves' opportunities for escape were few and risky, and large-scale insurrections were all but suicidal. But some were willing to try, and others were willing to help. The ingenuity and courage of Harriet Tubman, Levi and Catherine Coffin, and other committed abolitionists created the Underground Railroad, an informal network of secret routes and safe houses sheltering and aiding escaped slaves seeking freedom in the north. Estimates range as high as one hundred thousand for the number of escapes made possible by the Railroad.

Those valiant efforts made only a small dent in the slave population of the South – and organized slave rebellions in the South were rare, and never successful. The example of the successful slave uprising in the 1790s in the French Caribbean colony of Saint-Domingue (Haiti), which led to the murder or forced exile of thousands of former masters, had made a permanent impression upon the minds of southern slaveholders, and they were not about to permit something similar to happen on their soil, on their watch. The "moonlight and magnolias" view of antebellum southern slavery did not reckon with the underground river of suspicion and fear that coursed beneath the surface of everyday life.

The Nat Turner Rebellion in Southampton County, Virginia, in August 1831, was the most consequential uprising. Turner was a black field hand who was also a religious zealot, driven by prophetic visions to imagine that he was divinely ordained to lead a slave uprising. On August 22, 1831, Turner set out to do just that, with the intention of slaughtering as many as possible of the white neighbors who enslaved them. They began with Turner's master and wife and children, hacking them to death with axes, and then went on to successive farmhouses, repeating the process until, by the end of the next day, they had killed around sixty whites, mostly women and children. Bodies were thrown into bonfires or left for the wolves. The rebels were readily subdued the following day by units of white militiamen, although Turner himself eluded capture for more than two months. In the end, the state executed about fifty blacks, it banished others, and many more were killed by the militia without trial.

The ferocity of the Nat Turner Rebellion and its subsequent suppression dramatically altered the mental and moral climate of the South. It sent a chill of terror down the spines of white southerners, as rumors traveled far and wide about other such rebellions under way or in the making. There also were reports of violent white retaliation against blacks all over the South. Bloody violence was in the air, the civil order itself seemed threatened, and there was a tangible sense that a great divide was being crossed – or perhaps had already been crossed. The rebellion occurred just as the abolition movement in the North was gathering steam – Garrison's *The Liberator* published its first issue in 1831 – making its appeal on the basis of Christian moral values that southerners generally shared. And yet, it occurred at a moment when the South's investment in slavery as an economic institution seemed to have become too great to abandon. White southerners were still holding the wolf by the ear. They responded to the Nat Turner Rebellion by cracking down and tightening their control over the slave system, ensuring that no serious slave uprising would occur after this one.

Shortly afterward, in the 1831–32 session of the Virginia General Assembly, the state's legislators engaged in a far-reaching debate, occasioned by a flurry of some forty petitions, urging them to engage the problems associated with slavery. This was arguably the South's only full and free general debate over the status of the peculiar institution, and its tenor was surprisingly critical. Some called for outright emancipation, others for colonization, but none called for the protection of "perpetual slavery." Interestingly, although the delegates were divided about means, they did not differ about ends; many even saw Virginia's future as lying with the free-soil states to the north but differed only in the speed with which that end should be sought. None defended slavery in abstract terms; in fact, their compromise resolution did not hesitate to call slavery an evil and agreed that slavery would eventually end in Virginia. After vigorous debate, the members narrowly rejected, by a vote of 73 to 58, a plan for gradual emancipation and African colonization, proposed by a descendant of Thomas Jefferson. Instead, members declined to pass any such laws, deciding instead that they "should await a more definite development of public opinion."

That decision doomed to failure any hope that slavery would be abandoned in an orderly and peaceable way, for the window of opportunity for any such enlightened action was closing, and public opinion in the state was already running in the opposite direction. In fact, proslavery and antiabolitionist opinion rapidly overtook the alternatives in the years that followed, buttressed by arguments that had been previewed in the debate. The General Assembly passed legislation making it unlawful to teach slaves, free blacks, or mulattoes to read or write and restricting all blacks from holding religious meetings without the presence of a licensed white minister. Other slaveholding states across the South enacted similar laws restricting activities of slaves and free blacks. The institution of slavery was henceforth going to be even more closed, more devoted to total control, more bottled up, and more toxic than before. There was to be no loosening of the white South's uncomfortable grip on the wolf's ear.

Changes in ideas followed these changes in circumstances. The Turner revolt had forcefully given the lie to wistful myths about the harmonious benevolence of slavery. But it did so at a moment when the South's dependency on its peculiar institution was too great and too thoroughly entrenched to be abandoned – and at the very moment when the voices of northern abolitionists, although few in number and limited in influence, had suddenly become loud and threatening to southern slaveholders' ears. A defense had to be mounted. But how could one make a robust defense of an institution that one also regarded as an evil on the way to gradual extinction? Would it not be more effective if southerners were to steel their minds and hearts for the struggle ahead with the firm belief that this indispensable institution was actually a positive good and not merely a necessary evil? Instead of abandoning the paternalistic justification of slavery, masters chose to blame slave unrest on outsiders.

Hence the emergence of an unapologetically "proslavery" argument, and the source of no small part of its persuasiveness. But it was not merely an invention ginned up for the occasion to justify a dehumanizing economic institution that the prospering South could not, or would not, do without. It had deeper roots in the earliest sources of southern distinctiveness and clear elements of continuity with the neofeudal paternalist philosophy that had already been firmly in place in parts of the plantation South. But the proslavery argument had embraced this premodern, hierarchical vision and intensified a few notches, now couching it as a radical critique of modern capitalism that was startlingly similar in many respects to the critique then being offered by radical leftists like Karl Marx.

In the view of the Virginian George Fitzhugh, one of the more influential of the proslavery apologists in the 1850s, the paternalism of slavery was far preferable to the "wage slavery" of northern industrial society, in which greedy, profit-oriented capitalists took no responsibility for the comprehensive well-being of their workers but instead exploited them freely and then cast them aside like used tissues when their labor was no longer useful. Fitzhugh argued not only against capitalism but against the entire liberal tradition, including the ideas of such foundational thinkers as Locke and Jefferson, countering that free labor and free markets and other individual liberties only served to enrich the strong while crushing the weak. "Slavery," he wrote, "is a form, and the very best form, of socialism," the best counter to the rampant competitiveness and atomization of "free" societies. With Fitzhugh, we have come a very long way from the ideals of the American Founders.

It is hard to know how widespread acceptance of such a radical and unvarnished version of the proslavery argument was. What is clearer, though, is that its appearance on the scene, and its displacement of the more complex "necessary evil" argument in the minds of many elite leaders, including such powerful men as the influential South Carolina politician John C. Calhoun, were developments full of ominous portent for the future cohesiveness of the American nation. They were yet another sign of hardening cultural divisions, a sign that the South was charting its own course based on its own understanding of the nature of the American Founding. Even in the realm of religion, the southern Protestant churches developed a distinct theological orientation, adducing biblical precedents, such as the slaveholding of the Hebrew patriarchs or St. Paul's commands to slaves, to support the moral acceptability, and even desirability, of slavery. The Methodist and Baptist churches would divide into northern and southern denominations because of sectional disagreements over just such issues. For southern slaveholders, the model slaveholder became the biblical Abraham.

In myriad other ways, ranging from the seizure of the mails to prevent the transmission of abolitionist literature to the imposition in 1836 of a "gag rule" in the U.S. House of Representatives to suppress any discussion of petitions relating to slavery and abolition, the southern states seemed intent upon taking off the table, once and for all, any and all reconsideration of slavery, especially of the moral and political acceptability of slavery. The kind of open and frank discussion that took place in the Virginia General Assembly in 1831–32 had become, almost overnight, virtually impossible.

How rapidly things had changed. And this change, this defensive hardening of southern opinion, was a harbinger of things to come, none of them good.

CHAPTER NINE

THE GATHERING STORM

WHEN WE LOOK BACK TO A MOMENT IN THE PAST, IT IS hard not to read into it nearly everything that we know is to come after it. We can't help but see it as something carrying along with itself a future that we already know about, an awareness that gives us a perspective very different from that of the participants in that past moment.

In particular, it is hard to read about the United States of the early nineteenth century, and particularly about the emerging cultural gulf between North and South and the ever-festering wound of slavery, without thinking of the series of events culminating in the coming of the Civil War as if they were predictable stages leading to a preordained outcome. Like the audience for a Greek tragedy, we come to this great American drama already knowing the general plot. We anticipate the heavy tread of events, the steps leading down an ever-narrowing stairway toward a bloody inevitability. We naturally tend to structure our thinking about the past in that way, with every step along the way understood solely in light of the grim terminus toward which we know it to be leading. Behind even the most innocent moments is ominous background music, reminding us of what is coming.

That habit of mind should be resisted if we are truly to enter into the spirit of the past and to grasp the nature of historical change. History is only very rarely the story of inevitabilities, and it almost never appears in that form to its participants. It is more often a story of contingencies and possibilities, of things that could have gone either way, or even a multitude of other ways. Very little about the life of nations is certain, and even what we think of as destiny is something quite different from inevitability. Every attempt to render history into a science has come up empty-handed. The fact of human freedom always manages to confound the effort to do so.

What we can say, though, is that there were landmark moments along the way in which a blood-stained outcome became much more likely, and after which the alternatives to armed conflict and separation became far fewer and far less accessible. Chief among such moments along what we now see, in retrospect, as a road to American disunion was the Mexican War of 1846.

It is an event better remembered today by Mexicans (and Texans) than by most Americans. But the Mexican War had profound consequences for both countries, far out of proportion to its relatively short and decisive character. Above all else, the territorial gains it produced had the effect of destroying the uneasy peace over slavery that the Missouri Compromise had established and would lead to deeply unsettled circumstances that made an eventual conflict between North and South all but unavoidable. In more ways than one, the Mexican War provides support for the adage "be careful what you wish for."

Beginning in the 1820s, after Mexico had won its independence from Spain, it actively sought to attract immigrants from the American South who would settle and farm in its northern province of Texas. It more than got its wish, and got it more quickly than it could have imagined. Given the land hunger of so many westward-bound Americans, the vast and wide-open territory of the thinly settled Texas frontier was irresistible. By 1825, Stephen F. Austin, son of a Missouri banker, had brought three hundred settlers into Texas and thereby contributed the first trickle of what would quickly swell to a flood of migrants to the region. It didn't take long before these Anglo immigrants were the dominant demographic group. By 1830, newly arrived Americans, many of whom had brought their slaves with them, outnumbered the Mexicans by three to one. Texas was almost overnight becoming a part of the cotton kingdom. What began as migration was rapidly becoming cultural conquest.

Such rapid changes were certain to create discontent and conflict with existing residents, particularly given the sharp cultural differences between Protestant Americans and Catholic Mexicans. When the government of newly independent Mexico outlawed slavery in 1829 and insisted that the recent American immigrants convert to Roman Catholicism, it provoked intense resistance and open disobedience from the Americans, who were not willing to assimilate to what was rapidly becoming a minority culture. In response, in 1830, Mexico proceeded to close itself off to further American immigration; but that dictum went almost completely ignored, and the steady stream of incoming Americans continued essentially unabated.

Finally, with the rise to power in Mexico in 1834 of General Antonio López de Santa Anna, a haughty and eccentric leader who had moved to strengthen central authority and make himself a virtual dictator, the issue came to a head. When Santa Anna abolished the Mexican Constitution of 1824 and dissolved the state legislatures, he provoked a rebellion in Texas and several other Mexican states. In the case of Texas, this soon turned into a struggle for independence, in which the settlers were led by Sam Houston, a colorful and well-traveled Virginia native who had served as a governor of Tennessee and was an adoptive member of the Cherokee tribe, as well as an experienced Indian fighter. It soon became clear that the matter between Texas and Mexico could not be settled without a clash of arms.

The struggle began badly for the Americans, as Santa Anna's army of six thousand moved swiftly and brutally against the resistance, obeying Santa Anna's command that all survivors be summarily executed. After slaughtering a small but valiant American garrison holed up in the Alamo, an old Spanish mission in San Antonio that had been occupied by the rebels, the army proceeded to take the town of Goliad and to carry out a massacre of more than four hundred Texian prisoners of war. Santa Anna seemed on the verge of a great and bloody victory.

But the tide would soon turn. Less than a month later, at the Battle of the San Jacinto River, a largely untrained but fiercely motivated American force of volunteers, adventurers, and a few regulars under Houston's command would surprise the much larger Mexican Army, defeat it in a matter of minutes, and take Santa Anna prisoner. The Texas Revolution was a success, and in October 1836, Houston would be elected president of the newly independent Republic of Texas.

A month later, a plebiscite was held that indicated an overwhelming majority of Texans wanted their independent nation to become part of the United States by annexation. Accordingly, Houston appealed to the U.S. government to consider such a move. But Andrew Jackson, then in the last months of his second term as U.S. president, hesitated to go that route, for fear that it would mean a war with Mexico and would reignite the slavery controversy, because the admission of Texas as a state, or as several states, would almost certainly come with proslavery strings attached. Jackson quickly extended diplomatic recognition to the new Republic of Texas but otherwise quietly deferred the question of annexation, as did his successor, Martin van Buren. The matter drifted into the 1840s, unresolved.

In many ways, Jackson's and Van Buren's hesitation was entirely prudent. The country did not need the unsettlement of a war with Mexico. But southerners in particular were not happy with the status quo in Texas, because it left

Texas increasingly vulnerable to falling under British influence and then serving Britain as an attractive alternative source of cotton and tariff-free markets – in other words, a competitor and a magnet for runaway slaves. In addition to such practical considerations, there was a more powerful respect in which such hesitation was hard to sustain. It was out of step with an increasingly self-confident national mood, not confined to any one section or region, that envisioned steady westward expansion as the realization of what the journalist John L. O'Sullivan, in advocating for Texas annexation, called "the fulfillment of our manifest destiny to overspread the continent allotted by Providence."

Today, when we hear the term *Manifest Destiny*, our reaction is likely to be guarded. We may take it to be an expression of arrogance, a florid way of saying "step aside, we're taking over." And that reaction is not entirely wrong or unwarranted. But it reflects an incomplete understanding. It is important to recognize that O'Sullivan himself, and the Young America movement of which he was a part, did not envision this "destiny" merely as an imperialistic land-acquisition project. His vision was far more idealistic than that, a vision that had sprung from the spirit of Jacksonian democracy but that recalled American dreams of previous generations, of America as a land of hope. He said of his country that "we are the nation of progress, of individual freedom, of universal enfranchisement ... of the great experiment of liberty ... an Union of many Republics, comprising hundreds of happy millions, calling, owning no man master, but governed by God's natural and moral law of equality, the law of brotherhood."

A country embracing the great North American landmass, stretching "from sea to shining sea," from the Atlantic to the Pacific oceans: this was what they believed the United States was meant to be. Small wonder that even a figure like the poet Walt Whitman embraced the continent-spanning vision of Manifest Destiny with unbounded enthusiasm. The desire to incorporate Texas was a part of it; so, too, was the rising "Oregon fever" that was luring caravans of westward-bound wagons across the continent along the Oregon Trail to explore the lush green possibilities of the Columbia and Willamette valleys. Yes, there were economic and political motives involved; yes, there was arrogance and crusading zeal; but there were also generous democratic ideals being put forward. Like so many things in history, Manifest Destiny was a mixed bag.

In the end, these expansive forces proved too hard to resist, and Congress, in 1845, finally passed a joint resolution approving the annexation of Texas. As Jackson had anticipated, it led very soon to diplomatic trouble with Mexico. But the newly elected President James K. Polk, who took office after the resolution had passed, was determined to move ahead. Even as he was trying to settle the matter through negotiations, and finding that the Mexicans were unwilling even to receive John Slidell, the special minister whom Polk had sent, Polk ordered General Zachary Taylor to take his army to Corpus Christi, on the northern side of the Rio Grande, in disputed territory. After an incident in which the Mexican Army captured an American army patrol, killing or wounding sixteen men, Polk reacted by requesting, and receiving, congressional support for a war resolution on May 13, 1846.

Support for the war was overwhelming but not unanimous. Some northerners from the Whig Party, which had formed in the 1830s around opposition to Jackson's presidency, suspected that the war was meant merely to expand the number of slave states in the Union, and opposed it strongly, with figures such as John Quincy Adams willing to label it "a most unrighteous war." Daniel Webster, more the pragmatic defender of the national Union, feared that internal fragmentation might be the result. Yet the prospect of acquiring more land and the spirit of Manifest Destiny were irresistible, and their force even led some former opponents to change their position, on the basis that the addition of Mexican territory, being too arid for slavery-intensive agriculture, might actually promote the free-labor cause rather than inhibit it.

As for the strictly military aspect of the war itself, it turned out to be highly successful, a contrast in that regard to its predecessor, the near-disastrous War of 1812. It had a distinctly southern bent, with both southern soldiers and southern officers in the majority. General Taylor led his Rio Grande–based army into north-central Mexico, taking the city of Monterrey and then defeating a superior force under Santa Anna at Buena Vista in February 1847. Soon after, General Winfield Scott landed a force farther south at the coastal city of Vera Cruz and then marched west, first to Puebla, then to Mexico City, entering the latter in triumph on September 13. A contingent of marines raised the American flag as they occupied the national palace, the legendary "halls of Montezuma."

With the signing of the Treaty of Guadalupe Hidalgo on February 2, 1848, Mexico abandoned its claims to Texas above the Rio Grande and ceded California and the Utah and New Mexico territories to the United States. The result was yet another transformation of the American map, akin to a second Louisiana Purchase. If the newly annexed land of Texas is included in the total, the United States had just acquired nearly one million square miles of additional territory through the Mexican Cession. With the acquisition of the Oregon Territory two years before by treaty with Great Britain, the United States now had suddenly and dramatically achieved the dream of a transcontinental nation, including the acquisition of a new ocean coastline that featured the world-class harbors of San Francisco and San Diego. It must have seemed almost a culminating sign from on high when, in early 1848, at the same time that General Scott's troops were occupying the Mexican capital and the Treaty of Guadalupe Hidalgo was being negotiated, gold was found at Sutter's Mill in California, some forty miles northeast of Sacramento. The resultant gold rush would bring three hundred thousand people to California in the next seven years, transforming it almost overnight from a remote Mexican frontier into a thriving American state, the home of the first presidential candidate of the new Republican Party, John C. Frémont, in the election of 1856.

Many Americans exulted over the American defeat of Mexico as an event of world-historical importance, an affirmation of republicanism and democracy over the lingering authoritarianism and monarchism of the Old World, and a revitalization of patriotic sentiment. The conflict had supplied the nation with a whole new generation of military heroes to take the place of those of the Revolution. But more than that, it seemed to many that the country had "entered on a new epoch in its history," as a writer in *American Review* put it, an epoch that must "more than ever before, draw the world's history into the stream of ours." The discovery of gold in California seemed to be the crowning expression of divine favor; according to historian Robert W. Johannsen, "it was almost as if God had kept the gold hidden until the land came into the possession of the American republic." The way ahead seemed majestically clear and open.

But all this success and these giddy sentiments did not change the fact that the war had been deeply controversial, and that the amazing growth in the size and extent of the nation to come out of it was very soon going to prove to have been a deeply mixed blessing. As Jackson and other observers had predicted, the problem of slavery would have to reemerge, as decisions had to be made about whether to permit the extension of slavery into some, all, or none of the newly acquired lands. The delicately balanced Missouri Compromise that had been crafted in 1820 had calmed down the issue for the better part of three decades. But the 36° 30′ line extended only to the western boundary of the territory acquired in the Louisiana Purchase. Thus the Mexican Cession fell outside the boundary and raised anew, in more polarized times, the question of slavery's extension.

Even before the war was concluded, there were already efforts afoot to control its effects with regard to the expansion of slavery. In 1846, Pennsylvania congressman David Wilmot, while endorsing the annexation of Texas as a slave state, proposed that Congress forbid the introduction of slavery to any of the territories that might eventually be acquired in the Mexican War. His effort, dubbed the Wilmot Proviso and attached as a rider to an army appropriations bill, drew directly on the language and concepts of the Northwest Ordinance and repeatedly passed the House, only to be rejected by the Senate. However, versions of the same idea were proposed again and again in the ensuing years.

Yet, at the same time, vividly illustrating the widening cultural gulf between North and South, Senator John C. Calhoun of South Carolina responded to the Wilmot Proviso's antislavery intentions with undisguised disdain. Slaveholders had a constitutional right, he insisted, to take their slaves into the territories if they wished. The prohibition being proposed, he argued, would violate the Fifth Amendment to the Constitution, which ensured that no one could be deprived of life or property – and slaves were considered legal property – without due process of law.

Where was a middle ground to be found between two such antithetical positions, each of them claiming to draw on foundational sources? One way to manage the situation was to invoke the principle of "popular sovereignty," which was described by its chief proponent, Senator Lewis Cass of Michigan, as a system allowing the territories to "regulate their own internal concerns in their own way." Instead of having a great and polarizing national fight over the issue, it would allow for solutions to be arrived at piecemeal, region by region, permitting the decision in each instance to be made by those who were closest to the situation and knew it best. It was an idea with much superficial appeal to Americans, invoking as it did the fundamental idea of self-rule, and of allowing the people to decide the laws by which they would be governed. But it ran directly against the natural-rights philosophy embedded in the Declaration of Independence. Time would tell whether it could be effective in managing and mitigating the nation's growing divisions.

In the meantime, however, events were forcing the issue. The California gold rush, which had led to the largest mass migration in American history, had suddenly created a desperate need to organize a government to bring law and order to a disheveled and chaotic region suddenly overrun by ramshackle mining camps and shantytowns, permeated with rampant violence and crime. The situation bordered on crisis, and something had to be done. General Taylor, who had been elected president in 1848 on the strength of his military achievements, suggested that California be admitted immediately as a free state, skipping entirely the territorial stage. He did not believe that the newly acquired territory was suitable for slavery-intensive agriculture and that it was not in the interest of existing slaveholding states to press the issue in the territories. And in fact, by the end of 1849, the Californians themselves had already drawn up a constitution and created a state government that outlawed slavery.

Southerners were shocked and angered by this turn of events, because Taylor was himself a slaveholder and many of them had supported him because they fully expected him to defend the introduction of slavery into the territories, tooth and nail. They felt betrayed. And the stakes were very high, because

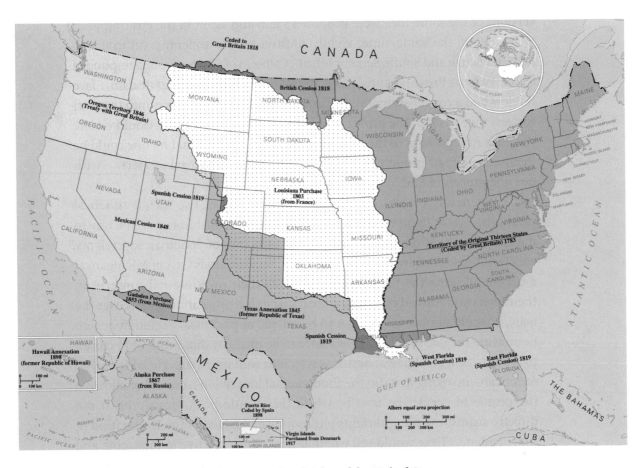

The historical expansion of the United States. National Atlas of the United States from the U.S. Department of the Interior.

the admission of California as a free state would undermine the balance between slave and free states in the Senate and consign the slave South to being a permanent and shrinking minority, a mere corner in the emerging continental American map. Small wonder that Congress found itself in an uproar, and there began to be serious talk of southern secession in the air.

Into this condition of high drama strode Henry Clay of Kentucky, the great deal-maker of the Senate, now in his seventies and in failing health. Clay was in some respects a tragic figure, having been repeatedly frustrated in his own ambitions for the presidency, and yet he was able to rise to the occasion and put aside a lifetime of disappointments for the sake of one last opportunity to preserve the Union. He took charge of the situation and fashioned a complex and multifaceted package of eight different resolutions that would, he hoped, settle "all questions in controversy between the free and slave States."

A great debate ensued, one of the greatest in the Senate's storied history, featuring lengthy and memorable examples of the oratory of Clay, Calhoun, Webster, William Seward, and a host of others. Clay and Webster favored compromise, while the proslavery Calhoun and the antislavery Seward opposed it. Thanks to the untimely death of Taylor, whose stubborn opposition had become an obstacle to the fashioning of an agreement, and the succession to the presidency of his more politically astute vice president Millard Fillmore, and thanks to the skillful political work of Stephen A. Douglas of Illinois, the measures making up what would become known as the Compromise of 1850 were passed individually, rather than as an Omnibus Bill, and by slim majorities in each case.

Chief among these measures were the admission of California as a free state, the leaving of the slavery status of the other territories arising out of the Mexican War to be decided by popular sovereignty, and the passing of a much-strengthened Fugitive Slave Law, which was to be the compensation for the unequal standing that the admission of California imposed upon the South. To put it even more simply, the heart of the deal was that the slave South would be induced to accept the likely permanent minority status it feared, on condition that the North agreed to measures that would protect, in an active and affirmative way, the operation of the "peculiar institution" that had come to be deemed essential to the southern way of life.

It was a sweeping effort, the last to be undertaken by the great generation of Clay, Calhoun, and Webster, to address the growing national crisis and secure the Union. Within two years, all three men would be dead. But the nation breathed a giant sigh of relief, as its politicians had moved back from the brink, and an outburst of patriotic harmony took hold for a time. "Let us cease agitating, stop the debate, and drop the subject," said Douglas, representing the next generation in the Senate. For a time, the overwhelming majority of Americans seemed inclined to agree.

In retrospect, it is difficult to see how anyone could have believed that such a compromise could hold. But we should make the effort to try to see the past as its actors saw it and understand the depth of their dilemma. More than ever, the country still had the wolf by the ear – and the great gains of the Mexican War had only augmented the size and ferocity of that wolf. The Compromise of 1850 did not effect any ultimate solutions, but it did buy time for the Union's future. It reduced political tension, quieted secession talk, and allowed perspective and breathing room for the emergence of other, better solutions. It would allow the country to turn its attention back to its real business, the taming and settling of a giant continent. Often in politics, problems are not solved so much as they are managed – and it is often in the unromantic work of preventing the worst from happening that statesmanship shows itself to best effect.

On the other hand, it is equally true that a festering wound does not heal itself, and the endless deferral of questions of principle may lead to a far worse reckoning when that reckoning must needs come. Moral reformers are sometimes disparaged as purveyors of "crackpot idealism," which is fair enough; sometimes they are unrealistic and blind in their demands. But there is also such a thing as "crackpot realism," a mistaken belief that the endless deferral of ideals is a more "realistic" political strategy than the effort, however difficult, to realize those ideals. It may be an especially fatal strategy for a land of hope. "What happens to a dream deferred?" asked the African American poet Langston Hughes. "Does it dry up / like a raisin in the sun? / Or fester like a sore – / and then run?.... Or does it explode?"

In any event, it soon became clear that the imposition of a strict fugitive slave law was not going to be acceptable to a significant number of northerners. The reason is not hard to find. It was one thing for northerners to accept the existence of slavery "down there," in circumstances that they did not have to confront in their daily life, and of which they did not have to approve but merely tolerate at a safe distance. Such acceptance was the acceptance of an abstraction. But the Fugitive Slave Law required far more of them than that. It required their active and direct support for the peculiar institution. It required them to be actively engaged in shoring up the institution, by cooperating in the tracking down, capture, and extradition of men and women who were merely seeking the conditions under which they could enjoy the life, liberty, and pursuit of happiness to which the Declaration said they were entitled.

Under such circumstances, toleration felt the same as complicity; as a consequence, the law was doomed to generate intense resistance and, ultimately, to be ineffective. The Wisconsin Supreme Court declared it unconstitutional, Vermont passed laws effectively nullifying it and assisting captured slaves, and Emerson denounced it as a "filthy enactment" that should be broken "on the earliest occasion." Abolitionist pastor Luther Lee of Syracuse, New York, declared simply, "The Fugitive Slave Law is a war upon God, upon his law, and upon the rights of humanity.... To obey it, or to aid in its enforcement, is treason against God and humanity, and involves a guilt equal to the guilt of violating every one of the ten commandments." Given such feelings, the appearance in 1852 of Stowe's *Uncle Tom's Cabin* could not have been more aptly timed, as a poignant and humanizing glimpse into the harsh realities of slave life and the perils faced by freedom-seeking slaves.

Meanwhile, another threat to the uneasy settlement of 1850 was brewing, but it would emerge from a somewhat unexpected quarter: the push for a

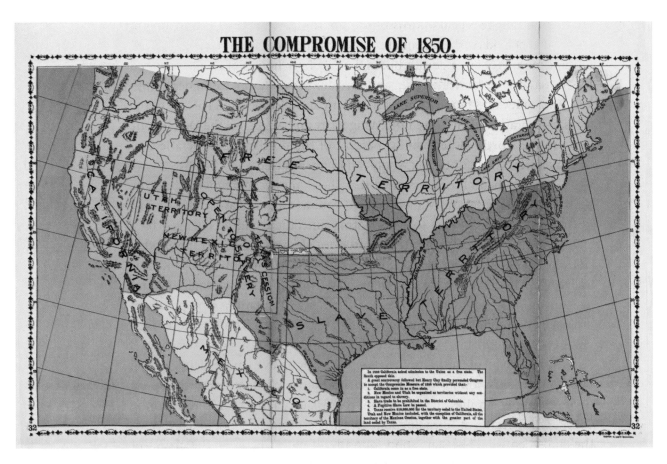

The territorial consequences of the Compromise of 1850, from a 1911 atlas in the Geography and Map Division of the Library of Congress.

transcontinental railroad that would link the two coasts. That such a rail line should be built was beyond question. But the question of where the line would be built, and where its eastern terminus would be located, became an enormous political football and very quickly devolved into two main rival proposals: a southern one, promoted by Jefferson Davis of Mississippi, and a north-central one, promoted by Stephen A. Douglas. To make his proposal more palatable to southerners, Douglas proposed that the land west of Missouri be organized into two territories, the Kansas Territory and the Nebraska Territory, with each being allowed to settle by popular sovereignty the question of whether slavery would be permitted.

This was a far more momentous proposal than it seemed. Because both the proposed territories were north of the 36° 30′ line established by the Missouri Compromise, Douglas's bill was opening up the possibility of introducing slavery into territory where it had previously been forbidden. He was, in effect, proposing to repeal the Missouri Compromise, the principal instrument that had kept a lid on the sectional conflict for three decades. The proposal led to three months of bitter debate, but in the end, both houses of Congress passed the Kansas–Nebraska Act of 1854, and President Franklin Pierce signed it into law. It was a reckless blunder, and it soon bore unwelcome fruit. Passage of the Kansas–Nebraska Act destroyed the Whig Party and weakened the Democratic Party in the North. More than 80 percent of the northern Democratic Congressmen who voted for the act would fail to be reelected.

Douglas had blithely assumed that the homesteaders moving into the Kansas territory from the Midwest would vote to exclude slavery. But he had not reckoned with the fact that the voting outcome could be changed by a change in the population and that proslavery elements had a strong motivation to do so. Slaveholders from adjacent Missouri began moving into Kansas and setting up homesteads partly in an effort to game the eventual vote and flip Kansas into a slave state. Such were the inherent limitations of popular sovereignty, even aside from its moral failings. Soon violent conflicts developed between the competing settlement communities, with a proslavery mob's attack on the town of Lawrence being answered by an even more vicious attack by the abolitionist John Brown and his sons, who hacked to death, in front of their screaming families, five men from a proslavery farm near Pottawatomie Creek. The spectacle of "Bleeding Kansas" was becoming a national disgrace, as the embattled would-be state soon found itself pulled between the claims of two competing governments and two rival constitutions. So much for popular sovereignty as a way to tamp down conflict.

Nor was the violence confined to Kansas in its effects. On May 20, 1856, Senator Charles Sumner of Massachusetts delivered an incendiary speech denouncing the Kansas–Nebraska Act on the floor of the U.S. Senate, decrying it as an instrument of "the Slave Power," designed for "the rape of a virgin Territory," with the aim of producing "a new Slave State, hideous offspring of such a crime." Sumner also went after specific individuals in a very personal way, including Senator Andrew Butler of South Carolina, whom he accused of having embraced "the harlot, slavery" as his "mistress," a loaded insult that seemed almost calculated to generate a fierce rejoinder. The response came two days later, when Butler's cousin, congressman Preston Brooks, confronted Sumner at his desk in the Senate chamber after an adjournment, denounced the speech as "a libel on South Carolina and Mr. Butler," and proceeded to beat him over the head with a gold-headed cane, nearly killing him.

The reaction to this incident was also telling. In the North, there were rallies in support of Sumner in Boston and a half-dozen other cities, and Emerson's comments were representative: "I do not see how a barbarous community and a civilized community can constitute one state. I think we must get rid of slavery, or we must get rid of freedom." But the southern view was different. The *Richmond Enquirer* praised the attack and asserted that Sumner should be caned "every morning." Brooks received hundreds of new canes in endorsement of his assault, and one of them was inscribed "Hit him again." Splinters of the cane became sacred relics.

By the time he delivered his fateful speech, Sumner had become a member of a new political party, the Republican Party, which had arisen in direct response to the Kansas–Nebraska Act. Drawing its membership from antislavery elements in the Democratic, Whig, and Free-Soil parties, the new party had unified around the issue of opposing the extension of slavery into the territories. By 1856, it had become the second largest party in the country; the largest, the Democratic Party, was struggling to avoid a splintering between its northern and southern elements, just as the Whig Party had already done before. The sectional crisis was producing new political alignments, and they were growing dangerously sectional in character; the Republican Party was from the start almost entirely a party of the North.

As the sole remaining national party, then, the Democrats expected to do well in the presidential campaign of 1856, with their highly experienced candidate, James Buchanan of Pennsylvania, who had served in both houses of Congress, as an ambassador to Russia and Great Britain, and as Polk's secretary of state. It would be the Republicans' first outing, and their candidate, the Californian John C. Frémont, was much younger, less well known, and completely without political experience. Nevertheless, in the election, Frémont won eleven states to Buchanan's nineteen, taking all of the northernmost states (though failing to carry California), while Buchanan was strongest in the solidly Democratic South. The Republicans campaigned on a platform that combined classic Whig issues, such as internal improvements (including a transcontinental railroad) and protective tariffs, with firm opposition to the expansion of slavery into the territories. It roundly condemned the Kansas–Nebraska Act and its disregard for the Missouri Compromise and what it called "those twin relics of barbarism – Polygamy and Slavery." It was the first time a national party had declared its opposition to slavery.

Buchanan, however, was a familiar face, elected to maintain the status quo in a turbulent time, and he believed that meant making conciliatory gestures and concessions toward the South: on states' rights, on territorial expansion, on popular sovereignty, and on slavery. The Republicans were a sectional party, the Democrats argued, and therefore a threat to the Union. Buchanan

The territorial consequences of the Kansas–Nebraska Act, from a 1911 atlas in the Geography and Map Division of the Library of Congress.

had been out of the country during the worst of the Kansas debate, so he was not tainted by association with it.

Yet before Buchanan could even get started on the Kansas issue, or anything else in his administration, something momentous came along to widen and deepen the chasm between the sections. A mere two days after his inauguration in March 1857, the Supreme Court handed down its decision in the long-awaited case of *Dred Scott v. Sandford*. And it was a blockbuster decision, one that would ratchet up the tensions between the sections by several orders of magnitude.

The case was a bit complicated. Dred Scott had been born a slave in Virginia. He had been sold to Dr. John Emerson, an army surgeon, who took him to Illinois, a free state, and to the Wisconsin Territory, also free, where Scott married and had two daughters. After his master's death in 1846, Scott sued in the Missouri courts for his freedom on the grounds that his residence in a free state and free territory had made him free. The case wended its way through the courts and finally was appealed to the Supreme Court, which was then presided over by Roger B. Taney, a Jacksonian Democrat from the border state of Maryland.

The court ruled against Scott. Taney, who wrote the majority opinion, was not content to decide the case narrowly; he wanted to resolve the issue of slavery in the territories once and for all. Far from doing so, his Court's decision blew up what little remaining national consensus there was.

There were three main thrusts of Taney's opinion. First, he dismissed Scott's claims, arguing that Scott did not even have legal standing to sue because he was not a citizen – and he was not a citizen because, he asserted, the Framers of the Constitution did not intend to extend citizenship rights to blacks. Second, he argued (distinctly echoing Calhoun) that Congress lacked the power to deprive any person of his property without due process of law, and because slaves were property, slavery could not be excluded from any federal territory or state. Third and finally, the Missouri Compromise was not merely rendered moot by the Kansas–Nebraska Act; it was *unconstitutional*, and had been all along, because it had invalidly excluded slavery from Wisconsin and other northern territories.

The explosive decision, only the second time in the Court's history that it had declared an act of Congress unconstitutional, appeared to doom the doctrine of popular sovereignty, since it would seem that, if the federal government could not exclude slavery from the territories, neither could a territorial government, which after all derived its authority from the federal government. With the Missouri Compromise in tatters, everything it had decided was now up for radical reconsideration, even overturning. Before the Court's decision, freedom had been the national norm, and slavery had been the regional exception. Now it appeared that matters would be completely reversed, as some radical southerners, emboldened by the decision, called for the establishment of a federal slave code to protect their property in human flesh. These radicals could feel the tide of events turning their way. They sensed, with good reason, that President Buchanan was on their side, perhaps even had known in advance of, and encouraged, the *Dred Scott* decision, and had hoped it would settle the slavery question once and for all. Northerners had similar suspicions of Buchanan: that he was a conscious tool of the southern slave-power conspiracy. His presidency was not going to be the instrument that would lead the nation out of its state of division. Leadership would have to come from elsewhere.

All eyes now turned to Stephen Douglas, the "Little Giant" of Illinois, the last remaining prominent Democrat who had national and not merely sectional sources of support, and whose campaign for reelection to the Senate in 1858 was likely to be a warm-up for his long-desired run for the presidency in 1860. If anyone could hold the Democratic Party together, and thereby the country, it was he.

But he would face a formidable challenge for that Illinois Senate seat from Abraham Lincoln, a rising star in the Republican Party who had been a successful trial lawyer and one-term Whig Congressman, and who had left politics for a time but had been goaded back into the fray by his fierce opposition to the Kansas–Nebraska Act. Lincoln had opposed Douglas from the very beginning of the controversy over that act, and he was the natural person to run against Douglas and his ideas.

Lincoln's life story would become the stuff of American legend, the tale of an uncommon common man born to humble frontier circumstances who rose in the world by dint of his sheer determination and effort. Born in Kentucky in 1809, his early life, he once said, could be summarized in one sentence: "the short and simple annals of the poor." Our knowledge of his early life is scrappy. We know that he moved from Kentucky to Indiana to Illinois, a typical pioneer farm boy, burdened with the tasks of hauling water, chopping wood, plowing, and harvesting. We know that he hated farmwork so much that he would seize the opportunity to do almost anything else. We know that he had almost no formal schooling yet was a voracious reader, with a great love of words and of oratory.

When young man Lincoln arrived in New Salem, Illinois, as, by his own description, "a piece of floating driftwood," he was a nobody. But he soon found employment as a clerk, insinuated himself into the life of the community, became popular, was appointed postmaster, ran for and on the second try was elected to the Illinois General Assembly, borrowed money to buy a suit, and then found himself thinking about a career in the law. As Lincoln said in announcing his candidacy for the General Assembly in 1832, he "was born, and [had] ever remained, in the most humble walks of life," without "wealthy or popular relations or friends to recommend" him. But he had been given unprecedented opportunity to realize his potential by the right set of conditions.

This was for Lincoln a kind of fulfillment of the spirit of the Declaration of Independence, which Lincoln revered and repeatedly recurred to, in its affirmation of the equal worth of all men and their equal entitlement to life, liberty, and the pursuit of happiness – and the equal right of all men to the fruits of their own labors, a declaration grounded not in the will of governments or men but in the dictates of Nature and Nature's God. Lincoln loathed slavery from his earliest youth – something he shared with his Baptist parents – but his deepest complaint about slavery seemed to be that it was a form of theft, which allowed one class of men to steal from another class the fruit of the latter's labors. The notion of economic equality was less important to him than the notion of limitless human opportunity – a priority that was much more in keeping with the ethos of the frontier.

So this son of the frontier seemed to have found his moment in the territorial controversy of the 1850s and in the newly founded Republican Party, with his Senate candidacy serving as a moral platform in opposition to Douglas's politically skillful but rather unprincipled opportunism, particularly to the moral relativism implicit in the doctrine of popular sovereignty. In July 1858, he challenged Douglas to a series of seven debates, and Douglas accepted the challenge.

The debates became classics of their kind and are worth poring over today, not only to gain a sense of the political discourse of the time, conducted at a very high level, but to illuminate some of the perennial dilemmas of modern democracies, particularly when they are faced with a choice between popular sentiments and enduring principles. To be sure, these also were political debates, with the rhetorical aggressiveness and crafty trap-setting that fact implies. Lincoln tried to make Douglas look like a radical proslavery, pro–*Dred Scott* southern sympathizer, something he was not. Douglas tried to make Lincoln look like a dangerous abolitionist and advocate for "race amalgamation," something he was not. Neither man, sadly, was able to rise above the sentiments of the crowd with regard to the principle of racial equality. Neither would pass the test of our era's sensibilities. But they also engaged the questions besetting the nation in a rational and surprisingly complex way, one that dignified and elevated the process of democratic deliberation. We would do well to recover their example. Our own era's content-free presidential "debates" are hardly even a pale imitation.

Even though Lincoln went on to lose the election to Douglas, the strength of his arguments endured and made the election a close one. Indeed, his strong showing in the Illinois Senate campaign had brought him to the attention of the whole nation and made him a formidable Republican candidate for president in 1860, a candidacy that was likely to improve dramatically upon what the little-known and inexperienced Frémont had been able to mount in 1856. And there were other suggestive political takeaways from 1858. All across the North, the Republicans made significant gains in the congressional elections, a development that raised the concerns of southerners, not only because of the party's antislavery commitments, but also because of its Whiggish economic program and its support for high tariffs. The Republican Party supplanted the Democratic Party as the party with the largest number of members in the House and, when all the ballots were counted, fell only four seats short of an absolute majority. An ascendant sectional Republican Party and a disintegrating national Democratic Party: these developments suggested trouble ahead for the Union itself.

Another, and perhaps the last, fire bell in the night came with John Brown's daring raid on the federal arsenal at Harpers Ferry, Virginia, on the night of October 16, 1859. Brown's hatred of slavery had only hardened and intensified in the years since his Pottawatomie Massacre, and he was more convinced than ever that it was God's will that he strike a powerful blow against the empire of slavery. His plan was to seize guns from the arsenal and use them to arm the slaves of the region and to fuel a slave uprising, which could lead to the creation in the Appalachian Mountains of a slave-run state within a state. His efforts failed, though not without the loss of fourteen lives, including the lives of two of his sons. Brown would be captured and hanged on December 2, but not before delivering a memorable speech in which he offered his life "for the furtherance of the ends of justice."

As with Preston Brooks, so with John Brown, the response to his actions and his execution were profoundly polarized. Southerners were horrified and took his violent rampage to be representative of the Republican antislavery program and a sure indication of what the North had in store for them. Northerners like Emerson, however, saw Brown as a martyr and saint, who "make[s] the gallows as glorious as the cross." Unfortunately, matters had come to a point where the extremists on both sides reinforced one another's perspective. There was not much room for moderates who saw slavery as neither an unalloyed good nor an irremediable evil but a problem that might eventually be solved by peaceful means.

By the time of the presidential election of 1860, the Democratic Party was finally splitting apart. Douglas was the likely nominee of the party's national convention, but he was unacceptable to southerners and Buchanan supporters, who eventually bolted from the party convention and nominated their own candidate, Vice President John Breckenridge of Kentucky. Douglas would be nominated by the remaining delegates on a platform of popular sovereignty and enforcement of the Fugitive Slave Law, but the Breckenridge Democrats would produce a platform calling for no restrictions on slavery in the territories and the annexation of slavery-rich Cuba. Other dissidents would form a new party, the Constitutional Union Party, which nominated John Bell of Tennessee and sought, through a deliberately vague platform, to encourage the moderation of passions and the enforcement of existing laws.

The Republicans nominated Lincoln, choosing him over the somewhat more radical William H. Seward, as an effort to win over any waverers. The profound divisions among the Democrats made the prospect of a Republican victory very likely – but also very problematic. For one thing, not one of the four candidates was capable of being a truly national candidate and mounting an effective national campaign. The election returns for November 1860 bore this out. Lincoln won 180 electoral votes from all eighteen free states – and from *only* those states. He got not a single electoral vote from the South. Douglas, the only candidate who might have been able to appeal to the nation as a whole, failed miserably, despite a frenetic campaign that took him down into the hostile Deep South states in a desperate quest for support. He received a pathetic twelve electoral votes, finishing a far-distant last in the four-way race.

Lincoln's election was momentous in a great many ways, but first and foremost, he was the first president elected to office on the basis of an entirely regional victory. Some southerners had warned in advance of the election that such an outcome could mean that the South would have no choice but secession from the Union. The "compact" theory of the Constitution, which had long been favored by many southerners, seemed to offer a constitutional basis for doing so. In this view, because the Constitution was a "compact" between preexisting states, those states had a right to withdraw from the compact, just as any contract can be revoked or terminated if sufficient cause for doing so can be adduced. In addition, many southerners strongly believed that any act of secession would be squarely in the tradition of the American Revolution, which had been justified on the grounds that the people have the right to overthrow or replace any government that fails to reflect the consent of the governed.

Soon after the election, South Carolina did just that, repealing its 1788 ratification of the Constitution and dissolving its union with the other states, citing the election of the antislavery Lincoln as justification. By February 1, 1861, six other southern states (Mississippi, Florida, Texas, Georgia, Louisiana, and Alabama) had followed suit and, by February 7, had formed themselves into the Confederate States of America, adopting a Constitution that was virtually identical to the U.S. Constitution, but with added limits on the government's power to impose tariffs or restrict slavery. It elected Jefferson Davis of Mississippi as president and Alexander Stephens of Georgia as vice president.

Even this impressive show of organization and strength would not have been enough to effect secession, however, had there been sufficient pushback from national leaders. For one thing, the immensely important state of Virginia, along with the other Upper South states, had made no commitment to secession, and it was possible that those states could be restrained from joining the others. Yet James Buchanan, in the four months of his lame-duck presidency, took a supremely passive posture toward the Confederacy's actions, believing that resistance would only exacerbate the South's sense of grievance and hoping that somehow the many ongoing efforts at reconciliation might succeed in bringing the country back from the brink of dissolution.

As a last, desperate move, Congress narrowly passed a constitutional amendment, which came to be called the Corwin Amendment, supported by Lincoln, Seward, and other Republicans, that would have explicitly protected slavery where it already existed. The text of the amendment read as follows:

> *No amendment shall be made to the Constitution which will authorize or give to Congress the power to abolish or interfere, within any State, with the domestic institutions thereof, including that of persons held to labor or service by the laws of said State.*

That stalwart antislavery men like Lincoln and Seward were desperate enough to support a measure so contrary to their own moral sentiments – and a measure as permanent as a constitutional amendment – speaks volumes about the sense of immense and immediate peril that had suddenly enveloped the land and the terrible abyss that seemed to be opening up before its leaders.

The amendment passed the House easily and passed the Senate by one vote above the required two-thirds majority on March 2, 1861, two days before Lincoln's inauguration. Had it gone on to be ratified by the states, it would have been the Thirteenth Amendment. But it was destined never to be ratified.

Instead, there would be secession and then four years of appalling war: a war to preserve the Union, but one that also would transform it in the process. Adoption of the Corwin Amendment might have bought some time, at best – just as the Missouri Compromise had. But it would have done so at enormous cost. It would have institutionalized the deepest moral wound in the nation's life, inscribed it explicitly in the Constitution, and rendered the cultural gulf between North and South permanently impassable. It would have made the ultimate reckoning even more horrific. It was not the solution that the nation needed.

In fact, matters had come to the point where it was no solution at all. Lincoln himself had predicted, in his "House Divided" speech of June 16, 1858, that the nation could not endure "permanently half slave and half free" but that it would have to "become all one thing or all the other." Events were in the process of proving him right.

CHAPTER TEN

THE HOUSE DIVIDES

P RESIDENT-ELECT ABRAHAM LINCOLN MOVED QUIETLY AND cautiously during the four months between the election and his taking office. As well he should have, since he would be faced with extraordinarily weighty and complex decisions from the moment he became president.

How active should he be in trying to prevent secession? How concilia-tory should he be toward the Southern states? Could conciliation persuade the states of the Upper South not to follow the Deep South into secession? And if secession occurred anyway, what would he do about it? Would he go to war and oppose secession by use of military force, or would he allow the Southern states to go in peace? If he did the former, how was he to go about fighting a war to force the antagonistic parts of a free nation to stay together? If he did the latter, might the United States be left so weakened and diminished by its dismember-ment, and so vulnerable to further disintegration, that its rising status in the world would soon end, and then be decisively reversed?

As Lincoln assembled his cabinet, a task at which he labored until the very day of his inauguration, he pondered all these things and more, and yet gave very few outward signs of what he was planning to do. Much of the public was nervous about the coming presidency of this lanky, awkward man of the prairies, and he disclosed little in his four-month waiting period to reassure them.

His initial thinking began to emerge more clearly in his eloquent First Inaugural Address on March 4, 1861. Its tone was, in the main, highly concilia-tory. The South, he insisted, had nothing to fear from him regarding his protec-tion of slavery where it already existed. He was willing to accept the Corwin Amendment, which had been passed by both houses of Congress and would institutionalize that protection, and he would enforce the Fugitive Slave Act, so long as free blacks were protected against its misuse. He promised not to use force against the South, unless the South were to take up arms in an insurrection against the government.

But secession was another matter. Lincoln was crystal clear about that: it would not be tolerated. The Union, he asserted firmly, was perpetual and indissoluble. Secession from it was impossible, particularly if undertaken by any individual state, acting "upon its own mere motion," that had not first sought to gain the consent of all other states to withdraw from their shared contract. Even by the logic of the compact theory of the Constitution, he was implying, what South Carolina and the other Deep South states were doing was wrong.

Still, despite the vein of iron he had revealed, Lincoln concluded his speech not with a rebuke or a threat but with a gentle and emotional appeal to unity and to the shared sentiments and experiences that had animated and bound together the United States for its eight and a half decades as a nation. "We are not enemies, but friends," he pleaded. "We must not be enemies." The passions of the moment "must not break our bonds of affection." It was not too much to hope that "the mystic chords of memory, stretching from every battlefield and patriot grave to every living heart and hearthstone all over this broad land, will yet swell the chorus of the Union."

Such splendid presidential oratory had not been heard in Washington since the days of Thomas Jefferson. In other respects, though, there was little practical difference between Lincoln's initial approach and Buchanan's. Lincoln's strategy would soon need to shift, however, once he faced his first crisis: the siege of Fort Sumter, a federal facility located on a small island in the harbor of Charleston, South Carolina, the white-hot center of secessionist sentiment. Secessionists in South Carolina had demanded that the fort be evacuated, something Buchanan had refused to do; but Buchanan's effort to resupply the isolated post had been driven away by Confederate artillery fire.

Such was the stalemated situation when Lincoln became president. When Sumter's commanding officer, Major Robert Anderson, declared that he and his sixty-nine men had only a few weeks' supplies left, Lincoln made the decision to attempt again to resupply him and the fort. Unwilling to permit this, the Confederates opened fire on the fort and, after more than thirty hours of shelling, forced its surrender in advance of the arrival of the resupply effort.

This was a seeming defeat for the Union. But actually the result was an important strategic triumph, for Lincoln had shown political and tactical shrewdness by maneuvering the South Carolinians into firing the first shots. If war was unavoidable, then it should be begun on terms favorable to the Union. He could easily have chosen other, more muscular measures. For example, he could have wasted no time in attacking the South Carolinian forces head-on.

But any such measures would have sacrificed the moral high ground, always important in modern warfare, and especially important in the conduct of a civil war whose success would depend on the direction of public opinion, and whose ultimate objective was not a conquest but a reconciliation of the warring factions. It was of inestimable value for him, and the federal forces, to be able to claim in truthfulness that they were not the ones to initiate the violence and that their response was one not of aggression but instead one of self-defense.

Immediately after the surrender of Fort Sumter, which produced an outburst of indignation in the North, Lincoln called on the Northern states to supply seventy-five thousand militiamen to help in the battle against the Confederacy, an effort to be followed by a blockade of Southern ports. These actions were viewed as an affront by Southerners, and that was enough to bring four Upper South states into the Confederacy, including the all-important Virginia, as well as Tennessee, Arkansas, and North Carolina. However, the border states of Kentucky, Missouri, Delaware, and Maryland did not join, and it would be an important strategic objective of Lincoln's, throughout the war, to keep the border states in the Union and out of the Confederacy.

And so the war began, with neither side expecting anything like the lengthy and destructive struggle that was to come. Even so, vital principles were in conflict, and the conflicts extended back many years. Southerners believed that Lincoln and the North were violating the important principle of state sovereignty by refusing to allow the Southern states to do as a majority of their citizens wanted to do, by means of a vote of delegates in the very same bodies, state conventions, that had ratified the Constitution. Lincoln, conversely, saw secession as a form of sheer anarchy, one that, by refusing to accept the results of a legitimate election, would serve to subvert and discredit the very idea of democracy itself in the eyes of monarchists and aristocrats around the world.

For Lincoln, the restoration and preservation of the Union was the chief goal of the war. All other objectives were subordinated to that one. It is important to stress this. It was not until well into the war that the overthrow of slavery became an important part of the Northern agenda. There could be no doubt that the existence of slavery was a central cause of the war; but there also can be no doubt that, as the war began, opposition to slavery was not the central reason why the North embraced a war against secession.

It might seem completely self-evident that, going into the war, the North enjoyed huge advantages in all the most important ways. It had the larger population (twenty-two million to nine million, with the latter number including four million slaves); held more states (twenty-three to eleven); had a larger economy; controlled the nation's banking and financial systems, most of the nation's industry, and most of its iron and coal; had huge advantages in transportation (more wagons, ships, and horses and 70 percent of the nation's railroads); had a decent-sized navy; and on and on. Totaling up the relative assets of the two sides, the South didn't seem to have had a prayer of success.

But wars are not won merely by comparing lists of material assets, and in this case, such lists would not adequately reflect some very real advantages that the Confederacy brought to the struggle. First and foremost, there was the fact that its war objectives were far simpler and far more easily met. The two sides needed to achieve very different things. To attain their objective of political independence, the Confederate states needed only to hang on to the territory they claimed for themselves, territory they already controlled. In other words, they had only to fight a defensive war on familiar and friendly territory to win, while the North had to conquer and occupy an unfamiliar and hostile area equivalent in size to Western Europe – and then convince the conquered section to reenter the nation. The Confederates were defending their homeland, the most potent of all military motivations, while the North was fighting for an abstraction, "the Union." In addition, many of the nation's most talented military leaders, men such as Robert E. Lee, Joseph E. Johnston, and Thomas J. "Stonewall" Jackson, were Southerners who had left the Union Army to join the Confederate cause. It seemed quite possible that with such leaders, and with the legendary marksmanship and fighting spirit of Southern soldiers, so visible in the Mexican War, the rebel force would be able to put up a compelling resistance.

The South also had other reasons for hope that did not seem unrealistic at the war's outset. It seemed entirely possible, for example, that European demand for Southern cotton might eventually induce one or another country to extend diplomatic recognition and financial support to the Confederacy, just as the support of the French in the American Revolution had led to the colonists' victory against all odds. In addition, it did not seem unreasonable to hope that the people of the North might tire of an extended war, particularly one to reimpose a Union upon people who no longer wanted it, a Union that seemed hopelessly broken and beyond repair. Lincoln faced a very complicated job, and although he came into office with some sources of popular support, he was a minority president whose support was neither deep nor wide. The successful conduct of the kind of war he was facing would be reliant on steadiness and patience in public opinion. Without a stable stream of conspicuous victories in the field of battle, the Northern citizenry might well become restless, lose patience with the war effort, and opt to force Lincoln into suing for peace through a negotiated settlement. That was precisely one of Lincoln's fears, and as we shall see, it turned out to have some considerable foundation in reality.

In addition, the Union was a long way from having a true national army. When Lincoln issued his call to the state militias in the wake of Fort Sumter, what arrived in Washington and other mustering locations was a motley assortment of men whose irregular uniforms reflected the natural diversity of what was still a highly decentralized and loosely organized republic. Some states had dressed their fighting men in blue, but others were in various combinations of gray, emerald, black, or red. The New Yorkers sported baggy red breeches, purple Oriental blouses, and red fezzes in tribute to the French Zouaves. One observer said that the first Union forces assembling in Washington looked less like a serious army than "like a circus on parade." It was not a condition that would last, but it was indicative of the obstacles that both Lincoln and his military leaders would face in welding together a capable fighting unit. It would take time.

The hope that the war could be concluded quickly, however, was widespread. Lincoln had signed up the first volunteers for enlistments of only ninety days. He hoped that a single effective stroke could end the South's ability to resist and allow the Union Army to march straight to the Confederate capital at Richmond, putting an end to the war. That hope would be shattered on July 21 by the first major land encounter of the war, the First Battle of Bull Run just south of Washington. Confederate General Jackson humiliated a force of thirty-seven thousand raw Union troops, sending them racing back to Washington in a panic, along with a contingent of curiosity seekers and observers. There would not be a single decisive stroke by the Union forces.

In the meantime, General-in-Chief Winfield Scott, who had been a hero in the War of 1812 and the Mexican War, but was now seventy-four years old and in poor health, was tasked with developing the overall Union strategy. He devised an approach that became known, irreverently, as the Anaconda Plan, named for the large tropical snake that defeats its prey by constricting and suffocating it. It was an appropriate image, however, despite its mocking intention, since the plan would rely heavily on the denial of trade and resources rather than on attacking and defeating the enemy in the field, to "squeeze" the Confederacy into submission. The Union would use the superiority of the Union Navy to blockade the Southern ports, which would have punishing effects upon the import-dependent Southern economy. In addition, the Union would take possession of New Orleans and the Mississippi River, which would allow it to control vital commerce on the river and to split the Confederacy in two.

It was a good strategy, and if it had been followed consistently, it could conceivably have led to a relatively bloodless and undisruptive outcome to the war. But it had one major defect: it took too long to have any visible effect. This was not a military defect, but it was a political one, as Lincoln recognized when he replaced the retiring Scott with General George C. McClellan, who confidently

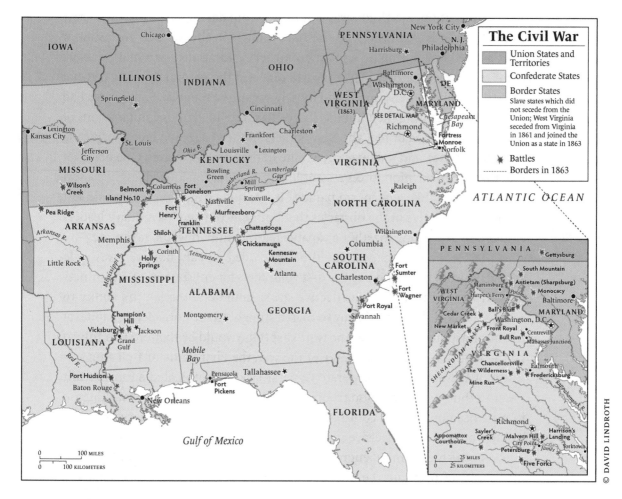

Major campaigns of the Civil War.

promised to push the battle forward as general-in-chief. The political pressure to make quick, visible progress in the field of battle, and eventually to march "Forward to Richmond," was so great that Lincoln could not afford to ignore it.

The haughty and fussy McClellan soon proved to be unsatisfactory to Lincoln, however. A stiffly professional West Point man who believed in thorough preparation, he insisted upon putting his troops through extensive training before going into battle, not moving on Virginia until March 1862. Lincoln's impatient complaints were brushed aside by the arrogant general, who made no secret of his disdain for the president's intelligence. Finally, McClellan devised an ingenious strategy for attacking the Confederate capital. Instead of attempting to advance southward over the difficult terrain of northern Virginia, he moved an army of 112,00 men down the Potomac River and the Chesapeake Bay to the neck of land between the James and York rivers, the peninsula containing Jamestown and Yorktown, with the ultimate intention of coming into Richmond from the southeast, by the back door.

This opening gambit of McClellan's Peninsula Campaign worked well and succeeded in placing his army within twenty-five miles of the Confederate capital. But then, in what became a pattern with him, McClellan hesitated and thereby frittered away the immediate advantage of his success. Through a series of tactically brilliant Confederate moves, many of them led by Robert E. Lee, McClellan's advance was repulsed, and he was eventually forced to retreat. Lee, buoyed by these triumphs and intent upon an even greater success, decided on a bold move of invading the North, specifically the enemy territory of Maryland and Pennsylvania. It would be risky, but Lee was willing to take the risk, considering the benefit that would come to the Confederate cause, especially in the eyes of potential European supporters, from a victory on the enemy's own turf.

It would be even riskier than Lee could have guessed, since he did not know that McClellan had obtained a copy of his secret orders detailing his battle plan for the next engagement with Union troops. McClellan exulted in this advantage, but he again failed to press it and gave Lee time to gather his forces. The two armies met at Antietam Creek in Maryland on September 17, 1862, and what ensued was the bloodiest single day of the entire war, with some twenty-two thousand men killed or wounded. Casualties of this magnitude had never before been seen on the soil of the United States.

The immediate result of the battle at Antietam was inconclusive. For all intents and purposes, it was a tactical standoff, despite the North's prior knowledge of Confederate plans and its possession of a two-to-one advantage in troop numbers going into the battle. True, the progress of Lee's army was stopped cold; his Northern-invasion ideas had been thwarted so far. But McClellan had failed to capitalize on this fact, something he easily could have done. He could have turned a standoff into a smashing victory simply by mobilizing his reserves and continuing to bring the fight to Lee, pushing him back to the Potomac River behind him and trapping him. All he had to do was seize the moment. But he didn't, and thanks to his indecision, the remnants of Lee's army were able to slip away and live to fight another day. Lincoln was furious. He had expected far better results from such favorable circumstances, and as a consequence, he curtly removed McClellan from command, replacing him with the more aggressive General Ambrose Burnside.

In fact, however, for all its disappointing aspects, the bloody standoff at Antietam Creek would turn out to be an important strategic victory for the Union. For one thing, it had denied the South a victory it had needed very badly. But perhaps even more importantly, Antietam had given the North a great opportunity, precisely the opportunity that it had failed to produce for the South: the right moment to make an appeal for the favorable attention of the world.

Even before Antietam, Lincoln had already been contemplating making moves to weaken American slavery. Even though he had not ever been an abolitionist in his politics, he had always regarded slavery as "an unqualified evil" whose eventual extirpation was an ultimate end for which he ardently wished. He was getting pressure from members of his own party and abolitionist groups to act. He knew that such a move on the part of his government would gain the Union cause much favor and support in foreign capitals and decisively counteract any strictly economic appeal of the Southern cause. Several concerns had been holding him back, though. Some were constitutional, some were military, and some were social or political. Some were questions of high principle, whereas others were questions of practical politics.

In the former category was the fact that the institution of slavery was protected under the Constitution, a fact that he himself had repeatedly stressed and even campaigned on. While it could be argued that the coming of the war changed the general context for his past remarks, it did not change the Constitution itself. Lincoln had an unusually high regard for the law in general and a respect bordering on religious veneration for the Constitution in particular. The strength of the Union depended on the nation's unflagging devotion to that document. If he were ever going to use his executive authority to restrict or inhibit slavery, it would have to be done in a way that entirely passed constitutional muster. And it would have to be done in a way that could not simply be overturned in the next election.

Lincoln had several other concerns on his mind. As mentioned before, he needed to keep the support of border states, such as his native Kentucky and Missouri, both of which were slave states that had not joined the Confederacy. A sudden move toward abolition would surely spell an end to that support and tip those states to the other side. Furthermore, it was not at all clear that a majority of Northerners would take well to abolition, and the end result of pushing ahead with it anyway might well be a division of the country, leading to a fatal undermining of the war effort. Lincoln needed to be careful not to get too far out in front of public opinion.

Nevertheless, it appears that by July 1862, he was convinced that the time had come for the national government to adopt a strongly antislavery position and that such a position could be justified both on military grounds (the freed slaves could participate in the war effort) and on diplomatic ones (to attract support from Europe). He would have preferred to see slavery abolished by the individual states through their own laws, with compensation for slave owners and federal aid for freedmen who wished to emigrate. But he had not enjoyed any success in persuading the border states to consider that approach and was now prepared to try to use the powers of his own office.

He had discussed the possibility of an Emancipation Proclamation with his cabinet and received a decidedly mixed response from them. Several feared anarchy in the South and a possible foreign intervention. His secretary of state, William Seward, favored the idea but advised him to wait to issue the Proclamation until there had been a significant Union victory, so that it would not appear that the Union was issuing a "last shriek of retreat." And so Lincoln would do. The Battle of Antietam, as an important if qualified victory, gave him the opportunity to make that bold move, in a way that showed strength rather than weakness. On September 22, 1862, just five days after the battle, he made public the first part of the Emancipation Proclamation, a preliminary statement that outlined the intent of the whole Proclamation, announcing that all slaves in Confederate-held "States and parts of States" as of January 1, 1863, would be "then, thenceforward, and forever free." The second part of the Proclamation would then be issued on that latter date. Theoretically, Confederate states and parts of states that ceased their rebellion by that date would have been allowed to keep their slaves.

That last item underscores something important about the Emancipation Proclamation: it was tailored as a war measure. Lincoln handled the matter this way out of his profound respect for the Constitution. He insisted that during peacetime, he had no legitimate power to abolish slavery where it already existed and already enjoyed constitutional protections. But in wartime, different considerations applied. He still could not abolish slavery by fiat. But as commander in chief of the nation's armed forces, he had martial powers under the Constitution to free slaves in rebel states "as a fit and necessary war measure for suppressing said rebellion." This meant that the four slaveholding border states in the Union, as well as the retaken parts of Tennessee and a few other areas, were exempted from the measure.

Many observers then and since have wished for a more resounding document, one comparable to the Declaration of Independence, that would mark the end of slavery dramatically and once and for all. The historian Richard Hofstadter disparaged the Proclamation by comparing it to a "bill of lading" and claiming that it did not free a single slave. But such criticisms miss the point of Lincoln's statesmanship. Yes, it can justifiably be claimed that Lincoln, though often soaring in his rhetoric, tended to be lawyerly in his ways. But that was because Lincoln wanted slavery abolished in the right way.

He was in no doubt that the Constitution's provision for slavery, while it had thus far been complicit in carrying forward the national wound wrought by that institution, was inconsistent with the Constitution's fundamental makeup, precisely because it was inconsistent with the Declaration's insistence upon the natural rights of all human beings. The remedying of that flaw would, he believed, render the Constitution more fully the instrument it was meant to be: a document of liberty, a "picture of silver" framing the "apple of gold," the Declaration. But the law could be corrected only by means of the correct use of the law, not by the overturning of the law – and there were legal means available for doing just that. The Thirteenth Amendment to the Constitution, not a second resonant Declaration, would be the proper way to accomplish it.

And one further observation about the Emancipation Proclamation: it had the effect of enlarging the war's purpose. Lincoln would make this point explicitly in the Gettysburg Address, a few months later in 1863. But it was now clear (if still mainly implicit) that, by putting the process of emancipation into motion, Lincoln had determined that the war was no longer just about the preservation of the Union.

After the upward turn of events at Antietam, the Union's fortunes quickly got worse. And Lincoln's generalship problems only grew. If McClellan had been an excessively cautious leader, General Burnside turned out to be the polar opposite: an incautious, emotional, even reckless one. When he attacked Lee's army at Fredericksburg, he sent in waves of men in traditional charges to be mowed down by Lee's well-entrenched units and suffered horrific casualties – twelve thousand to Lee's five thousand. The following day, a tearful Burnside withdrew his decimated forces and limped away from Fredericksburg, so to be replaced by General Joseph Hooker. As 1862 ended, the Union forces were stymied and demoralized, in a war that had been longer and far bloodier than anyone had expected, and with no end in sight.

Hooker, a pugnacious and vindictive man nicknamed "Fighting Joe," but better known for his overweening ambition, was unlikely to make things better. And he didn't. In May 1863, he encountered Lee's army in Chancellorsville, Virginia, with a force of 130,000, the largest Union Army so far, and yet, despite outnumbering the Confederates at least two to one, was badly beaten by Lee's tactical brilliance and his own inert and plodding leadership. A consolation for the Union, though, was that the Confederates paid heavily too, losing even more of their men (thirteen thousand casualties out of sixty thousand) than they had at Antietam, and losing the extraordinary General Stonewall Jackson, who died from accidental wounds produced by confused "friendly" fire from his own pickets in the darkness, which mistook his returning party for a Union cavalry unit.

It is hard to exaggerate the importance of Jackson's death and the grief elicited by it. He was arguably the most gifted and most beloved of all the Confederate generals, a deeply pious man who was also a brilliant tactician, the general whom Lee considered to be his irreplaceable "right arm." His loss was not only a military setback but a profound blow to the morale of the Confederate Army and its leaders, and to the Southern public.

The immediate Union reaction to Chancellorsville, too, was one of shock and disbelief. But the Confederacy's heavy losses, including the loss of the irreplaceable Jackson, were beginning to tell. In fact, the war's turning point was coming. In the first week of July 1863, the Confederacy suffered two colossal defeats, one in the West and the other in the East, that placed the Union well on the road to victory.

First there was Vicksburg. One part of the Anaconda Plan involved gaining control of the Mississippi River, and by spring 1863, that objective was nearly accomplished. New Orleans was under Union control, as was most of the river, and all that remained was the taking of the heavily fortified city of Vicksburg. General Ulysses S. Grant, who had been remarkably effective in securing the river, and had won an important early victory for the Union at Shiloh in Tennessee, would take Vicksburg easily, by means of a prolonged and punishing seven-week siege, on July 4. The Confederacy was now cut in two; Texas and Arkansas were isolated and, in effect, lost.

Then came Gettysburg. Robert E. Lee had once again decided to take the offensive and invade the North, hoping to strike while Northern morale was still low in the wake of Chancellorsville and the defeats of 1862. If he could win a great victory or capture a Northern city, that might yet induce a foreign country to intervene or move a sufficient number of discouraged Northerners to sue for peace. On July 1, the invading forces encountered Union units near Gettysburg in southern Pennsylvania and then began a three-day battle that would be the most important of the war. The Union Army under General George G. Meade had positioned itself on Cemetery Ridge, just south of the town, and repeated efforts by Lee's army, including a famously futile charge by General George Pickett's fifteen thousand infantry on July 3, failed to break his line or dislodge his army. Oddly, once again, Meade failed to follow up and crush the defeated Confederate force. But there could be no doubt that Lee had suffered a profound and unambiguous defeat.

Four and half months later, at the dedication of the Soldiers' National Cemetery near the Gettysburg battlefield, Lincoln delivered one of his greatest speeches, which read the Constitution through the lens of the Declaration of Independence. A masterpiece of reverent commemoration, the Gettysburg Address was also a crisp and memorable statement of national purpose and national identity, meant to provide a higher meaning for a war that cried out for such meaning, as it had grown into something far greater and far more destructive than had been imagined at its outset. Surely an ordeal so costly must, in some larger providential scheme, be procuring something very large – larger, perhaps, than the American people had hitherto realized.

In a sense, what Lincoln did in an address of fewer than three hundred words was to redefine the war not merely as a war for the preservation of the Union but as a war for the preservation of the democratic idea – "government of the people, by the people, for the people" – which America exemplified in the world. As such, it reached back to the nation's beginnings and echoed the words of Hamilton and other Founders, who saw in American history a larger purpose being carried out on behalf of all humankind. From its origins in 1776, it was to be a nation "dedicated to the proposition that all men are created equal," language that Lincoln took directly from the Declaration of Independence.

The current war, he said, was a time of testing for that idea, a time that had produced immense pain and suffering, and there was no end to it yet in sight. But Lincoln urged his listeners to be awed and inspired by the sacrifice that the dead soldiers had already made and to resolve that this immense sacrifice would not be in vain – resolve that they would go forward to finish the work the dead men had begun and bring the war effort to a victorious end. And in conclusion, it quietly but firmly asserted that this work included the commitment that he had already made in the Emancipation Proclamation, that the nation would, under the providence of God, see "a new birth of freedom" emerge out of these sufferings.

Reports vary widely as to the audience's reaction to the speech that day in Gettysburg. Some accounts suggest that it was overwhelmed by the much longer, more elaborate, and more learned speech by Edward Everett, the former governor of Massachusetts, president of Harvard, U.S. senator, and secretary of state. Others contend that its gemlike concentrated magnificence was fully appreciated on the spot. We can never know for sure. But we do know that it soon became regarded as one of the classic speeches in the English language, one that British prime minister Winston Churchill (no mean orator himself) would years later call "the ultimate expression of the majesty of Shakespeare's language."

With Grant's victory in Vicksburg, and a third brilliant performance at Chattanooga by Grant and generals under his direction, Lincoln felt he had finally found the fighting general for whom he had so long been looking. By 1864, Lincoln had brought him to Virginia and given him command of the Union Army. Grant was tasked with formulating a grand strategy for victory. There was nothing fancy about Grant's approach. It was a plan of brutal attrition, reflecting the outlook and tactics that had brought Grant success at Shiloh and Vicksburg. Wear the enemy down. Destroy his supply lines. Starve his army (and civilians, if necessary). Deploy massive blocks of troops to pound relentlessly at the resistance. Do not retreat. If necessary, abandon your own supply lines and live off the land, pillaging the enemy's crops and goods. Do not hesitate to incur significant casualties on your own side, so long as you are moving forward, and the enemy's capacity to fight is being degraded and, eventually, obliterated.

Such tactics would have been unthinkable just three years earlier, when no one could have imagined how long, wasting, and destructive the war would turn out to be. They were hardly ideal tactics for the conduct of a civil war that aimed at eventual reconciliation. But their ascendancy reflects another transformation that was being wrought by, and in, the war. Just as what began as a war for the Union was turning into a war for freedom, so what began as a more conventional war of armies clashing in the fields of battle was turning into a total war.

Hence the American Civil War became a first glimpse of what modern war would become in the twentieth century: the clash of whole societies, in which the mobilization of each society's total assets – its economy, its culture, its transportation system, its social cohesion and way of life, its morale – became a key element in the battle, as important as strictly military tactics. Accordingly, the goal of war was becoming not merely to defeat the enemy on the battlefield, let alone to win that one decisive battle that would change everything, but instead a relentless process of grinding and pounding, constantly challenging and destroying the enemy's ability and willingness to fight – and, in the process, obliterating the confidence of enemy civilians in the ability of their government to protect them.

Grant was about to become one of the most eminent generals of military history, but he certainly did not look the part. He was a completely unprepossessing-looking man, with a perpetual stubble on his face and a slovenly and unmilitary bearing. He was known for the cigar ashes that seemed a constant presence on the front of his unkempt uniform. There was not a hint of the great man about him; one of his biographers called him "a nobody from nowhere." He finished in the lower half of his class at West Point, and he compiled a respectable record in the Mexican War but then resigned from the army amid rumors of alcoholism. He was at a loss in civilian life and went on to fail at almost everything else he tried, finally ending up taking a position in his father's leather goods company in Galena, Illinois, then being run by his younger brothers.

And then the war came, and Grant was moved to seek recommissioning as an officer in the Union cause. The rest was history, a steady run of military successes that vaulted him into a preeminent role in the eventual Union triumph. But the man behind those achievements has always remained inscrutable. "Most men who saw U.S. Grant during the Civil War felt that there was something mysterious about him," wrote Civil War historian Bruce Catton. "He looked so much like a completely ordinary man, and what he did was so definitely out of the ordinary, that it seemed as if he must have profound depths that were never visible from the surface." Catton recalled that "even [General William Tecumseh] Sherman, who knew him as well as anybody did, once remarked that he did not understand Grant and did not believe Grant understood himself."

Be that as it may, his effectiveness was beyond dispute. In May 1864, he went back on the move, taking the 115,000 men of the Army of the Potomac south into eastern Virginia. There he engaged Lee's army in a series of bloody encounters, including the frightening Battle of the Wilderness on May 5–6, where the armies fought blindly through the woods, amid confusion and wildfires, with heavy casualties on both sides. In fact, the casualties were far heavier on the Union side. But in the aftermath, it was clear this would not be like Chancellorsville. There would be no interruption of Grant's drive southward. Even the battle at Cold Harbor a month later, in which Grant lost seven thousand men to an ill-fated frontal assault on Confederate positions, did not stop him. He did not stop until he arrived at Petersburg, south of Richmond and a vital railhead, where he trapped Lee's army and laid siege to it for the next nine months.

As part of the larger strategy, General Sherman set out from Chattanooga, Tennessee, with a force of nearly one hundred thousand men, bound toward Atlanta and then across Georgia to Savannah and the sea. In some respects, Sherman's March, as it became known, resembled the scorched-earth tactics of many generations of conquerors in ages past, going back at least to the legendary Roman destruction of Carthage. But there was a difference. This campaign of deliberate destruction was a textbook guide to the logic of total war, carried out calmly and methodically by a man who understood that logic better than almost anyone else.

Facing virtually no organized opposition, Sherman's army cut a swath of devastation sixty miles wide across central Georgia, confiscating food and farm animals, freeing slaves, destroying railroads and mills, and burning down the grand homes of planters (while usually sparing the humble houses of ordinary people), acts designed to terrorize the population into submission and destroy its capacity to fight. Sherman was explicit about psychological terror as his goal, and there was an edge of wanton cruelty in his voice: "My aim was, to whip the rebels, to humble their pride, to follow them to their innermost recesses, and make them fear and dread us." He added, in words that echoed a famous biblical saying, "Fear is the beginning of wisdom." There was more than a touch of hubris in such words. Small wonder that the name of Sherman would be loathed even more than that of Lincoln by generations of southerners to come.

In the midst of all the fighting, the American constitutional system required that another presidential election be conducted in November 1864. So the political dimension to all of these events could not be ignored, and certainly not by Lincoln, who could not take his reelection for granted, given that he had become a lightning rod for all of the public's dissatisfaction with a seemingly endless war. In his own Republican Party, while the majority supported him, the loud and articulate and morally insistent Radical wing viewed him as insufficiently abolitionist and feared he would allow the South back into the Union on overly lenient terms.

The Democratic Party, which of course here means only the northern remnant of it, was divided. The War Democrats supported the war effort but wanted only a restoration of the Union as it existed in 1860. Others, such as the Copperhead faction, so named in 1862 by Republicans to liken them to the poisonous snake, opposed the war and wanted an immediate end to the conflict on terms acceptable to the South. They thought of Lincoln as a tyrant, and some bordered on being pro-Confederate in their sympathies. The party nominated General McClellan as its candidate, which was another jab at Lincoln, although it also complicated the election, because McClellan himself did not entirely endorse his own party's platform.

Despite the Democratic divisions, though, there was the real possibility that Lincoln would not be able to prevail in the fall. In fact, in early 1864, before Grant's successful push to Petersburg and Sherman's taking of Atlanta and Savannah, the war effort had bogged down so much, and public morale was so low, as to convince Lincoln that he would indeed lose the election. It would have been an almost unimaginably bitter pill for him to swallow, to see all his labors, all the blood spilled, and all the treasure sunk into the war effort rendered naught and even thrown away.

We tend to forget about such things today. We forget, or are unaware of, the depth and breadth of Lincoln's unpopularity during his entire time in office. Few great leaders have been more comprehensively disdained or loathed or underestimated. A low Southern view of him, of course, was to be expected, but it was widely shared north of the Mason–Dixon line. As the Lincoln biographer David Donald put it, Lincoln's own associates thought him "a simple Susan, a baboon, an aimless punster, a smutty joker"; he was, in the view of the abolitionist

Wendell Phillips, a "huckster in politics" and "a first-rate second-rate man." McClellan openly disdained him as a "well-meaning baboon."

We need to remember that this is generally how history happens. It is not like a Hollywood movie, in which the background music swells and the crowd in the room applauds and leaps to its feet as the orator dispenses timeless words and the camera pans the roomful of smiling faces. In real history, the background music does not swell, the trumpets do not sound, and the carping critics often seem louder than the applause. The leader or the soldier has to wonder whether he is acting in vain, whether the criticisms of others are in fact warranted, whether time will judge him harshly, whether his sacrifice will count for anything. Few great leaders have felt this burden more completely than Lincoln.

But the string of military victories, which also included Admiral David Farragut's dramatic naval victory at the Battle of Mobile Bay in August 1864, turned the tide, and by the time of Lincoln's reelection, there was little doubt about the war's ultimate outcome and that its end would be coming soon. Although Lincoln still was a Republican, he ran as a candidate of the National Union Party, a name concocted to attract Democrats and others in the border states who would not vote Republican. For similar reasons, he chose the War Democrat Andrew Johnson of Tennessee, a border state, as his running mate. They won in a landslide.

The war was not yet done, though. In December 1864, Sherman finally arrived in Savannah, and after gathering his strength, in the new year, he marched north to Columbia, South Carolina, the very capital of secession, burning it and more than a dozen towns along the way. Then he headed to North Carolina, advancing relentlessly against Johnston's increasingly eroding army. Grant kept up the pressure against Lee's lines at Petersburg. The Confederates could smell defeat in the air.

On March 4, Lincoln was inaugurated into his second term and once again rose to the occasion to deliver an inaugural speech for the ages. In a relatively short but hauntingly eloquent text, he reflected on the larger meaning of this enormous conflict and began to lay the groundwork for the postwar settlement. We know from Lincoln's personal papers that he had been increasingly preoccupied with the problem of God's providential will, of discerning how He had steered these events and to what end, and it seems clear that Lincoln had searched the Bible and various theological writings for answers. The results of his meditations are evident in his Second Inaugural, a speech permeated with biblical themes and imagery.

Lincoln reiterated the observation that slavery was "somehow the cause of the war" but resisted the temptation to assign precise or exclusive blame to either side, while reminding his audience that the violent antagonists were brothers, part of the same culture. "Both read the same Bible and pray to the same God, and each invokes His aid against the other.... The prayers of both could not be answered. That of neither has been answered fully. The Almighty has His own purposes." Then Lincoln proceeded to invoke a stunning image: that the war had, perhaps, been an atonement for the nation's sin and that God had given "to both North and South this terrible war as the woe due to those by whom the offense [of slavery] came," and moreover that such an act of atonement would be fully consistent with our understanding of God's justice. Indeed, he went on, drawing on Psalm 19:9 of the King James Bible,

> *If God wills that [the war] continue until all the wealth piled by the bondsman's two hundred and fifty years of unrequited toil shall be sunk, and until every drop of blood drawn with the lash shall be paid by another drawn with the sword, as was said three thousand years ago, so still it must be said "the judgments of the Lord are true and righteous altogether."*

Yet the speech concludes in more hopeful and peaceful terms. "With malice toward none, with charity for all" – such words urged a spirit of reconciliation in the land, a spirit not of vengeance but of "bind[ing] up the nation's wounds" and "car[ing] for him who shall have borne the battle and for his widow and orphan," and the pursuit of a "just and lasting peace among ourselves and with all nations."

It is perhaps still surprising, even today, to see those luminous words "with malice toward none, with charity for all" uttered during the worst and most murderous war in American history. It should take nothing away from the generosity of those words to observe that Lincoln's use of them was also a sign that he knew the war was won, because only a victor can afford to be so generous. But it should also not escape our appreciation that Lincoln had never lost his clarity, even amid the turbulence of the preceding four years, about the chief purpose of the war. It was not to punish all wickedness and establish a realm of perfect justice. It was first and foremost to restore the Union. Lincoln remained clear that the perpetuation of the Union and of the constitutional order that upheld it was an essential prerequisite to the success of the liberty agenda that was on the verge of abolishing slavery. A postwar settlement dominated by malice and score settling, and lacking in the spirit of charity and forgiveness, could not ultimately succeed. The Christian virtues he was espousing in his speech were not only morally right but also practically right and politically wise.

A month later, on April 3, Richmond fell to the Union forces. On April 9, after a last flurry of futile resistance, Lee faced facts and arranged to meet Grant at a brick home in the village of Appomattox Court House to surrender his army. He could not formally surrender for the whole Confederacy, but the surrender of his army would trigger the surrender of all others, and so it represented the end of the Confederate cause.

It was a poignant scene, dignified and restrained and sad, as when a terrible storm that has raged and blown has finally exhausted itself, leaving behind a strange and reverent calm, purged of all passion. The two men had known one another in the Mexican War and had not seen one another in nearly twenty years. Lee arrived first, wearing his elegant dress uniform, soon to be joined by Grant clad in a mud-spattered sack coat, his trousers tucked into his muddy boots. They showed one another a deep and respectful courtesy, and Grant generously allowed Lee's officers to keep their sidearms and the men to keep their horses and take them home for the spring planting. None would be arrested or charged with treason.

Four days later, when Lee's army of twenty-eight thousand men marched in to surrender their arms and colors, General Joshua L. Chamberlain of Maine, a hero of Gettysburg, was present at the ceremony. He later wrote of his observations that day, reflecting upon his soldierly respect for the men before him, each passing by and stacking his arms, men who only days before had been his mortal foes:

> Before us in proud humiliation stood the embodiment of manhood: men whom neither toils and sufferings, nor the fact of death, nor disaster, nor hopelessness could bend from their resolve; standing before us now, thin, worn, and famished, but erect, and with eyes looking level into ours, waking memories that bound us together as no other bond; – was not such manhood to be welcomed back into a Union so tested and assured? . . . On our part not a sound of trumpet more, nor roll of drum; not a cheer, nor word nor whisper of vain-glorying, nor motion of man standing again at the order, but an awed stillness rather, and breath-holding, as if it were the passing of the dead!

Such deep sympathies, in a victory so heavily tinged with sadness and grief and death. This war was, and remains to this day, America's bloodiest conflict, having generated at least a million and a half casualties on the two sides combined: 620,000 deaths, the equivalent of six million men in today's American population. One in four soldiers who went to war never returned home. One in thirteen returned home with one or more missing limbs. For decades to come, in every village and town in the land, one could see men bearing such scars and mutilations, a lingering reminder of the price they and others had paid.

And yet, Chamberlain's words suggested that there might be room in the days and years ahead for the spirit of conciliation that Lincoln had called for in his Second Inaugural Speech, a spirit of binding up wounds, and of caring for the many afflicted and bereaved, and then moving ahead, together. It was a slender hope, yet a hope worth holding, worth nurturing, worth pursuing.

But the tender promise of that moment would not last. Only two days later, on April 14, Good Friday, the world would change again, as President Lincoln would be shot and killed by an embittered pro-Confederate actor in Washington while attending a theatrical performance at Ford's Theater. That one action would greatly complicate the task of national reconciliation and would throw the postwar settlement into chaos. And like the biblical Moses, Lincoln was cruelly denied entry into the promised land of a restored Union, denied the satisfaction of seeing that new birth of freedom he had labored so long and hard to achieve.

We can never know how well Lincoln's postwar leadership might have fared, had he been the one to oversee that process of national reunion. But what we do know for certain is that, in his absence, the factions he had managed to keep at bay for so long would no longer be held back by his reasonableness and constraining moderation. Winning the war was hard. Winning the peace was now going to be even harder.

CHAPTER ELEVEN

THE ORDEAL OF RECONSTRUCTION

THE REUNION OF THE NATION PRESENTED NUMEROUS challenges, and some of them were overwhelming in scope. First and foremost, there was the massive economic devastation that total war had wrought in the southern states, with the destruction of its cities, its railroads, and much of the rest of its physical infrastructure. Cities like Richmond and Columbia and Charleston had been reduced to barren wastelands, with rotting wharves and empty, unkempt streets lined with bombed-out, vacant buildings. Economic activity had ground to a halt. Factories had been destroyed or idled, while once-productive farmlands lay fallow and unattended. Property values had collapsed, Confederate bonds and other paper assets had been rendered worthless, and there was no investment capital flowing into the region to fuel a restart of business enterprise.

Nor were there any means to restart the southern agricultural machine, since the system of slave labor upon which the South had relied for much of its agricultural production was gone, and the wealth of planters and others who had counted their captive labor force as a capital asset was diminished overnight by a staggering $4 billion or more with the freeing of more than four million slaves. Cotton, tobacco, sugar, rice, hemp – the once-thriving businesses built around the production and sale of these commodities all were but shadows of their former status and would require decades to recover, if they recovered at all.

Most poignant of all was the displaced and disoriented state of emancipated slaves who found themselves wandering in a strange and unfriendly new world without familiar signposts, without capital, without land, without literacy or most other tools for participating in a free economy – possessing a freedom in name that fell very far short of being freedom in fact. Their prior condition had been, as Lincoln had said, one of the principal causes of the war. But now it was as if their present plight was forgotten, even by the abolitionists. "He was free from the old plantation," wrote Frederick Douglass of the liberated slave, "but he had nothing but the dusty road under his feet." The Freedmen's Bureau, established in March 1865, just before the war's conclusion, was a well-intentioned but inadequate attempt to use the War Department, in cooperation with private organizations like the American Missionary Association, to address some of these massive problems.

By contrast to the humiliated South, the North had prospered from the war in many respects. With the troublesome planters taken out of the political picture entirely for four years, the business community had been able to dominate Congress and promote the passage of legislation far more favorable to their interests than would have been the case in the past. The platform objectives of the Republican Party, such as protective tariffs (the Morrill Tariff) and free land for western settlers (the Homestead Act), were easily realized. The National Banking Act created a uniform system of banking and currency, and naturalization requirements for immigrants were eased. In addition, the much-controverted subject of the location for the first transcontinental railroad was easily settled in the North's favor; the north-central line would run from Omaha, Nebraska, to Oakland, California, with the golden "last spike" driven with a silver hammer at Promontory Summit, Utah, in May 1869.

The gaping inequality of the two sections, which proved a persistent problem well into the twentieth century, helped give rise to a view, classically expressed in 1927 by the historian Charles A. Beard, that the war had actually been a "second American Revolution," a social upheaval in which "the capitalists, laborers, and farmers of the North and West drove from power in the national government the planting aristocracy of the South." There was surely much truth in this, and it moreover is a view that accurately captures the fact that the America of the post–Civil War era was dramatically changed in many respects. But many of those changes have to do with political, social, and cultural issues that cannot be explained by economics alone.

There were, after all, numerous practical and moral issues to which to attend in thinking through the reunification of the nation. What would a just settlement look like? How should the Southern rebels be punished, for example? Should the leaders be imprisoned, charged with treason, put to death? What about their followers, including the Confederate officers whom Grant had allowed to return home after Appomattox with their sidearms and horses, or the infantry who had fought for them? And what about the demolished southern economy? Given the fact that the southern economy had depended so heavily upon slavery, the economy of the South would have to be restructured; but how? Who would do it? Who would pay for it? How could the freed slaves be equipped for life as free individuals, with the ability to participate in this economy? Would they be given their own land? Would they be treated as full equals in every respect?

To speak in broad generalities, there were two opposite dispositions among victorious northerners about how to proceed with the reunification of the fractured American nation. Some wanted to reincorporate the South with few complications and recriminations, maintaining as much of the former geographical, social, political, and economic structure as possible. Others felt that anything less than the administration of a severe punishment to the South, accompanied by a thorough transformation of the South into a completely different social and political order, would not be enough and would represent a betrayal of the war effort. It was a fairly stark alternative, both as a philosophical issue and as a practical matter. Were the Southerners to be treated as returning states or as conquered provinces?

Here is where Lincoln's absence from the scene may have made a crucial difference, for he had a firm and well-considered position on the subject. Even during some of the most turbulent parts of the war, with the uncertain outcome of the 1864 election facing him, Lincoln had been thinking deeply about the form that an effective reunification should take. He had concluded that, since secession was illegal, the states had never actually left the Union; and since they had never left the Union, it would be appropriate to demand only a very minimal standard of loyalty be met, as a condition for restoration to full membership in the Union. As early as December 1863, he had formulated a plan whereby pardons would be offered to those who agreed to swear an oath of loyalty to the Union and Constitution and who pledged to accept the abolition of slavery; then, under the Lincoln plan, states would be readmitted if 10 percent of the voters in that state had taken that loyalty oath. High officials and ranking military officers would be excluded from the pardon, but otherwise the offer was quite sweeping.

A very generous plan, indeed, and much too lenient in the eyes of many of his fellow Republicans in Congress, who feared that such a plan would do nothing to prevent the new states' governments from falling under the sway of disloyal secessionists and neo-Confederates. They were convinced of the need for a thoroughgoing reformation of southern society, one that would take apart the old southern class system and substitute something radically new in its place. Moreover, they were convinced that they, Congress, and not the president, had principal authority over such decisions in the first place. To these ends, they proposed and passed in 1864 the Wade–Davis Bill, which required not 10 percent but a majority of voters to swear loyalty and which required that only those who had never been loyal to the Confederacy would be able to vote for the new state constitutions.

Lincoln pocket-vetoed the bill, meaning that he refused to sign it and allowed it to expire unapproved. The Radical Republicans who supported the measure were outraged and accused Lincoln of usurping his presidential authority. In fact, the question of which branch of government was authorized to preside over the reincorporation of states was not easily answered from the text of the Constitution. But there was more going on here than a mere question of constitutional ambiguity. There were more fundamental questions about the very terms by which the national reunion would be effected.

Lincoln's final statement on the subject came in his last public address, on April 11, just two days after Lee's surrender at Appomattox. The subject at hand was whether Louisiana should be accepted back as a reconstructed state, based on a new constitution that abolished slavery and otherwise was sufficient to meet his standards, though not enough to please the Radical Republicans. A letter writer had complained to him that Lincoln was unclear about whether the seceding states were in or out of the Union; Lincoln waved the question away as a "pernicious abstraction" and then went on to explain his view in what can only be called a masterpiece of constructive evasion:

> We all agree that the seceded States, so called, are out of their proper relation with the Union; and that the sole object of the government, civil and military, in regard to those States is to again get them into that proper practical relation. I believe it is not only possible, but in fact, easier to do this, without deciding, or even considering, whether these States have ever been out of the Union, than with it. Finding themselves safely at home, it would be utterly immaterial whether they had ever been abroad. Let us all join in doing the acts necessary to restoring the proper practical relations between these States and the Union; and each forever after, innocently indulge his own opinion whether, in doing the acts, he brought the States from without, into the Union, or only gave them proper assistance, they never having been out of it.

And so matters stood three days later, April 14, the fateful day of Lincoln's assassination. That morning, during a meeting with his cabinet, Lincoln spoke, hauntingly: "I hope there will be no persecution, no bloody work, after the war is over.... Enough lives have been sacrificed. We must extinguish our resentment if we expect harmony and union. There has been too much of a desire on the part of some of our very good friends to be masters, to interfere with and dictate to those states, to treat the people not as fellow citizens; there is too little respect for their rights. I do not sympathize in these feelings." That night at around ten o'clock, at Ford's Theatre during a performance of *Our American Cousin*, his assassin, John Wilkes Booth, a pro-Confederacy Maryland-born actor, entered the president's box with a derringer in his hand. After firing a fatal shot into Lincoln's head at close range, he leaped onto the stage and shouted "Sic semper tyrannis," a Latin motto which means "Thus always to tyrants." Lincoln himself would become the first victim of the bloody work whose coming he had so greatly feared.

Never in history has a true-believing fanatic committed a heinous act that proved more injurious to his own cause. The South could not have had a better friend than Lincoln in enduring the arduous postwar years that lay ahead. True, the man from Illinois might or might not have been able to prevail in implementing his plans for a generous, mild peace between North and South. He was already facing stiff opposition to his 10 percent plan from his own party, and that might have intensified. But he also was experiencing a surge of popularity in the wake of the Union's final victory, and it is possible that he could have summoned the political support to overcome such opposition. It is also possible that his plan would have proved unworkable, even with him implementing it. We shall never know.

As it was, however, the national mood toward the South turned darker, harder, more angry, and more vengeful in the wake of Lincoln's brutal murder. It did not help matters that, in Andrew Johnson, who now rose to the presidential office, the country would be saddled with a president possessing little of Lincoln's political skill and even less of his eloquence and generosity.

Johnson had been added to the ticket in 1864 as a unity candidate from the border state of Tennessee, a War Democrat who opposed secession but had none of Lincoln's enthusiasm for a "new birth of freedom." Although he had been a congressman, governor, and senator from Tennessee, his origins were just as humble as Lincoln's. He grew up among the poor whites and yeoman farmers of North Carolina and eastern Tennessee, and he closely identified with them, while deeply resenting the planter oligarchs whom he held responsible for the calamity that had enveloped the South. These things were the driving force in his political career. He rose politically in Tennessee by championing the cause of poor whites in their conflicts with the wealthy planters. Republicans embraced him for that reason and anticipated being able to work well with him, perhaps more easily than with their own Lincoln. Surely he would want to punish the South, especially after the events at Ford's Theatre. Surely he would embrace the cause of social transformation in the South.

But they deceived themselves. They heard him inveigh against secession and wealth and assumed that meant he was one of them. They failed to see that Johnson's antagonism toward southern aristocrats was a reflection not of his generous disposition toward the marginalized but of his resentment of condescending and pretentious elites, who regarded themselves as his social superiors. He fully shared all of his white constituents' deepest prejudices against black people and had little or no objection to the institution of slavery. That was not what the Civil War was about, not for him. And he most emphatically did not share his Republican colleagues' desire to see the entire South humiliated. Only rich aristocratic planters.

Johnson was the wrong man for the job in other ways. The times called for a leader who was sufficiently self-confident and visionary to take the long view and not let the slings and arrows of everyday political debates upset him. But that was not Andrew Johnson. He was a mass of insecurities and hatreds, with a provincial, grudge-holding, narrow, and petty mind, emanating from a wounded and fearful soul. Historian Eric McKitrick described him as a quintessential outsider and "maverick" who was deeply convinced that "all the organized forces of society" were against him. If Lincoln provided a living illustration of the fact that a common man of unpromising background can rise to the heights of American politics, Johnson became a living illustration of the fact that not all common men can manage that rise successfully, no matter how ambitious they may be.

Johnson's problems began almost at the very beginning. In May 1865, he put forward a Reconstruction plan that was only slightly more demanding than Lincoln's, excluding from the general pardon property owners with more than $20,000 in taxable assets – an addition reflecting Johnson's prejudice against the wealthy. (Although there was also a provision for members of excluded groups to apply for pardons directly to Johnson, an avenue used by thirteen thousand individuals that year alone.) But these additions did not slow down the process of reorganizing the states, and by the time Congress reconvened in December, all eleven of the ex-Confederate states had met the criteria to be incorporated as functioning states of the Union. They had organized governments, ratified the Thirteenth Amendment to the Constitution (abolishing slavery), and elected senators and representatives. All that remained was for Congress to accept and seat them.

This was not going to happen. Radical Republicans in Congress recoiled at the prospect. For one thing, none of the southern states had extended voting rights to blacks as part of their new constitutions. And for another thing, there were former Confederate leaders, including generals, colonels, and cabinet members, among the new congressional delegations. Alexander Stephens, who had been vice president of the Confederacy, was elected U.S. senator from Georgia, even though he was still in prison, awaiting trial for treason! Furthermore, many legislatures were adopting "black codes" that regulated and restricted the rights and behavior of former slaves, in order to confine their movements and their ability to earn income off the plantation . Such codes varied from place to place but could include prohibitions on landownership and the widespread use of long-term labor contracts that were hardly distinguishable from slavery.

The Republicans might have been seriously divided among themselves between moderates and radicals, but their divisions did not extend to any willingness to tolerate such retrograde developments, which seemed to bespeak an attitude of southern defiance. Indeed, such defiance, along with still-fresh memories of Lincoln's assassination, tended to unite Republicans behind the Radical position. The Republicans in Congress rejected Johnson's approach to the readmission of states, refused to seat the new crop of senators and congressmen, and instead created a Joint Committee on Reconstruction to study the question.

The committee held public hearings that graphically highlighted evidence of the mistreatment of blacks under the new state regimes. It also examined the contested question of whether the Confederate states had ceased to be states but instead should be treated as conquered provinces, or, as the committee finally concluded, the states were entities that had continued to exist all along but, in seceding, had forfeited their civil and political rights under the Constitution. And most important of all, the committee concluded that Congress, not the president, was the appropriate authority to determine whether and when and how those forfeited rights could be restored. Up to this point, the process of reconstruction had been guided by the president; the committee was mapping out a future in which Congress would take the reins.

In the meantime, in early 1866, Johnson made things much worse for himself with two inflammatory vetoes. First, he vetoed a bill to extend the life of the Freedman's Bureau, arguing that it had been a wartime measure, but that since the war was over, the extension of the bureau into peacetime would be unconstitutional. His veto was sustained. Then he vetoed a Civil Rights Act that was designed precisely to counter the black codes and other forms of grossly unequal treatment being reinstitutionalized in the postwar South and that featured language establishing that "all persons born in the United States" were entitled to "full and equal benefit of all laws" (a tacit repudiation of one of the conclusions in the Supreme Court's *Dred Scott* decision).

Johnson justified his veto by saying that the act went beyond the proper scope of federal powers and would lead to racial disharmony and conflict. But this time, his veto was overridden – the first time in American history that a major piece of legislation had been enacted into law over the veto of a president. Shortly thereafter, a new Freedman's Bureau bill was also passed over Johnson's veto. It marked the beginning of a new era, both for Reconstruction and for presidential–congressional relations – and it marked the beginning of the end for Johnson's effectiveness as president.

To underscore the intentions behind the Civil Rights Act, and remove any doubt about its constitutionality, the Joint Committee recommended the creation of a new constitutional amendment, the Fourteenth, which was passed in June 1866 and declared ratified by the states by July 1868. The amendment was much more far-reaching than the Civil Rights Act, however, and more complex. It represented the first attempt to give greater constitutional definition and breadth to the concept of citizenship.

It did several different things. First of all, it declared that all persons born or naturalized in the United States and legally subject to its jurisdiction were citizens. It obligated the states to respect and uphold the rights of citizens, assured citizens they could not be denied "equal protection of the laws," and assured them that their rights could not be taken away without "due process of law." That portion of the amendment was significant because it extended to the individual states the requirement that they respect the rights of citizens, in just the way that the federal government was required to do within its own sphere. Thus the Fourteenth Amendment began a process, culminating in the 1920s, called *incorporation,* which refers to the extension of the protections of the Bill of Rights to the state constitutions and governments.

These provisions, all coming from the first section of the five-section amendment, had more long-term significance than other parts of the amendment. But those other parts had great, even explosive, significance in the immediate term. In particular, the second section was aimed directly at the southern states' refusal to grant voting rights to its black citizens. By the terms of the amendment, if a state kept any eligible person from voting, it would be penalized by having its representation in Congress and the Electoral College reduced accordingly.

As the fall elections of 1866 drew near, an angry and frustrated President Andrew Johnson decided to go for broke. He decided to make a "swing around the circle" of northeastern and midwestern cities, denouncing his Radical opponents as traitors and making opposition to the Fourteenth Amendment and support for his lenient approach to Reconstruction his central theme, along with support for his preferred candidates, most of them Democrats, in the upcoming congressional elections.

This was risky, even under the best of circumstances, because presidents did not do political campaigning in those days, and there were concerns that his doing so would seem undignified. At first the tour went extremely well, as Johnson stuck to his script and resisted the temptation to be spontaneous. In Cleveland, however, he lost his composure, had a shouting contest with a heckler, and made other injudicious remarks that were printed in the newspapers. In subsequent cities, matters only got worse, and by the end, in many places, spectators drowned out his efforts to speak.

Thus the swing around the circle ended up being a noose around Johnson's neck. Johnson himself later acknowledged that it did him much more harm than good. In the congressional elections that fall, the Republicans swept to landslide victories, leaving both houses of Congress with huge, veto-proof Republican majorities. Johnson would never again have any control over the agenda moving forward. The wresting of control over Reconstruction from the presidency by Congress was now mostly complete, and a new stage of Reconstruction was about to begin. With this change came a major shift in the structure of constitutional governance, since almost everything to come next would be imposed by Congress over the strenuous objections of the president and the Supreme Court. Never before had Congress reigned so fully over both; never before had any one branch of the federal government so completely dominated over the other two.

In early 1867, Congress passed three Reconstruction Acts, over Johnson's now-impotent vetoes, which in effect treated the South as a conquered province, abolishing the state governments for the time being, dividing the territory into five military districts, and placing it under military occupation. The requirements for readmission to the Union were also made much more stringent; the ex-Confederate states now had to ratify the Fourteenth Amendment and incorporate into their state constitutions measures that would ensure that all adult males, irrespective of race, would have the right to vote.

In addition, Congress passed in 1867 something called the Tenure of Office Act, which prohibited the president from removing a federal official from office without the consent of the Senate. The measure was probably unconstitutional, but its purpose was completely understandable in political terms: the Radicals wanted to ensure that Johnson could not fire the Radicals in his cabinet, such as Secretary of War Edwin Stanton, who oversaw the administration of the military governments in the South. The ever-stubborn and volatile Johnson took the bait, however, and went ahead and fired Stanton anyway. The House of Representatives responded to that act by impeaching Johnson on February 24, 1868, and seeking to remove him from office.

The stage was set for one of the great dramas of congressional history. Under Article I, section 3 of the Constitution, impeached presidents undergo trial in the Senate with the chief justice of the Supreme Court presiding and with a two-thirds vote of that body required for conviction. Johnson's trial lasted for three months of high drama and intrigue, playing to a packed gallery of onlookers. In the end, when the vote was taken, the margin was razor thin, owing to the defection of Republicans who feared the precedent established by Johnson's removal. The result came down dramatically to a single, unexpected vote against impeachment from Republican senator Edmund Ross of Kansas.

Johnson survived, but only by the barest margin, and his effectiveness as president was now at an end. He would be passed over for the Democratic nomination for president in 1868, and, as if to add to the repudiation, Edmund Ross would lose his bid for reelection to the Senate two years later. Bitter to the end, Johnson made his last act as president one that would sting his enemies: he issued a pardon to former Confederacy president Jefferson Davis. But that ineffectual gesture changed nothing. The Radical tide continued to sweep in and swamp all before it.

At their own 1868 convention, the Republicans chose General Ulysses S. Grant, a certified war hero who had no political experience. He was viewed as a sure vote-getter, in the way that Whig military heroes like Zachary Taylor had been. But Grant won the presidency by a surprisingly modest margin in the popular vote (3 million to 2.7 million), a fact that gave added impetus to the swift passage of the Fifteenth Amendment, which explicitly protected ex-slaves' right to vote. The 1868 electoral results showed the Republicans how important it would be to protect the votes of newly enfranchised African Americans, if they were to continue to prevail.

With the ratification of the Fifteenth Amendment, the Radicals had succeeded in getting their way in the South. Or had they? All the southern states were under Republican governments and had not only enfranchised blacks but, in some cases, actually elected blacks to public office, hence the rather misleading term "Black Republican" Reconstruction that is sometimes applied to this period. But in fact the actual government of those states was nearly always in the hands of whites, many of whom were northerners who had come to the region out of a wide variety of motives, ranging from simon-pure idealism to naked opportunism, and who were unaffectionately labeled "carpetbaggers" by white southerners who resented their intrusion. White southerners who had chosen to cooperate with Republican governments earned the even more disdainful epithet of "scalawags." The widespread use of such disparaging names gives a good sense of how ruled-over many white southerners felt themselves to be in the new era.

Leaving aside the names, though, how effective were such governments? More generally, how effective was the Reconstruction program being implemented by the Radical Republicans? The record is mixed, as are the opinions of historians. But it is fair to say, first, that there were many accomplishments, in areas such as civil rights, internal improvements, hospital building, and the creation of public school systems. There also were failures, evidenced both in the spread of corrupt practices in the awarding of state contracts and in the paucity of good and efficient political leadership – a problem that, arguably, afflicted the whole nation at the time, particularly the big cities of the North, just as much as it did the South. Under the circumstances, spectacular successes were too much to hope for; even a minor success was a major achievement.

What were conditions like for the freed slaves? They had not received the "forty acres and a mule" that they had hoped for at the war's end, which meant that for the foreseeable future, they would not have their own land and would still have to work for white landowners. And since the landowners needed the ex-slaves' labor, eventually systems of land tenancy, such as sharecropping and the crop-lien system, emerged that made this possible. In both systems, farmers received seed, tools, and necessities from their landlords in exchange for which the farmers would agree in advance to turn over a percentage (usually one-third to one-half) of what they produced. On the plus side for the freedman, share-cropping removed him and family members from the rigors of gang labor so characteristic of antebellum plantations. But because they were required to turn over so much of their crop to the landowner, and the rest of the crop was often committed to debt service, the resulting system often became a form of peonage that resembled slavery in a great many ways. There was no escape from the web of obligations, no way to accumulate capital and work toward independence.

In addition, although much progress was made in establishing the freedmen's community life – marital and family stability, schools, and independent churches for the newly emancipated ex-slaves, along with unprecedented access to the mainstream political system – there was also palpable and rising hostility toward them. By the time Grant had assumed the presidency, instances of anti-black sentiment and activity in the South were increasing, including the founding in 1867 of the Ku Klux Klan and other similar organizations whose members roamed the countryside, hidden behind masks and robes, issuing threats, scattering rumors, and occasionally perpetrating acts of savage violence and terrifying destruction, all measures designed to intimidate and suppress the black population and also any white Republicans who took the "wrong" side of things.

At Grant's insistence, Congress passed three Enforcement Acts in 1870–71, designed to combat these groups and their attacks and protect the suffrage rights of blacks in the South. But the acts suffered from weak and inconsistent enforcement, and the groups they were designed to inhibit did not stay inhibited; in fact, they only seemed to gather strength. Under this growing pressure, blacks began to stay home on election days; little by little, their political influence in their respective southern states waned away, and Democrats resumed control. The difference can be illustrated in a single stark example. In overwhelmingly black Yazoo County, Mississippi, in 1873, Republicans cast 2,449 votes, and Democrats cast 638; only two years later, Democrats received 4,049 votes, and the Republicans received 7. The terror campaign had succeeded. In state after state, white southern counterrevolutionaries, who became known as "redeemers," were taking control, a process that was complete by 1877. It was an astonishingly fast reversal of what had seemed a profound change.

Where was the North in all of this? It seems that the great reformist tide that had begun decades before with the antislavery movement, which had carried the cause of emancipation to its completion and then washed Andrew Johnson out of power, was now rapidly ebbing. Zeal was out; weariness and distraction seemed to be setting in. Weariness, in that after four years of horrifying war and nearly a decade of anxious and conflict-ridden "peace," and before that, decades of agitation and consternation over the slavery question, the problems of the South seemed intractable. Distraction, in that other matters were now occupying their attention: the distractions of settling a new continent and absorbing and exploiting the massive assets of a greatly enlarged American nation. This included such concerns as westward exploration and expansion, railroad construction, industrial development, Indian wars, and above all the eager pursuit of prosperity in the postwar economy, which often could involve corrupt bargains between business and the newly expanded government. Grant's administration proved to be riddled with corruption, as Grant himself showed a surprising weakness for employing and trusting thoroughly dishonest and unscrupulous men. Finally, a business panic in 1873, at the beginning of Grant's second term, produced a deep economic depression in which thousands of businesses went bankrupt, millions of people lost their jobs, and further blame was cast in Grant's direction. The condition of the South was the least of their worries.

Other additional and subtler forces were at work. As memories of the war itself began to fade, older loyalties began to reassert themselves. Yes, Virginia had been the North's enemy of late. But had it not been the case that George Washington and Thomas Jefferson were Virginians and national heroes of the highest order? That Andrew Jackson was a southerner? That Lincoln himself was a southerner by birth? The mystic chords of memory of which Lincoln spoke in his First Inaugural, the chords whose sounding would express the harmony of a reunited country, had not been silenced forever by war. With the growth of nationalism in Europe, a related desire for a greater measure of national reunification welled up, a desire that was hard to deny – even if it meant closing one's eyes to the lamentably incomplete social revolution of the South.

The final blow to Reconstruction came with the presidential election of 1876, which turned out to be one of the most corrupt and most controverted presidential elections in American history. The Republicans nominated Rutherford B. Hayes, governor of Ohio, a former congressman and a wounded Civil War veteran. The Democrats nominated Samuel J. Tilden, a wealthy corporate lawyer and reform-minded governor of New York who had actively opposed corrupt government in New York City and Albany.

The campaign itself made it obvious how thoroughly the tide of reform zeal had exhausted itself. Neither candidate supported the Radical agenda; both favored a more lenient approach to the South. Indeed, they disagreed on very few substantive issues, which meant that the campaign was mainly devoted to slurs and irrelevancies, with Democrats mocking the Republicans for their corruption and Republicans "waving the bloody shirt" at Democrats, taunting them with the charge that the Democrats had been the party of secession and the cause of the Civil War.

The electoral results were inconclusive. While Tilden won the popular vote by 250,000 votes, he was one vote short of a majority in the Electoral College, with several southern states still contested. There was a blizzard of claims and counterclaims by the two parties, and in the end, Congress, which was itself divided, set up an electoral commission to decide the outcome. Through various machinations, Hayes was able to carry the committee vote 8 to 7, along party lines. Democrats were outraged at this result and threatened to filibuster the results or to march on Washington to force the inauguration of Tilden.

But that was not to be, as cooler heads prevailed. An agreement, which became known as the Compromise of 1877, was worked out between the Republicans and a group of southern Democrats who were willing to defect, for a price. The deal was relatively simple. The Republicans would promise that Hayes, if designated as president, would withdraw the last federal troops from the South, allow the last two Republican state governments (Louisiana and South Carolina) to collapse, and commit to the construction of a southern transcontinental railroad. In return, the Democrats would drop their opposition to Hayes and agree to accept the three Reconstruction Amendments to the Constitution (the Thirteenth, Fourteenth, and Fifteenth). It was a bargain all parties were willing to accept.

With the Compromise of 1877, the era of Reconstruction came to an end. It is hard not to see it as having been an abject failure. Consider these words of a former slave named Henry Adams, who became a soldier in the U.S. Army and a landowner and community leader in Shreveport, Louisiana, but who reacted with undisguised dismay to the Compromise:

> *In 1877 we lost all hopes.... We found ourselves in such condition that we looked around and we seed [sic] that there was no way on earth, it seemed, that we could better our condition there, and we discussed that thoroughly in our organization along in May.*
>
> *We said that the whole South – every State in the South – had got into the hands of the very men that held us slaves – from one thing to another and we thought that the men that held us slaves was holding the reins of government over our heads in every respect almost, even the constable up to the governor. We felt we had almost as well be slaves under these men.*

Adams's anguished words reflected a bitter reality. There had indeed been a moment, a glimmer of hope for a better, different future. Over the next three decades, though, the protection of black civil rights in the South was crushed by the white "redeemer" governments' rise to power. The progress that had been made was soon forgotten. It gave way to a deep bitterness whose provenance seemed to stretch back to time immemorial, as if things had always been this way and should never have been disturbed.

And in a strange way, the earliest (and generally pro-Southern) chroniclers of Reconstruction, such as the followers of Columbia historian William A. Dunning, who saw Reconstruction as an unmitigated disaster, were of a similar disposition – even if they came to that disposition from an entirely different posture, one that was critical of Radical Reconstruction for attempting too much, rather than achieving too little. In their eyes, too, Reconstruction had been a failure.

Might these bleak testimonies, though, have understated the difficulty of the task, and the worthiness of the positive achievements brought about in those turbulent years – even if only as essential groundwork laid for better and more enduring solutions in a day yet to come? That is surely possible too. It is hard to reckon the balance in such matters, and each generation is likely to reckon the balance differently. The transformation of a culture is extremely long and difficult work, and even the best intentions can lead to unexpected and unwanted consequences. Hence the wisdom in Lincoln's poignant comments at his last cabinet meeting. He would not have approved Johnson's callousness or postwar southern defiance; but he also understood, better than the Radicals of his own party, that the humiliation of the white South was not going to produce the results he had sought, indeed, that it might produce entirely opposite results.

But amid all the arguments and counterarguments, one should not lose sight of the concrete benchmarks of achievement, the Thirteenth, Fourteenth, and Fifteen Amendments to the Constitution, changes in the structure of the nation's fundamental laws that ensured that, the next time around, the language of the law would be on freedom's side, just as Lincoln had wanted it to be.

One thing is certain. The deeply unsatisfying episode of Reconstruction left too much undone and a great many wounds unhealed. That work, and those wounds, would remain compelling tasks for other generations.

CHAPTER TWELVE

A NATION TRANSFORMED

W E HAVE JUST CONSIDERED THE CIVIL WAR'S EFFECTS ON the South, but it now remains to consider its more general effects on the nation as a whole. And those effects were enormous. It is no exaggeration to say that the Civil War marks the boundary between early America and modern America.

Like any great historical event, such as a revolution or technological innovation, the Civil War has been subject to all sorts of interpretations: it has been understood as a battle to preserve the Union, a crusade for freedom, a triumph for democracy, a tragic clash between incommensurable cultures, a failed war for Southern independence, a victory for capitalism, and so on. But in any event, it also needs to be understood as a historical watershed, a point of articulation after which almost everything about the country would be changed in some way. In economics, in political and social life, in culture, in the very texture of its self-consciousness, the nation would be altered in the aftermath of this conflict. The decentralized agrarian republic of the nation's earlier history was being left behind in favor of a new, larger, more unified, more consolidated, and more powerful nation-state. In the process, the country found itself in the grip of large and compelling new forces, exhilarating and full of promise, but also bewildering and even threatening.

Such great historical changes can be hard to depict compellingly. We lapse too quickly into using lifeless abstractions, expressed in large words like *industrialization, urbanization, nationalization, centralization, professionalization,* and so on. It is right and necessary to use them. But it can be hard to wrap our minds around them or to connect them with anything that we can see or feel. Sometimes a significant moment or thing is needed to make their meaning, as human experience, more vivid to us. And there was just such a significant moment at the very conclusion of the Civil War, a ceremonial occasion which we passed by in silence two chapters ago, but to which we shall now return.

That moment was the Grand Review of the Union armies, a solemn but celebratory procession ordered by the War Department for May 18, 1865, some thirty-nine days after Appomattox. The participants in the review were the men of the Army of the Potomac, under General George Meade, and of the combined western armies that had fought through Georgia and the Carolinas under General William Tecumseh Sherman. The resulting parade was an astounding spectacle: two hundred thousand men marching for two days through the streets of Washington, D.C., in a line stretching as far back as twenty-five miles, a steady flow of blue uniforms snaking its way through the city and past the shadow of the Capitol dome "like a tremendous python," as one observer put it. Walt Whitman was also there, enraptured by the panorama. "For two days now," wrote the poet, "the broad space of [Pennsylvania Avenue] along to Treasury hill, and so up to Georgetown, and across the aqueduct bridge, have been alive with a magnificent sight, the returning armies," marching in "wide ranks stretching clear across the Avenue." Spectators jammed the streets, sidewalks, doorsteps, windows, and balconies, craning their heads to watch, many having come from hundreds of miles away.

This excited response was a surprise. Few had expected that such a great rush of visitors would pour into Washington for the occasion and would stand and watch for hours, two days in a row, transfixed by what one journalist called "the greatest military pageant ever witnessed on this American continent." There were other celebrations in the land, but there had never been one even remotely like this one. There had been no such Grand Review at the end of the Revolution, or the War of 1812, or the Mexican War. The armies involved had been much smaller and had quickly dispersed in accord with the long-standing American distrust of standing armies and powerful central authority, melting back into the state-based militias whence they had come.

But the Grand Review was something new, a national pageant affirming the new primacy in American life of the American nation – of national power, national unity, national governance, and national consciousness. Whitman had called the marchers "returning armies," but they were not that, not technically. Their actual homes were from almost everywhere else but Washington: there were small-town Yankees from New England, midwestern farm boys, Irish city dwellers, freed Southern slaves who had joined the army in eagerness to serve. But in another sense, it *was* true. Wherever their homes, they had become transformed into national men, through modern war and through their integration into a modern, nationalized military organization. There was no more palpable sign of this change than that long river of blue uniforms flowing through the streets of Washington, the spectacle to which the eyes of the onlooking throngs were riveted.

What a contrast that sight must have seemed to anyone who remembered the motley garb of those first regiments responding to Lincoln's recruitment calls at the beginning of the war. That disorderly riot of diverse uniforms back in 1861 perfectly reflected an older America, with the diffuse cultures and regional loyalties of a far more loosely organized federal republic. Not so the Grand Review, which stilled the laughter and replaced it with awe, suitable for the installation of a new political order. The army visibly represented the welding together of inconsequential individuals into a grand and powerful unit, with great and lofty objectives.

And yet, one wonders how many souls, amid the cheering crowds lining the Washington streets those two days, were quietly harboring worries about what they were seeing, perhaps glimpsing in that invincible army something just as troubling as it was impressive: the possibility that their country was in the process of leaving behind altogether the simpler America of the Founding and moving into something else.

Think of the long refining process that had formed the characteristic Anglo-American institutions, since colonial times and especially since the Revolution, for which the central debates had been about how to divide power, divide authority, divide sovereignty among several competing entities, as a way of preventing the abuses of concentrated power. Were those questions now becoming moot, as the nation marched inexorably into a new era, in which the concentration of force was to be the decisive thing? Had Patrick Henry and the Anti-Federalists been right in their prediction that the Constitution would bring a centralization of power in a regime "incompatible with the genius of republicanism"? Indeed, the more important question of the era to come would be whether the Constitution was outdated: was the eighteenth-century document that had been sufficient for the needs of a small, decentralized, agrarian republic woefully insufficient to meet the needs of a major emerging industrial power?

For a major industrial power was precisely what the United States was becoming in the latter years of the nineteenth century, and it was doing so at breakneck speed. The country's industrial expansion was not exclusively a product of the war; it was already well under way before the war and continued during the war. If anything, the expansion probably would have occurred even more rapidly without the distractions and distortions caused by the sectional crisis and war. But the plain fact is that something utterly remarkable would happen in the mere thirty-five years between the end of the Civil War and the end of the nineteenth century. In 1865, the year of the Grand Review, American industrial power was inferior to that of any of the major European powers, but by 1900, the United States had become the leading industrial power in the world, as measured by the size of its gross national product (GNP; the total value of all goods and services produced by the citizens of the nation for a given year). The United States was manufacturing at such a prodigious rate that it had surpassed mature industrial powers like Great Britain, France, and Germany, and it seemed poised to grow even more.

It was a phenomenal leap forward on all fronts at once, reflecting the fact that postwar America was blessed with very nearly ideal conditions for rapid and sustained economic growth, which averaged around 4 percent per year, twice the pace of the British economy. It enjoyed the benefit of lavish natural resources, including abundant raw materials, such as coal, iron ore, timber, copper, and other forms of mineral wealth necessary to modern industry. It had a growing population (the population increased by nearly threefold in those years), which added to the size of the domestic market, and it enjoyed an abundant supply of inexpensive labor that was being steadily augmented by the arrival of hundreds of thousands of immigrants from Europe and Asia.

It had access to copious sources of capital, both domestic and foreign, as America came to be an irresistible place for profitable investment. It had an excellent transportation system, featuring extensive networks of railroad lines, waterways, and canals, as well as world-class harbors in its leading port cities. It benefited from numerous new inventions and technologies that steadily increased productivity, a process of inventiveness that was protected by a highly efficient patent system. And American businesses had the benefit of a friendly legal and political structure, one that respected private property, regulated and taxed business only lightly, and imposed protective tariffs to keep foreign competition at a minimum.

It was the era in which big business came into its own, and the first of the big businesses were the railroads, arguably the single most important drivers of American economic development of the time. Small wonder that railroad executives, not politicians, were among the most important people in the rankings of social status among postwar Americans. The railroads were impressive as an industry in their own right and grew with fearful rapidity in the immediate postwar era. In 1865, there had been 35,000 miles of railroad track; by 1900, that number had become 193,000 miles – more track than in all of Europe, including Russia.

The railroads were the first big business in several senses. They were the first American businesses to become a powerful magnet for well-heeled investors from all over the world, whose assets could be drawn on through financial markets and pooled to address the stupendous capital needs of building a railroad from the bottom up – from manufacturing and laying rails to constructing cars, building stations, and erecting telegraph lines, and a dozen other expensive stages of development and management that all have to be in place before a single train can roll or a single penny of income can be sought. A railroad was not something you could build piecemeal or organically; it was by its nature an all-or-nothing proposition. And it was expensive, costing as much as $36,000 per mile at a time when an average middle-class income was $1,000 a year.

Because of their size and complexity, and the sheer magnitude of their financial needs, the railroads burst the form of the individual- or family-owned business, and similar forms of business partnership, and instead adopted the form of the modern business corporation. The corporate form was a further iteration of the idea behind the joint-stock company, so important to the settlement of America, and it had many advantages. Unlike a business partnership, it was unaffected by the death of one or another partner, and unlike a partnership, it limited the liability of investors to what they had invested – a protection against financial ruin in the event of business failure and thus an encouragement of experimentation and risk taking. The corporate form also made it possible for the railroads to develop a large management bureaucracy to deal in a coordinated way with all the various aspects of running a railroad line smoothly, efficiently, and safely.

But these bureaucracies could only manage enterprises that individual initiative had put into motion. Like nearly all the most impressive and creative economic activity of the period, the development of the railroads was mainly a product of entrepreneurs, many of whom have very familiar names. One of the key figures was Cornelius Vanderbilt, a poor boy from Staten Island who started out running a ferry service in New York Harbor, enjoyed success in the steamship industry, and chose to shift his interests to railroading during the war years. He ended up consolidating and operating the New York Central rail line with forty-five hundred miles of track, connecting New York City with Chicago and other major midwestern cities.

Railroads stimulated the overall economy in a great many ways, directly and indirectly. They stimulated it by their purchase of goods from other industries, for example, the vast numbers of cars, locomotives, and tracks needed to operate, which in turn made them a major customer of the steel industry. In 1881, the railroads alone purchased 94 percent of the rolled steel manufactured in the United States. They were similarly a mainstay for the coal industry, as coal was an important locomotive fuel in the steam-engine era. Second, by creating a large and efficient national transportation network, it was possible for there to be a true national-scale market in almost any conceivable goods. This fact in turn stimulated the development of mass production directed at the mass consumption in those larger markets; it also allowed for a higher degree of economic specialization, since the production of niche goods – highly customized tools, for example – would be rendered more economically feasible when there was a larger population to draw upon in creating or finding the appropriate niche market for those goods. Railroads also stimulated growth in the undeveloped parts of the nation (for example, stimulating exponential growth of the steel industry in Alabama in the 1880s) and attracted settlers to locate in areas near the lines by selling the land to them cheaply.

Creation of an efficient national transportation system to make a national market possible necessarily meant achieving a high degree of standardization in the way the tracks were built and operated, and the railroaders themselves, with Vanderbilt in the lead, were the ones to establish such standards. In 1860, there had been 350 railroad companies in the United States, but there was as yet no national railroad system, in part because there was no universal standard for track gauge (the distance between the inner sides of the rails). That fact made it a major economic nuisance to ship outside one's own region of the country, because, since cars could not roll on tracks of the wrong gauge, a laborious, expensive, and time-consuming process of transferring goods from one train to another would be involved. By the 1890s, that problem would be successfully solved partly by the gradual consolidation of the industry under the leadership of Vanderbilt and a few others.

Even more consequential, and essential to the smooth operation of a transcontinental network, was the standardization of the measure of time. Before this period, time was reckoned by the position of the sun at any given place; noon was the moment when the sun was at its zenith. Obviously the "noon" at one place would not be simultaneous with the "noon" at another place down the road or across the country. But with only local time available, and without a standard grid allowing for the simultaneous reckoning of time across long distances, how would it be possible to schedule train trips over long distances? Particularly when several trains were using the same tracks, going in opposite directions? The solution was the adoption of standard time zones, in which clocks would be synchronized within a designated geographical area and thereby would establish a discrete standard for that whole area. A scheme to do so, based on the British system, was settled upon by the major American railroad executives meeting together in 1883 at the Grand Pacific Hotel in Chicago.

Several technological advances that facilitated the development of the railroads also deserve mention here. George Westinghouse's invention of the air brake, which allowed an engineer to brake all the cars in a train at the same time, made possible longer trains and higher speeds. The Pullman sleeping car made long-distance travel comfortable, even pleasurable, thus stimulating the growth of travel and tourism. The telegraph was an essential component of the railroads, serving as a kind of nervous system for the lines, a source of near-instant and reciprocal communication, indispensable for the command and control of the line's activity. The two were always built together, a sign that the relationship between them was symbiotic; the railroads could not have functioned efficiently without the telegraph, and the telegraph lines could not have been built without the cleared lands that had been prepared for the construction of the railroad lines.

Hundreds of thousands of patents were granted during this dynamic economic period of American history. There were too many important advances in technology in this era to be able to enumerate them all here, but a few deserve mention. An advance that occupies a category by itself involved the manufacture of steel, which is iron with 1–2 percent carbon added, a material that combines the hardness of cast iron with the toughness of wrought iron. Steel is superior to iron for most purposes, particularly railroad tracks, girders for tall buildings and bridges, and machine tools, but was too expensive to manufacture until the 1855 invention in Great Britain of the Bessemer process, which revolutionized steel production. The numbers tell the story; from 77,000 tons of steel produced in 1870, the number had made an astronomical leap to 11.4 million tons in 1900. By then, Pittsburgh had become the iron and steel capital of the United States, mostly due to the abundant coal deposits in the western Pennsylvania area. Its most prominent entrepreneurial figure was Andrew Carnegie, a poor Scottish immigrant who rose from working as a bobbin boy in a textile mill to becoming the titan of the steel industry.

An even more spectacular expansion was made by the petroleum industry, which did not even exist before 1859. At the end of the Civil War, about two to three million barrels of oil per year were being produced; by 1890, that number had increased to fifty million. At first, the petroleum was used mainly for its kerosene, which was burned in lamps as a cheaper and cleaner substitute for the whale oil or oil from coal that had formerly been used in lamps. By the 1870s, refiners learned how to alter the chemistry of petroleum by heating it, which not only increased the yield of kerosene but generated useful by-products, such as naptha, gasoline, and various lubricants and waxes.

Here the dominant figure was John D. Rockefeller, who got in on the ground floor of the business, seeing early on the potential profitability of refining oil. He incorporated Standard Oil Company of Ohio in 1870 and proceeded to buy out his competitors so that by 1879, he was controlling 90 percent of the nation's refining capacity. He soon became the richest man in America, often using harsh and cutthroat business tactics to get his way – in strange contrast to his Baptist piety. He was an early proponent of the idea of vertical integration, which meant that he attempted to control every aspect of the production of oil products, from their extraction to their refining to their distribution. To consolidate and coordinate the administration of all his scattered assets, he used legal instruments like trusts and the device of a "holding company" in ways that were innovative – but that also raised concerns about his holding what was essentially a monopoly over a central and indispensable feature of the economy.

A third major figure deserving of mention, and an inventor of sorts himself, was J. Pierpont Morgan, a wealthy, well-educated investment banker in New York whose firm played a key role in financing and stabilizing the fast-growing American industrial economy. Because giant corporations needed to raise huge sums of capital to function and expand, investment bankers became key players in the economy, and Morgan was the most prominent of them all. A large and forceful man who smoked dozens of cigars a day, Morgan's imposing personality and his ferocious eyes usually saw to it that he got his way; one contemporary said that after a visit from him, it felt as if "a gale had blown through the house."

Among Morgan's deepest beliefs, one he shared with Rockefeller, was his conviction that competition was wasteful and disorderly. Accordingly, he sought to bring order and stability, wherever he could, to the wild and often chaotic economy. He was, in short, a firm believer in the virtues of consolidation, and his fingerprints were on many of the most prominent efforts to consolidate entire industries, including most notably the steel industry, which led in 1901 to U.S. Steel becoming the world's first billion-dollar company. The process by which he acquired and consolidated companies, and then controlled them by placing his partners on their governing boards, became known as "Morganization," and by 1900, he and his partners had places on the boards of corporations accounting for a quarter of the nation's wealth. So wealthy and powerful did Morgan become that he twice (in 1895 and 1907) was called upon by a president of the United States to rescue the government and the national economy from financial panics.

Developments like that were shocking to many ordinary Americans. What had happened to their democracy? How could it be that their national government was so dependent on the private power of the House of Morgan – that is, ultimately, of one massively wealthy and powerful man – that the president himself would have to come, hat in hand, to beg for relief? But such concerns echoed again and again through the economy, through every business and every city and town, as the consolidation of vast quantities of new wealth in the hands of entrepreneurs with potentially monopolistic power gave rise to concerns about the subversion of republican government itself. Even without such concerns, it had to be conceded that big business itself had become a profoundly revolutionizing innovation, disrupting all the conventional and local ways of doing things, centralizing productive and financial power in the offices of a small group of corporate chieftains, giving the great mass of people unprecedented levels of prosperity and access to a wide array of cheap goods with one hand, while taking away much of their capacity for local self-rule and self-sufficiency with the other. It represented a formidable set of trade-offs, and it was not at all obvious which was the best way to go.

On balance, though, a taste of prosperity was a bargain a great many people were willing to strike. A wonderfully vivid example of what this new set of circumstances made possible would be the rise of the mail-order retail business, pioneered first by Montgomery Ward and then by Sears, Roebuck and Company. These companies used huge, lavishly illustrated mail-order catalogs to reach potential customers directly even in the most remote areas of the country. They then put the nation's transportation resources and postal services to good use in shipping the goods that customers wanted directly to their doors. Thus the often bleak and colorless lives of those living in rural isolation, such as the many pioneering farmers lured westward by the Homestead Act and the railroads, were greatly enlivened, their standard of living was raised significantly, and all the while the country was being knit together in a subtle but profound way. Buying goods from Sears, Roebuck was something that nearly every American could do; doing so made one part of an unprecedented and nationwide "community of consumption."

And yet there was a price paid for these new arrangements. Those mail-order companies were able to sell for less because they bought goods from their wholesalers in far larger quantities than any local general stores could. Their success had the potential to undermine the profitability and viability of local institutions. Local businessmen objected to mail-order arrangements and to the development of "chain stores" such as the A&P grocery stores, which operated two hundred stores around the country by 1900 (and more than sixteen thousand by 1930). It is a situation not unlike that faced today by local businesses that find themselves unable to compete with goods being sold at far lower prices by internet-based companies or giant high-volume retailers like Walmart.

It is virtually a law of economics, and perhaps of life itself, that every benefit comes with an attendant (and sometimes unanticipated) cost. The introduction of the railroad into rural communities meant that farmers were no longer restricted to the immediate vicinity of their farms but now had a larger area within which they could market their goods. But the same change made them vulnerable to a larger range of competitors, many of them invisible and distant and anonymous, and yet making their influence felt across the continent or even across the ocean. With the introduction of standard time, lives that had formerly been measured by, and entwined with, the seasonal local rhythms of agriculture, or by the hours tolled on the local church bells, were now made to conform to a national standard, set and maintained by people far away, for the sake of the railroad's efficiency. And they did not have any choice in the matter.

At the beginning of the nineteenth century, and well into the era of the Civil War, America was a nation of what have been called "island communities," more or less insular and self-contained towns and villages whose sense of connection to the larger world was abstract at best. By the end of the century, that was no longer true in a great many places. With the new world emerging, the sense of autonomy enjoyed by such places, for better or worse, had been penetrated and altered by the forces of political, economic, and cultural nationalization.

These economic changes were reflected in the changing conditions experienced by industrial wage laborers. First of all, there were many more of them: from about 885,000 in 1860 to more than 3.2 million in 1890. They benefited from the general rise in the standard of living produced by industrialization; not all the wealth was going into the pockets of the wealthy few, even if a disproportionate amount of it was. Upward mobility, that is, the movement from the lower to the higher ranks of social and economic standing, was common, and the long-term decline of commodity prices meant greater purchasing power for the wage earner.

But the down side of the move to intensified industrialization was a steep decline in the quality of the work environment, with sixty-hour workweeks and dangerous and exploitative conditions in factories being common. In the year 1913 alone, there were twenty-five thousand workplace fatalities in the United States and thirty times that number of serious employment-related injuries. The use of child labor was common; in 1880, one out of every six children in the nation, some of them as young as eight, was working full-time. Even aside from such considerations, under the best of circumstances, the setting of the modern factory was dehumanized and impersonal, with large numbers of workers working under the tyranny of the clock, engaged in highly repetitive and monotonous tasks that brought them none of the pride of workmanship for which smaller workplaces allowed.

Huge and vastly expensive machinery was the very core of the industrial enterprise, the machinery that propelled the steel mills, the oil refineries, the manufacturing plants. And it was the machinery that called the tune and controlled the pace of work, because in many respects, the machinery was far more important than the workers themselves. The steel mills had to be run twenty-four hours a day; they could not be stopped and restarted. So the work schedules of the actual laborers tending to them, which generally meant two crews working alternating twelve-hour shifts, had to adjust accordingly. The concentration of power made possible by the machine also came at a human cost.

Laborers had few effective ways of resisting these conditions. Even the passive-resistance tools used by slaves were not available to them, because they could easily be fired, cut loose, and replaced. Many changed jobs frequently, and about 20 percent would abandon factory work entirely. The best weapon industrial workers had at their disposal was the formation of unions, which allowed workers to organize, bargain as a group, and withhold their labor altogether in the form of a strike, as a way of countering the otherwise unchallengeable power of factory owners and managers.

But American workers were historically reluctant to join unions, for many reasons. The strong sense of individualism that prevails in American culture militated against it; so too did a lack of working-class identity among American workers, who tended to see their "hireling" status as temporary and hoped to rise eventually into the middle and upper classes, thus fulfilling the aspiration to be self-made men. Racial and ethnic tensions within the workforce also made unification difficult, particularly as the industrial workforce became more and more dominated by immigrants, whose cultural differences from native-born Americans and from one another often overshadowed their economic commonalities. The most successful unions were the craft unions associated with the American Federation of Labor, led by the feisty and tireless Samuel Gompers. But they had the advantage of being skilled workers, such as typographers or (like Gompers) cigar makers, and of being narrowly focused on higher wages, shorter hours, improved working conditions, and the like. For the large numbers of unskilled workers, who felt the need for more dramatic changes, there was no similarly effective organization or voice.

Nevertheless, the period from the early 1870s to the mid-1890s was a turbulent time for American labor, the most intensely violent such period in American history. Beginning with the quasi-terroristic activities of the Molly Maguires, directed against the mine owners of western Pennsylvania, through the violence and looting associated with the Great Railroad Strike of 1877, to the Haymarket riot in 1886, building finally to the Homestead steel strike of 1892 and the Pullman strike of 1894, labor suffered setback after setback, both in achieving its objectives and in winning over the American public to its cause.

Perhaps the only ray of hope for organized labor was the success of the Socialist Party, under the leadership of Eugene V. Debs, the tall, charismatic organizer of the American Railway Union, a rare union that embraced skilled and unskilled workers alike. Debs was a prominent figure in the Pullman strike and was jailed for his efforts, which contributed to his stature in the labor movement. He drew some of the discontented to his party's cause, to the extent that Debs was able, by 1912, to draw nearly a million votes in that year's presidential election. With socialist mayors in thirty-three cities, and a following developing among workers and farmers alike – the party was strong in highly agricultural Oklahoma, which gave almost 17 percent of its vote to Debs – it seemed that his party might have a future.

There is another -ization word that has to be invoked in understanding the disruptive nature of this period in American history. That word is urbanization: the growth of cities. And urbanization was disruptive not only because it took so many country people off the land but also because Americans have, for most of their history, lacked an urban ideal.

To put it another way, Americans have had a hard time reconciling what they think of as characteristically American aspirations with the actual life of modern American cities. The fierce attachment to ideals of individualism, self-reliance, self-sufficiency, and closeness to nature that we saw in the generation of Emerson and Thoreau does not always seem, for many Americans, to comport with the conditions of modern urban life. Perhaps that is because America, as historian Richard Hofstadter quipped, is a nation that "was born in the country and has moved to the city," while never entirely adapting to the city's mentality.

Resistance to urban identity goes back to the very beginnings of American history. At the turn of the eighteenth into the nineteenth century, there were only six places featuring populations of more than eight thousand, a number that is hardly a city by most present-day standards, and the combined population of these six was 183,000 in a nation of five million. Agriculture was not only the predominant mode of economic activity but the one held to be most exemplary, a sentiment most vividly expressed in Jefferson's famous encomium to "those who labor in the earth." Nor was Jefferson shy about extending the implications of this analysis to urban life: "The mobs of great cities add just so much to the support of pure government, as sores do to the strength of the human body." His fellow Virginian George Washington agreed: "the tumultu-ous populace of large cities are ever to be dreaded."

Such sentiments were not restricted to Virginians. Dr. Benjamin Rush, a Philadelphia civic leader, agreed on both counts, asserting that "farmers and tradesmen are the pillars of national happiness and prosperity," while cities, by contrast, are rightly compared to "abscesses on the human body, viz., as reservoirs of all the impurities of a community." And John Adams of Massachusetts, like Jefferson a zealous advocate for the American republican experiment, found much to be hopeful about in the new nation's dispersed cultural geography:

> In the present state of society and manners in America, with a people living chiefly by agriculture, in small numbers, sprinkled over large tracts of land, they are not subject to those panics and transports, those contagions of madness and folly, which are seen in countries where large numbers live in small places, in daily fear of perishing for want.

Urbanism did not come immediately thereafter for America, but when it did, it came in a rush, in tandem with all the other wrenching changes we have been exploring in this chapter. In 1790, 3.3 percent of the population lived in cities, defined as a population of eight thousand or more. By 1890, that number was 33 percent. The nation grew, but cities grew faster; the nation's population increased by 12 times between 1800 and 1890, but the population of cities increased by 87 times. By 1890, there were not merely six cities but 448 cities with greater than eight thousand in population. And there were six metropolises by 1900 with populations totaling more than a half million. Much of this growth took place in the postwar years; Chicago *tripled* its population between 1880 and 1900, while New York grew from two million to three and a half million in the same years.

Cities did not just get bigger, but as they did, they changed their character. Before roughly 1870, the American city was a "walking city," meaning that it consisted of a highly compact urban core of residential, commercial, and industrial buildings, along with churches and courthouses and other public buildings, all piled in together, with dependent rural farming in the surrounding countryside. If the city had a significant harbor, the downtown business district would be located near it, along with factories, banks, and the like: all side by side. Closeness to work was all-important, so that slum streets and fashionable streets were mixed together and different classes and ethnic groups lived in proximity to one another.

After 1870 and the dramatic economic changes we have been describing, all that changed quite noticeably. The modern segregated or segmented city came into being, a larger and more sprawling entity with an inner core of poverty surrounded by rings of rising affluence. Although there was no single cause for this development, it would not have been possible without the mechanically powered streetcar and variants such as cable cars and trams. With a network of streetcar lines in place, it became possible for people of sufficient means to live outside the city and commute in to work on a daily basis, and the very possibility of such a way of living worked a geographical transformation of the city in very short order. It was the first system of urban mass transit, and the result was an increasingly segmented and fragmented city, structured largely along socioeconomic lines, with wealth tending to move toward the city's edges and poverty tending to remain, and grow, in the city's core.

Living conditions in those urban cores deteriorated rapidly and could become dreadful. The poor increasingly lived in crowded tenement buildings, which maximized the number of living units but created unhealthy conditions that were a constant fire hazard and became breeding grounds for disease and crime. Infectious diseases, such as tuberculosis and measles, were rampant, as were gangs and street crime in chaotic and lightly policed neighborhoods. Public sanitation was very poor, with many places relying on cesspools rather than sewer systems to manage waste, resulting in water supplies being subject to pollution. Baltimore in summer, quipped H. L. Mencken, smelled like "a billion polecats," and he wasn't exaggerating. Those who could afford to had withdrawn from such conditions, understandably – and their withdrawal only made matters worse.

A new form of urban politics sprang up in such circumstances to address the needs of disoriented urban dwellers, many of whom were new not only to urban life but to the United States itself. Such individuals often found themselves in desperate need of the services of city government but were unsure how to gain access to them. Such matters were increasingly handled through powerful and well-positioned political "bosses" and their "machines," informal but highly disciplined networks of influence and officeholding, generally tied to the Democratic Party, which worked according to the age-old patterns of bribes and payoffs, patronage and graft, buying and selling votes. At bottom, it was an intricate system of mutual favors; I scratch your back, you scratch mine. It was thoroughly corrupt, and the bosses got rich from it. But at the same time, the political machines took care of urgent needs for their constituents – food for the poor, employment help, problems with City Hall, social clubs, immigration issues – and in return received their reward in money, favors, or other preferments: a far cry from the republican vision of the Founders, indeed, but at least providing a modicum of order, and humane concern for the needs of the poor and disadvantaged, in an otherwise disjointed and disorganized situation.

A great many of the urban dwellers who turned to the bosses for help were recent immigrants to America, and that fact constitutes a huge part of the post-war industrialization and urbanization story. The period of American history beginning in 1870 was a period not only of massive industrial expansion but also of massive immigration, on a scale unlike anything seen before in American history.

Immigration had, of course, always been a theme of American history, and the idea of America as an asylum for the world, a land of hope, had been firmly in place even before the nation's founding. What were the New England Puritans, after all, but a group of hope-filled immigrants seeking their Zion in the American wilderness? What was different about this new immigration was not only its scale but its ethnic and religious character.

Up to the 1870s, the bulk of American immigrants had come from Northern and Western Europe and were overwhelmingly from a British background, with Germanic and Celtic elements in the mix. In the pre–Civil War years, there was an uptick in Irish and German immigration, the former driven to emigrate by crushing poverty resulting from famines and crop failures, the latter consisting of political refugees fleeing the turbulence in the wake of the failed German Revolution of 1848. There was also a significant number of Asian immigrants, lured by news of the California gold rush; some twenty-five thousand Chinese had migrated there by the early 1850s. But after the Civil War, there was a big change, a change full of implications for American social history.

For one thing, the numbers of immigrants increased massively. Between 1880 and 1920, it is estimated that twenty million immigrants came to America, a number that probably understates the actual total. And for another thing, there was an increasing proportion of Latin, Slavic, and Jewish people in the immigrant ranks; by 1890, that proportion had become a majority. Now the bulk of immigration was coming from Eastern and Southern Europe, as well as Asia, with large numbers of Italians, Russians, Poles, Greeks, Slovaks, Czechs, Hungarians, Serbs, Croats, Rumanians, Japanese, and Chinese being among their numbers. Most of them were either Catholic or Eastern Orthodox or Jewish; most were emphatically not Protestants. Their numbers were unprecedented, their religions were different, their languages were different, their customs were different, their political experiences were radically different – indeed, almost everything about them was different, and that difference was changing the face of the country in ways no one could predict.

Why did they come? Some came for the same reasons that immigrants had always come to America: to escape the poverty, famine, and religious or political persecution of their native lands. But many more were pulled to America by its promise than were pushed to it by the conditions in their homelands. Those who had seen relatives become successful in America were inclined to follow in their wake, and in time whole extended families were affected. Real wages were relatively higher in the United States than in Europe, and burgeoning American industries, ever in need of fresh sources of unskilled labor, were only too happy to appeal to members of economically struggling groups in European countries with the promise of steady employment and an ability to rise in the world. Such companies sought out immigrants in their native lands and actively recruited them to come to America and work in the steel mills and on the railroads. Many did just that. Thus did the three great -ations converge – industrialization, urbanization, immigration – in the experience of these people.

There might be a fourth: *modernization*, because, in a sense, most of these people were dual migrants: not only were they migrating from Europe to America but they were migrating from Old World rural life to New World city life, and the adjustment was enormous. The immigration historian Oscar Handlin called these immigrants the "uprooted," a term that captures much about their experience, moving not only from country to country but from era to era, as if they were traveling in time as well as in culture, from feudalism to modernity in one great leap. They had left behind a form of rural life as it had been lived for many centuries, with primitive agricultural techniques that allowed for little more than scratching out a living, and with one's personal horizons severely limited by the conditions of one's birth. It took enormous courage, or desperation, to make the step into something completely unknown, and to shed so much that was familiar, for the sake of an opportunity that one could not yet see or touch, and to persist if they found themselves, as many did, in an unexpected and disorienting world of modernity, of those tenement slums located in the decaying urban cores of the disorderly new American cities.

And yet they did come, and did persist. Many of them passed through the famous reception center at Ellis Island in New York harbor after making long voyages in steerage compartments deep in the ships' hulls. In 1907, more than a million people passed through, an average of five thousand a day. Once released, they were likely to connect with family or friends clustered into ethnic neighborhoods, hence the ubiquity in the older American cities of Little Italy, Chinatown, Greektown, and other ethnic neighborhoods made up of Poles, Czechs, and Russian Jews. These neighborhoods were like beachheads and staging areas, or mediating zones between the world they had come from and the bewildering new world they were encountering. In them, they could preserve the old ways – the language, the foods, the religion, the family life – while shielding newcomers from culture shock and helping them reorient to life in a speeded-up, hyperpowered land of towering buildings, clattering streetcars, blazing electric lights, and crowds of transient strangers.

In that sense, the ideal of America as a melting pot was not realized in the short term; on the contrary, it was more of a salad for recent immigrants and a stew for the more acclimated, meaning that the distinct elements of immigrant groups retained their distinctiveness and did not melt immediately into the alloy of the larger culture. Indeed, a separateness bordering on clannishness that immigrant groups naturally fell into was one of the many reasons they were regarded with suspicion by many of the native-born. Their sheer numbers also made them impossible to ignore. In 1890, four out of five residents of New York City were foreign born. There were more Irish in America than in the city of Dublin. Chicago had the largest Czech population in the world and the second largest Polish population, second only to Warsaw. How on earth could such a diverse population of very different kinds of people be assimilated into a cohesive America, particularly if they seemed determined to hold on to their old ways?

It was a fair question, and many Americans of native birth began asking it. Some began to act on their concerns and seek to restrict immigration, with a mixture of motivations. Some felt their jobs threatened by cheap immigrant labor, a reason why Samuel Gompers and other labor leaders supported immigration restriction. Some thought that the immigrants threatened American culture, in light of their lack of exposure to American ideals of self-reliance; some distrusted Catholics for the same reasons that Protestants had always distrusted them, fearing their fealty to the pope and unquestioning devotion to the authority of their priests would make them bad republicans and unreliable citizens. Some believed in the genetic inferiority of the Slavic and Latin peoples or in their cultural predisposition to criminal behavior and drunkenness. Immigration restriction was not to come until the 1920s, but sentiment in its favor was building.

Some of these attitudes appear to us noxious and ugly, others (such as those of Gompers) understandable, even defensible. But for our purposes, it is important to draw back and look at the matter as broadly and historically as we can and to reserve our moral judgments. As the historian Herbert Butterfield once put it, the historian is of greater service when he is a recording angel rather than a hanging judge. What we can see is this: the massive waves of immigration in these years cannot be understood in isolation from the other massive -ations that were reshaping America, and the world, in the peculiarly troubled years after the Civil War. All these forces were so much greater than the power of any individual or group of individuals to resist them, and they had the effect of rendering what was known into something unknown, what had been familiar into something strange to them – natives and immigrants alike.

They all were part and parcel of a great unsettling, in a nation that was not unaccustomed to such things – indeed, a nation that had its very beginnings in a great unsettlement. And yet there was something especially grand and terrifying about this transformation, which unsettled and uprooted the lives of so many individuals, even as it was improving the lot of so many. We should not forget the countless human dramas that immigration entailed, the immense losses that came with every gain. Even assimilation, when it was successful, had its bitter side, in the experience of grandmothers and grandfathers who watched their progeny grow up, and away from them, into a culture and language they did not understand and could never enter into fully without denying their very identities – especially if those identities had been rooted in a world that no longer existed outside their memories. What more poignant experience of uprooting could there be than that?

But what of the great American West, that other mythic land of dreams? Had it been affected by these forces? With its great open spaces, its magnificent mountains and craggy canyons, its mighty rivers and verdant timberlands, surely it was majestically unconquerable, still resolutely the land of individualism and personal freedom so central to the American identity and way of life?

Maybe, but maybe not. The flow of migrants into the region after the Civil War was just as relentless as it was elsewhere, and the growing importance of the mining and cattle industries combined with the reach of the railroads was bringing the West into the more general range of the nation's consolidating forces. The heyday of the romantic cowboy, riding the open range and steering cattle drives of three thousand head or more northward to cow towns like Sedalia and Abilene, looms large in our imaginations. But it was actually quite brief, only a couple of decades between the end of the Civil War and the late 1880s, as farmers and ranchers began butting up against one another and settled property lines became a necessity. Ironically, the heavy involvement of the federal government in the western states, and federal ownership of roughly half the land of the West, would soon make the West the region least free of federal influence.

Nowhere was that truer than in Indian policy, where the national government's authority was paramount. Among the most tragic victims of the relentless drive toward national consolidation were the Plains Indians, some 250,000 of them, who faced constant encroachment on their lands. They fought back. Hundreds of battles took place on the Great Plains before these indigenous peoples were subdued. But they eventually lost everything. When the surrendering Chief Joseph of the Nez Perce tribe declared, movingly, "I will fight no more forever," he was not merely surrendering in combat; he was surrendering an entire way of life. To make matters even worse, he was turning that way of life over to the duplicities and ham-handed mercies of U.S. Indian policy, which sought to "Americanize" the Indians, notably through measures such as the Dawes Severalty Act of 1887, but succeeded only in uprooting them from all they had known. They, too, found their lives in the grip of forces larger than themselves and were left disoriented, displaced, and dispossessed.

Yet belief in the radical freedom and opportunity of the Western frontier continued to be something hard-wired in the American imagination, going back perhaps as far as the imaginations of its first settlers. That perhaps explains why the 1890 Census caused such a stir when it declared, in bland and bureaucratic language, that the western part of the country had so many pockets of settled area that "there can hardly be said to be a frontier line" anymore. More pungently stated, the Census – itself a quintessential agency of a consolidating national regime, a key tool for the administrative ordering of society – had declared that the age of the frontier was over. This was a shocking assertion. What were the implications of it? Could America endure as America without having a frontier? The Census did not answer; that was not its department.

More suited to the task, though, was a young historian from Wisconsin named Frederick Jackson Turner, whose 1893 essay called "The Significance of the Frontier in American History" went on to become one of the most influential works of American historical writing ever produced. The essay had its debut as a paper at 1893 Chicago's World Columbian Exposition, four hundred years after Columbus's first voyage to the New World. Turner's central contention in his paper and his essay was that the availability of free land on a Western frontier had "explained" American development, and he took care to link his inspiration directly to the heroic image of Columbus as explorer and discoverer, reminding the audience that ever since "the days when the fleet of Columbus sailed into the waters of the New World, America has been another name for opportunity."

Turner himself, as a Wisconsin native, was a man of the West by the standards of his day, and his historical vision reflected that fact. The West, he argued, was the most powerful agent of national consolidation, the region most progressive and democratic in its political and social life and most responsible for the "vitalizing of the general government," the cradle of the finest democratic statesmen, the source of America's "composite nationality," and the section that finally forced the nation to confront slavery – in fine, the only area from which the American national experience could be understood. Most important, he believed, the western frontier had given rise to the salient traits of the "American intellect" – its "coarseness and strength combined with acuteness and inquisitiveness," its "practical, inventive turn of mind," its "dominant individualism" with "that buoyancy and exuberance which comes with freedom," its "freshness, and confidence, and scorn of older society, impatience of its restraints and its ideas, and indifference to its lessons."

In Turner's view, the West played a necessary role in refreshing and purifying the country's outlook and morals, turning the United States away from Europe. While the material development of American society had streamed forth in an east-to-west direction, its moral development, which was linked to the purity of its Americanness, relied on a west-to-east eddying, a constant invigoration from the frontier source.

Indeed, Turner had a marvelously fresh and exciting view of the West's cultural effects. "The frontier," as he famously put it, "is the line of most rapid and effective Americanization. The wilderness masters the colonist. It finds him a European in dress, industries, tools, modes of travel, and thought. It takes him from the railroad car and puts him in the birch canoe." The wilderness was the place where "civilization" confronted the untamed elements of nature and where "the bonds of custom" were "broken," creating the possibility of a new life.

For Turner, the bold exploratory energy of Columbus's quest virtually defined the meaning of America. Hence his thesis is often read as the quintessential example of optimistic, forward-looking, triumphant American exceptionalism. But there was more to it than that. Turner's thesis was also a reflection of and comment on his own soul-searching times. Few works of the time better expressed the tension between a traditional vision of America as the land of boundless possibility and an emerging sense of America as a closed and finished nation, for which the cleanup job of consolidation was all that remained. There had been no more potent symbol of boundlessness than the frontier, and the process by which it had yielded to settlement and civilization – the process Turner attempted to describe – seemed to dramatize the nation's reckoning with consolidation and constraint.

Turner argued that, with the closing of the frontier, the factors that had shaped American development were now gone. Turner was understandably reluctant to speculate, before an audience of historians, about what the future might bring. Yet the essay's abrupt ending, with its bold proclamation that "the first period of American history" was over, tantalized its many readers with unanswered questions about the second period now getting under way. Would the American individualism nurtured by the frontier become a thing of the past now that the frontier was gone? Did the future now belong to the organized, the centralized, the consolidated, the nationalized – to the tramp, tramp, tramp of those endless boots marching down Pennsylvania Avenue? Or to save the Republic, would people have to look elsewhere for new frontiers to conquer outside the continent? One could only wonder.

New England theologian and preacher Jonathan Edwards (1703–58). Edwards was the first American thinker to earn a worldwide reputation for the power and originality of his writing. A Calvinist possessing a razor-sharp and far-reaching theological mind, Edwards also insisted upon the importance of the imagination and the affections in the religious life. His sermon "A Divine and Supernatural Light" (1734) expressed that importance in these mystical words: "This light, and this only, has its fruit in a universal holiness of life. No merely notional or speculative understanding of the doctrines of religion will ever bring to this. But this light, as it reaches the bottom of the heart, and changes the nature, so it will effectually dispose to a universal obedience."

Benjamin Franklin (1705–90), painted by the French artist Joseph Duplessis during Franklin's diplomatic service in France. The embodiment of the American Enlightenment and a senior figure in the American Founding, Franklin came into the world without pedigree or advantages, but rose steadily in the world through his resourcefulness and ambition.

A political cartoon attributed to Franklin,
Join, or Die, *was the first widely popular
image of British American colonial
unification. First created in 1754 to support
the French and Indian War, and later to
encourage consideration of the Albany Plan,
it was later deployed to promote colonial
unity in the Revolutionary era.*

*Although not an accurate depiction of the Boston Massacre, this Paul Revere engraving
called* The Bloody Massacre in King-Street *became a powerful tool of anti-British
propaganda.*

General George Washington (1732–99) at Trenton on January 2, 1777, on the eve of the Battle of Princeton, as depicted in a 1792 John Trumbull painting. Even in an age chronically suspicious of heroes, it is hard not to be awed by Washington's many virtues. Intrepid, courageous, charismatic, wise, tireless, and always learning, he commanded the instinctive respect of nearly all who knew him. He was known to be a man of exceptionally fine character who self-consciously modeled himself on the classical republican ideals of the unselfish, virtuous, and public-spirited leader who disdained material rewards and consistently sought the public good over his own private interest.

Thomas Jefferson (1743–1826) in the triumphant year of 1800, by Rembrandt Peale. Jefferson was a complicated man, with many paradoxes hiding behind his confident and direct gaze in this painting. An Enlightened intellectual of cosmopolitan sympathies who felt thoroughly at home in the salons of Paris, he nevertheless favored the rural agrarian way of life and held up the ideal of the yeoman farmer as a model of classical virtue. A man of lofty ideals, he also was a fierce and effective party leader who managed in his presidency to put the Federalist Party on a path to extinction. An eloquent proponent of liberty whose resonant words in the Declaration of Independence have influenced America and all the world in the years since 1776, Jefferson was at the same time deeply ambivalent about the institution of slavery, fully recognizing its evils and its incompatibility with the ideals of liberty, but unable, or unwilling, to free himself from involvement in it. By the time of the Missouri Compromise, though, he had begun to fear for the nation's future, as the conflict over slavery seemed beyond resolution.

ABOVE LEFT: *Pamphleteer extraordinaire Thomas Paine (1737–1809).*

ABOVE RIGHT: *James Madison (1751–1836), principal architect of the Constitution, by Gilbert Stuart. Though tiny in stature, Madison casts a large shadow over subsequent American history as a rare political man who was equal parts theorist and practitioner.*

RIGHT: *Alexander Hamilton (1755?–1804), the economic wizard of the nation's early history, by John Trumbull. Few stories of upward mobility in the nation's early history are more impressive than that of Hamilton. Born out of wedlock in the Caribbean island of Nevis, he was orphaned to a wealthy merchant. The boy's dazzling intellect and boundless energy became evident to all early on in life and would lead him, after being brought to America and educated at King's College (later to become Columbia University), into an early and fervent embrace of the Revolutionary cause and service as George Washington's personal aide. He went on to play a prominent role in the making of the new American nation, was instrumental in the creation and ratification of the Constitution, and was especially important in fleshing out its economic implications – though often in fierce conflict with Jefferson, who did not share Hamilton's vision of the nation's future.*

The brilliant, vain, honorable, quarrelsome, incorruptible, and ultimately lovable John Adams (1735–1826), in his official presidential portrait by John Trumbull.

Abigail Adams (1744–1818), John Adams's wife, confidante, advisor, and frequent correspondent, the other half of one of the great marriages in American history.

The L'Enfant Plan for Washington, D.C. Although the temperamental L'Enfant did not stay to see his project completed, the essence of his vision survived and created the underlying structure of the nation's capital city, which has since blossomed into one of the most beautiful cities in the world. Unlike the many American cities laid out as simple functional grids, L'Enfant's Washington would superimpose a graceful latticework of wide diagonal avenues that interconnected through circles and squares, providing for an endless array of dramatic and unexpected vistas as well as numerous park sites for the erection of statuary and monuments to celebrate and memorialize the unfolding national story. Under L'Enfant's plan, the area west of the Capitol was to be a garden-lined public promenade, a "grand avenue" open to all comers. Instead, it would become the National Mall, an expansive midcity park that is home to the Smithsonian Institution and numerous museums and is a premier site for public events and a haven for walkers and joggers.

Andrew Jackson (1767–1845), by Thomas Sully. The contrast between Jefferson and Jackson could almost be deduced from their portraits alone. Where Jefferson is elegant and patrician, even aristocratic, in bearing, Jackson here looks like the man of action who has just stepped off the battlefield, with his tousled hair and his chiseled, war-hardened looks. Jackson's great triumph in the Battle of New Orleans made him a national hero, at the very moment when an expanding American nation was looking for one. He became the nation's first populist leader, an appeal confirmed by his being denied the presidency by the political establishment of his day in the election of 1824, in which he received the largest number of popular and Electoral votes but failed to gain a majority. When Henry Clay's support tipped the result to John Quincy Adams, and Adams responded by making Clay his secretary of state, Jackson's supporters cried "corrupt bargain!" With their support, Jackson came roaring back to victory in 1828, knocking the elites back on their heels and setting the stage for a two-term presidency that remains controversial to this day.

RIGHT: *Abolitionist Frederick Douglass (1818–95). Author of a compelling narrative account of his own experience of slavery, and a spellbinding orator, Douglass was a living rebuke to the very idea of racial inequality.*

BELOW: *Harriet Beecher Stowe (1811–96), author of the epochal novel* Uncle Tom's Cabin *(1852).*

BELOW RIGHT: *Ralph Waldo Emerson (1803–82), transcendentalist sage and prophet of a new American culture. Oliver Wendell Holmes Sr., the father of the famous Supreme Court judge, referred to Emerson's lecture "The American Scholar" as the nation's "intellectual Declaration of Independence."*

Abraham Lincoln (1809–65) campaigning for the presidency in New York City, February 27, 1860, photographed by Mathew Brady. He was fifty-one years old at the time, but he appears younger in this photograph, having not yet acquired the beard that posterity associates with him. Although we find him formally dressed here, his rugged face and direct gaze are clear hints of his humble origins as a man of the prairie and frontier. As Lincoln said in announcing his candidacy for the Illinois General Assembly in 1832, he "was born, and [had] ever remained, in the most humble walks of life," without "wealthy or popular relations or friends to recommend" him. But the fact that a man in his lowly condition could win public office and rise in the world was, for him, confirmation of the spirit of the Declaration of Independence, a document that Lincoln revered with a near-religious awe.

A visibly war-weary President Lincoln on February 5, 1865, less than five years after the previous photograph. The war took an enormous toll on him. No one had anticipated the immensity of the conflict's destructive effects. As the casualties mounted, Lincoln had become increasingly preoccupied with the problem of God's providential will, of discerning how He had steered these events and to what end, and what it all meant. His Second Inaugural Address, delivered a month later, on March 4, was the fruit of that search, showing an immersion in biblical language and concepts that one had not seen before in Lincoln's oratory. Perhaps, he mused in that great speech, this war had come about because of the sins of the nation, and the need to atone for these sins. When Lincoln was assassinated by John Wilkes Booth on April 14 – Good Friday in the Christian calendar, the day that Jesus was crucified – it seemed to many Americans an event of enormous portent – as if Lincoln had himself taken on those sins. He was no longer merely a besieged politician; he was now a national martyr.

Harriet Tubman (1822?–1913), abolitionist and legendary "conductor" on the Underground Railroad. The Railroad was an informal network of secret routes and safe houses sheltering and aiding escaped slaves fleeing to the North. As many as one hundred thousand escapes were made possible by the Railroad. Tubman's abolitionist convictions were reinforced not only by her experience as an ex-slave but by her profound religious faith. Like so many African Americans in bondage, she saw their plight mirrored in the biblical story of the Exodus. The slave states were Egypt, and the North, especially Canada, was the Promised Land. Her friends called her "Moses," and she used the spiritual song "Go Down Moses" as a signal to warn fugitives to stay hidden. But when she led them across the border, she called out, "Glory to God in the highest. One more soul is safe!"

Lieutenant General Ulysses S. Grant (1822–85) at the battle of Cold Harbor, 1864. Rarely has an eminent general less looked the part than Grant did. As in this photograph, he generally had stubble on his face and a notably unmilitary bearing. Nor was there anything in his background that hinted at greatness. He finished in the lower half of his class at West Point, resigned from the army amid rumors of alcoholism, and went on to fail at everything he tried in civilian life, finally going to work for his father in Galena, Illinois. But when the war came, he sought recommissioning, and it soon became clear that he had found a powerful new focus for his life, as he rose to become Lincoln's favored general, the exponent of a brutally effective approach to fighting a war, one of the great generals of history.

The Grand Review of the Union Army, *as depicted in* Harper's Weekly (1865). *The participants in the review were the men of the Army of the Potomac, under General George Meade, and of the combined western armies that had fought through Georgia and the Carolinas under General William Tecumseh Sherman. The resulting parade was an astounding spectacle: two hundred thousand men marching for two days through the streets of Washington, D.C., in a line stretching as far back as twenty-five miles.*

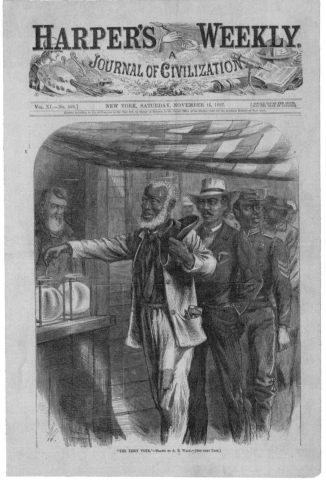

The First Vote, *drawn for* Harper's Weekly, *November 16, 1867, by A. R. Waud. In 1867, 105,832 freedmen registered to vote in Virginia, and 93,145 voted in the election that began on October 22, 1867. Twenty-four African Americans won election to the 1867–68 Virginia Constitutional Convention, which created the Underwood Constitution (named for John C. Underwood, the federal judge who was president of the convention) that granted the vote to African American men.*

These tenements lining Mulberry Street in the Lower East Side of Manhattan typified the lively yet densely settled and often unhealthy immigrant neighborhoods in New York and other major cities at the turn of the century.

A fearless workman nonchalantly bolts beams during the construction of the Empire State Building in a photograph by Lewis Hine, 1930. The Empire State was something of a miracle, being built in a mere 410 days at the depths of the Depression. It immediately became the most iconic image of the New York City skyline, the tallest building in the world and a symbol of American resilience.

Immigrants being served a free meal at Ellis Island, America's first federal immigration station, which opened in January 1892. Immigration officials reviewed approximately five thousand immigrants per day during peak times at Ellis Island, and the majority of those individuals came from eastern, southern, or central Europe. The peak year for immigration at Ellis Island was 1907, with 1,004,756 individuals processed. After the Immigration Act of 1924 was passed, only exceptional cases and refugees passed through the station, and it would eventually close in 1954 – only to reopen as a museum operated by the National Park Service. Small wonder that it would become a tourist attraction. Today, more than one hundred million Americans – about one-third of the population of the United States – can trace their ancestry back to Ellis Island.

Chief Joseph (1840–1904) of the Nez Perce tribe, who was compelled to surrender a way of life after leading his tribe in resisting forcible removal by the U.S. government from their ancestral lands in the Wallowa Valley of northeastern Oregon.

Emigrants Crossing the Plains *by German-born painter Albert Bierstadt, 1869.*

Theodore Roosevelt (1858–1919) as president, circa 1904, in a rare moment of inactivity. At the time he assumed the office of president, TR had already packed several lifetimes into a mere forty-two years on the planet. Born in New York City to a wealthy patrician family of Dutch extraction, and schooled at Harvard and Columbia universities, he developed a taste for adventure and challenge, a propensity that had been forged in his childhood experience of a successful struggle to overcome poor health. When he entered the arena of politics, he left his mark wherever he went as an intense, vigorous, idealistic, and reform-oriented activist – a quintessential Progressive.

William Jennings Bryan (1860–1925) in 1902. A silver-tongued orator with a radical populist agenda and a heart for the poor and disfranchised, Bryan was probably the most unabashedly religious major political candidate in American history.

Woodrow Wilson (1856–1924). Although a relatively unknown former professor of political science and president of Princeton University, the sum total of whose political experience was two years served as governor of New Jersey, Wilson became the presidential nominee of the Democratic Party in 1912. Thanks to the division among the Republicans, he was swept into office. Wilson too was a Progressive who had written extensively about American government and had been an important figure in the field of public administration, which dealt with the aspects of governance that were deemed to lie outside the realm of politics. Wilson sought to expand that realm and consign as much decision-making as possible to the authority of experts. He was an extraordinarily successful president on the domestic side, rapidly gaining most of his domestic agenda. Yet he often did so at the expense of the structure of governance that the Constitution had established, which he openly sought to reform, even overturn. He was notoriously stubborn and convinced of his own rectitude, traits that led to his disastrous mishandling of the controversy over American ratification of the Treaty of Versailles.

Calvin Coolidge (1872–1933) while governor of Massachusetts, 1919. Later, when he was Warren Harding's vice president, Coolidge received by messenger the news about Harding's death while staying in his childhood home of Plymouth Notch, Vermont. There, in that simple house, his father, who was a justice of the peace, administered the oath of office in the family parlor at 2:47 A.M. by the light of a kerosene lamp. It was a glimpse of an older and more rooted America, something Americans desperately needed after the turmoil of the Wilson and Harding years. Coolidge may be our most underestimated president. He managed to restore confidence in the office of the presidency and easily won election in his own right in 1924, setting the stage for an economic boom that lasted through his presidency. He also gave a profound speech on the 150th anniversary of the American Revolution, cogently articulating the enduring value of the Revolution's ideals.

Herbert Hoover (1874–1964). Few men as worthy and talented as Hoover have suffered so bitter a fate. He was a good man; a highly intelligent, competent, and accomplished public official; and a distinguished humanitarian with a cosmopolitan sensibility and an incomparable record of service to the nation and the world. In fact, it is hard to imagine any American of his day who had a more ideal résumé for service as president of the United States. He was a problem solver par excellence who combined an engineer's scientific insight with a social worker's benevolent intentions, and he had successfully tackled enormous tasks – relief efforts in war-torn Belgium, Russia, and Ukraine; the Mississippi Valley floods of 1927 – with skill and dedication. But the Great Depression defeated him completely and, in the process, caused him to present an image to the world of coldness and indifference toward his suffering fellow Americans. He would live for another three decades and do many more good things in public service. But he could never shake that image of ineptitude and sourness that history has affixed to him.

President Franklin D. Roosevelt, with British prime minister Winston Churchill. The picture speaks volumes about the two men. If Churchill looks cautious and reserved, Franklin Roosevelt seems full of geniality, goodwill, optimism, and openness to the future – the very image of the "first-class temperament" that Justice Oliver Wendell Holmes attributed to him, and even more, an image of the virtues that we think of as characteristically American. Yet the more suspicious temperament of Churchill meant that he took the measure of Soviet dictator Josef Stalin far more accurately than Roosevelt did.

Troops aboard an LCVP landing craft approach Omaha Beach on D-Day, the invasion of Normandy, June 6, 1944. D-Day remains the largest seaborne invasion in human history. These men knew that they would soon face heavy fire from gun emplacements overlooking the beaches and a shore littered with mines and covered with obstacles such as wooden stakes, metal tripods, and barbed wire. Casualties were heaviest at Omaha, because of its high cliffs.

This photograph of landing ships putting cargo ashore on Omaha Beach, at low tide during the first days of the D-Day operation, can only begin to convey a sense of the massive scope of the operation. Note the barrage balloons overhead and the Army "half-track" convoy forming up on the beach.

President Ronald Reagan (1911–2004) speaks to the veterans of Point du Hoc on the fortieth anniversary of their D-Day landing, June 6, 1984. Here is how he began his remarks: "We're here to mark that day in history when the Allied armies joined in battle to reclaim this continent to liberty. For four long years, much of Europe had been under a terrible shadow. Free nations had fallen, Jews cried out in the camps, millions cried out for liberation. Europe was enslaved, and the world prayed for its rescue. Here in Normandy the rescue began. Here the Allies stood and fought against tyranny in a giant undertaking unparalleled in human history."

President Harry S. Truman (1884–1972), in a photograph taken in June 1945, just a few weeks after his ascent to the presidency in the wake of FDR's death. Harry Truman could not have offered a more striking contrast to his urbane, well-born, and Harvard-educated predecessor. A simple, unpretentious midwestern man with only a high school education, blunt and down to earth, he was not a smooth operator but a feisty defender of the interests of the common people and the little guy. In addition, Truman was a decisive man who did not agonize over his choices. Just as he quickly resolved that it would be imperative to use the atomic bomb against Japan because its use would save countless lives, so he quickly moved to extend American support for the imperiled nations of postwar Europe, while doing all he could to prevent yet another ghastly and wasting world war.

President Dwight D. Eisenhower (1890–1969) in a photograph taken in 1954. A career army man who had, like Truman, come from out of the American heartland, Ike had been supreme Allied commander and the hero of D-Day in the Second World War. He brought to the political arena an aura of moderation and nonideological executive competence, qualities that spoke winningly to the country's postwar needs. Balance would be the watchword of his administration. While he favored a fiscally conservative approach to government spending, he did not challenge the essential architecture of the New Deal, either by contracting it or by expanding it. Although Ike was not known for his oratory, his Farewell Address has become one of the most important speeches of postwar American history, with its sage warnings about the damaging effects upon American democracy of a large military–industrial complex conjoined to governance by technocratic elites.

Martin Luther King Jr. (1929–68) at the March on Washington, August 28, 1963. It is fitting that King, a Baptist minister who became the greatest of a remarkable generation of African American civil rights leaders, should here be seen on the National Mall, the space that Pierre L'Enfant had intended for a democratic "grand avenue," with the Washington Monument in the background. King himself called it a "hallowed spot," and his greatest speeches, such as the one he delivered on this day in 1963, in support of the civil rights legislation then pending before Congress, his "I Have a Dream" speech, appealed for social change on the basis of the nation's foundational ideals, not in opposition to them.

The Apollo 11 moon landing, July 20, 1969, with astronaut Buzz Aldrin saluting the U.S. flag on the lunar surface. It is almost impossible for us in our technologically jaded era to comprehend the level of risk that the brave Apollo 11 astronauts faced. They had to entrust their lives to the perfect functioning of thousands of essential systems that were completely beyond their control. They also had to travel 250,000 miles through the vast emptiness of space, facing the genuine danger that they might miss the moon altogether and find themselves carried out into the void, far beyond any conceivable possibility of rescue. The risk level was so high that President Richard Nixon had a speech prepared in case they did not return.

President Richard Nixon (1913–94) meets with China's Communist Party leader, Mao Zedong, February 29, 1972. Nixon is probably the twentieth-century American president about whom historical opinion is most unsettled. Nixon himself predicted that it would take at least fifty years before his presidency could be properly assessed, and his prediction has, if anything, underestimated the problem. Like Truman, he was controversial and reviled by many in his time and left office under a cloud, with rock-bottom approval ratings, hated by his opponents. Like Johnson, he had none of the charm or charisma of a John F. Kennedy, and he suffered for it, an unloved leader who almost seemed uncomfortable in his own skin and who was openly mocked in the media for his chronic awkwardness and strange, lurching gestures. But the passage of time and the lessening of passions have led to significant reappraisals of Nixon's career, and there will likely be more in the years to come. In many respects, he was a talented and highly intelligent man who was consumed by the circumstances of the time: by the intractable war in Vietnam, by the terrible social divisions of the country, and by the outsized demands upon the presidential office. Yet this photograph reminds us of one of his greatest achievements in the realm of diplomacy, the "opening to China" that helped defuse many potential sources of conflict and advance American interests in the nation's relations with the Soviet Union. There was far more to Richard Nixon than Watergate.

NATIONAL OCEANIC AND ATMOSPHERIC ADMINISTRATION

The Italian tall ship Amerigo Vespucci, *named after the explorer and cartographer whose first name came to be used to name the New World, one of the tall ships from all over the world participating in the celebration of the nation's bicentennial year of 1976. In New York on July 4, an especially stately procession of tall ships from all over the world made its way from Staten Island, past Brooklyn and Governor's Island, past the Statue of Liberty, past the canyons of Wall Street, and up the Hudson to the northern tip of Manhattan, accompanied, as in this picture, by a flotilla of pleasure boats. It is estimated that five million people lined the shore to watch the event live that day, and many millions more watched on television.*

Official portrait of President Reagan and Vice President George H. W. Bush (1924–2018), 1981. Although they had been keen rivals for the 1980 Republican presidential nomination, and continued to have philosophical differences, Reagan and Bush made a strong and harmonious team as president and vice president, and the momentum of their partnership carried Bush to election as president in 1988. The two could point to a record of very significant achievement in restoring the strength of the nation's economy and its foreign policy. By the end of Bush's term of office, the Cold War was over, the Soviet Union had ceased to exist, and the power and dignity of the presidential office had been restored.

NATIONAL ARCHIVES AND RECORDS ADMINISTRATION, RONALD REAGAN PRESIDENTIAL LIBRARY

Urban search-and-rescue teams work to clear rubble and search for survivors at the World Trade Center, September 15, 2001. This attack of September 11, 2001, was the single deadliest such attack in American history. It was carried out by radical Muslim terrorists associated with the organization al-Qaeda, who flew two hijacked commercial airliners into the 110-story Twin Towers as part of a larger plan that included attacks on the Pentagon and other Washington government buildings, including possibly the White House or Capitol. Had they been fully successful, the concerted attacks could have paralyzed the U.S. government. As it was, they killed three thousand people, injured countless others, and did almost unimaginable damage to property in lower Manhattan, including the complete disintegration of the city's two tallest structures, while causing more than a hundred deaths, many injuries, and significant damage at the Pentagon. This picture represents a tiny portion of that swath of destruction.

The attack itself was a wake-up call to a country that had largely ignored or downplayed the terror threat during the 1990s. But more than that, it was a sign that the nation had entered a new era, one in which the protocols of the Cold War were a thing of the past and entirely new issues beckoned, requiring a reconsideration of America's place in the world.

CHAPTER THIRTEEN

BECOMING A WORLD POWER

E HAVE NOT HAD A GREAT DEAL TO SAY ABOUT AMERICAN foreign policy to this point, because it had not yet established itself as a theme of consistent importance in American history. In fact, beginning with the successful conclusion of the War of 1812 and lasting through nearly the rest of the nineteenth century, the United States enjoyed a long respite from any major involvement in the affairs of the rest of the world. That respite made it possible for the nation to direct most of its energies toward internal tasks: healing the sectional disputes that had erupted in the Civil War, while consolidating and developing the sprawling expanses that it had now acquired and making it all into a proper nation-state.

That of course didn't mean that the nation was ever completely cut off from the larger world. The familiar term *isolationism* nearly always represents an exaggeration of something far subtler. No country as energetic as the United States was, in the spread of commerce and trade and in the relentless search for new markets for its manufactured goods and agricultural commodities, could ever be completely isolated, or want to be. No country that welcomed so many immigrants from such a diversity of lands could help but have an abundance of ties, both personal and political, to the countries and cultures in the larger world. No country whose intellectual and high-cultural life remained so closely attentive to (and, as Emerson would lament, dependent on) cultural activity of Great Britain and other European societies would ever be isolated. But it remained the case that, for the time being, the United States was not involved in foreign wars or other serious military distractions, and there were very few foreign-relations controversies roiling the waters of American life during those eight decades. In that sense, it was indeed an interlude of relative apartness.

I have called it a respite, but many at the time believed it to be America's natural and permanent state, as a continental republic insulated from the world's woes by the protective buffer of two large oceans and endowed with a lavish array of natural resources, enough to make it largely self-sufficient for the foreseeable future. Such a conception of America could be said to have roots going back to the idea of being a "city upon a hill," although in this instance serving not as a religious exemplar but as a republican one, a model and inspiration for the ennoblement of the rest of the world. It was further upheld by the tenor of George Washington's much-revered Farewell Address, particularly by its insistence that the United States avoid contracting any permanent alliances or other enduring entanglements in the affairs of other countries – particularly not in the quarrelsome countries of Western Europe. A certain disposition toward apartness seemed to be part of the American character and the American mission.

Perhaps the most memorable statement of that view was offered by James Monroe's brilliant secretary of state, and a future President, John Quincy Adams, in an address celebrating the Declaration of Independence, delivered to Congress on July 4, 1821. The speech was long, eloquent, and intellectually ambitious, offering what amounted to an argument for American history as the greatest of all carriers of enlightenment and liberty for all of humankind. And yet, after reading the entire text of the Declaration and offering a thoughtful explication of it, Adams concluded with an apologia and a warning, both of which are worth quoting at some length.

Adams understood that in embracing a national disposition toward aloofness, America could convey an impression of self-satisfied indifference to the rest of the world. So, to those who posed the question, What has America done for the benefit of mankind? Adams's answer was this:

> America, with the same voice which spoke herself into existence as a nation, proclaimed to mankind the inextinguishable rights of human nature, and the only lawful foundations of government.... She has uniformly spoken among them, though often to heedless and often to disdainful ears, the language of equal liberty, equal justice, and equal rights.... She has abstained from interference in the concerns of others, even when the conflict has been for principles to which she clings, as to the last vital drop that visits the heart.... Wherever the standard of freedom and independence has been or shall be unfurled, there will her heart, her benedictions and her prayers be. But she goes not abroad in search of monsters to destroy. She is the well-wisher to the freedom and independence of all. She is the champion and vindicator only of her own.

"She goes not abroad in search of monsters to destroy." These were powerful words, adduced in the service of a compelling argument, one deep in the American grain as of 1821, and remaining so for many years to come. Adams could have chosen to build on those words and emphasize how difficult it is for any nation to remake the institutions of another. But instead, he chose to conclude with a warning that such endeavors would endanger the national soul of America herself:

> She well knows that by once enlisting under other banners than her own, were they even the banners of foreign independence, she would involve herself, beyond the power of extrication, in all the wars of interest and intrigue, of individual avarice, envy, and ambition, which assume the colors and usurp the standard of freedom. The fundamental maxims of her policy would insensibly change from liberty to force. The frontlet upon her brows would no longer beam with the ineffable splendor of freedom and independence; but in its stead would soon be substituted an imperial diadem, flashing in false and tarnished lustre the murky radiance of dominion and power. She might become the dictatress of the world: she would be no longer the ruler of her own spirit.

Such words also came from deep in the American grain, echoing the earlier warnings of Anti-Federalists such as Patrick Henry about the moral dangers of a powerful consolidated government. Yet the tone of the speech as a whole was overwhelmingly celebratory. It articulated the long-standing and deep-seated American preference for republican movements and constitutional institutions around the world, and pride in the belief that history was moving in their direction, with America leading the way. While Adams argued that direct American involvement in such movements would be counterproductive, and risk the corruption of America's own institutions, he added that America would always be cheering such movements on from the sidelines and serving as a friendly example to be drawn upon and imitated by them.

Still, these words stood in an uncertain relationship with others that Adams would articulate two years later in his drafting of the Monroe Doctrine. That document declared that the United States would not accept any further European colonization of the western hemisphere but would instead regard itself as the dominant power in that sphere of influence. The two perspectives are not entirely contradictory, but there is certainly a tension between them. How would the United States assert its hegemony over the western hemisphere without ever "going abroad," likely in a southerly direction, to support republicanism and perhaps destroy a few monsters in the process? What was to ensure that the principle of noninterference and American hegemony would not be interpreted as a right, and even an obligation, for the United States to intervene, if sufficiently provoked or encouraged? If so, how was that to be reconciled to America's founding principles?

Such questions would soon come to bedevil the American enterprise in the world. In any event, *respite* would turn out to be the right word after all. There had been an unusual and fortunate set of circumstances underwriting this period of apartness in the first century or so of the American nation's experience. There was a balance of power in post-Napoleonic Europe, during which time the British Navy, which was friendly to American interests, controlled the seas, thus postponing the need for the United States to have its own robust naval presence to support its large and growing maritime commerce around the world. Those conditions would not last forever, particularly as the growth of the American industrial economy would lead to more and more American shipping, both to export finished goods and import raw materials, and thus to more and more entanglement in the affairs of the rest of the world. A world-class U.S. naval force would eventually be needed, along with overseas acquisitions of harbors and coaling stations spanning the globe to support naval activity and protect far-flung American shipping.

Furthermore, the tensions beginning to be articulated in the 1820s would become posed more sharply as time went on. How would Adams's vision comport with the idea of America's Manifest Destiny, the belief that the nation was in some sense ordained by God to expand across the North American continent and bring democratic institutions to all the people and places therein? And what of Manifest Destiny itself, having reached its continental terminus? Was there any reason why the terms of that destiny had to stop at the water's edge? But if it did extend further, how would that be squared with Americans' traditions of republicanism, not to mention their view of themselves as the proud inheritors of the world's first great anticolonial revolution – the revolution whose public apologia was the Declaration of Independence? Was there a way for a nation to extend its influence in the world without such an action amounting to a form of imperialism?

The concept of imperialism was in the air, all around the world. Most of the major European nations, and a few minor ones, as well as Japan in the Far East, were frantically seeking out imperial acquisitions in Africa and Asia, driven by the desire for new sources of raw materials and new markets as well as the prestige and power associated with possession of an empire. Great Britain, France, Belgium, Germany, Italy, the Netherlands, and Spain: all were actively involved. In all of them, imperial ideas had taken hold among elite leaders and intellectuals, and all of them fiercely competed for the ever-diminishing number of available spaces on the map.

A few reflections on the words being used here. The word *imperial* and the *-ism* deriving from it ultimately come from the Latin term *imperium*, meaning "to command," as do the related words *empire* and *emperor*. As its Latin derivation implies, *imperial* describes something that existed and flourished long before the advent of the modern world. Empires, meaning political systems in which one central power, a country or people, exercised sovereign power over another country or people, or several of them, could be found everywhere in the ancient world, and the imperial concept reached a pinnacle in the empire of Rome itself.

It is common to distinguish imperialism from colonialism, on the basis that the latter word, which comes from the Latin word for farmer (*colonus*), involved a process of migration and permanent settlement, whereas imperialism involved the administration of power from afar. Thus Spanish colonization of Mexico and Peru was far more "imperial" in character than the British approach to the North American continent. This distinction is not always upheld in common usage, and the two concepts sometimes bleed into one another for good reasons. But nevertheless it is worth making the distinction for the sake of clarity. In very rough terms, *imperial* tends to refer to the activity of domination, while *colonial* tends to refer to the activity of settlement.

So imperialism was as old as human history, but it is also clear that its character and its potentialities had changed a great deal by the nineteenth century. One of the many factors that had undermined the Roman Empire was the sheer vastness of its extent, and the intrinsic difficulty of administering such a large imperium. But by the nineteenth century, owing to the multitude of technological breakthroughs in transportation and communications, this was less of a problem; it was far more feasible to maintain the central power's sovereignty over even very faraway and widely dispersed lands. Hence the growing interest in gaining political and economic control over parts of the world that had formerly been thought too remote from Europe.

Such practices placed the most advanced nations of the world on a collision course with liberal principles of inherent human equality and liberty, principles that were also on the rise in the civilized world. Some imperialists simply ignored those principles or declined to grant them universal status, often doing so by drawing on doctrines of "scientific" racism, which purported to ground their authority in Charles Darwin's notions of the "survival of the fittest," to argue for the inherent inferiority and incapacity of the "lesser" or "lower" races living in subordinate countries. "Superior" races were meant to rule, and other races were meant to follow; such was merely the way of nature itself.

But there was a different approach that seemed to reconcile these apparently opposed principles. It was the paternalistic concept of imperial rule as a "civilizing mission," in which a temporary period of political dependence or tutelage was deemed necessary in order to uplift backward or "uncivilized" societies to the point where they were capable of maintaining liberal institutions and self-government on their own. This approach was more palatable to Americans, because it was compatible with the idea that the Anglo-Saxon domination of the world might be generous rather than nakedly exploitative; it might even be intended for the world's good.

Such paternalism could even have religious dimensions, along with its political ones. So believed a Congregationalist minister named Josiah Strong, a proponent of the "Social Gospel," an influential strain of reformist Protestantism that emphasized the achievement of social justice through the active transformation of the world. Strong was particularly influential in pressing the view that the Anglo-Saxon peoples' superior character meant that they were "divinely commissioned" to "Christianize and civilize" the world. It should be added that Strong's understanding of "race" seemed to be more about culture than about biology, and he used the term "Anglo-Saxon" broadly to refer to all the English-speaking peoples of the world. It should also be added that he believed fervently that all "races" could be uplifted and brought to a saving knowledge of Christ. But he did believe that it was the peculiar responsibility of the Anglo-Saxons to be the "depositary" of the two great ideas of "civil liberty" and "a pure spiritual Christianity," and to carry those ideas forth into the larger world.

These ideas may have made imperial expansion more acceptable to the general public. But the driving force behind such expansion was a small but influential group of elite thinkers and public officials who came to believe, for a variety of reasons, that the acquisition of overseas possessions by the United States was a necessary next step in the national story. First and foremost among these was Alfred Thayer Mahan, a naval officer and strategic thinker whose 1890 geopolitical classic *The Influence of Sea Power upon History* made the case that the possession of a powerful navy was essential to national prosperity and great-power status in the modern world. His ideas were picked up by Senator Henry Cabot Lodge of Massachusetts, a committed expansionist who had already been advocating for a bigger navy, annexation of Hawaii, and the American domination of the Caribbean Sea. Other attentive readers were Theodore Roosevelt, then assistant secretary of the navy, who was working for naval expansion, and Indiana attorney Albert Beveridge of Indiana, whose soaring 1898 Senate campaign speech "The March of the Flag" expertly wove together all the elements – religious, strategic, humanitarian, commercial, national greatness – in the pro-imperial case:

Fate has written our policy for us; the trade of the world must and shall be ours. We will establish trading posts throughout the world as distributing points for American products. We will cover the ocean with our merchant marine. We will build a navy to the measure of our greatness. Great colonies governing themselves, flying our flag and trading with us, will grow about our posts of trade.

It remained to be seen whether those "great colonies" would see it the same way.

Asia was always a particular target of expansionists, who ultimately had their eyes on the limitless markets of China and the rest of the Far East, and the first steps toward expansion occurred in that direction. First was the acquisition of Alaska from Russia, through the diplomatic efforts of William Seward, President Johnson's secretary of state (inherited from Lincoln). Seward had been working on persuading the British Columbians to join their territory to the United States and stumbled on the Russian possibility, which he seized on, as a bargain at $7.2 million. Many scoffed at the time, calling it "Seward's Folly," but it was a farsighted choice whose wisdom would soon become apparent.

Next came the islands of Samoa and Hawaii. The former readily accepted an American naval base in 1878, but the latter was a stickier problem. The Hawaiian islands had been a united kingdom since the 1790s but had acquired a substantial number of American settlers, some of them missionaries but many more of them planters involved in creating what became a thriving sugar-production trade. But tensions and resentments seethed among the native Hawaiians and the Americans and ethnic Asians who had come to the island for the sugar production, and the Hawaiians resisted American rule and American annexation. Finally, the newly elected President William McKinley, citing "Manifest Destiny," and noting the growing Japanese interest in taking over the islands for themselves, decided to annex Hawaii by a joint resolution of Congress in 1898.

These were small steps, but a much larger step came in Cuba, which was still a Spanish colony, although one that was rocked periodically by unsuccessful revolts against increasingly ruthless Spanish rule. The United States looked on with interest, partly because of the proximity and strategic importance of Cuba, partly because of extensive American commercial interests in Cuba, partly because of the longtime American interest in acquiring Cuba, but also because the cause of Cuban independence was one for which Americans felt instinctive sympathy. When an insurrection broke out on February 24, 1895, and the Spanish government sent in troops, who turned on the civilian population in a brutal way – shooting and torturing rebels and herding all other inhabitants into the towns, which became disease- and starvation-ridden concentration camps – the American public was outraged.

Their curiosity was being fed by the intensive, even sensationalistic, coverage given to the atrocities in Cuba by the popular press of the time, particularly the dueling *New York Journal* and *New York World*, edited respectively by William Randolph Hearst and Joseph Pulitzer. Locked in a battle for dominance, the two dailies seized on the Cuban events as a source of pure circulation gold, and their often lurid and attention-grabbing approach to stories, which came to be known as "yellow journalism," most certainly moved public opinion far and wide. The new printing technologies allowed for the publication of as many as six daily editions, and rural delivery of mail could bring one of those editions daily to even the most remote villages and farms across the land. So the broader reading public was thoroughly caught up in the ongoing Cuban crisis and understood it as a humanitarian outrage. That said, one should not exaggerate the influence of the yellow press outside of the New York area; it was not the most salient factor in moving public opinion. But it is no exaggeration to say that public opinion was inflamed and that humanitarian concern with the plight of the Cubans was the source of that inflammation. If there were ever a monster worth going abroad to destroy, this seemed to be one.

Public outrage can be hard for public officials to ignore. Democratic president Grover Cleveland managed to avoid being pushed into direct involvement, beyond a few efforts to protect American interests on the island. But when the Republican McKinley was elected in 1896, as we have already seen from his actions in Hawaii, the tenor of American foreign policy changed. McKinley had in fact run on a platform advocating for Cuban independence from Spain, as well as the construction of a canal connecting the Caribbean with the Pacific. He was in negotiations with the Spanish over the situation and had sent the American battleship *Maine* to Havana as an expression of concern for the safety of American lives and property. But the public was in a state of anti-Spanish fever, after disclosure by the *Journal* of a stolen letter, written by the Spanish ambassador, that had disparaged McKinley as a *politicastro*, a small-time political hack who cared only about public acclaim. The ambassador resigned immediately, but that did little to calm the storm. Then, at 9:40 P.M. on the night of February 15, 1898, without any warning, the *Maine* suddenly erupted with a massive explosion, which sent her to the bottom of Havana harbor with a loss of 260 men, two-thirds of her crew, and many of the survivors badly injured.

The response was immediate. Interventionists accused Spain of having blown up the ship and called for war. Readers of the yellow press, who had been feeding on a diet of Spanish atrocity stories for weeks, knew right away that Spain had to be to blame. Responsibility for the blast was not clear at the time, and although a naval court of inquiry declared that a submarine mine was responsible, which would almost certainly have implicated the Spanish, more recent reviews of the evidence have suggested that the blast may have been caused by an internal explosion, ignited by a fire in the ship's coal bunker. We will almost certainly never know for sure, though looking at the matter with the 20/20 vision of retrospect, it seems highly unlikely that the Spanish government would have been so reckless as to perpetrate such an act, knowing that it would very likely bring American troops into Cuba.

In any event, McKinley now faced the heat of an inflamed American public opinion that wanted vengeance, as well as the outrage of detractors like Theodore Roosevelt, who called the sinking "an act of dirty treachery on the part of the Spaniards" and griped that McKinley "had no more backbone than a chocolate éclair." Yet McKinley prudently sought to avoid war, as did most of his supporters in the business community, and his caution brought down on him the wrath of much of the public, and a growing number of public officials, including Democrats who had in the past favored Cleveland's neutrality but were now reading the signs of the times. When McKinley submitted a restrained report on the *Maine* to Congress, he was excoriated for it by the Democrats, and his vice president, Garret Hobart, warned him that it was possible that Congress might declare war on its own, without his involvement, which would be a disastrous turn of events for the administration. He would very likely have no choice but to get out in front of the public passions or risk being bulldozed by them.

The Spanish sensed the perilous situation they were in and moved quickly to mollify the Americans, declaring a cease-fire in Cuba and then offering to the State Department a commitment to Cuban autonomy. But it was too late. By then the Cubans would settle for nothing less than full independence – and that was the one thing that the proud Spanish still could not bring themselves to grant, because it would have meant the collapse not merely of the current government but perhaps even of the monarchy, as punishment for the loss of the last remnant of their once-great American empire. Besides, McKinley had already given in to the pressure on him and had asked Congress for authority to use the armed forces "to secure a full and final termination of hostilities" in Cuba. On April 20, Congress recognized the independence of Cuba by joint resolution and authorized the use of the armed forces to drive out the Spanish, including in its measures an amendment by Senator Henry Teller that explicitly disclaimed any American designs upon Cuban territory. On April 22, McKinley announced a blockade of Cuba's northern coast and the southeastern port of Santiago. That was an act of war, and the Spanish promptly declared war in response.

The war itself was brief and one-sided, as disastrous for Spain as can be imagined. John Hay, who had once been Lincoln's personal secretary, and would serve McKinley as a distinguished secretary of state, called it "a splendid little war," a description whose aptness perhaps depends on one's point of view. But of the "little" there can be little doubt, because it lasted only 114 days. It marked the end of Spain's empire and the beginning of an American one. The latter of these two turned out to be a far more complicated matter than it appeared, going in.

The first action in the war took place not in Cuba but on the other side of the world, in the Spanish colony of the Philippine Islands. Before the conflict began, Theodore Roosevelt had used his position in the Department of the Navy to put on alert the Asiatic Squadron in Manila, under the command of Commodore George Dewey, and be ready to move on the Spanish base immediately if war came. Dewey was accordingly prepared, and when war came, he immediately steamed to Manila Bay and opened fire on the Spanish fleet, making five passes, starting at five thousand yards and closing with each pass, and when the smoke had cleared, all ten of the Spanish vessels had been sunk. Not a single American sailor had been killed. McKinley promptly dispatched eleven thousand troops to take Manila and hold the islands.

The second theater of operations was only a little more troublesome. While the U.S. Navy blockaded the harbor of Santiago, trapping the Spanish naval forces there, a contingent of American troops was landed nearby and managed to secure the commanding heights from which, to the west and south, it could easily bombard Santiago with siege guns. The Spanish Navy was pinned down and had no choice but to attempt to run the blockade. On July 3, their black-hulled ships, unfurled flags proudly flying, steamed out of the harbor and fled westward along the coast. They were pursued resolutely by five American battleships and two cruisers, which ran them down and destroyed every one of them. There was nothing left to do but admit defeat.

Soon there followed an armistice, specifying that Spain was to give up Cuba and that the United States should annex Puerto Rico and Guam and occupy Manila until the fate of the Philippines could be decided at a formal peace conference in Paris.

And so it was all over, just like that. It had indeed been splendid, if you weren't Spanish, and it had been short. It had produced a wave of American patriotic feeling that furthered reconciliation and healing between North and South, particularly since two of the principal generals involved in the war were Confederate veterans. And the results seemed utterly decisive. The United States was now elevated to the ranks of the certifiable world powers; Spain had lost that status, probably forever, through a war that became known to the Spanish for years thereafter simply as *El Desastre* (the Disaster). But the peace to follow would present the United States with far greater difficulties than it had imagined. This war that had been won at so little military cost was going to lead to other problems, far more vexing and costly than any that it solved.

To begin with, there was the problem of the Philippines. With the Spanish leaving, a power vacuum would be left behind, and it suddenly fell to the Americans, as the victorious party, to take responsibility for ensuring that the Philippines had stable and humane governance. It was not clear how that was to be done in a way that was consistent with American principles. The territory could not be given back to Spain or to some other country. Nor were the people of the Philippines sufficiently unified or prepared to rule themselves. No thought had been given to the idea of the United States annexing them before the war, but the idea began to appeal to expansionists, as they realized that the Philippines could serve as a perfect gateway into the continent of Asia and the markets of the Far East. Yet anti-imperialists were vehemently opposed to any such move, believing that such a step would imperil American democracy, in precisely the ways that John Quincy Adams had darkly predicted. The stage was set for a great national debate.

The anti-imperialists were extremely varied in their background and philosophy. Most of the northern Democrats and reform-minded eastern Republicans joined the anti-imperial cause in opposing annexation. Both Andrew Carnegie and Samuel Gompers were opposed, as were writers like Mark Twain and William Dean Howells, the philosopher William James, and the social reformer Jane Addams. Their reasons for opposing annexation were also quite varied, involving a mixture of idealistic and less-than-admirable motives. There were idealistic motives, flowing from the ardent belief that the Constitution should always follow the flag, and that it violated the spirit and letter of the Declaration of Independence for Americans to rule "over" another people and deprive them of government by their consent.

There were also racial and ethnic prejudices entangled with idealistic motives. For example, in the argument that annexation could not possibly lead to statehood, given the alienness of the Philippines' racial and cultural makeup. Instead, an annexed Philippines would live in a state of permanent oppression, permanent second-class status, inhabiting an American *imperium* whose very existence would have corrupting effects on the national ethos. In the words of Senator George Frisbie Hoar of Massachusetts, the United States would be acquiring "subject and vassal states" in "barbarous archipelagoes" and "trampling, as we do it, on our own great character which recognizes alike the liberty and the dignity of individual manhood." And there were also worries, particularly among labor leaders, about competition from foreign workers; as Gompers said, putting the matter rather nakedly, "if the Philippines are annexed what is to prevent the Chinese, the Negritos and the Malays coming to our country? How can we prevent the Chinese coolies from going to the Philippines and from there swarm into the United States and engulf our people and our civilization? . . . Can we hope to close the flood-gates of immigration from the hordes of Chinese and the semi-savage races coming from what will then be part of our own country?"

McKinley was not deaf to the anti-imperialists' arguments and agonized over the choice but finally concluded that there was no alternative to annexation. He did not believe that the people of the Philippines could be left to their own devices; the result, he feared, would be years and years of chaos and bloodshed, and he was not willing to allow that. By process of elimination, he concluded that he was left with only one viable choice. As he put it, "there was nothing left for us to do but take them all, and to educate the Filipinos, and uplift and civilize and Christianize them."

The trouble was that an indigenous anti-Spanish insurrectionary movement, led by Emilio Aguinaldo, which had been fighting the Spanish before the Americans arrived, had already created a republican government, complete with a constitution, and saw itself as the rightful successor to Spanish colonial rule. Under more normal circumstances, the United States would have agreed. But the logic of annexation militated against that, and when it became clear that the United States was not only not going to withdraw but was intent upon establishing control over the islands, the tensions between the two antagonists erupted into all-out war – a war that turned out to be far longer and less splendid than the war against the Spanish. The hostilities began in earnest in February 1899 and did not end until spring 1902. The conflict was mostly conducted as guerilla warfare, ugly, cruel, and bloody and marked by many instances of torture and other atrocities, as well as many civilian deaths. It underscored the unexpectedly high price of imperial expansion: there would be forty-three hundred American lives lost in the three years it took to crush the revolt, exponentially more than had been required to defeat the Spanish.

Fortunately, McKinley made an excellent choice when he appointed Judge William Howard Taft as the civil governor of the Philippines, a position for which the ebullient and likable Taft had just the right touch. He insisted on treating the Filipinos as partners and as social equals and rejected the racial assumptions that had consigned them to second-order status. He worked to improve the lot of Filipino farmers, even visiting the Vatican in the hope of persuading Pope Leo XIII to free up ecclesiastical lands for their use. These efforts would make a significant difference in the political climate, and very quickly. For his own part, Taft genuinely loved the Filipino people and turned down a much-coveted Supreme Court appointment out of a desire to stay with them a little longer and finish his work. By 1917, Congress would pass the Jones Act, which affirmed the American intention to grant the Philippines eventual independence in the foreseeable future. That would finally happen on July 4, 1946.

The Philippines were not the only problem facing the newly imperial United States. The clear principles of the Founding were being fudged left and right, as in the case of Puerto Rico, ceded to the United States by Spain, where an indeterminate and intermediate status, somewhere between colonial dependency and fully incorporated statehood, would be settled on. And what of Cuba, the original cause for the war? American policy faced some of the same kinds of problems there too, as a temporary American military occupation government clashed with rebel forces that had opposed the Spanish. Eventually the island was pacified, and the Cubans were given their independence. But there would be a catch. When a Cuban constitution was drafted in 1900, the Platt Amendment to a military appropriations bill passed by Congress was devised to restrict the independence of the new government. Among other things, it forced the Cubans to acknowledge the United States' right to intervene in Cuba whenever it deemed necessary "for the preservation of Cuban independence" and "for the maintenance of a government adequate for the protection of life, property, and individual liberty." In addition, Cuba had to promise that it would not conclude any treaty with a third power that would affect its independence and grant the United States the use of land for a naval base at Guantánamo Bay.

It is not hard to understand why the Cubans, after having fought a long war to free themselves of Spanish rule, deeply resented these impositions and would come to resent them more and more with passing years, even though the Platt Amendment was formally invoked only once, in 1906. Yet it is also not hard to understand why so many Americans, including most of the anti-imperialists, believed such measures to be necessary, given the chaotic state of postwar Cuba. Indeed, it was entirely plausible to argue that such measures should be extended to the whole Caribbean, which was filled with unstable and desperately poor countries, all seemingly in need of the steadying influence of a larger and more established neighbor.

When Theodore Roosevelt became president, he did just that. After stepping in to take charge of a parlous financial crisis in the Dominican Republic, which he reasoned was a responsibility incumbent upon the United States precisely because the Monroe Doctrine forbade European countries from doing it, he propounded this as a more general policy. Because of the chronic problems of the region, Roosevelt said, and its governments' proneness to "wrongdoing or impotence," the United States' adherence to the Monroe Doctrine would require it to exercise, "reluctantly," "an international police power." This became known as the Roosevelt Corollary to the Monroe Doctrine, presented by Roosevelt in a message to Congress delivered in December 1904. The policy worked very well in the Dominican instance. But like the Platt Amendment, it would cause resentments that would taint U.S. relations with Latin America for years to come.

Still, on balance, the American entry onto the world stage had been relatively auspicious, and its imperial record would be relatively benign, particularly when compared to some of the enormities committed by its European counterparts in the pursuit of their much more extensive and exploitative imperial enterprises in Africa and Asia. A useful point of comparison would be the American approach to China, a part of the world in which the United States' interest was now greatly heightened by its new stake in the Philippines. China was in considerable disarray at this time, having suffered such decline since its defeat in the Sino-Japanese War of 1894–95 that it had effectively lost its independence and become subject to the control of various outside governments. By the 1890s, the five great imperial powers (Russia, Japan, Great Britain, France, and Germany) had divided China into "spheres of influence," in which they enjoyed exclusive trading privileges and other forms of commercial exploitation. So weakened was China that there was even talk of carving up the country by partition among the great powers; and it was in the context of this foreign domination that the Boxer Rebellion, a failed antiforeign revolt by Chinese nativists, would erupt.

But in fall 1898, McKinley proposed the creation of an "open door" policy that would open the Chinese market to all trading nations, while recognizing the territorial integrity of China. Secretary of State John Hay worked tirelessly to advance the policy, and while it was never formally agreed to by the other powers, it became the basis of American policy in China for the next half-century. The policy was firmly in the American anti-imperial tradition, but it was not offered out of complete altruism. The United States wanted to be able to trade with Chinese cities and feared that a partition of China would likely end up cutting the United States out of China entirely. It was a far more generous position than that of the imperial nations, and the Chinese were appreciative of that fact. Yet it also had the effect of committing the United States to the preservation of China's territorial integrity, a commitment that would in turn influence U.S. relations with Japan in the years to come. It was yet another way that the American role in the larger world was becoming ever greater, sometimes almost despite itself.

There was always a divided heart in the American approach to imperial rule, which helps explain why most of the lands acquired in the Spanish–American War were soon devolved toward independent status. The great debate over the annexation of the Philippines went to a profound tension in the American experience, one that would only increase as the American role in the world became greater and greater. How to observe what was wise and proper in John Quincy Adams's admonitions, but at the same time recognize that the growth of American wealth and power naturally begot responsibilities for the well-being of rest of the world?

The answer, even if arrived at clumsily, and even if exasperatingly difficult to put into action, was well stated by Roosevelt's secretary of war, Elihu Root, when contemplating the problem of the Caribbean nations, in words that could apply just as well to the rest of the world: "We do not want to take them for ourselves. We do not want any foreign nations to take them for themselves. We want to help them." But helping them has always been a more complicated matter than it seems.

CHAPTER FOURTEEN

THE PROGRESSIVE ERA

HISTORIANS HAVE LONG REFERRED TO THE NEARLY TWO decades between the Spanish–American War and the American entry into the First World War as the Progressive Era. The term has its uses but can easily mislead. Yes, the years between 1898 and 1917 may have represented a high tide for a certain approach to reform, in which activist intellectuals and politicians, many of them associated with a loose movement that came to be called Progressivism, sponsored programs of far-reaching structural change to political and economic institutions. But it is not as if there were no reform ideas or efforts being promoted before 1898, and none again after 1917, and it was not as if those ideas were less sweeping or far-reaching than those of the people who are called Progressives.

What we call the Progressive Era was a more concentrated and widely influential phase in a longer and more general response to the great disruptions of industrialization, urbanization, national consolidation, and concentrated wealth and power. In that phase, the reformers achieved political power, even the presidency, and enacted significant portions of their reform agenda. Such responses were part of a larger quest for a new order, or at least for a new way of thinking about how American democracy and self-rule could survive and thrive under such dramatically changed conditions. We still struggle with some of those same questions today.

But the Progressive Era had an important prologue, which began with scattered visionaries who attracted large followings, offering radical innovations to solve the nation's problems. Some of their solutions were quite novel. The San Francisco journalist Henry George, in an 1879 book called *Progress and Poverty*, called for a single tax on land, termed a land value tax, as a way to equalize the alarming inequalities of wealth that he had observed in the cities. The many disruptions wrought by nineteenth-century industrialization also led to a rash of utopian novels, perhaps best exemplified by Edward Bellamy's fabulously best-selling 1888 fantasy *Looking Backward*, an effort to imagine a perfected postindustrial Boston, reconstituted as a socialist cooperative commonwealth in the year 2000. Far from celebrating individualism, Bellamy openly reviled it, proposing in its place a quasi-Christian "religion of solidarity" that would radically deemphasize the self and instead promote social bonds over individual liberty. The huge popularity of Bellamy's book – it was second only to *Uncle Tom's Cabin* as the best-selling book of the nineteenth century, and it gave rise to innumerable "Bellamy clubs" across the nation, where the reform-minded gathered and dreamed together – showed how many Americans were hungry for such alternative ideas.

Similar themes were sounded by Christian leaders drawn to the Social Gospel, such as Columbus's Washington Gladden and Rochester's Walter Rauschenbusch, both of whom argued that the essence of the Christian gospel was not in its supernatural aspects or its offer of salvation but in its implications for social and economic reform, for what Rauschenbusch called the "Christian transfiguration of the social order." Exemplifying such concern, urban reformers like Jane Addams and Ellen Starr moved into the most troubled neighborhoods in the new cities, seeking to establish "settlement houses" that could be sources of practical knowledge and material improvement in the lives of slum dwellers.

But the impulse for reform did not come only from the cities. Farmers, traditionally among the most self-reliant of citizens, found themselves experiencing a profound crisis in the latter years of the nineteenth century. Not only were they suffering from deeply depressed crop prices but now they found themselves struggling with bankers, railroads, grain-elevator operators, and a crowd of other middlemen and creditors, just to be able to get their livelihood. The simplicity of rural farm life was becoming a vanishing dream of the past.

But even if farmers' lives were becoming nearly as constrained as those of factory workers, they did not live and labor like factory workers. Being geographically dispersed and accustomed to living independently, they found it difficult to organize in order to change their condition. Nevertheless, by the 1890s, an agrarian protest movement was coming together, and farmers were being advised to "raise less corn and more hell." Eventually, a varied collection of movements coalesced into a third political party, called the People's Party or the Populists. The Populists formulated an ambitious platform, featuring calls for a graduated income tax, nationalization of the railroads, coinage of silver, direct election of senators, and the eight-hour workday, among many other items. It was more radical than anything on offer from the labor movement.

By the 1896 presidential election, the Populists had reluctantly joined forces with the Democrats in supporting the latter party's candidate, William Jennings Bryan, a two-term former congressman from Nebraska. Bryan was then only thirty-six years old but was a gifted and silver-tongued orator with the power to captivate audiences, using rhetoric with powerful and unabashed Christian and biblical overtones. When he spoke, he preached, and when he preached, it was on behalf of the poor, the disenfranchised, the debt-ridden farmers and small businessmen, and the laboring classes. In resonant tones and rolling cadences reminiscent of a revivalist, he could pull at the emotional strings of his audiences and bring them to their feet, weeping and cheering.

He did not promote the entire populist agenda, but his proposals included the free coinage of silver, an issue that had long been a populist favorite and had taken on great symbolic importance, following as it did directly upon lines of class division, separating the wealthy and the poor. But its importance was not merely symbolic. To monetize silver, and thereby depart from the conservative gold standard, would mean a significant inflation of the currency, which in turn would greatly help poor debtors (since they would be able to repay their debts in dollars that were worth less than the dollars they had borrowed) and disadvantage wealthy creditors (for the same reasons, and because inflation erodes the value of present assets). Bryan taunted the opposition for its hard-hearted ungenerosity in a time of such severe need, using an image that in such a robustly Christian culture would have to be regarded as the ultimate weapon: "You shall not press down upon the brow of labor this crown of thorns," he cried in his speech at the Chicago Democratic Convention of 1896. "You shall not crucify mankind upon a cross of gold." As he spoke those words, he raised his arms to his sides, offering himself as a veritable image of the crucified Christ. And the crowd went wild.

Bryan's tactics did not play equally well elsewhere. There were "gold" Democrats who could not support Bryan's currency ideas and did not much like his evangelistic manner; they bolted from the party. The campaign of Bryan's opponent, William McKinley, was able to paint Bryan as a wild-eyed anarchist, animated by a "communistic spirit," and in the end, despite Bryan's frenzied and effective cross-country campaigning, McKinley succeeded in beating back the Nebraskan's challenge. Bryan won the western interior and southern states, while McKinley took the Northeast, the Midwest, and most of the Pacific Coast. The margin of victory, while comfortable, was not of landslide proportions: about 51 percent to 48 percent in the popular vote.

Many historians have regarded the 1896 election as a climactic victory of urban and industrial values over the rural and agrarian values that Bryan was taken to represent, an election affirming the emergence of a new "modern" American status quo. This is entirely plausible. The election can indeed be read as a stamp of approval of the dramatic changes that had occurred since Appomattox, a stamp that would be made even more indelible two years later, with the Spanish war and the annexation of the Philippines. It could even be read as a conclusion to the Second American Revolution imagined by Charles Beard.

But how remarkable it was that a movement driven by radical protest had come so far, capturing the nomination of a major political party and losing the general election only by a modest and respectable margin. Bryan's 6.5 million votes amounted to the largest vote total achieved by any presidential candidate in American history up to that point – excepting only McKinley's 7.1 million, which sufficed to defeat him. If Bryan had somehow found a way of connecting with working-class Catholic voters in the Northeast and Midwest, the outcome could have been dramatically different. In short, there was no reason to think that the rising reform impulse in America could be undone by a single election.

Nor was it undone, but it would have to change its colors and shift its emphases to move ahead. The mantle of reform would be passed to a different cast of characters: the cast making up the Progressive movement. This movement had already begun in the 1890s but had so many different constituencies and was so diverse in character that it is probably a misnomer even to call it a "movement" or to attribute to "Progressivism" too strict a definition. But with those caveats in mind, we can make certain useful generalizations.

First, it can be said that while Progressives supported many of the very same measures that the Populists supported, they did so from a more urban and town-dwelling base. Progressivism was a middle-class movement, with its heartbeat in the small towns and growing cities of the upper Midwest, particularly in states such as Wisconsin, where Progressivism enjoyed a pinnacle of success. Its constituencies included a great many professional people and traditional pillars of the community – doctors, lawyers, ministers, bankers, shopkeepers – but also there were officeworkers and middle managers employed in government agencies and business corporations. Progressives tended to be educated, civic minded, religiously inclined, and morally earnest. They wanted not merely to help the poor and oppressed but to change the system that brought about those conditions: to correct the perceived abuses, inequities, and inefficiencies that the new industrial economy had created and, in doing so, to restore – and perhaps more fully realize – the preconditions of democracy. In that sense, they were both reformist and conservative: willing to endorse dramatic changes in the service of rescuing and recovering older values.

The impetus for Progressivism was, as in other reform efforts of the era, a perception that the economic and financial revolutions of the previous decades had distorted or displaced the institutions that ordered social and political life and that new ones needed to be devised to correct these abuses. Notable in feeding this perception were the great investigative journalists of the era, such as Henry Demarest Lloyd, Jacob Riis, Lincoln Steffens, and Ida Tarbell, whose slashing articles and books shed light on such ills as the monopolistic behavior of Standard Oil and other gargantuan corporations, the dire conditions of the urban slums, and the corruption of urban government. These writers became known, in a word that Theodore Roosevelt had borrowed from John Bunyan's religious classic *Pilgrim's Progress*, as "muckrakers." He did not mean it as a term of praise, since he felt that these writers were so fixated upon wallowing in the mud and "raking the muck" that they missed the better and more admirable aspects of life. But even he grudgingly acknowledged that they performed an important function, as indeed they did. They stirred things up, identifying problems and making them harder to ignore. As we will see, Roosevelt himself paid attention to them.

These writers enjoyed a national audience, but the movement itself began on the local level, in municipalities and states, before spreading to the national level, and it was focused on concrete structural reforms. The goals included not only the reining in of corruption but the creation of what they considered to be a more wholesome public life in its place. In Toledo, Ohio, the self-made millionaire Samuel "Golden Rule" Jones, a Christian Socialist who had been influenced by Henry George, brought Progressive ideas into his administration as city mayor, creating free kindergartens, parks and playgrounds, public baths, an eight-hour day for city workers, and other popular reforms. His successor, Brand Whitlock, also a Georgist, would continue in a similar vein. Cleveland's mayor Tom Johnson was an even more dramatic reformer, reforming almost every aspect of city government, from cleaning up the police department to establishing strict building codes, municipalizing functions such as trash collection, expanding public recreation offerings, promoting municipal ownership of streetcar lines and power utilities, and creating a spacious park called the Mall, meant as a grand public space open to all and expressive of the democratic ideal.

The control of utilities like electricity and water by the public rather than by private companies was an important and popular target in other Progressive cities as a way to break the often corrupt relationship between those corporations and the city bosses and return that power to the broader public. By 1915, two-thirds of American cities had publicly owned and operated water systems, and many cities had municipalized transportation systems, electrical power generation, and similar utilities affecting the entire public.

These reforms reflected one of the beliefs shared by nearly all Progressives: the view that there was something called "the public interest," above and distinct from the self-interests of any particular parties – particularly the Interests, so often capitalized, of the large business combinations whose rise troubled them so much – and that the pursuit of that larger public interest ought to be the chief concern of government, as it was the chief object of the most conscientious of Progressive reformers. The word *disinterested*, which we use today to mean "uninterested," was in those days a word that signified a very high ideal: the ideal of making decisions or allocating resources or rendering judgments without reference to one's particular interests but only with the public interest in mind.

Most of the more significant Progressive reforms proceeded from that motive of "disinterestedness." There was therefore a certain high-mindedness about the Progressives, which was a reflection of their religious formation. While they could be tough-minded in their efforts to promote reform, they ostensibly did not seek to aggrandize themselves, or to punish others, or otherwise to give quarter to the politics of self-interest. This was admirable; it also could be annoyingly self-righteous and self-deceiving, particularly when the term *public interest* was used to justify policies that did not appeal to those who did not share the Progressives' socioeconomic profile. More on that in a moment.

The ethic of disinterestedness carried over into the Progressive view of how governments should be structured. Progressives tended to distrust politics, which they found to be a dishearteningly grubby business of deal making and vote trading, or worse, and thought it better to entrust as much of governance as possible to those with the expert knowledge, and the disinterested position, to enable them to govern with purported objectivity and unquestioned authority. One expression of this view was the creation of the city-manager system of governance, pioneered by Dayton, Ohio, in which a nonelected professional city manager with certified expert knowledge was hired by the elected city council to run the various city departments, all of which would report to the manager rather than the council. By 1923, more than three hundred cities had adopted one form or another of that plan of government, and some of them still retain that form today.

On the state level, governors struggled with large corporate interests, such as railroads and insurance companies, and sought to institute changes in the legislative process, such as the introduction of initiative, referendum, and the party primary system, all ways that allowed ordinary citizens to circumvent the professional politicians and the deliberations of their smoke-filled rooms and take a direct hand in their own governance. The Progressives' interest in such reforms illuminates one of the paradoxes of their way of seeing things. On one hand, they took a very skeptical view of democratic political institutions and preferred the rule of professionals and accredited experts wherever it was possible to introduce it. On the other hand, they had an expansive faith in the people and their ability to initiate positive change in the public interest, operating outside the legislative frameworks that had been provided by their existing political institutions. Their heavy commitment to ballot reform, direct primaries, initiative, referendum, recall, and the like reflected their desire to increase citizen participation in government. They had great faith in democracy but far less faith in democratic institutions.

Yet there were places in which this combination of things seemed to work admirably well. Inspired and effective leadership made a big difference. In Wisconsin, the Progressive state par excellence, Governor (and later Senator) Robert La Follette (governor from 1900 to 1904) created something he called the "Wisconsin idea," a confluence of mutually reinforcing Progressive innovations and institutions in which an activist government, drawing on research conducted at the great state university in Madison and referred to a Legislative Reference Bureau, would enact "enlightened" policies based on the "science of governance," rather than the impure machinations of contending political factions, to produce good government, government in the public interest. Wisconsin under La Follette also embraced other classic Progressive innovations: direct primaries, railroad regulation, workman's compensation, natural-resources conservation, and other measures in the Progressive playbook. If there was a single place that was the best showcase for Progressive reforms, it was Wisconsin.

Progressives agreed on a great many other things, such as the outlawing of child labor in mines and factories and the protection of women in the industrial workforce. But one set of issues on which they did not entirely agree were those revolving around the matter of alcoholic beverages. Here it should be stressed that, as we have already seen in the mid-nineteenth-century rise of the temperance movement, the objections to alcohol on the part of Progressives were not merely prudish or pleasure-hating, as many today are likely to assume, but flowed in part from a concern about the ways that the excessive consumption of alcohol undermined the health, cohesiveness, living standards, and life prospects of working-class people. But the issues of temperance or prohibition produced something of an urban/small-town split. Big-city Progressives were wary of saloons, which they suspected not only as breeding grounds for crime and prostitution but as gathering places for the bosses and cronies who ran the corrupt urban political machines. But they were not drawn to the temperance movement, which would ultimately seek to ban the manufacture and distribution of all alcoholic beverages. More rural and small-town reformers, such as the members of the Anti-Saloon League, felt differently. For them, Demon Rum was an all-pervading enemy at the root of nearly all social and economic problems and needed to be attacked without ceasing.

The case of temperance provides an important window onto some of the underlying features of Progressive thinking. As we've observed, Progressivism was a middle-class movement, reflecting the legacy of Protestant moral and ethical teaching – although conspicuously lacking in the hard-edged doctrine of original sin. That was a key omission. The Progressive view of human nature saw humans as fundamentally good, and evil as a function of bad social systems and corrupted institutions, not something irremediably wrong or sinful deep in the souls of individual persons. There was no inherent limit to the improvability of the world. No problem was beyond solution.

The problems of the day would never, they thought, be corrected by a Madisonian system of raw competition, in which (as Madison said) ambition would be made to counteract ambition and interests to counter interests. Instead, they would be corrected through the exercise of scientific intelligence applied by disinterested experts. Hence the Progressive emphasis on the transformation and renewal of social and political institutions as the key to the renewal of the world. Hence the responsibility of government, acting as the "social intelligence" of an informed public, to order the community in a way that would order the souls of its members. Hence the central importance of schools and education, as the vehicles by which the findings of scientific research could be incorporated into the lives of families and individuals, for the betterment of all.

External change, then, would come before internal change. The deep social problems of the day, the unhappiness and insecurity of so many people whose lives had been upended by the new order of things – those problems could not be solved by religion, or the search for some other source of psychological "sense of wholeness." They could only be solved by the reordering of the social world along fresh lines, in a way that embraced the realities of modernity rather than seeking to negate or repeal them. The most eminent philosopher of the Progressive Era, John Dewey, expressed that idea in concise if somewhat dense form in his 1922 book *Individualism, Old and New*, as in the following paragraph:

> *For the idea that the outward scene is chaotic because of the machine, which is a principle of chaos, and that it will remain so until individuals reinstitute wholeness within themselves, simply reverses the true state of things. The outward scene, if not fully organized, is relatively so in the corporateness which the machine and its technology have produced; the inner man is the jungle which can be subdued to order only as the forces of organization at work in externals are reflected in corresponding patterns of thought, imagination and emotion. The sick cannot heal themselves by means of their disease, and disintegrated individuals can achieve unity only as the dominant energies of community life are incorporated to form their minds.*

Or, as Dewey goes on to say, "the disintegration of individuality" has come about because of a "failure to reconstruct the self so as to meet the realities of present social life." The rugged individualism that so many Americans celebrated? That was a thing of the past.

Not all Progressives would have agreed with, or even understood, every element of Dewey's formulation. But what one would find to be consistent is the sense that Progressivism was an outlook that cared deeply about the common people and knew, far better than they did, what was best for them. Who after all would determine when "the dominant energies of community life" had been properly "incorporated to form their minds"? Who would have the authority to say that the "reconstruction of the self" had succeeded in meeting "the realities of present social life"? Some superior person would have to be available to certify such things.

Thus there was always in Progressivism a certain implicit paternalism, a condescension that was all the more unattractive for being unacknowledged. But that was not the worst of its blind spots. Progressives also had very little comprehension of the situation of racial and religious minorities and in many cases failed to see that, for example, the propensity of Italian immigrants to have large families was a legitimate cultural difference and not a pathology. An interest in uplifting society could easily turn into a desire to remold or purify it; hence many Progressives came to support immigration restriction and racial segregation as a means to that end. A surprising number of Progressives even saw considerable merit in the theory and practice of eugenics, as a form of scientific human engineering that would over time eliminate "undesirable" or "unfit" elements from society. This could even turn into support for such noxious practices as selective infanticide, the sterilization of the "defective," population control, and the like, all in the name of social improvement.

To be sure, not all Progressives saw things this way. But no account of the Progressive years would be complete and accurate without some mention of them. Eugenics was not a fringe phenomenon in its time, and it was not confined to the most reactionary elements; it was endorsed by leading scientists and scientific organizations as well as by figures such as the feminist Margaret Sanger, the African American scholar W. E. B. Du Bois, the inventor Alexander Graham Bell, and Stanford University president David Starr Jordan and was actively supported by such respected organizations as the Rockefeller Foundation and the Carnegie Institute.

In the end, the scientific roots of Progressivism were likely to be incompatible with its religious ones. How could one reconcile the "purifying" impulse of eugenics, however much it might be sanctioned by the proclamations of "science," with the Christian requirement that respect be shown for all human life, as made in the image of God? How could the "gospel of efficiency" that Progressive business reformers like Frederick Winslow Taylor brought to the workplace, prescribing the exact motions and techniques to be used, automaton-like, on the assembly line to maximize productivity, be reconciled to a religious tradition that insisted upon the dignity of work and of the worker? It was Progressivism's fate to try to hold on to both sets of values at the same time – an impossible task.

The Progressives were not class-conscious radical socialists. They did not seek to overthrow modern industrial capitalism or to seize all private property. Indeed, they feared and fought against such radicalism. As middle-class reformers who drew on their Protestant religious traditions for moral instruction, they simply did not think that way. Nor did they seek to repeal the Industrial Revolution. Instead, they wanted to make modern capitalism more humane, soften its hard edges, heal its negative effects, improve its workplaces, and distribute its benefits more widely and fairly. Therefore the central task facing them, the one whose importance overshadowed all others, was the task of proper regulation. If the vast productivity of modern industry was not to be rejected and dismantled but was instead to be controlled and directed, made to serve the public interest and not private interests alone, then the chief question was how one was to do it.

To that question, there were basically two Progressive answers. Each would involve the vigorous use of government, but each would involve using government in nearly opposite ways. The first, which we shall call the antitrust method, would wherever possible use the power of government to break up the largest concentrations of corporate wealth and power, prevent the formation of monopolies, and endeavor to restore wherever it could a healthy competition between and among smaller entities within their respective spheres of the economy. The second approach, which we shall call the consolidation method, would accept bigness and concentration as an inevitable and even optimal feature of modern economic development, productive of stupendous efficiencies and economies of scale that could be matched in no other way. Instead of breaking up large combinations, it would actively and vigorously regulate them, with the public interest always in view.

Both approaches had already been introduced into political practice during the late nineteenth century. The Sherman Anti-Trust Act of 1890 had been an effort to take the first approach and ended up being used to break up the Northern Securities Company, the Standard Oil Company, and the American Tobacco Company, among others. The Interstate Commerce Act of 1887, on the other hand, was set up to regulate the railroad industry as a whole and involved establishing the first independent regulatory agency of the U.S. government. The question of which, if either, would come to dominate reform in the years ahead would be one of the most interesting underlying debates within the Progressive ranks. Either way, it was clear that Progressivism would grow into a national movement, addressing itself to national issues and proposing national remedies.

It soon became clear, too, that one of the burning questions raised by the Progressive movement would have to do with the status of the Constitution itself. Was it still the indispensable foundation of American law and life? Or had the new America passed it by and rendered it outmoded, a creaking eighteenth-century document no longer able to keep up with the needs of a twentieth-century world?

The presidential phase of Progressivism began in 1901 with the ascent to the office of Vice President Theodore Roosevelt upon the assassination of President William McKinley. Roosevelt had spent six restless months in the office of the vice presidency, an office without any power, affording him no outlet for his considerable energies. Members of his own party wondered if he was suitable for the office, and they were even more concerned when McKinley's death presented him with the presidency. McKinley's political mentor and friend Mark Hanna put it this way: "I told William McKinley it was a mistake to nominate that wild man at Philadelphia. I asked him if he realized what would happen if he should die. Now look, that damned cowboy is president of the United States!"

A cowboy was only one of the things that Theodore Roosevelt, or TR as he was widely known, had been during a career in which he had already packed several lifetimes into a mere forty-two years on the planet. We've encountered TR already in our story, as an unabashed imperialist favoring a war with Spain. But perhaps it is time for us to pause and give a more thorough introduction to one of the most fascinating characters in all of American history.

He was born in New York City in 1858, to a wealthy patrician family of Dutch extraction, and was schooled at Harvard and Columbia universities. But the most important thing about his younger life was his relentless struggle to overcome a weak and illness-prone constitution, a struggle that shaped his character decisively. He suffered from asthma and poor eyesight and had trouble with chronic headaches, fevers, stomach pains, and such, all of which made it difficult for him to exercise. But he attacked those disabilities with the intensity and determination that would become his trademark, and after an experience of being mistreated by two bullies on a camping trip, he was determined never again to be brought up short in his own self-defense. His father built a gym in their home, and the young TR worked relentlessly to improve himself, with a program that included weightlifting, gymnastics, wrestling, boxing, horseback riding, hiking, climbing, swimming, and rowing. His indomitable resolve won out, and he was able to build up a high degree of strength and physical stamina, which he was not reluctant to display to others, with an irrepressible boyish enthusiasm that charmed many and annoyed many others.

Homeschooled in his early years, "Teedy" (as he was then known) was clearly a prodigy, with strong historical and scientific interests. While in college at Harvard, he published his studies in ornithology and began writing a book on the naval war of 1812, based on careful research in the relevant U.S. Navy archives. That book was published in 1882 and remains to this day a standard study of the war. Athlete, scientist, historian: it seemed there was nothing he couldn't do.

But what he wanted was a career in politics. He was sufficiently wealthy that he did not need to work but chose instead to run for the New York State Assembly, a position he won, and went on to serve a total of three years. After his wife's unexpected and tragic death, he went west to North Dakota, to reconsider his life's direction, and learned to ride western style, rope, and mingle with the cowboys. When he returned in 1886, he was ready for a steady rise through the ranks of New York and national politics, from New York City police commissioner to assistant secretary of the U.S. Navy to governor of New York to vice president to president. Along the way, he developed elements of a distinctive governing philosophy.

First of all, he was an activist. Just as he could not be passive in his personal life so he could not see any reason to refrain from using the powers of government to make life better; so laissez-faire capitalism did not appeal to him. Nor, though, did socialism, which he distrusted as excessively radical. A balance between the two extremes was the position most congenial to him. That balance included, though, an expansive and vigorous view of the presidency, in which the president would set the legislative agenda for Congress. The activist power of the presidency had been relatively dormant ever since the death of Lincoln and the rise of congressional Reconstruction. Roosevelt would seek to restore it.

Second, and connected to the first, he was not inclined to be excessively deferential to the Constitution. As he said in his First Annual Message speech to Congress on December 3, 1901, "when the Constitution was adopted, at the end of the eighteenth century, no human wisdom could foretell the sweeping changes, alike in industrial and political conditions, which were to take place by the beginning of the twentieth century." The Constitution's plan was adequate for those times, but "the conditions are now wholly different and wholly different action is called for." Hence Roosevelt was pleased to make extensive use of independent executive power; he argued that he was permitted to do anything that was not expressly forbidden by the Constitution. This was a change from the Founders. He was now interpreting the Constitution as a charter, not of enumerated powers, but of enumerated prohibitions. This came to be known as his "stewardship" theory of the presidency: as the "steward" of the people, the president was permitted to do anything necessary for the well-being of the people.

By 1902, TR had already gotten his sea legs in the presidency and was endorsing the concept of a "square deal" for all. Roosevelt meant this to signify the promise that he, unlike presidents before him, would not routinely favor capital over labor but would seek to treat the two equally. An anthracite coal workers' strike in May 1902 gave him a chance to test out his ideas and leadership style. When the mine owners refused to negotiate, and it appeared that the country might head into a long, cold winter with a paralyzed coal industry, Roosevelt threatened to send in the army to operate the mines. Asked whether such an act would be constitutional, Roosevelt replied, "To hell with the Constitution when the people want coal!" The stewardship theory in action! But it worked, and the strike was soon settled.

Roosevelt was not eager to use the antitrust powers under the Sherman Act and did not seek to legislate further such powers. Although he has always had a reputation in American folklore as a "trust buster," that characterization is not entirely accurate. Roosevelt in fact tended to favor the consolidationist approach to regulation, a preference that would grow stronger over the years of his presidency. He did use his antitrust powers, as in the Northern Securities case, against what he regarded as "bad" trusts, those that, in his view, had abused their monopoly powers. "Good" trusts were left unmolested. How to decide between the good and the bad? It would be the responsibility of the executive branch of the national government, operating through the Bureau of Corporations in the new Department of Commerce and Labor, to decide which was which. Henceforth the government, TR said, must be "the senior partner in every business" – a stunning change to the most fundamental American conceptions about the relationship between business and government.

After winning election in his own right by a large margin in the 1904 presidential contest, Roosevelt stepped up his campaign for railroad regulation. After a bruising legislative battle, he managed in 1906 to get Congress to pass the Hepburn Act, which gave the Interstate Commerce Commission the power, for the first time, actually to set "just and reasonable" railroad rates as well as giving it power over bridges, ferries, and terminals.

Two other areas in which Roosevelt's second term had notable accomplishments were consumer protection and conservation, two issues that had never much concerned previous presidents. Activity in the first area was occasioned directly by the fierce public outcry stirred up by the writer Upton Sinclair's disturbing exposé of the meat-packing industry, a novel called *The Jungle* (1906). That same year saw two pieces of legislation passed in rapid response: the Pure Food and Drug Act banned the manufacture and sale of impure or fraudulent food and drugs, while the Meat Inspection Act provided that federal inspectors would visit meat-packing plants to ensure that meat shipped in interstate commerce met minimum standards of sanitation and came from healthy animals.

Conservation of natural resources was the second area of significant activity, and conservation soon became one of Roosevelt's signature concerns, forever thereafter associated with his name. Roosevelt was an outdoorsman, and his experiences in the Dakotas gave him a keen appreciation of the open spaces of the American West – and a concern that their wild and natural qualities be preserved as much as possible. He saw this preservation as a moral imperative: "We have fallen heirs to the most glorious heritage a people ever received," he said, "and each one must do his part if we wish to show that the nation is worthy of its good fortune." The nation's natural beauty could be thought of as a great common trust, one in dire need of benevolent protection and regulation to keep it whole and sound for generations to come. The scientific management of natural resources, such as forests and waterways, would be yet another opportunity for Progressive principles to bring order to what they feared was in danger of becoming chaotic and wasteful.

Roosevelt responded to this moral imperative with a wide array of actions. He established the U.S. Forest Service, signed into law the creation of five national parks, and signed the 1906 Antiquities Act, under which he proclaimed eighteen new U.S. national monuments. He also established the first 51 bird reserves, 4 game preserves, and 150 national forests, including Shoshone National Forest, the nation's first. The total area of the United States that he placed under federal control was approximately 230 million acres.

Roosevelt was said to be prouder of these measures than of anything else he ever did, and they certainly have brought him great honor in subsequent generations. Roosevelt and his friend Gifford Pinchot, the first head of the Forest Service, insisted on the careful stewardship of the land, with the needs of future generations always in mind. They are better understood as conservationists, then, rather than preservationists. As good Progressives, they sought to conserve nature for the sake of ongoing human benefit, striking a balance between exploiting nature heedlessly, on one hand, and treating it as sacred, on the other.

Not all agreed, as can be illustrated by their dispute with the naturalist John Muir, founder of the Sierra Club, over the creation of a water reservoir at Hetch Hetchy Valley in Yosemite National Park. Roosevelt and Pinchot favored the human needs of the city of San Francisco over the ideal of pristine nature that Muir favored. "The delight of the few men and women who would yearly go into the Hetch Hetchy Valley," said Pinchot, "should not outweigh the conservation policy, [which is] to take every part of the land and its resources and put it to that use in which it will serve the most people." Muir fired back, lambasting the two men as "temple destroyers" with "a perfect contempt for Nature," who, "instead of lifting their eyes to the God of the mountains, lift them to the Almighty Dollar." The dispute would echo through the century to come, even as the Hetch Hetchy Reservoir would became the principal source of water for the city of San Francisco.

By the end of 1907, buoyed by his successes and anxiously eyeing the imminent end of his term as president, Roosevelt turned up the heat even more and began calling for even more reforms, such as income and inheritance taxes, federal controls over the stock market, and stricter regulation of interstate corporations, among other things. His rhetoric also became notably more strident, as he denounced the "malefactors of great wealth" for their "predatory" behavior. Such proposals and such rhetoric still fell far short of a socialist vision, but they were strident enough to antagonize the conservative "Old Guard" of the Republican Party and ensure that the last months of TR's administration would not be very productive, even though his popularity remained high. Once out of office, TR immediately stormed off to Africa for a nearly yearlong expedition that combined game hunting with specimen-gathering for the Smithsonian Institution and the American Museum of Natural History.

Roosevelt chose William Howard Taft as his successor, based partly on his success in the Philippines and his loyal support for the Square Deal and Roosevelt's presidency. Taft easily won election in 1908 over William Jennings Bryan, who was taking a third unsuccessful run at the presidential office as the Democratic candidate. But Taft quickly turned out to have been an unsatisfactory choice in Roosevelt's eyes, being much more comfortable in the traditional Republican mold than the Progressive one. Although he dutifully tried to continue most of Roosevelt's policies, and in fact was far more of a trust buster than Roosevelt himself had been, he lacked Roosevelt's vigor and leadership ability and had deep qualms about Roosevelt's use of executive authority, which Taft regarded as bordering on illegality. Ultimately, he was not a Progressive at heart. And when he made the mistake of firing Gifford Pinchot over a controversy between Pinchot and Taft's interior secretary, a move that was seen as a betrayal of TR's conservation agenda, it was only a matter of time before Roosevelt turned against him.

It soon became clear that this was not just a personal squabble. The

Republican Party was dividing between its Old Guard and its Progressives, and Taft and Roosevelt were coming to represent the two factions. Not long after his return from Africa, Roosevelt delivered an important speech in Osawatomie, Kansas, in which he put forward a comprehensive plan for sweeping social legislation, which he called the New Nationalism. Invoking the memory of the Civil War and the Grand Army of the Republic, Roosevelt called for a Grand Review–like devotion to the ideal of the nation itself as the source and object of all loyalties. And he emphasized that it was futile to prevent large industrial combinations; the better path forward lay in "completely controlling them." More ominously for a great many old-line Republicans, Roosevelt began to talk enthusiastically about instituting new means of amending the Constitution much more easily – in effect, by majority vote, thus making an end run around the complex process laid out in the Constitution. He was eventually coaxed into standing for the Republican nomination.

Roosevelt failed to get the nomination, however, as Taft and his loyalists went all out to control the Republican Party convention in Chicago and defeat him. Disgusted Progressive supporters of Roosevelt walked out and formed the Progressive Party to support Roosevelt as an independent candidate. Roosevelt did not need much persuading; the cause was all-important, and he loved a good fight. "We stand at Armageddon," he cried, "and battle for the Lord!" The Progressive Party convention, also held in Chicago, was suffused with such openly religious rhetoric, and with the singing of songs like "Onward Christian Soldiers," as Roosevelt presented a "confession of faith" that included all of the classic Progressive regulatory reforms as counters to the "invisible government" of the special interests.

Meanwhile, the Democratic Party, meeting in Baltimore, took forty-six ballots to nominate Woodrow Wilson, a relatively unknown former professor of political science and president of Princeton University, the sum total of whose political experience was two years served as governor of New Jersey. On the central issue of regulation, Wilson was a convert to Progressivism, but of the antitrust variety. He came to call his platform the New Freedom, in deliberate contrast to Roosevelt's New Nationalism. The government should break up the great trusts, he argued, and establish the rule by which business should conduct itself, eliminate privileges of special interests, and then stand aside to allow renewed competition and free enterprise to assert themselves.

A tall, slender man with the angular face and overbearing manner of a tightly wound schoolmaster, Wilson may have lacked for political experience, but he did not lack for self-confidence. He had thought and written extensively about American government and was brimming over with ideas for reform. To begin with, he was, like Roosevelt, convinced that the U.S. Constitution was defective and inadequate. He favored something closer to the British parliamentary system, which would draw the executive and legislative branches together more closely and make the president as active in the legislative process as in the execution of the laws. In other words, like Roosevelt, he favored a very strong presidency. He found the constitutional system of checks and balances intolerably inefficient and complained that it diffused responsibility for errors and misdeeds: as he expressed it in his book *Congressional Government*, "how is the schoolmaster, the nation, to know which boy needs the whipping?"

Above all else, he thought that American government should be built on a more fluid and organically evolving basis rather than being tied to unchanging formal directives and protocols such as those contained in the Constitution. Governments arise to address the needs of their particular epoch and must be free constantly to adapt, just as Darwin had showed that the nature of organic life must constantly evolve in response to changes in climate and habitat. "Government does now," he remarked in his book *The State*, "whatever experience permits or the times demand." Even the natural-rights doctrines of human equality and fundamental rights stated in the Declaration of Independence were subject to this counterdoctrine of fluidity: "We are not bound to adhere to the doctrines held by the signers of the Declaration of Independence," he insisted in a 1907 speech. "We are as free as they were to make and unmake governments."

Wilson also thought and wrote extensively about the field of "public administration," a field of study that he helped to create. Wilson understood *administration* to denote the actual executive function of government, which he, being a typical Progressive, wanted to make ever more efficient. One way of doing so was to acknowledge that "administration lies outside the proper sphere of politics," that it was indeed something quite distinct from politics, and that one should seek to separate the two as much as possible. Administration was the sphere of scientific expertise, operating independently of the hurly-burly of everyday politics and above the winds of changing opinion. This separation is highly reminiscent of the separation envisioned by the city-manager system of municipal governance or by a highly professionalized and independent civil service. As such, it is a classic example of Progressive thinking.

Thus the stage was set for one of the more dramatic elections in American history, the only time so far in which a third-party candidate, Roosevelt, had a genuine chance to win. In the end, the split in the Republican Party was fatal to the chances of both Roosevelt and Taft, and Wilson was able to win easily, running up a commanding margin in the Electoral College (435 to 88 for Roosevelt and a mere 8 for Taft). It is worth noting one of the most extraordinary features of the election: that two of the three major candidates in the election were strongly Progressive and reformist in their sentiments; and if one adds the surprisingly strong nine hundred thousand votes for Eugene Debs, the Socialist candidate, we can say that of the fifteen million votes cast, eleven and a half million of them were for strongly reformist candidates. The public sentiment in favor of Progressive ideas and candidates was at high tide.

Once elected, Wilson went on, despite his inexperience, to enjoy one of the most impressive beginnings of any president in American history. Ever the activist, he moved quickly, putting his theories about a parliamentary-style presidency to the test. First he sought to lower tariffs, thereby fulfilling a campaign promise and, to compensate for revenues that would be lost by this change, introduced a bill creating a federal income tax, drawing upon the newly ratified Sixteenth Amendment to the Constitution. Then he proposed the Federal Reserve Act, which provided the country with a central banking system for the first time since Jackson's destruction of the Bank of the United States. The creation of a system of regional reserve banks gave activist government a key lever that could be used to regulate elements of the national economy. Finally, he enhanced the government's capacity for trust busting, using the newly strengthened Federal Trade Commission as its institutional home for such activity.

There were many other reforms in his first term: advances in labor organizing, creation of a system of federal farmland banks, a Federal Highways Act to stimulate road construction, child labor laws, an eight-hour workday for rail workers: in short, a dazzling array of legislative and executive accomplishment. In addition, the ratification in 1913 of the Sixteenth and Seventeenth Amendments, the latter being a measure to establish that senators be chosen by the direct election of the people and not by the respective state legislatures, seemed to betoken the dawning of a new and more streamlined, more efficient, more nationalized era. As he went, Wilson seemed more and more to shed the ideas of the New Freedom on which he had campaigned and to act in a way indistinguishable from the New Nationalism. In any event, it was a moment when Progressivism seemed triumphant.

Two serious concerns about the record of Progressivism remained and would reflect problems bedeviling the country in later years. First, as has already been mentioned, Progressivism generally tended to be indifferent to the plight of minorities, and in the case of black Americans living under the presidency of Woodrow Wilson, that indifference was closer to hostility. Here the contrast with Roosevelt is worth noting. Roosevelt was no crusader for racial justice, but his record was generally respectable, and he had expended considerable political capital in, for example, inviting Booker T. Washington, a leading black intellectual and educator, to the White House. Wilson, on the other hand, was a

Virginian who supported racial segregation and sympathized with the postbellum restoration of white rule in the South. He should, of course, be judged upon the totality of his record. But those facts about his views have to be considered as a part of that totality.

The second troubling problem is not unrelated to the first, and that was the Progressives' growing tendency to disparage the Declaration of Independence and the Constitution and their readiness to embrace radical changes in the very structure of the latter. It is always a temptation for well-meaning reformers to want to set aside the cumbersome restrictions that the rule of law places upon them. But Abraham Lincoln had built his entire presidency upon resisting any such temptation. He believed the preservation of those two foundational documents was essential to the enduring success of any serious attempts to reform American society. One can well understand the impatience that tugged at both Roosevelt and Wilson as they sought to address themselves vigorously to the titanic problems of their era. But it could prove a perilous matter to launch into a great project of national self-improvement while setting aside the two chief sources of American political continuity and moral guidance. G. K. Chesterton enunciated an important principle of reform: before you tear down a fence, be sure you first fully understand the use that the fence was erected to serve.

In any event, Progressivism's moment of unquestioned triumph was destined not to last much longer. Wilson had enjoyed phenomenal success in promoting his Progressive domestic agenda. That success was about to be tested in the larger and more unforgiving arena of world politics.

CHAPTER FIFTEEN

WOODROW WILSON AND THE GREAT WAR

THE FIRST WORLD WAR DESCENDED UPON EUROPE IN SUMMER 1914 like a violent thunderstorm shattering the stillness of a peaceful night. Or so it seemed to Americans, who had been paying little attention to the ominous rumblings in Morocco and the Balkans and other distant and obscure trouble spots of the world. They had other things on their minds. The conflict seemed to them a strictly European matter – so much so that it reminded them of why they'd wanted America to be a nation apart in the first place.

But Americans were not the only ones to find the war's origins to be tangled and incomprehensible. Nor were they the only ones to find that the nightmarish ferocity with which the war would be fought, using weapons of unparalleled destructiveness and cruelty, seemed out of proportion to the ambiguity of the war's causes and the vagueness of its purposes. So did many of their European contemporaries. What did it all mean, this breathtaking act of civilizational self-immolation? Surely if the Great War was a pivotal event in history, there had to be a self-evident explanation of where it was coming from and where it was going.

But some of the greatest events in human history are also among the most unfathomable. Today, more than a century later, there is no clear consensus among historians about the deepest causes of this devastating conflict that changed Europe and the world forever, ending a long period of unparalleled optimism and confidence and replacing it with persistent anxiety and doubt about the very idea of progress itself. Even today, the world has not fully absorbed and digested it all.

We can venture some generalizations, however. Ever since the unification of Germany in 1871 in the wake of the Franco-Prussian War, the balance of power among the great states of Europe had been in flux. All of the other great European powers had been expanding, competing all over the world for resources, for markets, for imperial acquisitions, for military eminence, for diplomatic advantage, for national prestige – and now a newly empowered Germany would be joining the field of contestants. This ceaseless jostling for advantage had given rise to an elaborate and shifting system of alliances, some of which were secret or contained secret clauses and all of which had been concluded principally for reasons of national security and mutual assistance in the event of an attack on the country or its colonial assets. By 1914, the great states of Europe had sorted themselves into two alliance blocs, the Triple Entente (Great Britain, France, and Russia) and the Triple Alliance (Germany, Austria-Hungary, and Italy). No one had planned it that way, and it was a tense and intrinsically dangerous situation.

The trouble began on the peripheries, in disorganized southeastern Europe. There the Ottoman Empire, long the dominant power in the region, was in the process of disintegrating after years of steady decline, leaving the whole region, and particularly the Balkan territories, in a state of confusion and insecurity. Among other sources of tension, the kingdom of Serbia was at odds with Austria-Hungary over the status of Bosnia, and more generally over the status of the Slavic peoples in the region, whose cause Serbia wanted to champion. It was in connection with this controversy that, on June 28, 1914, the Archduke Franz Ferdinand, heir to the Austrian throne, was assassinated in the Bosnian capital of Sarajevo by a Bosnian revolutionary who was associated with a Serbian nationalist organization.

This act of terrorism, though certainly serious and shocking, would seem at first glance to have had only minor regional significance. But it turned out to be the catalyst that set into motion all the treaty obligations that had tightly bound together all of the major nations of Europe. Within a few weeks, nearly all of them were at war. First Austria avenged itself on Serbia; then Russia as leader of the Slavic world came to the aid of the Serbians by opposing the Austrians; then Germany fulfilled its obligations to Austria by declaring war on Russia and France; then Britain declared war on Germany and Austria, Japan joined the alliance against Germany, and Turkey joined up with the Triple Alliance, now known as the Central Powers. (Italy managed to stay aloof and later joined up with the Allied powers, as the Triple Entente would become known.)

It was a royal mess, like a game of toppling and exploding dominoes. But the most important industrial power in the world quickly announced its unwillingness to take part in the game. The president of the United States, consciously following in the tradition of Washington and Jefferson, issued a solemn Declaration of Neutrality on August 4 and instructed the nation to remain impartial "in thought, as well as action" with respect to this unfolding conflict. Woodrow Wilson well understood that most of the inhabitants of his country could trace their ancestry back to one or another of the belligerent parties and that it was "natural and inevitable" that they should have their respective sympathies. But that only led him to impart to the speech a slightly threatening tone, directed at anyone who would presume to "excite passions" for one side or the other. His speech was meant as "a solemn word of warning" to such people, that they would "assume a heavy responsibility" in speaking out in such a manner. America was going to stay as far away from Europe as possible.

This hardly seemed to matter at first, because this war, like the American Civil War, was anticipated to be a brief one. As with the Civil War, that turned out not to be the case. Instead, it intensified quickly, fueled by the illusion that it could be ended quickly with a master stroke, and soon spun out of control, descending to levels of hellish mayhem and mass slaughter that were almost surreal in their enormity. Even more than the Civil War, this fitted the definition of total war. It would be a war in which the most civilized nations of the world introduced the commonplace use of terrifying weapons of war that had never been seen on such a scale, if ever at all: machine guns, poison gas, armored tanks, aerial bombing, flame throwers, land mines, and powerful long-range artillery, capable of reaching targets dozens of miles away (the Germans' "Paris gun" had a range of up to eighty-one miles).

On the Western front, things stalemated quickly and devolved into the squalid misery of trench warfare, through which it seemed nothing, not even tanks and poison gas, could effect a breakthrough. Attempts in 1916 to strike decisive blows escalated to unimaginable levels of bloodshed, achieving only inconclusive outcomes. In a battle near the small French city of Verdun, an unsuccessful German attack led to upward of a million casualties among the two sides combined. On the first day alone of the Allied offensive in the Battle of the Somme, on July 1, 1916, twenty thousand British soldiers were killed and forty thousand were wounded – the single worst day in the history of the British Army. When that battle finally ended in November, after 140 days of combat, the British Army (including Commonwealth members) had suffered 420,000 casualties, the French 200,000, and the Germans an estimated 500,000–600,000 – and the results seemed to have made little difference.

These numbers were, and are, almost too appalling to comprehend, as are the innumerable stories of woundings, mutilations, and shattered souls wrought by the war. And, from an American's point of view, to what end? Who could articulate the war's goals in a way that would explain, let alone justify, such carnage? Small wonder that most Americans wanted no part of this war, and Wilson's policy of neutrality was correspondingly popular. The divided sympathies of Americans provided yet another motivation to keep the country officially neutral, if at all possible, as long as possible, and to downplay these national divisions – even if a "warning" to remain neutral in "thought" seemed rather a lot to ask.

The policy of neutrality toward all belligerent parties would founder in the end, for the same reason it foundered in the time of the Napoleonic wars. The United States wanted to be able to trade with all parties, relying upon respect for the principle of "freedom of the seas" to protect its shipping. But such a policy had the effect of denying the British the full benefit of their superior naval power and would thereby in effect favor the Germans. The British could never agree to that. In fact, under these circumstances, nothing the Americans did could ever be completely impartial. That became even more clear when the United States began to allow American bankers to lend money to the Allies to enable them to continue purchasing the goods they needed to continue fighting the war.

Eventually, the Germans settled on a different tactic to challenge the Allies' control of the seas. They would unleash their submarine fleet to go after Allied shipping, launching their torpedoes without warning at merchant targets, including ships flying neutral flags. They announced this policy in February 1915, adding that any ship entering the war zone around the British Isles did so at its own risk. Wilson countered indignantly, declaring this policy to be "an indefensible violation of neutral rights" and warning that he would hold the Germans to "strict accountability" if anything were to happen to Americans' lives or property as a result of any such violations of neutral rights.

Then the inevitable happened: the sinking by a German torpedo of the British liner *Lusitania* on May 7, 1915, off the Irish coast, with a loss of 1,200 lives, including 128 Americans. The American public reacted to this incident with understandable outrage, and Wilson was forced to find a way to back up his earlier tough talk, without either leading the nation off the cliff into war or losing the respect of an angry public that might find him too passive in defending American interests and national pride. He stopped short of delivering an ultimatum but demanded that the Germans disavow their actions and indemnify the victims. Eventually he got his way, with the Germans pledging to stop targeting merchant and passenger ships, and so the issues subsided for the time being.

This careful finessing of these difficult issues paid him great dividends when it came to his reelection effort in fall 1916. He would need them, because he would be running against a reunited Republican Party, which fully expected to be able to resume its customary majority. To thwart them, he would need to find a way to move in opposite directions at once: both toward preparedness and away from war.

The *Lusitania* affair had contributed to a growing consensus among a wide range of Americans that a heightened and improved level of military preparedness was now an imperative task for the nation. After some resistance, Wilson himself was won over to this point of view and persuaded Congress to pass legislation to increase the size of the army to a (still very small) 175,000 and authorize the construction of some fifty new warships in the coming year. This buildup would help his campaign effort. But his major selling point in the fall election would be his commitment to keeping the United States from becoming a belligerent party and his success so far in making that policy work. "He kept us out of war!" became the Democrats' campaign slogan, and it spoke, simply and eloquently, to the gravest concern on the minds of voters.

Wilson won the election, running against Republican Charles Evans Hughes, a Supreme Court justice and former New York governor, who turned out to be a weak candidate with poor campaigning skills. But even so, Wilson did not win easily or commandingly. In fact, he won in a squeaker, carrying several crucial states by only the barest of margins. In California, for example, a state where Hughes committed a costly campaign gaffe, Wilson managed to win by only thirty-eight hundred votes out of a million cast; had the state's thirteen electoral votes gone to Hughes, so would have the election. Such an unimpressive victory by an incumbent president might well have been taken as a harbinger of problems ahead.

Wilson seemed undismayed, however, and with his characteristic self-confidence, he immediately launched into yet another effort to mediate a settlement to the war in Europe. He had tried this before, back in 1915, and had sent one of his chief aides to leaders in Paris, London, and Berlin, but with nothing to show for it. This time, he would step into the situation more personally and assert American moral leadership. First he sent a note to the belligerents, asking them to state the terms that they would need to have met to consider the possibility of a cease-fire. When he received an underwhelming response, he was not content to stop there. The next step would be something bold, even audacious.

On January 22, 1917, speaking to the U.S. Senate, Wilson gave an extraordinary speech, which he directed, not to the Senate itself, and even less to the leaders of the belligerent nations, but to "the *people* of the countries now at war." It was a classic Progressive move, a direct democratic entreaty, in which an empowered president, circumventing the constitutional "middlemen," appealed directly to – and spoke for – the populace itself.

Wilson began by stating that it was time to lay the foundations for peace, before the belligerents destroyed themselves utterly in the dogged continuation of such a brutal and wasting war, and that "it is inconceivable that the people of the United States should play no part in that great enterprise." But the settlement, he insisted, would have to be a "peace without victory," one that sought not just a new balance of power but a "just and secure peace ... a community of power," built upon the principles of democratic governance, the consent of the governed, the freedom of the seas, "moderation of armaments," and avoidance of entangling alliances in favor of a more general structure expressive of the "common interest."

Wilson was offering a first glimpse of visionary themes that he would be promoting more directly and explicitly in the years ahead. It was also a first glimpse of the *way* he would interject himself: not as a fellow combatant but as a force and authority standing above the mere combatants, like the schoolmaster descending upon the playground quarrels and breaking them up. But the world's reception of his words on this occasion would be cut short by decisions already made two weeks before he spoke. The Germans had decided that they would roll the dice and elect to undertake unrestricted submarine warfare of the most brutal and uncompromising variety. Eight days after Wilson's speech, the new policy was announced: beginning the next day, February 1, 1917, any and all ships in the war zone were vulnerable to being sunk without warning. So much for the freedom of the seas.

It was a roll of the dice because the Germans knew that they were now risking the likelihood of American entry into the war. But they took the risk, hoping for a quick and decisive blow and for a hesitant and balky mobilization on the American side. The resistance of Congress to Wilson's proposal for authorizing arms and measures to protect merchant vessels was an indication that the Germans might have guessed right. But the German tactics were not helped by the discovery of the Zimmerman Telegram, a message from the German foreign minister to his ambassador in Mexico, asking him to propose an alliance with the Mexican government. The idea was that, assuming the Americans entered the war, it would be helpful to have Mexican military actions divert the attention and resources of the Americans, in exchange for which the Mexicans would get back the territories lost in the Mexican War. This conniving naturally inflamed the American public, yet even that was still not enough to lead them to embrace war.

But the sinking of five unarmed U.S. merchant vessels in the first weeks of March was enough. Wilson was now ready to ask for a declaration of war, and did so on April 2, in a speech that decried Germany's submarine policy as "warfare against mankind" and declared that "the world must be made safe for democracy." It was lucky for Wilson that the Russian Tsarist regime had fallen to a democratic revolution just a few days earlier; this meant that he could couch the Allied cause in the purest and most lofty terms, as an effort undertaken by the world's democracies. The basis on which America entered the war would be different and more idealistic. "We act without animus," he asserted, "not in enmity towards a people or with the desire to bring any injury or disadvantage upon them, but only in armed opposition to an irresponsible government which has thrown aside all considerations of humanity and of right and is running amuck." On April 6, an overwhelming majority of Congress agreed and voted yes.

Now came the hard work of mobilization, which had to be accomplished quickly if Germany's gamble were to be thwarted. The race was on between American preparation and the knockout blow Germany hoped to administer. That mobilization was no small task, because the country was still monumentally unprepared for a war it had so ardently hoped to avoid. An army had to be raised, naval ships built, materiel produced, logistical problems mastered, food and munitions shipped to Allies in Europe. Because this was a total war, the entire economy would have to be mobilized and its elements coordinated to meet the blistering tempo that the circumstances demanded. In addition, there would need to be conscription to meet ambitious personnel goals, which would soon swell into the millions. It was a moment for "all hands on deck," and Wilson proved to be an excellent wartime leader, once he had accepted the fact that war was unavoidable.

The needs of mobilization created a plethora of wartime government agencies. The War Industries Board (WIB), led by the charming and debonair South Carolina–born Wall Street speculator Bernard Baruch, was the most important of these. The WIB was granted awesome powers. It set production quotas and allocated raw materials, encouraging companies to use mass-production techniques and product standardization to increase efficiency and decrease waste. It settled labor-management disputes resulting from increased demand for products, negotiating wages and prices and regulating strikes to prevent a shortage of supplies going to Europe. Under the WIB, industrial production increased a phenomenal 20 percent. For Progressives, it was exhibit A in illustrating the benefits a top-down coordination of the economy could bring.

Everywhere one looked, a bureaucracy was in charge of a sector of the economy. Herbert Hoover, an international mining engineer, took charge of the Food Administration, which encouraged wheat production and devised an effective voluntary food-conservation plan that avoided the need for rationing. The Fuel Administration undertook similar efforts to save coal, including the institution of Daylight Saving Time. The Railroad Administration took control of the coordination of rail traffic, and the National War Labor Board, headed by William Howard Taft, arbitrated disputes between workers and employers.

With nearly four million able-bodied men leaving the workforce for military service at its peak, even as the industrial economy was gearing up for accelerated wartime production, there would soon be a desperate shortage of workers at home. This hardship became a great opportunity for African Americans from the Deep South states, who were actively recruited by agents from northern firms and persuaded to migrate north in huge numbers – nearly half a million in five years – to take jobs in the war industries in cities like St. Louis, Detroit, and Chicago. Women too were recruited in significant numbers for unprecedented work in factories, machine shops, lumberyards, and railway crews. The war was creating a whole new domestic workforce.

The Wilson administration sought to do what it could to direct and uplift national morale, which meant having the ability to influence public opinion. Maintenance of public morale was yet another element in the comprehensive demands of total war; it was important that the public be brought to "think properly." This was a factor to which Wilson, as a former teacher, was acutely attuned, and it led him to form, immediately after the outset of war, the Committee on Public Information, headed by journalist George Creel from Denver. The Creel Committee went on to organize what was essentially a propaganda machine to drum up support for the war effort, using hundreds of speakers, including movie stars, artists, writers, and celebrity performers, to promote the sale of Liberty Bonds, food conservation, and other important elements of federal war policy. The committee supported the creation of films, posters, pamphlets, and the like that conveyed to the American people the worthiness of the war effort and the importance of their support for it. Each citizen got the message: you had to "do your bit."

The effort was a mixed blessing. Certainly it was important to try to establish as much national consensus as possible in support of American entry into the war. Certainly there was a strong case to be made for it. And yet, in presenting the war to the public as a crusade for democracy and freedom, speakers often in the process resorted to depicting the German people in a luridly negative way. A 1918 film called *The Kaiser, the Beast of Berlin* suggests the tone, as did the American Protective League's campaign slogan "Hate the Hun." There were stories in circulation of German savagery in the invasion of Belgium, including the wanton slaughter of children. German Americans found themselves under siege, irrespective of their views or their sympathies. Sauerkraut became "liberty cabbage," and symphonies refused to perform the music of German composers, such as Johann Sebastian Bach or Ludwig van Beethoven.

Even though the emphasis on propaganda was meant to sidestep the need for censorship and suppression, Wilson's desire to control thought and expression won out over such attitudes in his intolerance of dissidents who openly opposed the war and war-related policies. Two pieces of legislation had the effect of outlawing such dissent. The Espionage Act of 1917 prescribed fines and jail sentences for persons convicted of aiding the enemy or of obstructing recruitment for the draft. The Sedition Act of 1918 went even further, prohibiting anyone to "utter, print, write, or publish any disloyal, profane, scurrilous, or abusive language" about the government, the Constitution, or the armed forces. More than a thousand people were convicted under these two acts, including Eugene Debs, who was sentenced to ten years in prison for advocating resistance to conscription. Such convictions were upheld by the Supreme Court in *Schenck v. United States* (1919), in which Justice Oliver Wendell Holmes Jr. famously declared that the doctrine of free speech would not protect a man falsely shouting "fire" in a theater or in other incidents in which such speech presents a "clear and present danger."

Did Wilson overreact? Quite possibly so. The balance between maintaining protections for robust civil rights and precious personal liberties, on one hand, and seeing to the security needs of the nation in a time of war or other international conflict, on the other, has always been a difficult balance to strike. Thinking back to the Alien and Sedition Acts in the John Adams administration, it may even be the case that such overreaction may be a constant peril. That said, Wilson seemed to have an impatience with dissent and a reluctance to pay attention to contrary points of view, let alone compromise with them. That feature of his character would work against him in some of his most consequential decisions to come.

Progressive intellectuals and politicians had been very resistant to the war, but once it was under way, they began to warm to it. They believed that war was pulling the nation together, creating a sense of common purpose and national solidarity that would enable the conquest of social evils and the fostering of a deeper and more lasting sense of community. In short, it was achieving some of the very things that Progressives most earnestly coveted. Many looked to an influential 1910 essay by the late American philosopher William James, called "The Moral Equivalent of War," as way of thinking about the issue. James wondered if it would be possible to identify a shared objective that could elicit the same willingness to sacrifice for the whole, and the same disciplined ethos, as military conflict does – and yet direct that willingness and discipline toward entirely peaceful purposes.

Such a substitute would be the holy grail for Progressives. From Edward Bellamy's captivating vision of America in *Looking Backward* as a marching industrial army to present-day attempts to cast economic, social, public health, or environmental problems as the moral equivalents of war, the linkage of war imagery with the cause of social reform has popped up too often in the history of reform to be dismissed as a fluke. From a Progressive perspective, it speaks to a deep problem, one central to the successful operation of any free society. How can a liberal political culture, one grounded ultimately in the free consent of rights-bearing individuals, nevertheless be capable of purposeful public action when circumstances call for it? How can pluralistic societies find ways of marshaling their resources for great public exertions? How can they elicit from their citizens the acts of discipline and self-denial that are necessary to achieve such public goals? If not through the catalyzing effect of some crisis, preferably one that presents itself as the moral equivalent of war, then how is a nation of disorganized and separate units going to learn to act in concert?

This understanding of the problem, in turn, goes back to a fundamental conflict that we have already seen, between the centralizing, consolidating, harmonizing ideas at the center of Progressive thought and the competitive idea at the heart of the Constitution, which involved the channeling of conflict itself, through checks and balances, separation of powers, and other structures that protected against the dangers of concentrated power, and better suited the fallibility of the human condition. More importantly, it raised the question of whether there can be *any* equivalent to war, and if not, whether there was danger in using war as a guiding metaphor for distinctly different tasks of social organization.

The Germans' program of unrestricted submarine warfare started having its intended effect almost immediately. In the month of April 1917 alone, nearly one million tons of Allied shipping was sunk. The Germans also got a lucky break when a second successful Russian Revolution, this one carried out by the Bolshevik Communists under Vladimir Lenin's leadership, led to Russia's dropping out of the war completely and concluding a separate peace with the Germans, which in turn freed the Germans to redeploy their military resources to the Western front. The danger mounted that the American rescue effort would not arrive in time.

But good things were happening on the other side. The building of warships to serve as convoy escorts for oceangoing merchant vessels was proceeding at a rapid clip and having a notable effect by end of 1917. By April 1918, losses of Allied merchant shipping were down to under three hundred thousand tons, a large but manageable amount. Amazingly, the transporting of American troops across the ocean was managed without the loss of a single serviceman.

Moreover, the entry of the Americans into the war effort was a huge psychological boost to the exhausted Allies, who were depleted in resources but even more depleted in spirit. The injection of American energy and optimism, as expressed in the exuberant chorus of the popular song "Over There," written by the Irish American composer George M. Cohan, was of incalculable importance. The words were directed at American audiences, but their message could not have been more welcome to the bone-weary Allies as well:

> *Over there, over there,*
> *Send the word, send the word over there*
> *That the Yanks are coming, the Yanks are coming*
> *The drums rum-tumming everywhere.*
> *So prepare, say a prayer,*
> *Send the word, send the word to beware –*
> *We'll be over, we're coming over,*
> *And we won't come back till it's over, over there.*

If the Americans could be as good as their word, they could bring the great European nightmare to a close. But time was short. French premier Georges Clemenceau pleaded to a journalist, with clipped understatement, "Tell your Americans to come quickly."

The American Expeditionary Force (AEF) under General John J. Pershing did just that, arriving in Paris on July 4, 1917, as a kind of quick-deployment advance guard. Interestingly, Pershing did not yield any authority over his forces to his Allied counterparts but insisted on maintaining command of his troops as independent units. This insistence echoed Wilson's larger policy toward his cobelligerents, whom he never referred to as "allies" but instead as "associates." Such diction may have sounded a bit standoffish, but it faithfully reflected Wilson's desire that the American motive for involvement in the war be understood by all as a matter of an entirely different order than that of the belligerent nations. "We desire no conquest, no dominion," he declared. "We are but one of the champions of the rights of mankind." Wilson's America was not trying to get in on the spoils of war; he insisted that it had no such lowly or self-interested goals. And the claim was entirely credible.

As it turned out, the American "doughboys" did not see significant action until spring 1918, when the last big German assault came, fortified by masses of German soldiers transferred over from the Russian front. They enjoyed success at first and, by late May, had reached Château-Thierry on the Marne River, only fifty miles from Paris. But a successful counterattack by the AEF in early June drove the Germans back from Château-Thierry and Belleau Wood – small victories, but with a huge effect on Allied morale, because the victories provided a strong indication that the Americans might well be able to make the hoped-for difference.

In successive engagements, the Americans became more and more deeply involved, in greater and greater numbers. Finally, in late September, more than a million American troops drove west from blood-soaked Verdun along the Meuse River and then through the Argonne Forest. For a month of grisly, terrifying battle, the Americans crawled and slashed through the Argonne – rough, hilly terrain that the Germans had spent the past four years fortifying – while the French and British armies pushed against the Germans to the west, driving them back toward the German border. Finally, the Americans broke through on November 1, and the French Fourth Army was allowed the honor of recapturing Sedan (the site of a humiliating French defeat in the Franco-Prussian War). The Germans were forced to surrender and sign an armistice on November 11 – the day Americans now celebrate as Veterans Day.

It was over at last, but the extent of the losses and devastation was almost beyond comprehension. The Americans had suffered "only" 117,000 dead and 230,000 wounded, and of those deaths, only 53,000 were combat deaths; most of the others were from disease. But these numbers were tiny compared to the losses of other belligerent nations. The British Commonwealth death toll stood at nearly 1 million; the French 1.4 million, the Russian 1.7 million; the Italian 460,000; the German 1.8 million; the Austrian-Hungarian 1.2 million; and the Turkish 325,000. The total number of military and civilian casualties combined has been reliably estimated at about forty million, about 10 percent of Europe's entire population in 1900.

This was a pivotal moment for the European world. A decisive victory had been won, but in its wake came immense confusion, instability, and displacement; widespread starvation and deprivation; and fear for the future. Such were the fruits of a war that was supposed to end all wars. A huge portion of an entire generation of young men across the nations of Europe had been lost, with untold effects rippling through the lives of countless families, villages, and towns. The war had brought the collapse of four empires – Imperial Germany, Austria-Hungary, Tsarist Russia, and the Ottoman Empire – and would necessitate a redrawing of the map of Europe. It had also left behind an intense desire for vengeance as well as a widespread feeling of disillusionment and revulsion with the regimes that had survived. With communism on the rise in Russia, there was a militant ideology at large in the world that offered itself as a radical alternative, threatening to sweep all of Europe's corrupt and disintegrating bourgeois society aside in favor of a radical new international order such as the world had never seen.

Woodrow Wilson grasped all of this. He understood the gravity of the historical moment and brought to it an alternative vision to the task of postwar settlement – a vision that he believed could ensure that the Allied powers' costly victory would not turn out to have been in vain. And he was willing and eager to be the instrument by which that vision came to be reality. He had been busily consulting with experts in various fields about the optimal course of action to take when the time came to negotiate the peace treaty. He hoped that the resulting plan, his Fourteen Points, would be his most important achievement. His goal was the fashioning of a wholly new international order, a world "fit and safe to live in."

A quick review of the Fourteen Points, which Wilson outlined to Congress in a January 8, 1918, speech, discloses the magnitude of his ambition. There would be no more secret treaties; diplomacy would henceforth be entirely open and "in the public view." There would be "absolute" freedom of the seas. There would be few or no trade barriers. Armaments would be dramatically reduced. Colonial claims would be "adjusted," based in part on the wishes of the colonized populations. Most of the rest of the points dealt with redrawing the map of Europe, with a strong and consistent stress upon the principle of self-determination for all nationalities – an anti-imperial emphasis. But the final point, which was for Wilson the capstone of the whole enterprise, called for the creation of "a general association of nations" that would provide "mutual guarantees of political independence and territorial integrity to great and small states alike." The dangerous tangle of prewar alliances, often bilateral and secret, would never be allowed to be repeated again.

In many ways, the Fourteen Points appeared to be of a piece, calling for a new global order of free and self-governing nations that elected to submit to consensual collective decision-making rather than going it alone in the pursuit of narrow national interest. By being announced in January, they became an effective tool for encouraging Germany to accept defeat, in the knowledge that the Americans were not interested in a punitive settlement and the hope that American generosity would prevail.

But on closer examination, the Fourteen Points contained internal tensions and problems that ought to have been obvious. These pitfalls went beyond the inconvenient fact that the victorious powers had already cut secret deals with one another that they fully intended to follow through on and the near-certain fact that Great Britain would never accept the idea of "absolute" freedom of the seas. There were also problems arising out of the principle of national self-determination. In regions like the Balkans, and much of the rest of the former Austro-Hungarian Empire, consistent application of the principle of national self-determination was impractical, even impossible, because rival populations were too intermingled to be geographically separated. In addition, the idea of national self-determination inevitably fired the growth of nationalism – the very same force that Wilson and others felt needed to be tamped down in the postwar order.

The popular response to Wilson's plans seemed hopeful, but his Allied "associates" were manifestly unenthusiastic. In the end, Wilson concluded that only the force of his personality could prevail over the entrenched forces of inertia and cynicism, and he decided that he would go in person to Paris to lead the American peace delegation. Amazingly, it would be the first time that an American president had ever left the country during his time in office, and some of Wilson's opponents complained that he was violating the Constitution by doing so. It was a petty charge, but a more alert politician would have realized that there were warning signs embedded in it. A politician should never become so taken with the larger world that he forgets to tend to his home base. Wilson was about to provide one of American history's most potent illustrations of that truth.

Like so much else that Wilson did, the decision to go to Paris proceeded from a mixture of high-mindedness and hubris. He felt himself to be anointed to perform a great task for the world. But even historical giants must have their feet planted on the ground. While he was away in Europe for the first six months of 1919, his political coalition was coming unraveled, with labor grumbling about inflation and farmers about price controls. This came after the disastrous 1918 midterm elections, in which Republicans took control of both houses of Congress. An oblivious Wilson took off for Europe just a month after these crushing reversals and, perhaps most unwisely of all, failed to bring any Republican politicians with him as part of the delegation.

He arrived in Europe in December to a hero's welcome and briefly visited England, France, and Italy before arriving in France. Everywhere he was greeted by large, cheering crowds. He was confirmed in his conviction that the people of the world were with him. But once the conference got to work, none of that mattered. Although the conference included delegates from all the countries that had opposed Germany, the Big Four – Clemenceau of France, Lloyd George of Britain, Orlando of Italy, and Wilson of the United States – dominated it, and Wilson found it impossible to make much headway against the obstinacy and cynicism of the other three. There was an overwhelmingly strong sentiment in favor of punishing Germany and little taste for the more idealistic reforms expressed in the first five of Wilson's Fourteen Points. But there was a split between the French, who wanted to disable Germany entirely, and the British and Americans, who did not want to create the preconditions or pretexts for a new, avenging war. In the end, the conference agreed to a heavy burden of reparation payments by the Germans, some 132 billion gold marks, or the equivalent of around $33 billion in American dollars. Perhaps most fateful of all was the treaty's Article 231, often known as the War Guilt Clause, which served as the legal basis for the reparations:

> *The Allied and Associated Governments affirm and Germany accepts the responsibility of Germany and her allies for causing all the loss and damage to which the Allied and Associated Governments and their nationals have been subjected as a consequence of the war imposed upon them by the aggression of Germany and her allies.*

Nothing in the treaty would gall the Germans for years to come more than that clause.

Wilson also had to settle for a partial and inconsistent application of the self-determination principle, one that included the willful incorporation of German-speaking areas in Poland and Czechoslovakia, moves that would also have unfortunate later consequences. It came down to this: Wilson was in the end willing to sacrifice all else to gain the final of his Fourteen Points, the "association of nations," what became the League of Nations. All else, he believed, would be possible in due course if such an organization, committed to collective security and mutual accountability, could be established. Wilson was willing to accept that bargain.

It was clear almost from the start that he had made a bad choice. When he rolled out a draft of his plan for the League's structure on Valentine's Day 1919, it immediately encountered stiff resistance from Republicans. Senator Henry Cabot Lodge, an inveterate foe of Wilson's who was newly elected as chairman of the powerful Senate Foreign Relations Committee – and thus would be essential to the ratification of the treaty coming out of the Paris talks – not only opposed the League but got thirty-nine Republican senators or senators-elect to sign a "round robin" opposing it and demanding that the League issue be delinked from the treaty itself, to be decided separately. It was not an unreasonable position; and even if it had been, a prudent leader would have taken account of the fact that thirty-nine senators was more than enough to block the treaty from receiving the two-thirds vote needed for ratification. Nevertheless, Wilson brushed their demands aside contemptuously and vowed to "crush" all opposition. He was setting things up for a major confrontation and seemed entirely confident of prevailing.

Lodge would prove a formidable foe. A patrician in the old-line Boston Brahmin way – both the Lodges and the Cabots were dominant families in that city's ancestral elite – and a close friend of Theodore Roosevelt, he was learned, snobbish, and aristocratic in manner and disliked what he perceived as the insufferable moralism and empty preachiness of Wilson. He was no isolationist and had in fact, like Roosevelt, criticized Wilson for his reluctance to join the European war on the side of the Allies much earlier. But he had no qualms about putting the national interests of the United States first in his calculations and found Wilson's disavowal of national interest in the settlement of the war to be both naive and grating. He feared that Article X of the League Covenant, by committing member nations to mutual defense (at the discretion of the League's council) in the event of an attack was in effect a sacrifice of American sovereignty – and he was not about to let Wilson push the treaty into ratification over his objections. Wilson's decision to exclude Republicans from his deliberations was about to cost him dearly.

Several months of political wrangling followed, in which various groups arose, with various degrees of aversion to the League. There were about a dozen "irreconcilables" who were unwilling to consider entering the League under any terms. There was a similar number of "mild reservationists," who wanted small changes, mainly cosmetic in character. And there were the "strong reservationists," led by Lodge, who, although they did not oppose the League entirely, demanded major changes that would securely protect American sovereignty. But Wilson would not negotiate with any of them; he simply refused to consider any substantive changes, particularly to Article X.

It is often taken as a revelation of Wilson's almost pathologically inflexible character that he became so utterly rigid on this issue at this crucial point, when everything he had worked for was on the line. Perhaps so, although the same Woodrow Wilson had been hailed as a masterfully pragmatic politician in the halcyon days of his first term, just a half-decade before. It may also have been a sign of advancing illness or impaired mental capacity, since Wilson had suffered from poor cardiovascular health for most of his adult life and had experienced a number of minor strokes.

In any event, Lodge showed great political skill in holding these three factions together. Wilson, sensing at last that the tide was not going his way, chose to fight in a place where he believed he could win: the court of public opinion. He launched into a nationwide speaking tour that would rally support for his League and put pressure on the Senate to follow suit. But it was an exercise in futility. The barnstorming tour did nothing to affect the disposition of the Senate, and finally, after delivering a powerful address at Pueblo, Colorado, Wilson collapsed, having had a massive stroke that left him partly paralyzed. He was out of the public eye for two months as he recovered, and during that time, public opinion turned decisively against the League and the treaty, which were voted down.

It appeared, too, to have turned against Wilson himself – and perhaps to some extent against Progressivism as well. As a last-ditch effort, Wilson had called for the presidential election of 1920 to be a referendum on the question of the League. It is hard to know the extent to which voters were voting for or against the League, or Wilson, when they voted. There were many other issues on voters' minds by then. But the fact that the Republican candidate, Warren G. Harding, won a smashing victory, with over 60 percent of the popular vote – the first time in American history that any presidential candidate had reached the 60 percent mark – speaks volumes.

Harding had been a strong reservationist on the League, and he promised during his campaign that his focus would be on a return to American essentials: "not heroics, but healing; not nostrums but normalcy; not revolution, but restoration." The contrast he was drawing to the turbulent Wilson years was unmistakable. And that contrast was precisely what the voters wanted. It is hard to escape the conclusion that Wilson and his "nostrums" were being repudiated in Harding's unprecedented triumph. After eight years of Wilson, and twenty years of Progressivism, America was ready for something different.

CHAPTER SIXTEEN

FROM BOOM TO BUST

WARREN G. HARDING'S CALL FOR A "RETURN TO NORMALCY" has often been derided by historians as nostalgic and unrealistic. It was, they say, as if he were proposing that the country return to an idyllic state that never was, making a wistful retreat from the confusing complexity of the modern world into the homey simplicity of small-town life. Before we agree to go along with such a characterization, though, let us first try to understand what Harding might have meant in the context of his historical moment and why his words resonated so deeply with a huge majority of the voting public.

Begin with the postwar situation in Europe. Even as the Treaty of Versailles was being concluded, it was widely regarded, in Europe and America alike, as a self-evident mistake, bearing within itself the potential for even greater catastrophes than the one it was being created to settle. "They won the war, but lost the peace"; never was that adage more applicable, as a description of what the Allies had accomplished, and failed to accomplish, in their months of deliberations and machinations in Paris.

The economist John Maynard Keynes observed it all with sour resignation from his ringside seat as a British delegate to the Paris Conference. He firmly believed that the treaty's demands for German reparations had been set impossibly high and would almost certainly be counterproductive to the kind of general economic recovery needed to keep the peace and set a path for enduring recovery. In fact, he all but predicted that the burdens set by those reparations would lead to another and far worse war, "before which the horrors of the late German war will fade into nothing, and which will destroy, whoever is victor, the civilization and the progress of our generation."

It was a critical moment that called for the utmost wisdom – prudential wisdom like that of Lincoln, producing a settlement that might yet redeem the immense suffering and upheaval the war had brought. But there was no Lincoln to be found. Instead, Keynes found the Allies to be a spent force, with insufficient will to resist the brutal impulse simply to punish the vanquished. The prospect that Keynes saw lying ahead was unnerving:

> *In this autumn of 1919, in which I write, we are at the dead season of our fortunes. The reaction from the exertions, the fears, and the sufferings of the past five years is at its height. Our power of feeling or caring beyond the immediate questions of our own material well-being is temporarily eclipsed. The greatest events outside our own direct experience and the most dreadful anticipations cannot move us.... We have been moved already beyond endurance, and need rest. Never in the lifetime of men now living has the universal element in the soul of man burnt so dimly.*

Keynes did not make any exception for Woodrow Wilson, whom he dismissively compared not to Lincoln but to a provincial Presbyterian minister, badly overmatched by his worldlier European counterparts. Keynes had no more use for Wilson's high-flown idealism than he had for the others' short-sighted vindictiveness. To that hard-boiled realist, it was "stupid to believe that there is much room in the world, as it really is, for such affairs as the League of Nations."

Keynes's outlook no doubt reflected a particularly European form of world-weariness, but it would be fully echoed in the disillusionment felt by a great many Americans in the wake of the war. To be sure, the Americans had not suffered on anything like the scale that the European combatant powers had suffered. But they had lost more men than in any previous American war, aside from the Civil War, and had lived through a sudden and unprecedented disruption of their none-too-settled economy, all for a cause that now seemed dubious at best, a conflict that the nation could very easily have avoided. All the grand rhetoric from the presidential podium about the nation's noble war aims, making the world safe for democracy, self-determination, open agreements openly arrived at, freedom of the seas, and so on – all of it now rang pitiably hollow.

Some Americans even went so far as to suspect that American intervention in the war had occurred under false pretenses and was promoted primarily for the benefit of financial and banking interests associated with the munitions industry. These dark suspicions would grow steadily until, in the 1930s, a congressional committee chaired by Senator Gerald Nye would formally investigate the matter.

The roller-coaster ride of an unstable economy was another source of anxiety. Americans had become impatient with the drastic levels of regulation imposed to enhance wartime efficiency; but then they were equally upset by Wilson's abrupt decision to "take the harness off" and allow the necessary readjustments involved in the restoration of a peacetime economy to take place without any guidance from the government. The result was a disorderly mess. The vast U.S. Army, which had been so quickly swollen to wartime proportions, was now just as quickly demobilized, which led to returning veterans streaming home and finding no suitable employment available for them there. The railroads were restored to their private owners, war contracts were cancelled, and controls on business imposed by the WIB were eliminated in the blink of an eye.

Returning vets eager to get on with their lives found housing, autos, and consumer goods to be in very short supply, causing huge spikes in prices. These changes not only doubled the cost of living from what it had been before the war but led to widespread labor unrest, such as a general strike in Seattle and a giant strike at U.S. Steel, as unions sought to hold on to their wartime gains or otherwise cope in the savagely inflationary postwar environment. Some twenty-five race riots erupted in 1919 in cities around the country, notably a July riot in Chicago that left thirty-eight killed and more than five hundred injured. Although the immediate causes of violence were varied, the overflowing of ethnic and racial tensions in a fiercely competitive postwar labor and housing market was a common theme.

Often forgotten too amid the general pandemonium of the postwar environment was a public health calamity that took many more lives than the war. This was the 1918 Spanish influenza epidemic, which killed more than twenty-two million people around the world, including 675,000 Americans. While its exact origins are disputed, its spread was clearly facilitated by the extensive amounts of travel involved in wartime mobilization, especially when it resulted in the concentration of vulnerable populations in army camps and military hospitals, and in the carrying of particularly resilient forms of the disease by the returning servicemen in the United States. About 28 percent of the American population became infected. The effects on everyday life were profound and visible: people wearing surgical masks when out in public, closure of stores, theaters, dance halls, even churches and schools. So many people died that the city of Philadelphia used steam shovels to dig mass graves; 528 were buried that way on a single day.

On top of all this, there was the specter of the Bolshevik Revolution in Russia and what it might mean in the American context. Was all this social turbulence and upheaval on the American scene a harbinger of some more general wave of revolutionary violence, directed at a similar overthrow of the existing political and economic order in America? It was true that the number of radicals promoting such causes was tiny, but so too had been the number of Bolsheviks who carried out their revolution in Russia. Lenin had proved that it did not take many and that organized terrorism could be a potent political weapon. In April 1919, the U.S. Post Office intercepted thirty-six letter bombs addressed to prominent business and political leaders; then, on June 2, eight such bombs went off in different places, including one of them at the home of A. Mitchell Palmer, Wilson's attorney general. When the bomber turned out to be an Italian American radical, it gave credence to the connection of radicalism with the still largely unassimilated elements in the immigrant population and to the notion that a well-organized plot to foment a revolution might be afoot.

Palmer was convinced, in any event, and responded by putting into place the mechanisms for rapidly deporting radical aliens suspected of potentially seditious activity. His raids began in November 1919 with the apprehension of 650 members of a Russian anarchist group. Such "Palmer raids" were initially praised by the general public and the mainstream press; the *Washington Post* agreed that "there is no time to waste on hairsplitting over [the] infringement of liberty." So popular were they that Palmer continued them, eventually taking some six thousand people into custody, and even began to entertain the idea of running for the Democratic nomination for president in 1920.

Gradually, though, the fever subsided, and objections to the unconstitutionality of such raids began to break through and trouble the public's mind. So too did Palmer's reckless prediction of a May Day 1920 uprising, which, when the uprising did not occur, made Palmer look foolish and alarmist. The potential for Communist revolutions in Europe was gradually subsiding and, with it, the anxiety over an American revolution. The fears animating this "Red Scare," as it has been called, were soon diminished. But they did not spring merely from the overheated imagination of Palmer; they were prefigured in measures like the Espionage and Sedition Acts, which were centerpieces of the Wilson administration's wartime domestic policy.

All of these things – the sufferings of the war, the disillusionment over its botched settlement, the economic chaos, the widespread strikes and riots, a terrifying epidemic, and an upsurge in militant radicalism – all these things happened during the final years of the Wilson presidency. When Harding called for a "return to normalcy," he was offering the American public a time of respite from such things. Small wonder his message was so welcome.

Something else changed dramatically in the transition from the era of Wilsonian Progressivism to Harding's more business-oriented Republican rule. Presidential politics would no longer be as central to the story as they had been since the beginning of the Progressive Era. In many respects, the stars of the show for the next twelve years would be the American economy and the changing American culture, not the political leadership of the country. This is reminiscent of the country's experience of the last third of the nineteenth century, a time when America was mainly preoccupied with issues of economics and continental expansion. It is also consistent with the difference between Progressive philosophies of governance, which emphasized a large, vigorous, and highly directive political sector led by an activist president, and the new Republican governing class whose philosophy was, as Calvin Coolidge would put it, that "the chief business of the American people is business." Rather than seeking to make the world safe for democracy, as Wilson had proposed to do, the Republican leaders of the 1920s took on a more modest goal: making America safe for enterprise. In this, they would succeed beyond their wildest imaginings, at least for a time.

Things got off to a rough start for Harding, though, as he inherited a deep economic downturn beginning in July 1920 and lasting through 1921, during which time commodity prices, particularly for agricultural products, fell sharply and unemployment soared. Harding dealt with these challenges in a characteristically conservative fashion, closely following the advice of his secretary of the Treasury, the banker-financier Andrew W. Mellon. Soon after his inauguration, Harding called Congress into special session and asked it to approve higher tariffs, including tariffs on agricultural imports; lower income taxes; a reduction in federal spending; and aid to disabled soldiers and farmers.

Mellon was particularly insistent that the high wartime taxes be reduced without delay, since the country's problems would not be solved without rapid economic growth, and industry would not grow without fresh capital investment. Mellon believed that the weight of wartime taxes was inhibiting the flow of such investment. The tax cuts were largest for the highest incomes, from 77 to 24 percent, but even greater percentage-wise for low incomes, dropping from 4 to 0.5 percent. Mellon badly wanted to reduce the huge federal deficit from the war but reasoned that setting taxes too high would be counterproductive, since people of wealth would always be able to devise ways to shelter their wealth and avoid taxes. As Mellon wrote in a 1924 book on the subject, "the history of taxation shows that taxes which are inherently excessive are not paid ... [but instead] put pressure upon the taxpayer to withdraw his capital from productive business." Paradoxically, he argued, reducing taxes could actually serve to increase government revenues.

In addition, Harding sought to reverse the force of Wilson's regulatory agencies, not by eliminating them, but by appointing business-friendly men to the Interstate Commerce Commission, the Federal Reserve Board, and the Federal Trade Commission. Notably, too, he reversed Wilson's policy of excluding African Americans from federal positions and spoke out against the scandal of vigilante justice: "Congress," he declared to a joint session in 1921, "ought to wipe the stain of barbaric lynching from the banners of a free and orderly, representative democracy."

The Mellon economic policies did their work, and did it extremely well. By the end of 1922, real GNP was already inching up, and by 1923, it was up sharply and would continue to rise through most of the decade. It was the beginning of what would prove to be one of the most concentrated periods of economic growth and general prosperity in the nation's history. The economy grew 42 percent over the decade of the 1920s, with an average rate of GNP for the decade of 4.7 percent per year. In addition, Mellon's policies were successful in halving the national debt, from $33 billion in 1919 to $16 billion by 1929.

The sheer size of the American economy was simply astounding. It truly was becoming the economic colossus of the world. The United States was producing nearly half the world's output and possessed wealth equivalent to all of postwar Europe, wealth adding up to perhaps 40 percent of the world's total wealth. The Federal Reserve kept interest rates low, which helped to lubricate credit markets and provide a stimulus to growth. New construction almost doubled, from $6.7 billion to $10.1 billion, reflecting pent-up wartime demand. Wages rose, and unemployment never rose above the natural rate of around 4 percent. Average income rose from $6,460 to $8,016 per person.

Fueling this great expansion were a multitude of advances in manufacturing and industrial production, each creating economies of scale that vastly increased productivity and efficiency. The moving assembly line, which honed to perfection rational manufacturing methods pioneered in the late nineteenth and early twentieth centuries, exemplified the new developments. First put to use before World War I by Henry Ford in his automobile plants, by the 1920s, these methods – analyzing and breaking down complex processes into simple repetitive operations using standardized and interchangeable parts and employing the conveyor belt to move the work product steadily along the line, to worker after worker – had become widely used, with productivity gains in virtually every business in which they were applied. Ford's plants quadrupled in productivity over a ten-year period, a principal reason why Ford was able to sell his Model T cars for less than $300. By 1929, there were twenty-six million cars in the United States.

Automobiles became to the economy of the 1920s, and much of the twentieth century, what textiles had been early in the previous century and what railroads had been after the Civil War: a centrally important industry that was not only a big business in its own right but also a powerful economic multiplier that gave rise to important by-products, including additional big businesses, subsidiary industries, and various other ripple effects through the economy. In the case of automobiles, the by-products were items like rubber, tires, spark plugs, glass, paint, and, of course, the various petroleum products needed to operate an internal combustion engine – not to mention the extensive highway construction, some three hundred thousand miles of it between 1921 and 1929, to provide surfaces for those twenty-six million cars to travel on. And along with those new highways, there would be battalions of service stations, roadside restaurants, tourist attractions, and other businesses that would spring up like flowers after a summer rain, catering to travelers and commuters. The automobile was quickly beginning to transform the American landscape, changing the relationship between cities and suburbs and countryside and empowering individuals and families to move easily between and among them.

Henry Ford was perhaps the single most influential figure in the growth of the automobile industry and in many ways was more important than any American politician of the time. A farmboy and self-taught tinkerer from Michigan, Ford started out as an engineer for the Edison Illuminating Company but had an incurable fascination with gasoline engines. Eventually he was drawn into the burgeoning automobile business and, by 1903, had created his own company. In 1908, he introduced the Model T – simple, cheap to manufacture, easy to operate, easy to repair – with a blitz of nationwide publicity that made the car widely known to its full range of potential buyers. By relentlessly refining and simplifying and improving the manufacturing process, he was able to reduce the price every year. By 1925, he was manufacturing nine thousand cars a day.

Ford understood two absolutely vital things. First, he understood that if he could bring the price of a car down low enough, he could create a virtually unlimited mass market for it, hence his unceasing attention to cost cutting and productivity gains. Second, he realized that the nature of the work on his highly productive assembly lines could be boring at best, dehumanizing at worst, and so it would be necessary to pay his workers extremely well, to offset the grinding demands of the job – and to give the workers sufficient purchasing power to afford the products for themselves. Hence Ford's wages were as much as double that of the competition; he would also move to a forty-hour workweek to make it more attractive for his workers to stick with him. As a consequence, the turnover rate in his factories dropped by 90 percent.

Ford became a kind of national celebrity, a symbol of the potential for an American everyman to make it from rags to riches, while apparently maintaining his simplicity of character. He delighted in cracker-barrel aphorisms and was disdainful of high and mighty sophisticates who had the breeding and education he'd never gotten. In fact, like many outwardly simple people, Ford was actually a very complicated man, full of contradictions and hidden antipathies, often prone to act in headstrong and ignorant ways. His immense drive to succeed built an unparalleled business empire, but his defects as an executive threatened to undermine his success. For one thing, he took it upon himself to snoop around in his employees' private lives in ways that were inappropriate and near-oppressive in character. And his personality tics affected his business judgment. As competitors like General Motors came into the market, offering more commodious products directed at more affluent customers, he refused to change anything about the Model T until it was almost too late for the company, which, as a consequence of his hardheaded stubbornness, lost forever the industry dominance it had once possessed.

There were other oddities about Henry Ford. He was known for proclaiming that "history is more or less bunk" and dismissing history as unworthy of study, because it had no bearing on the present and there was nothing to be learned from it. But he also had a nostalgic passion for early Americana, exemplified by his creation of Greenfield Village, a living history museum meant to preserve vestiges of the older America – the very same older America that Ford's own great invention, the mass-produced automobile, was rendering more and more obsolete with each passing day. A very complicated man, Henry Ford, although his complexities were in many ways those of his own highly transitional times too.

Among those larger complexities were the changing faces of a burgeoning new national culture, bursting at the seams with nervous energy but going full tilt in several different directions all at once. The recovery and expansion of prosperity, and the scale of mass production of goods aimed at the individual consumer, soon transformed everyday life for most Americans in ways that the rapid expansion of automobile ownership and use only begin to hint at. Many historians consider the 1920s to be the first decade of "our times." What they mean by this is that a great many of the standard features of American life as we know it today – pervasive mass communications, personal automobiles, motion pictures, a consumer-oriented economy, professional sports, celebrity culture, readily available consumer credit, the widespread availability of cheap electrical power, and so on – first began to become commonplace during those years.

Consider a few humble examples, all of them involving the use of electricity. It was in the 1920s that the refrigerator began to become a typical feature of the American kitchen, replacing the cumbersome and inefficient ice box. In 1920, only about five thousand refrigerators were produced every year; by 1931, that number had jumped to one million. The variety of foods that urban and suburban dwellers would now be able to consume and safely store – dairy products, meats, fresh vegetable and fruits – would change the nation's diet and transform the dinner tables and grocery stores of the nation. Similarly, the arrival of such labor-saving devices as washing machines and vacuum cleaners would dramatically relieve the burdens of housekeeping.

Electronic transmission of words and music also became a constant feature of life. The first broadcast radio station in the nation – KDKA in Pittsburgh, Pennsylvania – began operating in 1920, carrying the election returns in that year's presidential election as part of its first broadcast. By 1929, 60 percent of American families owned radios. Along with the mass production of phonograph players, at a clip of five million a year by 1929, recorded music quickly became part of the lives of everyday people all over the land, including many without access to Broadway productions or concert halls. Sales of pianos and sheet music sagged as the electronic forms of musical reproduction replaced the parlor music of the Victorian era.

New and distinctively American forms of popular music, combining elements of jazz, blues, and conventional concert music, also began to emerge and find a large popular following. African Americans moving north during the First World War – figures such as Louis Armstrong and Duke Ellington – brought their musical arts with them, contributing to the development of a fresh American sound. White southern performers of traditional Appalachian music also found a home on the radio and on records, developing the first commercially viable expression of what is now known as country music. And from composers and lyricists from Broadway and Tin Pan Alley in New York, many of them the sons and daughters of Jewish immigrants, such as Jerome Kern, George Gershwin, and Irving Berlin, came the first entries in what would become known as the Great American Songbook, which would be, with jazz, one of the surpassing musical achievements of American culture.

And of course there were the movies. In 1900, the only comparable entertainment had been the crude nickelodeon; by 1929, the movies had taken the country by storm, moving quickly through a black-and-white silent period into "talkies," such as the breakthrough 1927 work *The Jazz Singer*, and featuring an array of celebrity "stars," such as Douglas Fairbanks, Greta Garbo, Mary Pickford, Charlie Chaplin, Buster Keaton, and Rudolph Valentino, whose doings on and off the set, skillfully amplified by press agents and image makers, became the stuff of newspaper columns and back-fence gossip all over the country. In many cities, movies were shown in "picture palaces," large, swanky urban theaters (often owned and run by the Hollywood studios themselves) that could seat as many as two thousand people at a time, places where common people could enjoy the numerous amenities and the ornate and exotic decorations.

Professional sports also came into their own as a mass-cultural phenomenon in the 1920s. For the first time in American history, large crowds gathered on a regular basis to watch spectacles of athletic competition – baseball, football, boxing – with many other Americans following along on radio and in newsprint and developing attachments to their city's teams. The 1920s produced some of the most famous athletes in American sports history – baseball's home-run king Babe Ruth; football's Red Grange, the "Galloping Ghost"; boxer Jack Dempsey, the "Manassa Mauler"; tennis players Bill Tilden and Helen Wills; swimmers Johnny Weissmuller and Gertrude Ederle; golfer Bobby Jones; and one could even include the racehorse Man O' War, still considered by many to be the greatest thoroughbred of all time.

Sports became a model of how the new mass communications media not only reflected events but created them, and created the buzz of excitement and aura of celebrity that surrounded them and the athletes taking part in them. But perhaps the most famous example of this new reality was not a sporting event or personality but Charles Lindbergh's 1927 airplane flight from New York to Paris, the first solo transatlantic flight in history.

A son of the American Midwest, Lindbergh was an early enthusiast for aviation and dropped out of college to pursue flight training. After honing his skills while barnstorming for nearly two years across the Midwest and South performing air stunts, he took a position as an Air Mail pilot operating out of Lambert Field in St. Louis, operating a regular route between that city and Chicago. But he was restless. Ever the adventurer, he chose to attempt the flight from New York to Paris in response to a prize offer from a New York hotel owner, to be awarded to the first pilot able to carry out this flight successfully. The prize of $25,000 (about $350,000 in 2018 dollars) had first been offered in 1919, but no one had yet claimed it. By 1927, in fact, four men had died trying, three were seriously injured, and two others went missing, while the prize still remained tantalizingly out of reach. Those who had failed were far more experienced pilots than Lindbergh. Yet the outwardly modest but inwardly tough Lindbergh was not to be deterred. Like David taking on the invincible Goliath, like Alexander the Great taming the wild horse Bucephalus, like King Arthur pulling the magic sword Excalibur out of the unyielding stone, so the unheralded and inexperienced Lindbergh would make a name for himself by doing the thing no other man had been able to do.

And he succeeded. When he landed his plane, named the *Spirit of St. Louis*, in Paris after a grueling, thirty-six-hundred-mile, thirty-three-and-a-half-hour flight, he was greeted by a cheering crowd of more than one hundred thousand French admirers. Later, on returning to New York, "Lucky Lindy" received a hero's welcome, with a ticker-tape parade from lower Manhattan up to Central

Park, where he was honored by the mayor and greeted by two hundred thousand people. It was a welcome far more grand than the returning soldiers of the First World War had received. He went on to tour ninety-two cities in forty-nine states, received the Medal of Honor and the Distinguished Flying Cross, and became a national spokesman for aviation.

It should take nothing away from our appreciation of Lindbergh's bravery to wonder why a single daring airplane flight, in an era of countless other wonders, should have excited such fervent and prolonged hosannas. Why were the parades in his honor even greater than those for the doughboys returning from the sacrificial perils of war? What possessed the editors of the *New York World* to call it "the greatest feat of a solitary man in the records of the human race"? Some part of the answer has to be found not only in the act itself but in the way that the new communications media allowed for the act to be amplified and made into a story, one with near-mythic overtones, to capture the nation's attention and fill newspaper column inches, magazine spreads, movie newsreels, and excited radio broadcasts. These events became elements in a shared national experience, one story among many others binding the nation together culturally in the ways that it was already being linked economically and politically.

This is mostly a positive development, even if it cries out for a constant process of reassessment and reweighting of the value of different achievements. But there was also always the danger that with enough spin applied, almost any occurrence could now be hyped up into being a significant *event* – or what Daniel Boorstin derisively called a "pseudo-event" – and that a celebrity could be a person who is famous not for his achievements, or any other particular thing, but simply for being well known. Such was the ambiguous power of the new communications technologies, just then coming into their heyday in the 1920s, for the mobilizing and manipulation of public opinion and popular sentiment. It is a subject to which we shall return.

For now, though, it is a subject that points us to one of the chief dangers of writing about recent history. It is sometimes said that journalism is a "first draft of history." This is a statement of which we should be wary. First impressions are not always the most accurate or the most perceptive source of historical insight. The passage of time is almost always necessary for us to have perspective on the past. But this is now harder to achieve than it used to be. The unprecedented forms of mass communications in the early decades of the twentieth century made it possible to produce journalistic "first drafts" that were captivating, vivid, and believable but that presented a sensational, one-sided, oversimplified, and misleading view of their subject, a view that historians need to apply with the utmost care.

We have already seen some preliminary indications of this problem. Consider the role that the mass-circulation daily newspapers had in sensationalizing the explosion of the *Maine* and inflaming public opinion against the Spanish, before the facts of the matter were known; or the productions associated with the Creel Committee, which used sophisticated communications technologies and techniques to convey a powerful, emotion-laden propaganda message in service to the national war effort. In both cases, it has taken us many years to overcome the powerful impressions made at the time by these messages and to see events in a different and more complex light. Seeing is believing, we like to say. But we also need to remember that things are not always as they seem.

The same techniques of propaganda and sensationalism that were refined in war also had their uses in peacetime, as ways of selling products and newspapers and magazines. Hence the 1920s were also the first great era of national advertising, which went hand in hand with the development of a national consumer economy. Advertising stimulated consumer spending, which was fueled in part by the increased availability of consumer credit, allowing for the easy purchase of automobiles, radios, and household appliances. Advertising also promoted spending on leisure activities like spectator sports and cinemagoing. The mass-circulation newspapers and magazines, radio broadcasting, and to some extent motion pictures all provided new media for advertisements to reach consumers. Events, media, credit, consumption – all were woven together in a tight web.

And it is to them, and to books like Frederick Lewis Allen's influential 1931 book *Only Yesterday*, which was in many respects a summation of the journalistic images of the Roaring Twenties, that we owe an image of those years as an age, in the words of historian Kenneth S. Lynn, of "jazz babies, speakeasies, sports worship, sex crimes, xenophobic politics, and governmental graft." The ability of the new mass-cultural mechanisms, and the "gargoyle journalism" (in Lynn's words) that they spawn, to fashion large and believable images of the past as it was being made was a powerful force, then and ever since. It is part of the strong countercurrent that historians must always struggle against in rendering an independent judgment of the past in its fullness.

A case in point is Allen's judgment that the 1920s saw a "revolution in manners and morals," a refrain that is echoed in nearly all textbook accounts of the decade, often using those very words. But he didn't base this judgment on careful empirical observation; he based it on what he found in the gargoyle journalism of the era. Allen makes the argument that the coming of the Jazz Age overthrew conventional morality and surrendered to "a widely pervasive obsession with sex," an argument he supports by referring to the enormous amount of space given over to sexual themes in the newspapers of the period. Or he found it in advertisements such as the film teaser that promised viewers that they would see "brilliant men, beautiful jazz babies, champagne baths, midnight revels, petting parties in the purple dawn, all ending in one terrific climax that makes you gasp" – in other words, in evidence drawn from media salesmanship.

This is not to say that Allen was entirely wrong. What is far more likely is that he was looking at one small portion of society, the sons and daughters of upper- and upper-middle-class backgrounds who could afford such explorations and indulgences and whose families had benefited disproportionately from the era's wave of prosperity. He was looking at the world of characters like the glamorous New Yorkers in F. Scott Fitzgerald's novels, notably *The Great Gatsby* and *This Side of Paradise*. He was not looking at the works of a writer like Indiana's Booth Tarkington, one of the most popular novelists of his time, whose *Alice Adams*, winner of the 1922 Pulitzer Prize for the Novel, deals with the aspirations and fundamental decencies of a lower-middle-class family in the Midwest. Nor was he looking at Fitzgerald's novels themselves very closely, since their characters, many of whom are displaced midwesterners, are filled with nihilism and foreboding about the possible moral consequences of the very prosperity their characters were craving and enjoying.

In other words, to the extent there was a revolution in manners and morals going on in the 1920s, we need to see it as a complicated thing, one in which class, social status, region, religion, race, and a dozen other considerations play a role, and in which revolution and counterrevolution were both going on at the same time. The 1920s were notable not only for their forward-charging modernity but also for their sharply reactionary or backward-looking aspects. It was a time of cultural bifurcation, in which action and reaction tracked with one another like the moving parts of a reciprocating engine.

It was a time of the most advanced experimentation and cosmopolitan modernism in the arts and literature, epitomized by the appearance of abstract painting, atonal music, free verse, stream of consciousness narrative and other techniques, and by the emergence of intellectual bohemias like Greenwich Village, New York, where the revolution in manners and morals was going full blast. But it was also a time that saw a resurgence of nativist sentiment, featuring the revival and rebranding of the Ku Klux Klan as an anti-immigrant, anti-Catholic, and anti-Jewish organization, in addition to its antiblack agenda, with a national following stretching from Oregon to Maine. Some of this sentiment was charged by the abrupt influx in the years between 1919 and 1921 of more than a million immigrants, many of them Catholics and Jews from Central and

Eastern Europe, adding to the competition for jobs and other pressures of post-war life. Congress responded by passing two laws, in 1921 and 1924, respectively, that established stringent quotas for immigration and effectively ended the era of mass immigration that had begun in the post–Civil War era.

It was a time in which the rise of liberal Progressivism and modernism in the urban churches was countered by the rise of a conservative Protestantism that insisted on a renewed commitment to key Christian doctrinal tenets, those deemed "fundamental" or foundational, hence the term *fundamentalism*. A controversy between fundamentalists and modernists had been percolating in the Presbyterian Church since the 1880s, but it came into the open in the 1920s, with a growing apprehension among conservatives that liberal theology undermined the authority of the Bible and led to, well, a revolution in manners and morals. William Jennings Bryan, who devoted much of his postpolitical career to religious causes, believed that Darwinism lent support to the "law of hate" in which the "strong" are allowed to prevail over the "weak" and that Darwinian thinking had influenced the militarism of Germany; "the same science that manufactured poisonous gases to suffocate soldiers is preaching that man has a brute ancestry and eliminating the miraculous and the supernatural from the Bible." For Bryan, Darwinism was to be resisted because it eliminated any basis for affirming the dignity of all human beings.

Bryan went on to spearhead an effort to ban the teaching of Darwinian evolution in the public schools and became involved in a test case in Tennessee, in which a young high school teacher named John Scopes challenged a state law, known as the Butler Act, outlawing the teaching of evolution. The resultant trial, held in summer 1925 in Dayton, Tennessee, was a blatant publicity stunt by the town fathers and became a frenzied media "pseudo-event," covered by two hundred reporters, including the famously acid-penned Baltimore critic H. L. Mencken, and featuring a rhetorical duel between Bryan and Scopes's attorney, the famous trial lawyer Clarence Darrow. Although Scopes lost the case, as it was always clear he would – there being no doubt that the textbook he used in his course taught Darwinian evolution – the cause of fundamentalism was decisively set back by the ridicule and negative publicity that the trial generated.

Recent historians of the trial, such as Edward Larson, have noted a complicating factor, however, in the textbook Scopes used in his class. George William Hunter's *A Civic Biology* was indeed an openly and unapologetically racist text, in line with Bryan's claims. It argued that "the civilized white inhabitants of Europe and America" were the "highest race type of all" and that eugenics should be used to improve "the future generations of men and women on the earth," which meant the elimination of such forms of "parasitism" as "feeble-mindedness" and other features of a "low and degenerate race." The Scopes trial does not yield today the same easy lessons that an educated observer might have drawn from it at the time.

Finally, we should make mention of the Eighteenth Amendment to the Constitution, the amendment that prohibited the manufacture, transportation, and sale of "intoxicating liquors," or alcoholic beverages. Prohibition is often presented as a feature of the "reactionary" or backward aspect of the 1920s. But there are two things wrong with that. First, it was passed under Wilson's administration, gaining congressional approval in December 1917, and after ratification by the states taking effect in January 1919. Second, it was a Progressive measure through and through, evincing most of the salient characteristics of such reforms. It concerned itself with improving the moral fabric of society; it was strongly supported by the middle classes; and it was aimed at controlling the "interests" (i.e., the manufacturers of alcoholic beverages) and their connections with venal and corrupt politicians in city, state, and national governments, seeking instead to establish the primacy of the public interest. Indeed, Prohibition pairs up nicely with the Nineteenth Amendment, ratified in 1920, which gave women the right to vote, since temperance had, ever since the antebellum period, been a "women's issue," championed by women for the sake of women and their families.

Herbert Hoover called Prohibition a "noble experiment," and in fact alcohol consumption in the country did drop dramatically, by as much as 50 percent, during the Prohibition years. But a noble experiment is not necessarily good public policy, and much of the social history of Prohibition revolves around the ways that the people of the United States sought to get around it. Enforcement of Prohibition was next to impossible, and a significant portion of the public, including the ethnic Catholic voters who had always resented the Progressive opposition to their saloon culture and felt targeted by the new law, was inclined to ignore it. A whole culture of illicit alcohol consumption arose, replete with speakeasies, bootleggers, bathtub gin, hip flasks, and cocktail parties. The illegal production and sale of alcohol became a very considerable business – in Detroit, it was second only to the auto industry – and a magnet for organized crime, which flourished thanks to this rich source of income and produced such icons of American crime history as Chicago-based "Scarface" Al Capone, who tooled around town proudly in his green custom-made armored Cadillac, complete with guns mounted on the sides, a veritable pirate-prince of the city and a law unto himself.

In short, Prohibition may have had noble intentions, but it turned out to be a disastrously unsuccessful experiment. It has been argued that Prohibition gave organized crime a foothold in American culture that it would never otherwise have attained. Such an assessment is impossible to prove or disprove, but it surely contains a fair portion of truth. What is perhaps worse, though, was the damage done in creating laws that a significant minority of Americans would be disinclined to obey, laws which moreover could never be seriously enforced. In doing so, the architects of Prohibition had seriously undermined respect for the law itself.

Harding's administration had been markedly successful in lifting the economy out of the postwar recession and getting it aloft. But it struggled in other respects. Harding was not a forceful or visionary leader and seemed to like nothing so much as his weekly White House poker game with his friends. Like the administration of U. S. Grant, another postwar president, his administration was honeycombed with incompetent and dishonest men, many of them associates from his days as an Ohio politician. Harding made some extremely good appointments, such as Mellon at Treasury, William Howard Taft as chief justice of the Supreme Court, and Herbert Hoover at the Commerce Department. But he made terrible appointments, notably Veterans Bureau head Charles R. Forbes, interior secretary Albert Fall, and attorney general Harry M. Daugherty. And the latter group brought his administration down.

There were scandals involving thefts and colossal mismanagement by Forbes at the Veterans Administration and Daugherty's fraudulent release of German assets seized during wartime. But the worst of these scandals involved an attempted theft of the nation's oil reserves, three oil fields set aside for strategic future use. Fall had leased two of the three – Teapot Dome in Wyoming and Elk Hills in California – to private interests, without competitive bidding, in return for a secret $400,000 payoff (about $5.5 million in 2018 dollars). It was arguably the worst scandal hitherto in American political history, and Fall went to jail for it, the first cabinet official to do so.

But by the time all of this chicanery became exposed, Harding was dead, having had a fatal heart attack in San Francisco on August 2, 1923, while on a western tour. His death was widely and deeply mourned, as the country had found in him a gentle, unpretentious ordinary man, perhaps all too ordinary, but who had been a relief to a nation weary of strutting and moralistic executive power. But once the depth of the scandals of his administration came to light, those tender thoughts disappeared and were quickly replaced by more negative ones. Harding's subsequent reputation has never recovered.

Fortunately for the country, though, he was succeeded by a man of extraordinarily high probity, a vice president who was much more suited to the presidency than the man he had served. The contrast with the squalor of the unraveling Harding administration could not have been more pointed. Calvin Coolidge was visiting his father at his childhood home of Plymouth Notch, Vermont, in a house which had neither electricity nor telephone, when he received by messenger the news about Harding's death. There in that house, his father, who was a justice of the peace, administered the oath of office in the family parlor at 2:47 A.M. by the flickering light of a kerosene lamp.

The scene offered a glimpse of an older and more rooted America, a reassuring prospect to the stunned nation. Their confidence was not misplaced. Coolidge managed to restore confidence in the office of the presidency after Harding's misjudgments and mismanagement but did so in a way that was fully in keeping with the small-government, pro-business ideal to which Harding and his party had been committed. He was a popular president and easily won election in his own right in 1924, running against the independent candidacy of Robert La Follette and against a Democratic Party so divided that it could not even agree on a resolution to condemn the Ku Klux Klan. He continued the taxation policies of Andrew Mellon, further reducing income tax rates and keeping spending low, in order to continue retiring the national debt. By 1927, income taxes affected only the wealthiest 2 percent of Americans; others paid no federal income tax. And the economy continued to thrive.

Because Coolidge was a man of few words, he has always been underestimated by historians, who miss his subtle wit. The stories about it are legion. His wife, the very elegant Grace Goodhue Coolidge, told a story about a young woman sitting next to Coolidge at a dinner party who confided to him she had bet she could get at least three words of conversation from him. Without looking at her, he quietly responded, "You lose." When emerging from church once, he was asked by a reporter about the sermon's subject. "Sin," responded Coolidge. What did the minister say about sin? "He said he was against it."

But there was far more to Coolidge than that, and when the occasion demanded, he could be both eloquent and profound. His speech delivered at Philadelphia commemorating the 150th anniversary of the American Revolution in July 1926 was a speech for the ages. It was a defense of America's founding principles against those, like Wilson and the Progressives, who believed that the massive social and economic changes that had taken place in American life had invalidated those founding principles and required that modern theories of government be introduced to take their place. It was a speech that stands in the line of great presidential speeches from Jefferson to Lincoln, a reminder to Americans then and now of the exceptional character of their own revolution and of the enduring importance of liberty and equality as natural rights. Here is a portion of it:

> About the Declaration there is a finality that is exceedingly restful. It is often asserted that the world has made a great deal of progress since 1776, that we

have had new thoughts and new experiences which have given us a great advance over the people of that day, and that we may therefore very well discard their conclusions for something more modern. But that reasoning can not be applied to this great charter. If all men are created equal, that is final. If they are endowed with inalienable rights, that is final. If governments derive their just powers from the consent of the governed, that is final. No advance, no progress can be made beyond these propositions. If anyone wishes to deny their truth or their soundness, the only direction in which he can proceed historically is not forward, but backward toward the time when there was no equality, no rights of the individual, no rule of the people. Those who wish to proceed in that direction can not lay claim to progress. They are reactionary. Their ideas are not more modern, but more ancient, than those of the Revolutionary fathers.

In keeping with his personal modesty and his rootedness in his New England origins, Coolidge chose not to run for a second term in 1928. He would be succeeded by Herbert Hoover, his commerce secretary, and Harding's, a former businessman with an interesting personal story. His life was a reminder that one still did not have to be born into great wealth to become president. He had come from a humble background in rural Iowa; was orphaned at the age of ten and raised in Oregon; and had worked his way through Stanford University, studying engineering and gaining the technical knowledge and background that would enable him to make a fortune as an international mining engineer, working in places as far-flung as China, Africa, Latin America, and Russia. When World War I broke out, he plunged into relief work for beleaguered Belgium and northeastern France and eventually ran Wilson's program for postwar economic relief in Europe. He attracted the keen admiration of John Maynard Keynes in that latter post, causing the often-caustic Briton to observe that "the ungrateful nations of Europe owe much more to the statesmanship and insight of Mr. Hoover and his band of American workers than they have yet appreciated or will ever acknowledge."

When he returned home, he was avidly sought by both political parties but eventually sided with the Republicans. In the Commerce post, he made his department into an important agency, using his engineer's acumen to devise economies and practices that saved the government more money than the entire budget of his agency. In the 1928 election, he cruised to victory, smashing the Democratic candidate Al Smith and riding the continuing wave of Coolidge prosperity. The Democratic Party seemed almost on the verge of electoral death.

But that was a deceiving appearance. Beneath the electoral surface, a realignment of American politics was beginning to take shape. Al Smith was an

Irish Catholic, the first Catholic ever nominated by a major political party, and an outspoken opponent of Prohibition. Working-class ethnic Catholics had already been swinging heavily toward the Democratic Party, and although Smith did not attract enough such voters to win, the potential for a new coalition of voters, including urban workers, farmers, and the states of the solid South, was taking shape. It was in some ways an improbable coalition, and as long as Coolidge prosperity prevailed, that coalition was unlikely to prevail. But let that prosperity slip, and anything was possible.

As Hoover took office in 1929, the stock market was booming. Indeed, the country was in the grip of a speculative mania, a bull market that had begun in 1927 and showed no signs of quitting. Many small investors had jumped into the market, often buying stocks "on margin" (i.e., on credit), betting that a rise in price followed by a quick sale would invariably net them a quick and easy profit. It seemed like a sure thing. Stocks became wildly overvalued, selling at prices far beyond any relationship to earnings or fundamentals. Caught up in a classic economic bubble, they forgot what every wise investor needs to remember: no boom lasts forever, markets fluctuate, and what goes up must eventually come down.

On September 3, those laws of nature asserted themselves, and the rise came to a halt. The market began a slow, quiet decline, which suddenly became a rout, even a plummeting fall. On October 24, nicknamed "Black Thursday," prices began to fall so fast that a group of New York's most influential bankers decided to pool their resources to support the market by propping up prices through strategic buys at above-current price levels. The strategy worked temporarily and allowed Hoover to inform the country that the economy was on a "sound and prosperous basis." But on the following Monday, October 28, prices again dropped, and then on the following day, Black Tuesday, the bottom fell out, as sixteen and a half million stock shares changed hands and prices collapsed. The slow melt of stock prices would continue for the weeks to come, until, by November 13, a share of U.S. Steel that had sold for $262 on September 3 had fallen to $150 and eventually would drop as low as $22. Montgomery Ward fell from $138 to $49 and finally hit bottom at $4. General Motors fell from $73 to $8. The Dow Jones Index had dropped from a September high of 381 to 198; three years later, that number would be 41 – less than one-ninth of its peak value.

It is important to understand that, although this great stock market crash was a herald of the coming Great Depression, and perhaps even marked its beginning, it was not its principal cause. Stock markets rise and fall, sometimes with extreme volatility, but their activity is largely self-corrective over time, like that of any market. This was the case even in 1929. Stocks would rally later in the year, and business activity did not begin to decline notably until spring 1930. But once depression had taken hold, it did not loosen its fierce grip, not until the Second World War had begun in Europe in 1939.

Even after nine decades of sustained and sophisticated analysis, there is no complete consensus on the causes of this Great Depression or the reasons for its persistence. But one can venture a few generalizations, to set the table for our account in the next chapter of how American leaders reacted to the problems they faced.

First, the Great Depression was a worldwide phenomenon, caused at least in part by imbalances in the world economy resulting from the Great War and its aftermath. Although it originated in the United States, the Great Depression caused drastic declines in output, severe unemployment, and acute deflation in almost every country of the world. In any serious analysis, it is difficult to isolate the American situation from the rest of the world. The problem of German reparations, for example, was intimately bound up in the American willingness to extend credit to Germans and open American markets to German goods. Policies that restricted either of those things, even if adopted for the sake of the perceived American interest, were likely to have an extremely adverse effect on the German economy – which would in turn affect the world economy and rebound upon the United States.

That said, there are basically two schools of thought about the causes of the Great Depression. There are those who place the principal blame on underconsumption, which means that there was a loss of broadly distributed purchasing power in the economy. Put more simply, in this view, too much of the wealth created by modern industrial capitalism was placed in too few hands, leaving the great mass of potential consumers unable to buy the goods that the ever more productive American economy was churning out. As unsold goods piled up, and inventories mounted, production had to be paused, leading to layoffs and other job loss, which in turn led to even less purchasing power, and thus the cycle continued in a downward spiral, with bank closures and collapsing agricultural prices joining in to make matters even worse.

Others blame bad government policy for turning an ordinary recession into a full-blown and persistent depression. In this view, the monetary policies of the Federal Reserve shrank the money supply severely between 1929 and 1932, by more than a third, and thereby produced a "Great Contraction," with declines in prices, income, and economic activity caused by an inadequate supply of money in circulation. Another related view places the blame earlier, arguing that during the entire decade of the 1920s, the Federal Reserve had pursued an overly liberal monetary policy, which led to an excessively credit-driven boom during the entire decade, a house of cards that was doomed to collapse.

There may well be some measure of truth in all of the competing theories. The global economic situation, rampant stock market speculation, uneven distribution of wealth, overuse of credit, overproduction of consumer goods, the weakness of the farming sector – the one part of the economy that had enjoyed almost none of the benefits of Coolidge prosperity – and bad government policies: all of these things seem to have played some role in the outcome. But the truth of the matter is that, as with the origins of the First World War, so with the Great Depression, we live in the immense shadow of a great event that remains, in some crucial respects, a mystery.

CHAPTER SEVENTEEN

THE NEW DEAL

W HAT IF CALVIN COOLIDGE HAD STILL BEEN PRESIDENT when the great stock market crash of October 1929 had occurred? What might he have done?

It is of course impossible to know for sure. But it seems likely that he would have responded by taking little or no governmental action to restore stock price levels. It also seems likely that he would have intervened as little as possible in the operation of the economy once recessionary forces had started to take hold in 1930. Aside from reducing federal spending and taxation further, he would likely have left the economic system to correct itself, much as it had in the 1920–21 recession, by allowing wages and prices to fall as necessary and allowing businesses to downsize or close until the economy found a healthy new footing, a firm foundation from which it could rally. Such measures would allow natural forces to "purge the rottenness out of the system," in the words of Andrew Mellon, and prepare a newly healthy economy for a fresh spurt of growth. Any propping up of shaky positions would, Coolidge might likely have concluded, only aggravate the problem, like a medicine that targeted symptoms rather than treating the disease itself. Propping up wages would only lead to sustained mass unemployment; propping up prices would lead to unsold surpluses. Better, he would have said, to swallow the bitter pill of a sharp but quick recession, as a way of resetting the economy and thereby setting the path for economic restoration.

We will never know whether such policies would have succeeded or failed, though, because they were never tried. It turned out that Herbert Hoover, even as secretary of commerce, had a very different outlook from that of his Republican predecessors on the economy and the role of government. Hoover's views reflected the can-do problem-solving spirit of his own profession of engineering, and his activist tendencies were far closer to the Progressive tradition than to the laissez-faire tradition embraced by Harding and Coolidge. Hoover had in fact been something of a restless soul during his tenure at Commerce, sometimes even working quietly at cross-purposes with the White House, but in any event showing an energetically activist bent that his two bosses did not share. That bent was clearly visible even before he became president.

During the 1920–21 recession, for example, Hoover began convening conferences between government officials and business leaders in which he advocated for fostering cooperation rather than competition between them, a governing philosophy that came to be called *associationalism*. Harding and Coolidge rejected most of his ideas, though they did permit Hoover to pursue an "Own Your Own Home" campaign, a collaboration with groups such as the Better Houses in America movement, the Architects' Small House Service Bureau, the Home Modernizing Bureau, and officers in banks and savings and loans, to promote the new long-term home mortgage, which in turn dramatically encouraged single-family home construction and therefore broad homeownership. Like the Progressives, Hoover was quite comfortable with the idea that government should play an active role in fostering a collective and coordinated response to public needs. When the stock market collapse came, he was not likely to sit by and do nothing.

Once the downward spiral of the economy gathered momentum, it seemed unstoppable, and its effects ramified out in every direction. Automobile output fell from 4.5 million units in 1929 to 1.1 million units in 1932, and Ford laid off seventy-five thousand workers, with similar ripple effects on auto-related industries, and reduction in the purchasing power of unemployed workers. More than thirteen hundred banks closed in 1930, thirty-seven hundred more in 1931 and 1932, depressing both consumption and investment in one stroke. People who had scrimped and saved for years to buy a house or send their children to college saw their hopes destroyed in the blink of an eye. The already weak agricultural sector was decimated, new investment in the economy dropped to one-tenth of what it had been before the crash, and national income dropped by a staggering 40 percent.

Unemployment rose to thirteen million by the end of 1932, which was about one in four workers; many more were underemployed in part-time jobs. Unable to meet their rents, some displaced workers crowded in with relatives, while others took to the open road, desperately seeking employment in the next town, or beyond. Parents in the cities regularly rooted around in garbage cans, searching for table scraps to feed to their children. Families that had just months before lived in decent and respectable housing now found themselves living in makeshift shanty towns, derisively dubbed Hoovervilles, with hovels made of cardboard and plywood for their dwellings.

How far things had fallen, and how dizzyingly fast! Hoover had come into office at the height of Coolidge prosperity and effused in his August 11, 1928, speech accepting the Republican nomination for president that "we shall soon with the help of God, be in sight of the day when poverty will be banished from this nation." Nothing in his experience could have prepared him for the awful spectacle now before him. What could he do about it?

Hoover responded energetically, drawing upon his activist belief in voluntary cooperation as a way out of the morass. He believed that the nation's economic structure was fundamentally sound and that the main problem now facing the nation was a debilitating loss of confidence. He gave a great many speeches devoted to this theme, even as he gradually developed a program for restoring the economy. In keeping with his associationalist ideals, he called for cooperative action by businessmen who would informally agree to keep their businesses operating, hold wages and prices steady, and avoid layoffs, while he asked union leaders to moderate their demands and refrain from striking. He sought tax reduction, public works projects to create jobs and stimulate the economy, federal aid to banks and corporations threatened with failure, aid to homeowners in danger of mortgage foreclosure, and a "limited revision" upward of the tariff to help beleaguered farmers and provide protection for textile mills and other depressed American industries.

Few of these measures seemed to make much of a difference. In fact, the "limited revision" of the tariff eventually turned into one of his most disastrous early decisions: his signing into law of the Hawley–Smoot Tariff of 1930. That ill-conceived measure – which Hoover himself opposed, even calling it "obnoxious," but felt he must sign out of party loyalty – boosted duties on a thousand different items, increases of up to 49 percent on foreign imports, in the hope of protecting American producers. This dramatic change brought little short-term benefit, however, and provoked a wave of retaliatory tariffs from America's trading partners in Europe, which had the effect of keeping American goods out of their countries' markets. Thus, over the longer term, the tariff had the effect of cutting American exports and imports in half and delivering a body blow to the economies of still-recovering Europe.

Somewhat more successful was the creation of the Reconstruction Finance Corporation (RFC) as a measure designed to prop up key institutions – such as banks, railroads, life insurance companies, building and loans, and farm-mortgage associations – that played a central role in the economy but were currently teetering on the brink of failure. The logic behind the RFC was that well-placed emergency federal loans designed to stabilize these strategically important institutions would in turn have benefits that would multiply out into the more general economy, shoring up the economic infrastructure, creating jobs, stimulating the flow of credit, and eventually helping needy individuals, as growing wealth in the upper reaches flowed down to the lower ones.

The plan enjoyed some limited success, but critics found it too favorable to the wealthy and well connected and strangely deaf to the immediate needs of the great mass of suffering people. It was a complaint that had some merit. The humorist Will Rogers, who often delivered himself of waggish political opinions in a down-home accent, put it this way:

> *The money was all appropriated for the top in the hopes that it would trickle down to the needy. Mr. Hoover was an engineer. He knew that water trickles down. Put it uphill and let it go and it will reach the driest little spot. But he didn't know that money trickled up. Give it to the people at the bottom and the people at the top will have it before night, anyhow.*

It was not the most sophisticated analysis, but it well described some of the disbelief that Hoover's policies elicited in those who were not seeing anything "trickling down" to them.

Hoover, in turn, although willing to do more than any predecessor to use the power of government to address the economic emergency that was facing the country, was committed to the idea that federal funds should not be used directly for the relief of individuals. This was an issue of fundamental importance to him. To do otherwise, he believed, would violate the constitutional limitations on the scope of the national government and allow it to preempt the roles of state and municipal governments, as well as private charitable organizations. Hoover was worried that doing so would "lead to the super-state where every man becomes the servant of the state and real liberty is lost." The RFC did not violate Hoover's principles, because it involved making loans to businesses that were productive and could be repaid eventually. The loans were, in that sense, commercial transactions rather than gifts, and they did nothing to touch the lives of individuals in a direct way. This, Hoover contended, was how it had to be.

At a time when millions were out of work, breadlines and soup kitchens were in business in every major city, and private charities were rapidly running out of the wherewithal to deal with the growing levels of desperate human need, such a position seemed, to a great many Americans, both blind and callous. The Democratic opposition (which had gained strength in both houses of

Congress from the 1930 midterms) took political advantage of that national mood, filing numerous bills proposing federal measures that would in fact provide direct relief to individuals. Hoover would not go that far, but he did yield slightly. In July 1932, he signed the Emergency Relief Act, which appropriated $300 million for relief loans to the states and supported a wide array of public works – all of which would presumably have benefits for individuals when implemented but did not cross that red line of authorizing direct federal cash payments to individuals.

Despite such efforts, Hoover's standing with the public only seemed to sink. This situation had tragic elements. Hoover was a good man; a highly intelligent, competent, and accomplished public official; and a distinguished humanitarian with a cosmopolitan sensibility and an incomparable record of service to the nation and the world. In fact, it is hard to imagine any American of his day who had a more ideal résumé for service as president of the United States. He was a problem solver *par excellence* who combined an engineer's scientific insight with a social worker's benevolent intentions, and he had successfully tackled enormous tasks – relief efforts in war-torn Belgium, Russia, and Ukraine; the Mississippi Valley floods of 1927 – with skill and dedication.

But the Great Depression defeated him completely and, in the process, caused him to present an image to the world of coldness and indifference toward his suffering fellow Americans. He would live for another three decades after leaving the presidency and continued to perform acts of great public service for the American people. But he never was able to shake the image of highhanded ineptitude and sour resentment that history has affixed to him.

The Depression deepened sharply in spring 1932, and with employment moving inexorably toward 25 percent, more and more homeless and rootless tramps were set loose, wandering the roads, riding the trains, living in Hoovervilles, and begging for work or food. Farmers were so disgusted by the low prices their crops were fetching in the market that they burned their corn for fuel. In June and July, some forty-three thousand marchers, seventeen thousand of whom were World War I veterans and their families, gathered together and descended upon Washington to demand early redemption of their World War I bonuses. They called themselves the Bonus Expeditionary Force, to recall Pershing's heroic AEF. When Congress said no to this disorganized Bonus Army, several thousand refused to leave and encamped in the Anacostia Flats on the south side of the city, keeping up the pressure. Hoover soon became alarmed by them, fearing that they had violent or criminal intent, or perhaps were Communist revolutionaries, and he sent in first police and then soldiers to disperse the crowd with rifles, bayonets, tear gas, and tanks. General Douglas MacArthur, who led the troops, made matters worse when he disobeyed Hoover's orders by driving directly into the encampment. In any event, it proved a fatal error for Hoover to allow himself to be seen as willing to send troops against honored American veterans. Influential senator Hiram Johnson, a fellow Republican, called the incident "one of the blackest pages in our history."

Hoover's fears were probably without much foundation in fact. But with such extreme discontent and despair running rampant, there was bound to be more and more talk of implementing radical economic and political solutions in the country. Mainstream labor leaders warned Hoover that unless the employment picture improved dramatically, and soon, the country might be faced with the prospect of open rebellion. One sign that they might be right was that the Communist Party, which had enjoyed very little popularity among American workers in the past, suddenly enjoyed a boomlet of interest, particularly among writers and intellectuals who openly included an out and out revolution as one of their objectives. Their membership shot up to one hundred thousand – still small, perhaps, but no longer insignificant.

As the 1932 election approached, Hoover and the Republicans seemed resigned to defeat. The economic triumphs of Republican rule had turned to ashes during the previous three years of deepening depression. Hoover seemed exhausted and overwhelmed by the intractability of the problems. His characteristic self-confidence had deserted him, leaving him sullen and pessimistic. That was not the outlook the country needed. The desire for change was in the air, and the Democrats were justifiably confident of victory.

They chose as their candidate the governor of New York, Franklin Delano Roosevelt, a distant cousin of TR. Unlike Hoover, Roosevelt had been born to great wealth and privilege, an only child pampered and cosseted by his mother; educated by governesses and tutors at the family's Hudson Valley estate; enjoying frequent trips to Europe; and then going on to the elite Groton School, Harvard College, and Columbia Law School. But like his patrician cousin, he was attracted to a life of public service and the rough-and-tumble of electoral politics. He rose quickly through the ranks, serving in the New York State Assembly, in Washington as assistant secretary of the navy (like his cousin TR), and then as the Democratic candidate for vice president in 1920. (Interestingly, he tried to persuade Hoover to run for president that year as a Democrat, with himself as the vice presidential running mate.)

Franklin Roosevelt had something else in common with his cousin Theodore: both had overcome physical disabilities by acts of sheer determination. TR had conquered his sickly constitution through a heroic program of physical culture. But Franklin (or FDR, as he would become known) had to face an even greater challenge. In 1921, at the age of thirty-nine, he was stricken while on vacation with a mysterious disease, then thought to be polio but now believed to have been Guillain–Barré syndrome, which left him permanently paralyzed from the waist down. It appeared his political career would be over. Roosevelt would not accept that fate, though. He put himself through a program of physical therapy, laboriously teaching himself to walk short distances while wearing iron braces on his hips and legs. But he would never regain the full use of his lower limbs; that was a limitation he would have to accept and forever have to work around. He took great care not to be seen using his wheelchair in public and avoided press coverage that would call attention to his disability. But he pressed on with his political ambitions, undeterred.

Unlike his cousin, FDR was not known for his intellectual gifts. While TR began writing his naval history of the War of 1812 during his college days, FDR was an inattentive student at Harvard, spending most of his time playing the social butterfly and editing the school newspaper. That lack of intellectual depth didn't change much as he got older. FDR's close presidential aide, Raymond Moley, said the following of him:

> His knowledge of political and constitutional history and theory is distinctly limited. During all the time I was associated with him I never knew him to read a serious book … [or to show] any appreciation of the basic philosophical distinctions in the history of American political thought.

But he had something equally important to compensate for that: a sunny and hopeful disposition, an unsinkable optimism and upbeat personality that were inspirational and infectious and gave the public reason to believe that, as his campaign song put it, "Happy Days Are Here Again," or would be soon. In short, he was a charismatic leader, capable of speaking to a mass following. Supreme Court justice Oliver Wendell Holmes put it well when he said that FDR possessed "a second-class intellect, but a first-class temperament." And given that the nation found itself enmeshed in an economic calamity that no one fully understood, a first-class temperament would likely be a far greater asset going forward. Roosevelt chose to wage a vigorous and grueling campaign, the rigors of which put to rest any qualms voters might have had about his physical strength or his endurance.

Without thinking much about it at first, Roosevelt introduced in his campaign speeches the theme of a "new deal for the American people." The term caught on and became his trademark. What exactly it meant was less clear. But the good-old-American ordinariness of a "deal," whether it referred to the business of contracts or the reshuffling of a deck of playing cards, implied that the changes he envisioned would be significant but would stop short of a being a cultural revolution. That read the public mood accurately. What Americans seemed to want was not a revolutionary panacea but a release from the stalled, stifled, thwarted mood of the Hoover administration and its replacement by a sense of moving forward. Roosevelt understood this too. As he said in a speech at Oglethorpe University in May 1932, "the country needs and, unless I mistake its temper, the country demands bold, persistent experimentation. It is common sense to take a method and try it: If it fails, admit it frankly and try another. But above all, try something. The millions who are in want will not stand by silently forever." Such experimentalism – try things until you hit on something that works – was very much in the American vein of unsystematic pragmatism. All Hoover could offer to counter it were sputtering warnings that Democrats in office would be reckless and make things worse, a warning that carried little weight under the circumstances.

But there were a few specific aspects of the New Deal taking shape in those speeches. First and foremost, Roosevelt was clearly not going to be bound by the limitations on federal power that Hoover had observed, if he believed that exceeding those limitations would advance the common good. He showed a willingness to incur small and short-term budget deficits to deal with emergency needs. He would seek to repeal Prohibition, which was also his party's official position. He would seek greater regulation of some public utilities and federal involvement in the development of electricity. In addition, in the Oglethorpe speech, he tentatively floated the idea that "national planning" would be necessary if the nation were to achieve its objectives.

In the election itself, Roosevelt's optimistic, hope-filled campaign won out, as expected, carrying all but six states and running up a 57–40 margin in the popular vote. Ironically, that was almost the same margin by which Hoover had beaten Al Smith four years earlier, an illustration of how volatile the nation's electorate had become in the past four years, and how willing they were to rethink their earlier commitments. It was also a sign that the new coalition hinted at in 1928, joining the Democratic strengths in the South with the support of urban workers in the north and angry farmers in the West, had become a reality.

In the four months between the November election and the March 1933 inauguration, the Depression descended to its worst depths yet, with a wave of bank failures that brought the economy to the edge of the abyss. By inauguration day, March 4, four-fifths of the banks in the country were closed, as was the New York Stock Exchange. Industrial production had fallen to just 56 percent of its 1929 level, at least thirteen million wage earners were unemployed, and farmers were in ever more desperate straits. Into these tense and challenging circumstances stepped Roosevelt. He would need to deliver an inaugural address that would honestly acknowledge the extent of the nation's problems and yet provide hope that they could be solved.

He succeeded brilliantly, though not without striking some troubling chords. He began with the poignant observation that "the only thing we have to fear is fear itself – nameless, unreasoning, unjustified terror which paralyzes needed efforts to convert retreat into advance." Above all else, the country needed to reject the psychology of depression and decline. He then went on to affirm the nation's enduring spiritual strength, using a biblical image to place the blame for the soured economy on the materialism and greed of bankers and businessmen. "The money changers have fled from their high seats in the temple of our civilization," he declared, echoing a famous event from the life of Jesus. "We may now restore that temple to the ancient truths." One might well wonder whether this rhetorical flourish was an honest description of the causes of the country's woes, and of the meaning of Roosevelt's election, or whether Roosevelt was using biblical language to pander to the people's need for an identifiable villain.

The speech concluded with two notable statements of purpose: first, that he would not hesitate to request "broad Executive power" from Congress to address the "national emergency" of the moment, and second, that this executive power would be used "to wage a war against the emergency, as great as the power that would be given to me if we were in fact invaded by a foreign foe." In other words, he would be drawing on the familiar Progressive language of the moral equivalent of war: "I assume unhesitatingly the leadership of this great army of our people," and we shall be "treating the task as we would treat the emergency of a war." It would remain to be seen whether that idea would fare better now than it had before – and what casualties this particular war might produce.

But the need for action was urgent, and Roosevelt set to work at an unprecedented pace. The new Congress, Democrat dominated in both houses, was eager to enact almost anything the president wanted, and in the following "Hundred Days" (between March 9 and June 16), there was virtually no opposition to the president's program. But what was that program to be? That was less clear. With the assistance of Raymond Moley, Roosevelt had assembled a brain trust of top experts in various aspects of public policy, but they all had different and sometimes conflicting ideas. Some wanted stricter enforcement of antitrust laws affecting commerce. Others wanted to see such laws waived, to make possible greater concentration and collaboration between the private sector and the government. Others wanted to see massive wealth transfers through social-welfare programs, to even out some of the grosser disparities in the society and enable the relief of suffering individuals and families.

Roosevelt characteristically did not choose one over the others in any definite pattern, so that his program often seemed a hodgepodge of conflicting tendencies. Some of this was for political reasons, due to the ungainliness of his coalition, which included the solid South, urban ethnics, farmers, and liberal / progressive types, all of whom had different priorities – and all of whom he needed to keep happy. This was particularly true of the southerners, who largely controlled the mechanisms of Congress. But much of it reflected Roosevelt's own mind and its unsystematic, unideological, and episodic way of proceeding.

In any event, certain concrete and immediate problems needed addressing. First and foremost, there was the banking system, the ultimate financial infrastructure in a capitalist economy, which was teetering on the brink of collapse. Roosevelt moved boldly by asking Congress to declare a bank holiday that would allow things to settle down in that sector and to pass certain other laws increasing his power over the operations of the Federal Reserve. He explained his actions immediately afterward with a radio "fireside chat," one of the most effective early uses of radio in American politics, a device to which Roosevelt would frequently turn and of which he was a master. It was such a dramatic contrast to Hoover's remoteness and diffidence, to have the president of the United States coming into everyone's home, with a combination of dignity and intimacy, with his gentle, reassuring, grandfatherly voice laying out the details of his actions. Nothing that Roosevelt did was more indicative of his political genius than those fireside chats.

It would require too much space for us to detail all the banking-related actions taken during the Hundred Days. But to cite the most significant, by the end of that first session, in the Banking Act of 1933, Congress had created the Federal Deposit Insurance Corporation, which would fully insure bank deposits up to $5,000, a way of reassuring depositors and preventing bank runs, and had also separated investment and commercial banking as a way of ensuring that investment banks would not raid the accounts of ordinary depositors and commercial banks would not be tempted to get involved in speculation.

Next came the problem of relieving the displacement and distress of individuals and families, an area in which Roosevelt was much more willing to experiment than Hoover had been. He created a wide array of structures designed to give a lift to those trapped in poverty. Again, we can only discuss the main ones here. The Civilian Conservation Corps was created to supply jobs to some three million unemployed young men working in parks, forests, and soil-conservation projects around the country. The Civil Works Administration employed another four million building bridges, roads, and schools. The Works Progress Administration (WPA), which built various public works, including some distinguished public buildings, and offered work for artists, actors, and writers, lasted until 1943 and employed at least eight and a half million during that time.

There were some worthy products of these programs, particularly of the WPA, which bequeathed to us such treasures as a set of travel guides to the states of the United States and the Federal Theatre Project's productions. But there was also a great deal of waste and public skepticism about these "make work" jobs. A popular song by the Mills Brothers, performed with jazz great Louis Armstrong, captured the mood in a satiric song called "WPA." Here is a sampling of its lyrics:

> *The WPA.*
>
> *Sleep while you work, while you rest, while you play*
> *Lean on your shovel to pass the time away*
> *T'ain't what you do; you can't die for your pay*
>
> *The WPA.*
>
> *Now don't be a fool; working hard is passé*
> *You'll stand from five to six hours a day*
> *Sit down and joke while you smoke; it's okay*
>
> *The WPA.*
>
> *I'm so tired, I don't know what to do*
> *Can't get fired, so I'll take my rest until my work*
> *Is through*
>
> *The WPA.*

Of course, there were also a great many heartfelt testimonies to the individual benefits wrought by the WPA and similar programs. But it must be conceded that these programs did very little to reduce unemployment in significant ways; the unemployment rate never dropped below 10 percent during the New Deal years. Was that because the idea of a massive public works program fueled by tax dollars and detached from the actual economy was an inherently bad idea, as some historians contend? Or was it, as others say, because Roosevelt was too timid, operated on too small a scale, and spent too little on these programs for them to have the requisite effect? Or do both such considerations miss the fact that the principal value of these relief measures was psychological, in fostering the perception that the country was no longer helpless before its problems? Debate over these matters continues to this day.

To stimulate the long-range recovery of industry and agriculture was an even more complex, but vitally important, task. To that end, Roosevelt devised two principal initiatives. The National Industrial Recovery Act (NIRA) would create the National Recovery Administration (NRA), under the direction of General Hugh Johnson. It authorized industrial and trade associations to establish production codes, set prices and wages, and otherwise cooperate (or as an antitrust skeptic might say, collude). The idea, borrowed from the WIB (with which Johnson had worked during the war), sought to tamp down "destructive competition" and establish an enduring basis for stable prices and fair wages. Membership was voluntary, but Johnson devised a blue-eagle emblem which would be displayed in the windows of cooperating businesses, with the slogan "We Do Our Part!" accompanying it, as a way that businesses could advertise their civic virtue and as a way to encourage widespread participation. Johnson was, for a time, lionized as a culture hero and was designated *Time* magazine's Man of the Year for 1933.

In one of his statements after signing the NIRA on June 16, 1933, Roosevelt clearly invoked the holy grail of sacrifice and community: "The challenge of this law is whether we can sink selfish interest and present a solid front against a common peril," he explained. Roosevelt specifically called upon the memory of the First World War: "I had part in the great cooperation of 1917 and 1918," he said, "and it is my faith that we can count on our industry once more to join in our general purpose to lift this new threat and to do it without taking any advantage of the public trust which has this day been reposed without stint in the good faith and high purpose of American business." FDR was hardly modest in his claims for the act: "It is the most important attempt of this kind in history. As in the great crisis of the World War, it puts a whole people to the simple but vital test: – 'Must we go on in many groping, disorganized, separate units to defeat or shall we move as one great team to victory?'" In another statement made that same day, he ventured to say that "history probably will record the NIRA as the most important and far-reaching legislation ever enacted by the American Congress."

That was not to be the case, however. The NRA enjoyed a few limited successes, but the agency very rapidly became completely unmanageable, overwhelmed with responsibility for enacting hundreds of codes of fair competition, formulating thousands of orders through which the codes were interpreted, issuing administrative orders, promulgating presidential executive orders, and so on. Imagine taking the burden of evaluating every price, every wage, every transaction, every rule of competition, every production quota, in a sprawling and ever-changing national economy. The job would be overwhelming. Every single decision made would have to take into account dozens of unforeseen and unforeseeable effects, because every economic decision has consequences ramifying out from it in dozens of directions. The problem is easy to understand. Raise the price of oil, for example, and one also raises the cost of transportation, the cost of food, and the cost of almost everything else in the economy, while diminishing disposable income available to consumers, which in turn diminishes the sales of many items, including manufactured goods such as automobiles and radios, which otherwise depresses those portions of the economy, possibly leading to layoffs and unemployment, and so on. Multiply that example by several hundredfold more examples, of prices and wages alike, with each one producing chains of effects drawn out as far as one can take them, and there you have the problem the NRA faced.

Given this morass, it was almost inevitable that the NRA's work would quickly became taken over by the dominant manufacturers in each industry, who used the codes to create sweet monopolies for themselves, to the detriment of the many small businesses that were being deprived of their competitive advantages. The process became so corrupt so quickly that by 1934, Johnson himself asked for the Senate to create a review board, headed by the lawyer Clarence Darrow, to investigate the agency. Darrow's conclusions were devastating: "the NRA was gotten up to help 'big business,' and they could not help big business very much unless they took the business away from the small fellows. We arrived at that conclusion from what seems to be perfectly obvious and undisputed evidence." It was almost an anticlimax when the NIRA was declared unconstitutional by the Supreme Court in 1935, in *Schechter Poultry Corporation v. United States.*

The Agricultural Adjustment Administration (AAA) was somewhat more successful. The chief problem with American agriculture had been that it was too productive for its own good, a fact that helped to produce the steady decline in commodity prices that had been farmers' bane for many years. The reasoning behind the AAA was simple: it sought to control agricultural prices by inducing farmers to reduce output, paying them for livestock that would not go to market or for taking some portion of their land out of cultivation and thereby reducing crop yields. The goal was to bring supply and demand closer to parity, or more simply, to raise prices by reducing supply. But it was counterintuitive, to put it mildly, for the government to induce farmers to be producing less during a time when starving people in American cities were standing in breadlines.

At first this program seemed to work, though the severe drought affecting the Plains states in these years, the so-called Dust Bowl years, may have had more to do with declines in production than the policies of the AAA. There is also evidence that many farmers saw their incomes rise because they pocketed their government subsidies and went ahead and planted at the same levels, sometimes double-planting in the available space. Perhaps more importantly, as in the NRA, the AAA favored the large and organized over the small and unorganized. Large producers thrived under the system, pocketing many thousands of dollars in subsidy, but smaller producers found it hard to compete. In 1936, the Supreme Court declared the AAA's funding source, a tax on companies processing farm products, to be unconstitutional; after a legislative fix in 1938, though, the program would resume.

Mention should also be made of several other programs of the early New Deal. The Tennessee Valley Authority (TVA) was a massive and ambitious experiment in regional planning, the main purpose of which was to supply government-subsidized electric power to citizens in that impoverished region. The Securities and Exchange Commission was created to regulate the stock market and limit the kind of speculative transactions that it was thought had led to the Crash of 1929. The Federal Housing Administration was created to insure bank loans for the construction and repair of houses, thus boosting the recovery of both building and mortgage banking.

However variable its measures were in the extent of their measurable success, the Roosevelt administration's amazing flurry of activity had produced one indisputable good effect: it lifted the nation's spirits, convincing Americans that their government cared about them and was determined to address the plight of its more vulnerable citizens. This was no small thing. The art of governing well is not only a matter of satisfying material needs but also one of supplying hope. The New Deal had done that, and the Democrats were accordingly rewarded with gains in the midterm elections of 1934, an unusual feat for any midterm presidency. But the hope began to give out when the Depression still showed no signs of lifting by the end of 1934. Roosevelt began to face more stringent criticism from critics both Right and Left, berating the ineffectiveness or wrongheadedness of his reforms.

From his Right, no less a personage than Herbert Hoover, in his 1934 book *The Challenge to Liberty*, was labeling the New Deal "the most stupendous invasion of the whole spirit of Liberty" the American nation had ever seen. Hoover's reaction could be dismissed as sour grapes. But it was not quite as easy to dismiss the American Liberty League, which arose to protest the steady growth of executive power and other extraconstitutional measures of the Roosevelt administration, and was a bipartisan group, featuring both John W. Davis, the 1924 Democratic presidential candidate, and Al Smith, the 1928 Democratic candidate, in its leadership. That Smith and Davis were both finding themselves moving in opposition to FDR is indicative of how much ground Roosevelt had traveled and how much he had moved leftward the center of gravity in the national discussion.

Nevertheless, Roosevelt flicked away the challenge from the Right fairly easily, while finding the discontent on the Left more troubling. "We were promised a New Deal," complained Milo Reno, an agrarian populist firebrand from Iowa who had supported Roosevelt in 1932, but instead "we have the same old stacked deck" and "the same old dealers." Reno would eventually declare his opposition to Roosevelt in the 1936 election, an ominous sign. If Roosevelt wanted to win reelection, he could not afford to lose many such supporters. And there were several prominent figures emerging on the scene who could plausibly supply a rallying point for distressed lower-class voters.

Perhaps the greatest threat to Roosevelt from the Left came from Huey P. Long of Louisiana, a governor and then senator from that state whose combination of generous populist policies, demagogic rhetoric, and unscrupulous control of the levers of power won him a large following – and the enduring enmity of governing elites. Long proposed his own plan for curing the Depression, the Share Our Wealth program, which would give every citizen a package of benefits, including a guaranteed annual income, financed by a net asset tax aimed at the personal fortunes of the rich. Long was a master of radio and used it to create a national organization, the Share Our Wealth Society, with seven and a half million members. In the discontented atmosphere of 1935, Long looked like a real contender to challenge FDR for the Democratic nomination, and if not that, a third-party candidate who could draw away enough votes to elect a Republican in the general election.

Nor was Long the only one peddling superficially attractive remedies. Dr. Francis E. Townsend of California, who himself had lost most of his money in the stock market crash, advocated giving a $200 per month pension for each elderly person in the country, with the only requirement being that they spend all $200 within a month. The Townsend Recovery Plan would thus at one and the same time take care of the needs of the elderly and jump-start the economy through increased economic activity. Father Charles Coughlin, a Roman Catholic priest from the Detroit area with a highly popular radio program – he was estimated to have as many as forty-five million listeners – promoted currency reform and coinage of silver, inveighed against capitalist greed, and condemned bankers in tones that gradually became more and more redolent of anti-Semitism.

Roosevelt was acutely aware of these political pressures coming from his Left and knew that he needed to counter them. The *Schechter* case gave him the pretext he wanted, prodding him into initiating a whole new flood of legislation, sometimes referred to as the Second Hundred Days or the Second New Deal. The centerpiece of the Second New Deal would be the Social Security Act of 1935, which FDR called the "cornerstone" of the New Deal. It was a direct response to the concerns that had activated Townsend's movement, setting up a system of old-age insurance financed partly by a tax automatically collected and levied equally on workers and employers and placed in a Social Security Trust Fund. When workers reached age sixty-five and retired, they would begin to draw a modest payment – Roosevelt insisted it would not be enough to live on, merely a supplemental income – for the rest of their lives. The act also established a state–federal system of unemployment insurance, similarly financed, and provided public assistance, also in a state–federal partnership, for those who were disabled and for families with dependent children and their mothers.

The passage and implementation of the Social Security Act was an enormously significant event, not least because it finally and unambiguously crossed the red line that Hoover had established of a program that brought the federal government into direct and ongoing relationship with individuals. One lesson the Democrats had drawn from the Great Depression had been that, given the complexity of modern industrial society, the individual is often at the mercy of forces incomparably greater than himself, and it is therefore reasonable to ask that government provide some minimal financial basis to ensure the individual's basic sustenance and well-being. The American people seemed to have accepted that premise and trusted Roosevelt when he said that, contrary to his critics, he wanted such changes in order to "save our system, the capitalistic system."

It is notable, too, that the program followed a very American pattern. It was modest, not intended to supplant the worker's own efforts to build a retirement nest egg. It would be the most minimal of safety nets. It was funded by worker and employer contributions, not (as in other countries) by the general operating funds of the federal budget, which meant that most recipients would not have to feel like charity cases, because they would have contributed their own funds to the Social Security Trust Fund over the entirety of their working lives.

There were two other significant legislative achievements in the Second New Deal. The National Labor Relations Act, often known as the Wagner Act after its sponsor, Senator Robert Wagner of New York, gave workers the right to join a union and bargain collectively and forbade employers from interfering with union organizing efforts. In addition, the National Labor Relations Board would supervise elections and certify unions as well as investigate employers for unfair practices.

The Revenue Act of 1935, which was popularly known as the soak-the-rich tax, raised tax rates on incomes above $50,000 (which was $920,000 in 2018 dollars) and raised corporate, estate, and gift taxes. This move helped to blunt the influence of Long's and Coughlin's populist appeal, although it made businessmen even more angry with Roosevelt than they already were. William Randolph Hearst called the tax "communism." The Chamber of Commerce, which had endorsed FDR in 1932, withdrew its endorsement in 1936. And in the end, its effects were mainly theatrical, since the taxes did not raise much new revenue.

The net effect of all these changes, though, was to clear the electoral battlefield of all other contenders and ensure Roosevelt's reelection in 1936. And what a reelection it was! As he was piling up the most commanding electoral triumph in American presidential history to date, defeating the decent but hapless Governor Alf Landon of Kansas, he was also fixing into place the coalition that had brought him victory in 1932, and adding to it. In addition to a solid base of southerners and ethnic northerners, he attracted western farmers who had been helped by his programs. Most momentously of all, he attracted the votes of African Americans, who had been firmly committed to the Republican Party since the postbellum years but now shifted a majority of their votes to the Democrats, even despite the presence in the party of the segregationist Democrats who ran politics in the southern states. Roosevelt won the popular vote by 60.8 percent to 36.5 percent, besting even Harding's commanding margin in 1920 and carrying all but two states, Maine and Vermont, in the Electoral College. And he would have a compliant Congress to work with, it seemed; the Republican presence in both houses was diminished to tiny minorities. Roosevelt was now in command, as no other American president had ever been.

Yet, as is so often the case in human affairs, pride goes before a fall. Roosevelt began his second term believing that the election was a giant affirmation of what he had been doing, and a call for more of it – more reform, more activism, more government. He had every intention of proceeding on to a Third New Deal, which would push his agenda even further. The only obstacle to him, the only branch of government he did not control, and had so far been unable to whip into shape, was the Supreme Court. Again and again, notably with his two major initiatives in the First New Deal, the NIRA and the AAA, the Supreme Court had obstructed him (and in the case of the NIRA, thwarted him completely). Legal cases against the Wagner Act and the Social Security Act were pending in the courts, and it was just a matter of time before those cases made their way onto the docket of the Supreme Court. And then what would happen? Was there any reason to believe that the Court would not act as it had in the past and strike down Roosevelt's laws?

Under the circumstances, Roosevelt felt he had to act, and given the size and scope of his electoral mandate, he felt supremely confident in doing so. He introduced legislation asking the Congress to increase the number of justices, then set at nine, ostensibly as part of a more general plan for reorganizing the judiciary, but really to give him the tools he need to dilute the power of the incumbent Supreme Court justices. The effort, which FDR's outraged opponents labeled a "court-packing" scheme, was immediately and intensely controversial, not only among Republicans but also among many liberals, who were deeply concerned about the precedent being set. Roosevelt discovered that, as great as his power was, it had distinct limits. In the end, the opposition was too heated, and he had to give up the battle. Ironically, he would get his way over the constitutionality of the Wagner and Social Security acts, which the Court chose not to overturn; and there are some indications that two key justices may have altered their position in response to the political situation. (This would come to be called "the switch in time that saved nine.") But Roosevelt's reputation would not survive the incident intact; the very attempt was seen as revelation of character: brazen, unprincipled, and too clever by half.

There was worse to come. A sharp recession in 1937, caused partly by Roosevelt's own policies of budget cutting and by the assessment of $2 billion in Social Security payroll taxes (with the attendant loss of disposable income for workers), and partly by business fears of the cumulative effects of the Wagner Act, minimum wage laws, and who knew whatever future changes might come with Roosevelt in such exclusive command – these led the economy down even below the depths of the early 1930s. It was fairly labeled the "Roosevelt recession," which was a way not only of identifying it but also of assigning blame for it. Not only did it reverse the gains that had been made since 1933 but it took the bloom off the rose with regard to the public's trust in Roosevelt's economic wizardry. It gave ample reason for economists to wonder, then and since, whether the Depression itself had in large measure been a policy-made disaster, a product of well-meaning but bumbling and counterproductive initiatives which prolonged rather than relived the misery. Might Andrew Mellon have been right all along?

The negative residual effects of the court-packing episode came back to bite Roosevelt in the controversies over the Executive Reorganization Act, introduced in 1937. The act would have freed executive branch officials from congressional oversight and created a much more powerful administrative state. It was resisted fiercely by Republicans and Democrats alike. Some of the influential newspapers were already calling Roosevelt a "dictator," with not only the court packing in mind but also the roughly contemporary Nazi seizure of power in the Weimar Republic of Germany. This new development only added to their anxieties.

Undaunted by his critics, Roosevelt responded with angry determination: he would rid his party of those who had opposed him – mainly southerners – and would remake the Democratic Party in the progressive image of the New Deal. This "purge" would mean that he injected himself into 1938 primary campaigns around the country, to see to it that his supporters were nominated and his opponents were defeated. Still riding high from his electoral triumph, Roosevelt had every confidence that he could pull it off. But it was a huge risk, since he was placing his own prestige in jeopardy, and expending precious political capital for an outcome that might well be beyond his reach. And indeed FDR failed, and incurred three costs: he turned a number of Democrats into enemies, he shattered the image of his own invincibility, and he contributed to the picture of himself as dangerously power hungry.

The elections of November 1938 would be a debacle for him, in ways that went beyond the numbers. Democrats lost six Senate seats and seventy-one House seats as well as a dozen governorships, including in such crucial states as Ohio, Michigan, and Pennsylvania. Democrats continued to hold their majorities in Congress, but these were no longer effectively pro–New Deal majorities. Democratic losses in the election had been concentrated among pro–New Deal Democrats, so that in the new Congress, the Senate was fairly evenly divided between pro– and anti–New Deal forces, and the "conservative coalition" of Republicans and conservative Democrats was in command in the House. As journalist Arthur Krock put it, "the New Deal has been halted."

For the most part, Krock would turn out to be right. Just two years after his epochal 1936 victory, Roosevelt was now faced with effective opposition on a scale he had never before experienced. How quickly his fortunes had turned. After November 1938, there would be no more Hundred Days explosions of legislative activity. Roosevelt's New Deal had made dramatic and permanent changes in the landscape of American life and had eased the effects of a very great economic calamity. His spirit and his words had restored the nation's spirit. But his policies had not solved the problems of the economy and had not returned the country to full employment. It would take, not the moral equivalent of war, but war itself to accomplish that.

CHAPTER EIGHTEEN

THE FINEST HOUR

World War II

THROUGH MOST OF THE 1930S, AMERICANS' ATTENTION remained riveted to their own massive internal challenges and the spirited internal debates about how best to address them. As we've seen, the problems of economic recovery and reform were elusive, with effective solutions hard to come by and hard to agree upon. These persistent facts alone would have been enough to ensure that the nation's energies would be largely directed inward during those years. But there was another important factor in play. The American public had a strong and lingering sense of regret over the country's involvement in the First World War, accompanied by a deep mistrust of any moves that might draw the country into making that same mistake again. The urgent need to solve problems at home coincided with an acute reluctance to go abroad in search of monsters to destroy.

The resulting national mood is frequently labeled as "isolationist," but that term can be a bit misleading. It is true that, in rejecting the League of Nations, the United States demonstrated an unwillingness to join a new multilateral organization that might infringe on its national sovereignty (as Article X of the League Covenant seemed to do). Although in that case, as we've seen, the rejection of the League need not have happened; it had less to do with "isolationism" than with Woodrow Wilson's extreme stubbornness in refusing to adapt the terms of the agreement by even so much as a particle, to meet the understandable concerns of its critics. A majority of senators, including Henry Cabot Lodge, would have readily supported the League, had their reservations, particularly those about the dangerous ambiguities of Article X, been addressed.

But even if one accepts this single example as a potential indicator, in most other respects, the United States during most of the interwar years was very far from being isolationist, if that term is taken to indicate a withdrawal from involvement in the larger world. To begin with, given its far-reaching commercial interests all around the globe, the United States was unlikely to be withdrawing from the world anytime soon. But there was more than that. The United States would play a leading role in promoting the cause of general disarmament, as in its sponsorship of the Washington Conference of 1921, which sought to limit the naval arms race among the major powers, and the Kellogg–Briand Pact of 1928, which sought to eliminate war as an instrument of national policy and attracted sixty-two nations as signatories. Whatever the wisdom or effectiveness of these actions, they were not the actions of an "isolationist" nation. It would be more accurate to say, instead, that in the interwar years, the United States was reverting to a traditional policy of acting selectively and unilaterally, with the national interest foremost in its mind. This meant acting in ways that were independent of the international security organization that the League was intending to create, or any other such systems of multilateral alliance. It meant an attempted return to the foreign-policy orientation of George Washington and John Quincy Adams.

It is also important to acknowledge that the interwar years saw a marked improvement in the relations of the United States with the countries of Latin America, relations that had suffered badly under TR and Wilson. Much of the initial groundwork for that improvement was laid by Republicans. In 1921, President Harding paid Colombia $25 million for the rights to the Panama Canal; later, President Coolidge would remove American troops from the Dominican Republic and Nicaragua, respectively; would eventually broker a peace settlement in the latter; and then would resolve a conflict with Mexico regarding American oil properties in that country. In 1928, Coolidge went to Cuba to open the Pan-American Conference; later that year, President-Elect Hoover would tour ten Latin American countries and, once in office, would generate considerable goodwill by signaling that the United States would not intervene in the region, a resolution to which he adhered as president. By the time FDR brought this era of improved relations to an even higher point, enunciating a "Good Neighbor Policy" that would take nonintervention and noninterference as its keynote, he could draw upon a pattern of more than a decade's improvements.

So things were steadily improving in the western hemisphere. But in the meantime, the world beyond American shores was sliding into dangerous instability, with the rise of authoritarian and expansionist regimes in Japan, Italy, and Germany, all of which seemed bent upon enlarging their sway by aggressive means. Japan had rapidly transformed itself into an impressive industrial power under the Meiji Restoration in the later nineteenth century. By the twentieth century, it was trying to build an empire to match those of the Western powers, seeking out resource-rich Asian territories that could supply Japan with the raw materials needed to support its modernizing economy. Italy had been humiliated by the Great War and the Treaty of Versailles, was embarrassed and demoralized by its chronic disorder and disunity, and found in Benito Mussolini and his governing philosophy of fascism a cultish form of highly centralized and authoritarian nationalism, a force that might weld together that fractious nation and restore to Italy the eminence that was once hers – the greatness of the Renaissance princes, the power and glory of ancient Rome.

Germany had been even more devastated by the War and the crushing burdens of war debt, not to mention the treaty's wound to German national pride. By 1933, the nation's valiant attempt to establish a liberal democracy, the Weimar Republic, had been overwhelmed by the forces of economic depression and political instability, and given way to the strongman Adolf Hitler and his Nazi Party. Upon being appointed chancellor in 1933, Hitler quickly assumed dictatorial powers and began to reorient Germany, both internally and externally. He openly defied the hated Versailles Treaty, pulled Germany out of the League of Nations, and began the task of rebuilding the nation's military strength.

As these three new aggressive powers came on the world stage, and their intentions began to emerge, one could almost hear a foreboding beat begin to sound, a low and menacing bass drum, starting quietly but becoming louder and louder with each act of wanton aggression – and as each transgression was met with only a feeble or negligible response from the exhausted and fearful Western democracies. The transgressions began in earnest in 1931 with the Japanese occupation of Manchuria, and then with its invasion and occupation of the Chinese port of Shanghai, as Japan brushed aside the treaty commitments it had made in the 1920s. Under Hitler, the Germans began rearming in violation of the Versailles Treaty and, by 1936, felt strong enough to bring troops into the Rhineland area of Germany, a flagrant treaty violation. That same year saw the beginning of the bloody Spanish Civil War, in which Spanish general Francisco Franco established a fascist-style dictatorship with extensive military assistance from Italy and Germany. In July 1937, Japan went to war against China and joined Germany and Italy in the Rome–Berlin–Tokyo Axis. The Japanese assault on China was markedly brutal; after capturing the then-capital city of Nanking (Nanjing), the army carried out what became known as the Rape of Nanking, with the massacre and torture of as many as three hundred thousand Chinese and the rape of tens of thousands of women.

In each case, the governments of the Western democracies did little or nothing, placing their hopes in a policy of appeasement, in which relatively small and regional acts of aggression and expansion would be tolerated in the larger interest of avoiding the possibility of large-scale open warfare.

Hitler was the most aggressive of the three and seized greedily upon the opportunities the weak appeasement policy provided him. He continued to press outward everywhere he could, using the Wilsonian pretext that he was merely reuniting the parts of an artificially fractured Greater Germany. He annexed Austria in 1938, then the ethnically German Sudeten territory of Czechoslovakia, soon to be followed in March 1939 by the rest of Czechoslovakia and parts of Lithuania. By then the pattern of his actions was unmistakable. As he began to prepare for a similar incursion against Poland, preparations that included the conclusion of a nonaggression pact with the Soviet Union, Britain and France warned that they would go to war if Poland were to be invaded by Germany. When the German invasion of Poland took place anyway, on September 1, 1939, the British and French had to make good on their promise, and so they declared war upon Germany. And so, once again, Western Europe was plunged into war. What had begun in China two years before had now become a globe-encircling world war.

As these tragic circumstances rippled through the decade of the 1930s, the United States stood back and assumed a position of neutrality, just as it had always tried to do in the past. American public opinion was vehemently opposed to any involvement in the European situation, an opinion that was reinforced by the disturbing findings of the Nye Committee, whose report provided strong evidence that bankers and munitions manufacturers had indeed made fortunes off the war effort, even if there was no evidence of their having been behind Wilson's war decision. Under pressure from a suspicious public, Congress passed and Roosevelt signed a series of neutrality acts, beginning in 1935, that were designed to inhibit trade with the warring nations and thus make it impossible for the United States to become pulled into the conflicts afflicting Europe, in the way it had been in the First World War. This reflected an overwhelmingly popular position. A Gallup poll in March 1937 found that 94 percent of its respondents preferred efforts to keep America out of any foreign war over efforts to prevent such wars from breaking out – a sentiment that can justly be described as "isolationist," since it meant forswearing any attempt by America to influence the flow of events in the world. Congress even came very close to approving a constitutional amendment, known as the Ludlow Amendment, which would have required a national referendum to confirm or overturn any declaration of war by Congress, except in cases in which the United States had been attacked first.

In hindsight, we can see that these neutrality measures played into the hands of the Axis powers. The militarists in the Japanese government could feel confident that the Americans would not intervene against them in China. Hitler knew he could count on a free hand in pursuing his goals in Europe, including the use of unrestricted submarine warfare in the waters around Great Britain and the prosecution of a proxy war in Spain, which provided him with a testing ground for some of the weapons and tactics he would soon employ in the rest of Europe. And yet, it was clear that there was still little inclination among Americans to back away from the neutrality policy, even though by the time the war in Europe was fully under way, the American public had come to deplore Hitler's despotic rule and wanted to see him defeated.

Events were conspiring to make that position more and more difficult to sustain. The German expansion was being driven by a seemingly unstoppable new military tactic that came to be called *Blitzkrieg*, or lightning war. It was designed expressly to circumvent the stalemates of World War I. In this highly mobile and mechanized approach to warfare, an attacking force, spearheaded by dense and rapidly moving columns of tanks and mechanized forces, with close support from military aircraft, would focus its destructive power on a narrow front. By puncturing the opponent's line of defense with short, fast thrusts designed to capture key targets (railheads, bridges, communications centers), this combined air–land attacking force spread confusion and havoc behind enemy lines. The effective use of air superiority and additional rapid thrusts by mechanized units kept the enemy off balance, and prevented the reorganization or reinforcement needed to mount a defense. Then, conventional German infantry units could encircle and capture the disoriented remnants of the enemy.

The Blitzkrieg had first worked its intense and pitiless fury in Poland, and then, after a deceptive lull of seven months, the Germans went on offense again in April 1940. First they overwhelmed Denmark and Norway in a matter of days. Next to fall were Belgium and the Netherlands, Luxembourg, and then it was on into France. It seemed that nothing could stop the Blitzkrieg. The French armies were soon shredded into insignificance by the German advance. By June 14, 1940, the capital city of Paris, which had eluded serious threat through the years of the First World War, was occupied by the Germans. The world could now see photographs of the Nazi swastika flag flying near the iconic Eiffel Tower. The world also could see Hitler forcing the French to accept his surrender terms in the same railroad car in which the defeated Germans had surrendered to the Allies in 1918. The bitter defeat, and the humiliation of Versailles, had now been fully avenged.

Such photographs expressed an exceedingly grim reality, a radical change in Europe's condition that had come about with lightning speed. In a matter of two months, between April and June, more territory had been gained by the remorseless efficiency of the Blitzkrieg than by all the mayhem of the First World War. All of Western Europe was now effectively in Hitler's hands, with the sole remaining holdout being Great Britain. Only Britain's small and vulnerable island stood between Hitler and his dream of complete European domination – and his appalling plans for the racial purification of the world. Only a miraculous evacuation of the fleeing British Expeditionary Force from the French seaport of Dunkirk, using a makeshift fleet of naval vessels and hundreds of civilian craft of all sizes to cross the English Channel, and thus to escape only narrowly the concentrated fury of the German forces, saved the British Army from being all but annihilated.

Nearly 350,000 Allied troops (minus their heavy equipment) had been rescued at Dunkirk, but the evacuation would be a hollow victory if further German advances could not be stopped. Britain now had to gird itself for the likely horror of an amphibious or airborne invasion. Its heroic prime minister, Winston Churchill, struggled to keep alive his nation's spirits with unforgettable oratory and a growling promise that "we shall never surrender." Americans were now beginning to awaken to the extent of the danger posed by the awesome Nazi war machine, not only to their cousins in Great Britain, but eventually to America itself. With the cooperation of Congress, Roosevelt initiated an American military buildup and began to make arms and airplanes available to the British. It was not yet an abandonment of neutrality. But Roosevelt now began also a long process of persuading, educating, cajoling, and maneuvering the American public into shaking off its isolationist suspicions and taking on a larger role of defending the Western democracies, and all that they stood for, against the Nazi aggressors.

As with the American Civil War, so with the Second World War. Because we all know how the war came out, we tend to underestimate the degree to which it was actually a very close-run thing, with the outcome deeply uncertain to those who had to live through those harrowing times. Americans in particular, having never had to contemplate the very near prospect of our country being overrun by intensely hostile foreign forces, need to use our imaginations if we are to appreciate what the world looked like to the British at this moment, as they faced the most fearsome military force in history, and faced it essentially alone.

Speaking to the British House of Commons, Winston Churchill expressed the stakes with a stirring exhortation:

> *The Battle of Britain is about to begin. Upon this battle depends the survival of Christian civilisation. Upon it depends our own British life, and the long con-*

tinuity of our institutions and our Empire. The whole fury and might of the enemy must very soon be turned on us. Hitler knows that he will have to break us in this island or lose the war. If we can stand up to him, all Europe may be freed and the life of the world may move forward into broad, sunlit uplands. . . . Let us therefore brace ourselves to our duties, and so bear ourselves, that if the British Empire and its Commonwealth last for a thousand years, men will still say, "This was their finest hour."

Hitler understood that a German amphibious assault on Britain would be very difficult, given the Royal Navy's command of the seas, and even the threat of one would not be plausible until the Germans had achieved decisive air superiority. So the defeat of the Royal Air Force became the focal point of the Battle of Britain.

If there are moments that we can single out as hinges of history, then the summer and fall of 1940 would have to be among them. It was a moment when much of the world held its breath, as the future of Britain, and perhaps of all Europe, hinged upon the outcome of this entirely airborne Battle of Britain – a strange and unprecedented kind of battle, like almost nothing that had ever come before it, in which the heroic and skilled pilots of the Royal Air Force managed to defeat the more numerous aircraft of the German Luftwaffe, and thwart their effort to gain control of the skies over Britain. Hitler was forced to shift strategy, abandoning the air war in favor of a saturation bombing of London, the so-called Blitz, hoping by those brutal means to demoralize the British and sap their will to fight.

But it was a clear victory for Britain, and this victory marked the first serious reversal of the hitherto unstoppable Nazi war machine. It forced the Germans to delay indefinitely an invasion of Britain and bought time for Roosevelt to supply American destroyers to the British for use against the German submarines that were wearing down the capacity of the Royal Navy. It also helped Roosevelt's efforts at reversing the isolationist tide of American public opinion, discrediting the views of those, like the U.S. ambassador to Britain Joseph P. Kennedy, who sneered to the *Boston Globe* that "democracy is finished in England" and strongly advocated against America's providing military and economic aid.

As we have seen, reversing that tide would not be easy. Indeed, by casting the destroyer transaction as a "trade" with the British in exchange for American use of a string of eight British naval bases from Newfoundland to the Caribbean, Roosevelt got around the legal and political delays that might have held up the deal if it had been structured in a more straightforward way. But such a clever diplomatic move on Roosevelt's part had the effect of reactivating the passionate debate between those advocating extensive aid to Britain and those who distrusted Roosevelt and feared that such a policy would inexorably lead to American involvement in the war. The interventionist–internationalist side was ably represented by groups like the Committee to Defend America by Aiding the Allies, led by Kansas journalist William Allen White; on the noninterventionist–isolationist side was the formidable America First Committee, with eight hundred thousand members at its peak, led by General Robert E. Wood of Sears Roebuck and Charles Lindbergh.

In fall 1940, Roosevelt ran for reelection to an unprecedented third term. The restriction of American presidents to two terms was a tradition established by George Washington, but Roosevelt and the Democrats felt that the critical nature of the times, with the war raging in Europe, justified a departure. The Democrats also wanted to keep their top campaigner at the top of the party's ticket. "Don't switch horses in the middle of the stream," they urged the country's voters. Interestingly, the Republican nominee, Indiana businessman Wendell Willkie, differed very little from Roosevelt in his policy views; he saw the Nazi threat clearly and strongly supported aid to the Allies, unlike more isolation-minded Republicans, many of whom had preferred Senator Robert Taft to him. In the end, Willkie vainly tried to draw contrasts by alleging that Roosevelt actively favored intervention and by criticizing Roosevelt's breaking of the two-term tradition. But neither of these was enough to carry the day for him, and Roosevelt would be reelected easily, though by a slightly smaller margin than in his two previous victories.

Encouraged by this win, Roosevelt ramped up his advocacy of support for the Allies, using a postelection fireside chat in December 1940 to explain how the American people could best support the war effort by serving as the "great arsenal of democracy," the chief provider of material support to the democracies' struggle. His purpose, he reassured his listeners, was the preservation of American national security, an effort "to keep you now ... out of a last-ditch war for the preservation of American independence." There would be no need to enter the fight ourselves. "The people of Europe who are defending themselves do not ask us to do their fighting. They ask us for the implements of war, the planes, the tanks, the guns, the freighters which will enable them to fight for their liberty and for our security. Emphatically we must get these weapons to them in sufficient volume and quickly enough, so that we and our children will be saved the agony and suffering of war which others have had to endure." Great Britain and the British Empire constituted "the spearhead of resistance to world conquest," and they were "putting up a fight which will live forever in the story of human gallantry." It would be America's task to supply them with the tools to prevail.

Roosevelt took a further step in the direction of intervention in two speeches in January. On January 6, 1941, in his annual message to Congress, Roosevelt attempted to give a definite shape to the war's aims, distilling them into a set of fundamental democratic commitments that he called the "Four Freedoms": freedom of speech, freedom of worship, freedom from want, and freedom from fear. These four values were universal in character and described a world "attainable in our own time," a world that was "the very antithesis of the so-called new order of tyranny which the dictators seek to create." Then, four days later, Roosevelt introduced the Lend-Lease Bill to the Congress, a measure providing that the president be given the power to lend or lease to the British – or to any other country whose defense he considered vitally important to the national interest – any war supplies that he deemed suitable. The program, which passed Congress on March 11, would constitute a massive involvement in the war; it would enable a battered and cash-starved Britain to have the means to carry on.

Isolationists like Robert Taft firmly opposed Lend-Lease, claiming it would "give the President power to carry on a kind of undeclared war all over the world." And Taft had a point. Lend-Lease was a popular measure, and its popularity seemed to mark a decisive shift in public opinion, toward aiding Britain at whatever cost. But its implementation would cast neutrality to the wind and would surely increase the chances of an American entanglement in the war. So too did the increasing American involvement in convoying and protecting American and British ships making their way across the North Atlantic, an endeavor that rapidly led to conditions approaching undeclared war. After the U.S. Navy destroyer *Greer* had been attacked on September 4 by a German U-boat, Roosevelt gave an order for American naval vessels thenceforth to "shoot on sight" any German or Italian raiders that they came across and to arm merchant ships traveling into dangerous zones. He did not disclose to the American people that the *Greer* had been shadowing the German U-boat and was reporting its position to the British – that it had, in a word, been actively helping the British war effort.

The United States was walking a knife's edge, hoping to help Britain and the other allies as much as possible without itself becoming a belligerent party. How long this constantly escalating but still undeclared and mostly secret war in the Atlantic could have gone on, without eventuating in outright war, is hard to know. But in any event, these undeclared hostilities were not to stay undeclared much longer. What changed matters decisively was something unexpected, coming from the other side of the world, an ocean away.

The Japanese incursion into China had become stalled by 1940, and as a consequence, Japanese leaders began to look to other East Asian territories as sources of vitally needed raw materials. They formulated the idea of a pan-Asian empire that would be called the "Greater East Asia Co-Prosperity Sphere," a bloc of Asian nations firmly under Japanese leadership, promoting the larger cause of Asian independence and self-sufficiency. And they looked to Southeast Asia – French Indochina, the Dutch East Indies, Malaya, and Burma – as sources for the oil, rubber, and other strategic materials they needed to flourish.

Japan remained dependent on American oil, however, and when the Japanese occupied French Indochina in July 1941, Roosevelt retaliated by freezing Japanese assets in the United States and embargoing shipments of U.S. oil to Japan. This was a potentially debilitating move, because the Japanese had only very limited reserves, and it was a provocation that Japan was not likely to stand for. Secretary of State Cordell Hull was in contact with Japanese diplomats and sought some kind of solution, which would include a withdrawal from China, as a means of lifting the embargo and resuming American trade. But the Japanese leadership would not give up its dreams of empire, and the dominant faction within the government opted for war instead. The Japanese were well aware of American reluctance to go to war in Europe and figured that a similar reluctance would prevail in the Far East.

Meanwhile, the United States intelligence services had broken the Japanese diplomatic code and knew that this change of policy had occurred. They knew in advance that a war was imminent. By November, they were certain that a surprise attack was in the offing, but they were not able to detect where it would occur. Perhaps it would be in the Dutch East Indies, perhaps the Philippines, perhaps Thailand. But almost no one suspected that on November 26, even as the Japanese ambassador continued to negotiate with the Americans, a massive Japanese aircraft-carrier fleet was steaming undetected across the North Pacific, bound for the American naval base at Pearl Harbor on the Hawaiian island of Oahu, preparing an audacious attack on the U.S. Navy's Pacific Fleet. With this bold move, the Japanese had hopes of striking a crippling blow to American sea power in the Pacific, one that would discourage the U.S. Navy from interfering with Japan's aggressive moves in Southeast Asia.

The attack largely succeeded in its immediate objectives. Early on the peaceful Sunday morning of December 7, Pearl Harbor was attacked by 353 carrier-borne Japanese warplanes – a mix of fighters, level bombers, dive bombers, and torpedo bombers – arriving in two separate waves. They caught Pearl Harbor completely unaware and battered it for two hours, leaving the Pacific Fleet in shambles. All eight U.S. battleships were either sunk or heavily damaged, while a dozen other vessels were put out of operational order, 188 planes were destroyed, and twenty-four hundred servicemen were killed. It was a shocking blow, and yet only a part of the vast Japanese plan, which over the course of seven hours included roughly simultaneous attacks on the United States in the Philippines, Guam, and Wake Island and on the British in Malaya, Singapore, and Hong Kong.

It was an ambitious and well-executed plan. But it would emerge in due course that the Japanese had overlooked some important things. For one thing, the U.S. Navy was supremely fortunate that its three Pacific-based aircraft carriers were all at sea at the time of the attack and were thus unscathed. As the Pearl Harbor attack itself illustrated, aircraft carriers were becoming the capital ships of the fleet, far more valuable and important than battleships for purposes of projecting power at a distance. In addition, the attacking planes neglected to destroy the oil tanks and support facilities that served the fleet, an omission that made it possible for the remnants of the fleet to stay in Hawaii rather than retreating to the West Coast and to recover far more quickly than would otherwise have been the case.

They also failed to reckon with the response of the American people. That was perhaps their greatest miscalculation. A country that had been furiously divided on December 6 became furiously united on December 7 and ready to do battle with the Japanese aggressor. There would be no more talk of neutrality. It is not hard to imagine why outside observers with entirely different cultural expectations would assume that a nation so outwardly divided would be unable to put aside its differences and unite so readily, even under attack. It would be hard for subjects of an authoritarian empire to understand that the genius of a free and self-governing society lies in the opportunity it affords men and women to form free and uncoerced loyalties, loyalties that allow for dissent and disagreement – loyalties that, fed by freedom, can be surprisingly intense and durable when circumstances draw upon them.

On December 8, Roosevelt delivered his war message to Congress, referring memorably to December 7 as "a date which will live in infamy," and he went on to lay out the treachery of the Japanese government in pretending to be in negotiations even as it was planning and launching this attack. He concluded by calling upon Congress to acknowledge the state of war that existed between the United States and Japan. Three days later, on December 11, Japan's allies Germany and Italy both declared war on the United States. The U.S. Congress responded immediately by declaring war on them too. Thus the European and Asian wars had become linked, a single global conflict with the Axis powers: Japan, Germany, Italy, and others, aligned against the Allied powers, which now included the United States.

The ranks of the Allies by now also included the Soviet Union, who had gotten its own taste of treachery from its former ally Hitler. The German leader had without warning renounced his nonaggression pact with the Soviets and turned his military machine eastward on them in June 1941. The operation reflected not only Hitler's distrust of the Soviet leader, Josef Stalin, but also the Nazis' goal of conquering the western Soviet Union to repopulate it with Germans, while seizing the oil reserves of the Caucasus. The German invasion of Soviet Russia turned out to be a colossal mistake and the single most important turning point leading to the failure of Hitler's war effort.

The incorporation of the totalitarian and thuggish regime of Stalin into the ranks of the Allied democracies would be awkward at best and would lead to intense problems in the postwar world. But that was all in the future, and present circumstances made an alliance absolutely necessary. As Churchill recognized from early on, it would likely be impossible to defeat Hitler decisively without the Soviets. And that was the first priority in his mind. "Hitler," he told his radio audience on June 22, "is a monster of wickedness, insatiable in his lust for blood and plunder." Hence, as Church quipped to his private secretary, "if Hitler invaded Hell, I would make at least a favourable reference to the devil in the House of Commons."

So the battle lines were now drawn, and it was time for Franklin Roosevelt, who had been elected in 1932 and 1936 primarily as a domestic-policy leader, to transform himself from Dr. New Deal to Dr. Win-the-War. Yet American domestic policy was not completely out of the picture, since the success of the Allied cause was going to depend so heavily upon the productive capacity of the U.S. industrial economy. American industry had struggled for more than a decade to emerge fully from the Great Depression, and its rapid transformation into a true arsenal of democracy would be a heavy lift. Could it do it?

In fact, it made the lift with surprising speed, exceeding all expectations and spearheading the Allied drive to victory. All the gloom and frustration of the past decade was set aside, as the moral equivalent of war gave way to the moral force of the real thing. Consider some statistics. By the end of the first year of American involvement in the war, American arms production had risen to the same level as that of Germany, Italy, and Japan put together. By 1944, it was *double* that amount. By the end of the war, the United States had turned out two-thirds of all the military equipment used by the Allies combined: a staggering 280,000 warplanes, 100,000 armored cars, 86,000 tanks, 8,800 naval ships, 2.6 million machine guns, 650,000 artillery pieces, millions of tons of ordnance, and 41 *billion* rounds of ammunition. Accomplishing all this, while putting into uniform 11 million soldiers, 4 million sailors, 700,000 marines, and 240,000 coast guardsmen, meant drawing into the industrial workforce a great many women and minorities, on an even greater scale than occurred in World War I. Depression-era unemployment rates were now a distant memory, as the factories of the nation whirred with activity.

As in the previous war, the U.S. government organized special agencies to coordinate military and economic resources, such as the War Production Board and the Office of War Mobilization. The Office of Price Administration regulated most aspects of civilian life, freezing prices and rents and handling the rationing of scarce commodities, such as meat, gasoline, and tires. As federal spending increased by 1,000 percent during the war years, deficits were pushed up to unheard levels, producing a national debt of $250 billion (five times what it had been in 1941), but also producing torrid economic growth, sometimes at a rate of as much as 15 percent per annum. Perhaps this was the great jolt of stimulus that the economy had been waiting for but would never have received in peacetime. As with the New Deal, though, the smaller corporations tended to lose out on government contracts, while the largest corporations led the recovery and pocketed the earnings, accounting for up to 70 percent of wartime manufacturing.

Numerous captains of industry played outsized roles in this great wartime expansion. The builder Henry J. Kaiser was one of the most important, a blustery, colorful entrepreneur with boundless energy, capable of going days without sleep when he threw himself into enormous projects, such as the construction of the Hoover Dam. Kaiser cared passionately about the war in Europe and involved himself in efforts to bring relief to victims of the Nazis as early as 1940. His chief contribution to the defeat of Hitler, though, was in inventing critically important techniques for the mass production of commercial and naval ships, such as the use of welding and subassemblies that allowed for Ford-like efficiency. He established the famous Kaiser Shipyard in Richmond, California, where he perfected the construction in a mere forty-five days of the homely but indispensable workhorse vessels known as Liberty ships, the first all-welded prefabricated cargo ships, later to be superseded by the larger and faster Victory ships. Other Kaiser shipyards produced the smaller "escort carriers," more than a hundred of them, deployed to protect convoys and otherwise project airpower in both the Pacific and Atlantic theaters of the war. All were produced in record time.

The war's effects were visible throughout the economy, and the social transformations it wrought were equally profound. Once again, women found themselves playing an indispensable role in the industrial labor force, while more than two hundred thousand women served in the military. Minorities were similarly afforded fresh opportunities. African Americans came north, as their forebears had done a quarter-century before, attracted by jobs in the humming and labor-hungry factories. In addition, a million young African American men joined the armed forces. The seeds of the postwar civil rights movement were planted by their experiences of discrimination endured at home while fighting for liberty and equality abroad. Civil rights leaders urged veterans to adopt the double-V slogan: one V for victory in Europe, and another V for victory in the struggle for equality at home. Native American "code talkers" helped ensure the security of tactical telephone and radio communications by devising ingenious forms of secret coding based on their Native languages. Mexican Americans also served in the military, three hundred thousand of them, and starting in 1942, Mexican *braceros* were allowed into the country to fill the labor shortage in agriculture.

There was one conspicuous exception to the pattern. Japanese Americans suffered grievously from their association with the nation's Pacific enemy, even though some twenty thousand Japanese Americans were serving honorably in the armed forces. The surprise Pearl Harbor attacks had produced a suspicious attitude toward Americans of Japanese descent, and there were even widespread fears of a Japanese attack on the West Coast of the United States. Succumbing to pressure from figures like California attorney general Earl Warren, President Roosevelt authorized the internment of over 110,000 Japanese Americans, mostly on the West Coast, and their relocation to camps in the nation's interior. They were forced to sell their homes and businesses at below market rates, see their lives uprooted, and then endure the supervision of armed guards in unpleasant settings, far away from everything that was familiar to them. It was a bitter injustice and a stain on the nation's otherwise admirable conduct during this war.

Now let us turn to the conduct of the war itself. Almost immediately upon American entry into the war, the Allies agreed that the defeat of Hitler ought to take priority. The ultimate offensive against Japan in the Pacific could be postponed, since the Japanese were not intent upon conquest of the American mainland. Hitler was the more formidable foe and the more immediate danger, and defeating him would be a more complicated and demanding task, with many stages and many dimensions to consider.

First of all, the German successes in submarine warfare against Allied convoys in the shipping lanes of the Atlantic would have to be stopped, or at least severely curtailed. In May 1942 alone, for example, 120 merchant vessels were sunk. Such a horrendous toll, a veritable Blitzkrieg of the seas, simply could not continue, or the war would be lost. By mid-1943, though, the situation had

The Second World War, European theater.

World War II in Europe

- Axis powers, 1942
- Axis allies
- Areas of Axis control, 1942
- Neutral countries
- ········· Front lines (at dates shown)
- ← Allied counteroffensives
- ✴ Major battles
- ── Political boundaries, 1942

0 ————— 500 MILES
0 ————— 500 KILOMETERS

been turned around, thanks to a number of innovations, technological and tactical. The development of radar and sonar technologies, which enabled the detection of submarines, and the effective bombing of German naval bases helped. Even more important was the deployment of naval escort vessels and patrolling aircraft to allow for convoys on the major sea routes. Unescorted merchant shipping operating out of the U.S. East Coast didn't have a chance against the U-boat menace, but once convoys began operating effectively in tandem with air support from both land- and escort carrier–based aircraft, and were supplied with intelligence intercepts of U-boat activity and communications, the menace was brought under control.

Then, the Germans had to be driven out of their advance positions in North Africa before a Mediterranean invasion of the European continent could be undertaken successfully. Once that had been accomplished in May 1943, under the leadership of British general Bernard Montgomery and U.S. general Dwight Eisenhower, the next step was a July invasion and occupation of the island of Sicily, preparatory to an assault upon the Italian peninsula itself in September. Churchill had imagined that Italy would be the "soft underbelly of the Axis," but U.S. general Mark Clark had it closer to the truth: it was, he said, "one tough gut." Mussolini had fallen from power by this time, but that only meant that the more formidable German troops now controlled much of the country and put up fierce resistance, taking every advantage of the rocky, challenging terrain. Movement up the peninsula was a matter of costly, inch-by-inch advances, and it would not be until June 4, 1944, that Mark Clark would take Rome, and many months more before the country could actually be cleared. The Italian campaign was a hard victory that weakened the Germans by tying up twenty-three of their army divisions – but it was not the dramatic breakthrough that had been hoped for.

Nor was there a ready solution to be found in the growing use of strategic bombing, the military term for sustained aerial assault on railways, harbors, urban and industrial areas, and other strategic targets in enemy territory, generally carried out by fleets of heavy, long-range bombers. Military theorists between the two world wars had pondered the potential uses of airpower in future conflicts, and some argued that strategic bombing could be highly effective in breaking down civilian morale and avoiding ground stalemates like that of the First World War. Such arguments seemed to make sense, and strategic bombing would thus be used by both sides in the war, notably by the Germans against the British during the Blitz of London and by the Allies against Germany, especially in the final year of the war. But strategic bombing would always remain controversial. Tactically, it was controversial, because its effects registered only gradually and cumulatively, wearing down the enemy by pounding away at him rather than taking him out in dramatic and visible strokes. Morally, strategic bombing was controversial, because it nearly always entailed civilian deaths and collateral damage on a massive scale – a moral issue that made its use weigh on the consciences even of the fiercest Allied leaders.

Meanwhile, all of this time, the Soviets had been complaining, and not without justice, that they were being forced to bear a disproportionate amount of the suffering and death in the bloody battles on the Eastern front. They had wanted to see the opening of a second front in the West at the earliest opportunity, to divert some portion of the enemy's full force away from them. The Italian invasion had not accomplished that; something else was needed. Finally, by summer 1944, the other Allies agreed that the right time had arrived for such a major new opening. On the morning of June 6, 1944, the D-Day invasion at Normandy established the long-awaited Western front to press in upon Hitler and relieve the burden in the East.

D-Day was, and remains, the greatest invasion of its kind in military history. In a stupendous feat of logistics and bravery, the invasion landed 326,000 men, 50,000 vehicles, and 100,000 tons of supplies in a single week, overcoming extensive German defensive preparations, including a seemingly unassailable set of fortifications on the French coastline. Despite its massiveness and complexity, and the many ways that things could have gone wrong – and, in a few cases, did go wrong – D-Day proved an unqualified success and provided the dramatic breakthrough that the Allies had needed. The story is not only a masterwork of large-scale military and logistical planning but also a mosaic of countless individual acts of unbelievable valor and daring.

Forty years after D-Day, an American president, Ronald Reagan, stood on that site and paid tribute to the remaining survivors of one of the most heroic such acts, the taking of the sheer cliffs of Pointe du Hoc by 225 U.S. Army Rangers:

> The Rangers looked up and saw the enemy soldiers – the edge of the cliffs shooting down at them with machine guns and throwing grenades. And the American Rangers began to climb. They shot rope ladders over the face of these cliffs and began to pull themselves up. When one Ranger fell, another would take his place. When one rope was cut, a Ranger would grab another and begin his climb again. They climbed, shot back, and held their footing. Soon, one by one, the Rangers pulled themselves over the top, and in seizing the firm land at the top of these cliffs, they began to seize back the continent of Europe. Two hundred and twenty-five came here. After 2 days of fighting, only 90 could still bear arms.
>
> Behind me is a memorial that symbolizes the Ranger daggers that were thrust into the top of these cliffs. And before me are the men who put them there.
>
> These are the boys of Pointe du Hoc. These are the men who took the cliffs. These are the champions who helped free a continent. These are the heroes who helped end a war.
>
> Gentlemen, I look at you and I think of the words of Stephen Spender's poem. You are men who in your "lives fought for life … and left the vivid air signed with your honor."

By June 24, the Allies had landed more than a million men and controlled a beachhead sixty miles wide and as much as fifteen miles deep, a large chunk of Normandy and Brittany. Their foothold on the continent was secure now. After a dramatic advance by General George Patton's Third Army, the Americans were able to swarm across France, while up from the Mediterranean came the Seventh Army under General A. M. Patch. Paris would be freed by August 25, the culmination of a liberatory campaign whose restorative sweep would mirror the rapidity with which Hitler had captured France in 1940.

In retrospect, it is clear that D-Day broke the back of the Nazi effort. By September, American and British troops had crossed into Germany and begun to push toward the capital city of Berlin from the west, even as Russian troops advanced toward Berlin from the east. The Germans launched an impressive and determined counterattack in Belgium in December 1944, in an effort known as the Battle of the Bulge, but it only delayed the inevitable and further depleted Germany's diminishing reserves. The race was on to Berlin.

Meanwhile, the question of who would get to Berlin first had begun to take on genuine importance. Winston Churchill had always been more deeply realistic about the character of Josef Stalin and the Soviets than was Roosevelt, and he urged Roosevelt to ensure that Eisenhower and the Americans should be the ones to get to Berlin first, to forestall the possibility that the Soviets would use their occupation as a source of leverage in shaping the postwar settlement according to their own self-interest. At the Big Three summit meeting of the three principal Allied leaders, held February 4–11, 1945, at the Crimean resort of Yalta, the leaders had decided that postwar Germany would be divided into four occupation zones, one for each of the Allies (including the French), with Berlin similarly divided and jointly occupied. Stalin had promised to respect the future of free government in Poland – whose freedom and independence, remember, was the cause of British and French entry into the war in 1939 – and the other countries of Eastern Europe. But Churchill did not trust him to follow through. "I deem it highly important," he told General Eisenhower, with characteristic wit, "that we shake hands with the Russians as far to the east as possible." The Soviets had been their allies, yes, but as soon as the war was over, all would be changed, he predicted, and they would become "a mortal danger" to the free world.

But Eisenhower disagreed and made the fateful decision to ignore this advice, and allow the Soviets to take Berlin, deeming the occupation of the German capital a "prestige objective" not worth the cost in American soldiers' lives that might be entailed in getting there. His objective was the destruction of the enemy's armed forces, not the taking of political targets. He assumed that the Yalta plan for division of the postwar German state would hold and would ensure a peaceful transition into the future.

Meanwhile, the war in the Pacific was unfolding, and there as in Europe, the eventual outcome was by no means predetermined. In fact, in the days and months after Pearl Harbor, it appeared that there would be a steep and perilous path forward. The lightning strikes of December 1941 had set the Allies back on their heels and presaged a steady stream of Japanese military successes. By early 1942, the Japanese controlled much of East and Southeast Asia, occupying Korea, eastern China, Hong Kong, the Philippines, Burma, Malaya, French Indochina, the Dutch East Indies, and most of the Pacific islands west of Midway Island, including Guam, Wake Island, and the Gilbert Islands. As was the case with the Germans mowing their way across Europe in 1940, so the Japanese military machine seemed nearly invincible in those early days of the war.

Like the Germans, they found the air of victory to be intoxicating and lost any sense of when to stop or where their limits lay. Flush with success, they made the decision to push into the South Pacific, seeking to cut off Australia and prepare the way for a second strike at Hawaii to finish off the American Pacific Fleet before it had time to recover.

Their advance would be abruptly stopped, however, in two critical naval battles between carrier-based aircraft, first at the Coral Sea (May 4–8, 1942) and a month later, even more decisively, at Midway (June 4–7, 1942), which the Japanese hoped to use as a launching pad for their renewed assault against Hawaii. Once again, though, American intelligence had cracked the Japanese naval code and knew in advance what the Japanese were planning, so that when the Japanese fleet arrived near Midway, it would be met by a well-prepared American force. The resulting battle was a brilliant success for the Americans and a calamity for the Japanese, who lost four carriers – all four of which had participated in the Pearl Harbor raid – and many of their most experienced aircrews. These losses, especially the loss of so many extraordinarily skillful Japanese pilots, would prove enormously consequential. It was, wrote historian John Keegan, "the most stunning and decisive blow in the history of naval warfare" and must be counted one of the war's turning points. Without any ability to contest American air superiority, the Japanese were never again able to launch a major offensive in the Pacific theater.

But that result could not be known at the time, and Midway, though a smashing win, was only one victory after many defeats. The Allies had not yet been able to put together a successful offensive, and they would need to do so, if they were to create any momentum against the Japanese. Hence they chose to follow up the triumph at Midway with a move to expel the Japanese from the Solomon Islands, a move that would have strategic importance for the defense of Australia. The action ended up being focused on a swampy island called Guadalcanal, where the Japanese had built an airstrip that could be used to

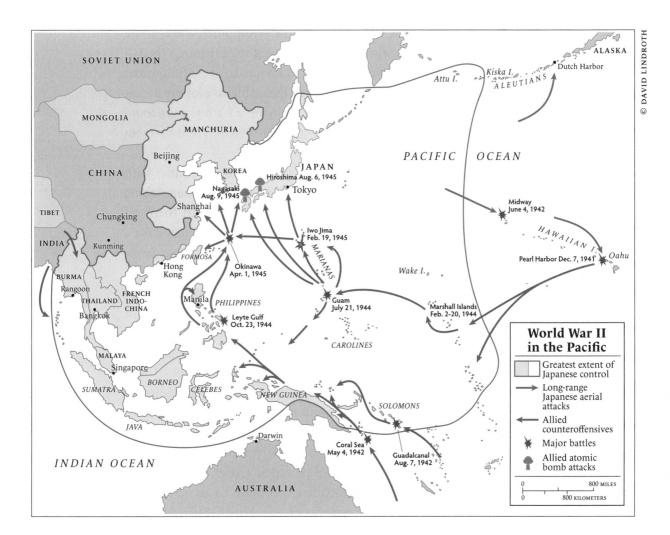

The Second World War, Pacific theater.

harass Allied shipping to Australia and New Zealand. The campaign that followed was a fiercely contested, six-month-long struggle on air, land, and sea, in which the Allies eventually prevailed. As the first major American combat operation of the war, it attracted excellent journalistic coverage, notably the on-the-scene reporting of Richard Tregaskis of the International News Service, whose powerful 1943 book *Guadalcanal Diary* was one of the finest accounts to come out of the Pacific War.

Having thus blunted the Japanese advance at Midway and removed the Japanese presence from the Solomons, the United States and its allies in Australia and New Zealand began their long counteradvance across the Pacific, using a two-pronged offensive strategy, with the two prongs eventually converging on the Japanese islands. In the southwestern Pacific, General Douglas MacArthur would move across northern New Guinea toward the Philippines, while in the central Pacific, Admiral Chester Nimitz would push westward through the Gilbert Islands, the Marshalls, the Marianas, and then on to the Philippines. Thanks to Americans' command of the skies, they were able to employ a strategy called *leapfrogging* or *island hopping*, in which Japanese strongholds could be neutralized by being bypassed in favor of less fortified islands and then cut off from resupply.

Once New Guinea and the Marianas were secured, Roosevelt met with MacArthur and Nimitz, and they decided the next move would be the retaking of the Philippines. Knowing the loss of the Philippines would cut them off from access to the raw materials of the East Indies, the Japanese prepared for a ferocious fight, concentrating their naval forces for three huge battles at Leyte Gulf in October 1944. In three battles, known collectively as the Battle of Leyte Gulf, the largest naval engagement in history, the Japanese were soundly defeated and their navy rendered all but nonexistent. After Leyte Gulf, there was no question in anyone's mind about the eventual outcome of the war.

But getting to that final outcome would be another matter. Ominously, Leyte Gulf saw the introduction of a new and terrifying instrument of war: kamikaze suicide pilots who would crash their explosives-laden planes into the American carriers. Such tactics echoed profound spiritual traditions (the word *kamikaze* means "divine wind") deeply ingrained in Japanese military culture, traceable back to the Bushido ethic of the samurai warrior: the honor entailed in loyal service to their Emperor would take precedence over life itself. The events at Leyte Gulf also suggested that Japanese resistance to an actual invasion of their homeland might be unimaginably fierce and costly. Such an apprehension was only reinforced by the ensuing ferocity of the eighty-two-day-long battle for Okinawa, the single bloodiest battle of the Pacific War, a "typhoon of steel" lasting from April to June 1945, which not only featured a new wave of some fifteen hundred kamikaze sorties but almost *a quarter of a million* deaths, many of them Okinawans used as human shields by the Japanese.

By the time Okinawa was secured, the war in Europe had ended, but not before an ailing Franklin Roosevelt had died on April 12, 1945, of a cerebral hemorrhage, as he was resting at his retreat in Warm Springs, Georgia. Sadly, although he lived to be reelected in November 1944 to an unprecedented fourth term, he did not live long enough to taste the victory he had worked so hard to achieve. Nor did his rival Hitler live to taste in full the bitter destruction that he had brought upon his people. He committed suicide on April 30, as the advancing Red Army was closing in on Berlin. On May 2, Berlin fell to the Soviets, and

German forces in Italy surrendered to the Allies. On May 7, the chief of staff of the German armed forces signed an unconditional surrender to the Allied forces. The following day, May 8, would mark the end of the war in Europe: V-E Day.

There would be celebrations everywhere, but their mood was dampened, not only by the sadness of Roosevelt's recent death, but by horrifying news beginning to filter out of American soldiers' discovery of abandoned German concentration camps, the ultimate sites of Hitler's campaign to exterminate the Jews of Europe. First to be discovered was the Ohrdruf camp, found on April 5, and toured a week later by Generals George Patton, Omar Bradley, and Dwight Eisenhower. They found thirty-two hundred naked, emaciated bodies in shallow graves. Even the hard-boiled Patton found himself nauseated, unable to bear the camp's sights. Eisenhower was shown a shed piled to the ceiling with bodies and equipped with various torture devices, as well as a butcher's block used for smashing the mouths of the dead and extracting gold fillings from their teeth. The old soldier's face turned white with shock at what he beheld, but he insisted on seeing the entire camp. He promptly issued an order that all American units in the area were to visit the camp. "We are told that the American soldier does not know what he was fighting for," he stated grimly. "Now, at least he will know what he is fighting against."

Further dampening any mood to celebrate V-E Day was the awareness that there was still a Pacific War to be won – a victory that, given the evidence of Okinawa, was going to involve a range of horrors all its own. Estimates of likely Allied casualties from an invasion of the Japanese mainland hovered at around 250,000 American casualties, and many more Japanese ones; but some estimates from respectable sources predicted as many as a million deaths, and some went even higher, numbers that, although staggering, did not seem beyond the range of possibility. (And such numbers did not include the likely execution, in the event of an invasion, of some one hundred thousand Allied prisoners of war then held in Japan.) The resistance mounted by the Japanese was likely to be intense. As the historian Paul Dull explained, "plans were already being formulated that if Japan herself were invaded, every Japanese man, woman, and child would be organized as *teishin butai* (Volunteer Corps) to meet the invaders, even though the Japanese might only be armed with sharpened bamboo spears." The determination to fight on at whatever cost, the brutalities inflicted on the Okinawans, the proliferation of new weapons, such as the *kaiten* suicide submarines and suicidal rocket-powered *baka* bombs – all these things seemed to point toward a truly horrifying task ahead.

By this time, however, a possible alternative was emerging. The United States had developed a new weapon, the atomic bomb, which was the product of the top-secret Manhattan Project. Research had begun in 1940 at Roosevelt's direction, after he had been alerted to the possibility of such a weapon by a personal letter from the physicist Albert Einstein. A refugee from Hitler's Germany, Einstein feared the possibility that Germany might develop such a weapon first and use it to devastating effect. Such a weapon would derive its power from the energy released by the fission of uranium atoms in a nuclear chain reaction, resulting in a bomb more powerful than tens of thousands of tons of TNT. So secret was the development of this weapon that the new American president, Harry S. Truman, had not been informed of its existence until becoming president after Roosevelt's death, and now he was the one who had to make the fateful choice whether to use it against Japan – and if so, how to do so.

Truman was a blunt, straightforward, and decisive man who did not agonize over his choices, and he quickly decided that it would be imperative to use this new weapon as something that would save lives, particularly in light of the experience in Okinawa and what it portended for a conventional invasion and occupation of Japan. But how best to use it? Given the fact that only two bombs were then available, and given the very real possibility of their failing to explode properly, it did not make sense to announce a demonstration explosion in some uninhabited area, to prove the weapon's awesome power. For one thing, the detonation might fail entirely and make any American threats look hollow. Even if a demonstration bomb did explode, it might not have the desired effect anyway. And how could Truman possibly justify to the world his declining to use this weapon, if that declining resulted in hundreds of thousands of unnecessary deaths? He concluded that the only realistic choice open to him was to demand Japanese surrender in the starkest and most threatening terms, with a deadline attached, and, when the deadline passed, to drop one of the bombs without warning on a valuable Japanese target.

That is what he did. There was a warning on July 26 to surrender or face the grim reality that "the alternative to surrender is prompt and utter destruction." Then, when there was no surrender forthcoming, early on the morning of August 6, a lone B-29 bomber dropped the first bomb unannounced on the port city of Hiroshima, a major naval and war-industrial center. It exploded as designed, with a blinding flash of light, followed by a towering fireball, shock wave, firestorm, and cyclone-force winds. Its destructive power was even greater than its creators had suspected; it killed eighty thousand people almost instantly and flattened four square miles of the city into rubble. Three days later, the second bomb was dropped on Nagasaki, with similar damage.

The second bomb convinced the Japanese Emperor that they were now up against an irresistible force, and he surrendered, although he was allowed to keep his titular status as head of state. General MacArthur would receive the Japanese surrender formally aboard the battleship *Missouri* in Tokyo Harbor on

September 2, 1945 – six years and one day after the German invasion of Poland, and eight years after the Japanese invasion of China.

Thus ended the most destructive war in human history, a conflict whose many facets and repercussions are almost impossible to grasp, let alone to hold together all at once in one's mind. The vast geographical sweep of the war, the immense scale of the casualties, the disorienting changes in the methods and textures of warfare, the disruptive influence on the various combatant peoples, the changes good and bad that it wrought in American society and culture, its effect on our conceptions of human rights and human dignity, all the way down to the revolutions effected by the uncanny array of innovations the war spawned, from radio navigation and computers and atomic energy to penicillin and jeeps and M&Ms candies – all of these things and more count as part of the war's legacy.

No contemporary could ignore the immense brutality of this war, from the massacres and tortures inflicted by the Japanese in Nanking to the horrors of the Holocaust in Europe and the civilian carnage caused in the strategic bombing of German and Japanese cities, including not only the two atomic bombs but the Allied firebombing of cities like Dresden and Hamburg, resulting in hundreds of thousands of civilian deaths and incalculable devastation. As in the First World War, so in the Second: the idea that humankind was riding a wave of inevitable progress was given a rude shock, from which it is still yet to recover.

But for our present purposes, one consequence of the war stands out above all the others: the permanently transformed status of the United States. Never again would it be able to return to anything like the remote and decentralized bucolic agrarian empire it once was; never again would isolation from the world be possible, let alone desirable. Nor could it ever again look to Europe in the way that a child looks to its parent. All that was changed. The mantle of world leadership had passed to it now, indeed had been thrust upon it, in a way it could no longer refuse. That mantle came to the United States not only because of its preeminent military and economic power but because of the generous way it had employed that power in the world's hour of desperate need. Without the sacrifice of blood and treasure by the United States and its allies, the world would not have been able to elude the awful fate of domination by the Axis powers. No thoughtful person can contemplate that prospect without a shudder, followed by a wave of gratitude. It was certainly one of America's finest hours.

"Forty summers have passed," said President Ronald Reagan in his speech to the veterans of Pointe du Hoc gathered once again at the windswept French cliffs on June 6, 1984, "since the battle that you fought here."

You were young the day you took these cliffs; some of you were hardly more than boys, with the deepest joys of life before you. Yet, you risked everything here. Why? Why did you do it? What impelled you to put aside the instinct for self-preservation and risk your lives to take these cliffs? What inspired all the men of the armies that met here? We look at you, and somehow we know the answer. It was faith and belief; it was loyalty and love.

The men of Normandy had faith that what they were doing was right, faith that they fought for all humanity, faith that a just God would grant them mercy on this beachhead or on the next. It was the deep knowledge – and pray God we have not lost it – that there is a profound, moral difference between the use of force for liberation and the use of force for conquest. You were here to liberate, not to conquer, and so you and those others did not doubt your cause. And you were right not to doubt.

In the postwar world, the idea of America as a land of hope acquired new layers of meaning. No longer merely a refuge, or a frontier, or an exemplar, the United States now found thrust upon it a role as a self-conscious leader for the world. It was an unaccustomed role, one that did not rest easily with many aspects of the American past. Would it represent a departure from everything that the nation had been and aspired to be, from its earliest days as a people self-consciously set apart? Or would it be a logical development of the American idea, a form of organic growth fully in continuity with the American past – perhaps even the fulfillment of a destiny? The answer remained to be seen.

CHAPTER NINETEEN

ALL THOUGHTS AND THINGS WERE SPLIT

The Cold War

NOTHING LIKE THE GRAND REVIEW WAS POSSIBLE AT THE conclusion of the Second World War. There could not have been a similarly concentrated gathering-in of the nation's forces after a conflict that had literally encompassed the globe, and whose conclusion found the U.S. military and its allies present in almost every corner of the planet. But that did not stop a multitude of exuberant celebrations from erupting in the streets everywhere across the American continent, often giddy and impromptu affairs – snake dancing in Salt Lake City, parades of honking autos in Indianapolis, riotous sailors in San Francisco, leather-lunged crowds in New York's Times Square, and everywhere an epidemic of public kisses between happy friends and strangers alike.

Happiest of all were the American soldiers and sailors, relieved to know that they would not have to put their lives on the line in an invasion of Japan. They whooped for joy, fired colored flares into the air, careened their wildly honking jeeps through the streets of Manila, and broke out their special caches of whiskey, reserved for the occasion. The country, in the words of *Life* magazine, "went on the biggest spree in American history," as it was released at last, or so it seemed, from the anxieties and deprivations of the war years.

Not only the war years, but the demoralizing shadow of the Depression years too. It had been sixteen long years since the prosperity of the 1920s had come tumbling down, and after many false starts and deferred hopes, it seemed that at last happy days might really be here again. Thanks to the massive economic stimulus of ramped-up wartime military spending – federal expenditures increased 1,000 percent between 1939 and 1945, resulting in a then-whopping $250 million national debt – the American industrial economy seemed to have recovered its footing. There would of course be anxieties looking forward, just as there had been in 1918 and 1919, about the problems of postwar demobilization; and this demobilization would be much, much larger. Would the returning soldiers and sailors be able to find jobs and housing? Would there be a wave of strikes and urban riots? Would the removal of price controls lead to inflation and loss of consumer purchasing power? And the greatest fear of all: would the return of the nation to a peacetime footing mean an end to the fleeting economic recovery that the war years had brought, and a return to depressed conditions of the 1930s?

Those concerns could be set aside for the time being, though, to savor the moment of victory. What a stirring spectacle it would be for the American servicemen packed onto ships returning from Europe, as they passed through the narrows and gradually came into sight of the Manhattan skyline! Many of them had only days before walked the rubble-strewn streets of war-torn Berlin and Frankfurt and observed the charred ruins of venerable old churches and public buildings in those once beautiful cities. Now they saw a contrasting vision unfolding before them. As Jan Morris has written, "Untouched by the war the men had left behind them," the great architectural jumble of Manhattan "stood there metal-clad, steel-ribbed, glass-shrouded, colossal and romantic – everything that America seemed to represent in a world of loss and ruin." The lofty, tapering silhouette of the Empire State Building, then the world's tallest building, towered in solitary splendor over all the lesser buildings around it, much as a resurgent United States stood tall and self-confident amid the wrecked and dispirited nations of Europe and Asia, allies and enemies alike.

Many of the fears about demobilization were borne out in the short term. There was a sharp but brief postwar recession. There were serious labor and housing shortages; there were major strikes in the auto, steel, and coal industries; there was inflation and other sources of distress and dislocation. But these concerns proved fleeting, and when they came and went, it became clear that a wholesale return to the stagnant conditions of the Depression was simply not in the cards. America had made it through its hard times and was coming out the other side.

Americans had accumulated considerable savings during the commodity-poor war years; incomes rose during the war, and it was not hard to save money when there were so few consumer goods available anyway. But now Americans were ready to spend, and the revived economy would provide the means for them to do so. The United States was embarked on the path of a new prosperity and would soon be enjoying the highest standard of living of any society in history to that point. "The Great American Boom is on," predicted the confident editors of *Fortune* magazine, writing in 1946. And what a boom it would turn out to be.

In the quarter-century between the end of the war and the year 1970, GNP more than doubled, from $355 billion in 1945 to $723 billion in 1970, while per capita income before taxes increased from $1,870 to $3,050 (all quantities measured in steady 1958 dollars). One element in this rising postwar prosperity was continued government spending at relatively high rates, particularly in the areas of defense and military research. But even more important was the flood of consumer spending, flowing out of the demand for housing, household appliances, automobiles – almost anything for which wartime restrictions had created a strong pent-up need. In addition, new inventions, such as televisions, washing and drying machines, lawnmowers, deep freezers, high-fidelity stereos, and countless other products oriented toward home use for individual consumers, whetted the public appetite.

The auto industry in particular continued to be a key element moving multiple sectors of the economy, as eight million new cars per year (as of 1970) were being manufactured, eight times the number produced during the war, a pace of production that consumed one-fifth of the nation's steel and two-thirds of its rubber and lead. Highway construction followed auto manufacturing, and in 1947, Congress authorized the construction of 37,000 miles of highways; then, in 1956, the nation launched into the construction of the 42,500-mile interstate highway system, a network of limited-access high-speed highways that would be the largest road construction project in American history and transform the nation's landscape, making long-distance automobile travel a staple of American transportation and commerce.

Along with the mobility supplied by the automobile, and the highway capacity to make automotive travel easy and efficient, there soon came an explosion of growth in brand-new housing springing up in suburban areas – so much growth that, by 1970, ten million more Americans lived in suburbs than lived in conventional central cities. Entrepreneurs like the developer William Levitt created whole new communities – Levittowns – featuring small, highly affordable new homes with lawns and other modest amenities designed for the young families of returning veterans and other young Americans just beginning to form families and take their place in the workforce. As remarkable a change in the national geography as suburbanization represented, it was a continuation of the same forces that had transformed the walking cities of antebellum America into the more segmented cities of the early twentieth century, a transformation that had been made possible mainly by the development of the streetcar. In the postwar years, a similar transformation was being wrought by the automobile and the highway transportation system coming along with it, which greatly expanded the reach of suburbanization and placed the possibility of homeownership within the reach even of people of relatively modest means.

The twelve million returning veterans received an additional form of support from their federal government that would ease their return to civilian life. The Serviceman's Readjustment Act of 1944, commonly known as the GI Bill of Rights (*GI*, or "government issue," being a slang term for military personnel), provided veterans with an impressive array of benefits, including the opportunity to attend college or job-training school at the government's expense, an opportunity that some eight million of them took. The result was an almost overwhelming boom in college enrollments, which swelled from 160,000 graduates in prewar America to 500,000 in 1950 and helped encourage the view that a college education, rather than being an option for the upper classes, was a source of opportunity that could be open to all Americans. The GI Bill also provided low-cost mortgage loans to veterans, which enabled about five million of them to buy houses, even if they were too financially strapped to afford a down payment.

All these developments gave support to a surge in new family formation, often referred to as the "baby boom" of the postwar years. The reasons for that boom, though, were not only material but also psychological. During the economic uncertainties during the Depression years of the 1930s, and the upheaval of the war years in the 1940s, a great many young people understandably decided to hold off from parenthood, even delay marriage, since the time did not seem propitious and the future did not look bright. How was one to justify bringing children into such a troubled world? But things now looked different, with the exuberant sense of possibility emerging in the postwar years. Now such couples felt confidence in the future and decided that the moment was right for making up for lost time. The result was phenomenal. Between the end of the war and the year 1960, the American population increased by 30 percent, an increase almost entirely due to internal growth, that is, the baby boom.

Yet all was not as well as it seemed. This happiness, this joy, this sense of relief, had to coexist with terrible anxieties that were not easily dispelled and perils that could not be ignored.

In the first place, there was the fact that the development and use of the atomic bomb seemed to have opened a new chapter in human history. As James Agee wrote in *Time* on August 20, just two weeks after the Hiroshima bomb had been dropped, and six days after peace terms had been reached, the bomb itself was "an event so … enormous that, relative to it, the war itself shrank to minor significance":

> With the controlled splitting of the atom, humanity, already profoundly perplexed and disunified, was brought inescapably into a new age in which all thoughts and things were split – and far from controlled.... The power of good and of evil bordered alike on the infinite.

Agee, and many others, feared that, as in the story of Frankenstein's monster, or the sorcerer's apprentice, a force had been let loose in the world that human ingenuity could not control and that would give added strength to the evil impulses to which humanity was so clearly susceptible.

The returning GIs, who were grateful that the bomb had saved their lives, were less likely to see the bomb in quite the way Agee did. But many of them would return from the great triumph with split thoughts of their own. Lauded as heroes, they also faced immense personal and financial challenges, disintegrating marriages, exploding family expenses, and what then was called "shell shock" but today would be called posttraumatic stress disorder (PTSD), a condition that rendered them nervous, bitter, or plagued by nightmares and other difficulties. Audie Murphy, despite being one of the country's most celebrated and decorated combat heroes, and a celebrated movie actor as well, returned from the war plagued with nightmares and depression and felt compelled to sleep with a loaded gun under his pillow.

His case was unusual, but a great many of the returning GIs had trouble readjusting to a prosperous and well-functioning country that seemed dramatically different from the war-torn world that they had just experienced – a country that, in fact, seemed almost to have benefited from the war more than it had been damaged. It all seemed a bit unreal. Moving from the moral chaos and mayhem of modern warfare into the smooth and orderly life of, say, a large business corporation in peacetime could be utterly disorienting, a change dramatic enough to give one vertigo.

In one of the most famous books of the 1950s, *The Man in the Gray Flannel Suit* (1956), author Sloan Wilson vividly described the postwar life of his main character, Tom Rath, a veteran of the European theater who had returned to a white-collar job and a socially ambitious wife. Rath was overwhelmed with the sense that he lived in

> a disconnected world, a lunatic world, where what is true now was not true then; where Thou Shalt Not Kill and the fact that one has killed a great many men mean nothing, absolutely nothing, for now is the time to raise legitimate

children, and make money, and dress properly, and be kind to one's wife, and admire one's boss, and learn not to worry, and think of oneself as … a man in a gray flannel suit.

Tom had killed seventeen men in the Italian campaign and could not forget having done so. Nor could he forget that he had lived for a time with an Italian girl named Maria and had left her behind, pregnant with his child. But how could the people who had not been in such a chaotic place possibly understand the experiences of those who had? How could he even talk to them? How could he assimilate in his own mind what he had experienced over there and incorporate it into the life he was now living over here? In Wilson's novel, Rath's gray flannel suit became a symbol of the cloak of denial behind which the postwar world went on with its routines and its work.

But the single most compelling reason for postwar split-mindedness was the fact that, just as the war against Germany and Japan was concluding successfully, and the champagne corks were popping – and just as fifty nations who had joined in opposing the Axis powers met in San Francisco, on April 25, 1945, to draw up the Charter of the United Nations, the world's hope for future peace – the victorious alliance between the United States and the Soviet Union was falling apart, with wartime suspicions being replaced by open hostility and by the genuine possibility of a serious military confrontation between the two most powerful nations in the postwar world. The Cold War, as it became known, would be especially frightening, because, thanks to the existence of nuclear weapons, it offered the possibility of a war between the former allies with destructive consequences too awful to contemplate.

So what the postwar era provided was a confusing mixture of the best of times and the worst of times: the best of times, with a surging economy accompanying high levels of domestic optimism, with the worst of times, in which even the winning of an unprecedented victory over the Axis powers seemed to offer no end to the nation's anxieties and obligations. In fact, the flow of events in the postwar period seemed to be ramping up those anxieties and obligations even further. One historian has called the state of affairs in postwar America a "troubled feast": an awkward and paradoxical term that nevertheless neatly captured the strange juxtaposition of promise and peril that ran through these years.

Harry S. Truman, who had succeeded to the presidency after FDR's death, found himself plunged abruptly into the awesome task of leading the nation through one of the most challenging times in its history. "Boys, if you ever pray, pray for me now," he confessed to reporters shortly after assuming office. "When they told me yesterday" about FDR's death, "I felt like the moon, the stars, and all the planets had fallen on me." Truman had been kept out of the major decisions of the administration during his short tenure as vice president, and now he would have to preside over some of the biggest and most consequential decisions ever made by an American president, as the United States tried to come to terms with its expanded role in the world – and the global ambitions of its determined ideological foe.

A small, bespectacled, and undistinguished-looking country boy who had been born and raised on his family's farm near Independence, Missouri, Harry Truman could not have offered a more striking contrast to the urbane, well-born, and Harvard-educated FDR. A product of an ordinary midwestern public high school, Truman did not go on to seek a college degree but instead kicked around at a variety of jobs, first as a timekeeper with the Santa Fe Railroad and later taking clerical jobs with banks and newspapers. It was not until the time of the First World War, when he joined the army and eventually ended up serving with distinction as an artillery officer with the AEF in Europe, that Truman discovered that he had a knack for leadership.

After returning from the war, and encountering failure in trying to run a men's clothing store, he turned to a career in politics, gradually working his way up the political ladder the hard way, without any family wealth or connections to fall back on. He attached himself to the powerful and unscrupulous Kansas City political boss T. J. Pendergast and parlayed a series of successes, beginning with a county judgeship, into election in 1934 to the U.S. Senate. Although immediately branded by his foes with the disparaging name "Senator from Pendergast," a connection that hurt him in running for reelection in 1940, particularly after Pendergast was imprisoned for income tax evasion, Truman was eventually able to transcend his political origins and outgrow any lingering image as a "political hack."

In particular, his dedicated work chairing a bipartisan Senate special committee, popularly known as the Truman Committee, with the task of investigating waste and fraud in military spending, brought him to the respectful attention of the nation, and of Roosevelt, who began to think of him as a possible fourth-term running mate. Mindful of the public suspicions aroused by the Nye Committee's report on World War I munitions profiteering, Truman doggedly sought out instances of corruption. Beginning with Fort Leonard Wood in his home state of Missouri, he drove his personal car (a modest Dodge) to military installations around the country, ten thousand miles of travel, to uncover cases of millions of government dollars going to well-connected military contractors under lucrative cost-plus contracts, without procedures to ensure the proper quality of the goods delivered.

This kind of dauntless, untiring dedication captured the public's emerging image of Harry Truman: a simple, unpretentious midwestern man, blunt, down to earth, incredibly hardworking, decisive, and thoroughly honest, not a smooth operator but a gallant and feisty defender of the interests of the common people and the little guy. If FDR had been formed in the well-pedigreed political tradition of Jefferson and Wilson, Truman was a product of the great unpedigreed tradition of Jackson and Lincoln, both of them uncommon common men in the American mold who rose to the presidency from unprepossessing beginnings, relying on audacity, ambition, talent, and sheer grit to make it to the top, but never forgetting the roots from which they had sprung.

Nevertheless, on the home-front side of the job, Truman would find the presidency very tough going. He was an enthusiastic New Dealer when it came to domestic affairs and in fact hoped to extend the New Deal into questions of national health insurance and ensuring full employment. But the Democrats had been in power for more than a decade; voters had had a bellyful of them and were now ready for a change. In the midterm elections of 1946, the Republicans won majorities in both houses of Congress – their slogan was "Had Enough? Vote Republican!" – and quickly put a stop to most of Truman's ambitious domestic program. Instead, the Republicans overrode a Truman veto to pass the 1947 Taft–Hartley Act, a significant revision of the Wagner Act of 1935 designed to pare back the power of labor unions by a number of measures, such as outlawing the "closed shop" (union membership as a precondition of any employee being hired), permitting states to pass "right to work" laws outlawing mandatory union membership, and various measures designed to inhibit unions' ability to strike and prevent the infiltration of labor unions by Communists and other radicals.

But the truly consequential work facing Truman was in the area of foreign relations, in discerning the American role in restoring a shattered world, as well as negotiating the minefield of postwar relations with the Soviet Union. The conditions with which he would have to deal had extremely complex origins, the needs were great, and his room to maneuver was often very constricted.

The three Allies who won the Second World War together, Great Britain, the United States, and the Soviet Union, were an unlikely and strange group, held together only by a shared opposition to the Axis powers and already showing signs of discord well before the end of the war. In point of fact, American relations with the Soviet Union had never been good, going back to the Revolution of 1917 establishing a Communist regime in Russia. The Soviet Union was viewed as a standing ideological threat to capitalist countries, and it was not until 1933 that the United States even was willing to grant it diplomatic recognition.

The events of 1941, with Hitler's surprise invasion of the Soviet Union and Japan's attack on Pearl Harbor, changed matters tactically, but they did not produce an atmosphere of trust or mutual support, only a temporary liaison of convenience. In spring 1945, as the Red Army began to occupy large portions of Eastern Europe, the Soviets began installing puppet governments in those countries, in essence establishing the basis for a Soviet empire. Such actions were flagrant violations of the terms of the agreement that had been reached between the Allies at the Yalta Conference of February 1945, in which the Big Three agreed that, apart from a portion of Poland ceded to the Soviets, they would sponsor free elections, democratic governance, and safeguards for fundamental liberties in all the rest of Europe. The Soviets were openly disregarding that commitment.

By March 5, 1946, not even ten months after the conclusion of the war in Europe, Winston Churchill was issuing this resonant warning to an American audience at Westminster College in Fulton, Missouri:

> From Stettin in the Baltic to Trieste in the Adriatic an iron curtain has descended across the Continent. Behind that line lie all the capitals of the ancient states of Central and Eastern Europe. Warsaw, Berlin, Prague, Vienna, Budapest, Belgrade, Bucharest and Sofia; all these famous cities and the populations around them lie in what I must call the Soviet sphere, and all are subject, in one form or another, not only to Soviet influence but to a very high and in some cases increasing measure of control from Moscow.

Churchill's "iron curtain" speech was a clear sign that a Cold War between the Soviet Union and the West, particularly the United States, was now under way.

The reasons for our conflicts with the Soviets have always been a source of controversy, but a few obvious points can be made. First, it is important to recall that the Soviets had strong grievances against the Allies. It was they who had borne the brunt of the battle and the bulk of the casualties in the fight against Hitler, during years in which Churchill and Roosevelt had repeatedly put off Stalin's demand for a decisive invasion from the West. Stalin believed that such an invasion would establish a second front that could take some of the heat off the East and spread the sacrifices of the war effort more equitably. This was not unreasonable. By some estimates, as many as half of all deaths in the Second World War were of Soviet combatants and civilians. For all Stalin's tendency toward deviousness and bad faith, some acknowledgment has to be made of the enormous extent of those concerns. It also needs to be recognized that, given Russia's history of suffering invasions from the West, most recently at the hands of Adolf Hitler, the Soviet desire for a protective buffer zone to the West was understandable.

But it is an entirely different matter to excuse the unmistakable pattern of Soviet deceptions, manipulations, and broken promises as, one by one, between 1946 and 1948, Soviet-controlled Communist regimes came to power in Poland, Romania, Bulgaria, Albania, Hungary, and Czechoslovakia. The expansion did not end with the creation of these "satellites." The four-way division of Germany prescribed at Yalta was to be temporary, but no sooner did the Americans turn the eastern zone of Germany over to the Soviet occupation than the Soviets began the process of erecting yet another Communist satellite state, the German Democratic Republic, meant to govern the zone permanently. The United States wanted to see a reunited Germany that would be economically strong; the Soviets, on the contrary, wanted to see a permanently divided Germany, to ensure a permanently weakened Germany.

Nor was this all. The Soviets seemed to be increasingly expansion minded, reflecting both Marxist–Leninist ideology and the conditions of the times. Postwar Europe was in a highly vulnerable economic and political state, with fragile regimes tottering on the edge of dissolution, making them prime targets of opportunity. The expansion of Soviet influence into the eastern Mediterranean, the Middle East, and even western Europe itself was a looming possibility. The Soviets challenged Turkey to allow their shipping to pass at will through the Turkish Straits connecting the Black Sea and the Mediterranean, a direct affront to Turkish sovereignty that could easily escalate into military conflict. In Greece, a Communist insurgency threatened to overthrow the Greek monarchy, which had lost the protection of a war-weakened British Empire. If either of these two countries fell under Soviet influence, the other would soon follow, and the Soviets would then be able to control the eastern Mediterranean and threaten the Suez Canal, the lifeline to Middle Eastern oil.

In the meantime, George F. Kennan, an American diplomat posted at the American embassy in Moscow, was formulating a strategic doctrine by which the United States could understand and respond to the increasingly alarming Soviet threat. An elegant writer and subtle analyst, Kennan was able to draw not only on his extensive knowledge of Russian history and Soviet institutions but also on his understanding of the psychological makeup of the Soviet regime. He found it permeated with internal instability and insecurity, which in turn helped to fuel a ceaseless drive toward expansion, even as it tended to make for a certain cautiousness in pursuing those ends.

Kennan concluded that the best way for the United States to respond to the Soviet threat would be by occupying a well-considered middle ground. It should not try to appease the Soviets by declining to resist them, nor should it attempt aggressively to roll back the Soviets' areas of established domination and risk cataclysmic war. Instead, Kennan recommended a "long-term, patient but firm and vigilant *containment* of Russian expansive tendencies," one that would have to subordinate the desire for visible victory but could do so in full confidence that the Soviet system "bears within it the seeds of its own decay, and that the sprouting of those seeds is well advanced."

This outlook corresponded roughly with the emerging outlook of President Truman and his advisors. On March 12, 1947, Truman appeared before a joint session of Congress and, after making a powerful and moving case for the perilousness of the Greek situation and the depth of the Greeks' need for assistance, requested a $400 million economic-aid package for Greece and Turkey. The action represented a fairly pure expression of the containment ideal. Aware of the precedent being set, Truman carefully set forward the principles by which the provision of such aid would be guided in the future:

> I believe that it must be the policy of the United States to support free peoples who are resisting attempted subjugation by armed minorities or by outside pressures.
>
> I believe that we must assist free peoples to work out their own destinies in their own way.
>
> I believe that our help should be primarily through economic and financial aid which is essential to economic stability and orderly political process

The economic vulnerabilities of the postwar world were at the heart of its perils. "The seeds of totalitarian regimes," he argued, "are nurtured by misery and want. They spread and grow in the evil soil of poverty and strife. They reach their full growth when the hope of a people for a better life has died. We must keep that hope alive."

The reaction to Truman's speech was generally positive, although there were criticisms. The influential journalist Walter Lippmann noted that the policy committed the country to a struggle that had no tangible object, only the vague hope that Soviet power would implode over time. Kennan himself would, years later, complain that Truman extended the containment doctrine much further and more aggressively than he had intended; others complained that it was too passive, too willing to accept the status quo, and that a "rollback" of Communist rule was the only acceptable response.

Yet what Truman and his advisors saw all over Europe was a critical situation, in which economic problems loomed even larger than military ones. Industrial production was nil, transportation systems were at a standstill, food production was grossly inadequate, coal shortages made many homes uninhabitable, and weather conditions of drought and extreme cold greatly exacerbated all these problems. In both Italy and France, the Communist Party was making serious inroads in the hearts and minds of a discouraged, desperate electorate. It was possible to imagine Soviet-aligned Communists coming to power through the ballot box in those countries. Only the United States, Truman stated in his address, could supply the help that could make a difference.

Following along these same lines, General George Marshall, now Truman's secretary of state, used his Harvard University commencement address in June 1947 to outline an ambitious plan for the recovery and rebuilding of Europe. The worst enemy, he said, was not any particular ideology but rather "hunger, poverty, desperation, and chaos." The goal of postwar American policy should be "the revival of a working economy in the world so as to permit the emergence of political and social conditions in which free institutions can exist." The Marshall Plan, as it came to be known, would extend aid to all European countries, including the Soviet Union. In the end, the Soviets would decline to participate, labeling the plan an "imperialist" scheme, and would force their satellite states to decline as well.

In fact, Stalin had no desire to see the free economies of Europe recover their strength. In the end, however, they did, and with remarkable speed. How much of this was due to the Marshall Plan and how much was due to general economic recovery is impossible to say. But a total of some $13 billion in American dollars was infused into the European economy, and it seemed to have just the effects that Truman and Marshall hoped it would. It strengthened the economies of the Western European powers so that they would not be vulnerable to seeing their democratic institutions subverted. It also helped the United States, both by furthering its foreign-policy objectives in Europe and also by creating markets for American exported goods. It thus was both a highly generous act and a very self-interested one on the part of the United States.

It did nothing, however, to bridge the chasm that had opened up between the United States and the Soviet Union. That relationship only worsened. In 1948, when the three non-Soviet sectors of occupied Germany announced plans to unite as "West Germany," the Soviets retaliated by blocking land access to Allied-occupied West Berlin, which was located in the heart of Soviet-dominated East Germany, hoping either to force a reversal of the Western German unification or to force the Western powers to relinquish control over West Berlin. Truman hung tough, though, and, instead of initiating armed conflict, chose to resupply West Berlin by a massive airlift, flying in thirteen thousand tons a day of food, medical supplies, coal, and other necessary items. The blockade, and the airlift, continued until May 12, 1949, when the Soviets finally lifted the blockade. Containment had triumphed.

Meanwhile, the decline in Allied–Soviet relations had given rise to a formal military alliance, the North Atlantic Treaty Organization (NATO), created in April 1949 and uniting twelve nations, including the United States and Canada, in a mutual-defense pact. In signing the NATO treaty, the signatory parties were agreeing to regard an attack on any one of its members as equivalent to an attack upon itself, and to respond accordingly. Truman appointed General Dwight Eisenhower as NATO's first supreme commander and stationed American troops in various parts of Western Europe as protection against possible Soviet invasion. For the United States, such a commitment was a striking departure from the tradition founded by George Washington's Farewell Address, which recommended against any permanent alliances for the United States. But there was near-universal agreement that such a mutual-defense commitment was needed, and NATO went on to become one of the most successful military alliances in history, an effective and durable check against Soviet aggression and a central institution for the West's policy of containment.

Finally, one should mention yet another event in Truman's action-packed first term as president: his decisive role in the creation of the modern state of Israel. The Jewish people of the world had for centuries been compelled to exist in diaspora, a term for scattering or dispersion, meaning that wherever they lived, they existed as minorities, at the mercy of the majority culture, since they lacked a geographical country of their own. The Zionist movement begun in nineteenth-century Europe set out to rectify this situation and sought the eventual achievement of a national homeland for the Jewish people.

Many Zionists began to migrate to Palestine, which they revered as the biblical Holy Land, and they found a haven there from the anti-Semitic pogroms and persecutions of Europe and Russia. Palestine had been under the rule of the Ottoman Turks, who were Sunni Muslims, until the First World War, but after the war ended and the Ottoman Empire disappeared, the League of Nations made Palestine a British mandate. The British had long been officially sympathetic to the Zionist idea, and with their encouragement, and the strong support of American Jews and much of the international Jewish community, Zionists began to envision Palestine as the destined location for a modern Jewish state.

The matter passed to the fledgling United Nations as successor to the League, and it tried in late 1947 to put forward an understanding that would partition Palestine into Jewish and Arab states and leave Jerusalem under an international trusteeship. But that proposition encountered strong Arab resistance, and matters were left stalemated as fighting broke out between Arab and Jewish factions. Finally, on May 14, 1948, David Ben-Gurion, head of the Jewish Agency for Israel, declared the independence of Israel. Eleven minutes later, Truman announced U.S. recognition of the new state of Israel. He had strongly supported such a move for many years and knew in advance what Ben-Gurion planned to do, and he wanted the United States to be the first nation in the world to grant official diplomatic recognition to the new nation of Israel.

Most of Truman's aides opposed the move, fearing that it would damage American national interests by seeming to disparage the concerns of Arab oil states. Indeed, Israel immediately found itself at war with its neighboring Arab states, and continued to be for many of the subsequent years. But Truman's reasoning in the matter was simple and direct:

> *Hitler had been murdering Jews right and left. I saw it, and I dream about it even to this day. The Jews needed some place where they could go. It is my attitude that the American government couldn't stand idly by while the victims [of] Hitler's madness are not allowed to build new lives.*

The reasoning clearly echoed his thinking in propounding the Truman Doctrine: it was up to the United States to stand for simple justice when the vulnerable and besieged were being set upon by tyrannizing outside forces. Such things moved his thinking even more than questions of geopolitical calculation.

Despite all these accomplishments, Truman would have an uphill fight in winning the presidency in his own right in fall 1948. The hangover of 1946 was still in the air, and the electorate still seemed to lean Republican in its mood. To make matters worse, his own Democratic Party was coming apart, splintering into three factions. As the party mainstream began to move away from its historical stance opposing black civil rights in the South, a southern "Dixiecrat" contingent left the party in opposition and nominated its own candidate (Strom Thurmond of South Carolina) for president, and a Progressive faction for which Truman and the mainstream did not go far enough did the same, nominating Henry A. Wallace as the Progressive Party candidate. Truman hardly seemed to stand a chance.

And yet, thanks to the lackadaisical campaigning of his Republican foe, New York governor Thomas E. Dewey, and thanks to Truman's own stupendous thirty-one-thousand-mile "whistle stop" campaign tour of the country by train, he pulled off a great upset, winning the election by more than two million votes and by a 303–189 margin in the Electoral College. Now the nation would see what Truman could do, elected in his own right. What they knew now about him, beyond a shadow of a doubt, was that he was a fighter.

As in his first term, foreign-policy concerns would dominate Truman's attention, and the going would be just as tough as before. In fact, the early months of his new term saw a series of setbacks, including a new crop of troubles in Asia.

First there was China, which had been in a state of civil war since the 1920s, when Chinese Nationalist forces had been fending off a challenge from Communists under the leadership of Mao Zedong for control of the country. That conflict was interrupted by the war with Japan but resumed in late 1945. Although the Nationalists, under Chiang Kai-shek, had the support of the United States, they were widely perceived by the Chinese people (and by some American military commanders on the ground) to be corrupt and oppressive, and Chiang did not enjoy much popular support. The Communists, on the other hand, were seen as a patriotic anticolonial force that stood for Chinese political and cultural independence over against foreign domination, whether that of Japan or of European colonizers such as Britain or France. The Communists had won over the peasantry, who expected to benefit from the large-scale land reforms that, under Mao Zedong, they promised to implement.

By the end of 1949, the Communists had won the war and had pushed the Nationalists off the Chinese mainland onto the large coastal island of Formosa (later renamed Taiwan). This was seen as a stunning setback for Truman's approach to foreign policy and a humiliating and unnecessary "loss" of China, for which Truman's Republican opponents did not hesitate to denounce him. It was true that Truman seemed to have suffered from an uncharacteristic indecisiveness regarding American policy in China. But his indecision was partly due to the complexity of the situation. Containment could not work in Asia as well as it had in Europe, precisely because of the extent to which the Communist cause came to be linked with the intense desire of many Chinese to be free of domination by foreign influences, a desire that had already manifested itself vividly in the Boxer Rebellion of 1899–1901 and had only grown during the years of brutal Japanese occupation. In Eastern and Central Europe, however, where containment meant the preservation of national independence against Soviet encroachment, the opposite was the case.

In any event, the most populous nation on earth, a people with whom Americans had long had friendly relations, and with which the United States had been aligned in the war against Japan, was now a Communist-ruled country and a near-certain antagonist, as the Nationalist remnant on Taiwan survived and continued to be recognized by the United States as the sole legitimate Chinese government. It was an enormous shock to find the tables turned so suddenly and massively. To make matters worse, at just the same time that Mao's revolution was succeeding, the Soviet Union successfully exploded an atomic bomb, bringing to an end America's brief monopoly over nuclear weapons. Finally, in 1950, Stalin and Mao signed a Sino-Soviet Treaty of Friendship and Alliance, which created a massive Communist bloc and gave powerful credence to the fear that Communism was an ideology bent upon world domination, and that its time had arrived.

Small wonder that so sudden and alarming a reversal of fortunes would give rise to national soul searching and executive rethinking. One of the immediate fruits of that rethinking was NSC-68, a confidential study of Cold War strategy produced by the National Security Council, an organization that had been created just after the war to advise the White House on matters of national defense. NSC-68 proposed a massive increase in spending on defense, along with a willingness to form alliances with non-Communist countries around the world, as pillars of American policy moving forward. Both, of course, represented dramatic changes from American military doctrine since the nation's beginning. Both the republican aversion to standing armies and the Washingtonian aversion to entangling alliances were being set aside.

In addition, fears of foreign subversion, coming from Communists and other radicals both outside and inside the government, manifested themselves much as they had in the Red Scare of the post–World War I era. The Truman administration instituted a loyalty program in the federal government, leading to the dismissal or resignation of hundreds of federal employees. Eleven leaders of the American Communist Party were jailed under the Smith Act of 1940, with their convictions upheld by the Supreme Court. The House Committee on Un-American Activities, first formed during wartime to ferret out Nazi sympathizers, was reactivated to seek out Communists and Communist influence, not only in government but also in the film industry and other institutions of civil society. Most notoriously of all, Senator Joseph McCarthy of Wisconsin carried on a one-man campaign against purported Communist influences and sympathies in the government, using the weapon of often baseless accusations to create an atmosphere of fear in the country, particularly among those of left-leaning sympathies.

In retrospect, this second "red scare" seems excessive to many historians and other observers, and "McCarthyism" remains to this day a byword for reckless, evidence-free, reputation-staining accusation. But not all of his concerns were groundless, and when considered in the setting of its times, in the context of a nation that still was emerging into an entirely new role after a long period of relative detachment, the reaction may not seem quite so excessive. In addition, we know much today that we did not know at the time, thanks to the opening of Soviet archives and the release of decoded secret diplomatic cables to researchers, and we know now that espionage was a serious problem and that there *were* foreign communist agents active in the U.S. government. We know that a series of sensational espionage cases raised legitimate concerns about the security of vital national secrets. We know that in the case of figures like atomic scientist Klaus Fuchs and Julius and Ethel Rosenberg, secrets relating to the Manhattan Project and the development of the atomic bomb were passed along to Soviet agents, treasonable acts that almost certainly helped to speed the development of such weapons and thereby aid a deadly enemy.

The Cold War turned hot in 1950, when the United States found itself again at war – this time on the Korean peninsula, confronting a communist foe. Japan had occupied the peninsula during the Russo-Japanese War and had annexed it in 1910. But after the defeat of Japan in 1945, a vacuum had been created. Soviet troops had streamed in to occupy the northern portion of the peninsula, even as American forces occupied the southern portion. There had never been any plan for a permanent division. But the evolving situation in postwar Germany would soon be repeated in postwar Korea as the Soviets established a communist government in the north and the Americans a Western-style democracy in the south. The dividing line between the two became the thirty-eighth parallel, with no plan for unification in sight.

It was an uneasy situation not destined to stay peaceful for long. On June 25, 1950, a wave of eighty thousand North Korean troops swept down into South Korea. It is not clear whether they did so at the direct bidding of Moscow, though it is hard to believe that Soviet encouragement was not somehow involved, and Truman certainly had no doubts on that score. When told of the invasion by his secretary of state, the suave Yale-educated diplomat Dean Acheson, Truman responded without hesitation and with characteristic bluntness: "Dean, we've got to stop the sons-of-bitches no matter what." Here was a prime test case for containment in Asia. But rather than approach the conflict as an Americans-only action, with a full declaration of war, Truman took a different path. He took the matter to the United Nations (UN) and sought its approval of a "peacekeeping" force that would fend off the North Korean assault. The Security Council agreed, and the U.S. Congress supported the idea, accepting a characterization of the intervention as a "police action" by the UN rather than a war by the United States. But in the end, it was primarily an American effort, with General Douglas MacArthur in command, although fourteen other nations contributed.

The war went very badly at first, partly due to the element of surprise. The South Korean army was not battle ready, and only five hundred American advisors were on the ground on June 25. The North Koreans drove their enemy all the way down the peninsula to Pusan, at the southernmost tip, occupying the South Korean capital of Seoul on the way. But then MacArthur countered on September 15 with a brilliantly effective amphibious invasion at Inchon,

Seoul's port city, well behind the lines of the advancing North Korean intruders. He cut off the invaders, retook Seoul, and began pushing the remnants of the North Korean army northward, seeking (with UN approval) to reunify the country by force.

MacArthur proceeded almost to the Chinese border in the north, ignoring Chinese warnings against such encroachment. Then, on November 25, a wave of more than a quarter million Chinese troops swept across the border, overwhelming the UN forces and pushing them back into South Korea, with the battle line finally stabilizing around the thirty-eighth parallel. It had been yet another dizzying reversal in this seesaw conflict.

At this point, MacArthur and Truman locked horns over what to do next. MacArthur claimed that with the Chinese intervention, it was a "whole new war" and a prime opportunity for the United States to rid the world of a dangerous Communist China before it consolidated power fully. He wanted to go after the Chinese full force, even making use of the nation's nuclear weapons, using naval superiority to enforce a blockage of Chinese ports and unleashing the Nationalists from Taiwan in an invasion of the mainland. Truman strongly disagreed, as did his advisors, and thought that a war with China would be a "booby trap," a fatal temptation that the United States needed to avoid at all costs.

It did not take long for the general, who had an ego the size of Asia itself, to overstep his bounds. He had taken to making policy statements on his own, without clearing them with Washington, and often directly contradicting presidential positions. When MacArthur took it upon himself to criticize Truman in an official letter to the House minority leader, proclaiming that "there is no substitute for victory" – a direct rebuke to the "containment" policy, and the related policy of "limited war" – Truman felt he had no choice but to fire him for insubordination, which he did on April 11, 1951. It was a politically costly act for Truman, because MacArthur was a war hero, much beloved, and the containment policy was always a difficult and unsatisfying one to pursue. When MacArthur returned to the country, his first return home to the United States since 1937, he received one of the largest ticker-tape parades in New York's history, a nineteen-mile-long affair winding through the streets of Manhattan and viewed by at least seven million cheering spectators. Meanwhile, Truman's personal popularity sank like a stone and remained low, going down to 22 percent in the early part of 1952, which remains the lowest mark ever recorded by an American president since Gallup began polling for approval ratings in the 1930s. No American president had been more deeply unpopular for a longer period of his time in office than Truman, and he knew better than to attempt to run for a second full term.

Yet no American president has seen his reputation rise more steadily in the years since his time of service. Over time, the American people have come to understand and appreciate the fact that Truman's actions prevented another world war, whereas MacArthur's preferred path would have embraced one, with consequences beyond imagination. Truman had the burden, a burden he shouldered honorably and wisely, of shepherding the nation through times of great changes, and many of the results were unwelcome or unsatisfying in the short term. Statesmanship is often like that, as many previous episodes in American history, such as the controversy associated with Jay's Treaty at the nation's beginnings, or with Lincoln's leadership in the Civil War, serve to illustrate.

There is no prettifying the fact that the end result of the Korean War was a stalemate which became a truce, and there was never a final peace conference capped by a settlement and a treaty. In effect, there was never really an end to this undeclared war, only a cessation of hostilities, with de facto recognition of a line slightly north of the thirty-eighth parallel as the boundary between the two hostile Koreas – a single people divided by happenstance, with a narrow demilitarized zone, a no-man's land, separating the two parts.

The situation remains largely unchanged in 2019, at the time of this writing. More than thirty-three thousand Americans, some one million Koreans, and an unknown number of Chinese died to preserve that separation. It was a success for containment, yes, but a coldly rational success at best, like that of a sports team that plays only for a tie, and a confirmation of Walter Lippmann's warning about containment's difficulties arising out of its lack of a tangible object.

By the time an uneasy truce had been established in 1953, the United States had a new president. Republicans had been alive with anticipation at the prospect of electing one of their own as president to succeed the unpopular Truman and end the Democrats' twenty-year domination of the presidency. They ended up nominating a national war hero who was not a politician and whose wide appeal could attract independent and crossover voters, including patriotic southern Democrats. General Dwight David Eisenhower, a career army man from the American heartland, had been supreme Allied commander and the hero of D-Day in the Second World War and brought to the political arena an aura of moderation and nonpartisan executive competence. At the time the Republicans recruited him to run for president, he was serving as the first supreme commander of NATO forces, an indication right out of the gate of his commitment to the new postwar order, in contrast to the lingering isolationist tendencies of some in his party.

In his campaign, Eisenhower promised to "clean up the mess in Washington" and to secure an "early and honorable" peace in Korea. Given his history, voters felt that this was a man who could in fact get the job done. His unequaled record of achievement and his tone of general managerial competence, combined with a winning smile and great personal amiability – "I Like Ike" was perhaps the best campaign-button slogan ever – made him unbeatable, particularly against the Democrats' candidate, the witty but relatively unknown governor of Illinois Adlai Stevenson, who could not generate popular enthusiasm for his candidacy and, in the end, could not even win his home state. It was said that the Democrats' slogan should be "Sadly for Adlai."

There was a decided shift in tone with the new president. Eisenhower favored a more fiscally conservative approach to government spending, and budget balancing was, after many years of deficit spending, high on the domestic agenda. In general, however, he did not challenge the essential architecture of the New Deal, either by contracting it or expanding it, although in a few cases – such as the extension of Social Security disability benefits – he extended the reach of programs. He filled his administration with business executives, such as his secretary of defense, Charles Wilson of General Motors. As a military man who was accustomed to the extensive use of top-down chain-of-command authority, and the extensive delegation of duties along the lines of the organizational chart, Eisenhower had a different management style and was less visible to the public and less accessible to the press than his immediate predecessors had been. This low-key style led many contemporary journalists to underestimate his leadership abilities, which were considerable but exercised discreetly and indirectly, using persuasion rather than force – a "hidden-hand presidency," as the political scientist Fred Greenstein dubbed it.

Indeed, if there is a single word that could encompass what the Eisenhower administration excelled in accomplishing, that word might be consolidation, using that word not in the Founders' sense but to describe a process by which changes are accepted and absorbed into a more settled condition. He brought a degree of composure and unity to the new circumstances in which the United States found itself, a sense of order after decades of disruption. This was as true in foreign policy as it was in domestic policy; in neither case did Eisenhower seek to overturn the key precedents set by his Democratic predecessors. Instead, he sought to improve their implementation and bring their costs under control.

Using shrewd pressure tactics, Eisenhower achieved an armistice in Korea, with the return of American prisoners of war. He worked behind the scenes to bring to an end the reckless career of Senator McCarthy. He continued, and expanded, Truman's program for ensuring government security, insisted that Soviet espionage remained an ongoing concern, and refused to stay the execution of the nuclear spies Julius and Ethel Rosenberg. Despite occasional talk coming from his secretary of state, John Foster Dulles, of "rolling back" Communist influence and using aggressive "brinksmanship" (including the brandishing of nuclear weapons) to achieve foreign-policy goals, Eisenhower tried his best to continue the fundamentally cautious and defensive policy of containment that Truman had established and the far-flung role in the larger world that the United States now seemed destined to play.

But the growing reliance on the deterrent effect of nuclear weapons, which both sides of the Cold War now possessed in growing power and numbers, produced a curious, though predictable, side effect. Because the possibility of a nuclear face-off between the United States and the Soviet Union was so unthinkable – it would be, as the strategists said, "mutual assured destruction" – the action of the Cold War found its way into more remote and particular channels, "brushfire" wars in the undeveloped or developing nations of the world, which were beginning to be called the Third World, to distinguish them from the Western capitalist democracies and the Communist bloc dictatorships, respectively. As the colonial empires of France, the Netherlands, and Great Britain all began to break up, new countries began to form – India, Pakistan, Indonesia, Ghana, and many others – and became pawns and proxies in the contest of the two contending superpowers. Governments, including that of the United States, turned to unconventional forces, including the use of covert forces, to accomplish their foreign-policy goals.

Such secret actions in Latin America, Asia, and Africa often took the form of morally questionable acts that cut against American traditions and led to longer-term resentment and distrust of the United States. For example, the U.S. Central Intelligence Agency (CIA) helped to overthrow a leader in Iran who had attempted to seize the holdings of foreign oil companies and supported the return of the Iranian monarch, Reza Pahlavi, who became a staunch American ally. It was a short-term success for American policy but one that would have far less favorable longer-term consequences in subsequent years. One of the goals of American Cold War policy was the effective positioning and projection of American power, in ways meant to contain Communism, but another goal was winning the hearts and minds of inhabitants of Third World countries, whose struggles with poverty and hopelessness were precisely the struggles that George Marshall had described in his Harvard commencement. Often the effective pursuit of the first goal made pursuit of the second goal difficult to impossible.

Much of Eisenhower's busy administration was preoccupied with the management of a profusion of foreign-policy challenges, too many for us to discuss in detail here. But three deserve particular attention.

The first involved the fall of French Indochina. The French had lost their Southeast Asia colony to Japan during the Second World War and had unwisely chosen to fight against anticolonial independence movements to regain it. As in China, the anticolonial cause in Indochina became championed by Communists, notably the Communist leader Ho Chi Minh, and thus was assimilated into the larger Cold War fabric. In 1954, the French forces were decisively defeated and chose to give up Indochina, which was divided by a settlement reached in Geneva into three independent nations: Laos, Cambodia, and Vietnam. As in Korea, and in Germany, Vietnam came to be temporarily divided at the seventeenth parallel, occupied in the north by Communist forces and in the south by pro-Western or anti-Communist ones, including many Catholics.

Eisenhower had tried to keep the United States out of this situation. He had refused the French request for intervention in 1954 and only reluctantly aided the emerging South Vietnamese regime, under Ngo Dinh Diem, a Vietnamese Catholic who had opposed both the French and the Communists. Eisenhower provided advisors who helped with the training of troops and law enforcement personnel but drew the line at American troops – and insisted that Diem establish democratic norms and enact land reforms to help the desperately poor peasantry. But Diem did not follow through on his end of the bargain and even refused to allow an election in 1956, as had been prescribed in the Geneva accords, to reunify the country. Eisenhower was stuck with a corrupt and unreliable ally, but one deemed essential to preventing a Communist takeover of the region.

Another important foreign-policy event occurred in the Middle East, where the chief challenge to American policy was balancing the American commitment to Israel with the need for good relations with the oil-rich Arab states, most of which were hostile to Israel's very existence. When Egyptian general and pan-Arab nationalist Gamal Abdel Nasser came to power in 1956, he actively sought to exploit the superpower rivalry. When the United States refused to help him build the Aswan Dam, he went to the Soviet Union for help. Then Nasser took the bold move of seizing the Suez Canal, which ran through Egyptian land but was jointly owned by the British and French. The British and French, in cooperation with Israel, responded with military force and retook the canal. But Eisenhower, sensitive to American standing in the Arab world, turned in anger against his former allies and insisted that they withdraw, even initiating a UN resolution condemning the action. And the forces withdrew.

This incident was important because it firmly established for all the world to see something that was already plain after the end of the Second World War: the United States now called the tune when it came to the foreign policy of the Western democracies, and its allies did not have the liberty to act independently, particularly when it came to their colonial or quasi-colonial holdings. The Indochinese situation, and the Greek situation before it in the Truman years, had illustrated a similar point: it was up to the United States to take care of the entities to which the now defunct colonial empires of the great European powers could no longer attend.

Finally, there was the disturbing loss of Cuba to a Communist dictatorship. The United States had a long and often tense relationship with Cuba, going back to the early nineteenth century, when it was a wealthy Spanish colony. During most of the 1950s, the United States had supported the dictator Fulgencio Batista, who in turn was widely accommodating to a range of US business interests (including networks of organized crime), which he allowed to dominate the island's economy. Nevertheless, when Fidel Castro, a young revolutionary who successfully fought a guerrilla war against Batista's regime, came to power in 1959, Eisenhower quickly extended diplomatic recognition to the new government, and many Americans applauded Castro and hoped he would be an instrument of democratic reform. They miscalculated badly. Instead, Castro declared himself a communist and made it clear that he was hostile to the United States and welcomed Soviet support. He began enacting land reforms and nationalizing foreign-owned businesses and properties in Cuba, and exiles streamed out of the country into southern Florida. By the time Eisenhower left office in early 1961, diplomatic relations with Cuba had been suspended, and the problem of what to do about Castro would be left to Eisenhower's successor.

In this chapter, we have concentrated on foreign relations in the postwar era, touching on domestic affairs mainly to remark upon the economic recovery and general prosperity of the postwar years. But there was a major development on the domestic scene in the postwar era that we shall reserve for a full treatment in the next chapter but that warrants mentioning in this context – the emergence of one of the great social movements of American history, the logical successor to abolition: the movement to secure full civil rights for African Americans.

It is no coincidence that the civil rights movement, whose beginnings are traceable back to the earliest years of the century, began to gather steam in the years immediately after the conclusion of the Second World War, a war that was fought abroad in the name of ideals that were not being fully embodied or lived out at home. At some point, a contradiction of that magnitude becomes hard to ignore. Returning American GIs of all colors brought back stories of Nazi racialist atrocities. Returning black American GIs who had risked their lives for their country, only to find themselves consigned to ride in segregated railroad cars to return to their segregated towns, did not need the war to bring home to them the reality of racial discrimination. But other Americans perhaps did need a shock of recognition to bring the contradiction home to them.

As in the case of Alexis de Tocqueville, the insights of a foreign observer proved especially helpful to Americans' ability to see themselves more clearly. The Swedish sociologist Gunnar Myrdal, in a massive and highly influential 1944 study called *An American Dilemma*, formulated it in this way: there was a deep contradiction at the heart of American society, a contradiction between American ideals and American practices. Myrdal introduced the idea that there was what he called the "American Creed," a set of informal but binding affirmations that holds Americans together and defines their social and political order. The Creed was based on a belief in universal human equality, freedom, and opportunity; but the condition of American race relations stood in glaring contradiction to that belief. In this respect, too, America at midcentury was a time when all thoughts and things were split.

But Myrdal did not counsel despair, because the struggle was not an unfamiliar one. In fact, "America," he concluded, "is continuously struggling for its soul." The struggle was the burden imposed by the nation's outsized aspirations; being a land of hope meant always being willing to shake off the weight of fatalism and push ahead. Myrdal read American history hopefully, as "the gradual realization of the American Creed" that defined the nature of American society. One or the other had to give; either the Creed had become empty, or the practice of racial subordination had to come to an end. Which would it be? Finding the answer would be one of the most important items on the American agenda in the second half of the twentieth century.

CHAPTER TWENTY

OUT OF BALANCE

The Turbulent Sixties

ISENHOWER FINISHED HIS SECOND TERM ENJOYING considerable popularity. The American people still liked Ike. His moderate demeanor and policies had succeeded in bringing a degree of calm and "normalcy" to the nation's life, buffering the currents of change and instability that continued to make their presence felt, much as the rolling power of the ocean's swell is felt by a ship's passengers. Ike had settled the controversial status of the New Deal programs and had fully embraced a sprawling international presence for the United States that none of its Founders would ever have dreamed either possible or desirable. He had managed to restore a measure of decorum and dignity to public discourse and, most importantly of all, to keep the country out of war. He could probably have won a third term, had the recently adopted Twenty-Second Amendment to the Constitution not barred that from happening. Ironically, it was the Republicans who had pressed for the amendment to avert the possibility of another multiterm FDR; they would be the first ones to pay the price for it, a good lesson in the perils of constitutional tinkering.

Among other things, Eisenhower restored George Washington's model of a full two-term presidency, an example that had not been emulated in the forty years since the end of the Wilson administration. Eisenhower also followed his great Virginian predecessor by delivering a Farewell Address to the nation, presented on January 17, 1961, just three days before he would leave office. Washington's address had been offered to the nation as both a benediction and a warning, at a time of profound transition. Eisenhower would attempt to use his speech to do the same things. He began working on it in 1959 and meant it to be weighty and thought provoking, summing up the insights he had gained in his many years of public service, and his informed assessment of the dangers facing the nation in the years ahead. It was not unsuccessful in that regard, and many observers in subsequent years have regarded it as prophetic, especially in its warnings.

His tone was by turns confident and optimistic, but also sober, even somber. While recognizing and celebrating the achievements and prosperity of the present moment, Eisenhower also warned Americans that they must be more mindful of the needs of future generations, not only in material terms, but in spiritual terms as well. With the prospect of a growing national debt in mind, he advised Americans to

> *avoid the impulse to live only for today, plundering for our own ease and convenience the precious resources of tomorrow. We cannot mortgage the material assets of our grandchildren without risking the loss also of their political and spiritual heritage. We want democracy to survive for all generations to come, not to become the insolvent phantom of tomorrow.*

There also were warnings that applied with special force to the unprecedented conditions of the Cold War. He warned that the vastly expanded scope of government, and particularly the need to maintain a high and constant level of military preparedness under the current and foreseeable circumstances, could distort the character of the nation's institutions. "In the councils of government," he said, in what became the speech's most famous sentence, "we must guard against the acquisition of unwarranted influence, whether sought or unsought, by the military–industrial complex," by which he meant the combination of a large military establishment and a large armaments industry to supply it – neither of which had ever been a feature of peacetime American life. "We must never let the weight of this combination endanger our liberties or democratic processes." Nor, he cautioned, should we let the process of scientific research become the prisoner of government funding – or let democratic governance become captive to a technocratic elite ruling class.

It was a surprising speech, coming from one of the greatest generals in American history – a speech warning solemnly against the possibility of an excessive military predominance in American society. And yet its warning hearkened back to the ideals of the early American republic, in which the military ideal was that of the citizen-soldier and militiaman, not of a large standing armed force, which was always viewed as a temptation to corruption and abuse of power.

This seemed an inconsistency. Eisenhower had presided over years in which America was changing in the direction of what critics would call a "warfare–welfare" state, in which the demands of expensive New Deal social programs and a high degree of constant military readiness together dictated a sprawling federal governing presence as far as the eye could see. Ike had accepted and normalized these changes. And yet here he was, warning against the potential corruptions that those very changes were likely to bring about, without intense vigilance coming from the citizenry. But the seeming inconsistency was easily explained. The venerable American ideals from two centuries before, and ultimately the ideal of self-rule itself that was so deeply rooted in the origins of American society, represented precious and fundamental values that he was not willing to part with, and that he was not willing that his countrymen should forget either.

In that sense, then, the speech was far more than a personal good-bye and in fact was surprisingly devoid of personal flourishes, or even personal pronouns, a feature that reflected Eisenhower's admirably modest character. He did not want the speech to be about him but about the future of America and the world. As such, the speech did something far more important than saying good-bye. It was an important contribution to democratic reflection, a salutary effort to wrestle publicly with the most important problems facing American democracy, such as the concentration of power, the relationship between the public and private sectors, the proper role of science, and the importance of balancing prudence and generosity in the conduct of American foreign policy. Fittingly, while he described the problems, Eisenhower did not seek to prescribe the solutions, because that was for Americans to decide for themselves.

Above all, there was the problem of how one went about reconciling the urgent demands of the present with the more abiding values embodied in the nation's founding institutions and affirmations. For Eisenhower, the key would be captured in the word *balance*, a word he used ten times in his speech, and whose spirit well captured the underlying goal of his presidency. It was also a concept profoundly important to the Framers of the Constitution, who recognized that good governance meant the management of conflict, and of conflicting goods and conflicting claims on the public's attention. But balance is hard to prescribe in the abstract. Sometimes it can only be found by testing its limits and by risking periods of imbalance. Such testing and risking would become major themes of the years to come.

The election of 1960 to determine Eisenhower's successor would inevitably be partly a referendum on the success of Eisenhower's balancing act. The

Republicans nominated Richard M. Nixon, a forty-seven-year-old former congressman and senator from California, who had been Ike's vice president for both terms. Nixon came to the task with impressive credentials. He has been called the "first modern vice president" because of the unprecedented degree to which he played an active part in administration policy making. He attended NSC and cabinet meetings and took on a highly visible role in diplomatic matters, including travels to Asia, Europe, and South America. He raise his profile as a statesman in his famous impromptu "kitchen debate" in Moscow with Soviet premier Nikita Khrushchev over the relative economic merits of capitalism and communism. He was already a familiar face in American politics even before Ike selected him as a running mate in 1952, for his record as a strongly anti-Communist legislator and particularly for his role in the exposure of Alger Hiss, a former State Department official, as a Soviet spy.

The Democrats nominated an even younger and far more fresh-faced candidate, the forty-three-year-old senator John F. Kennedy of Massachusetts, whom it was hoped could make up in energy and charisma what he lacked in experience. He outdistanced a field of Democratic worthies, including such luminaries as Hubert Humphrey of Minnesota and Senate majority leader Lyndon B. Johnson of Texas, to win the nomination. Then, in a very competitive race with Nixon, in which Kennedy's cause was helped by his superior performance in four televised debates – the first such debates in American political history – he won the presidency by a razor-thin margin of only one hundred thousand votes in the popular tally (the edge was a somewhat more decisive 303 to 219 in the Electoral College).

Although it is risky to draw sweeping conclusions from such a slender margin of victory, it seemed that the American people were once again ready for a change, and this time in the direction of energetic youth. Although Nixon was himself only forty-seven, he was heavily identified with Ike, who was seventy years old and in fragile health; that was the downside to Nixon's being the candidate of continuity. Kennedy, by contrast, was charming and handsome, with a glamorous young wife and two small children, an eloquent speaker with a forward-looking vision. He capitalized on the contrast, using as one of his campaign slogans the admonition "Let's get this country moving again!" He ran on a platform that he named the "New Frontier," an image meant to recall Frederick Jackson Turner's assertion of the frontier's central importance to American life as a place of exploration and renewal, extending that vision of "frontier" to such fresh possibilities as the exploration of space and the conquest of poverty and disease.

His inauguration took place on a brilliantly sunny day in snow-blanketed Washington, January 20, 1961, with Presidents Truman and Eisenhower both in attendance, and the eighty-six-year-old poet Robert Frost present to read a poem for the occasion. The contrast could not have been more plain. It was as if a line of demarcation were being drawn between the end of an old era and the beginning of a new one, a feeling that was echoed in Kennedy's finely crafted and stirringly delivered inaugural address, which quickly became one of the classics of the genre. "Let the word go forth from this time and place," the new president declared, "that the torch has been passed to a new generation of Americans." For any foreign listeners who thought this changing of the guard might mean America's gradual withdrawal from worldwide responsibility, he had this bracing warning: "Let every nation know, whether it wishes us well or ill, that we shall pay any price, bear any burden, meet any hardship, support any friend, oppose any foe to assure the survival and the success of liberty. This much we pledge – and more."

Kennedy made it clear: he intended to prosecute the Cold War vigorously – indeed, without limit – as an unrelenting ideological struggle on behalf of freedom and free institutions. His efforts would be targeted not only at the nations of the Communist bloc but also at the hearts and minds of the struggling post-colonial Third World. The "new states" formed by the breakup of empires, the "people in the huts and villages of half the globe struggling to break the bonds of mass misery," were very much on his mind. "In the long history of the world, only a few generations have been granted the role of defending freedom in its hour of maximum danger. I do not shrink from this responsibility – I welcome it." The defense of freedom would henceforth be the cause that would galvanize and animate the American nation. "And so, my fellow Americans, ask not what your country can do for you – ask what you can do for your country."

Such an openly self-confident burst of energy and call to duty from an appealing young leader excited much of the nation, and the early days of Kennedy's tenure seemed to bear out the immense promise of America's youngest president ever. Part of it was the Kennedy style, the glamour of a photogenic presidential couple that brought arts and culture and taste into the White House as never before. But there were more substantive reasons too. Kennedy had gathered into his administration some of the most talented and widely respected figures of the times, including a clutch of leading academics from Harvard and other top universities and innovative businessmen, such as the "whiz kid" Ford Motor Company president Robert S. McNamara. Seemingly, it would be an administration stocked with a highly credentialed, elite group, the best and brightest that American civilization had to offer.

There was more than a whiff of Progressivism in it all, the desire to make government the place where the best and brightest could be empowered to apply their superior educations and skills to devising and implementing solutions to the country's problems. Kennedy's administration added to this Progressive impulse a highly analytical, dispassionate, and pragmatic style, reliant not on emotion or ideology or piety but on cool rationality and sober applied intelligence. "What is at stake in our economic decisions today," Kennedy told an audience at the 1962 Yale Commencement exercises, "is not some grand warfare of rival ideologies which will sweep the country with passion, but the practical management of a modern economy."

Yet Kennedy found it very rough going in the early months of his term. For all his charisma, he lacked a sure hand in dealing with Congress, and his ambitious proposals for aid to education, urban renewal, health care for the elderly, mass transit, and a large tax cut all languished. He was more successful in getting new forms of foreign assistance enacted, such as the Alliance for Progress, directed at Latin America, and the Peace Corps, a volunteer program designed to provide technical assistance to less-developed countries around the world and to foster intercultural understanding. But a great many of Kennedy's domestic initiatives would be stalled during his administration and would have to be revisited later by his successors.

He was, however, very effective in a few areas. Notably, he enjoyed great success in stimulating the economy, and he did so by departing from the Keynesian orthodoxy of much of his party. The example of Great Britain had convinced Kennedy that excessively high rates of taxation were actually counterproductive, stifling economic growth and thereby reducing the amount of revenue available to the national treasury. "An economy hampered by restrictive tax rates will never produce enough revenue to balance the budget," Kennedy declared, "just as it will never produce enough jobs or enough profits." Slashing income tax rates both at the top and the bottom of income levels had a startling effect: over the next six years, personal savings and business investment both rose sharply, GNP increased by 40 percent in two years, job growth doubled, and unemployment was reduced by a third. Even Kennedy's economic advisors who had opposed the tax cut, and whose advice he had overridden, were astounded and had to admit that he had been right.

Another arena in which Kennedy enjoyed a measure of success was in expanding the scope of American efforts to explore outer space. For Kennedy, the exploration of space was not only an important scientific and technological enterprise but also an arena of competition with the Soviet Union. The Soviets had pulled far ahead of the United States in that category, launching the first Earth-orbiting satellite, called Sputnik, in 1957, and then sending the first human into orbit in April 1961. Both achievements alarmed many Americans, who suddenly feared being overtaken by Soviet scientific and technological prowess, and the latter event, which occurred early in Kennedy's administration, led him to proclaim, boldly, that the United States would establish a goal of placing a man on the moon before the end of the decade. By setting such an ambitious goal, Kennedy galvanized the country's formidable technological and economic resources into action, and his ambitious goal would be achieved, with the landing of the Apollo 11 capsule on the moon, on July 20, 1969. Kennedy received, and deserved, much of the credit for this great moment.

Yet these successes were overshadowed by some of the foreign-policy problems that Kennedy had inherited, nearly all of them related to the conduct of the Cold War. First there was the problem of Cuba and its increasingly pro-Soviet revolutionary leader Fidel Castro, whom Kennedy fiercely opposed. His opposition to Castro was so intense that it led him to consider undertaking the assassination of the Cuban "Maximum Leader." It did lead him to support an ill-considered CIA operation whose initial planning had begun under Eisenhower, to train and equip a small army of some fifteen hundred Cuban exiles to undertake an invasion of their homeland. Planners hoped that the invasion, launched from Guatemala and landing at the Bay of Pigs on the southern side of the island, would spark a general Cuban revolt that would overthrow Castro. But in fact the invasion was a complete fiasco and was over in three days, in no small part due to Kennedy's inexplicable decision to renege on an earlier promise of U.S. air cover for the invading force, a move that made the invaders into easy targets for Castro's forces. Kennedy fired CIA director Allen Dulles and other top officials, but it was clear to all that he himself bore the lion's share of the blame for this ill-conceived and poorly executed scheme. The robust and self-confident tone of his inaugural address now sounded like a young man's bluster. The Soviet Union took careful note.

Two months later, Kennedy met in Vienna with the Soviet premier Nikita Khrushchev, a bluff, forceful, vain, and temperamental man who had taken Kennedy's measure and found him wanting. Convinced that Kennedy was little more than a privileged and untested youth who had no idea what he was doing, Khrushchev treated Kennedy with undisguised contempt – "he savaged me," Kennedy told columnist James Reston – and threatened to cut off Berlin, as Stalin had done, if Kennedy did not remove American troops from West Berlin. When Kennedy called up the army reserves and national guard in response, Khrushchev countered by erecting the Berlin Wall, a structure separating Communist East Berlin from free West Berlin and preventing discontented East Germans from migrating to the West through Berlin. Although Kennedy visited the wall in 1963 and gave a stirring speech to assure Berliners of continued American support, he did not challenge construction of the wall, which remained in place for more than a quarter-century.

Matters came to a head with the Cuban Missile Crisis in fall 1962, which emerged after American reconnaissance planes discovered that the Soviets were secretly installing medium-range missiles that could be used to attack the United States. Khrushchev was in part responding to Kennedy's decision to install ballistic missiles in Turkey and Italy, a move he found threatening. But Kennedy saw the installation of Soviet missiles a mere ninety miles away from the United States as an unacceptably dangerous state of affairs and a clear intrusion into a part of the world that had been, ever since the Monroe Doctrine, regarded as an American sphere of influence. A tense standoff ensued, in which Kennedy chose to impose a naval blockade on Cuba and wait out the Soviets. The risks were enormous. Any attempt by the Soviet Navy to challenge the American blockade might well result in a catastrophic nuclear exchange between the two nations. The confrontation lasted for thirteen days.

But in the end, the Soviets backed down, recognizing that their naval forces could not contend successfully with the powerful U.S. Navy, and agreed to remove the missiles. It was a victory for the containment doctrine and a much-needed personal victory for Kennedy. But as a near-brush with calamity, it also had a sobering effect on both sides, leading to the establishment of a "hotline" that would facilitate rapid and direct communication between Moscow and Washington in the event of a similar future crisis.

Kennedy inherited one other foreign-policy headache, in Southeast Asia. The Diem government in South Vietnam that Eisenhower had reluctantly supported continued to be a source of discord and controversy. But South Vietnam was still seen as an essential bulwark against Communist expansion in the region, so Kennedy supported it, sending in sixteen thousand American military personnel to bolster its military effort and train its armed forces. By 1963, however, Kennedy and his advisors had concluded that the Diem regime was hopeless and could never command the loyalty of the people it ruled. When a group of disaffected South Vietnamese military officers set out to orchestrate a coup d'etat to remove Diem from office, the United States signaled its approval. The coup proved successful, but it did not solve the problem of instability and did not bring into power a higher caliber of leadership, preferable to Diem. The issue remained troubled, with no solution in sight. The status quo was obviously unacceptable. But was the answer further escalation, or withdrawal?

What Kennedy might have done next in Vietnam will be forever shrouded in mystery, however. On November 22, 1963, he was brutally assassinated by a lone gunman while riding in a presidential motorcade through Dealey Plaza in Dallas, Texas. His murder shocked and horrified the nation, and the memory of that day would be seared into the consciousness of nearly every American who lived through it. For all of the ways that Kennedy had proved an inconsistent and less-than-optimal leader in the actual facts of his governance, the vigor, glamour, and élan that he brought to the office had endured, and its effects on the national mood had been positive: uplifting and infectious, in much the same way that Franklin Roosevelt's presidency imparted fresh spirit to his own time. Now all of that had come to an abrupt end, an open door had slammed shut, and it felt to many Americans like the end, not just of a presidency, but of an era.

Prominent among the elements of unfinished business left behind in Kennedy's death were unfulfilled promises in the area of civil rights for African Americans. Kennedy had campaigned for the presidency in 1960 in support of racial integration and full civil rights for black Americans, but once he became president, he quietly tabled or deferred those promises, recognizing that southern Democrats held the balance of power in Congress. Kennedy did not wish to risk incurring the implacable opposition of southern white Democrats who opposed integration and whose support was essential to him. Several incidents in his administration, including controversies in Mississippi and Alabama over the admission of black students to state universities, forced him to use federal power in support of integration, but he always did so reluctantly. Civil rights leaders, such as the Reverend Dr. Martin Luther King Jr., soon found themselves losing patience with him, derided his reluctance as timidity and "tokenism," and began to devise ways to force the hand of him and other politicians.

That they could do so indicated the extent to which the cause of civil rights had gone beyond being merely political. In fact, it was a cause to which political institutions had been largely unresponsive. During the postwar era, it had gradually become transformed into something greater: a social movement for social and moral reform, a movement pregnant with religious overtones and dimensions, one that confronted the balkiness of political institutions with powerful appeals to conscience.

That moment had been a long time in the making, however, and many different elements played a role in its emergence. In the beginning, there were legal challenges. As early as the 1930s, groups like the National Association for the Advancement of Colored People (NAACP) had sought to use the courts to promote the desegregation of schools, colleges, and professional schools. With the Supreme Court's unanimous 1954 decision in *Brown v. Board of Education of Topeka, Kansas*, they scored a great victory, as the Court ruled that "in the field of public education the doctrine of 'separate but equal' has no place." But enforcement of the ruling proved extremely difficult, as Deep South states refused to follow it, and 101 members of Congress signed a "Southern Manifesto" that denounced the Court's decision as an "abuse of judicial power."

Clearly legal challenges by themselves, though necessary, would not be enough to alter ingrained attitudes. An essential role would be played by the direct actions of courageous and principled individuals who developed a strategy of combating racial inequality through nonviolent resistance, including nonviolent disobedience to unjust laws. One of the most notable such actions was the 1955 Montgomery Bus Boycott, led by King, then the twenty-six-year-old pastor of a local Baptist church in that highly segregated Alabama city, and soon to be perhaps the most eloquent and emblematic of a whole generation of black American clergymen who became civil rights leaders. The boycott was successful in breaking down the segregationist practices that had dictated the operation of the city bus system, using a unique weapon: what King called the "weapon of love."

Born in Atlanta as the son and grandson of Baptist clergymen, but educated in part at Boston University, King managed to fuse the deep biblical piety of his southern black church upbringing with a modern passion for social change, all the while borrowing heavily from the ideas and techniques of Indian reformer Mohandas Gandhi about the power of nonviolent resistance to awaken the conscience of the oppressor and appeal to the better angels of his nature. In refusing to return violence for violence, the nonviolent protestor held a mirror up to his opponent and helped him see his actions for what they were – actions that betrayed the deepest values that the opponent claimed to believe in. King repeatedly linked the goals of his movement with the American Dream, the Christian moral tradition, and the great American political heritage of the Declaration and the Constitution – and then asked, how can the African American quest for rights and recognition be seen as anything other than a fulfillment of that dream, that tradition, that heritage? The movement he led was not the repudiation of those things but the full realization of them. The goal of nonviolent resistance was not, King said, the defeat or humiliation of the opponent but the achievement of reconciliation and fellowship with him.

Such was the character of the civil rights movement in the 1950s and early 1960s – determined, dignified, and peaceful, but also provocative, seeking to challenge injustice by flouting unjust laws, and seeking integration into the American mainstream. In February 1960, four black college students in Greensboro, North Carolina, sought to break the barrier of segregation in public facilities by peacefully "sitting in" at a lunch counter labeled "whites only." Their success gave rise to dozens of similar sit-ins in nine different states and to "freedom riders" who sought to test a federal ruling that forbade segregation on buses and trains. The freedom riders encountered hostility and occasional violence in their efforts, and even Kennedy privately expressed the wish that the leaders would "call it off" – but his brother Robert, as attorney general, provided federal marshals to protect the riders.

This phase of the movement reached a kind of pinnacle in 1963, with two events. First, a series of peaceful King-led demonstrations in Birmingham, Alabama, were set upon by police, who used dogs, firehoses, cattle prods, and tear gas in a harsh and excessive response – one that a national television audience viewed with horror. That audience also witnessed the nonviolent heroism and unresisting dignity of the protestors, and as a consequence, national support for their movement swelled, and sympathy for their opponents evaporated. The response in turn pushed Kennedy to act more strongly and put his full public support behind a Civil Rights Bill that would abolish discrimination in public facilities and ensure voting rights for black southerners.

Second, in August 1963, in part to keep the pressure on Kennedy for passage of the Civil Rights Bill, King and other leaders organized a massive March on Washington, attracting more than two hundred thousand participants to the National Mall. Gathered by the Lincoln Memorial and Reflecting Pool, they heard one of most memorable speeches of the country's history: King's "I Have a Dream" speech, which perfectly expressed the hopeful spirit that had animated the movement to this point, a reconciling spirit that sought not to disparage the promise of America but to embrace it even more fully:

I say to you today, my friends, so even though we face the difficulties of today and tomorrow, I still have a dream. It is a dream deeply rooted in the American dream.

I have a dream that one day this nation will rise up and live out the true meaning of its creed: "We hold these truths to be self-evident: that all men are created equal."

I have a dream that one day on the red hills of Georgia the sons of former slaves and the sons of former slave owners will be able to sit down together at the table of brotherhood.

I have a dream that one day even the state of Mississippi, a state sweltering with the heat of injustice, sweltering with the heat of oppression, will be transformed into an oasis of freedom and justice.

I have a dream that my four little children will one day live in a nation where they will not be judged by the color of their skin but by the content of their character.

I have a dream today.

I have a dream that one day, down in Alabama, with its vicious racists, with its governor having his lips dripping with the words of interposition and nullification; one day right there in Alabama, little black boys and black girls will be able to join hands with little white boys and white girls as sisters and brothers.

I have a dream today.

Such powerful oratory, mingling the emotional style of the evangelical preacher with the hopeful determination of the political visionary, and drawing throughout upon the most central affirmations of American history, proved an irresistible force. Kennedy had feared that the March on Washington would make the Civil Rights Bill harder to pass, but he was wrong. Although he did not live to see it, the Civil Rights Bill would pass in 1964, followed in 1965 by a Voting Rights Act. These did not solve the problem of racial inequality and bigotry in America, but they were a huge step in that direction.

By the time the Civil Rights Bill had passed Congress, Kennedy's vice president, Lyndon Baines Johnson, or LBJ as he would become known, had succeeded him in the presidency. It was a difficult and uncomfortable transition, not only because it came in the wake of assassination, but for other reasons besides. The two men had not had a good working relationship. The more experienced and more qualified Johnson resented having been beaten by Kennedy in the contest for the Democratic nomination, and he knew he had been added to the ticket only for regional balance, not because of any affinity between the two. Moreover, the contrast between the two men could hardly have been greater. Johnson was a large, rough-hewn, and unsophisticated man from the Texas hill country, a graduate not of Harvard but of Southwest Texas State Teachers College, possessing none of the charm and refinement of the Kennedys and their circle.

But Johnson made up for these disadvantages with the colossal extent of his raw ambition, and through a long and relentless climb up the political ladder, he fashioned himself into one of the most skilled politicians ever to walk the halls of Congress. *Ruthless, conniving, deceitful, unscrupulous* – all these words have been applied to him. His somewhat ungenerous biographer Robert Caro described him as a man "unencumbered by even the slightest excess weight of ideology, of philosophy, of principles, of beliefs." Yet this is an inadequate and one-sided view of an immensely complex man. Perhaps because of his own rough origins, Johnson had a heart for the underprivileged, for those who had been marginalized or shunted aside by society. Such views made him an ardent New Dealer and led to him breaking with his own heritage as a southern Democrat to become perhaps the greatest civil rights president in American history.

Early on, Johnson signaled that he would continue Kennedy's program, seeking swift passage of an expanded version of the Civil Rights Bill and of the Kennedy income tax cuts. When he spoke publicly of Kennedy, it was with the utmost respect. But there was already evidence that he intended to go further, and act boldly, even audaciously, in precisely the areas in which Kennedy had been cautious, even timid. Employing once again the idea of the moral equivalent of war, Johnson declared in his 1964 State of the Union message that "this administration today, here and now, declares unconditional war on poverty in America," and that this would entail initiatives in schools, health care, housing, and job training and require the coordinated efforts of all levels of government. This, even as Johnson boasted that the budget he submitted to Congress was "the smallest budget since 1951." Later that year, he began to speak in even grander terms, declaring in speeches at Ohio University and the University of Michigan that "we will build a Great Society . . . a society where no child will go unfed, and no youngster will go unschooled," a society that would remake the cities, preserve the nation's natural beauty, and countless other things. How would he be able to do all these things at once?

In any event, before he could proceed very far in forming his own agenda for the Great Society, he would have to be elected president in his own right, in fall 1964. His Republican opponent, Senator Barry Goldwater of Arizona, was a staunch conservative harkening back to the pre-Eisenhower party, a libertarian-leaning small-government advocate who opposed much of the New Deal and the programs it had created, such as Social Security and the TVA, and even sought an end to the income tax and a slashing of foreign aid. Criticized even by fellow Republicans as an "extremist," the blunt and fearless (and often injudicious) Goldwater flung the word back at his critics in his speech accepting the Republican nomination, borrowing words from the great Roman statesman Cicero: "I would remind you that extremism in defense of liberty is no vice. And let me remind you also that moderation in the pursuit of justice is no virtue." Such stirring words brought the convention crowd to its feet, but it did nothing to still the sense of alarm among many members of Goldwater's own party.

Goldwater's presidential candidacy brought into the open a split in the Republican Party between its "conservative" wing in the increasingly important "Sunbelt" states of the South and West and the more moderate or liberal wing based in the Northeast, often called Rockefeller Republicans, in tribute to the relatively liberal New York governor Nelson B. Rockefeller, one of Goldwater's chief rivals for the nomination. Goldwater's small-government conservatism, with its fiscal stringency and militant anticommunism and antiglobalism, would, it was feared, fail to appeal to the majorities needed to win a national election. Goldwater and his following, however, thought the reverse: that the party had suffered under the control of a provincial eastern establishment that did not reflect the range of views in the party and had become "me too" Republicans, almost indistinguishable from Democrats.

Running against a divided Republican Party, carrying the legacy of a martyred President, Johnson seemed unlikely to lose. But what may have clinched the election for Johnson was Goldwater's penchant for careless rhetoric, especially concerning the use of nuclear weapons, which he frankly regarded as weapons that could and should occasionally be used rather than merely serving as deterrents. This had the effect of frightening many voters and made him easily portrayed as a dangerous figure by the Democratic opposition. The Goldwater campaign's slogan was "In your heart, you know he's right," an appeal to the values of a hidden conservative majority that his followers ardently believed could be coaxed out of hiding by a candidate bold enough to speak to and for their needs. But that slogan was cruelly and effectively parodied by Democrats: "In your guts, you know he's nuts."

In the event, Johnson won the election by a genuine landslide, the widest popular-vote margin in American history: 61.1 percent of the vote to Goldwater's 38.5. The results in the Electoral College were only slightly less overwhelming, at 486 to 52. Johnson had received from the country a clear popular mandate for change and a Congress in which both houses were controlled by a better than two-thirds majority. He intended to use these advantages without delay. It is worth noting, however, that there were two consoling aspects of the election for Republicans, features that, though not clearly visible at the time, would have longer-range consequences. First, the Goldwater campaign had created an energetic new conservative movement and introduced a new conservative superstar in the person of actor Ronald Reagan, who would soon be elected to the first of two terms as governor of California. That movement, and that superstar, were not going away anytime soon. Second, forty-seven of the fifty-two electoral votes that Goldwater received had come from five Deep South states, none of which had ever previously supported a Republican candidate. This was a strong indication that the Democratic Party's longtime grip on the solid South was slipping away and that voters' habitual party identifications might also be changing with it. There might yet be good news for Republicans coming from the South, which had almost entirely shut them out during the party's entire history.

As a knowledgeable veteran of the law-making process, Johnson was well aware that majorities can be fleeting and that he had little time to spare. So he set right to work, addressing himself to an astoundingly lengthy and weighty domestic legislative agenda. As the new eighty-ninth Congress got itself settled in early 1965, Johnson began to bombard it with proposals. Given the large majorities enjoyed by Democrats, and Johnson's general popularity, the bulk of the proposals were able to pass without much resistance. The list seems almost endless: expansion of the federal food stamp program, creation of the National Endowments for the Humanities and the Arts, Medicare health insurance for the elderly, Medicaid funding for the poor, the Elementary and Secondary Education Act, the Higher Education Act, the Immigration Act (which abolished discriminatory quotas based on national origins), the Child Nutrition Act, funding for mass transit, public housing, rent subsidies, two new cabinet departments (Transportation and Housing), and for good measure, the Highway Beautification Act. Not least, there was the Voting Rights Act of 1965, which followed upon the Civil Rights Act and removed obstacles to African Americans' ability to register and vote in southern elections, where they had long been disenfranchised. More than 250,000 new voters had registered by the end of 1965.

These, then, were some of the principal programmatic features of Johnson's Great Society. How successful was it? The jury is still out even today on many aspects of that question, but a few facts can be adduced. Perhaps the best evidence of success was the fact that the nation's poverty rate dropped from 22 percent to 13 percent between 1963 and 1970; the drop in the African American poverty rate was even more striking. But the war on poverty was by no means won, and other Great Society programs saw similarly mixed triumphs, along with unexpected consequences. Medicare, for example, addressed the health care needs of the elderly, but did so in a way that failed to contain costs, which soared as a result. Welfare programs addressed the needs of the poor but did so in ways that promoted dependency on cash supports, rather than moving people into productive work. Indeed, in some cases, such as the program for Aid for Families with Dependent Children, the net effect was to weaken families by disincentivizing marriage and family intactness, a development that would have especially disastrous effects upon minority families in urban environments. In general, the gap between the Great Society's promises and its results was large, and that gap tended to fuel skepticism, particularly among conservatives and Republicans, about the efficacy of the whole.

The Great Society also suffered from unfortunate timing, arriving as it did at precisely the moment when the civil rights movement, just after its moment of triumph, was beginning to change its tone and lose its unity, as well as its commitment to dignified nonviolence. In Los Angeles on August 11, 1965, a black motorist's roadside confrontation with police escalated into six days of rioting in the predominantly African American neighborhood of Watts. Other cities followed a similar pattern and boiled over in the following two years, including Chicago, Cleveland, Omaha, Newark, Detroit, Washington, D.C., and Baltimore. This epidemic of urban riots represented a repudiation of King's strategy of nonviolent integration and reflected an impatience with squalid living conditions and dismal life prospects in the northern industrial cities, whose problems were different from those of the more agrarian South.

Even before the riots, the black power movement had arisen as a vigorous counterstrategy, one that sought to empower African Americans for self-determination and the creation of a self-sufficient economy and disdained the desire for entry into the American mainstream, preferring a form of racial separatism that eerily resembled the very racial segregation against which King and others had fought. Yet this movement had a powerful rationale; it sought to instill pride in people who had been, as black power advocate Malcolm X often argued, taught to hate themselves and to hang too much upon the good opinion of whites. In any event, however, the growth of such separatist and black nationalist sentiment was reflected in the nihilistic anger behind the racial violence of the urban riots, even if it did not cause them. Such developments made the goal of a more unified and integrated nation, the underlying goal of the Great Society, seem ever more elusive and less feasible.

The other impediment to the success of the Great Society was the steadily escalating American commitment to a steadily deteriorating situation in South Vietnam. President Diem's assassination, which took place just two weeks before Kennedy's, left a power vacuum in the country, one that Johnson did not think he could afford to tolerate. Seizing on a naval skirmish between an American destroyer and three North Vietnamese torpedo boats in the Gulf of Tonkin as the pretext he needed, Johnson requested and received authorization from Congress, in a nearly unanimous vote, to use "all necessary measures" to guard American forces and American interests in the country and to take "all necessary steps, including the use of armed force," to assist the non-Communist states of Southeast Asia.

The Gulf of Tonkin Resolution was, critics said, providing Johnson with a blank check, virtually unlimited power, and time to prosecute a war in Vietnam as he pleased. And after his smashing victory in the November 1964 election, he proceeded to do just that, rapidly escalating the American involvement to include heavy bombing of the North and the steady introduction of American combat troops. By the end of 1965 there were almost 200,000 American troops in Vietnam; that number would eventually reach an astonishing 542,000 by 1969. One in four of those serving in Vietnam had been drafted, often young men barely out of high school, lifted out of their hometowns to fight in a war that many Americans could not understand.

Why did Johnson place such great value on the defense of tiny, fractious South Vietnam? The thinking of Johnson and that of his military advisors, was in line with the understanding of containment that had developed since the late 1940s. The United States had, since Truman's time, been pledged to resist the expansion of Communism anywhere in the world. Advisors such as Secretary of State Dean Rusk believed that the fall of South Vietnam would be the first step in the direction of a Communist takeover of Southeast Asia; countries such as Thailand and Burma would "fall like dominoes," one after the other, unless a firm line were taken in Vietnam.

Yet the same vulnerabilities of the containment doctrine that MacArthur had identified in Korea reappeared in the case of Vietnam. Despite the overwhelming superiority of the United States in men and materiel, political considerations dictated that the war could not be fought in an all-out way, because it was essential to keep the Soviets or Chinese from intervening directly and thereby provoking a major superpower confrontation. Hence Vietnam would have to be, contrary to the wishes of Senator Goldwater and other "hawks," a limited war, a war that *by design* was not going to yield a "victory" in any traditional or common sense of the term but would instead content itself with depriving the enemy of a victory and forcing a negotiated settlement. Hence strategic planning would involve making careful calibrations of the minimum amount of force needed to achieve limited goals. It would constantly be a question of applying the *least* amount of force needed to discourage the enemy from continuing the fight – and no more than that.

The problems with such an approach, particularly when telegraphed to the enemy, should have been obvious: it defied the logic of war itself, and attempted to reduce the violence and existential terror of warfare to a sterile costs-and-benefits calculation. Combatants would find it hard to be persuaded to fight and die for something far short of a clear-cut victory over the enemy. And the North Vietnamese enemy could see clearly that a foe intent on fighting a limited war, with only incremental increases in the application of force, could eventually be exhausted by a sufficiently patient commitment always to push back a little more, then a little more, then a little more. The determination of a combatant who lacked the will to win could always be overcome by the determination of an enemy who lacked the will to surrender.

This was particularly true in a democratic society that required robust popular support for any sustained military engagement if it were to be successful. When Johnson's escalation did not produce the promised results, the Vietnam War quickly became widely unpopular and the target of congressional hearings and of a large and vocal antiwar movement. The carnage of the war was visible on television, up close and personal, and many viewers were appalled at what they saw. A steady diet of such images wore away at the American desire to continue the fight, particularly given that this effort was not directed toward a clear and definable victory.

The administration's constant claims of progress in the war, some of which were based on false or faulty data, were consistently being undermined by facts on the ground. Many Americans objected to the expenditure of vast sums of money on the war effort, money that could be used to better effect to address the problems of the cities and the "war on poverty," and thereby advance the Great Society. Students on college campuses, many of whom faced the possibility of being drafted when they graduated, turned against the war with a vengeance. Many of them were persuaded by America's pursuit of what they considered an immoral war to entertain radically critical views of American society and history, with some even expressing outright support for the Communist enemy in Vietnam.

The antiwar sentiment flowed, along with the unhappiness with the nation's racial inequities, into a more general disaffection with the American status quo that had been building in some quarters for years, and was already manifesting itself in various ways, particularly among college and university students. Activist organizations like Students for a Democratic Society (SDS), which had been founded in 1962, protested the transformation of the university into a "depersonalized, unresponsive, bureaucracy" and sought to create a New Left, one that rejected the foreign policy of the Cold War and sought to inject a greater degree of participatory democracy into American politics. Other movements were more specific, taking their cues, and in some cases their methods, from the success of the civil rights movement. A revived feminist movement, inspired by Betty Friedan's 1963 book *The Feminine Mystique*, and groups organized to pursue Hispanic rights, Native American advancement, and gay rights, rose up in protest of the status quo. So, too, did conservative groups, such as the Young Americans for Freedom, which sought to bring together traditionalists and libertarians to counter the influence of organizations like SDS.

Distinct from all of these, but also an element in the more general current of disaffection, was the emergence of a "counterculture," a more apolitical form of rebellion that embraced long hair, colorful clothing, rock music, use of mind-altering drugs, and experimental living arrangements, such as communes and rural homesteading. Although clearly a by-product of American society's new wealth, it was paradoxically opposed to what it saw as the pervasive materialism of American life. Openly hedonistic, the countercultural impulse rejected the insistence on hard work and delayed gratification as the prerequisites of civilized life; such inhibitions were viewed as pinched middle-class preoccupations that stood in the way of a fuller and more joyous existence. Although often speaking a communitarian language, members of the counterculture tended to behave as radical individualists.

The counterculture took many forms, and it was often easy to make fun of it, as, for example, when it manifested itself in the deadbeat listlessness of stoned-out hippies. But it could also include a serious awakening to questions of religion – one scholar called the 1960s the "Fourth Great Awakening" for that reason – and it promoted welcome reflection on the proper ends of the sometimes-frenzied American pursuit of technological innovation and "progress," and the proper relationship of human activity to the delicate natural environment that sustained it. In that respect, as improbable as it might seem, one can say that it harkened back to some of the same themes that Eisenhower had touched upon in his Farewell Address.

The concerns about Johnson and the war crystallized into political opposition as the prospect of Johnson's reelection in 1968 came into view. By November 1967, Senator Eugene McCarthy of Minnesota had announced that he would challenge Johnson for the Democratic nomination for president. McCarthy was a witty, somewhat mercurial man, and although his candidacy was a rallying point for antiwar opposition to Johnson, it did not seem at first to present serious opposition. But two things changed that. First, the Tet Offensive on January 31, 1968, a fierce assault on American and South Vietnamese forces throughout the country, extending even to a brief occupation of the American embassy grounds in the South Vietnamese capital of Saigon, seemed to give the lie to the administration's claims of steady progress. In large part, this impression was the product of inaccurate media reporting; in the end, the Tet Offensive was actually a military failure. But it was a public relations success, to the extent that it further depressed American willingness to press the fight.

Second, there was a stunning result in the March 12 New Hampshire primary, in which Johnson only barely defeated McCarthy by a 48–42 margin. It was a humiliatingly poor showing for an incumbent president – the very same incumbent who had just four years before swept to an unprecedentedly lopsided triumph. What was worse, on March 16 Robert F. Kennedy, the late president's brother, announced that he too would be a candidate for the nomination. Kennedy would make a far more formidable opponent than McCarthy, and things looked to get even worse for Johnson in the primaries to come. The president faced the real possibility that he could lose the nomination or lose the election to the Republican candidate in the fall.

How the mighty had fallen. Disconsolate, isolated, angry, wounded, and bitter, Johnson came to the conclusion that the time had come for him to step down. On March 31, he surprised the nation with a television address in which he announced that he would suspend bombing of North Vietnam – a significant backtracking in his Vietnam objections – and then, almost as an afterthought, announced that he would not seek, and would not accept, renomination for president.

But these developments were only the beginning of the upheavals of

1968, an exceptionally violent, troubled, and fearful year for the American nation. After the Tet Offensive and the withdrawal of Johnson, there was another assassination, this time of Martin Luther King Jr., who had come to Memphis, Tennessee, to support a sanitary workers strike. King's murder shocked the world and triggered destructive riots in some sixty cities across the country. And then there was yet another assassination of a high-profile political target. On June 5, Robert Kennedy, just moments after winning a huge victory in the California primary, was gunned down at the Ambassador Hotel in Los Angeles by Sirhan Sirhan, a Jordanian of Palestinian Arab extraction who opposed Kennedy's strong support for Israel in the June 1967 Six-Day War.

Given this horrifying wave of assassinations, the massive antiwar protests, the stepping-down of Johnson, and the racial animosities let loose in the land, it seemed to many observers that the nation was coming apart. That sense was only heightened by the chaotic Democratic Convention in Chicago, in which the nomination of Hubert H. Humphrey, Johnson's loyal vice president and a representative of the party's establishment, was contested by youthful protestors who swarmed in the streets of Chicago, and clashed repeatedly with Chicago police.

After the debacle of Chicago, it seemed it would have taken a miracle for Humphrey to be elected. In addition, many working-class Democrats (and some Republicans) were drawn to the independent populist candidacy of Alabama governor George C. Wallace, a former arch-segregationist who had found a national following in voicing a general resentment against the politics of the Washington establishment. Wallace hoped to attract enough votes to deprive the two mainstream candidates of Electoral College majorities, which would throw the election to the House of Representatives and give him bargaining power.

Meanwhile, the Republicans, meeting in Miami, nominated Richard Nixon, who had returned from his time in the political wilderness with a fresh image and hopeful message, presenting himself as a figure of centrist stability in a troubled time, a spokesman for the values of orderly and law-abiding "Middle America." Nixon was studiedly unspecific about his plans for Vietnam, except to aver that he intended to end the war rapidly, achieving "peace with honor." The message was resonant with the voters, and Nixon won the election relatively easily, despite a rally in the final days by Humphrey. The margin in the Electoral College was 301–191, with 46 votes to Wallace, although the margin in the popular vote was tight, with Nixon prevailing by a mere five hundred thousand votes.

One can read these results in a variety of ways, but a salient point arises out of a consideration of the popular vote. It is true that the popular-vote margin between Nixon and Humphrey was small. But most of the ten million votes that went to Wallace would surely have gone to Nixon in a strictly two-way race. When the popular-vote totals for both Nixon and Wallace are combined, they constitute 57 percent of the ballots cast. Clearly a solid majority of American voters were ready to pull back from the frenzied pace of innovation and change that had come with Johnson's tenure, and recover some peace and stability after the bruising and disturbing years just past, particularly the terrible year of 1968.

It had, after all, been only a little more than seven years since Eisenhower's Farewell Address. So much had changed, and so quickly. It was far from clear to many Americans that the balance of the change had been for the better. They were hoping that with Nixon, they would regain some of the balance that had been Eisenhower's trademark achievement. It was an understandable wish – but it remained to be seen whether they would get it.

CHAPTER TWENTY-ONE

FALL AND RESTORATION

From Nixon to Reagan

OF ALL THE PRESIDENTS OF THE TWENTIETH CENTURY, THE one about whom historical opinion is most unsettled, and is likely to remain so for the foreseeable future, is Richard Nixon. Nixon himself predicted that it would take at least fifty years before his presidency could be properly assessed, and his prediction has proven accurate. Like Truman, he was controversial and reviled by many in his time and left office with rock-bottom approval ratings, hated by his opponents. Like Johnson, he had none of the charm or charisma of a John Kennedy, and he suffered for it, an unloved leader who almost seemed uncomfortable in his own skin and who was openly mocked in the media for his chronic awkwardness and strange, lurching gestures. We even have an adjective in the English language, *Nixonian*, used to describe politicians who are devious and secretive by nature, as Nixon himself seemed to be.

But the passage of time, and the lessening of passions, have led to significant reappraisals of Nixon's career, and there will likely be more in the years to come. In many respects, as we shall see, he was a talented and highly intelligent man who was consumed by the circumstances of the time: by the intractable war in Vietnam, by the terrible social divisions of the country, and by the outsized demands upon the presidential office. His presidency evoked passions that are still alive today. He provides us with a good example of why it becomes more and more difficult to write about history with perspective and balance the more closely one's subject matter approaches the present day.

Born in 1913 into a lower-middle-class Quaker family in southern California, Nixon was the son of a struggling grocer, forced to grasp hold of his opportunities and successes through extremely hard work. As a high school student, he rose every day at 4:00 A.M. and drove to the Seventh Street market in Los Angeles, where he bought vegetables, delivered them to his father's business, washed and displayed them, and then went for a full day of school, at which he was always an outstanding student. Such an exhausting round of dutiful burdens and responsibilities were the abiding themes of a remarkably joyless and careworn youth.

That hard school of experience fueled his immense drive and characteristic opportunism and also gave him a particular sympathy for people without pedigree, the ones he would later call the Silent Majority. "Even when he achieved positions too exalted for general attention to the less fortunate," his biographer Conrad Black writes, "his heart and his thoughts ... were always for those who had little, who struggled, who had been shortchanged.... He identified with them."

After law school at Duke, several years of legal practice, and service in the U.S. Navy during World War II, Nixon returned to California and entered into politics, making a name for himself as a hardball politician and a tough-minded anti-Communist concerned about foreign spying in the government. Elected first to the House, then in 1950 to the Senate, and then on to the vice presidency at the age of thirty-nine, Nixon was a rapidly rising star of the Republican Party. He would experience setbacks, but his relentless ambition was not to be denied. A mere eight years after his disappointing defeat of 1960, and six years after an even more humiliating defeat for the California governorship in 1962 – after which he angrily informed the press corps that "you don't have Nixon to kick around anymore because, gentlemen, this is my last press conference" – he had turned it all around and had ascended to the pinnacle of American politics.

I have said that Nixon was a hardball politician, and although that is true, it is only part of the story. One of Nixon's greatest political skills, paradoxically, was his remarkable talent for compromise and coalition building. The Republicans had been bedeviled for nearly four decades by a liberal–conservative divide, beginning with the split between Theodore Roosevelt and William Howard Taft and later continued in the ideological split between Rockefeller establishment liberals and Goldwater insurgent conservatives. Nixon managed to be different from either side but conversant with both. He was not an ideologue and would make a political career out of skillfully walking a political tightrope between the two sides, often doing unexpected things in the process. Balancing an assertive and consistently anti-Communist national-security policy with largely moderate social and economic policies, Nixon was always able to put together effective electoral combinations and eventually brought his formerly embattled party within hailing distance of majority status. On matters of principle, however, he was not always so clear.

In any event, getting elected was the easy part. Upon coming into the White House, he found a mountain of unfinished business piled on his presidential desk, problems left behind by his predecessor. Most pressing of all was a new approach to the deep and bloody gash that had been opened up by the ongoing American involvement in Vietnam. Nixon had campaigned on the promise of ending the conflict, and now he would have to find a way to make good on the promise. He did not shrink from the task. "The greatest honor history can bestow," Nixon proclaimed in his inaugural address, "is the title of peacemaker. This honor now beckons America.... [It] is our summons to greatness."

First, though, he would have to do something about the half million American troops in Vietnam – and the three hundred American soldiers who were dying every week. How to reduce that number, rapidly and visibly, without the action being seen as an American capitulation? How was he to achieve the oft-promised "peace with honor"? For Nixon, the answer was to seek the withdrawal of American forces, but in so seamless a way that South Vietnam could remain secure. To that end, he quickly formulated a strategy he called "Vietnamization," a systematic plan that would gradually replace American troops with loyal and competently trained South Vietnamese ones and turn the war effort over to the South Vietnamese themselves. The plan worked well, and by the end of 1972, the total number of American military personnel in Vietnam was fewer than twenty-five thousand.

Meanwhile, Nixon sought a settlement on the diplomatic front with equal energy, deploying his suave and brilliant German-born national-security advisor Henry Kissinger to conduct secret meetings with North Vietnam's Lê Đúc Thọ. After some back and forth between the two sides, including a premature announcement by Kissinger in fall 1972 that "peace is at hand," followed by the use of heavy bombing attacks against the North to force a settlement, the antagonists finally arrived at an armistice, the Paris Peace Accords of 1973, which allowed the United States finally to withdraw its troops and to get back more than five hundred prisoners of war. Unfortunately, the agreement did not require the withdrawal of a sizable number of North Vietnamese regulars from the South – a sticking point on which the North Vietnamese had been adamant – and that would prove in time to be a fatal mistake. Still in the short term, Nixon had achieved his fundamental object, and on March 29, 1973, the last American combat troops left Vietnam. Kissinger and Lê Đúc Thọ were awarded the 1973 Nobel Peace Prize for their efforts. The cease-fire seemed unlikely to hold, but that was a problem for another day.

There was another important, and far more enduring, diplomatic break-through to come from the Nixon administration. U.S. foreign policy had hitherto failed to take advantage of the fact that, during two decades of conflict and competition, a bitter rivalry had emerged between the two great Communist nations of the world, the Soviet Union and the People's Republic of China (PRC). American loyalty to the democratic regime in Taiwan had dictated that the United States had not recognized the PRC and had forsworn any relations with it. The strong anti-Communism of the time, particularly in Nixon's own party, militated against any change of that state of affairs. But Nixon himself had already hinted before the election that this isolation of the "Red" Chinese was misguided and counterproductive, a policy that needed to be revisited, if not ended altogether. For one thing, both Nixon and Kissinger grasped that improving relations with China was an essential step if the Chinese rivalry with the Soviets was to be made to work to the United States' benefit. Why not play them off against one another? But to do that effectively, better relations with China were an absolute imperative.

Keenly aware of the sensitivity of the matter, Nixon first sent Kissinger to conduct secret talks with the Chinese and then, in July 1971, made the stunning announcement that he would be traveling to China and meeting with Chinese leaders the following February. In an intricately choreographed and highly publicized weeklong visit, accompanied by more than a hundred journalists, Nixon and Kissinger laid the groundwork for diplomatic recognition, sidestepping for the time being the status of Taiwan. In turn, the developing relationship with China had the desired effect on the Soviet Union, which, suddenly fearing the possibility of an American–Chinese alliance, took steps to improve relations with the United States, including working toward an agreement on the limitation of strategic nuclear weapons. Once again, Nixon made a surprise visit to Moscow and repeated a spectacle similar to the one they had enacted in China. Nixon and Kissinger's grand playing-off strategy had worked extremely well.

It has been said, rightly, that only a president with Nixon's conservative and anti-Communist credentials could have made the opening to China without major pushback. But there was more to it than that. Nixon and Kissinger were exponents of "realism" in foreign policy, and their position entailed some revision of the containment doctrine and a reversal of Kennedy's exuberant world-spanning ambition, which had promised to "pay any price, bear any burden, meet any hardship, support any friend, oppose any foe to assure the survival and the success of liberty." Nixon disagreed. The United States could not be the world's policeman, he believed, and it could not "undertake *all* the defense of the free nations of the world." The Nixon Doctrine, which under-girded the philosophy of Vietnamization, posited that the United States would continue to assist in the support of allied nations, but *not* to the extent of committing its own military forces. The deciding factor in any foreign-policy commitment would be the national interest of the United States: "our interests must shape our commitments, rather than the other way around." The effort to establish improved relations with both the Soviet Union and the Chinese flowed from that view.

On the domestic front, Nixon faced greater challenges. The deck was stacked against him. The Democrats held majorities in both houses of Congress, and Nixon's ability to work with a variety of ideological bedfellows and antagonists would be put to the test. In fact, the Democratic Congress was able to get its own way repeatedly, passing a flood of Great Society–like bills such as the Occupational Health and Safety Act, the Clean Air Act, the Federal Election Campaign Act, the Endangered Species Act, the National Environmental Policy Act, increased funding for Social Security and food stamps, plus other similar legislation. Nixon was largely helpless to stop the flood and did not try very hard.

In addition, Nixon surprised everyone in his approach to the weak and troubled economy, lurching from right to left unpredictably. The smooth and steady hand Nixon brought to foreign affairs was not evident in these matters. To be sure, the problems left on his desk were considerable and limited his options. The efforts by the Johnson administration to have both "guns and butter" – to expend vast sums of money both on the war in Vietnam and on large and lavish social programs, without imposing commensurate tax increases – had led to large deficits and soaring inflation. A recession in 1970, partly brought on by Nixon's clumsy efforts to raise interest rates, had added to the economic woes. Nixon had also tried reducing the deficit by raising taxes and cutting the budget, but the congressional Democrats would have no part of the latter.

Finally, in 1971, in an act of desperation, Nixon abandoned free-market orthodoxy altogether and imposed temporary wage and price controls on the economy, something he had previously vowed he would never do. This move had the effect of curbing inflation by freezing existing prices in place, but the effect was only temporary and fleeting, because it treated the symptoms rather than the underlying disease. Nixon also ended the convertibility of dollars into gold, effectively establishing "fiat" currency, unbacked by a precious metal. These moves became known as the Nixon shock, and they were politically popular in the short run and widely applauded by economists. But the experts were wrong; such measures proved economically ineffective and only set the stage for much more severe problems later in the decade.

The mired-down economy, undergoing both high inflation and no-growth stagnation at the same time, would force economists to invent a new word, *stagflation* – a word as ugly and ungainly as the thing it denoted – to describe it.

Most economists had thought such a condition was not possible, because they believed there was a stable inverse relationship between inflation and unemployment, meaning that higher inflation would always mean a growing economy, which would in turn mean lower unemployment. But actual economic conditions were not cooperating with economic theory: both inflation and unemployment were high and on the increase at the same time. Once again, the experts were wrong and were inadvertently providing evidence that the dream of a micromanaged economy was not likely to work out as planned.

In economic matters, then, Nixon was far from conservative, and such actions enraged his conservative supporters. Yet, in other respects, Nixon was able to steer the public mood toward conservatism in small but significant ways that could manifest themselves more fully in the decades ahead. One of his successes in this regard was in implementing policies that he called the New Federalism, an attempt to reverse the steady centralization of government in Washington that had begun in the Progressive years, accelerated under the New Deal, and moved to breakneck speed in the Johnson years. Nixon attempted to move power back to the states and municipalities through *revenue sharing*, in which up to $30 billion in federal funds would be block-granted to the states and cities to be used for their own purposes.

It was not the same thing as the Constitution's original federalism, in which the states and localities were able to operate independently of the national government, empowered to make their own taxing and spending decisions without any involvement from Washington. But it was a sensible innovation that many conservatives welcomed, and it was acceptable to Democrats: an example of politics as the art of the possible, under conditions of divided government.

In any event, then, despite the lingering economic uncertainties, and despite the challenges of dealing with a Democratic Congress, Nixon's overall record heading into the 1972 elections was surprisingly strong. He had enjoyed spectacular successes in his dealings with China and the Soviet Union, he had wound down the American commitment to Vietnam without incurring the humiliation of defeat, he had brought a measure of peace and stability to a troubled nation, and he had at least shown energy and flexibility in his approach to the economy. His Democratic opponent, Senator George McGovern of South Dakota, was in a sense the Democrats' Goldwater, a principled man of honesty and decency, but far too ideologically liberal ever to win a national election, with a campaign too feckless and amateurish to show him in a favorable light.

On election day, Nixon won a huge victory, mirroring Lyndon Johnson's smashing triumph eight years before, gaining 60.8 percent of the popular vote and 520 electoral votes, compared to a pathetic 17 for McGovern. Unlike Johnson, he would still have to deal with a Congress dominated by the other party; Democrats continued to hold on to their solid majorities in both houses and even managed to increase it slightly in the Senate. But a closer analysis of the overall vote showed that the party realignment that had begun to be visible in 1964 was now fully under way. With the steady flow of Sunbelt and suburban voters into the Republican Party, and with Nixon's image as a consummate diplomat abroad taking hold, the Republicans stood on the brink of achieving majority-party status for the first time since the 1920s.

But that was not to be. Nixon's penchant for hardball politics, even in an election that he was almost guaranteed to win, got the better of him and proved to be his undoing. McGovern had complained during the campaign of a pattern of "dirty tricks" in the Nixon campaign, such as wiretaps, false claims about adulteries and racist comments, and forged documents, all designed to harass and embarrass opponents. His complaints were mostly ignored as the sour grapes of a losing campaign. But one incident stood out and eventually attracted attention. There had been an odd occurrence in June 1972 in which five intruders had been caught breaking into the Democratic Party's national headquarters at the Watergate office complex and attempting to plant bugging devices to enable eavesdropping on telephone communications. The trial of these five Watergate burglars led to revelations that the Nixon administration had been connected in some manner to the operation – one of the burglars, John McCord, was the chief of security for Nixon's reelection campaign committee – and that the administration was going to great lengths to cover up that connection and ensure the silence of the five, fearing that such a revelation would endanger the president's reelection prospects.

A nearly two-year-long battle ensued, as government investigators and journalists tried to uncover the nature of this connection and the Nixon administration stubbornly resisted them. In the process, it began to become clear that there were many far more disturbing abuses of power emanating from the Nixon White House than the Watergate break-in. Nixon was concerned, as all leaders are, by the leaking of confidential government information to the press or the larger world. That concern had become heightened in the stormy environment of the Vietnam years, when details about secret military operations were often being spilled out onto the front pages of major American newspapers. But Nixon had responded to that challenge by resorting to the use of illegal wiretaps on the phones of journalists and government employees who were suspected of the leaking. Moreover, it turned out that the "dirty tricks" had not been figments of McGovern's imagination but were part of a larger effort to sabotage the campaigns of Nixon rivals. Most disturbing of all was the possibility that Nixon might have used, or considered using, agencies of the federal government, such as the Federal Bureau of Investigation (FBI), the CIA, or the Internal Revenue Service, to derail opponents.

As the effort to "cover up" these illegal acts began to unravel, more and more individuals associated with the administration, including the president's own legal counsel John Dean, began to cooperate with the investigators. A Senate select committee was empaneled to investigated matters more fully. The investigation might have gone nowhere, however, were it not for two fortuitous developments. First, reporters for the *Washington Post* were fortunate to have the benefit of copious leaking from a disgruntled FBI official, Mark Felt, who had access to the FBI's files and was angry at Nixon for repeatedly passing him over as FBI director. Second, there was the casual disclosure in one of the committee's hearings that the Nixon White House used a taping system to record all conversations and telephone communications. This was a potential gold mine for investigators. Such tapes would show clearly whether there had ever been conversations about a cover-up.

Nixon resisted handing over the tapes to investigators, citing executive privilege. But when the Supreme Court ruled unanimously that he had to hand them over, and at the same time the House Judiciary Committee recommended three articles of impeachment for various abuses of power, Nixon knew that the game was up. On August 9, 1974, he resigned from the presidency rather than face near-certain impeachment and removal from office.

It was a sad ending to a promising presidency, one that was not without its extraordinary achievements, even if the long shadow of Watergate made it difficult to perceive those achievements clearly or to credit them for their true worth. But it had ramifications even beyond Nixon himself. It also cast a shadow over the office of the American presidency itself. The steady growth of federal power, and particularly the power of the executive branch, which had begun in earnest in the Progressive Era, grown during the New Deal and the subsequent years of war and Cold War, and the ever more expansive state that had come with those things – it now seemed to Americans of all stripes, liberal as well as conservative, that these developments carried real dangers with them.

Historian Arthur M. Schlesinger Jr., a close advisor to John F. Kennedy and an ardent defender of New Deal liberalism – and an impassioned Nixon foe – reflected the mood of the moment in a 1973 book called *The Imperial Presidency*. In it he argued that the American presidency was out of control, having exceeded its constitutional limits and, like a metastasizing cancer, threatened to destroy the very structure of constitutional democracy if it was not brought under control. Interestingly, Schlesinger was especially critical of what he called "indiscriminate global intervention," or more pungently, "messianic globalism," which strained the use of American power beyond its constitutional limits. This was precisely the expansive feature of American foreign policy that Schlesinger's hero Kennedy had sought to expand even further and that the "realists" Nixon and Kissinger had sought to rein in. It is worth noting, too, that one of Nixon's chief domestic innovations was the New Federalism, an effort to move power away from the federal government and the executive branch.

But the general point that Schlesinger made was nevertheless a valid one, and one that spoke to abiding concerns of the moment. Had the genius of the U.S. Constitution – its ability to limit the abuses of power of any one individual or entity by placing it in conflict with other, countervailing forces – been compromised by the growth of the size and scope of the presidential office? And might we not need to return to the earlier forms?

To do so would mean taking on a very different view of American history. Ever since the onset of the Progressive Era, many reformers had argued that the Constitution was obsolete, with too many barriers to the decisive use of power, and that greater and greater centralization and coordination of power was essential. A vigorous and assertive chief executive had been an essential part of that vision. But perhaps this had been entirely wrong. Didn't the case of Nixon show why constitutional restraints were more important than ever? After all, the constitutional system had worked in the case of Nixon; the combination of a free press and a vigorous legislative branch had seen to it that his abuses were called to account. But would it always work so well in the future? Might there be future presidents who would cover their tracks more skillfully than Nixon did? Might it not be necessary to do things to restrain such future presidents, even to weaken their office? The War Powers Act, passed over Nixon's veto in 1973, was an important reform of presidential war-making power, restoring constitutional accountability to Congress that had been lost since the days of the Gulf of Tonkin Resolution. Would more measures like this have to be adopted?

All of these were worries trailing in the wake of what became known, somewhat oversimply, by the single word *Watergate*. And as if that were not enough to worry about, there was another worry, one that crossed the minds of those who knew something about American history and remembered the example of Andrew Johnson. For three decades after Johnson's impeachment and near-removal, the presidency suffered from a diminished role in American governance. Could this happen again? Had Watergate not only shown the limits of the imperial presidency, but left the presidency too damaged to perform its legitimate and proper functions? This too was a distinct possibility.

Nixon's vice president and successor, longtime Michigan Republican congressman Gerald R. Ford, had an unenviable task in carrying on, after the unprecedented resignation in office of an American president. He carried it off as well as could be imagined, with modesty and humor. "I am a Ford, not a Lincoln," he humbly submitted, and his easygoing middle American demeanor was a welcome contrast to Nixon's tightly coiled intensity. Two years into Nixon's second term, Ford inherited a basketful of near-insoluble problems, including a rapidly deteriorating situation in Vietnam, continuing stagflation, and the threat of a Middle Eastern oil embargo. Nevertheless, he came into office as the beneficiary of a great deal of public goodwill.

First of all, though, he had to stanch the bleeding from Watergate. Nixon was still potentially liable, as a private citizen, to criminal prosecution for his misdeeds, and Ford reasoned that this could keep the controversy going endlessly, with untold damage to the nation. So he made the decision to use his presidential power to pardon Nixon of any crimes that he might have committed. Instantly, Ford's standing with the public evaporated, and his approval ratings dropped like a stone. The pardon made it difficult to imagine that Ford could ever hope to win the presidency in his own right in 1976. Yet today most historians would agree that the pardon was the right thing to do, for the sake of the country, and even that it was a heroic and sacrificially patriotic act on Ford's part.

In any event, the price of Watergate, and the diminution of presidential power, were visible enough elsewhere. The Democratic majorities in both houses of Congress had swelled in response to Watergate and continued stagflation; in the House, the Democrats picked up a whopping forty-nine seats. Thus emboldened, the Democrats were in no mood to accommodate Ford or to do what was necessary to uphold the peace agreement Nixon and Kissinger had brokered in Vietnam. By 1974, the South Vietnamese government was under intense attack from Communist forces and desperately in need of American aid if it were to survive. But Congress drastically cut that aid, from $2.8 billion in fiscal 1973 to $300 million in 1975. Once the aid had been cut, it took the North Vietnamese only fifty-five days to finish off the South Vietnamese and reunify the country under Communist rule.

At the same time, the U.S.-supported government in Cambodia was overthrown by the Communist Khmer Rouge, a radical Maoist-influenced group that proceeded to massacre a million of its own people in an effort to eliminate "Western" influences. Both these developments produced a flood of refugees to the West, particularly to the United States. In the meantime, the economic situation at home worsened steadily, with both the inflation rate and the unemployment rate approaching 10 percent. It was a dark time for America's standing in the world, and American morale at home was heading for rock bottom.

At this low point in the nation's fortunes came an obligatory moment of national celebration, a great national milestone: the commemoration of the nation's two-hundredth anniversary, on July 4, 1976. Under the troubled circumstances, the requirement to observe the American Bicentennial might have seemed tinged with irony, even a touch of sadness. Yet attention had to be paid; the event had been years in the making, with an elaborate set of events – speeches, exhibitions, radio and television shows, a nation-spanning American Freedom Train, fireworks in the skies above major American cities – planned for the occasion. Perhaps such events could begin to shift the national mood and impart a fresh perspective, reminding Americans of how far they had come. As the novelist John Dos Passos wrote, "in times of change and danger when there is a quicksand of fear under men's reasoning, a sense of continuity with generations gone before can stretch like a lifeline across the scary present." Sometimes it is important to look back, in order to be able to look forward.

In fact, the Bicentennial was a great success. But one event in particular stole the show: the Parade of Ships organized by Operation Sail, an international gathering of magnificent tall-masted sailing ships in New York Harbor on Independence Day (and then in Boston about one week later). OpSail 76, as it was called, was the creation of Frank Braynard, a museum curator and ship enthusiast from New York who also was involved in planning the city's South Street Seaport project, which transformed the derelict East River waterfront into a vibrant historical showcase and festival marketplace.

The "tall ships" came from Italy, Norway, Denmark, Poland, Chile, Ecuador, Germany, Panama, Portugal, the Soviet Union, Spain, Colombia, Romania, Argentina, Japan, Turkey – all over the world, though each flew a banner bearing the tricolor star insignia of the Bicentennial. Gathering on the edge of New York Harbor, they made their way in a stately procession from Staten Island, past Brooklyn and Governor's Island, past the Statue of Liberty, past the canyons of Wall Street, and up the Hudson to the northern tip of Manhattan. Alongside and behind them came a flotilla of other vessels: pleasure boats, schooners, yawls, ketches, sloops, military vessels, frigates and destroyers, submarines, amphibious vessels, plus a Chinese junk and a Spanish galleon, just for good measure. Each one was a magnificent and unforgettable sight – a glimpse of a bygone age, but also something timelessly beautiful and captivating in its own right. It is estimated that five million people watched the event live that day, and television coverage, and photographs of the ships appearing in magazines, captured the experience and fired the imaginations of Americans everywhere.

Why? What on earth did a stately procession of old ships, trailed by newer ones, have to do with anything? Why did those who saw it not only enjoy the spectacle but feel uplifted and reinvigorated by it, as so many testified then and since? Perhaps the answer is that there was something restorative, at a time of confusion and change, in being able to reach back to the solidity and beauty of the past, to feel a sense of connection to its grace and nobility, to be lifted out of the ordinariness of everyday life, and to do it all together. It should be noted, too, that New York City itself was experiencing extreme financial and social problems at the time, with rampant crime in the streets and the prospect of fiscal collapse and bankruptcy looming over it. OpSail 76 was a harbinger of hope for the city itself, at a time when it was in even more dire straits than the country as a whole.

The fall presidential election also offered a hopeful political prospect. Out of a crowded field of Democratic contenders, there emerged a fresh face, a little-known peanut farmer, naval officer, and former governor of Georgia, Jimmy Carter. Running against the corruptions of the Washington establishment, which included not only the transgressions of Watergate but the deceptions and misjudgments of those who created and directed the Vietnam War, Carter pledged himself to a standard of simple and direct honesty: "I will never tell a lie to the American people." Carter was an avowed evangelical Protestant and arguably the most openly religious presidential candidate since William Jennings Bryan. As a pro–civil rights white southerner, he could attract both white and black support and give the Democrats a shot at winning back some southern states from the Republicans.

Ford, conversely, had an uphill battle even to win his own party's nomination. He was strongly challenged by former California governor Ronald Reagan, who had the support of the Goldwater conservatives in the party. They had become restive under Ford, finding him too willing to accede to Soviet domination of Eastern Europe and faulting him, perhaps unfairly, for the loss of South Vietnam. Nor did they care for the fact that Ford had appointed Nelson Rockefeller as his vice president, even though his running mate in 1976 was combative Senator Bob Dole of Kansas. Ford was an unelected president and as such made for an unusually vulnerable incumbent. Reagan was energetic and charismatic and had the enthusiastic Goldwater troops solidly behind him. Nevertheless, Ford squeaked out a nomination victory.

Carter started the campaign with a huge advantage, but by election day, the vote was surprisingly close. Carter's inexperience started to become evident, and he performed poorly in the first presidential debates. He was helped by Republican blunders in the ensuing debates, in which Ford made injudicious comments about there being "no Soviet domination of Eastern Europe," and Dole, in a first-ever vice presidential debate, blamed "Democrat wars" for American military casualties, a barbed comment that seemed ungracious, even coming from a wounded World War II veteran like Dole. In the end, Carter was able to hang on and win relatively narrowly, 50–48 percent in the popular vote, in an election marked by low (53 percent) voter turnout – a mark of the general skepticism and disaffection from politics still afflicting much of the populace.

From the start, Carter was intent upon singlehandedly repealing the imperial presidency. He tried to signal this with even the smallest gesture. After his inaugural address, he and his wife, Rosalynn, chose to walk up Pennsylvania Avenue holding hands, from the Capitol to the White House, rather than making use of the usual limousine. He conspicuously insisted on carrying his own luggage and wore jeans and cardigan sweaters when giving televised "fireside chats." But after a while, the folksiness began to seem contrived, and the immense problems facing the presidency began to bear down on him. Washington insiders observed that Carter depended too much on his inner circle, a group of Georgians who knew how to campaign, but not much else.

Carter's talent for gesture showed in his offer of amnesty to those who had dodged the draft for Vietnam – controversial at the time, but a positive move toward national reconciliation after a bitter national defeat. But large-scale matters consistently defeated him. He attempted to grasp the nettle of energy policy, the reform of which had become central to the well-being of the nation, by devising a huge, comprehensive plan, emphasizing conservation in a coming era of scarce and high-priced oil and a shift from natural gas and oil to coal, nuclear power, and solar energy. Warning of a bleak future, praising conservation, appealing to patriotism, and criticizing the "special interests," the president gave a televised address, wearing his iconic cardigan sweater and referring to the energy challenge as the "moral equivalent of war" – a familiar, if demonstrably ineffective, appeal.

What he had not done, however, was attend to the basic politics of including key political and industry leaders in his deliberations, both to get the benefit of their knowledge and perspective and to secure their "buy in" in support of the bill that emerged. Practical politics is the art of the possible, but Carter disliked that sort of thing and more generally had a distaste for the wheeling and dealing involved in much practical politics. His provincial and inexperienced aides were ill equipped to deal with the subtle ways of Washington. As a result, his bill became altered beyond recognition by the legislative process. One of his aides said, by the time the bill passed in 1978 as the National Energy Act, that it looked as if it had been "nibbled to death by ducks."

Carter also had no luck in controlling inflation, which steadily rose during his administration, from an already high 5.2 percent when he took office in January 1977 to a frightening 14.76 percent in March 1980. Unemployment leveled out at just below 8 percent, but there were few signs of general economic recovery. His foreign-policy thinking did not resonate with many Americans either. For example, his decision to reorient American foreign policy toward an emphasis on promoting human rights fit his evangelical temper but seemed at odds with some of his own rhetoric about limiting the American role in the world and seemed to move back from the chastened "realism" of Nixon toward the idealism of Kennedy, and even further, of Woodrow Wilson. His decision to transfer operation of the Panama Canal to the Panamanian government struck many Americans as a needless "giveaway" of a precious national asset.

Carter did enjoy a partial triumph, however, in brokering a treaty between Egypt and Israel, known as the Camp David Accords, a major development that owed much to the visionary courage of Egyptian president Anwar el-Sadat. To be sure, though, significant parts of the agreement, particularly those related to the Palestinian refugee situation, unraveled as soon as it was signed, and Sadat was branded a traitor by Islamic extremists and assassinated by them for his brave acts. The loss of Sadat alone was an incalculable blow. But it still represented a breakthrough, leading to Egyptian recognition of Israel, though not to a hoped-for breakthrough in regional peace.

However, Carter's final undoing came from Iran. Resentment of American foreign policy there had been intense ever since the 1950s, when the CIA and its British counterpart had installed Reza Pahlavi in place of the country's elected leader. In early 1979, a revolution led by Shi'ite Muslim clerics overthrew the Shah and installed Ayatollah Ruhollah Khomeini as a theocratic leader of revolutionary Iran. When Carter allowed the deposed Shah to come to America for cancer treatments, the response, on November 4, 1979, was a seizure of the American embassy in Tehran by militant revolutionary "students," holding more than fifty embassy personnel as hostages. It was a difficult situation, with no easy solution. Carter tried appealing to the UN, tried freezing Iranian assets in the United States, tried sanctions, tried a commando raid (which had to be aborted), and nothing worked. Meanwhile, television crews recorded the taunts and threats of the militants and the display of the helpless hostages, all directed at an American audience and at a president who seemed impotent to act. This state of affairs continued for 444 days, making for a steady drip-drip erosion of Carter's credibility.

It only added to Carter's foreign-policy woes that, in December 1979, the Soviet Union invaded Afghanistan in an effort to gain greater control over its southeastern border. Despite his human-rights emphasis, Carter had also been offering a somewhat softer and more accommodating face to the Soviet Union and China, seeking additional arms-limitation treaties with the former and revoking recognition of Taiwan to accommodate the wishes of the latter. Carter had already signaled a changed American view by speaking, in a 1977 commencement speech at Notre Dame, of America's being "free" of an "inordinate fear of communism."

With the invasion of Afghanistan, though, along with the revolutionary situation in Iran, the fears of the past no longer seemed so obviously inordinate. Carter imposed sanctions on the Soviets, cancelled American participation in the Moscow Summer Olympic Games, and began to be much more hawkish in his statements while initiating the rebuilding of the American military after its post-Vietnam decline. Under the circumstances, these were the right and requisite things to do. But it was too late for him to recover from the public's impression of him as a well-meaning but inept leader who had been overwhelmed by circumstances. The question lingered in many minds, though, whether the failure of a good, intelligent, honest, and dedicated man like Carter might mean that the presidency itself had become an impossible job, too great a task for any one man.

Or perhaps we had the wrong kind of people serving in the office. The liberal political scientist James MacGregor Burns, in a 1978 book *Leadership*, posited that there were two kinds of leaders, "transactional" ones and "transforming" ones. Jimmy Carter (he said) was the first kind, someone who merely dealt with the exchange of existing goods, playing the game within the existing boundaries, rather than speaking to the deeper needs of people, and calling forth fresh political possibilities for the realization of those needs. Burns's book was a clear call for a different kind of Democratic politician, one perhaps more in the vein of Franklin Roosevelt or the late Robert Kennedy. Ironically, though, the leader who best fit Burns's prescription turned out not to be a Democrat at all. It was Ronald Reagan.

The aftereffects of the failed 1964 campaign of Barry Goldwater continued to reverberate through the 1970s, as the intellectual currents he set into motion continued to gather strength and as an intellectual alternative to the dominant liberalism of the 1960s continued to take shape. By the late 1970s, the structure of a conservative alternative to elements of Democratic orthodoxy was clearly emerging.

Not all views would be shared in every way by every self-described conservative. This was and would remain a coalition. "Social" conservatives who were concerned about the strict enforcement of drug laws might well clash with "libertarian" conservatives who wanted to see all such laws abolished. Some conservatives wanted to see an American withdrawal from the UN, from all multilateral treaties, and from world leadership more generally; others insisted that American leadership was indispensable to the furtherance of world order and an essential part of the nation's self-understanding. Not all were of the same mind about the importance of religion, and not all agreed about whether programs like Social Security should be kept or abolished.

But there was rough consensus on principles of smaller government with lower taxes, a relatively free economy with a minimum of regulation, and opposition to Communism. These were essential points of agreement. On all of these points and more, the burgeoning movement found a winsome spokesperson in Ronald Reagan, whose presidential time had at last come in 1980, after several previous attempts.

Reagan was far more than just a vehicle for other people's ideas, however. Ideas never translate automatically into politics; they have to be embodied in people. And Reagan's persona gave a particular cast to the ideas he espoused. He was a superbly gifted speaker whose years as a movie actor and television performer had given him an instinctive feel for the requirements of the television age, to an extent that no politician before him, and few since, have had. His speeches were extraordinarily well crafted and well delivered, spiced with humor and presented with timing that could rival that of the best stand-up comedian. He had the benefit of Hollywood good looks and a manner that was genial, witty, generous, and comforting, with none of the dour eat-your-broccoli harshness that many people associated with conservatism. He had been a liberal Democrat himself in his younger days, and even when he had come to reject many of the policies of the New Deal and Great Society, he never rejected the example of Franklin Roosevelt or neglected the great lesson of Roosevelt's presidency: a democratic leader's essential role, above all else, is to be a purveyor of hope and a prophet of possibility. That was what Burns meant by a "transforming" leader, and it was why historian Alonzo Hamby would call Reagan the "Roosevelt of the Right," a shrewd name that captures much of what Reagan was about and rightly places him in a longer stream of modern American history.

That was not all there was to him, of course. He was a clear and unapologetic conservative. During his years as governor of California, he developed a national reputation as a tough and decisive leader by staring down the student protestors on college campuses. And yet the part of that reputation that included an image of him as a hardheaded ideologue in the mold of Goldwater – that was not quite accurate. He was also a bit like Nixon: far more principled and focused than Nixon, but like Nixon, a coalition builder, who succeeded in joining together groups – the newly politicized evangelicals making up the so-called Religious Right; the blue-collar and urban-ethnic Catholics who were dismayed by the Democrats' embrace of social liberalism, including approval for unrestricted abortion rights; and the economic libertarianism of antiregulation businessmen and free-market enthusiasts – that might not naturally be nesting in the same place.

At the same time, Reagan made establishment Republicans, particularly those of the Rockefeller stripe, very nervous, in ways they hadn't been since 1964. Many of them opposed his nomination, and the rest tended to be lukewarm at best. Their preferred candidate was George H. W. Bush, a well-pedigreed and experienced former Texas congressman who had served in various administrative posts in the Nixon and Ford administrations. But a self-confident and battle-ready Reagan easily swept past Bush, and past his other Republican rivals, and the establishment was finally forced to swallow him, however grudgingly. As a concession to them, and a gesture toward party unity, he made Bush his running mate.

Carter would prove to be no match for Reagan either in the 1980 campaign – not only because Carter's own record in office was so poor, or because of the incessant coverage of the hostages in Iran, but because Reagan offered a vision of the future that was so much more hopeful than Carter's increasingly gloomy one. On the two critical issues driving the election – the economy and America's standing in the world – it was Reagan who conformed most closely to Burns's definition of a transforming leader, someone who was willing to speak to the whole person and present the problems of the economy and the world in terms that ordinary people can grasp, and grasp hold of in their lives. He concluded his campaign by asking his television audience a simple question: "Are you better off now than you were four years ago?" It would be hard for most viewers to say yes to that question. Carter was finally driven to caricature Reagan as an ideologue, but the desperate expedient did not work; Reagan could flick such attacks away with a gentle and expertly delivered quip: "There you go again."

Television pundits were saying the election was "too close to call," but in the end, it wasn't close at all. Reagan won by a landslide, carrying forty-four states and receiving 489 electoral votes. Just as importantly, he had "long coattails," meaning that his success redounded to the benefit of Republicans running in congressional elections, particularly in the Senate, where the Republicans gained twelve seats and achieved a clear majority for the first time since 1954, while picking up thirty-four seats in the House. Reagan would come to Washington with many of the pieces in place for some truly transformative change. Meanwhile, on the very day in January 1981 that he was inaugurated, the Iranians released the fifty-two hostages in Tehran as a last pointed humiliation hurled at Jimmy Carter. It was a reminder to Reagan and the nation that, in some sense, the dignity and standing of the American presidency were going to be at stake in the coming years.

In his inaugural address, Reagan blamed government itself for many of the nation's current problems and proposed that with a more open, less heavily regulated and less heavily taxed economy, growth would surge and government revenues would increase. The argument that lower tax rates would in fact increase revenues was hardly new and had been successfully demonstrated as recently as the Kennedy administration. Even so, it remained disfavored by most mainstream economists, who remained committed to the Keynesian idea of using carefully managed government spending to boost demand and incomes in times of economic sluggishness. Reagan proposed that reductions in taxes and government spending would free up capital for investment by the private sector, which would in turn lead to business expansion, job creation, and general prosperity.

To accomplish this, the Economic Recovery Tax Act of 1981 featured a 25 percent decrease in personal income taxes, phased in over the course of three years. The top tax rate was reduced to 28 percent, and small investors were allowed to invest on a regular basis in tax-deferred individual retirement accounts. There were also cuts in corporate, capital gains, gift, and inheritance taxes and significant reductions in domestic budget items such as funding for mass transportation and social-welfare benefits. However, Reagan also came into office promising a rebuilding of America's military power, and increased spending on defense offset the budgetary gains from cuts. Would the resulting deficits be reduced by economic growth? That was a question mark, even for supporters of Reagan's general outlook.

Democratic critics found much to fault in Reaganomics, as his approach became labeled, and most of all they objected to the ways that these proposals, while benefiting all, were especially favorable to the wealthy. In any event, it appeared at first that Reagan's policies were going to fail on their own terms. By 1982, the country had entered a steep recession, partly brought on by tight money policies from the Federal Reserve meant to break the back of inflation, but which also stalled growth and pushed unemployment up to 11 percent. Reagan even faced calls from Republican lawmakers to raise taxes, cut defense spending, and otherwise respond. But Reagan stayed the course; the recession turned out to be sharp but brief; and by early 1983, the economy was in recovery and humming along by mid-year, just as predicted. Meanwhile, inflation had dropped to under 4 percent and would reach 2.5 percent by July. The economy grew by 4.6 percent in 1983, 7.3 percent in 1984, and 4.2 percent in 1985.

Public confidence was buoyed by this startlingly rapid restoration of prosperity, and the Reagan–Bush ticket would be reelected in 1984 by a truly mammoth margin, carrying forty-nine states and winning 525 electoral votes, the most electoral votes won by any candidate in American history. The economic figures by the end of Reagan's second term were truly impressive: twenty million new jobs created, inflation stabilized at 4 percent, unemployment at 5.5 percent, GNP growth of 26 percent, interest rates down from 21.5 percent in January 1981 to 10 percent in August 1988. Growth in government spending slowed from 10 percent in 1982 to 1 percent in 1988. And even with the tax cuts, total federal revenues doubled from just over $517 billion in 1980 to more than $1 trillion in 1990. In constant inflation-adjusted dollars, this was a 28 percent increase in revenue. The economic gloom of the 1970s, which seemed as if it would go on forever, was suddenly a thing of the past. "It's morning in America," crowed Reagan's reelection campaign advertisements, and for once, the extravagant claim seemed plausible.

But for those whose eyes were not dazzled by the morning light, there was still the same dark cloud looming on the horizon: rampant deficit spending, which had only grown despite Reagan's efforts to rein it in. The cloud continued to grow. By the end of his second term, the national debt had grown from $900 billion to nearly $2.7 *trillion*. Behind that was what Reagan himself confessed to be his greatest failure: his inability, despite all his rhetoric to the contrary, to reduce the size and scope of government. Blame for the mounting deficits could be spread around widely. Reagan's tax cuts and sharply increased defense spending (up 50 percent during the Reagan years) of course bore some part of the responsibility, but so did the relentless growth of social spending; means-tested entitlement programs rose by 102 percent, and spending on defense was always dwarfed by domestic social spending. In any event, this massive national debt was an unwanted and ominous aspect of the otherwise highly successful Reagan economic program.

The other principal goal of the Reagan administration was rebuilding the nation's standing in the world, after the humiliations of Vietnam and Iran, and waging the Cold War with the Soviet Union more effectively and decisively. No president since Kennedy had proposed to conduct the Cold War competition in so vigorous and aggressive a manner; in fact, the forceful and unapologetic anti-Communism of Reagan's rhetoric made Kennedy's language look tame by comparison. Reagan didn't want merely to gain ground; he wanted to end the Cold War in victory. In 1977, he candidly told a visitor, "Here's my strategy on the Cold War: we win, and they lose." That view never changed, though the details filled themselves out in changing and sometimes unexpected ways. In his 1984 reelection campaign, as a bookend to "Morning in America," Reagan used an extremely effective advertisement called "Bear," which depicted a rampaging bear wandering through a forest, using the familiar national symbol of Russia to remind voters of the continuing threat posed by the Soviet "bear in the woods."

At times, particularly in the early part of his first term, his expressions recalled the morally charged language of Woodrow Wilson: the Soviet Union was, he said, an "evil empire" and "the focus of evil in the modern world." He lambasted and pitilessly mocked Communism for its many failures: its cruelty, its disdain for human rights, its economic incompetence, its atheism, its drabness. In a speech at Notre Dame in 1981, he subtly signaled that even the containment doctrine had reached its sell-by date, at least in his estimation: "The West will not contain Communism," he declared, "it will transcend Communism." He didn't use the word "defeat," but it was clear that the goal was no longer accommodation or coexistence.

If he was to accomplish these things, the commitment would have to go beyond tough words. And it quickly did. First and foremost, Reagan increased spending on defense, continuing the trend that Carter had already begun after the invasion of Afghanistan. There were new weapons systems, such as the B-1B bomber and MX Peacekeeper land-based ballistic missile, the Bradley armored fighting vehicle, and the Abrams tank. There was the building of a near-invincible six-hundred-ship navy, including new Ohio-class ballistic-missile submarines, Los Angeles–class attack submarines, and Nimitz-class supercarriers, plus recommissioned Iowa-class battleships. Most intriguing of all was the Strategic Defense Initiative (SDI), an antimissile defense system designed to intercept and destroy enemy missiles in space using lasers and particle beams. Critics of SDI called it "Star Wars" and worried that it would not work and could only fuel another round of the arms race in space. Yet it seems as likely, in retrospect, that Soviet leaders understood that they did not have the economic or scientific means to match the American efforts and that the effective deployment of SDI could render the United States virtually invulnerable to their existing weapons.

Reagan proceeded then to confront Soviet aggression around the world, with varying degrees of effectiveness: in Poland, where he supported the Solidarity labor movement in its struggle against the Communist government; in Central America, where he attempted to stem Communist influence in El Salvador and Nicaragua; and in the Caribbean island of Grenada. A crucial development was his firm decision in 1983, in the face of massive and near-hysterical opposition from media and organized pressure groups, to press for NATO's deployment of American cruise missiles and Pershing 2 medium-range ballistic missiles in Western Europe to counter the Soviet deployment during the

Carter years of SS-20 ballistic missiles aimed at European cities and NATO air bases in Great Britain. The Soviets sought to shatter NATO, but failed. The West German Parliament approved the deployment on November 22, 1983, and the American missiles began arriving the next day.

Reagan's handling of the "Euromissile crisis" was, in retrospect, a great breakthrough. In 1985, with the ascent of Mikhail Gorbachev to general secretary of the Communist Party, there was a conspicuous and dramatic change in tone from the Soviet leadership. Gorbachev wanted to reform Soviet life, with a view toward greater freedom and openness (*glasnost*) and a restructuring (*perestroika*) of the Soviet economy to remove the dead hand of top-down control and allow some free-market practices to flourish in it. Gorbachev understood that the Soviet economy was a shambles, unable to provide a decent material existence for its own people, and that the Soviet Union could no longer afford an arms race with the United States.

Reagan grasped the opportunities opened up by these changes, and responded favorably, with a willingness to negotiate. But he was insistent that words be followed by deeds. In a 1987 visit to West Berlin, in a speech delivered in front of the Berlin Wall and the Brandenburg Gate separating East and West Berlin, two of the most powerful symbols of the Cold War, he addressed Gorbachev and urged him,

> We welcome change and openness; for we believe that freedom and security go together, that the advance of human liberty can only strengthen the cause of world peace. There is one sign the Soviets can make that would be unmistakable, that would advance dramatically the cause of freedom and peace. General Secretary Gorbachev, if you seek peace, if you seek prosperity for the Soviet Union and Eastern Europe, if you seek liberalization, come here to this gate. Mr. Gorbachev, open this gate. Mr. Gorbachev, tear down this wall!

Gorbachev did not oblige him in that regard. But he did negotiate with Reagan a treaty to abolish intermediate-range (three hundred to three thousand miles in range) nuclear missiles (INFs), the first time that the two nations had agreed to eliminate an entire class of weapon – a move that would have been unthinkable without Reagan's firmness in the Euromissile confrontation just eighteen months before. In 1988, Gorbachev began to withdraw Soviet troops from Afghanistan and joined with the United States in diplomatic initiatives, such as the effort to end the war between Iran and Iraq. Was the end of the Cold War in sight? At long last, it was realistic to hope so.

Historians will argue for many years about the relative importance of Reagan and Gorbachev in the vast improvement of Soviet–American relations.

Both were transformational leaders. But in some sense, both needed one another. There had to be a man like Gorbachev, a reform-minded leader who was willing to break through the ossified structure of an inert and dehumanizing Soviet system to try for something better. But there had to be a Reagan, too, whose clarity and determination, and whose success in restoring the American economy and its military strength, limited the options that were open to Gorbachev.

There can be little argument, though, about the success of Reagan in restoring the dignity and élan of the office of the presidency, which had been in steady decline since the Kennedy assassination; in restoring the productivity of the American economy; and in restoring national self-confidence in a people whose sense of hope had been badly bruised by the reversals of the previous quarter-century. Whether that restoration could be carried forth into the new era that seemed on the verge of dawning was yet to be seen. But for the time being, there was a lot less talk about the presidency being an impossible job.

CHAPTER TWENTY-TWO

THE WORLD SINCE
THE COLD WAR

A S OUR TELLING OF THE AMERICAN STORY DRAWS CLOSER and closer to the present day, the problems inherent in creating a reliable account of current history become acute. It is too difficult to separate out our own partisan sympathies, the rooting interest that we feel in the success or failure of certain causes, and to achieve the level of detachment necessary to provide a general account that is both balanced and insightful. Often the grand passions of the moment prove to be of no enduring significance, while small things that are almost unnoticed in their day take on greater importance at a later date, when they are suddenly seen for their full worth. The events of the recent past have the advantage of being fresh in our minds, but part of the discipline of thinking historically is developing the ability to be skeptical of what we think we see plainly before our eyes and of what "everyone is saying" in the present moment. There can be no substitute for the passage of time, if we are to be able to gain proper perspective on those events. If history teaches us anything, it is that we only rarely have the power to grasp the meaning of events as they are occurring. Live long enough, and you will find out how true that is.

Therefore, in this final chapter, our approach will be slightly different. Rather than providing a close narrative of events, we'll try to draw back for a larger view, looking first at the final conclusion of the Cold War and then considering in a very general and broad-brush way the outlines of the quarter-century that has passed since the conclusion of that war, paying attention less to the multitude of events flowing through those years, or to the succession of presidencies and Congresses, than to the characteristic problems and issues that have emerged and that seem likely to enlist the energies of rising generations in the years to come. As will soon become clear, in many respects, the United States and the world are still engaged in a search for a post–Cold War order that has so far eluded their grasp.

Life was never going to be easy for a Republican successor to Ronald Reagan. George H. W. Bush would have to struggle mightily, much as Harry Truman did, to emerge from his predecessor's long shadow. Which is not to deny that Bush was an exceptionally accomplished man, not only an excellent vice president but an experienced politician with an impressive résumé of public service, including stints as UN ambassador, CIA director, and China envoy. Bush had reservoirs of experience, especially in foreign affairs, that other candidates could only envy.

Bush did not, however, have Reagan's immense rhetorical gifts and magnetic personality and did not attract an impassioned popular following. He could be eloquent when he needed to be, but it did not come easily to him. His speech was often stumbling and strangely inarticulate. He seemed more comfortable speaking prosaically and casually, often in shorthand phrases and sentence fragments that could easily become misinterpreted, and he was disdainful of what he called "the vision thing" – the very ability that Reagan had to evoke thoughts of a better future in the minds of his audiences. In fact, his eight years of playing second fiddle to a larger-than-life transformational president led many observers to underestimate him badly, and as he began to run for the presidency again in 1988, journalists openly speculated whether what they called the "wimp factor" could be his downfall as a candidate.

Such speculation was silly and groundless, and Bush showed it to be so by trouncing his Democratic opponent, Governor Michael Dukakis of Massachusetts, winning by a margin of seven million votes. Such a strong victory was an augury of a largely successful presidency. Although the fact is often forgotten, in the end, it was Bush rather than Reagan who would preside over the end of the Cold War and oversee the first beginnings of a transition into a putative post–Cold War world order. For the most part, Bush guided the nation smoothly and expertly through a series of foreign-policy shocks that would have flummoxed many, even most, other leaders. He deserves far more credit for this than he receives.

By the time Bush came into office, Reagan and Gorbachev had changed the chemistry of world politics, and challenges to Communism were popping up all over the world, not only in the Soviet bloc. The Communist government in mainland China was challenged in spring 1989 by pro-democracy demonstrations that were so large and general as to threaten the stability of the regime. The government was able to hang on to power by finally putting the demonstrations down with appalling brutality, using tanks to subdue unarmed crowds in Beijing's famed Tiananmen Square. But the Soviet empire in Russia was steadily coming unraveled. Starting in Poland in that same year, the Communist Party lost power in each of the Warsaw Pact countries, climaxing on November 9 in East Germany, where leaders found themselves powerless to stop gleeful crowds in East and West Berlin from uniting to tear down the Berlin Wall with sledgehammers, pickaxes, and chisels. Within a year, East Germany would vote to reunite with West Germany, without Soviet objection. In the blink of an eye, the Soviet presence in Eastern and Central Europe had essentially vanished.

In the sprawling empire that was the Soviet Union itself, the same disintegration was under way, and in 1990, the captive Baltic states (Estonia, Latvia, and Lithuania) declared their independence. After a failed last-gasp coup attempt against Gorbachev by a faction of hardline Communist political and military leaders, the other republics dissolved the Soviet Union as of December 1991. The Communist Party was abolished, and statues of Lenin and Stalin were toppled by enthusiastic crowds. With surprising speed, Bush and Gorbachev produced and signed agreements to reduce nuclear weapons as a form of mutual recognition that the world had changed dramatically, and the threat of a Soviet invasion of Western Europe was no longer credible. As an additional good-faith gesture, Bush also offered economic aid to the shattered Russian economy.

Bush's demeanor through all these changes was so sober and cautious that some observers wondered why he was not more excited about them. Wasn't this a tremendous victory for the West and a great breakthrough for freedom? When the press wondered about his lack of enthusiasm over the collapse of the Berlin Wall, Bush responded by stating, "I am not an emotional kind of guy." When Bush's advisors urged him to visit Berlin to celebrate the occasion – something that President Reagan very likely would have done, and something that would have made for marvelous political theater – Bush dismissed the idea stiffly: "What would I do, dance on the wall?" Instead of joining the celebration, and reaping the political benefits, Bush thought it far more important to remain vigilant and stay in the background, doing what he could quietly to assure Gorbachev, and West German leader Helmut Kohl, that he was there to help them through this extremely delicate and perilous passage.

It was admirably sound governance, even if it did not make for particularly good domestic politics. Bush's refusal to gloat in public about victory in the Cold War probably helped to reduce the possibility of a backlash from the defeated hard-liners in the Soviet Union and Eastern Europe. But it was also surely true that he, like so many others, could sense that with the end of the

Cold War, there would be profound changes coming, many of which would be hard to predict. There would be great opportunities but also great risks. Hence it was prudent to move as cautiously as possible.

The realization was gradually dawning on more and more Americans that the end of the Cold War would affect a great deal more than just the geostrategic balance of power in the world. For all that had been terrifying about it, the Cold War had been an ordering principle, a solar center around which nearly all the most important aspects of American foreign policy, and many aspects of American domestic life, even the nation's self-understanding, had revolved for nearly a half-century. It had been a tense and difficult order at times, featuring white-knuckle moments like the Cuban Missile Crisis, and it had required Americans to accept adaptations to, even distortions of, their spending priorities and their constitutional system itself to make the nation able to perform its larger role in the world. But it had been an order, after all – and now it was gone. What was going to take its place?

The question moving forward, then, was not only whether those adaptations, such as the creation of a greatly enlarged national-security state, would continue to be necessary. The answer to that question depended on prior ones: How would the post–Cold War world reorder itself? Would the new order be an American-led world striving toward the universal spread of liberal-democratic values? Would it be a harmonious association of diverse, peace-loving nations, eventually living under the aegis of a UN that could at last, for the first time in its existence, operate free of the acrimony of the bipolar superpower rivalry? Would such a new world order be a cosmopolitan one, in which a global economy would supersede all merely national ones, capital and population would move freely in accordance with shifting needs, national boundaries would all but disappear, and the primacy of national cultures and national identities would disappear along with them? Or would the world revert to the nation-state, to something like the old balance-of-power national politics that had ordered Europe for much of the nineteenth century?

There were sure to be new and unprecedented sources of conflict in the world; what would they look like? What about the relatively new problems of global terrorism and "rogue states" that acted as renegades intent upon destabilizing the modern world order? Would the United States still need a huge, expensive, and intrusive national-security establishment, one that had been built up primarily with the menace of the Soviet Union in mind but that would need to be deployed to deal with unconventional and "asymmetrical" threats emanating from nonstate actors using unprecedented weapons?

All these questions were suddenly highly pertinent, especially the question about whether America's proper role in the world would need to be rethought. Bush was keenly interested in the fashioning of a new world order that would be peaceful, prosperous, law abiding, and democratic. Even as the Soviet empire was imploding in Europe, another conflict was unfolding in the Middle East, one that, though unexpected, fit rather neatly the pattern that Bush had in mind. In August 1990, Iraq's president Saddam Hussein suddenly invaded and occupied the small oil-rich kingdom of Kuwait. Not only was this act a potential threat to Western oil supplies but the invasion violated the rules of international relations that Bush hoped the new world order would observe and could enforce. The UN condemned the act, but their words had no effect. It was going to be necessary to respond forcefully and to remove Iraq from Kuwait – and America would have to lead the effort.

After an unsuccessful effort to impose economic sanctions on Iraq, Bush received congressional approval for an invasion, to be called Operation Desert Storm, which would include some five hundred thousand American troops as well as troops from twenty-eight other countries. Some members of Congress, mindful of the Vietnam experience, were opposed. Senator Ted Kennedy warned of "eighty thousand body bags" returning home from the Persian Gulf. But Bush and his military men were mindful of Vietnam, too, and did not want to repeat the mistakes made there. They designed an invasion that used overwhelming force, had a clearly defined goal, and defined a clear exit strategy. The invasion, which began in January 1991 with five weeks of air strikes, followed by a ground invasion, was brilliantly planned and perfectly executed and resulted in a rapid and complete Iraqi defeat. Bush chose to stop short of occupying Baghdad, the Iraqi capital, reasoning that the war had been premised upon the limited goal of evicting the Iraqis from Kuwait, not the overthrow of the Iraqi regime. Such thinking reflected the containment doctrine that had been in place for so many years during the conflict with the Soviet Union.

If the invasion of Kuwait was a blatant violation of the terms of the emerging new world order, then the work of Desert Storm was a model for the proper response. In many ways, the action reflected a world picture that corresponded to the influential musings of political scientist Francis Fukuyama, who wrote in 1989, at the very time that the Cold War was ending, that its end marked an "end to history." By this startling phrase, he meant not that all historical events were about to cease but that the long, steady process of historical progress, by which human institutions had moved through various phases of development, had now reached a terminal point, and that with the failure of Communism, all the possible alternatives to Western-style liberal-democratic capitalism had been exhausted.

It was appropriate, therefore, that America was taking the lead in Kuwait, not as sole actor but as organizer of an impressive "coalition of the willing" enforcing the rules of the new world order that was aborning. But this view, envisioning Western modernity on a steady march of global triumph, was far from being the only view of the emerging post–Cold War world order. In 1993, a much more detailed and far less optimistic view was put forward by Harvard scholar Samuel Huntington in an article in *Foreign Affairs* called "The Clash of Civilizations?" In it, and in a more detailed book that would follow, Huntington argued that the end of the conflict between the United States and the Soviet Union, which he understood as an *ideological* conflict, would likely be followed by conflicts, not between ideas or countries, but between *civilizations*. "The most important distinctions among peoples are [no longer] ideological, political, or economic," he wrote. "They are cultural," by which he meant that they are conflicts between distinctly different ways of life, historically rooted and religiously motivated. The chief conflicts in the future, he posited, were likely to be between Western civilization (meaning the United States, Europe, the British former colonies, and Israel), the Muslim world of the Middle East and Asia, and the Sinic world of China and its ancillaries.

Huntington's thesis was highly controversial, and he was at great pains to make it clear that he was not somehow *advocating* this coming era of civilizational conflict but merely *describing* what he believed to be in the offing. He cited wars such as those in the Balkans following the breakup of Yugoslavia and between India and Pakistan as evidence for the coming era of civilizational conflict that he was predicting. He also argued that the widespread Western belief in the universality of the West's values and political systems was naive and ethnocentric and that continued insistence on the imposition of democracy and other "universal" norms as a condition for participation in the world economy would have the opposite effect of stirring up resentment in those other civilizations.

The debate that has ensued over the succeeding quarter-century has included a great many other voices but has not greatly improved upon the formulation of alternatives that was generated by Huntington and his many critics and opponents. We still are in the process of working out how the post–Cold War world should be ordered and what the United States' place in it should be. Is the world headed ineluctably toward a global future, in which the independence and importance of nations, ethnicities, tribes, and cultures are destined to be submerged beneath the new realities of global travel, global finance, global trade, global problem solving, and global governance? Or will those particularities of human association reassert themselves, as Huntington predicted, as culture and historical identity prove to be more powerful than economics?

Or, more likely, will there continue to be an interplay among all these factors, as the nation struggles to formulate anew its role in the world? If the past thirty years are any indication, such interplay is likely to continue in the years ahead. Consensus about such matters still seems far away.

Indeed, if one sweeping generalization can be made about the texture of American political life in the years since the end of the Cold War, it would be precisely this: how elusive, and difficult to sustain, our moments of national consensus have become. The historian Daniel T. Rodgers has argued that we are living in an "age of fracture," in which all shared narratives are called into question, and we have abandoned the search for common ground in favor of focusing on the concerns and perspectives of ever smaller groups and more exclusive categories of experience. The broad and embracing commonalities of old seem to have fragmented into a thousand subcultural pieces.

We often imagine that the past was more unified than the present; such nostalgia can often mislead us. But it does seem that the all-encompassing status of the Cold War, which, while it lasted, represented a genuine existential threat to the nation's survival, had the effect (despite the controversies it engendered) of submerging and concealing other potential sources of conflict beneath its weighty mantle. Since its conclusion, that mantle has been thrown off, and new conditions prevail. One can see this reflected in the increasingly polarized and conflict-ridden state of American politics and the relative ineffectiveness of three successive presidential administrations to rise above such conflict and make decisive progress in solving immensely pressing national problems. The extent of the dysfunction can be well illustrated by a brief tour of those years.

An event on February 26, 1993, just weeks before the appearance of Huntington's article, seemed to give advance confirmation to his thesis. The World Trade Center in New York City was the target of a terrorist bombing attack by Islamic militants associated with the radical terror group al-Qaeda. The attackers hoped to bring down at least one of the Twin Towers, then the tallest buildings in New York and a symbol of the globalized world economy, with a giant truck bomb exploded at the building's base. Their ostensible motive in the attack was revenge against the United States for its support of Israel in the Middle East. Although their attempt failed, the incident could also be seen as an indication of a future pattern of threats to the safety and security of the United States.

By the time of the World Trade Center bombing, however, a new president was in the White House whose interests ran in a different direction: former Arkansas governor Bill Clinton, who had defeated George H. W. Bush's bid for reelection in 1992 in a stunning upset. Bush's strength had been in foreign policy; he had enjoyed approval ratings of 91 percent just the year before, in appreciation for the Desert Storm success and his skillful approach to the end of the Cold War. But his handling of domestic issues was far less skillful. He raised taxes despite promising never to do so, and a steep economic recession put him in electoral jeopardy. Clinton was a young, energetic, articulate, and charming politician with Kennedy-like appeal, along with a Carter-like ability to win both white and black southern votes. He was able to run a winning campaign by focusing like a laser beam on the economy as a decisive issue.

Clinton's victory felt a bit like a generational transition, much as Kennedy's victory in 1960 had felt. Unlike Kennedy, though, Clinton wanted to focus primarily on domestic issues, and in this respect, he reflected the public mood, especially its desire to leave behind the responsibilities and expense of Cold War overseas commitments and cash in the "peace dividend" that came with an end to that conflict. There was a bit of the spirit of the early 1920s in the air. Foreign policy and the terrorist threat would get very little attention in the Clinton years.

Clinton started his term with a very ambitious agenda: an economic stimulus, campaign-finance reform, environmental bills, antidiscrimination rules protecting gays in the military, and, above all, a program for universal health care coverage, whose drafting was commandeered by Clinton's ambitious and energetic wife, Hillary. But success eluded Clinton. Nearly all of these measures foundered and died, in a massive display of Republican opposition and Democratic incompetence. Clinton's most notable achievement, the North American Free Trade Agreement (NAFTA), which created a free-trade zone with Canada and Mexico, passed chiefly because of the strong support of Republicans, and did so over the objections of organized labor, one of the Democratic Party's most important and loyal constituencies. Clinton had not yet seemed to get his footing.

In the midterm elections of 1994, discontent with Clinton led to a debacle: Republican majorities in both houses of Congress, including a gain of fifty-four seats in the House, leading to a GOP takeover of the House for the first time in forty years. Under the leadership of Congressman Newt Gingrich of Georgia, the Republicans had cleverly nationalized the congressional elections, producing a ten-point Contract with America that offered a list of specific objectives that they promised to enact in the first hundred days of the new Congress. Gingrich became speaker of the House, and Clinton found himself facing a dismal two years and a likely repudiation in running for reelection.

But Clinton did not roll over and die. He accommodated the Republicans to the extent he could and worked with them to pass a sweeping welfare reform bill, which added work requirements, time limits, and stricter controls on eligibility and eliminated the controversial Aid to Families with Dependent Children, which many believed was a contributing factor in the rise of illegitimate births in poor urban environments. And he cleverly fought Republicans by twice cornering them into causing government shutdowns, which damaged their image with the public and enhanced his. Clinton pursued a strategy of "triangulation," tagging Republicans with extremism when he could, while taking over their most popular positions, such as welfare reform, and claiming them for his own. By the 1996 election, Clinton had managed something quite extraordinary in the postwar environment: a balanced budget, the first since 1969. The feat was owed partly to solid economic growth and partly to spending discipline that his Republican opponents had imposed upon the process. Clinton managed to make all these things work for him.

After winning reelection easily in 1996, Clinton could have basked in the growing prosperity of the times. Much of the debate in Washington was over the relatively pleasant problem of how to spend the surplus revenues now flowing into the Treasury, projected to be more than $4 trillion by the end of the twenty-first century. This could have provided for a moment of national consensus. But Clinton continued to be embattled, as the intense partisan struggle that had begun with the Watergate era, and continued through Reagan's administration, also came to inflame and dominate an investigation of Clinton's ethical lapses. An independent prosecutor, similar to the one appointed in Watergate, found that Clinton had lied under oath to a grand jury about his sexual relations with a young female intern working at the White House. Clinton was charged and impeached by the House of Representatives and placed on trial before the Senate. Yet the Republicans had overplayed their hand and were unable to prevail. Clinton's approval ratings remained high; the public, pleased with the economy, chose to overlook Clinton's misdeeds; and the effort to remove Clinton failed. He finished out his term amid rancorous feelings on all sides.

Adding immeasurably to the national acrimony was the 2000 election. A clear pattern of partisan polarization in American politics was emerging. With relatively close and shifting margins between the two parties, often accompanied by divided government, divisions of power made productive activity difficult and partisan bitterness near-constant. Former Texas governor George W. Bush, son of the previous president Bush, became the Republican nominee in 2000, ran against Albert Gore, a former senator from Tennessee who had served as Clinton's vice president. The electoral result was a virtual tie, with Bush having a razor-thin margin in the decisive Electoral College, while Gore had a slight edge in the popular vote. In a denouement that reminded many observers of the corrupt 1876 election, weeks of wrangling and recounts in the politically divided state of Florida finally led to an intervention by the U.S. Supreme Court, in effect deciding the matter in Bush's favor – an outcome that left Democrats seething and inclined them to view the Bush presidency as illegitimate.

Bush's administration had great difficulty in rising above the acrimony. It did so for a short time, however, thanks to the unified national response to a horrifying event: the successful attack of September 11, 2001, on the World Trade Center Twin Towers in New York City by al-Qaeda terrorists flying hijacked commercial airliners into the buildings, a suicide attack that killed three thousand people and did untold damage to property in lower Manhattan. In addition, a third hijacked plane was flown into the Pentagon in Washington, and a fourth was headed for the White House and the Capitol, only to be forced to the ground in rural Pennsylvania by heroic passengers. These attacks of September 11, or 9/11 as the day soon became known, were a wake-up call to a country that had largely ignored the jihadist terrorist threat. To an amazing extent, the divided American public rallied around its political leadership, largely supporting Bush in his efforts to respond effectively to the attacks.

But the political harmony did not last very long. When Bush resolved to adopt an aggressive posture toward potential sources of terror, including the use of "preemptive" attacks to stop the acquisition of weapons of mass destruction (WMDs) by terror organizations or their state sponsors, Democrats cried foul; and when an invasion of Iraq in 2003, prompted by the belief that Saddam Hussein was stockpiling WMDs, became bogged down and threatened to destabilize the entire region, Bush's approval ratings plummeted and never came back up. By 2005, some of the same people who had cheered his response to 9/11 were calling for his impeachment.

Bush's approval ratings went as low as 25 percent by 2008, for another reason: the Great Recession of 2007–8, an event of immense complexity, the causes of which are traceable back to a pervasive pattern of unsound mortgage lending and reckless real estate speculation, matters for which Bush's immediate responsibility was very limited but for which he, as president, had to take the rap in the public mind. But there was bipartisan blame to go around, and many Americans felt that those who were most responsible did not suffer any of the consequences. The spectacle of government bailouts for the improvident and possibly criminal behavior of large bankers and insurance companies would leave a deep impression in the minds of many Americans. It would further a growing disaffection with both parties, and distrust of government itself, and of the elite classes whose interests the government seemed to serve.

Finally, the election of 2008 was epochal in bringing into the presidency the first African American to hold that office: Senator Barack Obama of Illinois, a young, fresh-faced, relatively inexperienced lawyer and former community organizer who possessed a commanding podium style and a vibrant message of hope and change. Running as the Democratic candidate against a confused and indecisive Republican Arizona senator John McCain, Obama cruised to victory, the recipient of enormous goodwill even from those who had not voted for him but wanted to see his success redound to the country's favor and aid the cause of racial equality and reconciliation. Obama had long coattails, too, and brought solid Democratic majorities to both houses of Congress.

The glow wore off quickly. Obama, too, would soon find his options delimited by intense partisanship. For all his inspirational talk about hope and change, Obama was a surprisingly ineffective leader when matters got down to specifics. For one thing, Obama's proposals themselves turned out to be not particularly innovative. His economic stimulus package of $787 million was a standard Keynesian approach, a grab bag of projects that did little to stimulate growth, improve infrastructure, or create new jobs. His effort to restructure the health care system, legislation that attracted not a single Republican vote, and was actually a variation on the approach pioneered by Republican governor Mitt Romney of Massachusetts, was deeply unpopular not only with Republicans but with the most progressive elements in his own party, and ultimately with the general public, all of whom complained that it had failed to address the problems of high cost and accessibility that it set out to solve.

By 2010, the opposition to "Obamacare," to the growing national debt, which had already skyrocketed under George W. Bush and was now rising even faster under Obama, and to a whole passel of other issues, including the post-2008 government bailouts of improvident banks and reckless investors, had given rise to a spontaneous and loosely organized popular movement called the Tea Party. The Tea Party activists were more libertarian than conservative and were in many cases just as disgusted with the Republican Party as with the Democratic. They opposed incumbents of both parties, and the energy of the Tea Party helped flip enough seats to give Republicans a decisive House win in the midterm elections of 2010 while reducing the Democrats' Senate total to fifty-three, including two independents. From that point until the end of his second term in early 2017, Obama found his administration stymied legislatively, caught in a partisan deadlock and unable to move a significant agenda that could command the support of the nation as a whole.

The 2016 election brought one of the most surprising electoral victories in American history, with the election of billionaire real estate developer and television celebrity Donald J. Trump, a brusque and often bombastic political neophyte, over the highly experienced former New York senator (and former secretary of state, and former First Lady) Hillary Clinton, who had been universally favored to win the election. Relying on his remarkable grasp of modern mass media, and speaking to feelings of discontent that had been ignored by both major parties, Trump conducted a campaign like none other, eschewing campaign consultants and conventional packaging, and yet succeeding in spite of, or perhaps because of, his unconventionality. Trump promised to reverse many of the policies of both Obama and Bush, such as their embrace of free-trade agreements like NAFTA and virtually unrestricted immigration, policies that, he argued, had had catastrophic effects on working-class Americans, both by sending their jobs abroad and by importing cheaper immigrant labor as their replacements at home. The margin of his surprising victory came partly from working-class voters in traditionally Democratic industrial states in the upper Midwest who objected to those policies and resonated to those promises.

To such prospective supporters, Trump promised to "Make America Great Again," to encourage economic growth and job creation, deregulating the economy wherever possible, particularly in the energy sector, and seeking a better climate for business in the country. As of this writing in 2019, he seems to have enjoyed considerable success in that regard, posting economic numbers in his first two years – record low unemployment, particularly for minority groups; wage growth; GDP growth in excess of 4 percent – that would be the envy of any president. Yet Trump has also proved to be an intensely polarizing figure with a talent for enraging his opposition, and his administration has, as of the time of this writing in 2019, divided the nation almost equally between supporters and detractors.

It is too far early at this juncture to make any judgments or predictions about his eventual success or failure. But two things can be said with relative confidence. First, while Trump seems highly unlikely to be the architect of a fresh national consensus, he has brought to the fore certain ideas, notably the emphasis on a strong sense of nationalism, that appear to be on the rise in much of the world, as in Great Britain and Italy. The post–Cold War order, at least as expressed in the globalization of economic life and the empowerment of supranational organizations like the European Union and NATO, appears for now to be weakening. And second, his election itself and the brutal, nonstop political combat that has ensued since it are symptomatic of the growing distrust of established American political and governmental institutions felt by a significant portion of the American public. Thus, even as the idea of the nation-state enjoys something of a revival, the condition of the American nation-state is deeply fractious. As the politicians continue to quarrel, and fail to do the people's business, the people's confidence in them and in their nation's established institutions continues to weaken.

One can hardly miss the latter pattern. The Gallup organization provided strong evidence in 2016 that Americans' average confidence in fourteen key American institutions – Congress, business, television, newspapers, labor unions, the medical system, the police, banks, and educational institutions – has plummeted in the ten years since 2006 and overall stands at just 32 percent. It is significant, too, that, beginning in 2007, more Americans identified as independents than as Republicans, and by 2013, more identified as independents than as Democrats. By 2017, a full 37 percent of registered voters refused to identify with either of the mainstream political parties. There are many reasons for this disaffection, but distrust of both of the established political parties is surely chief among them.

It is not the first time in American history that the inability of the nation's political leaders in Washington to work together to solve the country's problems has been so flagrant. But the examples of the past suggest that often it takes the hard, rude shock of implacable events, and the urgent need to respond to them, to bring about constructive action. Will it be the same for us? Let us hope not. But wishful thinking alone will not make it so.

The country faces a huge number of difficult problems that are not only not yet being solved, but are exacerbated by the dysfunctional condition of Washington. Let's conclude with just one example, picked precisely because it is a thoroughly bipartisan problem, a problem sitting in plain view, but about which neither political party and no organized part of the electorate seems inclined to do anything. And that is the mounting national debt, and the consequent imperilment of the nation's public credit, all fed by a seemingly endless and unstoppable parade of annual budget deficits – deficits that have by now reached astronomical proportions.

It was not until 1981 that the United States accumulated its first trillion dollars of cumulative debt. At the time of this writing, the debt is $21.6 trillion, paired with a $20 trillion GDP, which means that the U.S. has a debt-to-GDP ratio of 106%. Which means that the nation's debt is now larger than its economy. This is not a problem if it happens only occasionally, in response to war or other emergency; and it has happened once before in U.S. history, just after World War II. But it becomes a problem if it persists year after year, for no compelling reason. Since the early 2000s, billions of dollars have continued to be added to the national debt by the budget deficits of each passing year, and the nation is not (as of this writing) experiencing a financial or military crisis. Projected deficits from the present through 2021 come to over a trillion dollars for *each year*.

In addition, no one doubts that the current trends, unless changed dramatically, will soon place the United States in a condition in which each year's budget outlays could be eaten up entirely by servicing of the debt, leaving governmental functions paralyzed. The Congressional Budget Office reported in July 2014 that this unhappy condition – with federal debt held by the public exceeding 100 percent of GDP, and continuing to rise – would be reached in the year 2039 simply if the laws and programs currently on the books are implemented. A significant increase in interest rates, which will surely happen at some point, would get us there even faster. So would additional spending initiatives or declines in revenue. Nor would the effects be merely internal. A country that is perceived to be so fiscally unsound as to be at risk of defaulting on its debt-service obligations loses its social, economic, and political power in the world. This, in turn, makes the national debt a national security issue and turns debt into a potential agent of inexorable national decline.

Of course, it is always a fallacy to assume that current trends will continue unabated. But by the same token, it is always a mistake to imagine that those same trends cannot get worse, and unexpectedly so. And this problem of our addiction to debt is not a particularly controversial one. Unlike other issues, such as immigration, trade, economic growth, education, health care, environmental protection, and the like, the issue of the national debt is one about which there is little fundamental disagreement. Everyone who understands it knows it is a serious problem whose ramifications are immense. The evidence of the past suggests that the problem can be successfully addressed. And yet nothing is done about it. All the old adages about the consequences of living beyond our means seem to lie in wait, eager to prove their continuing relevance.

That is not a justification for despair, though, or even for pessimism. Such emotions are luxuries that a democracy cannot afford to indulge, if it is to stay one. But it is a reason for increased civic attention. It is said that we get the government we deserve, and in the long run there is truth in the saying. We like to blame the politicians, but it is important to remember that in the end, politicians must be responsive to their constituencies if they are to stay in office. And with total household debt in America rising to over $13 trillion in 2017, an all-time high and the fifth consecutive year of growth, it is clear that pervasive debt is not just a problem in Washington. It is a problem for each and every one of us. To recover the capacity for self-rule, we will need among other things to recover the wisdom of our predecessors regarding the corrupting effects of pervasive debt, both public and personal, and the importance of cultivating virtue, both civic and individual, as an essential precondition for the self-governing life. This is an awesome task, but it is not beyond our power.

One of the chief uses of the study of the American past, the task we have taken up in this book, is precisely for the examples it provides and the inspiration it imparts. American society has in fact faced far worse crises than the ones that now confront it, and we can take heart and gather strength and determination from that very fact. The study of the past should not be a merely ornamental thing. Instead, if approached rightly, it should be a fortifying thing, and an enlarging thing, providing us with the sense that we are part of a longer and larger story, a great story to which we owe a great portion of who and what we are.

We close this historical survey, though, with an air of uncertainty, both about where we are and about where we are going. That's why you should turn back and reread the passage from John Dos Passos reprinted as the epigraph with which this book begins. There is no need to paraphrase it; Dos Passos expresses his ideas far better than any summary ever could. But take especial note of this striking phrase: "the idiot delusion of the exceptional Now that blocks good thinking." We should be brought up short by these words, because they describe so many of the unconscious assumptions of our times. We suffer from just such delusions. Above all, we suffer from the assumption that our time, our Now, is so different from all other past times that we have nothing to learn from them. Not true, he says. In fact, it is at just the moment when "old institutions are caving in and being replaced by new institutions" that we most need to look backward as well as forward. He was right about that.

THE SHAPE OF
AMERICAN PATRIOTISM

A S WE CONCLUDE THIS INVITATION TO THE AMERICAN PAST, your faithful scribe has a few closing thoughts about the proper uses of our study of the subject and a related confession to make. Let the confession come first. The book you have just read attempts to tell the story of the American past, some of it anyway, in as objective a manner as I could, while being fair and generous to all legitimate positions. Mindful of Herbert Butterfield's insistence that the historian should strive to be a recording angel and not a hanging judge, I have tried my best to be guided by that dictum. But while trying to be objective, I have not claimed to be neutral in all respects. There is a crucial difference between the two. And although it is important to do one's best to be objective, even when it involves confronting unpleasant and shameful things in our past, I cannot pretend to be neutral when the larger cause of America and American history is involved. This is part of what it means to say, as we did at the outset, that history always begins in the middle of things. Those who write about history are also in the middle of it.

This book is offered as a contribution to the making of American citizens. As such, it is a patriotic endeavor as well as a scholarly one, and it never loses sight of what there is to celebrate and cherish in the American achievement. That doesn't mean it is an uncritical celebration. The two things, celebration and criticism, are not necessarily enemies. Love is the foundation of the wisest criticism, and criticism is the essential partner of an honest and enduring love. We live in a country, let us hope, in which our flaws can always be openly discussed, and where criticism and dissent can be regarded not as betrayals or thought-crimes but as essential ingredients in the flourishing of our polity and our common life. We should not take these aspects of our country for granted. They have not been the condition of most human associations through most of human history. They do not automatically perpetuate themselves. Hence they are among the very things we must be zealous to guard and protect, rather than leaving them to chance.

There is a strong tendency in modern American society to treat patriotism as a dangerous sentiment, a passion to be guarded against. But this is a serious misconception. To begin with, we should acknowledge that there is something natural about patriotism, as an expression of love for what is one's own, gratitude for what one has been given, and reverence for the sources of one's being. These responses are instinctive; they're grounded in our natures and the basic facts of our birth. Yet their power is no less for that, and they are denied only at great cost. When the philosopher Aristotle declared that we are by nature "political animals," he meant that we are in some sense made to live in community with one another. It is in our nature to be belonging creatures. One of the deepest needs of the human soul is a sense of membership, of joy in what we have and hold in common with others.

Much of the time, though, the way we Americans talk about ourselves takes us in the opposite direction. We like to think of the individual person as something that exists prior to all social relations, capable of standing free and alone, able to choose the terms on which it makes common cause with others. We have an endless fascination with romantic culture heroes from Emerson and Whitman to the current crop of movie stars and pop musicians, all of whom sing the praises of nonconformity and the song of the open road, again and again, in strikingly similar ways. Even our own battered but still-magnificent Constitution, with its systemic distrust of all concentration of power, assumes that we are fundamentally self-interested creatures. This does capture some part of the truth about us.

But only a part. For among our deepest longings is the desire to belong, and it is an illusion to believe that we can sustain a stable identity in isolation, living apart from the eyes and ears and words of others. Patriotism, to repeat, is an utterly natural sentiment whose primal claims upon our souls we deny at our peril. But we should not take it in the initial form in which it is given to us. An instinctive and unthinking patriotism is not good enough. Like every virtue, patriotism is something we must work upon, refine, and elevate, if we are to make it what it should be.

For Americans, this becomes an especially complicated task, because American patriotism is not a simple thing. America can be hard to see because America itself is more than one thing. We have illustrated that fact repeatedly in the preceding pages. There are at least two distinct ways of understanding American patriotism, and each one has its valid place.

To illustrate the point, consider, as one small example from the relatively recent past, the passing controversy over the naming of the U.S. government's Department of Homeland Security after the 9/11 attacks in 2001. The use of the term *homeland* generated complaints almost from the start, and the reasons had to do with a clash in fundamental perceptions about American national identity. *Homeland* seemed all wrong to some. It was insular and provincial. Some heard in it an echo of the German concept of *Heimat*, a fatherland of blood and soil.

That was not America, they argued. Americans' attachment is not to something geographical or ethnic, but to a community built around widespread assent to a universal civic idea of "freedom." In other words, they urged, America is best understood not as a country in the usual sense but as an idea, or rather as the embodiment of a set of ideas – a nation dedicated to, and held together by, a set of propositions. A creed rather than a culture.

Furthermore, this argument goes, those ideas have a universal and all-encompassing quality, so that the defense of the United States is not merely the protection of a particular society with a particular regime and a particular culture and history, inhabiting a particular piece of real estate, whose chief virtue is the fact that it is "ours." It is something far greater and more inclusive than that. American society is built not on our shared descent but on our shared consent, meaning that every individual is created equal and is equally provided with the opportunity to give his or her assent to the values for which the nation stands. It doesn't matter where you came from, as long as you can say yes to those propositions, those ideas, that creed.

This is a very powerful view. Its power is reflected in the fact that the United States has, for so much of its history, been so welcoming to immigrants. For one is, in this view, made an American not so much by birth as by a process of agreeing to and consciously appropriating the ideas that make America what it is. Converts are always welcome. In fact, in this view of America, we are a *nation* of converts, every one of us. The use of the term *homeland* seemed to the critics to be a betrayal of precisely this core meaning, the openness and vitality at the heart of the American experiment.

As we saw in chapter 5, there is evidence for this view at the very beginnings of the history of the United States, provided by Alexander Hamilton's contention in *Federalist* 1 that the American nation was marked by historical destiny to be a test case for all humankind, deciding whether it is possible for good governments to be constituted by "reflection and choice" rather than relying on "accident and force." Such a mission, Hamilton added, being universalistic in character, should join "the inducements of philanthropy to those of patriotism" in the hearts of those hoping for the success of the American experiment. In other words, Hamilton was saying that the success of the American experiment then being launched would contribute to the well-being of the whole world. The particular mission of America is part of the universal quest of humanity.

There can be no doubt that, on some level, this view is correct in stressing that a strong sense of American universalism is a key element in the makeup of American national self-consciousness, and therefore American patriotism. But it is far from being the only element. There is in the United States, as there is in all nations, an entirely different set of considerations also in play. Those considerations are particular, not universal. They are *not* best understood as matters of blood and soil, or race, or biology, or any such determinant. Instead, as the French historian Ernest Renan insisted in his 1882 lecture "What Is a Nation?," a nation should be understood as "a soul, a spiritual principle," constituted not only by present-day consent but also by the dynamic residuum of the past, "the possession in common of a rich legacy of memories" which form in the citizen "the will to perpetuate the value of the heritage that one has received in an undivided form."

In this view, shared memories, and the passing along of them, are what form the core of a national consciousness. They are what make us an "us."

"The nation," Renan explained, "like the individual, is the culmination of a long past of endeavours, sacrifice, and devotion. To have common glories in the past and to have a common will in the present, to have performed great deeds together, to wish to perform still more – these are the essential conditions for being a people.... A nation is therefore a large-scale solidarity, constituted by the feeling of the sacrifices that one has made in the past and of those that one is prepared to make in the future."

As I've said, Renan strongly opposed the idea that nations should be understood as entities united by racial or linguistic or geographical or religious or material factors. None of those factors could account for the emergence of this "spiritual principle." What binds them instead is a shared story, a shared history. The ballast of the American past is an essential part of American national identity, and it is something quite distinct from the "idea" of America. But it is every bit as powerful, if not more so. And it is a very *particular* force. Our nation's particular triumphs, sacrifices, and sufferings – and our memories of those things – draw and hold us together, precisely because they are the sacrifices and sufferings, not of all humanity, but of us alone. In this view, there is no more profoundly American place than Arlington National Cemetery or the Civil War battlegrounds of Antietam and Gettysburg and Shiloh.

This quality of particularity is, in its own way, a different kind of universal. It is simply the way we are. It is part of the human condition and is something that we share with the peoples of nearly all other nations. It is universal precisely because it is not universalistic, just as the love of one's own parents or one's family or one's spouse is universal precisely in its particularity. All parents love their children, but *my* parental love and obligations are directed at my own. And that is as it should be. All enduring civic affections must be built from the inside out.

Something similar holds true for countries and for patriotism, even American patriotism. Yet this aspect of American patriotism is not always well articulated, particularly in academic settings. One will have better luck finding it in popular culture, in songs and fictions where one can find the more primal aspects of American patriotism expressed with great directness and vividness. Consider the words of the classic American patriotic songs, where the senses of "home" and shared suffering are ever-present. "The Star-Spangled Banner" speaks not of the universal rights of man but of the flag, and like all revered symbols it recounts a very particular story, recalling a moment of national perseverance in time of war and hardship during the War of 1812. "America the Beautiful" mingles wondrous invocations of the American land with reverent memories of military and religious heroes of the past and calls to virtue and brotherhood. Lee Greenwood's anthem "God Bless the USA" is not a disquisition in political science but a tribute to the land and to "the men who died" to preserve freedom. And there is little else but images of land and echoes of *Heimat* in Irving Berlin's song "God Bless America" – "Land that I love!" and "My home sweet home!" – which has enjoyed a surge of popularity in the years since 9/11.

Nearly all Americans love this song, but most of them have no idea that its composer, one of the formative geniuses of American popular song, was born in Tsarist Russia with the name Israel Beilin. This is, of course, both amazing and entirely appropriate. Even immigrants who shared neither descent nor language nor culture nor religion could find a way to participate in the sense of America as, not an idea, but a home, a place where they could be "born again." Not only could they participate in that sense but they could become among the most articulate exponents of it. This astonishing feature of American life illustrates a quality about the United States that sets it apart from every other nation in the world. It also serves to illustrate the immense distance between the actual form taken by American patriotism and the "blood and soil" nationalisms to which it is so often inaccurately compared. America can be hard to see.

So there is a vital tension in the makeup of American patriotism, a tension between its universalizing ideals and its particularizing sentiments, with their emphasis upon memory, history, tradition, culture, and the land. The genius of American patriotism permits both to coexist, and even to be harmonized to a considerable extent, therefore making them both available to be drawn upon in the rich, but mixed, phenomenon of American patriotism. It would be a mistake to insist on one while excluding the other. They both are always in conversation with one another, and they need to be. And that conversation, to be a real and honest one, must include the good, the bad, and the ugly, the ways we have failed and fallen short, not merely what is pleasing to our national self-esteem. But by the same token, the great story, the thread that we share, should not be lost in a blizzard of details or a hailstorm of rebukes. This is, and remains, a land of hope, a land to which much of the rest of the world longs to come.

Abraham Lincoln showed an instinctive understanding of this complexity in American patriotic sentiment, emphasizing first one, then the other in his oratory, as circumstances dictated. In his First Inaugural Address, pleading against the rising tide of secession, he appealed not to principle but to memory, expressing his hope that "the mystic chords of memory, stretching from every battle-field, and patriot grave, to every living heart and hearthstone, all over this broad land, will yet swell the chorus of the Union, when again touched, as surely they will be, by the better angels of our nature."

These are familiar words, so familiar that we may not notice in them the careful and dignified blending of the local with the national, the public with the private. Those "mystic chords of memory" are understood to emanate not only from the earth's fallen heroes but also from the hearts of living individuals and the hearthstones of living families. The choice of the word *hearthstone* was especially inspired, because it invokes in a single word the whole universe of local and particular loyalties and intimacies that are the stuff of ordinary human life – the warm and welcoming center of a beloved family home. Lincoln hoped that by sounding the notes of the local and particular, one could also reinvigorate the larger chorus of the national.

At other times, though, Lincoln's oratory took on a different and more expansive tone, attributing universal meaning to the survival of the American experiment. In his second annual message to Congress in 1862, he envisioned the United States as "the last best hope of earth," as did Jefferson before him and Ronald Reagan after him. In the Gettysburg Address of 1863, Lincoln speculated that the war's outcome would test for the world whether a stable and enduring nation built upon the twin commitments to freedom and equality was even possible – words that recall Hamilton's words in *Federalist* 1. Yet he was not being inconsistent. All of the meanings he tapped into were part of the complex web of sentiments and meanings making up American national identity. All made sense.

The mixed patriotism that the United States has brought into being is one of the bright lights of human history, and we should not allow it to be extinguished, either through inattention to our ideals or through ignorance of our story. So we have a responsibility before us. We must know both, not only our creed but also our culture. We need to take aboard fully all that was entailed in our forebears' bold assertion that all human beings are created equal in the eyes of the Creator and that they bear an inherent dignity that cannot be taken away from them. But we also need to remember, and teach others to remember, the meaning of Lexington and Concord, and Independence Hall, and Gettysburg, and Promontory Summit, and Pointe du Hoc, and Birmingham, and West Berlin, and countless other places and moments of spirit and sacrifice in the American past – places and moments with which the American future will need to be conversant and will need to keep faith. I hope this book can be helpful in carrying out these important tasks.

ACKNOWLEDGMENTS

For a book like this one, the acknowledgments could run on forever, since a book like this one is almost entirely dependent on the accumulated work of many generations of brilliant and dedicated scholars, only a few of whom are mentioned in the text or in the suggested readings at the end of the book. In addition, over the course of some thirty years of teaching, I have accumulated many more debts than I can even remember, let alone adequately discharge. But I would like to express particular thanks to the mentors and colleagues I've known along the way, in several different institutions, whose intellectual and personal friendship have made the study of the past into an inexhaustible source of joy and satisfaction. These include Kenneth Lynn, William W. Freehling, Jack P. Greene, and John Pocock from Johns Hopkins; Thomas Haskell of Rice University; Sam Ramer, Rick Teichgraeber, and Dick Latner from Tulane; and Ted McAllister, Gordon Lloyd, and Pete Peterson from Pepperdine.

I am particularly grateful to my current colleagues and friends at the University of Oklahoma, a wonderful institution lacking only for a football team worthy of its faculty. I'm singularly blessed to be there, and any virtues this book possesses owe much to the climate I've found there, an air made sweet with the unfeigned love of learning. The list of names for this part alone could be especially long, but let me be disciplined about it and single out a few special people. First, my thanks to Provost Kyle Harper for his unwavering support and his inspiring scholarly and pedagogical example – and for his deer chili. I'm exceedingly fortunate to have David Anderson as a colleague, a man who has forgotten more about English literature (among countless other important subjects) than I will ever know and yet is as gracious and gentle as he is learned. Andrew Porwancher is a blazing force of nature, a happy warrior possessing such energy as a scholar and such ebullience as a teacher that he puts the rest of us to shame. And Luis Cortest is a wise man with the soul of a Spanish mystic in the body of a Kansas Chicano, and with the pianistic hands of the great Bill Evans thrown into the bargain. And I cannot possibly say enough good things about my wonderful assistant Amber Murray, a veritable fountain of intelligence, invention, and good sense.

Although I greatly fear inadvertently leaving out some of their names, I also want to thank some of my students, who generally taught me far more than I taught them: at Tulane, Garnette Cadogan, Noam Scheiber, Rich Cohen, Chris Suellentrop, Jessica Lepler, Danton Kostandarithes, Andrea Hamilton, Bob Brandon, Roxane Pickens, and especially Cory Andrews and Michael Andrews; at the University of Tennessee at Chattanooga, Jason Morgan, Connie Cloud, Matthew Bailey, John Exum, Scott Greer, and especially Lynn Ireland; at the University of Rome, Giuseppe Sorrentino and Fulvia Zega; at Pepperdine's School of Public Policy, Monica Klem, Ben Peterson, Ashley Trim, and Miriam Grunert; and my students at Oklahoma – well, I hardly know where to begin with them, so I won't. I'll save that list for an appendix to the second edition. That will be something to look forward to. I also want to thank the dozens of dedicated teachers who have taken part in my "Visions of America" summer institute over the past five years at OU; they have been an utter joy, and working with them every summer has been one of the privileges of my position.

Special thanks go to Lucien Ellington, my friend and colleague at UTC, an indefatigable Mississippian who is the obvious successor to James Brown as the hardest-working man in show business. When I was at UTC, Lucien and I founded the Center for Reflective Citizenship, dedicated to the improvement of education about American history and civics. In the years since I left, Lucien's energy and vision have turned CRC from a fledgling start-up into a game-changing enterprise. I also want to thank my friend and former student Mike Andrews and everyone else associated with the Jack Miller Center for Teaching America's Founding Principles and History, including Jack Miller himself, a self-made millionaire who decided to dedicate his wealth to the improvement of the country he loves – another *Mensch* of a very high order. I've been privileged to be associated with Jack and JMC since its beginnings, and he is making a difference in the way we go about educating the young.

I also want to thank several hardy individuals who read drafts of all or part of the manuscript with painstaking care at various points in its development: Donald Yerxa, Robert Paquette, Mark McClay, Robert Jackson, and Danton Kostandarithes. Every one of them deserves a medal, and in a couple of cases more than one. Not to mention my wife, Julie, without whom I doubt I would be able to write anything at all, her incomparable sister, Pamela Luhrs, and my mother-in-law, Barbara Holt, the Empress, a great soul and omnivorous reader who also has a wicked talent for spotting typos. I'm also grateful to my talented daughter, B. D. McClay, aka The Blue Pencil, whose marvelous writings are a constant source of both pride and inspiration for me, and to my son Mark, a rising classicist who took time out from his dissertation writing to read these pages. These individuals get much credit for what is good in the book, and none of the blame for what is bad. Similar credit is due to my dear friends Fr. Patrick and Rhea Bright, for reasons too numerous to specify, but very much including their gently Canadian perspective on things American. Parts of this book were written at their home in West LaHave, Nova Scotia (see if you can figure out which ones). I'm fortunate to have had the benefit of the steady, patient, intelligent, and unfailingly competent work of the staff at Encounter Books, including Katherine Wong, Vanessa Silverio, Sam Schneider, Lauren Miklos, and Roger Kimball, who were a dream to work with. All authors should be so lucky.

Finally, I am especially honored to be able to dedicate the book to the memory of my late friend Bruce Cole, a splendid art historian and extraordinary American patriot whose inspired service as chairman of the National Endowment for the Humanities was a great and enduring gift to our national life.

FOR ADDITIONAL READING

This work is heavily indebted to the labors of a great many others, a long succession of worthy interpreters of the American national experience. The following list of books, most of which I have drawn upon in some way in composing this text, is an attempt to acknowledge that debt. The list no doubt reflects the author's idiosyncrasies – I neglect some subjects and include some rather old books – and it is nothing even remotely resembling a complete bibliography. But any such bibliography would be overwhelming and would therefore utterly defeat the purpose. After all, this book is meant to be an invitation, and an invitation is meant to be the beginning of something, a foretaste rather than a comprehensive meal plan. What I hope for is that all those who are new to the subject and have come along with me this far will be sufficiently intrigued or curious to explore the rich and various fare that awaits them in these works and authors.

Adams, Henry. *The Education of Henry Adams: An Autobiography*. New York: Modern Library, 1996. First published 1918.

Adams, Henry. *"The History of the United States in the Administrations of Thomas Jefferson"* and *"History of the United States of America in the Administrations of James Madison."* New York: Library of America, 1986. First published in nine volumes between 1889 and 1891.

Allen, David Grayson. *In English Ways: The Movement of Societies and the Transferal of English Local Law and Custom to Massachusetts Bay in the Seventeenth Century*. New York: W. W. Norton, 1982.

Ambrose, Stephen E. *D-Day: June 6, 1944 – The Climactic Battle of World War II*. New York: Simon and Schuster, 1994.

Ambrose, Stephen E. *Undaunted Courage: Meriwether Lewis, Thomas Jefferson, and the Opening of the American West*. New York: Simon and Schuster, 1997.

Appleby, Joyce Oldham. *Relentless Revolution: A History of Capitalism*. New York: W. W. Norton, 2011.

Armitage, David. *The Declaration of Independence: A Global History*. Cambridge, Mass.: Harvard University Press, 2007.

Bailyn, Bernard. *Voyagers to the West: A Passage in the Peopling of America on the Eve of the Revolution*. New York: Knopf, 1986.

Baker, Kevin. *America the Ingenious: How a Nation of Dreamers, Immigrants, and Tinkerers Changed the World*. New York: Artisan, 2016.

Barry, John M. *The Great Influenza: The Epic Story of the Deadliest Plague in History*. New York: Penguin Books, 2004.

Beisner, Robert L. *Twelve against Empire: The Anti-Imperialists, 1898–1900*. Chicago: University of Chicago Press, 1985.

Blight, David W. *Frederick Douglass: Prophet of Freedom*. New York: Simon and Schuster, 2018.

Blight, David W. *Race and Reunion: The Civil War in American Memory*. Cambridge, Mass.: Harvard University Press, 2001.

Bodnar, John. *The Transplanted: A History of Immigrants in Urban America*. Bloomington: Indiana University Press, 1985.

Boorstin, Daniel J. *The Image: A Guide to Pseudo-Events in America*. New York: Vintage, 1992.

Bowen, Catherine Drinker. *Miracle at Philadelphia: The Story of the Constitutional Convention, May to September 1787*. New York: Bantam Books, 1968.

Brookhiser, Richard. *Founding Father: Rediscovering George Washington*. New York: Free Press, 1996.

Bryce, James. *The American Commonwealth*. Indianapolis, Ind.: Liberty Fund, 1995.

Buel, Richard, Jr. *America on the Brink: How the Political Struggle over the War of 1812 Almost Destroyed the Young Republic*. New York: Palgrave Macmillan, 2005.

Bunting, Josiah, III. *Ulysses S. Grant*. New York: Times Books, 2004.

Chace, James. *1912: Wilson, Roosevelt, Taft and Debs – The Election That Changed the Country*. New York: Simon and Schuster, 2004.

Chambers, Whittaker. *Witness*. New York: Random House, 1952.

Chappell, David L. *A Stone of Hope: Prophetic Religion and the Death of Jim Crow*. Chapel Hill: University of North Carolina Press, 2004.

Conkin, Paul K. *The New Deal*. New York: HarperCollins, 1967.

Craven, Avery. *The Coming of the Civil War*. New York: Charles Scribner, 1942.

Davis, David Brion. *Inhuman Bondage: The Rise and Fall of Slavery in the New World*. New York: Oxford University Press, 2006.

Davis, David Brion. *The Problem of Slavery in Western Culture*. Ithaca, N.Y.: Cornell University Press, 1969.

Delbanco, Andrew. *The War before the War: Fugitive Slaves and the Struggle for America's Soul from the Revolution to the Civil War*. New York: Penguin Press, 2018.

Delbanco, Andrew. *The Abolitionist Imagination*. Cambridge, Mass.: Harvard University Press, 2012.

Dewey, John. *Individualism Old and New*. Carbondale: Southern Illinois University Press, 1984.

Dos Passos, John. *The Ground We Stand On*. Boston: Houghton Mifflin, 1941.

Douglass, Frederick. *Autobiographies*. New York: Library of America, 1994. Includes Douglass's three major autobiographical works, *The Narrative of the Life of Frederick Douglass, an American Slave* (1845), *My Bondage and My Freedom* (1855), and *Life and Times of Frederick Douglass* (1881, revised 1892).

Du Bois, W. E. B. *Writings: "The Suppression of the African Slave-Trade"/"The Souls of Black Folk"/ "Dusk of Dawn"/Essays and Articles*. New York: Library of America, 1986.

Ellison, Ralph. *Invisible Man*. New York: Random House, 1952.

Emerson, Ralph Waldo. *Essays and Lectures*. New York: Library of America, 1983.

Engel, Jeffrey A. *When the World Seemed New: George H. W. Bush and the End of the Cold War*. Boston: Houghton Mifflin Harcourt, 2018.

Fischer, David Hackett. *Albion's Seed: Four British Folkways in America*. New York: Oxford University Press, 1989.

Fitzgerald, F. Scott. *The Great Gatsby*. New York: Charles Scribner, 1925.

Foner, Eric. *The Fiery Trial: Abraham Lincoln and American Slavery*. New York: W. W. Norton, 2011.

Foner, Eric. *Reconstruction: America's Unfinished Revolution, 1863–1877*. New York: HarperCollins, 1988.

Fox-Genovese, Elizabeth, and Eugene D. Genovese. *The Mind of the Master Class: History and Faith in the Southern Slaveholders' Worldview*. New York: Cambridge University Press, 2005.

Franklin, Benjamin. *Franklin: Autobiography, Poor Richard, and Later Writings*. New York: Library of America, 2005.

Freehling, William W. *Prelude to Civil War: The Nullification Crisis in South Carolina, 1816–1836*. New York: Harper and Row, 1965.

Freehling, William W. *The Road to Disunion*, vol. 1, *Secessionists at Bay, 1776–1854*. New York: Oxford University Press, 1991.

Gaddis, John Lewis. *The Cold War: A New History*. New York: Penguin Press, 2005.

Genovese, Eugene D. *Roll, Jordan, Roll: The World the Slaves Made*. New York: Vintage, 1976.

Genovese, Eugene D. *The Slaveholders' Dilemma: Freedom and Progress in Southern Conservative Thought, 1820–1860*. Columbia: University of South Carolina Press, 2003.

Gordon, John Steele. *An Empire of Wealth: The Epic History of American Economic Power*. New York: Harper Perennial, 2005.

Gordon, Sarah H. *Passage to Union: How the Railroads Transformed American Life, 1829–1929*. Chicago: Dee, 1998.

Greene, Jack P. *Peripheries and Center: Constitutional Development in the Extended Polities of the British Empire and the United States 1607–1788*. Athens: University of Georgia Press, 1986.

Guelzo, Allen C. *Abraham Lincoln: Redeemer President*. Grand Rapids, Mich.: Eerdmans, 2003.

Guelzo, Allen C. *Fateful Lightning: A New History of the Civil War and Reconstruction*. New York: Oxford University Press, 2012.

Guelzo, Allen C. *Lincoln's Emancipation Proclamation: The End of Slavery in America*. New York: Simon and Schuster, 2004.

Hamby, Alonzo L. *Liberalism and Its Challengers: From F.D.R. to Bush*. New York: Oxford University Press, 1992.

Hamilton, Alexander, John Jay, and James Madison. *The Federalist*. Indianapolis, Ind.: Liberty Fund, 2001.

Handlin, Oscar. *The Uprooted: The Epic Story of the Great Migrations That Made the American People*. Boston: Little, Brown, 1951.

Hanson, Victor Davis. *The Second World Wars: How the First Global Conflict Was Fought and Won*. New York: Basic Books, 2017.

Hartz, Louis. *The Founding of New Societies: Studies in the History of the United States, Latin America, South Africa, Canada, and Australia*. San Diego, Calif.: Harcourt Brace and World, 1964.

Hawthorne, Nathaniel. *Nathaniel Hawthorne: Collected Novels*. New York: Library of America, 1983.

Hayward, Steven F. *The Age of Reagan: The Conservative Counterrevolution, 1980–89*. New York: Crown Forum, 2009.

Herman, Arthur. *Freedom's Forge: How American Business Produced Victory in World War II*. New York: Random House, 2013.

Herring, George C. *America's Longest War: The United States and Vietnam, 1950–1975*. New York: Knopf, 1986.

Higgs, Robert. *Crisis and Leviathan*. New York: Oxford University Press, 1987.

Hofstadter, Richard. *The Progressive Historians: Turner, Beard, Parrington*. New York: Knopf, 1969.

Howe, Daniel Walker. *The Political Culture of the American Whigs*. Chicago: University of Chicago Press, 1998.

Howe, Daniel Walker. *What Hath God Wrought: The Transformation of America, 1815–1848*. New York: Oxford University Press, 2007.

Israel, Jonathan I. *The Expanding Blaze: How the American Revolution Ignited the World, 1775–1848*. Princeton, N.J.: Princeton University Press, 2017.

Jaffa, Harry V. *Crisis of the House Divided: An Interpretation of the Issues in the Lincoln–Douglas Debate*. Garden City, N.Y.: Doubleday, 1959.

James, William. *Pragmatism*. New York: Dover, 1995.

Johanssen, Robert W. *To the Halls of the Montezumas: The Mexican War in the American Imagination*. New York: Oxford University Press, 1985.

Johnson, Paul. *A History of the American People*. New York: Harper Perennial, 1997.

Johnson, Paul E. *A Shopkeeper's Millennium: Society and Revivals in Rochester, New York 1815–1837*. New York: Hill and Wang, 2004.

Joyner, Charles W. *Down by the Riverside: A South Carolina Slave Community*. Urbana: University of Illinois Press, 2009.

Kamen, Henry. *Empire: How Spain Became a World Power, 1492–1763*. New York: HarperCollins, 2003.

Kazin, Alfred. *On Native Grounds: An Interpretation of Modern American Prose Literature*. Garden City, N.Y.: Doubleday, 1956.

Kazin, Michael. *A Godly Hero: The Life of William Jennings Bryan*. New York: Knopf, 2006.

Keegan, John. *The Second World War*. New York: Penguin Books, 2005.

Kouwenhoven, John Atlee. *The Beer Can by the Highway: Essays on What's "American" about America*. Baltimore: Johns Hopkins University Press, 1988.

Larson, Edward J. *Summer for the Gods: The Scopes Trial and America's Continuing Debate over Science and Religion*. New York: Basic Books, 1997.

Lawrence, D. H. *Studies in Classic American Literature*. New York: T. Seltzer, 1923.

Lemann, Nicholas. *The Promised Land: The Great Black Migration and How It Changed America*. New York: Knopf, 1991.

Limerick, Patricia Nelson. *The Legacy of Conquest: The Unbroken Past of the American West*. New York: W. W. Norton, 1988.

Lincoln, Abraham. *Speeches and Writings*. New York: Library of America, 1994.

Lind, Michael. *Land of Promise: An Economic History of the United States*. New York: Harper, 2012.

Lockridge, Kenneth A. *A New England Town: The First Hundred Years—Dedham, Massachusetts, 1636–1736*. New York: W. W. Norton, 1970.

Lukacs, John. *Historical Consciousness; or, The Remembered Past*. New York: Schocken, 1988.

Lynn, Kenneth S. *The Air-Line to Seattle: Studies in Literary and Historical Writing about America*. Chicago: University of Chicago Press, 1984.

Maier, Pauline. *American Scripture: Making the Declaration of Independence*. New York: Random House, 1998.

Martin, Albro. *Railroads Triumphant: The Growth, Rejection, and Rebirth of a Vital American Force*. New York: Oxford University Press, 1992.

McClay, Wilfred M. *The Masterless: Self and Society in Modern America*. Chapel Hill: University of North Carolina Press, 1994.

McCullough, David. *1776*. New York: Simon and Schuster, 2005.

McCullough, David. *John Adams*. New York: Simon and Schuster, 2001.

McCullough, David. *Truman*. New York: Simon and Schuster, 1992.

McDonald, Forrest. *Novus Ordo Seclorum: The Intellectual Origins of the Constitution*. Lawrence: University Press of Kansas, 1985.

McDougall, Walter A. *Freedom Just Around the Corner: A New American History, 1585–1828.* New York: HarperCollins, 2004.

McDougall, Walter A. *Promised Land, Crusader State: The American Encounter with the World since 1776.* New York: Houghton Mifflin, 1997.

McPherson, James M. *The Battle Cry of Freedom: The Civil War Era.* New York: Oxford University Press, 1988.

Merrell, James H. *The Indians' New World: Catawbas and Their Neighbors from European Contact through the Era of Removal.* New York: W. W. Norton, 1989.

Miller, Perry, and Thomas H. Johnson, eds. *The Puritans: A Sourcebook of Their Writings.* 2 vols. New York: Harper and Row, 1963.

Morgan, Edmund Sears. *American Slavery, American Freedom.* New York: W. W. Norton, 2003.

Morgan, Edmund Sears. *The Genius of George Washington.* New York: W. W. Norton, 1980.

Mumford, Lewis. *The Golden Day: A Study in American Experience and Culture.* New York: Boni and Liveright, 1926.

Noll, Mark A. *America's God: From Jonathon Edwards to Abraham Lincoln.* New York: Oxford University Press, 2005.

Novick, Peter. *That Noble Dream: The "Objectivity Question" and the American Historical Profession.* New York: Cambridge University Press, 1988.

Paulsen, Michael Stokes, and Luke Paulsen. *The Constitution: An Introduction.* New York: Basic Books, 2015.

Pestritto, R. J. *Woodrow Wilson and the Roots of Modern Liberalism.* Lanham, Md.: Rowman and Littlefield, 2005.

Peterson, Merrill D. *The Great Triumvirate: Webster, Clay, and Calhoun.* New York: Oxford University Press, 1987.

Peterson, Merrill D. *Lincoln in American Memory.* New York: Oxford University Press, 1995.

Rahe, Paul. *Republics Ancient and Modern.* Chapel Hill: University of North Carolina Press, 1992.

Reed, John Shelton. *Minding the South.* Columbia: University of Missouri Press, 2003.

Remini, Robert V. *Andrew Jackson and the Course of American Democracy 1833–1845.* London: Harper and Row, 1984.

Remini, Robert V. *Andrew Jackson and the Course of American Freedom 1822–1832.* London: Harper and Row, 1981.

Remini, Robert V. *Henry Clay: Statesman for the Union.* New York: W. W. Norton, 1991.

Riesman, David, Nathan Glazer, and Reuel Denney. *The Lonely Crowd.* New Haven, Conn.: Yale University Press, 1950.

Rodgers, Daniel T. *Age of Fracture.* Cambridge, Mass.: Belknap Press of Harvard University Press, 2011.

Rosenberg, Rosalind. *Beyond Separate Spheres: The Intellectual Roots of Modern Feminism.* New Haven, Conn.: Yale University Press, 1982.

Santayana, George. *The Genteel Tradition in American Philosophy and Character and Opinion in the United States.* Edited by James Seaton. New Haven, Conn.: Yale University Press, 2009.

Shain, Barry Alan. *The Declaration of Independence in Historical Context: American State Papers, Petitions, Proclamations, and Letters of the Delegates to the First National Congresses.* Indianapolis, Ind.: Liberty Fund, 2014.

Shain, Barry Alan. *The Nature of Rights at the American Founding and Beyond.* Charlottesville: University of Virginia Press, 2013.

Shlaes, Amity. *Coolidge.* New York: Harper Perennial, 2013.

Shlaes, Amity. *The Forgotten Man: A New History of the Great Depression.* New York: Harper Perennial, 2007.

Storing, Herbert. *What the Anti-Federalists Were For: The Political Thought of the Opponents of the Constitution.* Chicago: University of Chicago Press, 1981.

Stowe, Harriet Beecher. *Three Novels: "Uncle Tom's Cabin; or, Life among the Lowly"; "The Minister's Wooing"; "Oldtown Folks."* New York: Library of America, 1982.

Taylor, Alan. *American Revolutions: A Continental History, 1750–1804.* New York: W. W. Norton, 2016.

Thoreau, Henry David. *Henry David Thoreau: A Week on the Concord and Merrimack Rivers / Walden; Or, Life in the Woods / The Maine Woods / Cape Cod.* New York: Library of America, 1989.

Tocqueville, Alexis de. *Democracy in America.* Translated by Harvey Mansfield and Delba Winthrop. Chicago: University of Chicago Press, 2000.

Twain, Mark. *Mississippi Writings: "Tom Sawyer," "Life on the Mississippi," "Huckleberry Finn," "Pudd'nhead Wilson."* New York: Library of America, 1982.

Ulrich, Laurel Thatcher. *Good Wives: Image and Reality in the Lives of Women in Northern New England, 1650–1750.* New York: Knopf, 1982.

Ulrich, Laurel Thatcher. *A Midwife's Tale: The Life of Martha Ballard, Based on Her Diary, 1785–1812.* New York: Knopf, 1990.

Walther, Eric H. *The Fire-Eaters.* Baton Rouge: Louisiana State University Press, 1992.

Washington, Booker T. *Up from Slavery: An Autobiography.* New York: Cambridge University Press, 2014.

West, Thomas G. *The Political Theory of the American Founding: Natural Rights, Public Policy, and the Moral Conditions of Freedom.* Cambridge: Cambridge University Press, 2017.

White, Richard. *The Republic for Which It Stands: The United States during Reconstruction and the Gilded Age, 1865–1896.* New York: Oxford University Press, 2017.

Whitman, Walt. *Leaves of Grass and Other Writings.* Norton Critical Editions. New York: W. W. Norton, 2002.

Wilentz, Sean. *No Property in Man: Slavery and Antislavery at the Nation's Founding.* Cambridge, Mass.: Harvard University Press, 2018.

Wilentz, Sean. *The Rise of American Democracy: Jefferson to Lincoln.* New York: W. W. Norton, 2005.

Wood, Gordon S. *The Creation of the American Republic: 1776–1787.* Rev ed. Chapel Hill: University of North Carolina Press, 1998. First published 1969.

Wood, Gordon S. *Empire of Liberty: A History of the Early Republic, 1789–1815.* New York: Oxford University Press, 2009.

Wood, Gordon S. *The Radicalism of the American Revolution.* New York: Knopf, 1992.

Woodward, C. Vann. *The Old World's New World.* New York: Oxford University Press, 1991.

Woodward, C. Vann. *The Strange Career of Jim Crow.* New York: Oxford University Press, 1955.

Wright, Richard. *Later Works: "Black Boy (American Hunger)," "The Outsider."* New York: Library of America, 1991.

Yarbrough, Jean. *Theodore Roosevelt and the American Political Tradition.* Lawrence: University Press of Kansas, 2012.

Yirush, Craig. *Settlers, Liberty, and Empire: The Roots of Early American Political Theory, 1675–1775.* New York: Cambridge University Press, 2011.

The letter *m* following a page locator denotes a map.

the, 207, 255–56, 394; supremacy clause, 113–14; TR's interpretation of, 251–52; uniqueness, 69

construction industry, 281

consumer economy, 287

consumerism, 213, 343

consumer protections, 252–53

Continental Army, 53–54

Continental Congress, 46, 48, 53, 60–61, 86

Contract with America, 415

Coolidge, Calvin, 280, 291–94, 296–99, 317

Coolidge, Grace Goodhue, 292

Cooper, James Fenimore, 130

Copperhead Democrats, 185

Coral Sea naval battle, 334

Cornwallis, Charles, 57–58

Corruption in government
FDR administration, 309; Harding administration, 291; Nixon administration, 392–93; Teapot Dome scandal, 291; World War II, 347

Cortés, Hernando, 20

Corwin Amendment, 170–71

cotton economy, 107, 140, 142

Coughlin, Charles, 311, 313

counterculture, 381–82

Crawford, William, 111

credit, consumer, 287

Creel, George, 266

Creel Committee, 287

Crockett, Davy, 116

Cromwell, Oliver, 33

Crusades, 8

Cuba, 168, 231–34, 237, 363

Cuban Missile Crisis, 371–72, 411

Currency Act, 43

Daniels, Jonathan, 141

Darrow, Clarence, 289, 309

Dartmouth College v. Woodward, 96

Darwin, Charles, 229, 256

Darwinism, 289–90

Daugherty, Harry M., 291

Davis, Jefferson, 161, 169, 199

Davis, John W., 310–11

Dawes Severalty Act, 223

Daylight Saving Time, 265

D-Day invasion, 332

Dean, John, 393

Debs, Eugene V., 216, 257, 267

Declaration of American Rights, 46

Declaration of Independence
actions underlying, 49, 106; adoption of, 48; aspirations of, 58, 166; endurance of, 49–50; fulfilling the spirit of, 166; "Gettysburg Address" and the, 181–82; goal of, 49; influence of, 49–50; natural-rights philosophy, 157; opposition to, 52; popular sovereignty doctrine vs., 157; Progressive position on, 258; questions raised, 49–50

Declaration of Neutrality, 261

Declaratory Act, 44–45

deficit spending. *see* national debt

Deism, 41, 121

Democracy in America (Tocqueville), 117–18, 120

Democratic Party
African American vote, 313; beginnings, 111; Civil War position, 185; Compromise of 1877, 202; FDR election and administration, 304–6, 314–15; Kansas–Nebraska Act effect, 162; Nixon administration, 390–92; political machine, 218; weakening of the, 162–63, 166–68, 292; Wilson administration, 255, 263

Dempsey, Jack, 285

Department of Commerce and Labor, 252

Department of Homeland Security, 425

Dewey, George, 234

Dewey, John, 247–48

Dewey, Thomas E., 354

Dias, Bartolomeu, 10, 11

Dickinson, John, 47, 48, 52

Diem, Ngo Dinh, 362, 372, 380

discrimination
in education, 373; immigrant, 221; racial, 70–71, 373–74; disease, 21; disinterestedness ethic, 245

diversity, 69, 79

"Divine and Supernatural Light, A" (Edwards), 38

divine right of kings, 33

Dix, Dorothea, 127

Dole, Bob, 397, 398

Dominican Republic, 237

Donald, David, 185

Dos Passos, John, 396

Shays, Daniel, 62–63
Shay's Rebellion, 62–63
Sherman, Roger, 64, 67, 73, 109
Sherman, William Tecumseh, 184–86, 206
Sherman Anti-Trust Act, 249, 252
"Significance of the Frontier in American History, The" (Turner), 223
Silent Majority, 387
Sinclair, Upton, 253
"Sinners in the Hands of an Angry God" (Edwards), 38
Sino-Japanese War, 238
Sino-Soviet Treaty of Friendship and Alliance, 355–56
Sirhan, Sirhan, 384
Sixteenth Amendment, 257
Slater, Samuel, 107
slave codes, 70
slavery
    abolitionist movement, 127–29, 147–48; Civil War and, 173, 178–79, 186–87; Constitution on, 72–73, 179–80, 195; economics of, 71, 140–41, 190; Fugitive Slave Act, 171; Fugitive Slave Law, 159–60, 168; history of, in America, 70; as institution, 50, 70, 71–72; in Mexico, 152; Missouri Compromise and, 108–10; Northwest Ordinance prohibiting, 61; Southern, 143–50; Wilmot Proviso opposing, 156–57
slave society, 143–45
slaves, emancipated, 70, 190–91, 200
slave uprisings, 146–47
Slidell, John, 155
Smith, Adam, 36–37
Smith, Al, 293, 304, 311
Smith, Hyrum, 124
Smith, John, 24–25
Smith, Joseph, Jr., 123–24
Smith, Sidney, 130
Smith Act, 356
Social Gospel, 230, 241
Socialist Party, 216
Social Security, 360, 377, 390, 401
Social Security Act, 312–14
Social Security Trust Fund, 312
"Sometimes I Feel Like a Motherless Child," 146
South, the
    class structure, 140, 143–44, 195; cotton economy, 140, 142; culture of, 139–42; emergence of the, 139; slavery in the, 140–41, 143–50
South Carolina, 29, 57, 70–72, 115
South Carolina Exposition and Protest (Calhoun), 114
Southerner Discovers the South, A (Daniels), 141
Soviet Union. *see also* Communism
    Afghanistan invasion, 399–400, 405–6; in China, 355, 358, 362, 409–10; Cold War, 361–63; in Cuba, 371–72; end of the, 410; expansionism, 350–52, 355–57, 372, 380–81, 405; Germany divided, 371; rivalry with China, 389; space exploration, 370–71; in World War II, 331–32
space exploration, 370–71
Spanish–American War, 238, 243
Spanish Civil War, 318
Spanish colonialism, 20–23, 34, 62, 229, 231–34
Spanish exploration, 11–12
Spanish influenza, 278
Spender, Stephen, 332
Spirit of St. Louis, 285
Square Deal, 251–52, 254
stagflation, 390–91, 395
Stalin, Josef, 327, 333, 349, 352, 355, 371, 410
Stamp Act, 43–45
Standard Oil Company, 212, 249
Stanley, Ann Lee, 126
Stanton, Edwin, 198
Starr, Ellen, 241
"Star-Spangled Banner, The" (Key), 103, 427
State, The (Wilson), 256
states rights, 60–61, 65, 68, 113–15
"Steal Away to Jesus," 146
steamboat technology, 107
steel manufacture, 211, 215
Steffens, Lincoln, 244
Stephens, Alexander, 169, 196
Steuben, Friedrich Wilhelm von, 56
Stevenson, Adlai, 360
Story, Joseph, 134
Stowe, Harriet Beecher, 128–29, 141, 146, 160, 241
Strategic Defense Initiative, 405
Strong, Josiah, 230
Students for a Democratic Society (SDS), 381
submarine warfare, 329–30

259–60; civil rights protections, 267; disillusionment following, 277; economy, 295; economy post-, 278, 280; effects following, 270; end of, 270; FDR's use of, 308; intensification, 261; peace talks, 272–73, 276; public position on, 316, 319; submarine warfare, 262, 264, 268; U.S. entry into, 264–70

World War II
Allied response, 329–33; atomic bombing, 338–39; casualties, 336, 337, 349; celebrations post-, 341–42; D-Day invasion, 332; demobilization, 342; economy, 295, 327–29, 342; end of, 336–39; European theater, 330*m*; events leading up to, 317–19; industrialization, 327–29; internment camps, 329; legacy, 338–39; minority involvement, 329, 363; Pacific theater, 334–37, 335*m*; postwar world, 339–40; postwar years, 342–46; public position on, 319, 323–24, 326; recovery and rebuilding post-, 351–52; relief programs, 328; strategic bombing, 320–22, 331; submarine warfare, 329–31; U.S. entry into, 325–27; U.S. involvement pre-entry, 322–25

"WPA" (Mills Brothers), 307
Wright, Elizur, Jr., 127

Yalta Conference, 333, 349–50
yellow journalism, 232
Young, Brigham, 124
Young Americans for Freedom, 381

Zimmerman Telegram, 264
Zionist movement, 353

A NOTE ON THE TYPE

LAND OF HOPE has been set in Le Monde Livre. Designed in 1997 by Jean-François Porchez, Le Monde Livre adapts for book typography the award-winning 1994 type family Porchez created for France's Le Monde newspaper, types now called Le Monde Journal. While the Journal types were specifically intended to be used at small sizes, the Livre family is suitable for larger, less dense settings planned for longer reading. The family was subsequently expanded with a more decorative variation (Le Monde Classic) and a sans-serif (Le Monde Sans). Graced with both style and readability, all of the Le Monde types display Porchez's considerable skill as a designer of typefaces and his deep knowledge of typographic history, particularly the rich heritage of French types from the sixteenth through nineteenth centuries. ¶ The display type is Hypatia Sans designed by Thomas W. Phinney for the Adobe Originals collection of types.

DESIGN & COMPOSITION BY CARL W. SCARBROUGH